Th
se
C

Introduction to C++

is book is primarily for students who are taking a course on the C++ language, for those who wish to lf-study the C++ language, and for programmers who have experience with C and want to advance to :++. It could also prove useful to instructors of the C++ course who are looking for explanatory programming examples to add in their lectures.

The focus of this book is to provide a solid introduction to the C++ language and programming knowledge through a large number of practical examples and meaningful advice. It includes more than 500 exercises and examples of progressive difficulty to aid the reader in understanding the C++ principles and to see how concepts can materialize in code.

The examples are designed to be short, concrete, and substantial, quickly giving the reader the ability to understand how to apply correctly and efficiently the features of the C++ language and to get a solid programming know-how. Rest assured that if you are able to understand this book's examples and solve the exercises, you can safely go on to edit larger programs, you will be able to develop your own applications, and you will have certainly established a solid fundamental conceptual and practical background to expand your knowledge and skills.

Introduction to C++

George S. Tselikis

CRC Press
Taylor & Francis Group
Boca Raton London New York

CRC Press is an imprint of the
Taylor & Francis Group, an **informa** business

First edition published 2023
by CRC Press
6000 Broken Sound Parkway NW, Suite 300, Boca Raton, FL 33487-2742

and by CRC Press
4 Park Square, Milton Park, Abingdon, Oxon, OX14 4RN

CRC Press is an imprint of Taylor & Francis Group, LLC

ISBN: 9781032136066 (hbk)
ISBN: 9781032136080 (pbk)
ISBN: 9781003230076 (ebk)

DOI: 10.1201/9781003230076

Typeset in Times
by KnowledgeWorks Global Ltd.

This book is dedicated to my family.

Contents

Preface   ix
Acknowledgements   xi
About the Author   xiii

1   Introduction to C++   1

2   Variables, Constants, and Arithmetic Conversions   11

3   Data Input/Output   31

4   Operators   45

5   Program Control   71

6   Loops   99

7   Arrays   133

8   Pointers   169

9   Characters   217

10 Strings   227

11 Functions   265

12 Searching and Sorting Arrays   343

13 Structures and Unions   365

14 Memory Management and Data Structures   403

15 Preprocessor and Macros   453

16 More about Functions   471

17 Classes and Objects   509

18 Operator Overloading   559

19 More about Classes   595

20 Inheritance   637

21   More about Inheritance   **689**

22   Exceptions   **717**

23   Class Templates   **745**

24   Files   **773**

25   Namespaces, Type Cast Operators, and Smart Pointers   **805**

26   Introduction to Standard Template Library   **835**

27   Application Example   **861**

Epilogue   871
Annex A: Precedence Table   873
Annex B: ASCII Table   875
Annex C: Hexadecimal System   877
Bibliography   879
Index   881

Preface

This book is primarily addressed to students who are taking a course on the C++ language, to those who wish to self-study the C++ language, as well as to programmers who have experience with C and want to move on to C++. It could also prove useful to instructors of the C++ course, who are looking for explanatory programming examples to add in their lectures.

This book aims to introduce the reader to the basic principles of C++ and the philosophy of object-oriented programming. It does not present all the technical and syntax details of the language, but tries to present the fundamental concepts of the language in a simple and understandable way. So, this book is not a reference book; its goal is to make the reader understand how to use a feature and not to describe every syntax or technical detail of the feature. Understanding the technical details comes with time and practice. After all, you don't have to know all the details of C++ to write C++ programs.

Also, this book does not present in detail the services of the Standard Template Library (STL). It just provides an overview of its most important features. A detailed presentation of STL would require an entire book. However, because learning STL is an integral part of learning C++, you should, after reading this book, read an STL reference book in order to get familiar with the numerous useful services and tools that STL offers.

So what, exactly, differentiates this book from the others in the field? This book tests the skills of the reader by providing a solid introduction to the C++ theory enriched with tips and advice accompanied by a large number of difficulty-scaled examples and solved programming exercises showing how concepts can materialize in code. When I first encountered the C++ language as a student, I needed a book that would introduce me to in a smooth way to the fundamentals of the C++ language, to provide a robust foundational understanding of its principles, a book with a focus on providing inside information and programming knowledge through practical examples and meaningful advice. That is the spirit that this book aims to capture.

It presents in a compact and substantial way the essentials of the C++ language and contains a large number of explanatory examples and solved exercises of scaling difficulty. Through them, language pitfalls are frequently discussed, in order for the reader to understand the little tweaks and hidden traps which a programmer – especially novice but not only – usually bumps into. There are trap holes the reader is lured to fall into. There are examples on how things that look normal can nevertheless go wrong. Be sure that if you are able to understand the book's examples and solve the exercises, you can safely go on to edit longer programs, you'll be able to read more complex programs, and you'll have certainly established a solid fundamental conceptual and practical background to expand your knowledge. The source code of the exercises is available at www.cplusplus.gr.

To the question if you need to know C or some other programming language to read this book, the answer is no. This book introduces C++ from scratch. No prior programming experience is required. Also, in the question if one needs to learn C before C++, my opinion is to start with C++. C++ is more secure, very powerful, with much more expressive and technical capabilities. Is it an easy language? No, it contains a lot of difficult concepts, which require lot of practice in order to understand them and apply correctly and efficiently in your programs. C++ is not learned (if at all) in a week or in a year; it is an intrinsically hard language to master and even at a later stage of the learning curve, there will always be reasons to go back to the fundamentals. Therefore, even an advanced programmer, may get benefited to browse this book from times to times.

For all of you who intend to deal with computer programming, a little bit of advice coming from my experience may come in handy:

- Programming is a difficult task that among other things it requires clear mind, calmness, patience, self-confidence, and luck as well. Don't write code when you are in a bad mood (e.g., certainly not if your favourite team lost the game), tired, or stressed.
- When coding, try to write in a simple and comprehensive way for your own benefit and for those who are going to read your code. Always remember that the debug, maintenance, and upgrade of a code written in a complex way is a painful process.
- Hands-on! To learn the features of any programming language, you must write your own programs and experiment with them.
- Programming is definitely a creative activity, but do not forget that there are plenty of creative, pleasant, and less stressful activities in life. Do not waste your life in front of a computer screen, searching for infinite loops, dangling pointers, thrown exceptions, buffer overflows, and buggy conditions. Program for some time and then have some fun. Keep living and do not keep programming.

Enjoy the C++ flight; it would be safe, with some turbulence, though.

Acknowledgements

I would like to thank S. Stamatiadis, N. Tselikas, and, particularly, I. Karali and A. Kotaras, whose comments, fruitful suggestions, and criticisms contributed to the improvement of this book.

About the Author

Dr. George S. Tselikis received both his Dipl.–Ing. degree and his PhD from the School of Electrical and Computer Engineering of National Technical University of Athens (NTUA). In 1998, he joined the Department of Electrical Engineering at Columbia University, New York, and worked as a postdoc research associate. He was a founding member of 4Plus S.A. (1999–2014), where he worked in the development of network protocols and services. He has a long working experience in the telecom area, and his main research interests focus on software specification, development, and testing of network protocols and services in wired and wireless networks. He has participated in many European research projects and he has collaborated with several companies in the telecom industry. Since 2004, he has been a visiting lecturer in several Greek universities teaching courses related to network technologies, protocols and communications, and programming languages.

Introduction to C++

1

Before getting into the details of C++ language, this chapter presents, in brief, its history, evolution, and strengths. Then, we'll discuss some basic concepts that we'll need in order to write our first program.

SOME BRIEF HISTORY

C++ is one of the most popular languages and it has been used for the development of many widely used applications. Although it is one of the older programming languages, C++ is steadily ranked among the most widely used and most powerful programming languages. C++ is not specialized for a specific application field; on the contrary, it is used for an impressive range of applications. For example, C++ is widely used to develop gaming applications, web applications, operating systems, networking applications, financial, browsers, compilers, embedded systems, and many more. A great number of popular applications that we all use in our daily life are written in C++. Also, it is more effective than many other languages for developing applications across a different range of computing systems and environments, such as personal computers, workstations, tablets, and mobile phones.

C++ originally derives from C, which was developed at Bell Labs in the early 1970s by Dennis Richie and others. The rapid expansion of the C language and its increased popularity led many companies to develop their own C compilers. However, due to the absence of an official standard, features that were not clearly described could be implemented in different ways. As a result, the same program could be compiled with one C compiler and not with another. In parallel, the C language continued to evolve with the addition of new features and the replacement or obsolescence of existing ones. The need for the standardization of C language became apparent. In 1983, the American National Standard Institute (ANSI) began the development of the C standard that was completed and formally approved, in 1989, as ANSI C or Standard C. The ANSI C standard also defines a library that every ANSI C implementation must support. C++ also supports that library.

The design and development of C++ began at Bell Labs in the early 1980s by Bjarne Stroustrup as an extension of the C language. Stroustrup had several reasons to base C++ on C, such as C's brevity, high performance, portability, and widespread popularity. In fact, the name C++ comes from the C increment operator ++, which increments the value of a variable by one. According to Stroustrup, the name signifies the evolutionary nature of the changes from C.

Essentially, with a few exceptions, C++ is a superset of C. C is a relatively simple language. Its key components are control flows, iterations, arrays, pointers, functions, and structures. These are the basic tools available to a C programmer to write programs. In C++, the tools are much more. At conceptual level, the most important features added are data hiding, polymorphism, inheritance, support of generic programming, and the standard library that provides a large number of tools to the developer. At design level, C++ supports *procedural* programming based on the use of control flows, iteration statements, and calls to functions to execute a set of actions when called, *abstract* programming based on the design of types that hides implementation details, *object-oriented* programming based on the design

DOI: 10.1201/9781003230076-1

of classes hierarchies and objects that represent the entities with which the program deals, and *generic* programming based on the use of templates and generic algorithms that allow the programmer to write type-independent code. The ability to combine all these programming design techniques when writing programs highlights the flexibility and strength of C++. Yes, I'd say enough programming services for a single language.

Furthermore, a major goal of C++ is to continue to be close to the hardware like C providing efficient memory usage and high performance of low-level functions, as well as to enable the developer to define own types with the same syntax support, application range, and performance with the basic types. This combination has enabled the spread of C++.

C++ began to spread and, as in the case of C, the publishing of a standard to describe its characteristics was necessary. C++ was initially standardized in 1998 as ISO/IEC 14882:1998, which was then amended by the C++03, C++11, C++14, and C++17 standards. C++03 was primarily a technical revision of C++98, aiming at fixing bugs and reducing ambiguities. Since C++03 didn't add new features, C++98 is often referred to as C++98/C++03. Next versions add new features to the language. C++ still continues to evolve and at the time of this writing, C++20 is underway.

This book covers C++98 thoroughly and presents several C++11/C++14/C++17 features. Any references to C++11/C++14/C++17 are clearly identified. I could describe the language in a uniform way without any special references to the standards, I just preferred the distinction for readers who may have some experience with C++98 and would like to see the changes separately, as well as for historical reasons, in order to show the evolution of the language and the needs that a new feature covers. Also, because you may run into code which uses older features that may have been removed by now, it is helpful to know how they work in order to be able to read that code. This book assumes that you have no prior knowledge of C. Any reference to C concerns ANSI C and not subsequent versions. In case you know C, it is a good opportunity to refresh your memory and test again your skills.

Notice that this book is not intended to be a complete C++ reference; a detailed coverage is beyond its scope. The main goal is to introduce you in the fundamental concepts of the C++ language and show how to apply them in your programs through lots of examples and programming exercises.

PROGRAM LIFE CYCLE

The life cycle of a C++ program involves several steps: write the code, compile the code, link the object code produced by the compiler with any code needed to produce the executable file, and run the program. Usually, a C++ compiler provides an Integrated Development Environment (IDE) that allows us to perform this set of operations without leaving the environment.

WRITING A C++ PROGRAM

To write a C++ program, you can use any available text editor to create the source code file. An editor is often integrated with the compiler. When naming the source file, you must use the proper extension to identify that the file is a C++ file. The extension depends on the compiler you are using. The most common extension is .cpp, although other extensions such as .cc and .cxx are also used to identify a C++ source file. Typically, a C++ program consists of many source files; then, each file is compiled separately.

OUR FIRST C++ PROGRAM

Our first program will be a "rock" version of the program that most programmers begin with. Instead of the classical *Hello world* message, our first program displays on the screen the classical song of *Ramones*, *Hey Ho, Let's Go.* Play it loud, and let's go.

```cpp
#include <iostream>
int main()
{
        std::cout << "Hey Ho, Let's Go\n";
        return 0;
}
```

Before explaining the lines of the program, let's briefly discuss about the standard library.

Standard Library

The word *library* refers to a collection of software resources (e.g., functions), usually written by others, that we can use in our programs. The standard library occupies a large part of the C++ standard and provides a large collection of components that facilitate the work of the programmer. For example, the string class is one of these components and makes it easier for the programmer to manage strings. Every C++ compiler must support the standard library.

The standard library is defined in a separate namespace, which is called std. We'll talk about namespaces in a short. The services of the standard library (e.g., display data on the screen) are provided through special files. These files are typically called *header files* and are provided with the compiler. One of them is the iostream file. As we said, the C++ library includes the C library. For each X.h header file of the C library there is the corresponding cX header in the C++ library. The letter c indicates that the header file is part of the C library. For example, the corresponding file of stdio.h is the cstdio file. Although their contents might be the same, the cX format is most suitable for C++ programs. In particular, the inclusion of the cX file places the names defined in this file in the std namespace. Note that you may read programs that include the iostream.h file instead of iostream. iostream.h is an older version of iostream and is not supported by the C++ standard any more.

The #include Directive

C++ uses a software program called preprocessor. The preprocessor is typically a part of the compiler and its role is to process the program before it is compiled. The preprocessor communicates with the compiler through directives. A preprocessor directive instructs the compiler to act accordingly. For example, with the #include directive, the preprocessor instructs the compiler to include the contents of the iostream file in the program before it is compiled. Regarding syntax, directives always begin with the # character and do not end with a semicolon (;) or some other special marker. We'll see more preprocessor directives in Chapter 15.

The iostream file, where the letter i corresponds to *input* and o to *output*, contains information about classes and functions that are necessary in order to read and display data. If we do not include this file, the compiler will not recognize the cout and the compilation will fail. To include a file of the standard library, such as iostream, we place the file name in brackets <>. An included file may also contain

#include directives and include other files. In general, when we are using components of the standard library in our program, we should include the corresponding header files. For example, if we are using the string class we need to include the string file. The order in which the files are included does not matter. The common practice is to put the #include directives at the beginning of the file.

When you get familiar with the C++ language, you may edit your own header files and include them in your programs. To include your own header file you place its name in double quotes (" ").

When the program is compiled, the compiler searches for the included files. The searching rules depend on the implementation. Typically, if the file name is enclosed in <>, the compiler searches in pre-defined directories that contain the headers of the standard library. If it is enclosed in double quotes (" "), the compiler usually begins with the directory that contains the source file, then it searches the predefined directories. If the file is not found, the compiler will produce an error message and the compilation fails. The file name may include relative or full path information. For example:

```
#include "d:\projects\serial.h" // DOS/Windows path.
#include "/usr/include/serial.h" // Linux/Unix path.
#include "..\projects\test.h" // Relative path.
```

However, it'd be better to avoid including path or drive information, because if your program is transferred to another system its compilation might fail.

Once you become familiar with the language, you may open the included files (e.g., iostream) and read them. Don't rely on them only as a source of some mystic knowledge that hides unseen secrets. They are text files that exist on your computer. Find them and see their content. It is an excellent source of extra knowledge and information.

The main() Function

Each C++ program must contain a function named main(). The word main() must be written in lowercase characters. The code of the program, or else the body of the function, must be enclosed in braces ({ }). A statement is a command that will be executed when the program runs. Statements are typically written in separate lines and, almost always, each statement ends with a semicolon. Although the compiler does not care about the layout of the program, proper indentation and spacing make your program easier to read. Braces are used to group declarations and statements into a block or else a compound statement that the compiler treats as one. Besides functions, we'll use braces in control statements and loops.

The main(), as its name implies, is the main function of any program. We'll talk about functions in Chapter 11. Simply put, a function is a series of declarations and statements that have been grouped together and given a name (e.g., main()). A function is called by its name to perform a specific task and may optionally return a value. The main() function is called *automatically* by the operating system when the program runs. The execution of the program begins with the first statement of main() and ends when the last statement of main() is executed, unless an exit statement (e.g., return) is called earlier. Of course, if a severe error occurs during the execution of the program, such as a division by 0, the program will terminate abnormally. The keyword int indicates that main() must return an integer to the operating system when it terminates. This value is returned with the return statement; the value 0 indicates normal termination, while non-zero values indicate some sort of failure. This declaration of main() is fairly common. However, you may see other declarations such as:

```
void main()
```

As we'll see in Chapter 11, the keyword void indicates that main() does not return any value. Although a C++ compiler may accept this declaration, it is not conforming to the standard because main() must return a value. Another common declaration is:

```
int main(void)
```

The word `void` explicitly states that `main()` does not accept parameters; however, its use is unnecessary because the empty parentheses `()` indicate the same. In Chapter 11, we'll see another declaration of `main()`, where `main()` takes parameters. Note that the `return` statement can be omitted. If it is omitted, the program will automatically return the value `0`. Although the result is the same, my preference is to use the `return` statement so that it is clearly shown.

`cout` is an object that is declared in the `std` namespace and it is associated with the predefined standard output (e.g., screen). `cout` knows how to display a variety of data including strings, numbers, and individuals characters. In C++, a series of characters enclosed in `""` is called a *string literal*. The ≪ notation indicates that the string is sent to `cout`. As we'll see in Chapter 3, the new line character\n moves the cursor to the beginning of the next line. The main reason I add\n at the end of the string is that messages like *Press any key to continue*, which may be displayed by some compilers after the program is finished, appear on the next line.

Writing Style

Regarding the syntax of the program, the braces `{}` do not have to be placed in separate lines. For example, we can add the {next to `main()` and write `main(){` or the} next to the `return` statement. Also, it is not necessary to indent the code. As you guess, there are many ways to write the program. For example, we could write `main(){` and put the code in a single large line; however, that option would make our program illegible. A line may contain multiple statements. For example, it is legal to write:

```
std::cout << "Hey Ho, Let's Go\n"; return 0;
```

Aside from the preferences that anyone may have, what really matters is that a program should be written in such a way that it is easy to read not only by the person who wrote it, but also by others who are going to read it. For better readability, the writing style I prefer is always to put the {} in separate lines, each statement in one line, and indent the code.

Namespaces

Let's make a short introduction to namespaces. C++ allows the grouping of data (e.g., classes, functions, variables, ...) in a common namespace. Thus, the namespace is a part of the program, in which certain names (e.g., variables) are declared. These names are not known outside of this area. For example, all the names of the standard library are defined in a namespace called `std`. As we'll see in Chapter 25, in order to access an element of the namespace, we must write the namespace followed by the scope resolution operator `::`. For example, when we write `std::cout` we access the `cout` object that is declared in the `std` namespace. If we want to make available all the names of the `std` namespace, we write:

```
using namespace std;
```

Now, we don't need to add the prefix `std::` before the names we use, that is, we can write:

```
cout << "Hey Ho, Let's Go\n";
```

Alternatively, we can make available only the names that we use. This is achieved by using corresponding `using` declarations. For example:

```
using std::cout;
```

Now, we don't need to add the prefix `std::` when we use the `cout`, while we have to add it when using other `std` names. The convention I usually follow is to put separate `using` declarations for the names I use or, if these names do not appear many times in the program use the prefix, as I did in the first program with `std::`. The reason I prefer to use separate `using` declarations rather than the entire namespace is to make clear what elements I use from that namespace. Occasionally, if the names used are many, for greater ease in writing and reading the code, I'll make the whole namespace available. If in some programs I declare the entire `std`, although the names are not many, it is for formatting the pages of this book to save some lines. We'll talk more about namespaces in Chapter 25. For now, it is enough to know that with the namespaces C++ allows different spaces to contain elements (e.g., variables) with the same names, which can be used in the program without creating a conflict between them.

Adding Comments

Adding comments improves the readability of the program and makes it easier to understand how it works. A comment begins with // and ends at the end of the line. The compiler ignores the comments, so the comments do not increase the size of the executable file, do not affect the operation of the program, nor do they increase the execution time. For example, two comments are added:

```
// The program displays a message on the screen.
#include <iostream>
using std::cout; // We'll use the cout object.

int main()
{
        cout << "Hey Ho, Let's Go\n";
        return 0;
}
```

C++ also supports the use of /* */ to insert comments. The compiler ignores anything included between the /* */. If a comment extends to more than one line, we can use // at the beginning of each line or /* */. It is a matter of personal preference. My preference is to use // for one-line comments, while to use /* */ for multiple lines. For example:

```
/* The purpose of the first program is to display a message on the screen,
and then terminate. */
```

Nested comments are not allowed. For example, the following code is illegal, and the compiler will raise an error message:

```
/*
/* Another comment. */
*/
```

Adding comments is a must when writing programs. An explanatory program saves you time and effort when you need to modify it, and the time of other people who may need to understand and evolve your program. The person who most probably will benefit from the comments is you, when you come back to that code sometime in the future and don't remember exactly why you wrote the code the way you did. In fact, I've regretted many times in the past when in non-obvious parts of my programs I did not add comments, because I thought that I'd always understand what I was writing. I was wrong, and I paid the price with the time I wasted to understand what I've done.

On the other hand, I've read comments that made it more difficult for me to understand the intentions of the programmer. Better not exist. Besides the tricky points of the program, I'd suggest that you add comments to describe the purpose of each file, as well as the purpose of important functions, entities (e.g., classes), or variables (e.g., global). And, when you add a comment, don't rush to write it down to continue writing the code. It is very important that the comment is substantial, explanatory, and understandable.

Let's do an exercise. Based on what you've learned so far, can you tell me what does the following program output? Read the program carefully and do not rush to see the answer.

```cpp
#include <iostream> // Example 1.1
using std::cout;

int main()
{
//      cout << "That is ";
        cout << "the first"; /* A program with multiple outputs
        cout << " trap"; /* That's the last one. */
        return 0;
}
```

Did you notice the `//` and answered `the first trap`? Yes, but you didn't notice that the comment starting with the `/*` in the second line ended at the end of the third line. Therefore, the program outputs: `the first`.

 Be careful when using `/*` `*/` to add comments, because the compiler ignores anything between them.

And yes, that was the first trap. There will be several in this book, I'll ask you questions, sometimes give you misleading suggestions, and wait for you to fall into. Watch out!

COMPILATION

After writing the program, the next step is to compile it. The compiler is a software program that translates the program to a language that the machine can interpret and execute (*machine language*). Essentially, this language is a sequence of bits with values 0 and 1, which the system can execute. Many compilers provide an IDE together with an editor and other facilities for the development of C++ programs. For example, *Microsoft* provides compilers for *Windows* environment. For *Unix/Linux* environments, the most popular compiler is g++, which is freely available from the Free Foundation Software. There are many free compilers available which you can find with an online search. To run the programs of this book, you'll need a compiler that conforms to the C++17 standard.

The way we compile a program depends on the operating system and the compiler. For example, suppose that the code of the program is saved in a file named *first.cpp*. In order to compile it in a *Unix/Linux* system with the g++ compiler we write in the command line:

```
$ g++ first.cpp
```

If we are using a compiler for *Windows*, the IDE typically provides a menu command such as *File-> New-> Source_File* to write the program, a command like *Build->Compile* to compile it and a command like *Build->Execute* to execute it. Let's see an example using the Microsoft Visual C++ compiler.

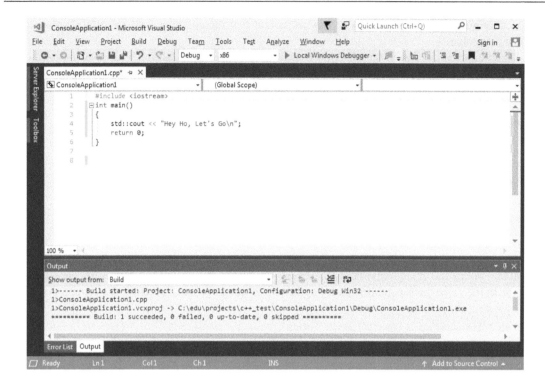

When we compile and run the program the output console is displayed.

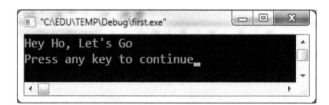

When the program is compiled, the compiler checks if the syntax of the program is according to the language rules. If the compilation fails, the compiler informs the programmer for the fail reason(s). If it is successful, the compiler produces an object file that contains the source code translated in machine language. By default, it has the same name as the file that contains the source code and its extension is. *obj* or. *o*, depending on the operating system. For example, the name of the object file would be *first.obj* (*Windows*) or *first.o* (*Unix/Linux*).

LINKING

After the successful compilation, the linker links the object code produced in the previous step with library code that the program uses and other necessary information. The library code contains the machine code of classes and functions used by the program. This code is contained in library files that are supplied with the compiler and usually have the .lib extension. For example, the code of the sqrt() function is found in such a file.

To make it clear, both header files and library files are supplied with the compiler; a header file contains information about the components of the program (e.g., function declarations), while a library file contains the implementation code (e.g., function definitions) in machine language. Also, in some cases the necessary libraries must be explicitly loaded. For example, if you are using the *g++* compiler and your program (e.g., *test.cpp*) uses a math function (e.g., `sqrt()`), you might need to load the math library by writing: *g++ test.cpp –lm*. In an integrated environment, a menu command with the name *Build* or *Make* is typically found, which performs program compilation and linking in one step.

If the linking is successful, an executable file is created. For example, the default name of the executable file produced by the *g++* compiler is `a.out`, while a *Microsoft* compiler produces an executable file having the same name with the source file and extension *.exe*.

An executable file is generated for a specific system, that is, an executable created on a *Windows* system cannot be executed on a *Mac*. What about the source code? If the code can be successfully compiled on a variety of systems without any modifications, we say that the program is *portable*.

RUN THE PROGRAM

There are several ways to run a program. For example, if the executable file was generated by the *g++* compiler, type in the command line:

```
$ a.out
```

If an error message like `No such file or directory` or `command not found` is displayed, write:

```
./a.out
```

so that the file is searched in the current folder. In an IDE, a menu command like `Build->Execute` is typically found to run the program.

ERRORS

Errors may appear in all stages of the program development. Errors reported by the compiler are called compile-time errors, errors reported by the linker are called linker errors, and errors that emerge when the program runs are called runtime or logical errors. As you guess, the latter is the worse type of errors.

The most common compile-time errors are syntactic. For example, if you write < in the `cout` instead of ≪ or omit the double quotes or you don't add the ; at the end, the compilation fails and the compiler will display error messages. Spelling errors are very common, as well. For example, if you write `mein` the compilation fails. C++ is a case-sensitive language, meaning that it distinguishes between uppercase and lowercase letters. For example, if you write `Cout` instead of `cout`, the compilation fails.

If the compiler displays many errors, fix the first one and any obvious errors and recompile the program. Often, a single error can cause the compiler to display more errors than actually exist. The new compilation may show less errors, even none. Also, notice that an error detected by the compiler may not occur in the indicated line, but in some previous line, most likely the immediately preceding one.

Apart from the error messages, the compiler may display warning messages. If there are only warning messages, the program will be compiled. However, don't ignore them; it may warn you against the potential malfunction of your program. In fact, for better control of your program it'd be safer to set the warning level at the maximum level supported by your compiler in order to catch all of them.

It is very important to understand that the compiler detects errors due to the wrong use of the language and not logical errors that may exist within your program. The compiler is not "inside your head" to know what you intend to do. Therefore, a successful compilation does not mean that your program would operate as you expect. I write this again, especially for novice programmers. *If your program is compiled it does not mean that it will work as you want.* For example, if you want to write some code that displays the word Less if the value of the integer variable a is less than 5, and you write:

```
if(a > 5)
      cout << "Less\n";
```

then, although these lines will be compiled successfully, the code won't display Less. This type of error is a logical error *(bug)* not detected by the compiler. The use of the word *bug* as a synonym of a programming error is credited to the mathematician and computer scientist Grace Hopper, when she discovered that a hidden bug inside her computer caused its abnormal operation.

If the program does not operate as you expect, you are in trouble. The depth of trouble you are in depends on the size of the source code. If it extends to some hundreds of lines, you'll probably find the logical errors in a short time and the debugging procedure won't take long. But if your program consists of thousands of lines, the debugging may become a time-consuming, painful, and very stressful procedure, particularly if your supervisor hangs over your head demanding immediate results. To avoid such troublesome situations, always remember my advice: try to write simple, clear, readable, and maintainable code.

READING THIS BOOK

As for the linguistic expressions of this book, I'd say that there is nothing special. If some code is marked as *program behaviour is undefined*, it means that the program may continue to run, crash, or produce unexpected results. All scenarios are possible. What is the most likely scenario? According to Murphy's Law, to work normally during the development phase and crash when you perform a public demonstration. Also, even if your program works normally with a compiler it may fail with some other or with a next version of the same compiler. So, avoid what may cause *undefined behaviour.*

If some code is marked as *the result depends on the implementation* or *it is platform dependent*, it means that if you compile your program with another compiler or transfer it to another system and compile it, that code may produce different results. As you can imagine, debugging a program that runs normally on one system and not on another is a very painful process. So, if you want your program to be portable, do not write code that depends on the system in which you work.

In my experience, the first step to learn a programming language is through coding examples. You'll find many examples throughout this book. Some are just code snippets, while others are complete programs that help you understand the material. After understanding (and not just reading) a topic, the next step is to write code in order to test your knowledge. You cannot learn a programming language by just reading a book; you must write code. For that reason, each chapter provides many programming exercises. A program may be written in several ways. When reading an exercise, my advice is to hide the answer and write your own version. Then, compare the solutions. Pay extra attention to all questions of type "What is the output of the following program?" Don't rush to see the answer; hide it and give it some time. Each chapter ends with a number of unsolved exercises for more practice. Always try them to test your skills and understanding of what you've learned, before continuing to the next chapter. Remember, to learn any programming language, you must write your own programs and experiment with them; hands on, that is the only way.

C++ is a powerful language with many features, rules, and concepts. So, don't be disappointed if some text or examples in this book make it difficult for you to understand. It's normal to feel that way. The best way to overcome such difficulties is to write small, simple programs and experiment with them so that you gradually become familiar with the features of the language and how they work.

Oh yes, almost forgot, as you "heard" in our first program, you'll need a pair of speakers …

Variables, Constants, and Arithmetic Conversions

2

In this chapter, we'll learn the basic data types and see how we can use them in order to declare variables in our program. As we move on to the next chapters we'll learn how to build composite types that are based on the basic types, such as arrays and structures. This chapter also discusses arithmetic conversions and constant variables.

VARIABLES

The computer's RAM (Read Access Memory) consists of millions of successive memory cells that are used to store data. The size of each cell is one byte. For example, a PC with say 8GB (gigabytes) of RAM would have $8 \times 1024\,MB = 8 \times 1024 \times 1024\,KB = 8 \times 1024 \times 1024 \times 1.024$ bytes $= 8.589.934.592$ memory cells.

A *variable* is a memory location with a given name (e.g., i). The value of a variable is the content of its memory location (e.g., 10). When we want to access that value we use the name of the variable (e.g., i).

Naming Variables

There are some basic rules for naming variables. These rules also apply for function names. Be sure to follow them or your code won't compile:

1. The name or else the identifier can contain letters, digits, and *underscore characters* _. The language does not set a limit on the length of the name.
2. The name must begin with either a letter or the underscore character.
3. C++ is *case sensitive*, meaning that it distinguishes between uppercase and lowercase letters. For example, the variable sum is different from the variables Sum or sUM.
4. The following keywords cannot be used as variable names because they have special significance to the C++ compiler.

and	const_cast	friend	or_eq	template	volatile
and_eq	continue	goto	private	this	wchar_t
asm	default	if	protected	throw	while
auto	delete	inline	public	true	xor
bitand	do	int	register	try	xor_eq
bitor	double	long	reinterpret_cast		
bool	dynamic_cast		return	typedef	
break	else	mutable	short	typeid	
case	enum	namespace	signed	typename	
catch	explicit	new	sizeof	union	
char	extern	not	static	unsigned	
class	false	not_eq	static_cast	using	
compl	float	operator	struct	virtual	
const	for	or	switch	void	

DOI: 10.1201/9781003230076-2

C++11 also reserves the following keywords:

```
alignas alignof constexpr char16_t char32_t decltype noexcept nullptr
static_assert thread_local
```

Also, the word `export` is reserved, while the words `final` and `override` have a special meaning, as we'll see in Chapter 20. The word `asm` enables the programmer to add code written in *assembly* language. This book explains the meaning of each keyword, except `thread_local`. Just to know, `thread_local` is used to declare local variables in threads. This book does not discuss about threads. Once you read a book that describes Standard Template Library (STL), you'll learn about multi-thread programming.

5. In order to avoid name conflicts, don't choose names that begin with one or two _ characters, because these choices are reserved for use in the standard library. Also, don't use names that the compiler uses, such as names of library functions or variables (e.g., `cout`). Their use is allowed, but it is confusing and dangerous. Therefore, it is safer to handle predefined names as if they were reserved words.

In addition to the rules given earlier, there are a few conventions that are good to follow when naming your variables. While these are not enforced by the compiler, these "rules of thumb" will tend to make your programs easier for you to understand, as well as for those who have to read your code.

Use descriptive names for variables (of course, the same applies to functions, types, …). It is much easier to read a program when the names of the variables indicate their intended use. For example, if you use a variable that holds the sum of some numbers, give it a name like `sum` rather than an irrelevant name like `i`. Many programmers prefer to use lowercase letters when naming variables and uppercase letters when defining macros or constants. Short names (e.g., `i`) are usually used as indexes in arrays or loops. Don't give names to variables that are slightly different (e.g., `more` and `More`); it is very easy to make a mistake and use one variable in place of the other.

When necessary, don't be afraid to use long names to describe the role of a variable. If a variable name consists of words, the usual practice is to separate them with the underscore character _ for better readability. For example, you might call a variable that holds the number of days `days_number`, instead of `daysnumber`, or something less readable. In general, whatever approach you choose, it is good to be consistent and apply it throughout the program.

Data Types

C++ provides a set of data types. Each variable must have a type. The type determines the amount of memory allocated to the variable, the range of values that can be assigned to it, and the kind of operations that can be applied to it. The size of the types is implementation dependent, that is, it can vary among different systems. The data types and their usual size in a 32-bit system are shown in Table 2.1.

C++11 adds the following types:

`char16_t`: Used to store 16-bit character sets, such as UTF-16.
`char32_t`: Used to store 32-bit character sets, such as UTF-32.
`long long int`: Used for very large integers (e.g., at least 64 bits). It is valid that `sizeof(long) <= sizeof(long long int)`.

The memory space that a data type reserves may vary from one system to another. For example, the `int` type may reserve two bytes in an embedded or an older system, four bytes, or eight bytes in a modern system. To learn the number of bytes a data type reserves on your system, use the `sizeof` operator, as discussed in Chapter 4.

TABLE 2.1   Data types

DATA TYPE	USUAL SIZE (BYTES)	RANGE OF VALUES (MIN-MAX)
bool	1	false/true
char	1	−128 ... 127
wchar_t	2	−32.768 ... 32.767
short int	2	−32.768 ... 32.767
int	4	−2.147.483.648...2.147.483.647
long int	4	−2.147.483.648...2.147.483.647
float	4	Lowest positive value: $1.17*10^{-38}$ Highest positive value: $3.4*10^{38}$
double	8	Lowest positive value: $2.2*10^{-308}$ Highest positive value: $1.8*10^{308}$
long double	12, 16	
unsigned char	1	0 ... 255
unsigned short int	2	0 ... 65535
unsigned int	4	0 ... 4.294.967.295
unsigned long int	4	0 ... 4.294.967.295

The `char`, `short`, `int`, and `long` types are used to store integer values, which can be either signed or unsigned. If we add the word `unsigned` the variable has no sign bit and it may store only positive values or zero. The word `int` can be omitted. For example, `long` instead of `long int`. Also, the words can be mixed in any order. For example, the declaration `unsigned long int a;` is the same as `int long unsigned a;`.

With the exception of the `char` type, all other types are signed by default. In signed types, the leftmost bit is reserved for the sign. If the number is negative its value is `1`, `0` otherwise. The advantage of using `unsigned` types is that they have a higher upper limit than their signed counterparts, since they don't need to account for negative values.

Characters are represented by specific numeric codes. The `char` type is typically used to store the numeric codes of the characters of the basic character set, such as the ASCII set (e.g., it includes characters that appear on the keyboard such as digits, letters, punctuation marks, …). The `wchar_t` type is used to store the numeric codes of the characters of a larger character set, such as the Unicode.

The `char` type may be signed or unsigned, it is implementation dependent. Therefore, if it is important for your program, you should explicitly write `signed char` or `unsigned char` instead of `char`. For example, if we write:

```
char a = 255;
int b = a;
```

the value of b is unspecified. In one system where the `char` type is signed b becomes -1, while in another where the `char` type is unsigned b becomes `255`.

The `bool` type has two possible values, `true` and `false`. The literal `true` converts to `1` when converted to a value and `false` converts to `0`. Conversely, non-zero values convert to `true`, whereas a zero value converts to `false`. For example:

```
bool b = 2; // b becomes true.
int i = false; // i becomes 0.
```

Typically, a `bool` variable is used to store the result of an action, such as whether a value is found in an array or not.

The `float`, `double`, and `long double` types are used to store values with a fractional part, that is, floating-point numbers. Unlike integer types, floating-point types are always signed. Although the `long double` type normally provides the highest precision, it is rarely used because the precision of the `float` and `double` types is usually sufficient.

Although C++ allows each implementation to set its own sizes for the data types, it places some restrictions on their minimum sizes. Specifically, the size of the `char` type must be at least 8 bits, the size of the `short` at least 16 bits, and the size of the `int` at least equal to that of the `short`. The size of the `long` type must be at least 32 bits and at least equal to that of `int`. The following order applies: `sizeof(char) <= sizeof(short) <= sizeof(int) <= sizeof(long)`. The size of the `wchar_t` type depends on the implementation; however, it applies: `sizeof(char) <= sizeof(wchar_t) <= sizeof(long)`. If it is important to save memory and the values fit, use `short` instead of `int`, because its size is usually smaller. A typical example is when you have a large array of integers.

For floating-point types, C++ specifies that the size of the `long double` type must be at least equal to that of the `double`, and the size of the `double` type must be at least equal to that of the `float`. If you want to learn the sizes of the integer and floating-point types that your system supports use the `sizeof` operator. If you want to find out more about the type limits, read the `climits` and `cfloat` header files. Also, you can use the `limits` header file and get type information. For example, the next statement displays the maximum value of the `int` type:

```
std::cout << "Max value of type int is " << std::numeric_limits<int>::max();
```

To get the minimum value we replace `max()` with `min()`. If you want to get the maximum values for other data types, replace the `int` type in the angled brackets with the desired type.

 If you don't care about precision use the `float` type, because it usually reserves less bytes and calculations with float numbers tend to be executed faster.

Let's run the following program. The `==` operator in the `if` statement compares the value of a against 3.1. What do you think the program will display, `Yes` or `No`?

```cpp
#include <iostream> // Example 2.1.
int main()
{
        float a = 3.1;

        if(a == 3.1)
                std::cout << "Yes\n";
        else
                std::cout << "No\n";
        return 0;
}
```

Although the obvious answer is `Yes`, did the program output `No`? Surprise! And the reason is due to the limited capacity of the `float` type to represent precisely the number 3.1. As we'll see later, by default, the type of a floating constant (e.g., 3.1) is `double`.

When using floating-point variables in comparisons, it is safer to declare them as `double` or `long double` rather than `float`. For example, if you use these types, the program would most probably display `Yes`. But in general, when you test the value of a floating-point variable for equality, you can never be sure about the result of the comparison, as there is a possibility that the number cannot be represented with the accuracy of the type. If it can be represented, the result of the comparison is valid. For example, if instead of 3.1 we compare to 0.5, the comparison is successful and the program displays Yes, because the number 0.5 can be represented with the accuracy of the `float` type without losing decimal digits.

In general, if you have to test two floating-point values for equality don't write `if(a == b)`, it is not safe. You may insert a hard to trace bug, as I did once. A simple, though, safer approach is to check not whether the values are exactly the same, but whether their difference is very small. For example, we could write: `if(fabs(a-b) <= accuracy)`. `fabs()` is a library function declared in `cmath` and calculates the absolute value of the argument, that is, the difference between a and b. For the value of `accuracy`, you may choose any value you consider it approaches their equality. There are other more efficient solutions, but it is out of scope to expand further.

To sum up, because floating-point variables can only store a certain number of significant digits, and any additional significant digits are lost, be aware of the possibility of rounding errors that may affect the behaviour of your program.

You may think that this discussion should have been later in this book and not so early. You may be right, but I prefer to discuss it now that I'm discussing about the types and draw your attention here, rather than add it somewhere else that you may not notice.

For simplicity, I've made some assumptions throughout this book. I assume that the type character-istics supported by the compiler are those shown in Table 2.1, that one byte contains eight bits (yes, it can have more), and the system uses the most common method to represent signed numbers, that is, the two's complement. Also, I assume that the underlying character set is the ASCII set. When using floating-point values in our programs, we'll use both `float` *and* `double` *variables, in order to get familiar with both types.*

Before concluding this section, I'd like to point out that C++ supports *static type control* in the sense that the validity of the use of types is done during the compilation and not during the execution of the program. That is, if we do an action that the type does not support, the compiler will generate an error message. Static type control is fundamental to the effective use of language, as errors can be detected before running the program. Later in this book we'll see that we can use the basic types to create other types (e.g., pointers) using operators. We'll also learn to create our own types, such as structures and classes.

Declaring Variables

Variables must be declared before used in the program. The declaration informs the compiler about the name of the variable and its type. We've already seen some examples of declarations in the previous section. To declare a variable we write:

```
data_type variable_name;
```

The `variable_name` is the name of the variable and the `data_type` its type. As we said, C++ is a statically typed language, in the sense that the compiler must know the type of every entity (e.g., variable) at the point of its use. The type of the entity determines the operations we can perform on it. For example, to declare an integer variable named i and a floating-point variable named j, we write:

```
int i;
float j;
```

Variables of the same type can be declared in the same line, separated with a comma. For example, instead of declaring the variables i, j, and k in three different lines:

```
int i;
int j;
int k;
```

we can declare them in the same line and save space: `int i, j, k;`

Once a variable is declared, the compiler reserves the bytes in memory that it needs in order to store its value. For example, as shown in Table 2.1, the `char` type reserves one byte, while the `double` type reserves eight bytes. Also, the compiler saves the name of the variable and its memory address, so, whenever a variable is used within the program, the compiler uses the name to retrieve the corresponding address and access the content. For example, with the statement `i = 10;` the compiler stores the value `10` into the memory location corresponding to the name `i`. As we'll see in Chapter 8 we can use the `&` operator to retrieve the memory address of `i`. Note that the value `10`, like any other value (e.g., float, character, ...), is stored in memory in binary as a sequence of bits `0` and `1`.

Next, we'll see that we can specify more properties when declaring a variable, such as the type quali-fier and the storage class (we'll discuss about it in Chapter 11). Although they may appear in any order, the typical practice is to specify the storage class first, then the qualifier, and last the data type. For example:
`static const unsigned int a;`

Until we reach Chapter 11, we are going to declare all our variables within `main()`. Those variables are called *automatic*, in the sense that their lifespan ends when the program terminates. Their initial value is indeterminate (i.e., garbage), that is, the initial value of a variable is whatever happened to be at its memory location. For example, the following program displays the initial value of `i`:

```cpp
#include <iostream> // Example 2.2.
int main()
{
    int i;

    std::cout << i;
    return 0;
}
```

In general, using variables that have not been initialized is very dangerous and can cause the pro-gram to behave unpredictably. Most likely, the compiler will warn you of such use, but you should also be careful.

A variable can be declared anywhere in the program. Many prefer to declare the variable when it is to be used. In most cases, I prefer to declare all the variables at the beginning of each function, so that some-one who reads the code can quickly get an idea of the complexity of the function and the type of variables it uses. Also, I find it more convenient to have them all together in one place, so that when you want to see the type of a variable you don't have to search for its declaration point. On the other hand, there are cases where it is more efficient to declare the variable after checking certain conditions. Here is an example to avoid an unnecessary memory allocation:

```cpp
void f(int a)
{
    if(a == 0)
        return;

    int arr[10000]; /* First the condition is checked and then the
variable arr is declared. The variable arr is an array and, as we'll see in
Ch.7, the compiler reserves memory for 10000 integers when declared. This
memory will be reserved only if needed, that is, if the condition is
false.  */
    ...
}
```

As a matter of style, I use a blank line to separate the declarations of variables made at the begin-ning of the function from the rest of the code. In general, indentation, alignment, spaces, and blank lines, improve the readability of the program. For example, I always indent declarations and statements to make it clear that they are nested inside the function. Also, I use blank lines to divide the program into logical blocks, making it easier for the reader to understand the structure of the program.

Before ending this section let's briefly explain the terms *declaration* and *definition*. A declaration is a statement that introduces a name (e.g., variable) into a scope. A declaration that also sets aside memory is called definition. Therefore, when we write:

`int i;` this declaration is also a definition since memory is reserved for the variable. However, not all declarations are definitions. For example, we'll see such declarations when we discuss about `extern` variables in Chapter 11.

Assignment of Values

The traditional way to assign a value to a variable is by using the assignment operator =. For example, the following code assigns the value 2 to a:

```
int a;
a = 2;
```

Alternatively, a variable can be initialized together with its declaration:

```
int a = 2;
```

We could also write `int a = {2};` As we'll see in the next chapters, the braced {} syntax is usually used to initialize the elements of an array or structure. The braces can be left empty, in which case the variable in initialized to 0.

We can also initialize more than one variable of the same type when declared. For example, the following statement declares the a, b, c, and d variables and initializes the first three with the values 2, 3, and 4, respectively. The variable d is initialized with a garbage value.

```
int a = 2, b = 3, d, c = 4;
```

We could even write:

```
int a = 2, b = a+1, d, c = b+1;
```

The assignments take place from left to right, meaning that first a becomes 2, then b becomes 3, and then c becomes 4. Here is another way:

```
int a(2), b(a+1), c(a+2);
```

Their values become 2, 3, and 4, respectively. As you can see there are many alternatives to initialize a variable. For better readability, my preference is to initialize each variable in a separate statement right after its declaration. In some examples I'm not consistent and initialize it when declared; the reason is to save space.

In an assignment, the expression on the right side can be a number, a variable, or a more complex expression, such as an expression that uses arithmetic operators. The value of the expression is first evaluated and then assigned to the variable. Also, the same variable can be used on both sides of =. For example:

```
int a = 2;
a = a-5; // a becomes -3.
```

The value assigned to a variable should be within the range of its type. For example, the statement:

```
unsigned char a = 260;
```

does not make a equal to 260 (100000100 in binary), because the maximum value that can be stored in an `unsigned char` variable is 255. Only the 8 lower bits will be stored, that is, 00000100, and a becomes 4. In general, for unsigned types, the assigned value is the unsigned remainder of dividing the integer (e.g., 260) by 2^n, where n is the number of bits required to represent the type (e.g., 8). If an out-of-bounds value is assigned to a signed type, the result is undefined. Note that the compiler will most likely not display a message to warn you for an overflow. So, always pay attention to the ranges of your variables! For example:

```
short int s = 32767; // The maximum value is assigned.
s = s+1; /* The new value of s is undefined. For example, it may be -32768 in
one system and something different in another system. */
```

C++11 supports initialization with a value list within {}, without using the =. For example:

```
int a{5}; // a becomes 5.
vector<int> v{1, 2, 3}; /* Initialization of a vector with integers. We'll
talk about vectors in Ch.7. */
```

An advantage of this format is that the compiler informs the programmer for conversions that may cause information loss. For example:

```
int a = 5.2; /* a becomes 5. The compiler may not inform the programmer for
the information loss. */
int a{5.2}; /* The compiler informs the programmer for the conversion of the
float number to an integer. */
```

An empty value list {} is used to assign a default value. For example, the default value for an integer or float type is 0, and for pointers (we'll see them in Chapter 8) the `nullptr`:

```
int a{}; // a becomes 0.
char *p{}; // p becomes nullptr.
```

Type Specifiers

As we said, when a variable is declared, its type must be specified. C++11 provides alternative ways to specify the type using the `auto` and `decltype` identifiers.

When using the word `auto` it is not needed to declare the type of the variable (e.g., `int`), as long as the compiler can deduce it from the initialization value. For example:

```
auto a = 5; // The type of a is int.
auto d = 1.2; // The type of d is double.
auto v = i+j; /* The type of v is inferred from the type of the result i+j.
For example, if i and j are double, the type of v is double. */
auto k = f(); // The type of k is the return type of f().
```

For simple declarations, such as the above, there is no benefit to use `auto`. The `auto` identifier is very useful for simplifying complicated declarations, such as those in generic programming, where the type identification can be lengthy, complex, and hard to find. In these cases it is very convenient to use `auto`, since instead of trying to find the type we let the compiler do it. We'll see such examples in Chapter 26. To infer the type, an `auto` variable must be initialized when declared, that is, it is an error to write:

```
auto a;
```

As with simple types, we can use `auto` to declare multiple variables. The initial values must correspond to the same type. For example:

```
auto a = 5, b = 6; // OK, the type of a and b is int.
auto c = 5, d = 6.12; /* Wrong, inconsistent types for c and d. First int,
then double. */
```

As for the `decltype` you'll understand better its use when we'll talk about functions and references. Keep reading to get an idea. As with `auto` the usual use of `decltype` is in generic programming. Sometimes we may want to declare a variable with a type that the compiler infers from an expression. The expression can be a simple variable or something more complex, such as the return value of a function. For such cases C++11 introduces the `decltype` identifier. Its syntax is `decltype(expression)` and it returns the type of the `expression`. For example:

```
int i, j;
int& r = i;
const int c = i;

decltype(i) d1; // The type of d1 is int.
decltype(r) d2 = j; // The type of d2 is reference and it refers to j.
decltype(r) d3; /* Wrong, since the type of d3 is reference it must be
initialized. */
decltype(c) d4 = j; // The type of d4 is const int.
d4++; // Wrong, d4 is const int.
```

The type of the variable declared with `decltype` is that of the `expression`. Note that in case of d3, its type is reference but it does not refer to the variable that the operand refers to (e.g., i). This is the reason that d3 must be initialized, as an ordinary reference variable.

Note that if the variable name is enclosed in double parentheses, the return type is a reference to the variable type, not the variable type. For example:

```
int i, j;
decltype(i) d1; // The type of d1 is int.
decltype((i)) d2 = j; // The type of d2 is reference to integer.
decltype((i)) d3; /* Wrong, since the type of d3 is reference it must be
initialized. */
```

When `decltype` is applied to a non-variable expression, the return type is the type of the expression. The compiler only evaluates the expression to infer its type, it does not execute it. For example:

```
int i, j;
decltype(i+j) d1; // The type of d1 is int.
decltype(f()) d2; // The type of d2 is the return type of f()
```

The compiler does not call `f()`, it just makes the type of d2 the same as the return type of `f()`.

ARITHMETIC CONSTANTS

The integer numbers we've used in our examples (e.g., 5) are *decimal* constants. An integer constant can be written in decimal, octal, hex, or binary notation; they are nothing more than alternative ways of writing the same number. By default, `cout` displays the values in decimal form. A decimal constant contains the digits of the decimal system 0-9, but must not begin with 0. If it begins with 0, it is interpreted as an *octal* constant. An octal constant contains the digits 0-7. For example:

```
int a = 0123;
```

The value of a does not become 123 in the decimal system, but 83, since 123 is interpreted as an octal number. Since each digit corresponds to a power of 8 we have $123_8 = 3 \times 8^0 + 2 \times 8^1 + 1 \times 8^2 = 83_{10}$.

A constant that begins with 0x or 0X is interpreted as *hexademical* constant. A hexademical constant contains the digits 0-9 and hex letters. For example:

```
int a = 0x2f;
```

The value of a becomes 47, since $2f_{16} = 47_{10}$. The letters may be either uppercase or lowercase. Annex C provides a brief introduction to hex system. Typically, the hex notation is used in applications that communicate with the hardware.

C++14 allows an integer to be written in binary form. The syntax uses the 0b or 0B prefixes. For example:

```
int a = 0b1111; // a becomes 15.
```

Of course, no matter how you write a number (e.g., 12), that is, 12, 014, 0XC, or 0b1100 it will be stored in the computer memory as a binary value. Note that all notations can be combined in one expression. For example, the following statement assigns the value 80 to a:

```
int a = 10 + 020 + 0x30 + 0b110;
```

The type of an unsuffixed constant is the smallest of the `int`, `long int`, and `long long int` types that can represent its value. For example, the type of 200000 is `int` in a system with 32-bit integers, while it is `long int` in a system with 16-bit integers. If it is suffixed by l or L (e.g., 10L, 0x121), its type is the first of the `long int` and `long long int` types that can hold its value, while if it is suffixed by ll or LL its type is either `long long int` or `unsigned long long int`. If it is suffixed by u or U (e.g., 200U), its type is the first of the `unsigned int`, `unsigned long int`, and `unsigned long long int` types. If the suffixes are combined (e.g., 100UL), its type is the first of the `unsigned long int` or `unsigned long long int` that can hold its value. The order of L and U does not matter, nor does their case.

A character constant is a character or a series of characters enclosed in single quotes. For example:

```
char ch = 'a';
```

The type of the constant is `char`. As we'll see in Chapter 9, the value of a character constant depends on the character set that the system supports. For example, if the ASCII set is used, the value of 'a' is 97, and that will be the value of ch.

A floating constant is a value with decimal digits. Notice, that we use dot (.) for the decimal part, and not comma (,). For example, we write 1.23, not 1,23:

```
double a = 1.23;
```

A floating constant can be written in scientific notation using the letter E or e that corresponds to base 10 and an exponent with a positive or negative sign. For example, we can write a = 123E-2; which means that 123 is multiplied by 0.01. Similarly, we can write a = 0.123e1;. Scientific notation is most useful when the number is very small or very large to make it easier for the programmer to read and write. By default, the compiler treats a floating constant (e.g., 1.23) as double. Because of that, if we declare a as float in our example, the compiler would most probably issue a type incompatibility warning message such as: *'initializing': truncation from 'const double' to 'float'*. To make the compiler store the constant as float, we can add the letter f or F at the end (e.g., 1.23f), or the letter l or L to store it as long double (e.g., 1.23L).

As we'll see in Chapter 4, when both operands are integers the division operator / cuts off the fractional part and produces an integer result. For example:

```
int i = 8;
double j = i/5;
```

Since both operands are integers, the result of i/5 is integer. Therefore, the value assigned to j is 1, regardless of the type of j. A common mistake is to assume that because j is double, the value to be stored will be 1.6. No, the type of the variable to which the result is assigned (e.g., j) plays no role.

If either of the operands is floating-point, the fractional part is not truncated. For example, if i is declared as floating-point variable, j will be 1.6. The same happens if we write 5.0 instead of 5, since the divisor is a floating-point constant.

Since C++14, the single-quote character ' may be used as a digit separator in both integer and floating point constants. This can make large numbers easier to read. For example:

```
int a = 1'000'000'000;
double b = 0.0'123'456'2;
int c = 0b1'0011'1000'0001;
```

ARITHMETIC CONVERSIONS

C++ allows different data types to be mixed in the same expression. For example, adding an int and a double value. In such cases the compiler performs type conversions according to the rules that we'll see below. In general, the goal of a conversion is the type of the result to be produced to be that of the wider operand. The arithmetic conversions are applied to binary operators that expect operands of arithmetic type, such as arithmetic, relational, and equality operators. The conversion of one type to another is done either *implicitly* or *explicitly*. Implicit conversion is caused by the compiler, explicit by the programmer.

Implicit Conversions

When implicit conversion is performed, the compiler, without the programmer's intervention, promotes the type of the operand with the "narrower" type into the "wider" type capable of storing its value. We examine two cases:

1. If either operand has a floating type. In this case, the operand whose type is narrower is promoted in that order: float->double->long double. That is, if one operand is long double, the other is converted to long double. Otherwise, if one operand is double, the other is converted to double. Otherwise, if one operand is float, the other is converted to float. Notice that these rules also apply in case of an integer operand. That is, if one operand is double and the other is int, the int operand is converted to double.

2. If neither operand has a floating type. First, integral promotions are applied in both operands. Specifically, the `bool`, `char`, `signed char`, `unsigned char`, `short int`, and `unsigned short int` types are promoted to `int` or to `unsigned int` in case the `int` type cannot represent all the values of the original type. In particular, `true` is promoted to 1 and `false` to 0. The `char16_t`, `char32_t`, `wchar_t` types, and the scoped enumeration type (we'll discuss about it in Chapter 4) are promoted to the first of the `int`, `unsigned int`, `long int`, `unsigned long int`, `long long int`, or `unsigned long long int` types that can represent all the values of the original type.

Then, the operand with the narrower type is promoted in that order: `int->unsigned int->long int->unsigned long int->long long int->unsigned long long int`.

   a. That is, if one operand is `unsigned long long int`, the other is converted to `unsigned long long int`.
   b. Otherwise, if one operand is `long long int` and the other is `unsigned long int`, then if the `long long int` can represent all the values of the `unsigned long int`, the `unsigned long int` is converted to `long long int`. If not, both operands are converted to `unsigned long long int`.
   c. Otherwise, if one operand is `unsigned long int`, the other is converted to `unsigned long int`.
   d. Otherwise, if one operand is `long int` and the other is `unsigned int`, then if the `long int` can represent all the values of the `unsigned int`, the `unsigned int` is converted to `long int`. If not, both operands are converted to `unsigned long int`.
   e. Otherwise, if one operand is `long int`, the other is converted to `long int`.
   f. Otherwise, if one operand is `unsigned int`, the other is converted to `unsigned int`.
   g. Otherwise, the type of both operands is `int`.

Let's see some conversion examples:

```
bool b;
char c;
short int s;
int i;
unsigned int u;
float f;
double d;
long double ld;


i = c+s; // The types of c and s are converted to int.
i = i+b; // The type of b is converted to int.
u = u+i; // The type of i is converted to unsigned int.
d = d+i; // The type of i is converted to double.
d = d+f; // The type of f is converted to double.
ld = ld+d; // The type of d is converted to long double.
```

Pay attention that when signed and unsigned types are mixed, the conversion rules may produce unexpected results. For example, what does the following program output?

```
#include <iostream> // Example 2.3.
int main()
{
        int a = -20;
        unsigned int b = 200;
```

```
    if(a < b)
        std::cout << "Yes\n";
    else
        std::cout << "No\n";
    return 0;
}
```

Although we'd expect the program to output Yes, it outputs No. Here is why. Since a and b operands have different types, the applied conversion rule says that the type of a is promoted to unsigned int before the comparison. Therefore, the value of a will be converted to a large positive number greater than b (in a 32-bit system, it is $2^{32}-20$). As a result, the program outputs No.

 Be very careful when mixing signed and unsigned operands or, even better, don't mix them at all, in order to avoid unpleasant surprises.

Implicit arithmetic conversions may also occur in assignments when the type of the expression on the right side does not match the type of the variable on the left side. The applied rule says that the type of the expression is converted to the type of the variable. If the type of the variable is at least as wide as the type of the expression, there will be no loss of information. For example:

```
char c;
short s;
float f;
long double ld;

s = c; // The type of c is converted to short.
f = s; // The type of s is converted to float.
ld = f; // The type of f is converted to long double.
```

In a similar way, the statement double d = 10; is equivalent to: double d = 10.0;, because the compiler converts the integer constant 10 to the type of d, that is, double.

However, there are conversion cases where information may be lost. These are called *narrowing* conversions. For example, when a floating-point value is assigned to an integer variable:

```
int i;
double d = 11.999;
i = d; // i becomes 11.
```

The fractional part is truncated and i becomes 11. Notice that the assigned value is not rounded to 12. Loss of precision may also occur when a bigger floating-point type is assigned to a smaller one (e.g., double to float) or a bigger integer type to a smaller one (e.g., long to int).

As you guess, narrowing conversions can be the cause of unexpected errors; the compiler most probably will issue a warning message to inform the programmer. At the initialization, C++11 prevents narrowing conversions with the {} syntax as we saw earlier.

Explicit Conversions

Besides the implicit way where the compiler performs the conversion, the programmer can explicitly convert the type of one expression to another type using the cast operator. The cast expression in the traditional way, that is, before the introduction of special operators, has the following syntax:

```
(data_type)expression or data_type(expression)
```

The first syntax is inherited from C. The type of the `expression` is converted to the `data_type`. For example, after declaring the following variables:

```
double a, b, c = 1.23;
```

the expression:

```
a = (int)c;
```

casts temporarily the type of c from `double` to `int` and a becomes 1. Notice that the cast does not change the value of c, that is, c remains 1.23. The term "temporarily" means that the compiler treats next c as `double`. In a similar way, the statement:

```
b = int(c+3.7);
```

casts the result of the addition to `int` and assigns that result to b. Therefore, b becomes 4.

Let's look at this example. What will be the value of d?

```
int d = (int)2.99 * 20;
```

To answer this question we need to know if the type cast precedes the multiplication. Therefore, we must consult the precedence table in Annex A. Because the cast operator has higher precedence than the * operator, d becomes 40. If the expression were enclosed in parentheses, that is (2.99 * 20), d would become 59.

Besides the traditional method, C++ provides special operators to perform explicit conversions. We'll talk about them in Chapter 25. For example, the `static_cast<>` operator can be used for converting values from one numeric type to another:

```
d = static_cast<int>(c); // double to int.
```

The variable to be converted (e.g., c) is enclosed in parentheses and the new type in brackets (e.g., `int`). The type of c is temporarily converted to `int` and the integer value is assigned to d.

As Chapter 25 discusses, the main reason for using special cast operators is for more safety, in order to avoid castings that may cause problems in the operation of the program. Also, with a simple search of the operator name (e.g., `static_cast`) in the program we can quickly find all the castings, resulting in better control of the program. On the contrary, in the traditional way, we've to search the program line by line and waste much more time to find the castings, since there is no special mark to identify them.

CONSTANT VARIABLES

Besides the type of a variable, we can specify additional properties. For example, sometimes we may want to declare a variable whose value remains constant during the program execution. Such a variable is called *constant*. To declare a constant variable, we use the `const` keyword. A `const` variable must be initialized when it is declared and it is not allowed to change its value thereafter. For example:

```
const int a; // Wrong, it is not initialized.
const int a = 5; // OK, it is initialized when the program is compiled.
const int a = f(); /* OK, it is initialized with the return value of f() when
the program runs. */
```

An attempt to change the value of a later in the program (e.g., a = 20;) will produce a compile error. A `const` variable can participate in expressions like a non-`const` variable, as long as no attempt is made to change its value. For example:

```
float a = 1.23;
const float b = a; // OK, it does not matter that a is not const.
float c = b; // OK, it does not matter that c is not const.
b = a*c; // Wrong, it is not allowed to change the value of b.
```

The most common use of `const` is to declare a constant that is used many times in the program. For example:

```
int main()
{
        const int RATE = 50;
        int a, b, c;

        a = 3*RATE;
        b = RATE-20;
        c = -RATE/30;
        ...
}
```

The compiler replaces all the occurrences of RATE with the value 50. Thus, the values of a, b and c become 150, 30, and -1, respectively. In order to distinguish the `const` variables from the ordinary variables, many programmers prefer to name them with all uppercase letters. Don't forget to use descriptive name for the constants you declare, to help the reader understand their role. In large programs where the same constants can be used in multiple source files, the common practice is to put them in a header file, which becomes `#include` in whichever source file needs them.

Okay, one might ask, is it necessary for RATE to be declared as `const`, why not declare it as a simple integer variable? Of course we can do it, nevertheless, it is much safer to make it `const` in order to avoid an unintentional change of its value.

In order to make the program more flexible, a good practice is to use constants to represent values that appear many times within the program. If you ever need to change the value of a constant you only need to change it in one place.

For example, let's write the previous program without declaring the RATE constant:

```
int main()
{
        int a, b, c;

        a = 3*50;
        b = 50-20;
        c = -50/30;
        ...
}
```

If we ever need to change the value 50 we would have to make three replacements instead of one. It may seem simple in a small program, but imagine having to change every value in a program that is thousands of lines long! And to be precise, we have to find the right occurrences of 50 that really need to change, because the number 50 can be used in other cases that must not change. Therefore, it is much faster and safer to declare a constant and change its value to a single point, if necessary. This makes the program much easier to maintain and control. Also, the name of a constant may indicate its role more expressively than a plain value (often referred to as *magic constant*) and make the program easier to read.

Alternatively, we can use the `#define` directive to declare a constant. The `#define` directive is used to define a macro. In most cases, a macro is a name that represents a numerical value. To define such a macro, we write:

```
#define macro_name value
```

For example, instead of the constant RATE, we can define a macro named RATE, as follows:

```
#define RATE 50
```

When the program is compiled, the preprocessor replaces each occurrence of RATE with 50. RATE looks like a variable, but it has nothing to do with a variable. It is just a name that will be substituted with 50, before the code is compiled. As with `const` variables, it is a common practice to use all uppercase letters for macro names. Unlike ordinary statements, notice that the `#define` directive does not end with a semicolon ;.

Although both `const` and `#define` can be used to create names for constants, there are significant differences between them. We can use `#define` to create a name for a numerical, character, or string constant. However, we cannot specify the data type of the constant. On the other hand, we can use `const` with any type, such as arrays, pointers, and classes. Second, the `const` constants are subject to the same scope rules as the ordinary variables (we'll discuss them in Chapter 11), whereas `#define` constants are not. Thus, the scope of a `const` can be limited in a particular function or file. Another difference is that the names of the `const` constants can be viewed in the debugger; whereas the `#define` constants cannot, since the preprocessor has replaced the names with their values. These are some of the reasons why it is recommended to use `const` or `constexpr` (since C++11), instead of `#define`.

We'll see other uses of the `const` qualifier in the next chapters. For example, `const` is usually used for protection when passing data to functions, as we'll see in Chapter 11.

Additionally, C++11 introduced the `constexpr` qualifier to declare a constant. The main difference between them is that a `const` variable is not required to be initialized at compile time, that is, it can be initialized at runtime (i.e., when the program runs), whereas a `constexpr` variable must be initialized with a value that is known at compile time. The main idea for `constexpr` is to improve the performance of the program since the computations are performed at compile time rather than runtime. If the initialization value is not a constant expression or, in general, if the compiler cannot initialize the variable, the compilation fails. Let's see some examples:

```
int i = 3;
constexpr int a = 5; // OK.
constexpr int b = a+2; /* OK, the a+2 is a constant expression. The value of
b is calculated when the program is compiled. */
constexpr int c = i; // Wrong, i is not a constant.
constexpr int e = f(); /* OK, only if f() is a constexpr function. We'll talk
about constexpr functions in Ch.16. */
void h(int d)
{
        constexpr int g = d; /* Wrong, the value of d is not known at compile
time. */
}
```

EXERCISES

C.2.1 What is the output of the following program?

```cpp
#include <iostream>
int main()
{
        int i = 100;

        i = i+i;
        i = 2*i;
        std::cout << i+i << ' ' << i << '\n';
        return 0;
}
```

Answer: The value of i initially becomes equal to i = i+i = 100+100 = 200 and then i = 2*i = 2*200 = 400. Therefore, the program displays: 800 400.

C.2.2 Find the errors in the following program and fix them, so that the program runs and displays Nice.

```cpp
#include <iostream>
int main()
{
        int j = 4.5;
        unsigned float i = 1.23;
        double j = 6.7;

        k = 10;
        cout << "Nice << '\n';
        return 5;
}
```

Answer: Assigning a floating-point value to an integer variable is not wrong, the fraction part will be truncated and j becomes 4. The declaration of i is incorrect, because a floating-point variable cannot be declared unsigned. The declaration of j is incorrect, because the name j has already been used. The use of k is another error, because it hasn't been declared. Another error is the missing " next to Nice. A program may return to a non-zero value, so the return statement is acceptable.

C.2.3 Write a program that declares two integers, assigns to them the values 50 and 20, and displays in separate lines their sum, difference, product, the precise result of their division (i.e., 2.5), and the remainder (i.e., 10). To find the remainder use the % operator. Use a single cout statement.

```cpp
#include <iostream>
int main()
{
        int i = 50, j = 20;

        std::cout << "Sum:" << i+j << "\nDiff:" << i-j << "\nProd:" << i*j <<
"\nDiv:" << (double)i/j << "\nRem:" << i%j << '\n';
        return 0;
}
```

Comments: As we'll see in Chapter 4, the `%` operator is used to find the remainder of the division of two integer operands. The other operators are used as in math. If we omit the cast of `i` and write `i/j`, the program would output the integer result of the division, that is, 2.

C.2.4 What is the output of the following program?

```cpp
#include <iostream>
int main()
{
        bool b = 18;
        int i = b+2;
        double d = i+1.99;

        i = d*2;
        std::cout << i/010 << '\n';
        return 0;
}
```

Answer: The declarations make `b` equal to 1, `i` becomes 3, the type of `i` is converted to `double` when added to `1.99`, so `d` becomes `4.99`. Then, `i` becomes 9 and the program displays the result of the division by 8 (`010` is 8 in the octal system), that is, 1.

C.2.5 Write a program that assigns a two-digit positive value to an integer variable and displays the sum of its digits. For example, if the assigned value is 35, the program should display 8. Don't use the `%` operator.

```cpp
#include <iostream>
int main()
{
        int i, j, k;

        i = 35;
        j = i/10;
        k = i - (10*j);
        std::cout << j+k << '\n';
        return 0;
}
```

Comments: The term `i/10` calculates the tens of `i`. Notice that we could omit the declarations of `j` and `k`, and write: `std::cout << i/10+(i-(10*(i/10)));`

C.2.6 What is the output of the following program?

```cpp
#include <iostream>
int main()
{
        int k;
        float i = 3.9, j = 1.2;

        k = i + (int)j;
        std::cout << k - (int)((int)i + j) << '\n';
        return 0;
}
```

Answer: Since the value of `(int)j` is 1, we have k = 3.9+1 = 4 (not 4.9, because k is `int`). Similarly, we have `(int)((int)3.9+1.2)` = `(int)(3+1.2)` = `(int)(4.2)` = 4. Therefore, the program outputs 0.

C.2.7 Write a program that declares two floating-point variables (e.g., i, j), assigns to them two positive values (e.g., 3.45 and 6.78) and swaps their integer parts (i.e., i becomes 6.45 and j becomes 3.78). For casting, use the static_cast<> operator.

```cpp
#include <iostream>
int main()
{
    int k;
    float i = 3.45, j = 6.78, dec;

    dec = i - static_cast<int>(i); // Get the decimal part.
    k = static_cast<int>(i); /* Save the integer part, before changing its
value. */
    i = static_cast<int>(j) + dec;

    dec = j - static_cast<int>(j);
    j = k + dec;
    std::cout << i << ' ' << j << '\n';
    return 0;
}
```

UNSOLVED EXERCISES

U.2.1 Write a program that uses a single cout to display the following pattern.

```
*    *
  *
*    *
```

U.2.2 Find the errors in the following program and fix them, so that the program runs and displays the value of m.

```cpp
include <iostream>
int mein();
(
    int m;
    a = 10
    m = 2a+100
    std:cout < M < \n;
    return0;
)
```

U.2.3 Find the errors in the following program and fix them, so that the program is compiled successfully.

```cpp
#include <istream>
#define NUM 30;
int main{}
{
    const int a;
    int i = f;
    float f = 1,23;
```

```
              a = 10;
              NUM = i+2;
              retern 0;
        }
```

U.2.4 Write a program that assigns two negative values into two integer variables and uses these variables to display the corresponding positives.

U.2.5 Write a program that assigns two positive values into two integer variables and displays the remainder of their division without using the % operator. Use only two variables.

U.2.6 Write a program that assigns two positive values into two float variables and displays the integer part of their division and the fractional part. For example, if they are assigned the values 7.2 and 5.4, the program should display 1 and 1.8, since 7.2 = (1×5.4)+1.8.

U.2.7 Write a program similar to C.2.5 for a three-digit positive value. For example, if the assigned value is 123, the program should display 6.

Data Input/Output

3

In this chapter, we'll learn various methods of formatting the output using the `cout` object. We'll also learn how to use the `cin` object in order to get input from the user, store that input in variables, and use it in our programs. We won't cover every aspect of data input/output, but you'll get enough of what you need, in order to read and output data.

DATA OUTPUT WITH cout

In C++, data input and output is accomplished via *streams*. The term stream refers to a data source or destination. For example, an output stream may be associated with the screen, a file, or an output device (e.g., printer). C++ provides a set of classes declared in the `iostream` and `fstream` header files to support data input/output operations. We'll discuss classes and objects in Chapter 17. For now, it is enough to know that a class is a data type that the programmer defines and it represents a logical entity. An object is an instance of a particular class and it is created according to the description of the class. A class contains variables and functions that determine the operations that can be performed on objects of that class. For example, the `ostream` class contains functions that are responsible for data output.

`cout` is an object of the `ostream` class. By default, the `cout` object is associated with the predefined standard output (e.g., screen). For those who know C, `cout` corresponds to `stdout`. The `cout` is followed by the `<<` operator and the expression we want to display. By default, the values written in `cout` are converted to a sequence of characters. For example, if we write:

```
cout << 35;
```

the characters 3 and 5 are inserted into the output stream. Before we continue, a parenthesis for those who know from C that the `<<` is the left shift operator. The same applies for C++. It's just that the `ostream` class overloads it and changes its behaviour. When used in this way, the `<<` operator sends the data on its right to `cout`. The `<<` visually suggests that the direction of the data flow is from right to left. When we get to Chapter 18 and discuss operator overloading, you'll see how we can change the behaviour of an operator.

If you are familiar with the C input/output system and the functions declared in `stdio.h` (e.g., `printf()`), you can also use them in C++ programs to display data. However, the format and syntax of `printf()` is more complex, since the type of each variable must be specified. Also, `printf()` is not scalable to print user-defined types (e.g., there is no specific identifier for displaying all the members of a class), nor it is secure in the sense that it does not check the types and arguments passed to it. For example:

```
int i;
printf("%s", i); /* Wrong, it should be %d instead of %s. The code is
compiled successfully. However, this error may cause the program to behave
unpredictably. */
```

C++ provides flexibility, security, and simplifies the data output, since the `cout` and the `<<` operator know how to handle each data type.

DOI: 10.1201/9781003230076-3

31

The data written to `cout` are not sent directly to the destination, but are stored in a buffer area in memory. When it becomes full, the program flushes the buffer and the data are sent to the destination. The use of that memory is especially useful when the output stream is connected to a peripheral device, such as a file on the hard disk, since one large transfer is much more efficient and increases the program performance than many individual transfers. In case the output is directed to the screen, things are simpler, since the program does not have to wait until the memory is full. Typically, writing a new line character or waiting for data entry causes the memory to be flushed. Also, as we'll see below, the use of `endl` and `flush` manipulators has the same effect.

C++ provides several ways to format the output. We'll describe them briefly in a short. Before that, let's discuss escape sequences.

Escape Sequences

In C++, there are characters that have a special meaning. For example, the " delimits a string, that is, a sequence of characters enclosed in double quotes, so we cannot add an extra " within it. Also, there are characters that we cannot enter directly from the keyboard. For example, you cannot add the new line character in a string by pressing *Enter*. If you press *Enter*, you'll start a new line in your source code file.

For the representation of non-printable characters (e.g., backspace) and characters with special meaning (e.g., "), C++ provides special notations, called *escape sequences*. An escape sequence consists of a backslash (\) followed by a character. Although these sequences look like two characters, they represent only one. For example, when we write \n the compiler interprets it as a new line instruction and not as the character n. Table 3.1 lists the escape sequences and their meaning.

TABLE 3.1   Escape sequences

ESCAPE SEQUENCE	MEANING
\a	Audible alert.
\b	Backspace.
\f	Form feed.
\n	New line.
\r	Carriage return.
\t	Horizontal tab.
\v	Vertical tab.
\\	Backslash.
\'	Single quote.
\"	Double quote.
\?	Question mark.
\ooo	Represents the character that corresponds to the octal number (one to three octal digits). For example, according to the ASCII set in Annex B, the value '\143' corresponds to 'c', because $143_8 = 99_{10}$. The sequence ends if either three digits have been used or a character other than octal digit is met. For example, the string "\142k" contains the characters '\142', that is, 'b', and 'k'. The octal number does not have to begin with 0.
\xhhh	Represents the character that corresponds to the hexadecimal number (h is a hex digit or letter). For example, according to the ASCII set in Annex B, the value '\x6d' corresponds to 'm', because $6d_{16} = 109_{10}$. The standard does not set a limit on the number of h. The sequence ends if a character other than hex digit is met.

If the character after \ is not supported, the behaviour is undefined. The escape sequences are divided into *character escapes* and *numeric escapes*. The character escapes can represent common ASCII control characters (e.g., new line), while the numeric escapes, which are the latter two in Table 3.1, can represent any character. Let's see the following program:

```
#include <iostream> // Example 3.1
using std::cout;

int main()
{
    cout << '\a';
    cout << "Check\b\b\b back\n";
    cout << "Test\rCR\n";
    cout << "\53\n\x2d\n"; /* The octal number 53 (decimal 43) corresponds
to the character + and the hexadecimal number 2d (decimal 45) to -. */
    cout << "T\"ree\'\n";
    cout << "Check\t\t\\point\\\n";
    return 0;
}
```

As we'll see later, besides the \n, we can also use the endl manipulator to change line. The first statement creates a beep, while the second one deletes the last three characters of the word Check, prints back and the \n moves the cursor to the beginning of the next line. On the third, the \r moves back the cursor to the beginning of the line and the word CRst is displayed. The next one outputs the + character, changes line and outputs –. The next one outputs T, then a ", and then the word ree'. The last one outputs the word Check, adds two tabs, and prints the word \point\. To sum up, the program outputs:

```
(Hear a beep)
Ch backspace
CRst
+
-
T"ree'
Check            \point\
```

Note that if we want to display a single character we can also use single apostrophes (e.g., cout << 'd'). If you want for better readability to expand the format string of cout to several lines, one way is to use the backslash\. For example, the following cout is written over three lines, but the output will appear on one line:

```
cout << "This statement extends in three lines, \
but the message is displayed \
in the same line";
```

Format Flags

The format flags are used to specify the output format. The flags are declared in the ios_base class and are divided into two categories: those that operate individually and those that belong to groups. Individual flags can be turned on or off independently of the other flags. These flags are shown in Table 3.2.

TABLE 3.2   Format flags

FLAG	MEANING
boolalpha	Reads/writes boolean values using the words `true` and `false`.
showbase	Prefixes octal numbers with `0` and hex numbers with `0x`. No prefix for decimal-base values.
showpoint	Displays the decimal point for floating-point values.
showpos	Prefixes positive numerical values with `+`.
skipws	Discards whitespace characters (i.e., spaces, tabs, newlines) when reading data from an input stream.
unitbuf	The associated buffer is flushed after each output operation.
uppercase	Displays the `e` of scientific notation and the `x` of hex notation in uppercase.

The `ios_base` class provides the `setf()` function to activate flags. Because the `ostream` class derives from the `ios_base` we can use the `cout` object to call `setf()`. For example, the statement:

```
cout.setf(ios_base::showpos);
```

sets the `showpos` flag. As we'll learn in Chapter 17, because these flags are declared in the `ios_base` class we must use the class name (or a class that inherits it) and the scope operator `::`. That is, we have to write `ios_base::showpos`, not just `showpos`. The expression `ios_base::showpos` refers to the `showpos` constant declared in the `ios_base` class.

A flag remains activated until it is disabled. To deactivate a flag we can use the `unsetf()` function. For example:

```
cout.unsetf(ios_base::showpos);
```

All flags correspond to integer values. C++ uses the name `fmtflags` (usually, it is an alias of the `long` type) to store values. Specifically, each flag is an integer with only one bit set to one. Thus, we have the ability to use the bit operator `|` (we'll discuss it in Chapter 4) and enable more than one flag in the same `setf()` call.

The second category includes the selective flags as shown in Table 3.3.

The `ios_base` class provides a second overloaded version of `setf()`, which takes two arguments and allows flags to be turned on and off at the same time. This second version is typically used to handle these

TABLE 3.3   Selective flags

FLAG	GROUP	MEANING
dec	basefield	Reads/writes integer values in decimal format.
hex		Reads/writes integer values in hex format.
oct		Reads/writes integer values in octal format.
fixed	floatfield	Writes floating-point values in fixed point notation.
scientific		Writes floating-point values in scientific notation.
internal	adjustfield	The output is padded up to the field width. For numerical values fill characters are inserted between the sign and the number. The predefined fill character is the space.
left		The output is aligned to the left by inserting fill characters at the end.
right		The output is aligned to the right by inserting fill characters at the beginning.

selective flags. The first argument specifies which flag will be activated and the second which flag(s) will be deactivated. For example:

```
#include <iostream> // Example 3.2
using namespace std;

int main()
{
        int i = 100;

        cout.setf(ios_base::showbase|ios_base::uppercase);
        cout.setf(ios_base::hex, ios_base::basefield);
        cout << i << '\n';
        return 0;
}
```

The first setf() activates the showbase and uppercase flags, while the second deactivates the basefield group flags and activates the hex flag. Therefore, the values are displayed in hex and the program displays 0X64.

In C++, the precision for the floating-point values depends on the selected mode. If the fixed or scientific mode is selected, the precision specifies the maximum number of digits after the decimal point. If no mode is selected, the precision specifies the maximum number of all digits. The default precision for all modes is six digits. In the scientific mode the value is displayed with an exponent and one digit before the decimal point. To return to the default mode we can write:

```
cout.setf(0, ios_base::floatfield); or cout.unsetf(ios_base::floatfield);
```

If you know the conversion characters specified in C for printf(), it is helpful to know that the fixed mode corresponds to %f, the scientific mode to %e, and the default mode to %g. In case of a cut-off digit, if its value is greater than 4 the output value is rounded up, otherwise down. Let's see the following program:

```
#include <iostream> // Example 3.3
using namespace std;

int main()
{
        double i = 12345.689;

        cout << "Default mode: " << i << '\n';

        cout.setf(ios_base::fixed, ios_base::floatfield);
        cout << "Fixed mode: " << i << '\n';

        cout.setf(ios_base::scientific, ios_base::floatfield);
        cout << "Scientific mode: " << i << '\n';

        cout.unsetf(ios_base::floatfield);
        cout << "Default mode: " << i << '\n';
        return 0;
}
```

The program outputs:

```
Default mode: 12345.7 (since the default precision is six digits and the cut-off digit is 8, which
    is greater than 4, the output value is rounded up).
Fixed mode: 12345.689000
Scientific mode: 1.234569E+004 (the letter E corresponds to base 10).
Default mode: 12345.7 (the mode is reset to the default mode).
```

Manipulators

A more convenient way than `setf()` to format the output is to use manipulators. The manipulators are declared in the `std` namespace. Table 3.4 shows the most frequently used standard manipulators.

C++11 added the `defaultfloat` manipulator, which sets the floating-point numbers in the default notation, and the `hexfloat` manipulator, to output the floating-point numbers in hex notation.

TABLE 3.4   Manipulators

MANIPULATOR	OPERATION
endl	Inserts a new line character into the output. The difference with \n is that endl guarantees that the buffer will be flushed and the output will be immediately displayed, while you don't get that guarantee with \n.
ends	Inserts the null character '\0' into the output.
dec	setf(ios_base::dec, ios_base::basefield)
hex	setf(ios_base::hex, ios_base::basefield)
oct	setf(ios_base::oct, ios_base::basefield)
internal	setf(ios_base::internal, ios_base::adjustfield)
left	setf(ios_base::left, ios_base::adjustfield)
right	setf(ios_base::right, ios_base::adjustfield)
fixed	setf(ios_base::fixed, ios_base::floatfield)
scientific	setf(ios_base::scientific, ios_base::floatfield)
boolalpha	setf(ios_base::boolalpha)
noboolalpha	unsetf(ios_base::boolalpha)
showbase	setf(ios_base::showbase)
noshowbase	unsetf(ios_base::showbase)
showpoint	setf(ios_base::showpoint)
noshowpoint	unsetf(ios_base::showpoint)
showpos	setf(ios_base::showpos)
noshowpos	unsetf(ios_base::showpos)
skipws	setf(ios_base::skipws)
noskipws	unsetf(ios_base::skipws)
ws	Extracts and discards leading whitespace from an input stream.
uppercase	setf(ios_base::uppercase)
nouppercase	unsetf(ios_base::uppercase)
flush	Flushes the output buffer.
setfill(c)	Sets the fill character of the stream to c. If an output value does not fit in the width of the field, the remaining positions are filled with the character c.
setprecision(n)	Sets the precision digits to n. The precision remains in effect for subsequent operations.
setw(n)	Sets the width parameter to n. If n is less than the characters required to display the field is ignored. The width remains in effect only for the next field.
setiosflags(n)	Sets the format flags specified by n.
resetiosflags(n)	Unsets the format flags specified by n.
setbase(n)	Sets the numeric base to n.
unitbuf	Sets the unitbuf flag. The associated buffer is flushed after each output operation.
nounitbuf	Unsets the unitbuf flag.

As shown in Table 3.4, some manipulators perform the same operation as the format flags by calling the corresponding setf() and unsetf() functions. For example, the noshowbase manipulator calls unsetf(ios_base::showbase), while the dec manipulator calls setf(ios_base::dec, ios_base::basefield). Some of the manipulators (e.g., setw) are declared in the file iomanip. The following program displays integer and floating-point values in various formats:

```cpp
#include <iostream> // Example 3.4
#include <iomanip>
using namespace std;

int main()
{
        int i = 100;
        double j = 100.536;

        cout << i << oct << '\t' << i << hex << '\t' << i << endl;
        cout << scientific << j << '\t' << fixed << j << endl;
        cout << setprecision(2) << j << '\t' << setprecision(0) << '\t' << j
<< endl;
        cout << showbase << uppercase << i << '\t' << 1.4999 << '\t' <<
showpos << dec << i << endl;
        return 0;
}
```

The endl flushes the output buffer and inserts a new line. Regarding my preference between\n and endl, I prefer to embed the\n within a string; this is often more convenient than using endl. For example, I prefer to write cout << "\nCheck\n"; than cout << endl << "Check" << endl;. Also, note that endl may affect the performance in case of many flushing requests.

Note that it is not necessary to use one cout for each print. cout is smart enough to concatenate output. We just use the << operator before what we want to display. You'll understand better the sequential use of << when we discuss operator overloading in Chapter 18. The program outputs:

100 144 64 (the number 100 is equivalent to 144 in octal and 64 in hex. The values are one tab away).

1.005360e+002   100.536000

100.54 101 (the value is displayed with two precision digits. Because the cut-off digit is 6, that is, greater than 4, the value is rounded up. Then, the precision becomes 0 and, as before, because the cut-off digit is 5 the program displays 101).

0X64 1 +100 (because the hex manipulator is still active the value is displayed in hex. Similarly, because the precision remains 0 and the cut-off digit is 4 the program outputs 1. The dec manipulator is activated and the + sign prefixes the value).

In essence, the manipulators are functions, while the format flags are integers. For example, we can write:

hex(cout); instead of cout << hex. In my view, the second syntax looks easier and clearer to write. In practice, the ostream class overloads the << operator so that the second syntax becomes equivalent to hex(cout);. Note that most manipulators are sticky (e.g., hex), which means that they persist until we tell the stream otherwise.

Let's look at an example with different field widths and output alignment:

```cpp
#include <iostream> // Example 3.5
#include <iomanip>
using namespace std;

int main()
{
        int i = 200;
        double j = 1.23497654;

        cout << setw(10) << setfill('*') << i << '\n';
        cout << setw(2) << i << ' ' << setw(7) << fixed << j << '\n';
        cout << setw(8) << setprecision(3) << left << j << '\n';
        cout << setw(7) << showpos << setfill('#') << internal << i << '\n';
        return 0;
}
```

The program outputs:

*******200 (since the width is set to ten characters and the default alignment is to the right, the first seven positions are filled in with the fill character, i.e., *).

200 1.234977 (to display i three characters are required, while the specified width is 2. Therefore, this value is ignored. To display j eight characters are required; one for the integer part, plus one for the dot and six for the digits of the predefined accuracy. Since the width value is less it is ignored. The output value is rounded up).

1.235*** (to display j five characters are required; one for the integer part, plus one for the dot, and three for the precision digits. The output value is rounded up. Since the width is set to eight characters and the alignment to the left, the first five positions are filled with the value and the remaining three with the fill character).

+###200 (when internal alignment is set the fill character is inserted between the sign and the value).

Member Functions

Another way to format the output is by using cout member functions, as shown in Table 3.5.

TABLE 3.5   Member functions

FUNCTION	MEANING
flags()	Returns the value of the format flags.
fill()	Returns the fill character.
fill(c)	Sets the fill character to c.
precision()	Returns the precision digits.
precision(n)	Sets the precision digits to n. The precision remains in effect.
width()	Returns the value of the field *width*.
width(n)	Sets the value of the field *width* to n. The new width may remain in effect only for the next field, and then reset to its default value.

Let's see an example:

```
#include <iostream> // Example 3.6
using namespace std;

int main()
{
        double i = 12.428, j = 5.67321;

        cout.precision(2);
        cout.width(7);
        cout.fill('*');
        cout << fixed << i << '\t' << j << '\n';
        return 0;
}
```

The program outputs: **12.43   5.67. As you can see, the precision remains in effect for both variables, while the width is applied only to display i.

DATA INPUT WITH cin

In this section we'll learn how to get data from an input stream, store that data in variables, and use it in our programs. For example, an input stream may be associated with the keyboard, a file on the hard disk, or a peripheral device (e.g., modem). cin is an object of the istream class. By default, the cin object is associated with the standard input device (e.g., keyboard). For those who know C, cin corresponds to stdin. The type of the variable after the >> determines the type of the input data that will be read and stored in that variable. Just as the ostream class overloads the << operator, the istream class overloads the >> right shift operator to read the data. When used in this way, the >> operator extracts the data from the input stream and stores it into the indicated variable. The >> visually suggests that the direction of the data flow is from left to right. Both istream and ostream classes are defined in the iostream file.

The istream class provides several functions to get the input data. For now, we'll read numeric values and store them in appropriate variables. We'll use other types of variables (e.g., pointer) in the next chapters. Also, we'll see in Chapter 18, that we can use cin to get data for user defined types (e.g., class) in the same way we use it with basic types (e.g., int). Let's see an example:

```
#include <iostream> // Example 3.7
using std::cout;
using std::cin;
using std::fixed;

int main()
{
        int i;
        double j;

        cout << "Enter number: ";
        cin >> i; // Read an integer and store it into i.
        cout << "Enter number: ";
        cin >> j;
        cout << i << '\t' << fixed << j << '\n';
        return 0;
}
```

When the `cin` statement is executed, the program waits for the user to enter a value. Usually, a `cout` statement precedes `cin` to indicate to the user what kind of data to enter. Once the user enters an integer and presses *Enter*, this value will be stored into `i`. Because the value is not stored before pressing *Enter*, the user can change it. For example, if the user enters the value 5 and presses *Enter*, `i` will become 5. Then, the program waits for the user to enter a new value. For example, if the user enters the value 1.23 and presses *Enter*, `j` will become 1.23. Like `cout`, `cin` is a smart object. It converts input, which is a series of characters typed in the keyboard, into a form that fits to the variable receiving the data. For example, in case of `i`, the input is converted to an integer.

Note that we can use the `>>` operator many times in the same `cin` statement to enter multiple values. For example, we can write `cin >> i >> j;`. In this case the input values must be separated from each other by one or more spaces in order to distinguish. For example, if the user enters the values 5 and 1.23, `i` will become 5 and `j` will become 1.23. As with the data written to `cout`, the data read from an input stream, such as the keyboard, are stored in an intermediate memory. Normally, a C++ program flushes this memory when *Enter* is pressed. Notice that if the user enters values that do not correspond to the types of variables, for example, two float values or first a float value and then an integer, incorrect values will be stored in `i` and `j`.

The `>>` operator skips any white characters (i.e., spaces, tabs, or new line characters) that may exist before the numeric value and continues until it encounters a non-white character. If it encounters a character that does not match the type of the variable, it stops reading. The unread characters are left in `cin`. For example, if the user enters the values 5 and 1.23ABC, the ABC characters will remain in `cin` and A will be the first character to be read with the next `cin` statement.

If we want to specify the numbering system of the integer to be read we can use the `hex`, `oct`, and `dec` manipulators. For example, if we write:

```
int i;
cout << "Enter number in hex: ";
cin >> hex >> i;
```

and the user enters f, `i` will become 15.

For those who are familiar with `scanf()` from C, you can also use it, but its use, like `printf()`, is complex, unsafe, and not scalable. Here is an example of a common error:

```
int i;
scanf("%d", i); /* Wrong, it should be &i instead of i. The code compiles
successfully, however it won't run properly. */
```

My advice for those who still prefer to use `printf()`/`scanf()` than `cout`/`cin`, even if you know all their peculiarities, it's time to stop using them. Put them in the drawer of your programming memories.

Read Specific Input Format

Usually, a program just asks the user to enter some values. However, there are cases where the user may be asked to enter the data in a specific format. For example, a program that requires the date to be entered in day/month/year format. One way to get the values we are interested in and assign them to corresponding variables is to use extra variable(s) in order to extract the characters we are not interested in. For example, the variable `ch` is used to extract the / character:

```
char ch;
int d, m, y;
cout << "Enter date in the form d/m/y: ";
cin >> d >> ch >> m >> ch >> y;
```

In this example, the user must enter the date in the expected form (e.g., 13/5/2030), otherwise this code won't work.

Check Input Stream Status

Without going into details, it is useful to know that you can check if the input data caused the `cin` statement to fail. One way is to use the member function `good()`. If no error occurs, it returns a non-zero value. If an error occurs you can use the `clear()` member function to restore the stream's state. For example, the following program checks the return value of `good()` to ensure that an integer value is stored into `i`. Do not be scared with the program, take a look at it, but you'll be able to understand it only after learning the basics of the language.

```cpp
#include <iostream> // Example 3.8
#include <cstdio>
using std::cout;
using std::cin;

int main()
{
        int ch, i;
        while(1)
        {
                cout << "Enter number: ";
                cin >> i;
                if(cin.good())
                        break;
                cin.clear();
                while((ch = cin.get()) != '\n' && ch != EOF)
                        ; // Clear the unread characters.
        }
        cout << "Input number: " << i << '\n';
        return 0;
}
```

For example, if the user enters the value `z123`, `good()` will return zero and the inner loop will clear the characters left in `cin` in order to read the new value. Note that there are several code variants to handle not acceptable input values; this is just a simple example.

For simplicity, we'll assume that the user input would be valid and we won't check the state of the input stream throughout this book. However, remember that a robust program should always check it to verify that no read failure occurred. We'll discuss more about that in Chapter 24.

The `istream` and `ostream` classes provide many alternatives to read and output data. A complete description of all its capabilities is beyond the scope of this book. For more details, consult your compiler's documentation.

EXERCISES

C.3.1 The following program reads three integers and displays their average. Is it written correctly?

```cpp
#include <iostream>
using namespace std;

int main()
{
        int i, j, k;

        cout << "Enter three integers: ";
        cin >> i >> j >> k;
        cout << fixed << "Avg: " << i+j+k/3 << '\n';
        return 0;
}
```

Answer: No, there are two errors. The first one is that the sum is not enclosed in parentheses. As shown in Annex A, because the division operator / has priority over the addition operator +, the division k/3 is performed first and then the additions. So, we fix this bug by writing (i+j+k). The second error is due to the operands of the division. Because their types are integers, the result is integer. A quick way to fix this is to write 3.0 instead of 3.

C.3.2 Write a program that reads two positive numbers, a float and an integer, and displays the remainder of their division. For example, if the user enters 5.67 and 3, the program should display 2.67.

```cpp
#include <iostream>
using std::cout;
using std::cin;

int main()
{
        int i, div;
        double d;

        cout << "Enter positives float and int (#0): ";
        cin >> d >> i;
        div = d/i; /* Suppose that the input values are 5.67 and 3. Since div
is declared as integer it becomes 1. */
        cout << d - div*i << '\n';
        return 0;
}
```

Comments: Note that we couldn't declare the variable div and write:

```cpp
cout << d - (int)d/i*i;
```

C.3.3 Write a program that reads two positive float numbers and displays the sum of their integer and decimal parts. Use only two `double` variables. For example, if the user enters 1.23 and 9.56, the program should display 10 and 0.79.

```cpp
#include <iostream>
using std::cout;
using std::cin;

int main()
{
        double i, j;

        cout << "Enter two positives: ";
        cin >> i >> j;
        cout << (int)i+(int)j << ' ' << (i-(int)i) + (j-(int)j) << '\n';
        return 0;
}
```

C.3.4 Write a program that reads three integers, stores them in three variables, and rotates them one place right. For example, if the user enters the numbers 1, 2, and 3 and they are stored in variables a1, a2, and a3, the program should rotate their values one place right, so that a1 becomes 3, a2 becomes 1, and a3 becomes 2.

```cpp
#include <iostream>
using std::cout;
using std::cin;
```

```
int main()
{
        int a1, a2, a3, tmp;

        cout << "Enter numbers: ";
        cin >> a1 >> a2 >> a3;

        tmp = a1;
        a1 = a2;
        a2 = tmp;

        tmp = a3;
        a3 = a1;
        a1 = tmp;
        cout << a1 << ' ' << a2 << ' ' << a3 << '\n';
        return 0;
}
```

C.3.5 Write a program that reads a three-digit positive integer, makes its hundreds units and vice versa and displays the new number. For example, if the user enters 123, the program should display 321. Use only one variable.

```
#include <iostream>
using std::cout;
using std::cin;

int main()
{
        int i;

        cout << "Enter number between 100 and 999: ";
        cin >> i;

        i = 100*(i%10) + 10*(i%100/10) + i/100;
        cout << i << '\n';
        return 0;
}
```

Comments: As we'll see in Chapter 4, the % operator is used to find the remainder of the division of two integer operands. The term (i%10) calculates the units of the number, the term (i%100/10) calculates its tens and the term (i/100) its hundreds.

C.3.6 Write a program that reads a positive integer and rounds it up or down to its last digit. For example, if the user enters 13, the program should display 10. If the input number is 6, the program should display 10, while, if it is 255, the program should display 260. For casting, use the static_cast<> operator.

```
#include <iostream>
using std::cout;
using std::cin;

int main()
{
        int i;
        float j;
```

```
        cout << "Enter positive number: ";
        cin >> i;

        i = i+5;
        j = i/10.0; /* Divide by 10.0 and not by 10, so that the fractional
part is not truncated. */
        i = static_cast<int>(j) * 10; // Cut off the decimal digit.
        cout << i << '\n';
        return 0;
}
```

UNSOLVED EXERCISES

U.3.1 Write a program that reads the number of students who passed and failed in the exams and displays the percentages. For example, if the user enters 12 and 8, the program should display:

```
Success Ratio: 60%
Fail Ratio: 40%
```

U.3.2 Suppose that a customer in a store bought some plates and cups. Write a program that reads the number of the plates and the price of one plate, the number of the cups and the price of one cup, and the amount the customer paid. The program should calculate and display the change.

U.3.3 Write a program that reads an octal number, a hexadecimal number, and a decimal integer and displays their sum in decimal. For example, if the user enters 20, 3f, and 5, the program should display 84.

U.3.4 Write a program that reads an integer that corresponds to seconds and analyses it in hours, minutes, and seconds. For example, if the user enters 8140, the program should display: 2h 15m 40s. Use only one variable.

U.3.5 Modify the exercise C.3.6, so that the program reads a positive integer and rounds it up or down to its two last digits. For example, if the user enters 40, the program should display 0. If the input number is 130, the program should display 100, while, if it is 4550, the program should display 4600.

U.3.6 Write a program that reads a two-digit positive integer and duplicates its digits. For example, if the user enters 12, the program should display 1122.

U.3.7 Write a program that reads a positive integer and analyses it in multiples of 50s, 20s, 10s, and units. For example, if the user enters 285, the program should display: 5*50, 1*20, 1*10, 5*1.

U.3.8 Write a program that reads two three-digit positive integers, swaps the hundreds of the first one with the units of the second one, and displays the new numbers. For example, if the user enters 123 and 456, the program should display 623 and 451. Use up to three variables.

U.3.9 Write a program that reads a four-digit positive integer (e.g., i) and a one-digit positive integer. The program should convert the value of i to a five-digit number by placing the one-digit integer in the middle. For example, if the user enters 1234 and 5, i should become 12534 and the program should display that value.

Operators

4

Now that you've been introduced to the concepts of data types, variables, and constants, it is time to learn how to manipulate their values. C++ provides a rich set of operators that are used to form expressions and perform operations on them. In this chapter, we'll present the arithmetic, relational, logical, and bit level operators. We'll also discuss about the `sizeof` operator, the comma operator, and the `enum` enumeration type. The rest operators will be introduced gradually over the next chapters.

THE = ASSIGNMENT OPERATOR

The = operator is used to assign a value to a variable. For example, the statement a = 20; assigns the value 20 to the variable a, while the statement a = b; assigns the value of the variable b to a. When used in a chained assignment, the assigned value is stored in all variables in the chain. For example:

```
int a, b, c;
a = b = c = 20;
```

the values of a, b, and c become 20. In particular, because the = operator is right associative as shown in Annex A, the rightmost expression is evaluated first and evaluation proceeds from right to left. Therefore, first c becomes 20, then c is assigned to b, and, finally, b is assigned to a.

An assignment such as a = 30; produces a result, which is the value of the left operand (i.e., a) after the assignment. For example:

```
a = 30;
c = a + (b = 10-a);
```

The result of the assignment b = 10-a is -20, so c becomes 10. Use separate assignments than mixing them together; it is much easier to read and control the code.

If the variable and the assigned value are not of the same type, the value is first converted to the variable's type, if possible, and then assigned. For example, what would the value of j be in the following code?

```
int i, *p;
float j;
j = i = 5.999; // OK.
i = p; /* Wrong. Their types are different and the type of p, that is int*
(it is a pointer variable as we'll see in Ch.8) cannot be converted to the
type of i, that is, int. */
```

Since the type of i is `int`, its value becomes 5, and this value is stored in j.

DOI: 10.1201/9781003230076-4

As we said in Chapter 2, if an overflow occurs in a computation with signed numbers, for example, if the outcome of an addition is too big to be stored into a variable, the result is undefined. If the numbers are unsigned, the result is defined as modulo 2^n, where n is the number of bits of the unsigned type. For example, if the size of the `unsigned int` type is 32 bits the result of `4000000000u + 1000000000u` is `705032704`.

 When performing arithmetic operations, be sure that overflow won't occur in order to avoid unpleasant situations.

For example, if we use the `new` operator to allocate memory, we'll see how in Chapter 14, and an overflow occurs in the computation of its size (e.g., we are using a `short` variable to hold the size), the size of the allocated memory won't be the one asked with unpredictable consequences on the program execution. To give you a hint, the basic idea to avoid an overflow is to check for a potential overflow before it happens. For example, suppose that all a, b, and c are integers and b is positive; before assigning the result of a+b into c, we could write:

```
if(a > INT_MAX - b) /* INT_MAX is defined in <climits>. It is a macro that
specifies the maximum value that an integer variable can hold. */
{
        cout << "Error: overflow case\n";
        return;
}
c = a+b;
```

For simplicity, I assume that the values used throughout this book's programs are within valid ranges and no overflow occurs.

Lvalues and Rvalues

The right operand is an expression that has a value, such as a constant value or a variable. The left operand must be an *lvalue*. An lvalue refers to an object stored in memory (e.g., a variable) in which we can store something. That is, the object should be addressable, which means that we can extract and use is memory address. It is not allowed to use a constant or the result of a computation. For example:

```
20 = a; // Wrong.
b-a = 30; // Wrong.
```

The compiler will produce an error message similar to *error '=': left operand must be lvalue*. Also, the lvalue must be modifiable. For example, we'll see in Chapter 8 that an array variable is not a modifiable lvalue. The complement of the lvalue concept is the *rvalue*. As a rule of thumb, an rvalue is an expression that is not lvalue, such as a constant value (e.g., 10), or an expression (e.g., a+b) or a function call that returns a non-reference type. In particular, an rvalue expression evaluates to a result that is stored only temporarily in memory. For example, if we write `c = a+b;` the result of the expression a+b is temporarily stored somewhere in the memory, only to be copied into c, and then that memory is discarded. Thus, the expression a+b is an rvalue. To sum up, an rvalue is an expression that evaluates to a temporary value, while an lvalue evaluates to a more persistent value which is addressable in memory.

When in doubt, a quick test to determine whether an expression is an lvalue or rvalue is to ask yourself if you can take and later on use its address (we'll learn how to do that with the & operator in Chapter 8). If you can, it is an lvalue. For example:

```
int f() {int c = 10; return c;}
int a, b;

int* p1 = &a; // Yes you can, so a is an lvalue.
int* p2 = &(a+b); // No you can't, so a+b is an rvalue.
int* p3 = &10; // No you can't, so 10 is an rvalue.
int* p4 = &f(); // No you can't, f() returns an rvalue.
```

ARITHMETIC OPERATORS

The arithmetic operators +, -, *, and / are used to perform addition, subtraction, multiplication, and division, respectively. If the operands have arithmetic type, the arithmetic conversions discussed in Chapter 2 are applied, if necessary.

When both operands are integers, the / operator cuts off the decimal part. For example, suppose that a and b are int variables with values 8 and 5, respectively. Then, the result of a/b is 1, not 1.6. If both operands are negatives the result is a positive number (e.g., -16/-3 = 5). If either of the operands is a floating point variable or constant, the decimal part is not truncated. For example, the result of a/16.0 is 0.5, because the decimal point makes the constant floating-point.

The % operator is used to find the remainder of the division of two integer operands. Both operands must be integers, otherwise the code won't compile. In our example, the result of a%b is 3. If the right operand of the / or % operator is 0, the result is undefined (e.g., the program may terminate abnormally).

Note that before C++11, if one of the operators was negative and the other positive, the result of the division was implementation dependent. For example, the result of -9/5 could be either -1 or -2, it depends whether the implementation rounded up or down the result. C++11 specifies that the result is rounded down (to 0), so, it is -1. Also, before C++11, if one operator was negative, the sign of the remainder was implementation dependent. For example, the result of -9%5 could be either 4 or -4, it depends on the implementation. C++11 specifies that the remainder's sign is the same as the divisor's, that is, the result is -4. As a final example, the result of -9/-5 is 1 and the result of -9%-5 is -4.

These five operators are called *binary*, because they require two operands. Also, C++ provides the + and – *unary* operators which require one operand. The unary + operator has no effect. The result with the unary – is the negative of its operand. When both unary and binary + and – operators are mixed, the compiler figures out how to apply them. For example:

```
int a = +30; // + has no effect.
a = -40; // - is interpreted as the unary operator.
int b = -(a-10); /* The inner - is interpreted as the binary operator and the
outer - as the unary. */
-a; /* This statement does nothing. Be careful, the value of a remains the
same. */
a = -a; // Now, the value of a changes.
```

The value of a becomes 40 and of b equal to 50.

By convention, most programmers add a space before and after the operators. Most times I do the same; less often with the arithmetic operators though.

THE ++ AND -- OPERATORS

The ++ increment operator is used to increment the value of a variable by 1. It can be added before (*prefix*) or after (*postfix*) the variable's name. The operand must be a modifiable lvalue, such as an ordinary variable. For example:

```
int a = 10;
a++; // Equivalent to a = a+1;
++a; // Equivalent to a = a+1;
(a+10)++; // Wrong.
```

The value of a is incremented twice and becomes 12.

If the ++ operator is used in postfix form, the increment is performed after the current value of the variable is used in an expression. For example:

```
int a = 10, b;
b = a++;
```

the current value of a is first stored into b, and then a is incremented. Therefore, a becomes 11 and b becomes 10.

If used in the prefix form, the variable's value is first incremented and the new value is used in the evaluation of the expression. For example:

```
int a = 10, b;
b = ++a;
```

a is first incremented, and then that value is stored into b. Therefore, both variables become 11.

The -- decrement operator is used to decrement the value of a variable by 1. For example:

```
int a = 10;
a--; // Equivalent to a = a-1;
--a; // Equivalent to a = a-1;
```

The value of a is decremented twice and becomes 8. When the -- operator is used in an expression it behaves like the ++ operator. For example:

```
#include <iostream> // Example 4.1
int main()
{
        int a = 10, b;

        b = --a;
        std::cout << a << ' ' << b << '\n';

        b = a--;
        std::cout << a << ' ' << b << '\n';
        return 0;
}
```

The current value of a is first decremented and the new value is stored into b. Thus, the program outputs: 9 9. Then, the value of a is first stored into b, and then it is decremented. Thus, the program outputs: 8 9. Another example:

```
double a = 1.23;
cout << ++a << '\n';
cout << a-- << '\n';
```

The current value of a is first incremented and the code displays 2.23. Then, the code first displays the value of a, that is 2.23, and then a is decremented. The ++ and -- operators can be combined in the same expression. For example, what does the following program output?

```
#include <iostream> // Example 4.2
int main()
{
        int a = 0, b = 1, c = 2;
        std::cout << (b++)-(--a)*(c--) << '\n';
        return 0;
}
```

With the operation b++ the value of b is first used and then increased. With --a, the value of a is first decremented and then used in the expression. With c--, the value of c is first used and then decremented. Therefore, the program outputs 1-(-1)*2 = 3 and the values of a, b, and c become -1, 2, and 1, respectively.

 If you apply the ++ and -- operators to change the value of a variable in an expression don't use the variable again in the same expression, because the evaluation order is undefined.

For example, the result of: a * a++; is implementation dependent. It depends on the compiler whether a is first incremented and then multiplied, or not. In most cases, as in this example, the compiler is free to evaluate the operators in any order. There are exceptions such as the &&, ||, ?: and the comma operator, where the evaluation order is specified, but generally the compiler can choose any order. Therefore, do not create expressions like the previous one, because their result is undefined.

RELATIONAL OPERATORS

The relational operators >, >=, <, <=, !=, and == are used to compare two operands and determine their relationship. As we'll see in the next chapters, the relational operators are mostly used in if statements and iteration loops. For example, with the statement:

- if(a > 5) we check if a is greater than 5.
- if(a >= 5) we check if a is greater than or equal to 5.
- if(a < 5) we check if a is less than 5.
- if(a <= 5) we check if a is less than or equal to 5.
- if(a != 5) we check if a is not equal to 5.
- if(a == 5) we check if a is equal to 5.

 An expression is considered true when it has a non-zero value. If it is zero, it is considered false.

The result that the relational operators produce is of type `bool`, that is, `true` or `false`. For example, the value of the expression (a < 5) is `true` only if a is less than 5, otherwise, it is `false`. A more difficult example, tell me what is the result of the expression: -10 < a < -3; Does it depend on the value of a?

Because the < operator is left associative (see Annex A), first the value of -10 < a is evaluated. The result is either `true` or `false`. Remember from Chapter 2 that `bool` values are promoted to `int` with a default value of 1 for `true` and 0 for `false`. So, the result of the comparison, that is, 1 or 0, is compared with -3. Therefore, the value of the expression is always `false`, no matter what the value of a is. As we'll see next, to test whether a value is within a given set, we use the && operator.

 A common mistake is to confuse the == and = operators. The == operator is used to check whether two expressions have the same value, while the = operator is used to assign a value.

For example, the value of the expression a == 5 is `true`, only if a is equal to 5, otherwise, it is `false`. The value of a remains the same. On the other hand, the expression a = 5; assigns the value 5 into a. We'll see more examples like this when presenting the `if` statement in the next chapter.

EXERCISE

C.4.1 What is the output of the following program?

```cpp
#include <iostream>
int main()
{
        int a = 4, b = 6, c;

        a = (a <= (b-2)) + (b > (a+1));
        b = (a == 2) > ((b-3) < 3);
        c = (b != 0);
        std::cout << a << ' ' << b << ' ' << c << '\n';
        return 0;
}
```

Answer: Since a is 4 and b is 6, the first expression becomes (4 <= 4) + (6 > 5), so a becomes 2. Since a is 2, the value of (a == 2) is `true`. Since b is 6, the value of ((b-3) < 3) is `false`. So, b = 1 > 0 = 1. Since b is 1, c becomes 1. As a result, the program displays: 2 1 1.

COMPOUND ASSIGNMENT OPERATORS

The compound assignment operators are used to shorten statements using the form: `exp1 op= exp2;`. This statement is equivalent to `exp1 = exp1 op (exp2)`. Notice that the compiler encloses the expression exp2 in parentheses for reasons of priority. Typically, the op operator is one of the arithmetic operators: +, -, *, %, /, though it can also be any of the bit operators: &, ^, |, <<, >>, as we'll describe later in this chapter. For example, consider the following program:

```cpp
#include <iostream> // Example 4.3
int main()
{
        int a = 1, b = 2;

        a -= 2;
        a *= 1-b;
        a += b+3;
        a /= b+2;
        a %= b;
        std::cout << a << '\n';
        return 0;
}
```

The statement a -= 2; is equivalent to: a = a-2 = 1-2 = -1.

The next statement is equivalent to: a = a*(1-b) = -1*(-1) = 1. Notice that the compiler encloses the expression 1-b in parentheses.

The statement a += b+3; is equivalent to: a = a+(b+3) = 1+5 = 6, while the next statement is equivalent to: a = a/(b+2) = 6/4 = 1.

Finally, the statement a %= b; is equivalent to: a = a%b = 1%2 = 1. Therefore, the program outputs 1.

When the expression is a long one, the compound operator can make the code easier to read and safer to write as well. For example, it is more convenient and safer to write:

```cpp
publisher[i].book[j].prc += 10;
```

than to write again this long expression on the right. Indeed, it is more convenient, but, why is it safer? Because, it is too easy to make a type error and write:

```cpp
publisher[i].book[j].prc = publisher[i].book[i].prc + 10;
```

and use i instead of j, in the book member in the right expression. As you'll learn in Chapter 7, this error may cause a crash!

 When using the compound assignment operators, be careful first to write the op operator, and then the =. If you switch the characters, you inserted a bug most likely.

For example, if you write a =- 5; the value of a becomes -5. In some chapter later on, there will be an exercise which contains such an oversight. Watch out!

LOGICAL OPERATORS

The logical operators !, &&, and || are used to form logical expressions. The ! operator is *unary*, while && and || are both binary. The logical operators produce either **true** or **false**, just like the relational operators. The logical operators are left associative, so the compiler evaluates the operands from left to right.

The ! Operator

The ! *not operator* is applied on a single operand. If an expression `exp` has a non-zero value, then the value of `!exp` is `false`. Otherwise, it is `true`. For example:

```cpp
#include <iostream> // Example 4.4
int main()
{
        int a = 10;

        std::cout << !(a-20) << '\n';
        std::cout << !!a << ' ' << !!!a << ' ' << a << '\n';
        return 0;
}
```

Since the value of the expression a-20 is non-zero, the program outputs 0. If a were 20, the program would output 1. Since a is 10, the value of !a is 0. So, the expression !!a is equivalent to !0 and the expression !!!a equivalent to !1. The value of a does not change, so the program outputs: 1 0 10.

As we'll see in the next chapter, the ! operator is mostly used in `if` statements to test whether the value of an expression is true or false. For example:

- the statement if(!a) is equivalent to if(a == 0)
- the statement if(a) is equivalent to if(a != 0)

The && Operator

The `&&` operator performs the logical AND operation. The value of the expression is `true`, only if both operands are true. Otherwise, the result is `false`. For example, if we write: a = (1 < 2) **&&** (3 == 3); a becomes 1, since both operands are true. If we write: a = (1 < 2) && (3 == 3) && (4 > 6); a becomes 0, since the last operand is false.

 The `&&` operator performs "short-circuit" evaluation of its operands. That is, if an operand is false, the compiler stops evaluating the other operands and sets the value of the entire expression to `false`.

For example, in the following program b is not incremented, because the first operand (a < 2) is false.

```cpp
#include <iostream> // Example 4.5
int main()
{
        int a = 5, b = 8, c;

        c = (a < 2) && (++b > 3);
        std::cout << c << ' ' << b << '\n';
        return 0;
}
```

Therefore, the program outputs: 0 8. Short-circuiting is often used to prevent the evaluation of right-hand operands that would otherwise fail. For example, if we write:

```cpp
if(a != 0 && (b/a > 1))
```

we do not need to worry about a possible division by 0, because if a is 0, the first operand will have a false value, and therefore the second one will not be evaluated.

If you need to test multiple conditions and some conditions execute faster than others, it'd be better to put them first. The same applies for the || operator. For example:

```
if(a > 0 && (a*a*a - 20*a > 35))
```

The second, more expensive, operand will be evaluated only if the first one is true.

The || Operator

The || operator performs the logical OR operation. The value of the expression is true, if either of its operands is true. If both operands are false the result is false. For example, if we write: a = (1 < 2) || (5 > 7); a becomes 1, since the first operand is true. If we write: a = (3 != 3) || (5 > 7); a becomes 0, since all operands are false.

 Similar to the && operator, the || operator performs "short-circuit" evaluation of its operands. If an operand is true, the compiler stops evaluating the other operands and sets the value of the entire expression to true.

For example, in the following program b is not incremented, because the first operand (a > 2) is true.

```
#include <iostream> // Example 4.6
int main()
{
        int a = 5, b = 8, c;

        c = (a > 2) || (++b > 3);
        std::cout << c << ' ' << b << '\n';
        return 0;
}
```

Therefore, the program outputs: 1 8.

EXERCISES

C.4.2 What is the output of the following program?

```
#include <iostream>
int main()
{
        int a = -2, b = 2, c;

        c = ((a+b) == !b);
        a = -((a < c) || (--b == c));
std::cout << (!(a != -c) && (b+a >= c) && ((a+c)%2 || (-a+c-b))) << '\n';
        return 0;
}
```

`Answer:` Since a is `-2` and b is `2`, the value of the expression `(a+b)` is false. Since b is `2`, the value of `!b` is false. Therefore, c becomes `1`.

Since a is `-2` and c is `1`, the value of the expression `(a < c)` is true. So, the second operand is not evaluated and b is not decremented. Therefore, a becomes `-1`.

Since a is `-1` and c is `1`, the value of the expression `(a != -c)` is false. So, the value of `!(a != -c)` is true. The value of `(b+a >= c)` is `1`, because 2-1 >= 1. The value of `(a+c)%2` is `(-1+1)%2`, that is, false. The value of `(-a+c-b)` is `-(-1)+1-2 = 0`. Since both operands are false, the value of the third operand is false. Since the third operand is false, the value of the entire expression is false and the program outputs `0`.

C.4.3 Write a program that reads the water consumption in cubic metres and calculates the amount payable according to the following table.

CONSUMPTION (CM)	COST (CM)
[0–5]	0
(5–30]	1.2
> 30	1.5

For example, if the consumption is `35` cm the final cost is calculated as follows: `cost = (30-5)*1.2 + (35-30)*1.5.`

```cpp
#include <iostream>
int main()
{
        float cost, a;

        std::cout << "Enter water consumption: ";
        std::cin >> a;

        cost = (a > 5 && a <= 30)*(a-5)*1.2 + (a > 30)*((a-30)*1.5 + 25*1.2);
        std::cout << "Cost: " << cost << '\n';
        return 0;
}
```

`Comments:` If the consumption is between 5 and 30, the expression `(a > 5 && a <= 30)` is true, while the expression `(a > 30)` is false. If the consumption is greater than 30, the opposite happens. The cost is calculated for the part of the consumption over than 5. If the consumption is less than 5, both expressions are false, so `cost` becomes `0`.

Isn't it a complicated solution? Yes, indeed. However, there's no need to worry. In the next chapter, you'll see how the `if` statement makes easy to solve such problems.

THE COMMA OPERATOR

The comma (,) operator can be used to merge several expressions to form a single expression. It is used like this:

```cpp
exp1, exp2, exp3, ...
```

Because the comma operator is left associative, `exp1` is evaluated first, then `exp2`, then `exp3`, through the last expression. The type and the value of the entire expression are those of the last expression evaluated. For example, since the expressions are executed from left to right the following code outputs 30:

```
int b;
b = 10, b += 20, cout << b;
```

Consider the following program:

```
#include <iostream> // Example 4.7
int main()
{
        int a, b, c;

        a = (b = 30, b = b/8, ++b);
        std::cout << a << ' ' << b << '\n';
        c = (b != 4);
        if(a, b, c)
                std::cout << "One\n";
        return 0;
}
```

The first two expressions make b equal to 3. The expression `++b` first increments the value of b, then stores that new value into a. Therefore, the program outputs 4 4. Since b is 4, the condition is false and c becomes 0. Next, since the value of the entire expression is the value of c, and because c is 0, the `if` condition is false and the program displays nothing.

 Because the precedence of the comma operator is the lowest, the parentheses in an assignment are necessary.

For example, if we write: `a = b+3, b-20;` the value of a will be equal to `b+3`, because the = operator has higher precedence than comma. The expression `b-20` is evaluated, but its value is ignored, not assigned.

Because the use of the comma operator may produce more complex code and harder to evaluate, it is not often used. As we'll see in Chapter 6, it is mostly used in the `for` statement. For example:

```
int a, b;
for(a = 1, b = 2; b < 10; a++, b++)
```

The first expression first assigns 1 to a, then assigns 2 to b. The third expression first executes `a++`, then `b++`.

Note that the comma we use to separate variables in declarations, values in initialization lists, and function arguments is not the operator, but just separator.

THE `sizeof` OPERATOR

The `sizeof` operator is used to compute the number of bytes required to store the value of a particular type, variable, constant, or expression. The type of the result is `size_t`, which is defined in the `cstddef` file as well as in other header files as an alias of some unsigned integer type (e.g., `unsigned int`).

For example, the following program uses the `sizeof` operator to display how many bytes allocate in memory the variables of the program:

```cpp
#include <iostream> // Example 4.8
int main()
{
        char c;
        int i;
        double d;

        std::cout << sizeof(c) << ' ' << sizeof(i) << ' ' << sizeof(d) << '\n';
        return 0;
}
```

In my environment, the program displays: 1 4 8. Notice that if we declare another variable, e.g., int j, and write `sizeof(i+j)`, the program will display again 4, because the type of the expression is integer. However, if we write `sizeof(i+d)`, the program will display 8, because, as we learned in Chapter 2, the type of the expression is `double`.

Note that if the operand is a type (e.g., `int`) parentheses are required, but if it is a variable it is not necessary. However, if you are not using parentheses the result of an expression such as `sizeof i*j` is not clear. `sizeof` applies first and then the multiplication or the other way round? Because you'll learn always to use parentheses in `sizeof` expressions, as I'm doing to avoid problems, I won't give you the answer. If you insist to get the answer, consult the precedence table in Annex A. Nevertheless, parentheses may give the wrong impression that `sizeof` is a function. No, it is not a function, it is an operator.

The `sizeof` operator is particularly useful in writing portable code. For example, as we'll see in Chapter 7, in order to find the size of the memory that an array allocates, we write:

```cpp
int arr[100];
...
int i = sizeof(arr);
```

Thus, we calculate the memory size regardless of the system in which the program runs and the size of the `int` type. In the next chapters, we'll see its usefulness with other data types, such as structures.

The next one is a quite easy example to introduce you in the `if-else` statement. What does the following program output?

```cpp
#include <iostream> // Example 4.9
int main()
{
        if(sizeof(int) > -1)
                std::cout << "Yes\n";
        else
                std::cout << "No\n";
        return 0;
}
```

Who cares about the `if-else` statement? I deliberately put it there to mislead you. Although the obvious answer is `Yes`, the program outputs `No`. I just told you that the type of the `sizeof` result is unsigned, didn't I? Therefore, when the `if` condition is evaluated, `-1` is promoted to an unsigned value greater than 4 and the condition becomes false.

THE `enum` TYPE

The `enum` type is used to define an enumeration type, which is a set of named integer constant values. The names must be different from each other as well as with the names of the variables in the same scope, but values need not be different. Typically, it is declared as follows:

```
enum tag {enumeration_list};
```

The `tag` is an optional identifier that identifies the enumeration list. For example, the statement:

```
enum Day_Parts {MORNING, AFTERNOON, EVENING, NIGHT};
```

defines the `Day_Parts` enumeration type and the enumeration constants `MORNING`, `AFTERNOON`, `EVENING`, and `NIGHT`. The names of the constants are subject to C++ scope rules. For example, if an enumeration is declared inside a function, its constants won't be visible outside the function. We'll discuss scope rules in Chapter 11. An untagged enumeration is used when we want to have a set of constant integers and we are not interested in declaring variables of this type.

The value of the first constant is `0` by default; though, we can set specific values when declaring the enumeration. For example:

```
enum Day_Parts {MORNING=5, AFTERNOON, EVENING=10, NIGHT};
```

If a constant is not explicitly assigned a value, it is initialized to the value of the last initialized constant plus one. Therefore, the values of `MORNING`, `AFTERNOON`, `EVENING`, and `NIGHT` constants in the first example become 0, 1, 2, and 3, while in the second one become 5, 6, 10, and 11, respectively. Note that the values don't have to be unique. For example, we could make `AFTERNOON` equal to the value of `MORNING`.

Recall from Chapter 2 that we can use the `#define` directive and the `const` qualifier to declare constants. Their main difference with `enum`, is that the `enum` type groups the constants, in order to form a set of values. That is, when we need a set of values to characterize an entity (e.g., day), the `enum` type is more representative. And if such a set is to be passed to a function, it is better to pass an enumeration variable, than a plain integer. For example:

```
void test(Day_Parts d); instead of void test(int d);
```

The first prototype tells the reader that the passed value should belong within a set. Therefore, it becomes easier for the reader to read and verify the code. On the other hand, the second prototype does not provide any information about the passed value.

In order to declare enumeration variables of a named enumeration type, we write:

```
tag variable_list;
```

For example, with the statement: `Day_Parts d1, d2;`

d1 and d2 are declared as enumeration variables of the type `Day_Parts`. For those who know the `enum` type from C, note that it is not needed to add the word `enum` when declaring enumeration variables. In C++, the name of the enumeration defines a new type that can be used just like a basic type. Alternatively, we may declare variables when the type is defined. For example:

```
enum Day_Parts {MORNING, AFTERNOON, EVENING, NIGHT} d1, d2;
```

In this example, if the tag `Day_Parts` won't be used later to declare extra variables, it can be omitted. However, even if it won't be used, my preference is always to use an enumeration tag, in order to become easier for the reader to realize the purpose of the enumeration.

We can treat enumeration variables like integer variables, but not always, because they are not really integer variables. In particular, enumeration variables are implicitly converted to integers, but integers are not implicitly converted to enumeration types. For example, consider the following program:

```
#include <iostream> // Example 4.10
using std::cout;
using std::cin;

int main()
{
        int i, next_part;
        enum Day_Parts {MORNING=1, AFTERNOON, EVENING, NIGHT} dp;

        cout << "Enter day_part [1-4]: ";
        cin >> i;

        dp = static_cast<Day_Parts>(i); /* Cast to the enumeration type is
needed. */
        if(dp == NIGHT)
                next_part = MORNING;
        else
                next_part = dp+1;

        cout << "Next day part: " << next_part << '\n';
        return 0;
}
```

The program reads an integer, stores it into the enumeration variable d, and displays the number that corresponds to the next part of the day. Since an integer is not implicitly converted to an enumeration type, cast is needed. Notice that the compiler does not check whether the value stored in an enumeration variable is a valid value for the enumeration. You have to check its validity. If a value other than its constants is assigned, the compiler may issue a warning.

C++11 defines a second type of enumeration, called the *enumeration class*. One difference with the enumeration we saw is that the scope of the names in an enumeration class is local to the enumeration. Thus, we are allowed to use the same names in different enumerations. For example, with a simple enumeration it is wrong to write:

```
enum Day_Parts {MORNING, AFTERNOON, EVENING, NIGHT};
enum Work_Shift {NIGHT, MORNING}; /* Wrong, the names NIGHT and MORNING have
been declared in the same scope. */
```

But if we use an enumeration class, which is created as before by adding the word `class`, there is no problem. For example:

```
enum class Day_Parts {MORNING, AFTERNOON, EVENING, NIGHT};
enum class Work_Shift {NIGHT, MORNING}; /* Because the scope of the names is
local, there is no name conflict. */
```

Because the scope is local we must use the scope resolution operator :: to access the names. For example:

```
int i = MORNING; // Wrong, MORNING is not visible in this scope.
```

Also, the values of the enumeration constants are not converted implicitly to integers, as with simple enumeration. That is, it is wrong to write:

```
int i = Day_Parts::MORNING; /* Wrong, the implicit conversion to int is not allowed. */
```

we should make a cast. For example:

```
int i = static_cast<int>(Day_Parts::MORNING);
```

Disallowing the implicit conversion to an integer, it may be helpful to avoid the potential of a wrong action. For example, with simple enumeration we can make an invalid comparison:

```
if(dp == 10) // We've made a type error and compare to a non valid value.
```

though, the code compiles. If `dp` were an `enum` class this code won't compile.

In general, the need for a cast and the fact that the enumeration class defines its own scope (we'll discuss scopes in Chapter 11), thus we avoid the potential of name conflicts, makes the `enum` class a safer and better choice over the simple enumeration.

BITWISE OPERATORS

Bitwise operators are typically used to access the individual bits of an integer variable or constant. A bit value is either `0` or `1`. The evaluation of an expression that contains bit operators is done by applying them to the corresponding bits of the operators.

 When using bitwise operators, it is safer to apply them on `unsigned` variables. If you choose not to, make sure you account for the sign bit when performing your calculations.

Bitwise operators are particularly useful in several applications. For example, I've used them in communication protocols, data encryption algorithms, and in low-level applications that communicate with the hardware. I'll show you some examples later.

The & Operator

The `&` operator performs the Boolean AND operation on all bits of its two operands. If both corresponding bits are `1`, the result bit is `1`. Otherwise, the bit is set to `0`. For example, the result of `23 & 11` is `3` (I use 8 bits for simplicity):

```
        00010111 (23)
&       00001011 (11)
        -----------
        00000011 (3)
```

The & operator is often used to make zero a number of bits. For example, the statement: a = a & 15; sets to zero all but the four lower bits of a.

 Don't confuse the && and & operators. For example, if a=2 and b=4, the result of a && b is 1, while the result of a & b is 0.

The | Operator

The | operator performs the Boolean OR operation on all bits of its two operands. If both corresponding bits are 0, the result bit is 0. Otherwise, the bit is set to 1. For example, the result of 23 | 11 is 31:

```
        00010111 (23)
|       00001011 (11)
        ------------
        00011111 (31)
```

The | operator is often used to set to one a number of bits. For example, the statement: a = a | 15; sets to one the four lower bits of a.

 Don't confuse the || and | operators. For example, if a=2 and b=4, the result of a || b is 1, while the result of a | b is 6.

The ^ Operator

The ^ operator performs the Boolean XOR operation on all bits of its two operands. If the corresponding bits are different, the result bit is 1. Otherwise, the bit is set to 0. For example, the result of 23 ^ 11 is 28:

```
        00010111 (23)
^       00001011 (11)
        ------------
        00011100 (28)
```

The ^ operator is often used in data encryption applications. For example, the following program reads an integer that corresponds to the cipher key and another integer that will be encrypted with that key. The encryption is performed by applying the ^ operator on them. Then, the program uses once more the ^ operator to decrypt the encrypted result and print it on the screen.

```cpp
#include <iostream> // Example 4.11
using std::cout;
using std::cin;

int main()
{
    int num, key;

    cout << "Enter key: ";
    cin >> key;

    cout << "Enter number: ";
    cin >> num;
```

```
        num = num ^ key;
        cout << "Encrypted: " << num << '\n';

        num = num ^ key;
        cout << "Original: " << num << '\n';
        return 0;
}
```

Since (a ^ b) ^ b = a, the result of the decryption is the input number.

The ~ Operator

The ~ complement operator is unary and performs the Boolean NOT operation on all bits of its operand. In particular, it reverses the 1s to 0s and vice versa. For example, the result of ~23 in a 32-bit system is:

```
~ 00000000 00000000 00000000 00010111 (23) =
  11111111 11111111 11111111 11101000
```

Shift Operators

The shift operators shift the bits of an integer variable or constant left or right. The >> operator shifts the bits to the right, while the << operator shifts the bits to the left. Both operators take a right operand, which indicates how many places the bits will be shifted. If it is negative or it has a value equal to or greater than the number of the bits of the type of the left operand, the result is undefined. It is the programmer's responsibility to make sure that the right operand has a valid value. For example, if the int type has 32 bits and a is int, it is valid to write a << 31, but not a << 32 or a << -1.

The expression i >> n shifts the bits in i by n places to the right. If i is positive or its type is unsigned, then the n high-order bits inserted on the left are set to 0. If i is negative, it depends on the implementation whether 1s or 0s are added. For example, what would be the value of a in the following code?

```
unsigned int a, b = 23;
a = b >> 2;
```

Let's write the number in binary to explain the shifting operation. For simplicity, we'll use 8 bits. Since 23 is 00010111 in binary, the result of 00100111 >> 2 is 00001001, and that will be the value of a (i.e., 9). In particular, the two rightmost bits 1 and 1 of the original number are "shifted off" and two zero bits are entered in positions 7 and 8. Notice that the value of b remains 23.

 Since a bit position corresponds to a power of 2, shifting a positive integer n places to the right divides its value by 2^n.

The expression i << n shifts the bits in i by n places to the left. The n low-order bits inserted on the right are set to 0. For example, what would be the value of a in the following code?

```
unsigned int a, b = 23;
a = b << 3;
```

Since the number 23 is 00010111 in binary, the shifting result of 00010111 << 3 is 00010111**000**, and that will be the value of a. In particular, the bits of the original number are shifted three places to the left and three zero bits are added in positions 1, 2, and 3. Therefore, a becomes 184, while b remains 23.

 If no overflow occurs, shifting a positive number n places to the left multiplies its value by 2^n.

When you use the << operator to store the shifting result into a variable, make sure the type of the variable is large enough to hold the value. For example, what would be the value of a in the following code?

```
unsigned char a = 32;
a <<= 3; // Equivalent to a = a << 3;
```

The statement a <<= 3 shifts the value of a three places to the left and inserts three zero bits at the right. Therefore, the shifting result is 100000000. However, since a is declared as unsigned char, it can hold only the value of the eight low-order bits. Therefore, a becomes 0 and not 256, as you might expect. If it were declared as int, its value would be 256. Let's see another example:

```
char a = 4;
a <<= 5;
```

the value of a is shifted four places to the left and becomes 10000000. If the char type is signed, the leftmost bit is reserved for the sign and a becomes -128. If a were declared as unsigned char, its value would be 128.

Remember, it is safer to perform bitwise operations on unsigned types.

Now that you've learned about the << and >> operators, you may wonder how are they used with the cout and cin objects? The answer is that when used like this they do not operate as shift operators. As we'll learn in Chapter 18, the ostream class overloads them and changes their behaviour. As far as the compiler is concerned, the way they are used is clear from the context.

ALTERNATIVE REPRESENTATIONS

The language provides a set of reserved words for the alternative representation of the following operators:

&&	&=	&	|	~	!	!=	||	|=	^	^=
and	and_eq	bitand	bitor	compl	not	not_eq	or	or_eq	xor	xor_eq

For example, the expressions:

```
bool a = (b && c) || !d;
int a = (b & c) | ~d;
```

are equivalent to:

```
bool a = (b and c) or not d;
int a = (b bitand c) bitor compl d;
```

My preference is to use the operators.

Although we'll discuss about the `if` statement in the next chapter, we'll use it in some of the following programs so that you can better understand the use of the operators.

EXERCISES

C.4.4 Write a program that reads an integer and displays a message to indicate whether it is even or odd. Use the `&` operator.

```
#include <iostream>
using std::cout;
using std::cin;

int main()
{
        int num;

        cout << "Enter number: ";
        cin >> num;

        if((num & 1) == 1) // We could also write if(num & 1)
                cout << "The number " << num << " is odd\n";
        else
                cout << "The number " << num << " is even\n";
        return 0;
}
```

`Comments:` To determine whether a number is even or odd we check its last digit. If it is `0`, the number is even; otherwise, it is odd. Suppose that the variable `num` is coded in binary as:

```
xxxxxxxx xxxxxxxx xxxxxxxx xxxxxxxx
```

where each `'x'` represents a bit of either `0` or `1`. Then, the result of `num & 1` is:

```
        xxxxxxxx xxxxxxxx xxxxxxxx xxxxxxxx
&       00000000 00000000 00000000 00000001
        ------------------------------------------------------------
        00000000 00000000 00000000 0000000x
```

Therefore, the result is equal to the value of the last bit. If it is `1`, the condition in the `if` statement is true and the program displays a message that the number is odd. If it is `0`, the condition is false and the program displays a message that the number is even.

    Notice that this solution is based on the assumption we've made in Chapter 2 that the system uses the most common method to represent negative numbers, that is, the two's complement. For a more generic and portable solution, you should use the `%` operator.

C.4.5 What is the output of the following program?

```cpp
#include <iostream>
using std::cout;

int main()
{
        unsigned int i = ~(~0 << 3);

        if(i >> 3)
                cout << "One\n";
        else
                cout << "Two\n";

        if((i << 2) == 28)
                cout << "One\n";
        else
                cout << "Two\n";

        cout << i << '\n';
        return 0;
}
```

Answer: According to the precedence table in Annex A, the ~ operator has higher precedence than the << operator; therefore, the expression ~0 is evaluated first, and then the result is shifted three places to the left. In a 32-bit system, the result of ~0 is the number with all 32 bits set to 1s. Therefore, the value of (~0 << 3) is the number: 11111111 11111111 11111111 11111000

Since the ~ operator is applied again, the value assigned to i is: 00000000 00000000 00000000 00000111, that is, 7.

Since the value of the expression (i >> 3) is 0, the first if statement displays Two. Notice that the if statement does not change the value of i to 0; it just tests whether i shifted three places to the right is 0 or not. The second if statement tests whether the value of (i << 2) is 28. Since it is true, the program displays One. As previously, i does not change, so the program displays 7.

C.4.6 Applications that get data from the hardware often need to retrieve the values of certain bits. For example, write a program that reads an integer and a bit position and displays the value of the respective bit. Assume that the user enters a bit position within [1, 32].

```cpp
#include <iostream>
using std::cout;
using std::cin;

int main()
{
        unsigned int num, pos;

        cout << "Enter number: ";
        cin >> num;

        cout << "Enter bit position [1-32]: ";
        cin >> pos;

        cout << "bit" << pos << " is " << ((num >> (pos-1)) & 1) << '\n';
        return 0;
}
```

C.4.7 Bitwise operators are often used in data coding in network communications. For example, some specific bits in the header of a Transport Control Protocol (TCP) packet are coded as follows:

bit8	bit7	bit6	bit5	bit4	bit3	bit2	bit1
		URG	ACK			SYN	FIN

FIN (bit1): If it is 1, it indicates the release of the TCP connection.

SYN (bit2): If it is 1, it indicates the establishment of the TCP connection. That's the famous bit responsible for Denial-of-Service (DoS) flooding attacks, but this is another story ...

ACK (bit5): If it is 1, it indicates the acknowledgement of data reception.

URG (bit6): If it is 1, it indicates the transfer of urgent data.

Write a program that reads the values of URG, ACK, SYN, and FIN bits and encodes this information in a program variable. Then, the program should decode the value of this variable and display the values of the respective bits.

```cpp
#include <iostream>
using std::cout;
using std::cin;

int main()
{
        unsigned int temp, urg, ack, syn, fin;

        cout << "Enter FIN bit: ";
        cin >> fin;

        cout << "Enter SYN bit: ";
        cin >> syn;

        cout << "Enter ACK bit: ";
        cin >> ack;

        cout << "Enter URG bit: ";
        cin >> urg;

        temp = fin + (syn << 1) + (ack << 4) + (urg << 5);
        cout << "\nEncoding: "  << temp << '\n';

        fin = temp & 1;
        syn = (temp >> 1) & 1;
        ack = (temp >> 4) & 1;
        urg = (temp >> 5) & 1;
        cout << "FIN:" << fin << " SYN:" << syn << " ACK:" << ack << " URG:"
<< urg << '\n';
        return 0;
}
```

C.4.8 Bitwise operators are often used in applications that communicate with the hardware. For example, a common configuration method used in asynchronous serial communication is eight-bit characters, with one *start_bit*, one *stop_bit*, and one *parity_bit*. The transmission of data is signalled with the *start_bit* set to 0 to inform the receiver for arrival of data. The *stop_bit* indicates the end of the transmission. For example, the data bits 10100 are encoded as follows:

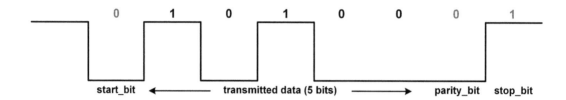

The sender may optionally transmit a *parity_bit*, which is used by the receiver to detect transmission errors. There are two variants of parity: even parity and odd parity. In even parity, the value of the *parity_bit* is calculated in a way that the total number of 1s in data plus the parity bit is even. In case of odd parity, the total number should be odd. In our example, we choose even parity. Therefore, since the number of 1s in data is two, that is, even, the *parity_bit* is set to 0.

Write a program that simulates the sender. The program should read the values of five data bits and use even parity to generate a 8-bit value.

```cpp
#include <iostream>
using std::cout;
using std::cin;

int main()
{
        unsigned char data, ones, bit1, bit2, bit3, bit4, bit5, parity_bit;

        ones = 0;

        cout << "Enter bit1: ";
        cin >> bit1;
        if(bit1 == 1)
                ones++;

        cout << "Enter bit2: ";
        cin >> bit2;
        if(bit2 == 1)
                ones++;

        cout << "Enter bit3: ";
        cin >> bit3;
        if(bit3 == 1)
                ones++;

        cout << "Enter bit4: ";
        cin >> bit4;
        if(bit4 == 1)
                ones++;
```

```cpp
        cout << "Enter bit5: ";
        cin >> bit5;
        if(bit5 == 1)
                ones++;

        if(ones & 1) // It means that the number of 1s is odd.
                parity_bit = 1;
        else
                parity_bit = 0;

        data = (bit1 << 6) + (bit2 << 5) + (bit3 << 4) + (bit4 << 3) + (bit5
<< 2) + (parity_bit << 1) + 1; // The last 1 represents the stop_bit.
        cout << (int)data << '\n'; /* The type cast is used to output the
integer value. */
        return 0;
}
```

OPERATOR PRECEDENCE

As shown in Annex A, each operator has a *precedence* that determines the order in which operators are evaluated. In an expression with several operators, the operators with higher precedence are evaluated first. For example, since the * operator has higher precedence than the + and - operators, the result of: 10-2*4+1 is 3.

When operators of equal precedence appear in the same expression, the operators are evaluated according to their *associativity*. For example, since the * and / operators have the same precedence and are *left associative*, the result of: 6/2*4/3 is 4, because the division 6/2 = 3 is executed first, then the multiplication 3*4 = 12, and last the division 12/3 = 4. In another example, do the following statements assign the same value to a?

```cpp
float a, b = 4, c = 3;
a = 2/3*b*c;
a = b*c*2/3;
```

Since the result of the division 2/3 is 0, the first statement assigns 0 to a. Since multiplications are performed first and the numerator is `float`, the second statement assigns 8 to a.

In another example, can you tell me what does the following program output? Consult Annex A.

```cpp
#include <iostream> // Example 4.12
int main()
{
        int a = 2, b = 6, c = 9;

        c = (a < c > b);

        a = b = c = c+5;
        std::cout << (a == b == c) << '\n';

        a -= b += c--;
        std::cout << a << ' ' << b << ' ' << c << '\n';
        return 0;
}
```

According to Annex A, the < and > operators have the same precedence and are left associative. Therefore, the expression (a < c) is first evaluated. Since a is 2 and c is 9, its value is true. So, the expression is equivalent to 1 > b, which is false because b is 6. Therefore, c becomes 0.

Next, all variables become equal to 5. Since the == operator is left associative, the expression a == b is first evaluated. Since a equals b, its value is true. Therefore, the expression a == b == c is equivalent to 1 == c. Since c is 5, this expression evaluates to false and the program outputs 0. If c were 1, the program would output 1. Note that the whole expression is enclosed in parentheses, because the << operator has higher precedence than the ==.

The compound operators are executed from right to left. Therefore, the expression is equivalent to a = a-(b += c--);. By itself, the expression (b += c--) is equivalent to b = b+(c--). Therefore, b = b+5 = 5+5 = 10, while c is decremented and becomes 4. As a result, the expression is equivalent to a = a-10 = 5-10 = -5 and the program outputs: -5 10 4.

Some operators have precedence other than the expected one or the one we'd like to have. For example, suppose that we want to shift a variable two places to the left and add 3. It'd be plausible to write: a = b << 2 + 3; assuming that the evaluation order is from left to right. Unfortunately, that would be wrong; the addition is performed first, because the + operator has higher precedence. To get the desired result, the expression b << 2 must be enclosed in parentheses. In another example:

```
if(a & 8 == 0)
        cout << "One\n";
```

Since the == operator has higher precedence than the & operator, the expression 8 == 0 is first evaluated, which is false, and then the value of a & 0, which is false for any value of a. As a result, this if condition is always false. To get the desired result the expression a & 8 must be enclosed in parentheses.

Note that you do not need to memorize the precedence and associativity of all the operators. If you are not certain about the evaluation order, use parentheses. In fact, the use of parentheses, even when it is not necessary to do so, increases the readability of code and clarifies the way that expressions are evaluated. For example, it is clearer to write: a = b-(c/d)+d; instead of a = b-c/d+d;

UNSOLVED EXERCISES

Don't use the if statement in any of the following exercises.

U.4.1 Write a program that reads two integers and displays the smaller.

U.4.2 Suppose that a customer in a store buys some things. If the total cost is less than $100, no discount is due, otherwise a 5% is offered. Write a program that reads the total cost and displays the amount to be paid.

U.4.3 Write a program that reads the minimum score required to pass the exams, the grades of three students, and displays how many of them succeeded. A grade to be valid should be <= 10.

U.4.4 Continue the previous exercise and find the average grade of those who passed the exams. Assume that one student succeeded, at least.

U.4.5 Write a program that reads two integers, it stores them into two variables, and uses the ^ operator and the equations (x^y)^x = y and (x^y)^y = x to swap their values. Use only two variables.

U.4.6 Write a program that reads an integer, it swaps the two quads of its binary digits and displays the new number. For example, if the user enters 10 (00001010_2), the program should display 160 (10100000_2). Assume that the user enters a number within [0, 255].

U.4.7 What is the output of the following program?

```
#include <iostream>
int main()
{
        unsigned char ch = 3;

        ch = ((ch&1) << 7) | ((ch&2) << 5) | ((ch&4) << 3) | ((ch&8) << 1) |
((ch&16) >> 1) | ((ch&32) >> 3) | ((ch&64) >> 5) | ((ch&128) >> 7);
        std::cout << (int)ch << '\n';
        return 0;
}
```

U.4.8 Write a program that reads an integer and displays the sum of the digits in the positions 2, 4, 6, and 8. For example, if the user enters 170 (binary: 10101010), the program should display 4. Use only one variable.

U.4.9 Write a program that reads a positive integer and another integer which represents a number of bytes (e.g., n). The program should rotate the input number n bytes to the right and display the new value. Assume that the size of the int type is 32 bits and the user enters a valid value for n within [1, 3]. For example, if the user enters 553799974 (binary: 00100001|00000010|01010001|00100110) and 1, the program should display: 639697489 (binary: 00100110|00100001|00000010|01010001).

U.4.10 Write a program that reads an integer in [0, 255] and the number of shifting bits (e.g., n). The program should display the sum of:

a. Shifting the input number n places to the left and add the "shifted-off" bits to the right of the number.

b. Shifting the input number n places to the right and add the "shifted-off" bits to the left of the number.

For example, if the user enters 42 (binary: 00101010) and 3, the program should display the sum of:

00101010 << 3 = 01010**001** = 81 (the shifted-off bits are: 001) and: 00101**010** >> 3 = **010**00101 = 69 (the shifted-off bits are: 010). The sum is 150.

U.4.11 Write a program that reads an integer, the positions of two bits and displays the value of the bits between them. The program should find the size of the int type; don't assume that it is 32 bits. For example, if the user enters 176 (binary: 10110000) and the values 6 and 4, the program should display the value of the bits between the positions 6 and 4, that is, the decimal value of the bits 110, which is 6.

U.4.12 Write a program that reads a positive integer and rounds it up to the next highest power of 2. For example, if the user enters 35, the program should display 64, since 35 < 64 = 2^6. If the user enters 16, the program should display 16.

Program Control

5

Up to this point we've seen that program's statements are executed from top to bottom, in the order that they appear inside the source code. However, in real programming, certain statements should be executed only if specific conditions are met. This chapter will teach you how to use the `if` and `switch` selection statements to control the flow of your program and make it select a particular execution path from a set of alternatives. It also introduces the conditional operator `?:`, which can be used to form conditional expressions.

THE `if` STATEMENT

The `if` statement controls program flow based on whether a condition evaluates to true or false. The simplest form of the `if` statement is:

```
if(condition)
{
        ... // block of statements
}
```

If the value of the `condition` is true, the block of statements between the braces will be executed. For example:

```
int x = -6;
if(x != 0)
{
        cout << "Yes\n";
}
```

Since x is not 0, the `if` condition is true and the code displays Yes.

 `if(x)` is equivalent to `if(x != 0)`

If the value of the `condition` is false, the block of statements won't be executed. For example, the following code displays nothing:

```
int x = -6;
if(x == 0)
{
        cout << "Yes\n";
}
```

DOI: 10.1201/9781003230076-5

if(!x) is equivalent to if(x == 0)

The position of the braces, not only in case of if, but also in the loop statements of Chapter 6, is a matter of personal preference. For example, many programmers prefer to add the { at the end of the statement:

```cpp
if (x == 0) {
        cout << "Yes\n";
}
```

The reason I don't prefer this style is because the left brace is not clearly shown. My preference is to put each brace in a separate line, so that someone who reads the code can clearly and quickly match them. You may choose the style you like more. However, the common practice, and this is what I strongly recommend, is to indent the inner statements in order to make clearer their grouping and easier to read the code. I use the same style for the loop statements in Chapter 6.

If the block of statements consists of a single statement, the braces can be omitted. For example, we can write the previous code like this:

```cpp
if (x == 0)
        cout << "Yes\n";
```

In general, the braces are used to group declarations and statements into a compound statement, or block, which is treated by the compiler as a single statement. As we'll see in Chapter 6, compound statements are also very common in loops.

Common Errors

A common error is to add a semicolon (;) at the end of the if statement, as we usually do with the most statements. The semicolon is handled as a statement that does nothing, that is, a *null statement*, and the compiler terminates the if. For example, in the following code:

```cpp
int x = 10;
if (x < 0);
        cout << "Yes\n";
```

the ; terminates the if statement, so the cout statement is out of the if. Therefore, this code outputs Yes regardless of the value of x.

Another popular error is to confuse the == equality operator with the = assignment operator. Remember from Chapter 4 that the == operator checks whether two expressions have the same value, while the = operator assigns a value to a variable. Also remember, that the assignment of a non-zero value to a variable corresponds to a true expression, while the assignment of zero value corresponds to a false expression. For example, the following code:

```cpp
int x = 10;
if (x = 30)
        cout << "Yes\n";
```

does not check if x is 30, but makes x equal to 30. Thus, the condition is true and the code outputs Yes. Most probably, the compiler will display a message to warn you about the potential error. In a similar way, this code:

```
int x = 0;
if(x = 0)
        cout << "Yes\n";
```

displays nothing since the assignment of 0 into x makes the condition false.

Although they are not protected when two variables are compared, some programmers prefer to write the constant first when a variable is compared against a constant. For example:

```
if(-10 == x) // Instead of if(x == -10)
```

The reason they prefer this syntax is that if they forget one =, the compiler would display an error message for illegal action since it is not allowed to assign a value to a constant. Personally, I prefer to forget one = and insert a bug, than using this style. After all, bugs are inserted to make the programmer happy when finding them.

Also, when using the == operator don't forget that floating-point comparisons may produce unexpected results due to potential rounding errors. Revisit the example C.2.1.

Another error is to write in reverse order the characters of the != operator in a comparison condition. For example, tell me what does the following program display?

```
#include <iostream> // Example 5.1.
int main()
{
        int i = 20;

        if(i =! 5) // Instead of !=
                std::cout << "One\n";
        else
                std::cout << "Two\n";
        std::cout << i << '\n';
        return 0;
}
```

Because the ! operator is applied to the constant value 5, i becomes 0, so the condition becomes false. Therefore, the program outputs Two and 0.

Another common error is to forget the braces when we want to execute multiple statements (e.g., if you are coming from another language that uses indention to group statements). For example:

```
if(i < 0)
        i = -i;
        cout << "Negative\n";
```

We would like the message to appear only if i is negative. However, as we wrote it, the message always appears regardless of the value of i. The right thing to do is to use braces and place the cout statement inside. That is:

```
if(i < 0)
{
        i = -i;
        cout << "Negative\n";
}
```

To avoid such bugs, which can be really hard to find, some recommend always using braces (as well as in loops) regardless of whether the statements are one or many.

As we said, if we want to check that some value is true we can write `if(i)`. Some may suggest writing `if(i == true)`. No, it is dangerous. For example, see the following code:

```cpp
int i = 20;
if(i == true) // Instead of if(i)
        cout << "One\n";
else
        cout << "Two\n";
```

If `i` is not `bool`, as it happens in this example, `true` is converted to the type of `i` before applying `==`. So it is as if we've written `if(i == 1)`, which is not the desired comparison and the code displays `Two`. In general, do not use `true` and `false` as operands in comparisons, because an error can easily occur if the comparison is made with a non `bool` variable.

THE `if-else` STATEMENT

As we saw in the previous example, an `if` statement may have an `else` clause:

```cpp
if(condition)
{
        ... // block of statements A
}
else
{
        ... // block of statements B
}
```

If the `condition` is true, the first block of statements is executed; otherwise, the second one. For example:

```cpp
int i = 10, j = -10;
if(i+j)
{
        cout << "One\n";
}
else
{
        cout << "Two\n";
}
```

Since the sum is `0`, the condition is false and the code displays `Two`. Since both blocks consist of a single statement, we could omit the braces and write:

```cpp
if(i+j)
        cout << "One\n";
else
        cout << "Two\n";
```

As in the case of `if`, a common error is to add the ; at the end of `else`. For example:

```
int i = 20, j = 10, max;
if(i > j)
        max = i;
else; // Be careful, don't add ;
        max = j;
cout << max;
```

Initially, `max` becomes 20, but then, because the ; terminates the execution of `else`, it becomes 10. Thus, the code displays 10.

Note that we can declare a variable within the condition. For example:

```
if(int a = f()) /* Declaration of a. f() is assumed to return an integer
value. If a is not zero, the condition is true. */
{
        ...
}
```

The scope of a extends to the end of the `if` statement. Then, as we'll see in Chapter 11, a ceases to exist. If there is an `else` branch, its scope extends to it as well. The common practice is to declare a before the `if` statement. However, some programmers prefer to make the declaration inside the condition, so that the code is more compact and the scope of the variable is limited to the block that it is used.

C++17 provides a new version which allows us to init the variable inside `if` and then test for a condition. The general syntax is:

```
if(init; condition)
```

For example, we can write:

```
int f(){return 10;}
if(int a = f(); a > 3)
        cout << "One\n";
else
        cout << "Two\n";
cout << a; // Error, a is out of scope.
```

As we'll learn in Chapter 11, `f()` is called, it returns the value 10, which is assigned to a. Since a is greater than 3, the code outputs `One`. If we use the ordinary syntax we'd write the same code as follows:

```
int a = f();
if(a > 3)
        cout << "One\n";
else
        cout << "Two\n";
cout << a; // OK, a is in scope.
```

The difference of the two `if` versions has to do with the scope of a. In the first version its scope is limited in the `if-else` block, which means that since a ceases to exist we can use the same name a next in the code to declare another variable. On the contrary, in the second version its scope continues after the block. The C++17 syntax may be useful when we want to test for a condition and keep the variable scope limited in the `if` statement, as we can do with the `for` statement (we'll see it in Chapter 6).

NESTED `if` STATEMENTS

An `if` statement may contain other `if` and `else` statements, which in turn may contain others, and so on. For example, what is the output of the following program?

```cpp
#include <iostream> // Example 5.2
int main()
{
        int a = -1, b = 0, c = 1;

        if(a < b && b < c)
        {
                if(!b)
                {
                        if(-a == c)
                                std::cout << "One\n";
                        else
                                std::cout << "Two\n";
                }
        }
        else
                std::cout << "Three\n";
        return 0;
}
```

Since the condition in the first `if` is true, the nested `if` is executed. Since b is 0, the condition is true and the next nested `if` is executed. Since the condition is true, the program displays One.

Because the `else` part is optional, an ambiguity may arise when an `else` is omitted from a nested `if` sequence (*dangling else*). To match `if` and `else` statements, the rule is that an `else` is associated with the closest unmatched `if` inside the same group of statements. For example, apply this rule in the following program and find the output:

```cpp
#include <iostream> // Example 5.3
int main()
{
        int a = 10;

        if(a != 10)
                if(a < 30)
                        std::cout << "1\n";
        else
                std::cout << "2\n";
        else
                std::cout << "3\n";
        return 0;
}
```

According to this rule, the first `else` is associated with the nearest `if`, which belongs in the same group of statements. This is the second `if`. The second `else` is associated with the first `if`. Therefore, since the first `if` condition is false the program outputs 3.

Note that I intentionally used this alignment to mislead you into thinking that the first `else` is related to the first `if`. By aligning each `else` statement with the matching `if`, indenting the statements, and adding braces even if you don't have to, the program becomes easier to read. For example, see how much easier is to read and control the code when aligning each `if` with the matching `else`:

```cpp
#include <iostream> // Example 5.4
int main()
{
        int a = 10;

        if(a != 10)
        {
                if(a < 30)
                        std::cout << "1\n";
                else
                        std::cout << "2\n";
        }
        else
                std::cout << "3\n";
        return 0;
}
```

Although the braces of the first `if` are not necessary, their use makes the code much clearer. To test a series of conditions, the typical choice is to use the following syntax:

```cpp
if(condition_A)
{
        ... // block of statements A
}
else if(condition_B)
{
        ... // block of statements B
}
.
.
.
else
{
        ... // block of statements N
}
... // next program statements.
```

There can be any number of `else if` clauses between the first `if` and the last `else`. The conditions are evaluated in order starting from the top. Once a true condition is found, the corresponding block of statements is executed and the remaining `else if` statements are ignored. The program continues with the execution of the next statement after the last `else`. For example, if `condition_A` is true, the first block of statements is executed. If it is false, `condition_B` is checked and so on. Note that the last `else` is optional. If it exists and all conditions are false, its block of statements will be executed. For example, the following program reads two integers and displays the result of their comparison:

```cpp
#include <iostream> // Example 5.5
using std::cout;
using std::cin;
int main()
{
        int i, j;

        cout << "Enter numbers: ";
        cin >> i >> j;
```

```
    if(i < j)
            cout << i << " < " << j << '\n';
    else if(i > j)
            cout << i << " > " << j << '\n';
    else
            cout << i << " = " << j << '\n';
    return 0;
}
```

As we said, the last `else` is optional. If it is missing and all conditions are false no action takes place; the program continues with the execution of the next statement after the last `else if`. For example, if we delete the last `else`, and the user inserts two same values, the program continues with the execution of the `return` statement and displays nothing. If you want to optimize the performance, that is, to minimize the number of the conditions being checked before the matching condition is met, an easy optimization is to put the conditions in frequency order, from the most likely to happen to least likely.

EXERCISES

C.5.1 Write a program that reads two floats (e.g., a and b) and displays the solution of the equation a*x + b = 0, if any.

```
#include <iostream>
using namespace std;

int main()
{
        double a, b;

        cout << "Enter numbers: ";
        cin >> a >> b;

        if(a == 0)
        {
                if(b == 0)
                        cout << "Infinite solutions\n";
                else
                        cout << "No solution\n";
        }
        else
                cout << "The solution is " << fixed << -b/a << '\n';
        return 0;
}
```

C.5.2 What is the output of the following program?

```
#include <iostream>
int main()
{
        int i = -3, j = 2, k = 3, m = 0;

        if(i = -1)
                m++;
```

```
        if(j = 4)
                m++;
        if(k = 5)
                m++;
        if(k = 0)
                m++;
        if(i < m < k)
                m++;
        std::cout << m << '\n';
        return 0;
}
```

Answer: This is another example of how the wrong use of the = operator instead of the == operator can produce unexpected results. In particular, the first four if conditions don't test the variables for equality, but the variables are assigned with the respective values instead. As a result, i becomes -1, j becomes 4, while k first becomes 5, and then 0. Since non-zero values are assigned to the first three if conditions they are true, while the fourth is false. Therefore, m becomes 3.

According to the precedence rules the < operator is left associative. Since i is -1 and m is 3, the expression i < m is true. Then, the expression 1 < k is evaluated, which is false, because k is 0. As a result, the program displays 3. Remember, when we want to check if the value of a variable is within an interval we use the && operator, that is, if(i < m && m < k).

C.5.3 To change the PIN code of a mobile phone, the user is asked to enter the current PIN code and the device compares that code with the one stored in the SIM card. If they are the same, the user is asked to enter the new PIN code twice for verification, and if the same number is entered twice, it is stored in the SIM card. Write a program that simulates this process. Assume that the current code stored in SIM is 1234.

```
#include <iostream>
using std::cout;
using std::cin;

int main()
{
        int tmp, new_code;

        cout << "Enter code: ";
        cin >> tmp;

        if(tmp == 1234)
        {
                cout << "Enter new code: ";
                cin >> tmp;

                cout << "Enter new code once more: ";
                cin >> new_code;

                if(new_code == tmp)
                        cout << "New code is stored\n";
                else
                        cout << "Different codes are entered\n";
        }
        else
                cout << "Wrong code\n";
        return 0;
}
```

C.5.4 Write a program that reads a man's height (in metres) and weight (in kilograms) and calculates his body mass index (*BMI*) using the formula bmi = weight/height^2. The program should display the BMI and a corresponding message according to the following table, as well as the lower and upper limit of the normal weight for the given height.

MASS INDEX	RESULT
BMI < 20	Lower than normal weight
$20 \leq$ BMI ≤ 25	Normal weight
$25 <$ BMI ≤ 30	Overweight
$30 <$ BMI ≤ 40	Obese
$40 <$ BMI	Extremely obese

```
#include <iostream>
using std::cout;
using std::cin;

int main()
{
        float bmi, height, weight;

        cout << "Enter height (in meters): ";
        cin >> height;

        cout << "Enter weight (in kgrs): ";
        cin >> weight;

        bmi = weight/(height*height);
        cout << "BMI:" << bmi << '\n';

        if(bmi < 20)
                cout << "Under normal weight\n";
        else if(bmi <= 25) /* Since the previous if checks values up to 20,
this statement is equivalent to: else if(bmi >= 20 && bmi <= 25). */
                cout << "Normal weight\n";
        else if(bmi <= 30)
                cout << "Overweight\n";
        else if(bmi <= 40)
                cout << "Obese\n";
        else
                cout << "Serious obesity\n";

        cout << "According to your height the bounds of normal weight are " <<
20*height*height << " and " << 25*height*height << '\n'; /* According to the
table, the BMI limits for normal weight is 20 και 25, respectively. */
        return 0;
}
```

C.5.5 Write a program that reads the prices of four products and displays the highest one.

```
#include <iostream>
int main()
{
        double i, j, k, m, max;

        std::cout << "Enter prices: ";
        std::cin >> i >> j >> k >> m;
```

```
        if(i > j)
                max = i;
        else
                max = j;

        if(k > max)
                max = k;
        if(m > max)
                max = m;

        std::cout << "Max: " << max;
        return 0;
}
```

Comments: To display the lowest price we change the > to <.

C.5.6 A water supply company charges the water consumption, as follows:

a. Fixed amount of $10.
b. For the first 30 cubic metres, $0.6/m³.
c. For the next 20 cubic metres, $0.8/m³.
d. For the next 10 cubic metres, $1.1/m³.
e. For every additional metre, $1.2/m³.

Write a program that reads the water consumption in cubic metres and displays the total cost. For example, if the consumption is 55 cm, the final cost is calculated as follows: cost = 10 + 30*0.6 + 20*0.8 + 5*1.1.

```
#include <iostream>
using std::cout;
using std::cin;

int main()
{
        float mtrs, cost;

        cout << "Enter meters: ";
        cin >> mtrs;

        /* I don't do the fixed multiplications, to show in detail the method
of the cost calculation. */
        if(mtrs <= 30)
                cost = 0.6*mtrs;
        else if(mtrs <= 50)
                cost = 0.6*30 + 0.8*(mtrs-30);
        else if(mtrs <= 60)
                cost = 0.6*30 + 0.8*20 + 1.1*(mtrs-50);
        else
                cost = 0.6*30 + 0.8*20 + 1.1*10 + (mtrs-60)*1.2;

        cost += 10;
        cout << "Cost: " << cost << '\n';
        return 0;
}
```

C.5.7 Write a program that reads the grades of three students and displays them in ascending order.

```cpp
#include <iostream>
using std::cout;
using std::cin;

int main()
{
        float i, j, k;

        cout << "Enter grades: ";
        cin >> i >> j >> k;

        if(i <= j && i <= k)
        {
                cout << i << ' ';
                if(j < k)
                        cout << j << ' ' << k << '\n';
                else
                        cout << k << ' ' << j << '\n';
        }
        else if(j < i && j < k)
        {
                cout << j << ' ';
                if(i < k)
                        cout << i << ' ' << k << '\n';
                else
                        cout << k << ' ' << i << '\n';
        }
        else
        {
                cout << k << ' ';
                if(j < i)
                        cout << j << ' ' << i << '\n';
                else
                        cout << i << ' ' << j << '\n';
        }
        return 0;
}
```

Comments: At first, we compare each grade with the other two, in order to find and display the lowest. Next, we compare the two remaining grades and display them in ascending order.

C.5.8 The 13-digit International Standard Book Number (ISBN) is a unique code that identifies a book commercially. The last digit is a check digit used to detect errors in the previous 12 digits. To calculate its value, each digit of the first 12 digits is alternately multiplied, from left to right, by 1 or 3. The products are summed up and divided by 10. The check digit is the remainder of the division subtracted from 10. If it is 10, it becomes 0. For example, assume that the first 12 digits are: 978960931961.

a. $(9*1 + 7*3 + 8*1 + 9*3 + 6*1 + 0*3 + 9*1 + 3*3 + 1*1 + 9*3 + 6*1 + 1*3) = 126$
b. check_digit $= 10 - (126\% \ 10) = 10 - 6 = 4$

Write a program that reads a 13-digit ISBN code and checks the last digit to verify if it is valid or not.

```cpp
#include <iostream>
using std::cout;
using std::cin;
```

```
int main()
{
        int dig1, dig2, dig3, dig4, dig5, dig6, dig7, dig8, dig9, dig10,
dig11, dig12, dig13, chk_dig, sum;

        cout << "Enter ISBN's digits: ";
        cin >> dig1 >> dig2 >> dig3 >> dig4 >> dig5 >> dig6 >> dig7 >> dig8 >>
dig9 >> dig10 >> dig11 >> dig12 >> dig13; /* Since a 13-digit number exceeds
the size of the int type, we use a variable for each digit. */
        sum = dig1 + dig2*3 + dig3 + dig4*3 + dig5 + dig6*3 + dig7 + dig8*3 +
dig9 + dig10*3 + dig11 + dig12*3;
        chk_dig = 10 - (sum%10);
        if(chk_dig == 10)
                chk_dig = 0;

        if(chk_dig == dig13)
                cout << "Valid ISBN\n";
        else
                cout << "Invalid ISBN\n";
        return 0;
}
```

C.5.9 Suppose that two PCs reside in the same IP network. Write a program that reads their IP addresses (version 4) and displays if they are configured correctly in order to communicate. The user must enter each IP address in the x.x.x.x form, where each x is an integer within [0, 255]. The value of the first octet of an IP address defines its class, as follows:

 a. Class A: [0, 127]
 b. Class B: [128, 191]
 c. Class C: [192, 223]

If the two IP addresses indicate different classes, the PCs cannot communicate. If they belong in the same class, we compare their network octet(s). The octet(s) to be compared are defined according to their class, as follows:

 a. Class A: first octet
 b. Class B: first two octets
 c. Class C: first three octets

If they are the same the PCs may communicate. For example, the PCs with IP addresses 192.168.1.1 and 192.168.1.2 may communicate, because they belong to the same class C and the first three octets that specify the network, that is, 192.168.1, are the same. For your information, the method we just described is referred to as classful addressing. For the more efficient management of the IP addresses the classless addressing was later introduced.

```
#include <iostream>
using std::cout;
using std::cin;

int main()
{
        char ch;
        int a1, a2, a3, a4, b1, b2, b3, b4;
```

```
        cout << "Enter first IP address: ";
        cin >> a1 >> ch >> a2 >> ch >> a3 >> ch >> a4;

        cout << "Enter second IP address: ";
        cin >> b1 >> ch >> b2 >> ch >> b3 >> ch >> b4;

        if(a1 < 128)
        {
                if(a1 == b1)
                        cout << "Class A: Correct Configuration\n";
                else
                        cout << "Class A: Wrong Configuration\n";
        }
        else if(a1 < 192)
        {
                if(a1 == b1 && a2 == b2)
                        cout << "Class B: Correct Configuration\n";
                else
                        cout << "Class B: Wrong Configuration\n";
        }
        else if(a1 < 224)
        {
                if(a1 == b1 && a2 == b2 && a3 == b3)
                        cout << "Class C: Correct Configuration\n";
                else
                        cout << "Class C: Wrong Configuration\n";
        }
        else
                cout << "Error: Wrong class\n";
        return 0;
}
```

Comments: Because the user enters the IP in the x.x.x.x form I used the variable ch, to get the dot.

C.5.10 In a course exam, each test is graded by two graders. If the difference of their grades is less than diff, the final grade is their average. Otherwise, the test is reviewed by a third grader, as follows:

   a. If the grade of the third reviewer is equal to the average of the first two grades, that is the final grade.
   b. If it is less than the minimum (e.g., min) of the first two grades, the final grade is min.
   c. Otherwise, the final grade is the average of the grade of the third reviewer and the one of the first two grades closest to it.

Write a program that reads the two grades, the difference diff and displays the final grade according to that procedure.

```
#include <iostream>
using std::cout;
using std::cin;

int main()
{
        double g1, g2, g3, fin_grd, avg, min, max, diff;

        cout << "Enter grades: ";
        cin >> g1 >> g2;
```

```
        cout << "Enter difference: ";
        cin >> diff;
        if(g1 < g2)
        {
                min = g1;
                max = g2;
        }
        else
        {
                min = g2;
                max = g1;
        }
        avg = (g1+g2)/2;
        if((max-min) < diff)
                fin_grd = avg;
        else
        {
                cout << "Enter third grade: ";
                cin >> g3;
                if(g3 == avg) /* For simplicity, we make a simple comparison.
However, this comparison is not safe as mentioned in Ch.2. */
                        fin_grd = avg;
                else if(g3 < min)
                        fin_grd = min;
                else
                {
                        if(g3 > avg) // The max value is closer.
                                fin_grd = (g3+max)/2;
                        else
                                fin_grd = (g3+min)/2;
                }
        }
        cout << fin_grd << '\n';
        return 0;
}
```

THE CONDITIONAL OPERATOR? :

The conditional operator ?: allows a program to perform one of two actions depending on the value of an expression. The conditional expression has the following form:

```
exp1 ?  exp2 : exp3;
```

Because the conditional operator takes three operands, it is often referred to as a *ternary* operator. If the value of exp1 is true, exp2 will be evaluated, otherwise exp3. The value of the entire conditional will be the value of the evaluated expression, that is, exp2 or exp3. To use the exp2 or exp3 in the conditional expression, their data types should be the same or in case of different types they can be converted to a common type. For example, if they have different arithmetic types, the conversions as discussed in Chapter 2 are applied and the common type is produced. The data type of the conditional expression is the common type. For example, if d is double and i is int, the type of:

```
(j > 0) ?  d : i;
```

is `double` regardless of the value of `j`. Simply put, a conditional expression is a sort of an `if-else` statement:

```
if(exp1)
        exp2;
else
        exp3;
```

For example, the following code displays two values in increasing order:

```
(i < j) ?   (cout << i << ' ' << j) : (cout << j << ' ' << i);
```

The value of a conditional expression can be stored to a variable. For example, the following code reads a student's grade and if it is within [5, 10] is stored into `i`. Otherwise, `i` is set to `0`.

```
float i, grd;
cin >> grd;
i = (grd >= 5 && grd <= 10) ?   grd : 0;
```

Typically, the conditional operator is used in place of an `if-else` statement, when it has a simple form. For example, the next `if-else` statement:

```
if(a < b)
        min = a;
else
        min = b;
```

can be replaced with: `min = (a < b)?   a: b;` The parentheses are not necessary, because the precedence of `?:` is very low. However, it is advisable to use them to make clearer the tested condition.

Conditional expressions can be merged by replacing the expression that follows the colon: with another conditional expression. In the following example, `exp3` is replaced with the `add1 ? add2 : add3;` expression:

```
k = exp1 ?   exp2 : add1 ?   add2 : add3;
```

If `exp1` is true, `k` will be equal to the value of `exp2`. If `exp1` is false, the value of `add1` is evaluated. If `add1` is true, `k` will be equal to the value of `add2`. Otherwise, it will be equal to the value of `add3`. The equivalent chain of `if-else` statements is:

```
if(exp1)
        k = exp2;
else if(add1)
        k = add2;
else
        k = add3;
```

For example, the following code outputs 2.

```
int a = 10;
(a > 100) ?   (cout << "1\n") : (a == 10) ?   (cout << "2\n") : (cout << "3\n");
```

Note that because the `? :` operator has a low priority, when the conditional expression is used in a larger expression it is very likely that you should enclose it in parentheses, as unexpected results may occur. For example:

```
int a = 10;
cout << (a > 20) ?   "Yes\n" : "No\n";
```

Although we would expect this code to display No, it displays 0. Let's see why. First, the cout <<
(a > 20) is executed, which displays 0. The << operator returns the cout (we'll see how in Chapter 18),
so the initial expression becomes equivalent to cout ? "Yes\n" : "No\n"; This expression does not
print something. It just checks the value of cout, and because it is true, the expression yields Yes. To
display the correct result we must use parentheses:

```
cout << ((a > 20) ?  "Yes\n" : "No\n");
```

EXERCISES

C.5.11 What is the output of the following program?

```cpp
#include <iostream>
int main()
{
        int a = 1, b = !a;

        if((b ?  a : -a) <= 10)
                std::cout << "One " << -a << '\n';
        else
                std::cout << "Two " << -a << '\n';
        return 0;
}
```

Answer: Since b is 0, the result of the conditional expression is -a, that is, -1. The value of a does not
change, it remains 1. Therefore, since the if condition is true, the program outputs: One -1

C.5.12 Write a program that reads the prices of three products and uses the ?: operator to display the
highest price.

```cpp
#include <iostream>
int main()
{
        float i, j, k;

        std::cout << "Enter prices: ";
        std::cin >> i >> j >> k;

        std::cout << "Max: " << ((i >= j && i >= k) ?  i : (j > i && j > k) ?
j : k) << '\n';
        return 0;
}
```

Comments: To display the lowest price we change the > to <.

C.5.13 Write a program that reads a student's grade and uses the ?: operator to display a corresponding
message according to the next scale:

    a. If grade is within [7.5–10], the program outputs: A
    b. If grade is within [5–7.5), the program outputs: B
    c. If grade is within [0–5), the program outputs: Next time
    d. If grade is out of [0, 10], the program outputs: Wrong input

Note: The right parenthesis ")" means that the right number is not included in the indicated set.

```cpp
#include <iostream>
int main()
{
        float grd;

        std::cout << "Enter grade: ";
        std::cin >> grd;
        std::cout << ((grd >= 7.5 && grd <= 10) ?  "A" : (grd >= 5 && grd <
7.5) ?  "B" : (grd >= 0 && grd < 5) ?  "Next time" : "Wrong input") << '\n';
        return 0;
}
```

THE switch STATEMENT

The `switch` statement can be used as an alternative to an `if-else-if` series, when we want to test the value of an expression against a series of values and handle each case differently. In the most common form, or at least the one I prefer, the syntax of the `switch` statement is:

```cpp
switch(expression)
{
        case constant_1:
        /* block of statements that will be executed if the value of the
expression is equal to constant_1. */
        break;
        ...
        case constant_n:
        /* block of statements that will be executed if the value of the
expression is equal to constant_n. */
        break;

        default:
        /* block of statements that will be executed if the value of the
expression is other than the previous constants. */
        break;
}
```

As a matter of style, there are several ways to write the `switch` statement. The most popular is to put the statements under the `case` label and the `break` statement some space(s) inner or aligned with the statements. My preference is to align each `break` with the `case` label and leave a space between each `case` and the preceding `break`.

The `expression` must be of an integral type (e.g., an integer variable or expression), or be a class type that provides an unambiguous conversion to integral type and the values of all `constant_1`, ..., `constant_n` must be integer constant expressions (e.g., 30 is a constant expression, and 30+40 as well) with different values. That is, you are not allowed to write:

```cpp
double i, j;
const int c = 10;
```

```
switch(i) // Wrong.
{
        case 1.23: // Wrong.
        case j:    // Wrong.
        case c:    // Fine.

}
```

Naturally, any constant_ must either be of the same type as the expression or be convertible to that type. The order of case does not matter. When the switch statement is executed, the value of the expression is compared with each case constant. If a match is found, the group of statements of the respective case will be executed and the remaining cases will not be tested. If no match is found, the statements of the default case will be executed. In any case, the break statement terminates the execution of the switch and the program continues with the next statement after the switch. We'll discuss more about the break statement in Chapter 6. switch statements may be nested, and a case or default clause is associated with the enclosing switch.

For example, the following program reads an integer and if it is 1, it outputs One; if it is 2, it outputs Two, otherwise, it outputs Other. In any case, the break statement terminates the switch and the program outputs End.

```
#include <iostream> // Example 5.6
using std::cout;
using std::cin;

int main()
{
        int a;

        cout << "Enter number: ";
        cin >> a;

        switch(a)
        {
                case 1:
                        cout << "One\n";
                break;

                case 2:
                        cout << "Two\n";
                break;

                default:
                        cout << "Other\n";
                break;
        }
        cout << "End\n";
        return 0;
}
```

Notice that the default case is optional; it may also appear anywhere in the list of cases and will be executed if there is no match. If it is present, my suggestion is to put it always at the end to make it clear. If it is missing and there is no matching case, no action takes place.

Let's make a parenthesis for the default case. Typically, it is used to report an "impossible" condition, a condition that shouldn't happen. One time, I've chosen to output the message *Panic: Wish you weren't here* paraphrasing the classical song of *Pink Floyd*. As you may guess, this wrong situation had never occurred during the testing phase. Can you imagine when it occurred? After the delivery of the application to the client, of course. As a matter of fact, I should expect that I'd be a victim of *Murphy's Law*. And believe me, it is not one of my favourite memories the moment when the client called me in "panic" to ask me about this message. I think I told him to listen to the song and relax. I should have known better; am sure that if I had chosen a happier song the bug wouldn't occur ... Something similar had happened to one of my colleagues, when a message with "inappropriate" content popped up on the screen during a live demonstration. Besides some light relief, the reason I mentioned these incidents is to warn you about the messages you choose to display, when others are going to use your program.

Besides the `break` statement, the `return` statement is often used to exit from the `switch` statement. For example, if we change the first case in the previous example to:

```
case 1:
        cout << "One\n";
return 0;
```

and the user enters 1, the program displays One and then the `return` statement terminates the program. Therefore, the message End won't be displayed. As we'll see in Chapter 11, the `return` statement not only terminates the `switch` but also the function in which it is contained.

Note that the presence of the `break` statement in each `case` is not mandatory. If it is missing from the matching `case`, the program will continue with the execution of the next `case` statements. In fact, the unintended absence of `break` is the most common error with `switch` statements. For example, consider the following program:

```
#include <iostream> // Example 5.7
using std::cout;

int main()
{
        int a = 1;

        switch(a)
        {
                case 1:
                        cout << "One\n";

                case 2:
                        cout << "Two\n";

                case 3:
                        cout << "Three\n";
                        break;

                default:
                        cout << "Other\n";
                        break;
        }
        cout << "End\n";
        return 0;
}
```

Since a is 1, the first `case` outputs One. However, since there is no `break`, the `switch` statement is not terminated and the execution falls through to the next cases, until the `break` is met. Therefore, the program outputs Two and Three. The `break` statement terminates the `switch` and the program displays End. If that `break` was missing, the program would also output Other. The last `break` can be omitted, since, the right brace} terminates the `switch` anyway. My preference is to put it, not only to keep a uniform style, but also to have it as a safe guard if some day another `case` is added below.

 Typically, the absence of `break` is a signal of potential bug. If you deliberately omit it, add a comment to state it explicitly, so that someone who reads your code or even you after a while won't wonder.

Alternatively, C++17 provides the `[[fallthrough]]` attribute, which can be used to inform the reader for that intended behaviour and also inform the compiler in order not to issue warnings for not having a `break` statement after a `case` label. For example, in the previous program we add it in the same place where we would otherwise put the `break` statement:

```
case 1:
        cout << "One\n";
        [[fallthrough]];
case 2:
        cout << "Two\n";
        [[fallthrough]];
```

If we want to execute the same block of statements in more than one case, we can merge them together. For example:

```
case constant_1:
case constant_2:
case constant_3:
/* block of statements that will be executed if the value of the expression
matches any of constant_1, constant_2 or constant_3. */
break;
```

For example, the following program reads an integer that represents a month (`1` for January, `12` for December) and displays the number of days:

```
#include <iostream> // Example 5.8
using std::cout;
using std::cin;

int main()
{
        int month;

        cout << "Enter month [1-12]: ";
        cin >> month;

        switch(month)
        {
                case 1:
                case 3:
                case 5:
                case 7:
                case 8:
                case 10:
                case 12:
                        cout << "31\n"; /* If the user enters one of these
values the program displays 31. */
                        break;
```

```
                case 4:
                case 6:
                case 9:
                case 11:
                        cout << "30\n";
                break;

                case 2:
                        cout << "28 or 29\n";
                break;

                default:
                        cout << "Error: Wrong input\n";
                break;
        }
        return 0;
}
```

Declaration of Variables inside Switch

As we said, when the code of the matching `case` is to be executed, the code that exists before that label is ignored. The question is, what if a variable is declared in this code? For example:

```
case 1:
        int i = 10; // Wrong.
        int j; // Correct.
break;

case 2:
        if(i > 5)
        {
        }
        j = 20; // Correct.
break;
```

The compiler does not compile this code. The reason is that if the code of the second `case` is executed and not that of the first `case`, i would be used with an uninitialized value and not with the value of 10 as the programmer might expect. To prevent this, the compiler displays an error message to inform the programmer about the disallowed initialization. If i is not initialized, like j, the code is compiled successfully. If we want to declare and use a variable in a specific `case` we can use the braces to define a block and place the declaration inside. The scope of the variable is constrained inside the block. For example:

```
case 1:
        {
                int i = 10; // Correct.
                ...
        }
break;

case 2:
        if(i == 20) // Wrong, the compilation fails because i is out of scope.
        {
        }
break;
```

This code fails to compile because i is visible only within the block.

As with the if statement, C++17 provides a new version of switch that allows us to add an initialization clause inside switch and then test for the condition. This syntax is similar to:

```
switch(init; condition)
```

For example:

```
int f(){return 10;}
switch(int a = f(); a+1)
{
        case 11:
                cout << "One\n";
        break;
        ...
}
cout << a; // Error, a is out of scope.
```

Since a becomes 10, the code outputs One. The scope of a is limited in the switch block. As with the new if version, this concise syntax may be used to initialize the tested variable and limit its scope inside the block.

switch versus if

The main disadvantage of the switch statement is that we can make tests only for equality, that is, to test whether the value of an expression matches one of the case constants. On the contrary, we can use if to test any kind of condition. In addition, the case constants are restricted to integers and the expression must be an integer variable or expression only. Because characters are treated as small integers they may be used, but floating-point numbers and strings are not permitted. On the other hand, if the number of the if conditions being tested is large, then the use of switch might be preferable in order to make the code easier to read and maintain. For example, a typical use of the switch statement is to handle user choices from a large menu of options. Also, switch might be faster than a long list of if conditions because the compiler may produce at compile time a jump table indexed by the values of the cases, and find right away the matching case when the program runs. This may be faster compared to the list of ifs, where each if condition should be evaluated sequentially to reach the matching one.

EXERCISES

C.5.14 Write a program that simulates a physical calculator. The program should read the symbol of an arithmetic operation and two integers and display the result of the arithmetic operation.

```
#include <iostream>
using std::cout;
using std::cin;

int main()
{
        char sign;
        int i, j;
```

```
        cout << "Enter math sign and two integers: ";
        cin >> sign >> i >> j;

        switch(sign)
        {
                case '+':
                        cout << "Sum: " << i+j << '\n';
                break;

                case '-':
                        cout << "Diff: " << i-j << '\n';
                break;

                case '*':
                        cout << "Product: " << i*j << '\n';
                break;

                case '/':
                        if(j != 0)
                                cout << "Div: " << (float)i/j << '\n';
                        else
                                cout << "Second number should not be 0\n";
                break;

                default:
                        cout << "Unacceptable operation\n";
                break;
        }
        return 0;
}
```

Comments: As we'll see in Chapter 9, the character constants are treated as integers and declared within single quotes ' '.

C.5.15 Write a program that reads a person's sex and height and displays the corresponding description for the height according to the following table.

SEX	HEIGHT (m)	RESULT
Male	< 1.70	Short
Male	≥ 1.70 and < 1.85	Normal
Male	≥ 1.85	Tall
Female	< 1.60	Short
Female	≥ 1.60 and < 1.75	Normal
Female	≥ 1.75	Tall

```
#include <iostream>
using std::cout;
using std::cin;

int main()
{
        int sex;
        float height;
```

```
        cout << "Enter sex (0:man - 1:woman): ";
        cin >> sex;

        cout << "Enter height in meters: ";
        cin >> height;

        switch(sex)
        {
                case 0:
                        if(height < 1.7)
                                cout << "Result: Short\n";
                        else if(height < 1.85) /* Since the previous if checks
values up to 1.7, this statement is equivalent to: else if(height >= 1.7 &&
height < 1.85). */
                                cout << "Result: Normal\n";
                        else
                                cout << "Result: Tall\n";
                break;

                case 1:
                        if(height < 1.6)
                                cout << "Result: Short\n";
                        else if(height < 1.75)
                                cout << "Result: Normal\n";
                        else
                                cout << "Result: Tall\n";
                break;

                default:
                        cout << "Error: Wrong input\n";
                break;
        }
        return 0;
}
```

C.5.16 Write a program that calculates the cost of transporting a passenger's luggage, according to the following table. The program should read the type of the passenger's class and the weight of the luggage and display the cost.

CLASS	WEIGHT (lb)	COST ($)
Economy	≤ 25	0
	> 25 and ≤ 40	1.50 for each pound over 25
	> 40	2.00 for each pound over 40
Business	≤ 35	0
	> 35 and ≤ 50	1.25 for each pound over 35
	> 50	1.50 for each pound over 50
VIP	≤ 60	0
	> 60	30 (fixed cost)

```cpp
#include <iostream>
using std::cout;
using std::cin;

int main()
{
        int clas;
        double cost, weight;

        cout << "Enter class (1-Eco, 2-Business, 3-VIP): ";
        cin >> clas;

        cout << "Enter weight: ";
        cin >> weight;

        cost = 0; // Covers all cases where the passenger pays nothing.
        switch(clas)
        {
            case 1:
                    if(weight > 40)
                            cost = 22.5 + 2*(weight-40); // 22.5 = 1.5*15
                    else if(weight > 25)
                            cost = 1.5*(weight-25);
                break;

            case 2:
                    if(weight > 50)
                            cost = 18.75 + 1.5*(weight-50); // 18.75 = 1.25*15
                    else if(weight > 35)
                            cost = 1.25*(weight-35);
                break;

            case 3:
                    if(weight > 60)
                            cost = 30;
                break;

            default:
                    cout << "Error: Wrong traffic class\n";
                return 0;
        }
        cout << "Cost: " << cost << '\n';
        return 0;
}
```

UNSOLVED EXERCISES

U.5.1 Write a program that reads the prices of three products and uses the ?: operator to display a message about whether one of them costs more $100 or not. Don't use an if statement.

U.5.2 Write a program that reads three integers and checks if they are in successive ascending order (e.g., 5, 6, 7 or -3, -2, -1).

U.5.3   Write a program that reads three integers and if the sum of any two of them is equal to the third one, it should display the integers within [0, 10]. Otherwise, the program should read another three integers and display how many of them are multiples of 6 or other than 20.

U.5.4   A factory produces small and big bottles. A small one costs $0.008 and a big one $0.02. For orders of more than $200 or more than 3000 bottles in total, there is an 8% discount. For orders of more than $600, the discount is 20%. Write a program that reads the number of small and big bottles ordered and displays the total cost.

U.5.5   Write a program that reads a student's grade and displays its corresponding description, as follows:

a. (18–20]: Excellent
b. (16–18]: Very Good
c. (13–16]: Good
d. [10–13]: Dangerous Zone
e. [0–10): Need Help

U.5.6   Each Ethernet network card is characterized by a unique 48-bit identifier, which is called MAC address. Typically, the MAC address is represented in hex form. To find the type of the address we check the value of the first octet at the left. If it is even, the address type is *unicast*. If it is odd, the type is *multicast*. If all octets are 0xFF, the type is *broadcast*. For example:

a. The FF:FF:FF:FF:FF:FF address is *broadcast*.
b. The 18:20:3F:20:AB:11 address is *unicast*, because 18 is even.
c. The A3:3F:40:A2:C3:42 address is *multicast*, because A3 is odd.

Write a program that reads a MAC address and displays its type. Assume that the user enters the MAC address in x:x:x:x:x:x form, where each x is a hex number.

U.5.7   Write a program that reads the grades of three students in the lab part and their grades in the theory part. The final grade is calculated as: lab_grd*0.3 + theory_grd*0.7. The program should display how many students got a grade between 8 and 10. Don't use more than three variables.

U.5.8   Write a program that reads an annual income and calculates the due tax according to the following table:

INCOME	TAX RATE (%)
0–12000	0
12001–14000	15
14001–30000	30
>30000	40

For example, if the user enters 18000, the tax due is: tax = (14000-12000)*0.15 + (18000-14000)*0.3.

U.5.9   Write a program that reads a four-digit positive integer and uses the ?: operator to display a message about whether it can be read the same in reverse order or not (e.g., the number 7667 can be). Don't use an if statement.

U.5.10 Write a program that reads a floating-point value (e.g., x) and displays the value of $f(x)$, as follows:

$$f(x) = \begin{cases} 8, & x < -5 \\ \dfrac{1}{x}, & -5 \le x < 3 \\ x^2 - 4, & 3 \le x < 12 \\ \dfrac{6}{(x-14)^2}, & x \ge 12 \end{cases}$$

U.5.11 Write a program that reads four integers and displays the pair with the largest sum. For example, if the user enters 10, -8, 17, and 5, the program should display 10+17=27. Don't use the && operator.

U.5.12 Write a program that reads the time in the h:m:s form and displays how much time is left until midnight (i.e., 24:00:00).

U.5.13 Use one cout statement and the ?: operator to write the program of U.5.5.

U.5.14 Write a program that reads a month number (1 for January, 12 for December), the day number (e.g., if the input month is January, the valid values are from 1 to 31) and displays the date after 50 days. In case of February, the program should prompt the user to enter its days, that is, 28 or 29. For example, if the user enters 3 for month, and 5 for day, the program should display: 4/24.

U.5.15 Write a program that reads three integers and the user's choice and uses the switch statement to support three cases. If the user's choice is 1, the program should check if the integers are different and display a message. If it is 2, it should check if any two of them are equal and display a message, and if it is 3, it should display how many of them are within [−5, 5].

U.5.16 Write a program that reads the numerators and the denominators of two fractions and an integer which corresponds to a math operation (e.g., 1: addition, 2: subtraction, 3: multiplication, 4: division) and uses the switch statement to display the result of the math operation.

U.5.17 Write a program that reads the current year, the year of a person's birth, and uses the switch statement to display the age in words. Suppose that the age has not more than two digits. For example, if the user enters 2020 and 1988, the program should display thirty-two.

U.5.18 Write a program that calculates the cost of renting a vehicle, according to the following table:

VEHICLE	CYBISM (cc)	COST PER DAY ($)		
		DAYS 1–2	DAYS 3–5	DAYS > 5
Moto	≤ 100	30	25	20
	> 100	40	35	30
Auto	≤ 1000	60	55	50
	> 1001	80	70	60

The program should read the type of the vehicle, the cybism, the days to rent it, and use the switch statement to display the cost. Also, the program should ask the user if an insurance coverage is desired, and if the answer is positive (e.g., the input number 1 stands for Yes), an extra 5% in the total cost should be charged.

Loops

6

Programs often contain blocks of code that must be executed more than once. A statement whose job is to repeatedly execute the same code as long as the value of a controlling expression is true creates an *iteration loop*. In this chapter, we'll discuss about the iteration statements: for, while, and do-while, which allow us to set up loops, as well as the break, continue, and goto statements, which can be used to transfer control from one point of a program to another.

THE for STATEMENT

The for statement is one of the three loop statements. The general form of the for statement is:

```
for(exp1; exp2; exp3)
{
        /* a block of statements (loop body) that is repeatedly executed as
long as the value of exp2 is true. */
}
```

The three expressions exp1, exp2, and exp3 can be any valid expressions. The execution of the for statement involves the following steps:

1. exp1 is executed only once. Typically, exp1 initializes a variable used in the other two expressions.
2. The value of exp2 is evaluated. Typically, it is a relational condition. If it is false, the loop terminates and the execution of the program continues with the statement after the closing brace. If it is true, the loop body is executed.
3. exp3 is executed. Typically, exp3 changes the value of a variable used in exp2.
4. Steps 2 and 3 are repeated until exp2 becomes false.

Generally, the loop terminates either when the exp2 condition becomes false or if a statement that terminates its execution is executed earlier, such as break or return. As with the if statement, if the loop body consists of a single statement, the braces can be omitted. The following program displays the numbers from 0 to 9:

```
#include <iostream> // Example 6.1
int main()
{
        int i;

        for(i = 0; i < 10; i++) // The braces can be omitted.
        {
                std::cout << i << '\n';
        }
        return 0;
}
```

Regarding the position of the opening {, a common practice is to put it at the end of the statement, like this:

```
for(i = 0; i < 10; i++) {
```

As I mentioned in the `if` statement, my preference is to put it on a separate line. Let's see the execution steps:

   a. The statement `i = 0;` is executed.
   b. The condition `i < 10` is checked. Since it is true, the program displays `0`.
   c. The `i++` statement is executed and `i` becomes `1`. The condition `i < 10` is checked again. Because it is still true, the program displays `1`. This process is repeated until `i` becomes `10`, at which point the condition `i < 10` becomes false and the loop terminates. As a result, the program displays the numbers from `0` to `9`.

Let's see another style. Some prefer to use the `!=` operator instead of `<` in the `for` condition. They also prefer the prefix form to change the step. For example, they write:

```
for(i = 0; i != 10; ++i)
```

The result is the same. And why do they prefer that way? The reason they prefer the prefix form is that the postfix form must save the current value. Since we do not need the current value there is no reason for this extra overhead. For basic types (e.g., `int`) the compiler will do the optimization and there will be no difference in performance. However, if the type is a complex one (e.g., iterator), then the prefix form may be more efficient than the postfix form, as we'll see in Chapter 18. As for the `!=`, this preference is probably related to generic programming. For example, as we'll see in Chapter 26 the `!=` can be applied to iterators to traverse library containers, while `<` may not be applicable. So, they always prefer this form, because it may be more efficient in case of complex types or in case the `<` operator cannot be used. I guess that this paragraph confused you, don't worry, you'll understand it when we get to Chapter 26.

Note that we can declare a variable in the first part of the statement. Its scope extends up to the closing }, that is, it is not visible and cannot be used outside of it. We'll discuss more about the scope of variables in Chapter 11. For example:

```
for(int i = 0; i < 10; i++)
{
        . . .
}
cout << i; /* The compiler will display an error message for undeclared variable,
because i has not been declared in this scope. The scope of i is up to } */
```

The expressions in the `for` statement may consist of more than one expression separated with the comma operator (,). For example:

```
int a, b;
for(a = 20, b = 10; a > 10; a-=2, b++)
```

The first expression assigns the values 20 and 10 into a and b, while the third expression decrements a by two and increments b. Note that we can declare multiple variables in the first part, as long as they are of the same type. For example:

```
for(int a = 20, b = 10; a > 10; a-=2, b++)
```

In general, I avoid using multiple expressions and prefer to use separate statements to make the `for` easier to read.

Because in several programs we'll need to generate random numbers, let's make a parenthesis to show you such an example:

```cpp
#include <iostream>  // Example 6.2
#include <cstdlib>
#include <ctime>
int main()
{
        int i, num;

        srand(time(NULL));
        for(i = 0; i < 5; i++)
        {
                num = rand();
                std::cout << num << '\n';
        }
        return 0;
}
```

The `rand()` function together with the `srand()` and `time()` functions is used to generate random integers each time the program runs. `rand()` returns an integer between `0` and `RAND_MAX`. The value of `RAND_MAX` is defined in `cstdlib`. The `srand()` function sets the seed for `rand()`. For example, if we want to generate random floating-point numbers in [0, 1], we write `(double)rand()/RAND_MAX`. To use these functions in our program we must include the `cstdlib` and `ctime` files. In practice, random numbers are often used, such as in gaming applications and applications that simulate experiments. Note that the standard library provides in the `<random>` file several functions that generate random numbers. If you ever write an application that needs random numbers with satisfactory properties (e.g., for cryptography) you should explore the `<random>` functions; `rand()` is not sufficiently random for demanding uses. For simplicity, we'll use the ones we just described.

Common Errors

Let's use the same example:

```cpp
for(i = 0; i < 10; i++)
        std::cout << i << '\n';
```

A very common error is to use = to check if the final value is reached. That is, it is an error to write `i = 10` instead of `i < 10`. Since this assignment makes the condition true, the loop becomes infinite and displays continuously `10`, significantly degrading the performance of the computer. It is also an error to write `i == 10`. In the first step, since `i` is `0`, the condition is false and the loop terminates; nothing is displayed on the screen.

As with the `if` statement, a common error is to add accidentally a semicolon `;` at the end of the `for` statement. For example, consider the following program:

```cpp
#include <iostream>  // Example 6.3
int main()
{
        int i;

        for(i = 16; i > 10; i-=3);
                std::cout << i << '\n';
        return 0;
}
```

As we said in the similar case with the `if` statement, the `;` represents the null statement, a statement that does nothing. Therefore, the compiler assumes that the loop body is only the `;`. Therefore, the `cout` statement does not belong to the loop; it will be executed only once, after the loop ends. Let's trace the iterations:

First iteration. Since `i` is `16`, the condition `i > 10` is true. Since the loop body is empty, the next statement to be executed is `i-=3` (`i = i-3 = 16-3 = 13`).
Second iteration. Since `i` is `13`, the condition is still true and the statement `i-=3` makes `i` equal to `10`.
Third iteration. Since `i` is `10`, the condition becomes false and the loop terminates.

Next, the program outputs the value of `i`, that is, `10`.

If it is indeed your intention to create an empty loop, it is advisable to put the semicolon on a line by itself, to make it clear to the reader. For example:

```
for(i = 16; i > 10; i-=3)
        ;
```

Now, the reader won't wonder if the semicolon was accidentally put.

As in case of the `if` statement, a common error is to forget the braces when we want to execute multiple statements. For example, in the following code, suppose that we want to output the value of `j` in each iteration:

```
int i, j;
for(i = j = 0; i < 4; i++) // We forgot to add braces.
        j = j + i;
        cout << j << '\n';
```

Since the `cout` statement does not belong to the body of the loop, it will be executed only once. Thus, this code displays `6`.

Due to potential rounding errors you should be very cautious when comparing the result of floating-point computations using operators such as `==`, `>=`, or `<=`.

We saw such an example in the C.2.1 program. Let's see another one. In the examples so far we use an integer variable (e.g., `i`) to control the loop. Let's use a float variable. What you think the following code outputs?

```
for(double i = 0; i <= 0.3; i+=0.1)
        cout << i << '\n';
```

Normally you should answer that it outputs `0`, `0.1`, `0.2`, and `0.3`. However, when I run it, it does not output the `0.3` value. Why is that? The loop ends when `i` becomes `0.2`, because when `0.1` is added to `0.2`, the result is greater than `0.3`. The reason for this is that the number `0.1` cannot be represented exactly as a binary floating-point value. That's why we have one iteration less than expected.

As you see, the comparison of floating-point numbers may introduce a bug very hard to trace. The safe is to use integers to control the loop. If we cannot do that, a solution is to change the condition to anticipate for rounding errors. For example, we can write: `i < 0.3 + 0.001`, where `0.001` is a sufficient number to add greater than the expected rounding error and less than the increment of `0.1`.

Omitting Expressions

The three expressions of the `for` statement are optional. In fact, we can omit any or all of them. For example, in the following code, because `a` is initialized before the `for` statement, `exp1` can be omitted.

```
int a = 10;
for(; a >= 3; a--)
```

Notice that the ; before exp2 must be present. In fact, the two ; must always be present even if exp1 and exp2 expressions are both omitted.

In a similar way, we can put exp3 in the loop body and remove it from the for statement. For example, in the following code, the third expression a-- is put inside the body.

```
for(a = 10; a >= 3;)
{
    cout << a << ' ';
    a--;
}
```

If the controlling expression exp2 is missing, the compiler treats it as always true, and the loop becomes infinite, that is, it never ends. For example, this for statement creates an infinite loop:

```
for(a = 0; ; a--)
```

Most programmers omit all three expressions in order to create an infinite loop. For example:

```
for(;;)
```

Infinite loops are used in many applications, such as programs that receive data continuously or monitor the operational status of some kind of systems. Next, we'll see how we can terminate an infinite loop. We'll also see later that if exp1 and exp3 are both missing, the for statement is equivalent to the while statement. For example:

```
for(; a >= 3;) is equivalent to: while(a >= 3)
```

C++11 introduces another form of the for statement, which is called range-based for. We'll discuss it in Chapter 7.

THE break STATEMENT

We've already discussed how a break statement terminates the execution of a switch statement. It can also be used to terminate a for, while, or do-while loop and transfer control out of the loop. For example:

```
#include <iostream>  // Example 6.4
int main()
{
    int i, j = 3;

    for(i = 0; i < 10; i++)
    {
        if(i == j)
            break;

        std::cout << i << '\n';
    }
    std::cout << "Out: " << i << '\n';
    return 0;
}
```

As long as i is not j, the `if` condition is false and the program displays the values of i from 0 to 2. When i becomes 3, the `break` statement terminates the loop and the program continues with the execution of the outer `cout` and displays Out: 3

As we'll see next, in case of nested `break` commands, each `break` terminates the execution of the loop or the `switch` statement in which it is contained. For example, can you find the output of the following program?

```cpp
#include <iostream> // Example 6.5
int main()
{
        int i;

        for(i = 1; i < 10; i++)
        {
                switch(i)
                {
                        case 2:
                        case 3:
                        break;

                        default:
                                if(i == 4)
                                        break;
                                std::cout << i << "* ";
                        break;
                }
                if(i == 5)
                        break;
        }
        return 0;
}
```

In the first iteration, the `default` case outputs 1* and the `break` terminates the `switch` statement, not the `for` statement. In the next two iterations the `break` of the first two `cases` terminates the `switch` and the program displays nothing. Be careful now, in the fourth iteration (i = 4), it is the `break` of the inner `if` that terminates the `switch` and the program displays nothing. The fifth iteration outputs 5* in the `default` case and since the condition in the outer `if` is true, the `break` terminates the loop. Therefore, the program outputs: 1* 5*.

And now that we remembered `switch`, here is a new challenge for you; can you tell me what does the following code output?

```cpp
for(i = 1; i < 12; i++)
        switch(i)
        {
                case 1: i += 2;
                case 2: i += 3;
                default: i += 4;
        }
        cout << i;
```

As you guess, I used on purpose this syntax to confuse you. Since the `for` has no braces, it contains only the `switch` statement. In the first iteration, since i is 1, the code executes the statement of the first `case` and continues with the next ones, since there is no `break`. Therefore, i becomes 10. In the second iteration, because i is now 11, only the `default` case is executed and i becomes 15. Next, i becomes 16, the loop ends, and that is the output value.

THE continue STATEMENT

The continue statement can be used only inside a for, while, or do-while loop. While the break statement ends the loop, the continue statement terminates the current iteration of the enclosing loop and causes the next iteration to begin. The statements after the continue are not executed for the current iteration. For example, consider the following program:

```cpp
#include <iostream> // Example 6.6
int main()
{
        int i;

        for(i = 0; i < 5; i++)
        {
                if(i == 2 || i == 3)
                        continue;
                std::cout << i << ' ';
        }
        return 0;
}
```

If i is 2 or 3, the if condition is true and the continue statement terminates the current iteration. The rest of the loop body, that is, cout, is skipped and the program continues with the next iteration i++. Therefore, the program outputs: 0 1 4

Note that we can avoid the use of continue by testing the reverse condition. For example:

```cpp
if(i != 2 && i != 3)
        std::cout << i << ' ';
```

However, my preference is to use the continue statement rather than reverse logic, in order to make clear to the reader which is the condition that triggers the next iteration. For example, it is easier to read and write the following code rather than using reverse logic:

```cpp
if(a < -3 || b == 10 || c >= 2)
        continue;
```

Unlike break, the continue statement does not apply to switch. It can appear inside a switch, only if the switch is contained in a loop. When executed, the continue triggers the next loop iteration. For example, in example C.6.5 of the previous section, what does the code output if we change the default case to:

```cpp
default:
        if(i == 4)
                break;
        else
        {
                continue;
                std::cout << i << "* ";
        }
std::cout << i << "* ";
break;
```

Since the continue statement causes the next iteration to begin, the program displays nothing.

EXERCISES

C.6.1 What is the output of the following program?

```cpp
#include <iostream>
using std::cout;
int main()
{
        int i = 2;
        unsigned int j = 2;

        for(i > j; i && (i+j == 4); i--, j++)
                cout << i << ' ';
                cout << j << ' ';

        for(j = i; j >= 0; j--)
                cout << "\nOne";
        return 0;
}
```

Answer: Since the `for` has no braces, the loop body contains only the first `cout`. I deliberately indented the second `cout` to make you think that it also belongs to the loop body. No, it does not, it is executed only once, after the end of the loop. The value of `i > j` is `0`; however, this does not affect the execution of the loop. Let's trace the iterations:

> *First iteration.* The first term of the condition, that is `i`, it is equivalent to `i!=0`, which is true. Since `i` is 2 and `j` is 2, the second term is also true, so the program outputs 2. Then, `i` and `j` become 1 and 3, respectively.
> *Second iteration.* The condition is true again and the program outputs 1. Then, `i` and `j` become 0 and 4, respectively.
> *Third iteration.* Since `i` is 0, the condition becomes false, the loop ends, and the second `cout` outputs the value of `j`. So far, the program has displayed: 2 1 4

Let's go to the next trap. Once `j` has been declared as an unsigned, its value will never become negative (e.g., -1). The number -1 will be converted to an unsigned value (e.g., in a 32-bit system it is 4294967295). Therefore, the second loop is infinite and the program displays `One` continuously.

C.6.2 Write a program that reads an integer and, if it belongs to [30, 50], the program should display the word `One` as many times as the value of the number, otherwise it should read 10 integers and use the `switch` statement to display how many times the user entered the values 1 and 2.

```cpp
#include <iostream>
using std::cout;
using std::cin;

int main()
{
        int i, j, k, num;

        cout << "Enter number: ";
        cin >> num;
```

```
if(num >= 30 && num <= 50)
{
        for(i = 0; i < num; i++)
                cout << "One\n";
}
else
{
        j = k = 0;
        for(i = 0; i < 10; i++)
        {
                cout << "Enter number: ";
                cin >> num;

                switch(num)
                {
                        case 1:
                                j++;
                        break;

                        case 2:
                                k++;
                        break;
                }
        }
        cout << j << ' ' << k << '\n';
}
return 0;
}
```

C.6.3 Write a program that reads an integer and displays its factorial. The factorial of a positive integer *n*, where *n* ≥ *1*, is defined as *1 × 2 × 3 × ... × n*, while the factorial of *0* equals *1 (0! = 1)*. Since factorials grow rapidly and may exceed very fast the capacity of the larger type don't enter a large integer.

```
#include <iostream>
using std::cout;
using std::cin;

int main()
{
        int i, num;
        unsigned long long int fact;

        cout << "Enter number: ";
        cin >> num;

        if(num >= 0)
        {
                fact = 1; /* This variable holds the factorial of the input
number. It is initialized to 1, to make the multplications. */
                for(i = 1; i <= num; i++)
                        fact = fact*i;
                /* If the user enters 0, the loop won't be executed because the
condition (i <= num) is false (i=1 and num=0). Therefore, the program would
display the initial value of fact, that is, 1, which is correct, since 0! = 1. */
                cout << "Factorial of " << num << " is " << fact << '\n';
        }
        else
                cout << "Error: Number should be >= 0\n";
        return 0;
}
```

`Comments:` The reason I declared `fact` as `unsigned long long int` is to maximize the range of the factorials that can be calculated. For example, had we used the `int` type, the program would have displayed correctly only the factorials of numbers from 0 to 12. Suppose that the user enters 20. Let's trace the first three iterations:

> *First iteration.* Since `i` is 1, the condition `i ≤ 20` is true and `fact` becomes `fact = fact*i = 1*1 = 1`.
> *Second iteration.* Since `i` is 2, the condition is true again and `fact` becomes `fact = fact*i = 1*2 = 2`.
> *Third iteration.* `i` becomes 3 and `fact = fact*i = 2*3 = 6`.

Therefore, the first three iterations calculate the product of $1 \times 2 \times 3$. In a similar way, the next iterations calculate the factorial of the input number. A reasonable question to ask is how do we calculate the factorial of larger numbers? To give you an idea, in case of larger factorials that cannot be hold in a variable, the idea is to make the multiplications as we've learned in school digit by digit and store each result digit in an array.

C.6.4 Write a program that reads a positive integer n (n > 0) and verifies the math formula: $1 + 3 + 5 + \ldots + (2n-1) = n^2$. The program should force the user to enter a positive integer.

```cpp
#include <iostream>
using std::cout;
using std::cin;

int main()
{
        int i, n, sum;

        for(;;) // Create an infinite loop.
        {
                cout << "Enter number > 0: ";
                cin >> n;
                if(n > 0)
                        break; /* If the user enters a positive integer the loop
terminates. */
        }
        sum = 0; /* This variable holds the sum of the terms. It is
initialized to 0, to make the additions. */
        for(i = 1; i <= 2*n-1; i+=2)
                sum += i;
        if(sum == n*n)
                cout << "Verified\n";
        else
                cout << "Not Verified\n";
        return 0;
}
```

`Comments:` Essentially, the left part of the formula calculates the sum of the odd numbers from 1 up to `2*num-1`. Suppose that the user enters 3. Let's trace the iterations:

> *First iteration.* Since `i` is 1, the condition `i ≤ 5` is true and `sum` becomes `sum = sum+i = 0+1 = 1`.
> *Second iteration.* Since `i` becomes `i+=2 = i+2 = 1+2 = 3`, the condition is true again and `sum` becomes `sum = sum+i = 1+3 = 4`.
> *Third iteration.* `i` becomes 5 and `sum = sum+i = 4+5 = 9`.

Since `i` becomes 7, the loop terminates and the formula is verified.

C.6.5 What is the output of the following program?

```
#include <iostream>
int main()
{
        unsigned char i;

        for(i = 4; (i && i-2) ?  i+1 : 0; i--)
                std::cout << (int)i << '\n';
        for(; ++i;)
                std::cout << (int)i << '\n';
        return 0;
}
```

Answer: The first loop ends when i && i-2 becomes false. This happens once i becomes 2. Therefore, the loop executes twice and the program outputs 4 and 3. Note that the expression i+1 has no effect, that is, it does not increment i. Let's see the second loop. The expression ++i is equivalent to ++i != 0. Will i ever be equal to 0? Yes, since the type of i is unsigned char, once it becomes 255 the next increment makes it 0. Therefore, the second loop outputs the values of i from 3 up to 255.

C.6.6 Write a program that reads two integers and displays the sum of the integers between them. For example, if the user enters 3 and 8, the program should display 22 because 4+5+6+7 = 22. The program should check which one of the two input numbers is the greater and act accordingly. Use a single for loop.

```
#include <iostream>
int main()
{
        int i, j, min, max, sum;

        std::cout << "Enter numbers: ";
        std::cin >> i >> j;

        if(i < j)
        {
                min = i;
                max = j;
        }
        else
        {
                min = j;
                max = i;
        }
        sum = 0;
        for(i = min+1; i < max; i++)
                sum += i;

        std::cout << "Sum: " << sum << '\n';
        return 0;
}
```

C.6.7 Write a program that reads the number of students in a class and their grades on a test. The program should display the average grade of the passed students, the average grade of the failed students, the minimum and maximum grade, and how many students got the same maximum grade. A student passes the exams with a grade ≥ 5. If the input grade is out of [0, 10] it should be ignored and the program should inform the user via a message, in order to enter a new value. Also, if the user enters -1, the insertion of grades should end.

```cpp
#include <iostream>
using std::cout;
using std::cin;

int main()
{
        int i, studs_num, suc, fail, times;
        float grd, sum_suc, sum_fail, min_grd, max_grd;

        cout << "Enter number of students: ";
        cin >> studs_num;
        if(studs_num <= 0)
        {
                cout << "Wrong number of students\n";
                return 0; // Program termination.
        }
        suc = fail = 0;
        sum_suc = sum_fail = 0;
        min_grd = 11;
        max_grd = -1;
        for(i = 0; i < studs_num; i++)
        {
                cout << "Enter grade: ";
                cin >> grd;

                if(grd == -1)
                        break;
                if(grd > 10 || grd < 0)
                {
                        cout << "Wrong grade, try again ...\n";
                        i--; /* If the input grade is out of [0, 10], the grade
is ignored and i is decremented to repeat the insertion. */
                        continue;
                }
                if(grd >= 5)
                {
                        suc++;
                        sum_suc += grd;
                }
                else
                {
                        fail++;
                        sum_fail += grd;
                }
                if(grd < min_grd)
                        min_grd = grd;
                if(grd > max_grd)
                {
                        max_grd = grd;
                        times = 1; // First appearance of the new maximum grade.
                }
```

```
                else if(max_grd == grd)
                        times++;
        }
        if(i)  // Check that at least one grade has been entered.
        {
                if(suc)
                        cout << "Avg(+): " << sum_suc/suc << '\n';
                else
                        cout << "Everybody failed\n";
                if(fail)
                        cout << "Avg(-): " << sum_fail/fail << '\n';
                else
                        cout << "None failed\n";

                cout << "Min: " << min_grd << " Max: " << max_grd << " (appeared "
<< times << " times)\n";
        }
        return 0;
}
```

C.6.8 Consider the following recursive formula:

$$a_n = 2 \times a_{n-1} - a_{n-2} + a_{n-3}, \text{ where } a_0 = 1, a_1 = 2, \text{ and } a_2 = 3.$$

Write a program that reads the value of integer n and displays the value of the n-th term. The program should force the user to enter a number greater than 2.

```
#include <iostream>
int main()
{
        int i, num, an, an1, an2, an3;

        for(;;)
        {
                std::cout << "Enter number [> 2]: ";
                std::cin >> num;
                if(num > 2)
                        break;
        }
        an1 = 3;
        an2 = 2;
        an3 = 1;
        for(i = 3; i <= num; i++)
        {
                an = 2*an1 - an2 + an3;
                an3 = an2;
                an2 = an1;
                an1 = an;
        }
        std::cout << "a[" << num << "] = " << an << '\n';
        return 0;
}
```

C.6.9 Write a program that reads an integer and displays a message to indicate whether it is a prime number or not. It is reminded that a prime number is any integer greater than 1 with no divisor other than 1 and itself.

```cpp
#include <iostream>
using std::cout;
using std::cin;

int main()
{
        int i, num;

        cout << "Enter number (>1): ";
        cin >> num;

        if(num > 1)
        {
                if(num % 2 == 0)
                {
                        if(num == 2)
                                cout << num << " is prime\n";
                        else
                                cout << num << " is not prime\n";
                        return 0;
                }
                for(i = 3; i <= num/2; i+=2)
                {
                        if(num % i == 0)
                        {
                                cout << num << " is not prime\n";
                                return 0; /* Since a divisor is found, it is not
needed to search for other divisors, so the program terminates. */
                        }
                }
                cout << num << " is prime\n";
        }
        else
                cout << "Error: Not valid number\n";
        return 0;
}
```

Comments: If the number is even other than 2, it is not prime and the program ends. If the number is odd, only the odd divisors are checked. Because any number *N* has no divisor greater than *N*/2, the program checks if any integer from 2 up to the half of the input number divides that number. If a divisor is found, the program ends.

Note that this solution is not the most efficient. It can be further improved. For example, we could check for divisors from 2 up to the square root of the input number, given the math fact, that, if a number *N* is not prime, it has at least two divisors greater than 1, and one of them is equal or less than $\sqrt{N}$. To find the square root, we can use the sqrt() function or else compare i*i with num.

NESTED LOOPS

When an iteration loop is included in the body of another loop, each iteration of the outer loop triggers the execution of the nested loop. We can nest loops within loops to any depth it is needed. Also, any loop may be nested within any other kind of loop. For example, we can nest a while loop inside a for loop inside a `do-while` loop, they can be mixed in any way we wish. I'll use `for` loops to explain the nested loops. Nested `while` and `do-while` loops are executed in a similar way. For example, let's trace the iterations in the following program:

```cpp
#include <iostream> // Example 6.7
int main()
{
        int i, j;

        for(i = 0; i < 2; i++)
        {
                std::cout << "One ";
                for(j = i+1; j < 2; j++)
                        std::cout << "Two ";
        }
        return 0;
}
```

First iteration of the outer loop (i=0): Since the condition (i < 2) is true, the program displays One.

First iteration of the inner loop (j=1): Since the condition (j < 2) is true, the program displays Two.

Second iteration of the inner loop (j=2): Since the condition (j < 2) is false the loop terminates.

Second iteration of the outer loop (i=1): Since the condition (i < 2) is true, the program displays One.

First iteration of the inner loop (j=2): Since the condition (j < 2) is false the loop terminates.

Third iteration of the outer loop (i=2): Since the condition (i < 2) is false the loop terminates.

Therefore, the program displays: One Two One

As we said, the `break` statement terminates the execution of the loop in which it is contained. For example, what is the output of the following program?

```cpp
#include <iostream> // Example 6.8
int main()
{
        int i, j;

        for(i = 1; i < 3; i++)
        {
                for(j = 0; j < i; j++)
                {
                        if(i+j == 1)
                                break;
                        std::cout << "Two ";
                }
                std::cout << "One ";
        }
        std::cout << i << ' ' << j << '\n';
        return 0;
}
```

First iteration of the outer loop (i=1): Since the condition (i < 3) is true, the inner loop is executed.
    First iteration of the inner loop (j=0): Since i=1 and j=0, the if condition is true and the break statement terminates the inner loop. Then, the program displays One.

Second iteration of the outer loop (i=2): Since the condition (i < 3) is true, the inner loop is executed.
    First iteration of the inner loop (j=0): Since j=0, the condition (j < i) is true. Since i=2 and j=0, the if condition is false and the program displays Two.
    Second iteration of the inner loop (j=1): Like before, the program displays Two.
    Third iteration of the inner loop (j=2): Since j=2, the condition (j < 2) is false and the loop terminates. Then, the program displays One.

Third iteration of the outer loop (i=3): Since the condition (i < 3) is false the loop terminates.

The values of i and j are 3 and 2, respectively. Therefore, the program displays:

One   Two   Two   One   3   2

EXERCISES

C.6.10 What is the output of the following program?

```cpp
#include <iostream>
int main()
{
        int i, j, k;

        for(i = 0; i < 2; i++)
        {
                std::cout << "? ";
                for(j = i+1; j; j--)
                {
                        std::cout << "! ";
                        for(k = i; k < j+1; k++)
                                std::cout << "* ";
                }
        }
        return 0;
}
```

Answer: Let's trace the iterations:

First iteration of the outer loop (i=0): Since the condition (i < 2) is true, the program displays ? and the inner loop is executed.
    First iteration of the inner loop (j=1): The condition j corresponds to (j != 0) which is true. Therefore, the program displays !.
    Execution of the inner loop (k=0): The loop is executed twice for k=0 and k=1 and the program displays two *.
Second iteration of the inner loop (j=0): Since the condition (j != 0) is false the loop terminates.

Next iterations are executed in a similar way. Finally, the program displays: ? ! * *?   ! * * ! *

C.6.11 Write a program that reads an integer which corresponds to a number of lines. The program should display in the first line a number of '*' equal to the input number and one less in each next line. For example, if the user enters 5 the program should display:

```
*****
 ****
  ***
   **
    *
```

```cpp
#include <iostream>
using std::cout;
using std::cin;

int main()
{
        int i, j, lines;

        cout << "Enter lines: ";
        cin >> lines;

        for(i = 0; i < lines; i++)
        {
                for(j = 0; j < i; j++)
                        cout << ' ';
                for(j = lines; j > i; j--)
                        cout << '*';
                cout << '\n';
        }
        return 0;
}
```

Comments: Suppose that the user enters 5. Let's explain the code by tracing the first two iterations of the outer loop.

First iteration of the outer loop (i=0): Since the condition (i < 5) is true, the inner loop is executed.
  Execution of the first inner loop (j=0): Since j=0 and i=0, the condition (j < i) is false and the loop terminates.
  Execution of the second inner loop (j=5): Since j=5 and i=0, the condition (j > i) is true and the loop displays *. This is repeated four more times. Then, a line change is made.

Second iteration of the outer loop (i=1): Since the condition (i < 5) is true, the inner loop is executed.
  Execution of the first inner loop (j=0): Since j=0 and i=1, the condition (j < i) is true, so the program displays a space.
  Execution of the second inner loop (j=5): Since j=5 and i=1, the condition (j > i) is true and the loop displays *. This is repeated three more times. Then, a line change is made.

So far, the program has displayed:

```
*****
 ****
```

and the next output is produced in a similar way.

C.6.12 Write a program that reads the grades of five students in three different courses and displays the average grade of each student in these three courses, as well as the average grade of all students.

```cpp
#include <iostream>
using std::cout;
using std::cin;

int main()
{
        const int LESSONS = 3;
        const int STUDENTS = 5;
        int i, j;
        float grd, stud_grd, sum_grd;

        sum_grd = 0;
        for(i = 0; i < STUDENTS; i++)
        {
                cout << "***** Student_" << i+1 << '\n';
                stud_grd = 0; /* This variable holds the sum of a student's
grades in all courses. It is initialized to 0 for each one. */
                for(j = 0; j < LESSONS; j++)
                {
                        cout << "Enter grade for lesson " << j+1 << ": ";
                        cin >> grd;
                        stud_grd += grd;
                        sum_grd += grd; /* This variable holds the sum of all
grades. */
                }
                cout << "Average grade for student_" << i+1 << " is " << stud_
grd/LESSONS << '\n';
        }
        cout << '\n' << "Total average grade is " << sum_grd/
(STUDENTS*LESSONS) << '\n';
        return 0;
}
```

C.6.13 Write a program that displays the integer solutions, if any, of: $4x - 2y + 3z = 20$, $xyz < 15$ and $x^2 + y^2 + z^2 > 8$, where x is an integer within [-10, 10], y is within [-3, 3] and z is within [2, 6].

```cpp
#include <iostream>
int main()
{
        int x, y, z, flag;

        flag = 1;
        for(x = -10; x <= 10; x++)
                for(y = -3; y <= 3; y++)
                        for(z = 2; z <= 6; z++)
                                if((4*x - 2*y + 3*z == 20) && (x*y*z < 15) &&
                                        (x*x + y*y + z*z > 8))
```

```
                        {
                                std::cout << "Solution: " << x << ' ' <<
y << ' ' << z << ' ' << '\n';

                                flag = 0;
                        }
        if(flag)
                std::cout << "No solution\n";
        return 0;
}
```

THE while STATEMENT

The while statement is the simplest way to create iteration loops. Its syntax is:

```
while(exp)
{
        /* block of statements (loop body) that is repeatedly executed as long
as the value of exp is true. */
}
```

As with the if and for statements, if the loop body consists of a single statement, the braces can be omitted. The value of the controlling expression exp is evaluated. If it is false, the loop is not executed. If it is true, the loop body is executed and exp is evaluated again. If it is false, the loop terminates. If not, the loop body is executed again. This process is repeated until exp becomes false. For example, the following program uses the while statement to display the integers from 10 to 1:

```
#include <iostream> // Example 6.9
int main()
{
        int i = 10;

        while(i != 0)
        {
                std::cout << i << '\n';
                i--;
        }
        return 0;
}
```

Note that we could write while(i) *instead of* while(i != 0). *Similarly,* while(!i) *is equivalent to* while(i == 0).

The for and while statements are closely related. In fact, the for statement:

```
for(exp1; exp2; exp3)
{
        statements;
}
```

is equivalent to:

```
exp1;
while(exp2)
{
        statements;
        exp3;
}
```

unless the `for` loop contains a `continue` statement.

To answer in the question whether to use the `while` or the `for` statement, given that both produce equivalent code, I'd say that it is mainly a matter of personal preference. Typically, the `while` statement is used when the number of the iterations is unknown or when a condition is directly tested without initializing a variable or using a step.

When the number of the iterations is known and a step is used, it is preferable to use the `for` statement, because its compact form makes the loop easier to read. However, there are cases where the `for` statement, although it may seem the best option, can produce "inelegant" code. The use of `for` in the exercise C.6.7 is such an example. If the user enters a wrong value, the step changes inside its body (e.g., `i--`), which is something that I consider "inelegant". If this `for` statement is replaced with a `while` statement, the code becomes more elegant. Do it and see the difference.

If `exp` is always true the loop is executed forever, unless its body contains an exit statement (e.g., `break`). For example, the following loop is infinite:

```
while(1)
        cout << "One\n";
```

By convention, most programmers use the value `1` or `true` to create an infinite loop. However, any non-zero constant can be used. Usually, when a program continuously reads data until a condition becomes true, I prefer to use an infinite loop. For example, let's read integers:

```
int i;
while(1)
{
        cout << "Enter number: ";
        cin >> i;
        ...
}
```

Others prefer not to prompt the user to enter data and put the `cin` statement in the `while` condition:

```
while(cin >> i)
{
        ...
}
```

In this way not only the value is entered but the condition of the `cin` is also checked. If something goes wrong, the condition becomes false and the loop ends. However, I prefer the first way, that is, first guide the user with an appropriate message about what to enter and then enter the value. If we want to check the state of the input stream, we can do it after the input. As I mentioned in Chapter 3, for the sake of brevity and simplicity, I omit such checks.

As with the `for` statement, a; at the end of the `while` statement declares an empty loop body. For example, putting a; after the parentheses:

```
int a = 1;
while(a != 10);
        a++;
```

makes the loop infinite, and the statement a++; will never be executed. A last example before we go to the exercises. What does the following program output?

```
#include <iostream> // Example 6.10
int main()
{
        int i = 6, sum = 0;

        while(i >= 0)
        {
                sum =+ 20;
                i = i-2;
        }
        std::cout << "Sum: " << sum << '\n';
        return 0;
}
```

Trace the iterations and be careful with the calculations, before you see the answer in the next page; should be easy for you.

Caught you sleeping? Is 80 your answer?

Who told you that the =+ is a compound operator? You were warned at Chapter 4 that the = in a compound operator comes second, weren't you? Therefore, the statement sum =+ 20; is equivalent to sum = +20;, which merely assigns 20 to sum, and that is the output value. Had I written sum += 20, the program would display 80 indeed.

Basically, the main purpose of this example is to show you that when reading code, even if it is a few lines, imagine tens of thousands, it is very easy to skip a simple bug. Sometimes, the easier you insert a bug, the harder is to find it. Just remember, when writing code you should be particularly concentrated, cautious, and in a good mood. Continue with the exercises; watch out for the next traps though.

EXERCISES

C.6.14 What is the output of the following program?

```cpp
#include <iostream>
int main()
{
        int i = 4, j = 3;

        while(i >> 1)
        {
                i--;
                while(!(j%i))
                {
                        std::cout << "One ";
                        j--;
                        if(i == 1)
                                break;
                }
                j += 2;
        }
        std::cout << j << '\n';
        return 0;
}
```

Answer: As with the nested for loops, each iteration of the outer while loop triggers the execution of the nested loop. Note that while(i >> 1) is equivalent to while((i >> 1) != 0), that is, it is checked whether the value of i shifted one place to the right is not 0. Also, while(!(j%i)) is equivalent to while(j%i == 0). Let's trace the first iteration of the outer loop:

   First iteration of the outer loop: Since i is 4, the condition is true, so, the inner loop is executed.
      First iteration of the inner loop: Since i and j are both 3 the condition (!(j%i)) is true, so the program displays One and j becomes 2. As we've said, the break statement terminates the loop in which it is contained.
      Second iteration of the inner loop: Since the condition is false, the loop terminates. Then, j becomes 4.

Eventually, the program outputs: One One One 6

C.6.15 Write a program that reads an integer and displays the number of its digits and their sum. For example, if the user enters 1234, the program should display 4 and 10 (1+2+3+4 = 10).

```cpp
#include <iostream>
int main()
{
        int num, sum, dig;

        sum = dig = 0;
        std::cout << "Enter number: ";
        std::cin >> num;

        if(num == 0)
                dig = 1;
        else
        {
                if(num < 0)
                        num = -num;

                while(num != 0)
                {
                        sum += num % 10; // We find the last digit and add it.
                        num /= 10; // Remove the last digit.
                        dig++;
                }
        }
        std::cout << dig << " digits and their sum is " << sum << '\n';
        return 0;
}
```

C.6.16 Write a program that reads an integer in [0, 255] continuously and displays it in binary. For example, if the user enters 32, the program should display 00100000. The program should also display the word Hi a number of times equal to the input number. If the user enters a number out of [0, 255], the program should display the total number of the displayed Hi, then terminate. It should also display the smallest and largest input number, as well as the average of the input numbers with a value in [8, 50]. Use while loops only.

```cpp
#include <iostream>
using std::cout;
using std::cin;

int main()
{
        int i, num, times, cnt, min, max, sum;

        times = cnt = sum = 0;
        min = 256;
        max = -1;
        while(1)
        {
                cout << "\nEnter number: ";
                cin >> num;
                if(num < 0 || num > 255)
                        break;
```

```
                        i = 7;
                        while(i >= 0) // Check each bit.
                        {
                                if((num >> i) & 1)
                                        cout << '1';
                                else
                                        cout << '0';
                                i--;
                        }
                        i = 0;
                        while(i < num)
                        {
                                cout << "\nHi";
                                i++;
                        }
                        times += num;
                        if(num >= 8 && num <= 50)
                        {
                                sum += num;
                                cnt++;
                        }
                        if(max < num)
                                max = num;
                        if(min > num)
                                min = num;
        }
        cout << "Total number of Hi is: " << times << '\n';
        cout << "Min: " << min << " Max: " << max << '\n';
        if(cnt)
                cout << "Avg: " << (float)sum/cnt << '\n';
        else
                cout << "No integer in [8, 50] is entered\n";
        return 0;
}
```

C.6.17 The sum of the series $1/1 - 1/3 + 1/5 - 1/7 + 1/9 - \ldots$ converges to pi/4. Write a program that finds how many terms should be added until the result converges to pi/4 with an accuracy of 0.001. Consider pi equal to 3.14. Use the fabs() function to check for the convergence.

```
#include <iostream>
#include <cmath>
int main()
{
        int i, terms;
        double a, val, sum, final;
        const double pi = 3.14, accuracy = 0.001;

        terms = sum = 0;
        a = 1;
        i = 1;
        final = pi/4;
        while(1)
        {
                terms++;
                sum += a/i;
                if(fabs(sum-final) < accuracy)
                        break;
```

```
                a = -a;
                i += 2;
        }
        std::cout << "Sum: " << sum << ' ' << "Terms: " << terms << '\n';
        return 0;
}
```

C.6.18 Write a program that continuously reads a month number (1=Jan, 12=Dec), the first day of the month (1=Mon, 7=Sun), and displays the calendar for that month. If the input month is February, the program should prompt the user to enter its days, that is, 28 or 29. If the given month is out of [1, 12], the program should terminate.

```
#include <iostream>
using std::cout;
using std::cin;

int main()
{
        int i, mon, mon_days, day, rows;

        while(1)
        {
                cout << "\n\nEnter month: ";
                cin >> mon;
                if(mon < 1 || mon > 12)
                        break;
                if(mon == 2)
                {
                        cout << "Enter Feb days: ";
                        cin >> mon_days;
                }
                else if(mon==4 || mon == 6 || mon == 9 || mon == 11)
                        mon_days = 30;
                else
                        mon_days = 31;

                cout << "Enter start day (1=Mon,7=Sun): ";
                cin >> day;

                cout << "Mon\tTue\tWed\tThu\tFri\tSat\tSun\n";
                for(i = 1; i < day; i++) /* Add some spaces up to the first day
of the month to format the output. */
                        cout << '\t';

                rows = 0;
                for(i = 1; i <= mon_days; i++)
                {
                        cout << i << '\t';
                        if(i == 8-day+(rows*7))
                        {
                                cout << '\n';
                                rows++;
                        }
                }
        }
        return 0;
}
```

Comments: The `if` statement in the last `for` loop checks whether the last day of the week is reached or not. If so, a new line character is added. The `rows` variable counts how many day rows have been displayed so far. For example, if the user enters 3 as the first month day (day = 3), the first new line character will be added when i becomes 8-day+(rows*7) = 8-3+(0*7) = 5. Next, `rows` becomes 1. The next new line characters will be added when i becomes 12, 19, and 26, respectively.

C.6.19 Write a program that simulates a theatre's ticket office. Assume that the seats are 300. The program should display a menu to provide the following choices:

1. Buy a ticket. The ticket price is $15 for the adults and $10 for the minors. There is a 10% discount for the purchase of more than three tickets.
2. Display the total income and the number of the free seats.
3. *Program termination.*

```cpp
#include <iostream>
using std::cout;
using std::cin;

int main()
{
        const int SEATS = 300;
        int sel, adults, tkts, rsvd_seats;
        float cost, tot_cost;

        rsvd_seats = 0;
        tot_cost = 0;
        while(1)
        {
                cout << "\nMenu selections\n";
                cout << "---------------\n";

                cout << "1. Buy Ticket\n";
                cout << "2. Show Information\n";
                cout << "3. Exit\n";

                cout << "\nEnter choice: ";
                cin >> sel;
                switch(sel)
                {
                        case 1:
                                cout << "\nHow many tickets would you like to
buy? ";
                                cin >> tkts;
                                if(tkts + rsvd_seats > SEATS)
                                {
                                        cout << "\nSorry, the available seats are
%d\n", SEATS - rsvd_seats;
                                        break;
                                }
                                while(1)
                                {
                                        cout << "\nHow many adults? ";
                                        cin >> adults;
```

```
                                     if(adults <= tkts)
                                          break;
                                     else
                                          cout << "Error: Wrong number of
persons\n";
                              }
                              cost = adults*15 + (tkts-adults)*10;
                              if(tkts > 3)
                                   cost *= 0.9;
                              tot_cost += cost;
                              rsvd_seats += tkts;
                              if(rsvd_seats == SEATS)
                              {
                                     cout << "\nNot available seats. Income: "
<< tot_cost << '\n';

                                     return 0;
                              }
                       break;

                       case 2:
                              cout << "\nFree seats: " << SEATS-rsvd_seats <<
" Income: " << tot_cost << '\n' << '\n';
                              break;

                       case 3:
                       return 0;

                       default:
                              cout << "\nWrong choice\n";
                       break;
                }
        }
        return 0;
}
```

THE do-while STATEMENT

Unlike the for and while statements where the controlling expression is tested *before* the execution of the loop body, the do-while statement tests the controlling expression *after* each execution of the loop body. Therefore, a do-while loop is executed at least once. It has the form:

```
do
{
     /* block of statements (loop body) that is executed at least once and
then repeatedly executed as long as the value of exp is true. */
} while(exp);
```

The loop body is executed first, then exp is evaluated. If it is false, the loop terminates. Otherwise, the loop body is executed again and exp is tested once more. If it is false, the loop terminates. If not, the loop body is executed again. This process is repeated until exp becomes false.

 A do-while statement must end with a ;.

For example, the following program uses the `do-while` statement to display the integers from `1` to `10`:

```
#include <iostream> // Example 6.11
int main()
{
        int i = 1;
        do
        {
                std::cout << i << '\n';
                i++;
        } while(i <= 10);

        return 0;
}
```

Although the braces around a single statement can be omitted I always use them, otherwise, the reader might be mistaken and consider the `while` part to be a separate `while` statement. For example:

```
        do
                std::cout << i << '\n';
        while(++i <= 10);
```

In practice, the `do-while` loop is used less often than the `for` and `while` loops, as it can be replaced by them. Typically, it is used to check the validity of the input values. Let's use `do-while` in the following exercises, although we could use `for` or `while` instead.

EXERCISES

C.6.20 Write a program that reads continuously an integer and displays the word `Hi` a number of times equal to the input integer. The program should force the user to enter a positive integer. If the user enters the same value sequentially the program should terminate. Use `do-while` loops only.

```
#include <iostream>
using std::cout;
using std::cin;

int main()
{
        int i, num, last;

        do
        {
                cout << "Enter number: ";
                cin >> num;
        } while(num <= 0);

        do
        {
                last = num;
                i = 1;
                do
                {
                        cout << "Hi\n";
                        i++;
                } while(i <= num);
```

```
            do
            {
                    cout << "Enter number: ";
                    cin >> num;
            } while(num <= 0);
    } while(last != num);

    return 0;
}
```

C.6.21 Write a program that a teacher can use to test if the students know the multiplication table. The program should generate two random values within [1, 10] (e.g., a and b) and display axb = (the smaller number should appear first). The program should prompt the student to enter the result and display an informative message to indicate whether the answer is correct or not. If the student enters -1, the program should display the total number of correct and wrong answers and then terminate.

```
#include <iostream>
#include <cstdlib>
#include <ctime>
using std::cout;
using std::cin;

int main()
{
        int i, j, num, fails, wins;

        fails = wins = 0;
        srand(time(NULL));
        do
        {
                i = rand()%10+1; /* rand() returns a random positive integer and
the % operator constrains it in [0, 9]. We add one to constrain it in [1, 10]. */
                j = rand()%10+1;
                if(i < j)
                        cout << '\n' << i << 'x' << j << '=';
                else
                        cout << '\n' << j << 'x' << i << '=';

                cin >> num;
                if(num != -1)
                {
                        if(num == i*j)
                        {
                                cout << "Correct\n";
                                wins++;
                        }
                        else
                        {
                                cout << "Wrong. The answer is " << i*j << '\n';
                                fails++;
                        }
                }
        } while(num != -1);

        cout << "Fails: " << fails << " Wins: " << wins << '\n';
        return 0;
}
```

C.6.22 Write a program that calculates the $\sin(x)$ according to the Taylor series: $\sin(x)$ = $x - x^3/3!$ + $x^5/5! - x^7/7! + x^9/9! - \ldots$ The program should read x in degrees, convert it to radians, and calculate the result until the absolute difference of two successive terms is less than 0.0001. Don't calculate factorials or raise to powers. In particular, to calculate a new term use the previous term and multiply it by an appropriate number. For example, to calculate $x^5/5!$ use the previous term $x^3/3!$ and multiply it by $x*x/4*5$. Consider pi equal to 3.14. Use the `fabs()` function to find the difference and the `sin()` function to compare the results.

```cpp
#include <iostream>
#include <cmath>
int main()
{
        int i, a;
        double x, sum, prev_term, cur_term;
        const double pi = 3.14, accuracy = 0.0001;

        std::cout << "Enter x in degrees: ";
        std::cin >> x;

        x = pi*x/180; // Convert degrees to radians.
        sum = x;
        a = 1;
        cur_term = x;
        i = 2;
        do
        {
                a = -a;
                prev_term = cur_term;
                cur_term = prev_term * x*x/(i*(i+1));
                sum += cur_term * a;
                i += 2;
        } while(fabs(cur_term-prev_term) >= accuracy);

        std::cout << "Sum: " << sum << ' ' << "sin: " << sin(x) << '\n';
        return 0;
}
```

THE goto STATEMENT

The `goto` statement is used to transfer control to another statement within the same function, provided that this statement has a label. Its syntax is:

```cpp
goto label;
```

When the `goto` statement is executed, the program transfers control to the statement that follows the label. A `label` is named like a variable and it must be unique in the function where the `goto` statement is used. Its name must be followed by a colon `:`. The scope of the `label` is the entire function. For example, in the following program, if the user enters `-1` the `goto` statement transfers the execution to the START label and the loop is repeated.

```cpp
#include <iostream> // Example 6.12
int main()
{
        int i, num;
```

```
START:
        for(i = 0; i < 5; i++)
        {
                std::cout << "Enter number: ";
                std::cin >> num;
                if(num == -1)
                        goto START; /* We could write i=-1; and get the same
result; it is just an example of how to use goto. */
        }
        return 0;
}
```

Usually, it is better to avoid the use of `goto`, because the transition of the program's execution from one point to another and then to another and so on leads to obscure, hard-to-read and complex code that is hard to maintain and modify. In fact, most programmers oppose its use, arguing that it has no place in a well-structured program. However, `goto` can be helpful in several cases such as to group a block of statements when something goes wrong. For example:

```
if(error_1)
        goto ERROR;
...
if(error_2)
        goto ERROR;
...
ERROR:
... // Error handling statements.
```

As another example, since `break` terminates only the `switch` or loop statement in which it is contained, `goto` can be helpful to exit from a nested `switch`, or from a `switch` inside a loop, or from a deeply nested loop. For example:

```
for(i = 0; i < 10; i++)
        for(j = 0; j < 20; j++)
                for(k = 0; k < 30; k++)
                {
                        if(condition)
                                goto NEXT;
                }
NEXT:
...
```

Although it should be rarely used, don't forget that `goto` can simplify coding in some situations. Ignore statements like "never use `goto`", "`goto` is only for rookies", "no place for `goto` in structural programming", and disparaging comments like these.

Before ending this chapter, I'd like to point out once more that it is very important to write clear and easy to read code, particularly in case of large applications. In fact, when a company wants to hire a programmer, it might be more useful to ask the candidate to write a short essay and test his writing skills, how he expresses himself, if the text is clear, concise, well structured, balanced, without repetitions, ..., than to ask him what is the type of `p` in a declaration such as `int *(*p[5])(int*)` (don't worry, we'll answer it in Chapter 11) or which version of an overloaded function template the compiler will choose. Even if he cannot answer similar questions, it is easy to get the knowledge. On the other hand, learning to organize his thoughts in a straight-forward, comprehensive, concise, non-repetitive way is a very tough task. In high-school, I underestimated the value of the course "How to Write an Essay"; as a programmer, I realized its importance.

UNSOLVED EXERCISES

U.6.1   Write a program that displays all numbers from 111 to 999, except those that begin with 4 or end with 6.

U.6.2   Write a program that reads integers continuously and calculates their sum until it exceeds 100. Then, the program should display the sum and how many numbers were entered.

U.6.3   What is the output of the following program?

```
#include <iostream>
int main()
{
        for(unsigned char i = 1; i <= 256; i*=4)
                cout << "One\n";
        return 0;
}
```

U.6.4   Write a program that reads the initial population of a country and its annual population growth (as a percentage). Then, the program should read the number of years and display the new population for each year.

U.6.5   Write a program that reads continuously daily temperatures and displays the percentage of those with a temperature equal, less, or more than 40°F. If the user enters 1000, the insertion of temperatures should terminate.

U.6.6   Write a program that reads up to 100 integers. If an input number is greater than the last entered, the insertion of numbers should terminate and the program should display how many numbers were entered.

U.6.7   Write a program that reads three integers (e.g., a, b, and c) one after the other, not all together. The program should force the user to enter the numbers in descending order (i.e., a > b > c).

U.6.8   Write a program that reads the initial height from which a ball is thrown and displays after how many bounces the ball reaches a height less than ¼ of the initial height. The program should prompt the user to enter the decrease height ratio (%). For example, the input value 0.1 means that each time the ball hits the ground it bounces up to a height 10% less than the previous one.

U.6.9   Write a program that reads integers continuously, until the user enters 0. Then, the program should display the largest positive and the smallest negative input numbers. If the user enters only positive or negative numbers, the program should display an informative message. Zero is not counted in either positive or negative numbers.

U.6.10 Write a program that it is mandatory to read ten positive numbers. If an input number is negative, the program should prompt the user to enter another one. The program should display how many negative numbers were entered, before it terminates. Use one `for` loop. Zero is not counted in either positive or negative numbers.

U.6.11 Write a program that reads ten integers and displays how many times the user entered successive values. For example, if the user enters: -5, 10, 17, -31, -30, -29, 75, 76, 9, -4, the program should display 3 due to the pairs: {-31, -30}, {-30, -29}, and {75, 76}.

U.6.12 How many terms should be added by the series:

```
S₁ = 4 + 10 + 16 + 22 + …
S₂ = 1 + 8 + 15 + 22 + …
```

so that S_2 becomes at least 100 greater than S_1. Use a `do-while` loop.

U.6.13 Write a program that reads an integer and displays the number of its bits set. For example, if the user enters 30 (in binary: 0000000000000000000000000011110), the program should display 4.

U.6.14 Write a program that reads eight bits (each bit is 0 or 1) and displays the corresponding unsigned integer, assuming that the bits are entered from left to right. For example, if the user enters 10000000 the program should display 128.

U.6.15 Write a program that uses rand() to generate the integers 0 and 1 in a random manner. The program should read an integer that corresponds to rand() calls and display the maximum number of successive 0 and 1 pairs in the generated sequence. For example, if the user enters 15, rand() should be called 15 times and if, let's say, the generated sequence is 010011**010**100100, the program should display 2, because that is the maximum number of pairs with successive 01.

U.6.16 What is the output of the following program?

```cpp
#include <iostream>
int main()
{
        int i, j, k = 100;

        for(i = 0; i < 2; i++)
        {
                std::cout << "One ";
                for(j = 0; k; j++)
                {
                        std::cout << "Two ";
                        k -= 50;
                }
        }
        return 0;
}
```

U.6.17 Write a program that reads an integer which corresponds to a number of lines. The program should display in each line a number of '*' equal to the line number. For example, if the user enters 5 the program should display:

```
*
**
***
****
*****
```

U.6.18 Write a program that reads an integer which corresponds to a number of lines. Suppose that the user enters 4. The program should add spaces and '*' according to the line number, as shown below (three spaces at left of one '*' in the first line, two spaces at left of two '*' in the second line, and so on). When the last line is reached, the program should display in each line one '*' less, and the spaces at the right of '*', until one '*' is displayed.

```
   *
  **
 ***
****
 ***
  **
   *
```

U.6.19 Write a program that reads two integers (e.g., M, N) and produces an M×N grid. Each grid cell should be 3×2 characters wide. For example, see a 3×5 grid:

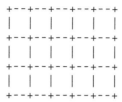

The three horizontal characters of each cell are: +-- and the two verticals are: +|

U.6.20 Write a program that reads a positive integer (e.g., N) and calculates the sum of:

$$\frac{5}{3} + \frac{25}{9} + \frac{125}{27} + ...$$

until it becomes greater than N. The program should display the last valid sum and the number of its terms, before it terminates.

U.6.21 Write a program that reads an integer (e.g., N) and displays the sum of:

$$\frac{1}{1 \times 3} + \frac{1}{3 \times 5} + \frac{1}{5 \times 7} + ... + \frac{1}{(N-2) \times N}$$

The program should force the user to enter an odd number greater than or equal to 3.

U.6.22 Write a program that reads an integer (e.g., N) and displays the sum of: $2^2+4^2+6^2+ \ ... \ +(2 \times N)^2$. The program should force the user to enter a positive integer less than 20. Use one loop only.

U.6.23 Write a program that reads 100 integers and displays the number entered the most successive times. If more than one number entered the same most successive times, the program should display the last one.

U.6.24 Write a program that reads 100 integers and displays the two largest different values.

U.6.25 Write a program that reads an integer and displays the prime numbers that are less than or equal to it. It is reminded that a prime number is any integer greater than 1 with no divisor other than 1 and itself.

U.6.26 Write a program that reads an integer and displays its digits in words. If the number is negative, it should begin with the word minus. The program should accept integers up to five digits. For example, if the user enters -12, the program should display minus one two.

U.6.27 Write a program that reads a positive integer and checks if it is an Armstrong number. An Armstrong number is a number that it is equal to the sum of its digits raised to the power of the number of digits. For example, the three-digit number 153 is an Armstrong number, because $1^3 + 5^3 + 3^3 = 1 + 125 + 27 = 153$.

Arrays

7

The variables we've used so far can store a single value. In this chapter, we'll discuss a new type of variable capable of storing a number of values. This type is called array. Essentially, an array is a data structure that groups elements of the same type in contiguous memory. It may contain basic type elements (e.g., `int`) or user-defined elements (e.g., structures). An array may be multidimensional. We'll discuss the most common form of arrays, which are the one-dimensional and two-dimensional arrays. To introduce you to arrays, we'll use basic types such as integers and floating-point elements. We'll also discuss the standard class `vector`, which is a more flexible and safer approach for grouping elements of the same type. We'll discuss other types of arrays, as well as their close relationship to pointers in later chapters. In Chapter 12, we'll describe some popular algorithms for searching a value in an array and sorting its elements.

ONE-DIMENSIONAL ARRAYS

An array is a data structure that contains a number of values, or else elements, of the same type. Each element can be accessed by its position within the array.

Declaration

To declare a one-dimensional array, we must specify its name, the number of its elements, and its data type, like this:

```
data_type array_name[number_of_elements];
```

The `number_of_elements`, or else the length/size of the array, is specified by a positive integer constant expression enclosed in brackets. All the elements are of the same type; it may be of any type (e.g., `int`, `float`, `char`, …). For example, the statement: `int arr[1000];` declares the array `arr` with `1000` elements of type `int`. To realize the importance of arrays, imagine that if C++ did not support this type of aggregate variable, we'd have to declare `1000` different integer variables.

 The length of an array cannot change during the program execution. It remains fixed.

That is, it is not allowed to add new elements to the array or delete elements from it. If the length of the array is used several times in the program, a good practice is to use a constant instead. If you ever need to change it, you just change the constant in only one place. Otherwise, you are under the risk of forgetting to change some of them. For example:

```
const int SIZE = 100;
double arr[SIZE]; /* The compiler creates an array of 100 elements of type
double. */
```

A common error is to use a variable to declare the length. For example:

```
int n;
cin >> n; // Suppose that the user enters the length of the array.
double arr[n]; // Wrong.
```

The C++ standard does not allow the size to be specified at runtime. As said, it must be a constant expression known at compile time. However, there are C++ compilers that allow the programmer to use a variable for the declaration. Thus, don't be surprised if the compiler you are using compiles the previous code.

When declaring an array, the compiler allocates a memory block to store the values of its elements. These values are stored one after another in consecutive memory locations. Typically, this memory block is allocated in a region called *stack* and it is automatically released when the function that declares the array terminates. For example, with the statement int arr[3]; the compiler allocates 12 bytes to store the values of the 3 elements. If we assume that the memory address of the first element is at position 100, the value of the first element is stored in positions 100-103, the value of the second element in positions 104-107, and the value of the third one in positions 108-111. To find the size of the allocated memory, we can use the sizeof operator. For example, the value of sizeof(arr) is 12.

 The maximum memory size that can be allocated for an array depends on the available memory in the stack.

For example, the following program:

```
#include <iostream> // Example 7.1
int main()
{
        double arr[300000];
        return 0;
}
```

may not run in your computer, unless the available stack size is large enough to hold the values. In Chapter 14, we'll see that we can allocate the required memory from a larger area, called *heap*.

 When memory is scarce, don't declare an array with more length than needed, in order to avoid waste of memory.

Accessing Elements

To access an element, we write the array's name followed by the element's index inside brackets []. The index specifies the position of the element within the array, and it must be an integer constant, variable, or expression. In an array of n elements, the first one is stored in position [0], the second one in position [1], and the last one in [n-1]. For example, the statement:

```
float arr[1000];
```

declares the array arr with 1000 elements of type float, that is, arr[0], arr[1], ..., arr[999]. An element can be used just like an ordinary variable. Here are some examples:

```
int i, j, a[10], b[10];
a[0] = 2; // The value of the first element becomes 2.
b[9] = a[0]; // The value of the last element becomes 2.
i = j = b[9]+1; // The values of i and j become 3.
a[i+j] = 100; /* Since i+j=3+3=6, the value of the seventh element becomes
100. */
b[2*i-1] = a[i%j]; // b[5] becomes equal to a[0], that is, 2.
```

Avoid side effects in indexing. For example, don't write something like this: b[i] = a[i--]; It depends on the compiler when i is decremented.

Let's see how to use an array. The following program reads five integers and stores them into an array. Then, it displays the array's elements in reverse order.

```
#include <iostream> // Example 7.2
int main()
{
        int i, arr[5];

        for(i = 0; i < 5; i++)
        {
                std::cout << "Enter number: ";
                std::cin >> arr[i];
        }
        for(i = 4; i >= 0; i--)
                std::cout << arr[i] << '\n';
        return 0;
}
```

Common Errors

A popular error of novice programmers is to forget that index numbering starts from zero. Remember, in an array of *n* elements, the first element is stored in position zero, not one, and the last one in position *n-1*, not *n*.

Another popular error. Suppose that we have two arrays of the same size and type and we want to copy the elements of the first one (e.g., a) into the second (e.g., b). It looks pretty natural to write b = a; However, this plausible assignment is illegal; it does not compile. In Chapter 8 and when investigating the close relationship between arrays and pointers, you'll see why. The simplest way to make the copy is to use a loop and copy the elements one by one or use a copy function, such as memcpy().

One more. Consider the a and b arrays and suppose that we want to check if the two arrays have the same values. It is logical to write if(b == a). No, it does not work as you'd expect, the elements are not compared. We'll see in Chapter 8 what is really compared. And the worse is that this misleading statement compiles and gives us the false impression that the arrays are truly compared. Be careful, it is a common pitfall.

And coming to the very serious error, which is the source of many program crashes.

> ⚠️ C++ does not check if the index is out of the array bounds. It is you task to make sure that its value is within the valid range of the array. If you use an out-of-range index to store data, the behaviour of the program is unpredictable.

For example, consider the following program:

```cpp
#include <iostream> // Example 7.3
int main()
{
        int i, a[3];

        for(i = 0; i < 4; i++)
        {
                a[i] = 0;
                std::cout << a[i] << '\n';
        }
        return 0;
}
```

Since a contains three elements, the valid indexes are from 0 to 2. Therefore, when i becomes 3 the statement a[3] = 0; assigns a value to an element out of the array's bounds. No, unfortunately, the compiler won't inform us about this major error. Even if we write a[-100] = 0; the code compiles. To continue, the value 0 overwrites the content of the memory just after a[2]. If this memory is allocated for i, i becomes 0 and the loop becomes infinite. Test it on your computer to see what happens.

Never ever forget, exceeding array's bounds poisons the program. Play loud *Strychnine*, kind of poison, from *Fuzztones* (original sound from *Sonics*) to stick it in your mind.

Initialization

Like ordinary variables, an array can be initialized when it is declared. Uninitialized elements get the arbitrary values of their memory locations, just like an uninitialized variable. In the most common form, the array initializer is a list of values enclosed in braces and separated by commas. The list is allowed to end with a comma. For example, with the declaration:

```cpp
int a[4] = {10, 20, 30, 40};
```

the values of a[0], a[1], a[2], and a[3] become 10, 20, 30, and 40, respectively.

If the initialization list is shorter than the number of the elements, the remaining elements are set to the default value of the element's type. The default value for integers is 0 and for floating-point types 0.0. For example, with the declaration:

```cpp
int a[4] = {10, 20};
```
the values of a[0] and a[1] become 10 and 20, while the values of a[2] and a[3] become 0. See another example. What will be the values of a?

```cpp
int i, a[10] = {0};
for(i = 0; i < 10; i++)
        a[++i] = 20;
```

When a is declared, its elements are initialized to 0. The statement a[++i] = 20; first increments i and then makes a[i] equal to 20. The `for` statement increments i once more. Therefore, the elements with even index, that is, a[0], a[2], ... remain 0, whereas the odd ones, that is, a[1], a[3], ... become 20.

The list of values must not exceed the number of the elements. For example:

```
int a[2] = {10, 20, 30}; // Wrong
```

If the array's length is omitted, the compiler will create an array with length equal to the number of the values in the list. For example, with the statement:

```
int a[] = {10, 20, 30, 40};
```

the compiler creates an array of four integers and assigns the values 10, 20, 30, and 40 to its elements.

If we want the values of an array, whether it is one-dimensional or multidimensional, to remain the same during program execution, we declare the array as `const`. A `const` array must be initialized when it is declared. For example, with the declaration:

```
const int a[] = {10, 20, 30, 40};
```

the a array is declared as `const`. If we attempt to change the value of any element the compiler will produce an error message. For example, it is illegal to write `a[1] = 5;`.

Since C++11 it is not necessary to add the =. For example:

```
int a[] {10, 20, 30, 40};
```

We can also use empty {} to initialize all elements with 0. For example:

```
int a[4] {}; // All elements are set to 0.
```

THE RANGED-BASED FOR STATEMENT

C++11 introduces a simpler form of the `for` statement to access a sequence of values, such as in an array or in a container (e.g., `vector`). This form of the `for` statement is called *range-for*. Its syntax is:

```
for(declaration : expression)
```

where the `expression` after: represents a sequence of values and the `declaration` specifies the variable to be used to hold the values of the elements of the sequence. For example:

```
int arr[] = {10, 20, 30, 40};
for(auto i : arr)
        cout << i << '\n';
```

In each iteration, from the first to the last element of the array, `i` becomes equal to the value of the corresponding element of the array, that is, its value is copied to `i`, and this is displayed. The loop traverses all the elements of the array. That is, `i` will be assigned the values 10, 20, 30, 40 sequentially. We could declare `i` as `int`, I just used the word `auto`, so that the iteration is written in a general way that does not depend on the type of the array. It is more flexible and convenient to let the compiler infer the type.

Note that the values of the array are assigned to `i`, which means that we cannot change their values by changing the value of `i`. In other words, `i` is a local copy of every element. For example, if we write:

```
for(auto i : arr)
        i += 5;
```

this code just adds 5 to i, it does not change the values of the elements. If we want to change the values of the elements we use a reference. We'll discuss references in Chapter 16, for now, it is enough to know that a reference is an alias of the variable to which it refers. For example:

```
for(auto& i : arr)
{
        i--;
        cout << i << '\n';
}
```

In each iteration, i is an alternate name for each element in the array. The value of the corresponding element is decremented by one, and this is displayed. Note that we can use a reference to access the elements, even if we are not going to change their values. In fact, this is the most efficient approach, in order to avoid copying which may be expensive on time. If we don't want to change any value, we make the reference const in order to prevent any unintentional change. For example, the following code calculates the product of the array's elements:

```
int mul = 1, arr[] = {10, 20, 30, 40};
for(const auto& i : arr)
        mul *= i;
```

Note that the ordinary for provides more abilities than the for range statement. For example, with a for range we cannot change the values of two elements at the same time. Typically, the for range is used in simple loops to traverse all the elements of standard containers (e.g., vector). Since it does not use a counter as an index to access the elements, we avoid the possibility to exceed the array's bounds and insert a bug as in example C.7.3. For more complicated loops, we use the ordinary for.

THE vector CLASS

As we'll see in Chapter 26, the Standard Template Library (STL) contains a large collection of containers, iterators, function objects, and algorithms that offer a great variety of ways to organize and access your data. Like an array, a container can store a number of elements. For example, the standard vector class is a container used to store elements of the same type contiguously in memory. The vector class is one of the most useful STL containers, probably the most useful. This section provides a short description of its features.

Unlike arrays, we can specify the initial size of a vector object dynamically, and the most important, its size can grow dynamically whenever required. That is, the vector class supports dynamic memory management that allows elements to be added or deleted while the program is running. Adding or deleting elements at the end of the vector is done at a fixed cost, that is, the time required does not depend on the number of elements. Adding or deleting elements at the beginning or in the middle of the vector is done at a linear cost, that is, the time required depends on the number of elements.

To use the vector class we must include the vector file. To create a vector object we use the template syntax <type> to specify the type of elements it will contain. The vector class supports several constructors to create objects. We'll discuss classes, objects, and constructors in Chapter 17. Until then, read this section to get an idea. Let's look at some examples of declaring vector objects:

```
vector<int> vec; // Create an empty vector of integers.
vector<int> vec(3, 20); // Create a vector of three integers set to 20.
vector<int> vec{1, 2, 3, 4}; /* Create a vector of four integers with the
respective initial values. */
```

```
int num;
cin >> num;
vector<double> vec(num); // Create a vector of num doubles.
```

The following program reads a number of students, creates a `vector` object that contains their grades and a second one with their names. Then, it displays the names and the grades of the students with a grade greater than or equal to the average grade.

```cpp
#include <iostream> // Example 7.4
#include <string>
#include <vector>
using namespace std;

int main()
{
        int i, num;
        float avg, sum;

        cout << "Enter number of students: ";
        cin >> num;

        vector<float> grd(num);
        vector<string> names(num);

        sum = 0;
        for(i = 0; i < num; i++)
        {
                cout << "Enter grade: ";
                cin >> grd[i];
                cin.get();

                cout << "Enter name: ";
                getline(cin, names[i]);

                sum += grd[i];
        }
        avg = sum/num;
        for(i = 0; i < num; i++)
                if(grd[i] >= avg)
                        cout << names[i] << ": " << grd[i] << '\n';
        return 0;
}
```

We'll discuss the `string` class in Chapter 10. For now, consider that each name is stored in a `string` object. Thus, the `names` object contains `num` elements of type `string`. Note that we use the `[]` operator to access the vector elements, as we do with arrays. In fact, as we'll learn in Chapter 18, the `vector` class overloads the `[]` operator. Also, the `vector` class provides the `at()` function, which takes as an argument the index of the element. For example:

```cpp
for(i = 0; i < num; i++)
        cout << names.at(i) << ": " << grd.at(i) << '\n';
```

The difference with the `[]` operator is that `at()` checks for exceeding the bounds of the vector and in such a case it creates the `out_of_range` exception (we'll discuss exceptions in Chapter 22). Therefore, if you care about safety, use `at()` and check for exceptions. On the other hand, if you are sure that your code will never exceed the limits, use `[]` for greater speed.

In addition to the dynamic definition of the `vector` size, it is very useful that the size of the initially allocated memory can dynamically increase by adding new elements. For example, the following program reads ten numbers and stores them in a `vector` object that is initially empty:

```
#include <iostream> // Example 7.5
#include <vector>
using namespace std;

int main()
{
        int i, num;
        vector<int> vec;

        for(i = 0; i < 10; i++)
        {
                cout << "Enter number: ";
                cin >> num;
                vec.push_back(num);
        }
        cout << vec.size() << ' ' << vec.capacity() << '\n';
        return 0;
}
```

push _ back() adds the integer to the end of the `vector` object. Exercise C.7.2 is a similar example.

Let's see how memory is managed. Typically, the compiler initially allocates more memory than needed to avoid successive memory allocations each time a new element is added. If the available memory runs out, then the compiler allocates new memory to store new elements. Its size depends on the implementation, where a typical size is half the original. The allocation of new memory may not be a simple extension to the adjacent memory, as this memory may be used for other purposes. In such a case, the compiler allocates new memory in another area and copies the contents of the original memory to the new one. Remember that `vector` elements are always stored in consecutive memory locations. The `capacity()` function returns the number of elements that can be stored in the allocated memory, while the `size()` function returns the number of elements that are already stored. For example, the above program with the compiler I used shows 10 and 16.

Besides the `at()` function, another way to securely manage a `vector` object is by using the `begin()` and `end()` functions. `begin()` returns an iterator that refers to the first element of the object, while `end()` returns an iterator that refers to the next position after the last element. For now, consider that an iterator behaves like a pointer. For pointers, we'll discuss in Chapter 8. See the following example to get an idea and you may look it again after reading Chapter 8:

```
vector<int> vec(10);
vector<int>::iterator iter;

for(iter = vec.begin(); iter != vec.end(); ++iter)
        *iter = 200;
```

Like any container, the `vector` class declares an iterator type. The `iter` variable is declared as iterator. As shown, we use `iter` as a pointer and the value 200 is assigned to all elements of the `vec` object. The use of `begin()` and `end()` functions along with an iterator to traverse the vector is a safe practice, as it ensures that the limits of the vector will not be exceeded.

By using iterators we can delete or add elements into it. For example, the `erase()` function takes as arguments two iterators that specify the part to be deleted:

```
vec.erase(vec.begin(), vec.begin()+3);
```

The first iterator specifies the beginning of the part to be deleted, while the second one its end, without including this position. Therefore, this statement deletes the first three elements, from `vec[0]` to `vec[2]`. If we call `size()` to display the number of elements we'd see that it is 7 indeed. In another example, if we write:

```
vec.erase(vec.begin()+1, vec.end());
```

all the elements of the `vec` object are deleted, except the first one. That is, `size()` returns 1. The `vector` class supports an overloaded version of `erase()`, which takes as an argument an iterator and deletes the element it refers to. For example, the statement:

```
vec.erase(vec.end()-1);
```

deletes the last element of the object. If we want to add a new element we use the `insert()` function. For example, the statement:

```
vec[3] = 20;
vec.insert(vec.begin()+3, 50);
```

inserts the value 50 just before the position indicated by the iterator, that is, before `vec[3]`. Therefore, the value of the new element `vec[3]` is 50, while the value of `vec[4]`, stored as `vec[3]` before the insertion, is 20. The `vector` class supports an overloaded version of `insert()` to add a number of elements. Its arguments are three iterators. Let's say their names are `pos`, `first`, and `last`. The new elements are inserted before the element at the position pointed by `pos`. The function copies all the elements between `first` and `last`, including the element pointed by `first` but not the one pointed by `last`. That is, the copy range includes all elements in the interval [`first`, `last`). Usually, this version of `insert()` is used to copy elements from one `vector` object to another. For example:

```
vector<int> v1(3, 20);
vector<int> v2(3, 10);
v1.insert(v1.begin()+1, v2.begin()+1, v2.end());
```

The content of `v1` becomes: 20 10 10 20 20

The `vector` class provides the `swap()` function and overloads several operators, such as the = and ==. For example:

```
vector<int> v1(3, 20);
vector<int> v2(5, 10), v3;
v1.swap(v2);
v3 = v1;
if(v3 == v2)
if(v3 != v2)
if(v3 < v2)
```

The `swap()` function exchanges the contents of two objects and, if necessary, allocates more memory to store the elements. Therefore, the elements of `v1` become five with a value of 10, while the elements of `v2` become three with a value of 20. The = operator assigns the elements of `v1` to `v3`, while the == operator compares the two objects. If they are the same, that is, if they have the same number of elements and their values are equal, the return value is `true`.

On the other hand, as we've said, if `v1` and `v3` were ordinary arrays it'd be illegal to write `v3 = v1`. To copy the elements we'd need to use an iteration loop or some copy function. You'll also see in Chapter 8 that it is wrong to write `if(v3 == v2)` to check if the two arrays have the same values.

One may ask, wouldn't be better to present the `vector` class later on after we've learned about classes and templates, so that we can better understand it? Before answering, let's discuss a bit about some very important differences between arrays and `vector`. The main weakness of an array is that it does not support out-of-bounds checks, and, as we said, if that happens, the consequences for the program may be catastrophic. In contrary, the `vector` class supports secure access to its elements. Second, the size of the array remains fixed, which means that we cannot add or delete elements from it. Instead, the size of a `vector` object can dynamically change by adding or deleting elements whenever we want. Third, when using an array, we have to write the code to manage it and support various functions, such as to search for a value within it. With `vector`, the code is ready and we just call the appropriate functions. For example, we saw `erase()` and `insert()`, there are many more.

As you see, the `vector` class is easy to work with and provides greater security and flexibility than the array. This is the reason why I decided to discuss `vector` in this chapter and not later on. The earlier you learn to use it the better for you; we'll use `vector` in several programming exercises in order to get familiar with it. C++11 has added the `array` class, which is also an easy-to-use and safer option compared to the array. Due to lack of space I won't present it. For more information about the `vector` and `array` classes, consult a standard library reference.

Nevertheless, because arrays existed long before standard containers and are still quite popular in production code, especially in older code, it is very important to learn their semantics and to use them well and safely, since it is almost certain that either you'll have to use them or meet them in existing code written by others. For example, in Chapter 8 we'll discuss arrays and pointers.

EXERCISES

C.7.1 What is the output of the following program?

```cpp
#include <iostream>
int main()
{
        int i, sum, a[] = {5, 6, 7, 8, 9};
        double b[] = {3.1, 1.9, 0.5, -4.1, -0.9};

        sum = 0;
        for(i = 0; a[i] = b[i]; i++)
                sum += a[i];
        std::cout << sum << '\n';
        return 0;
}
```

Answer: The condition `a[i] = b[i]` is equivalent to `(a[i] = b[i]) != 0`, which means that the elements of b are copied to the respective elements of a as long as `a[i]` does not become 0. If it does, the loop terminates. Since the type of a is `int`, only the integer parts of the b elements will be stored into the respective a elements. Therefore, when the value `0.5` is copied, `a[2]` becomes 0 and the loop terminates. The values of `a[3]` and `a[4]` remain the same. As a result, the program outputs the sum of `a[0]` and `a[1]`, that is, 3+1=4.

C.7.2 Write a program that an instructor can use in order to get grade statistics. The program should read the grades of the students continuously and store in one `vector` object the grades within [5, 10] and in a second one the grades within [0, 5]. If the user enters -1, the insertion of grades should end and the program should display the worst grade, the best grade, and the average of the grades stored in each vector. The program should force the user to enter grades within [0, 10] or the value -1.

```cpp
#include <iostream>
#include <vector>
using std::cout;
using std::cin;
using std::vector;

int main()
{
        int size;
        float grd, sum_suc, sum_fail, min_fail, max_fail, min_suc, max_suc;
        vector<float> suc, fail;

        sum_suc = sum_fail = 0;
        min_fail = min_suc = 11; // Initialize with a value greater than 10.
        max_fail = max_suc = -1; // Initialize with a value less than 0.
        while(1)
        {
                cout << "Enter grade: ";
                cin >> grd;
                /* There are several ways to check whether the input grade is
valid. In next exercises I use do-while. */
                while(1)
                {
                        if((grd >= 0 && grd <= 10) || (grd == -1))
                                break;
                        cout << "Error - Enter grade: ";
                        cin >> grd;
                }
                if(grd == -1)
                        break;
                if(grd >= 5 && grd <= 10)
                {
                        sum_suc += grd;
                        suc.push_back(grd);
                        if(grd > max_suc)
                                max_suc = grd;
                        if(grd < min_suc)
                                min_suc = grd;
                }
                else
                {
                        sum_fail += grd;
                        fail.push_back(grd);
                        if(grd > max_fail)
                                max_fail = grd;
                        if(grd < min_fail)
                                min_fail = grd;
                }
        }
        size = suc.size();
        if(size != 0)
                cout << "\nSuccess_Avg: " << sum_suc/size << " Best: " <<
max_suc << " Worst: " << min_suc << '\n';
        else
                cout << "\nAll students failed";
```

```
        size = fail.size();
        if(size != 0)
                cout << "\nFail_Avg: " << sum_fail/size << " Best: " <<
max_fail << " Worst: " << min_fail << '\n';
        else
                cout << "All students passed\n";
        return 0;
}
```

Comments: This program is an example of the great flexibility that the `vector` class provides. If we were using arrays to store the grades (e.g., `suc` and `fail`), we'd not know their exact size because the number of the students who passed and failed in the exams is unknown. Thus, we declare two empty vectors and memory will be allocated only if grades are stored in them.

C.7.3 Write a program that reads an integer and displays the digits that appear more than once and the number of their appearances. For example, if the user enters `1868`, the program should display that digit `8` appears twice. If no digit appears more than once, the program should display a related message.

```
#include <iostream>
using std::cout;
using std::cin;

int main()
{
        bool flag;
        int i, dig_times[10] = {0}; /* This array holds the appearances of each
digit. For example, dig_times[0] indicates how many times digit 0 appears. */
        cout << "Enter number: ";
        cin >> i;
        if(i == 0) // Check if 0 is entered.
                dig_times[0] = 1;
        else if(i < 0)
                i = -i;
        while(i != 0)
        {
                dig_times[i%10]++;
                i /= 10;
        }
        flag = 0;
        for(i = 0; i < 10; i++)
        {
                if(dig_times[i] > 1)
                {
                        cout << "Digit " << i <<  " appears " << dig_times[i] <<
" times\n";
                        flag = 1;
                }
        }
        if(flag == 0)
                cout << "No digit appears multiple times\n";
        return 0;
}
```

C.7.4 Write a program that reads integers continuously and stores them in a `vector` object. If the user enters -1, the insertion of numbers should terminate. Then, the program should check if the vector is symmetric, that is, if the value of the first element is equal to the last one, the value of the second one is equal to the value of the last but one, and so on. If it is not symmetric, the program should check if there is a duplicated value and, if so, it should terminate. If not, the program should display a message that all values are different.

```cpp
#include <iostream>
#include <vector>
using std::cout;
using std::cin;
using std::vector;

int main()
{
        bool flag;
        int i, j, size;
        vector<int> v;

        while(1)
        {
                cout << "Enter number: ";
                cin >> i;
                if(i == -1)
                        break;
                v.push_back(i);
        }
        size = v.size();
        flag = 1;
        for(i = 0; i < size/2 ; i++)
                if(v[i] != v[size-1-i])
                {
                        flag = 0;
                        break; /* Since we found out that the vector is not
symmetric, the loop ends. */
                }
        if(flag)
                cout << "Symmetric\n";
        else
        {
                cout << "Not symmetric with ";
                for(i = 0; i < size; i++)
                {
                        for(j = i+1; j < size; j++) /* This loop checks if there
is another element with the value of v[i]. */
                        {
                                if(v[i] == v[j])
                                {
                                        cout << "same values\n";
                                        return 0; /* Since we found out that two
elements have the same value, the program terminates. */
                                }
                        }
                }
                cout << "different values\n";
        }
        return 0;
}
```

Comments: If one wonders what happens if the number of elements is odd, the code is still valid, since the middle element is not compared with any other element.

C.7.5 Write a program that reads an integer and displays it in binary. Use an array to store the bits of the number. To display the bits of a negative number use the two's complement technique. For example, if the user enters -5:

    a. convert it to positive (i.e., 5).

    b. reverse its bits (i.e., 101_2 becomes $11111111111111111111111111111010_2$).

    c. add 1 (i.e., the number becomes $11111111111111111111111111111011_2$ and that should be the output value).

```cpp
#include <iostream>
using std::cout;
using std::cin;

int main()
{
        int i, j, tmp, bits[32]; /* This array holds the bits of the number,
that is 0 or 1. The size is 32, because we assume that the size of an integer
is 32 bits. */
        unsigned int num;

        cout << "Enter number: ";
        cin >> tmp;
        if(tmp < 0)
        {
                tmp = -tmp;
                tmp = ~tmp;
                tmp++;
        }
        num = tmp; // It is stored as positive.
        i = 0;
        /* Successive divisions by 2 and store each bit in the respective
array position. */
        while(num > 0)
        {
                bits[i] = num & 1;
                num >>= 1; // Equivalent to num /= 2.
                i++;
        }
        cout << "Binary form: ";
        // Display the bits from left to right.
        for(j = i-1; j >= 0; j--)
                cout << bits[j];
        return 0;
}
```

Comments: The reason I used the shift operator is to improve performance. However, it is unnecessary most likely, because the compiler would optimize the operation by itself.

C.7.6 What is the output of the following program?

```cpp
#include <iostream>
int main()
{
        int i, a[] = {-1, 5, 7}, b[] = {5, 4, -1};
```

```
        for(i = 0; i < 3; i++)
               a[a[i]-b[2-i]]++;
        for(--i; a[i]; i--)
               std::cout << a[i] << '\n';
        return 0;
}
```

Answer: Let's trace the iterations of the first loop:

> *First iteration* (i=0). a[a[0]-b[2]]++ = a[-1-(-1)]++ = a[0]++ = 0.
> *Second iteration* (i=1). a[a[1]-b[1]]++ = a[5-4]++ = a[1]++ = 6.
> *Third iteration* (i=2). a[a[2]-b[0]]++ = a[7-5]++ = a[2]++ = 8.

Therefore, a[0], a[1], and a[2] become 0, 6, and 8, respectively. In the second loop, i first decrements and becomes 2. The condition is equivalent to a[i] != 0. Since a[0] is 0, the loop outputs the values of a[2] and a[1], that is, 8 and 6, and then it terminates.

C.7.7 Write a program that reads products' codes and stores them in an integer array of 50 places. The program should store a code in the array only if it is not already stored. If the array becomes full or the user enters -1, the program should display the stored codes and terminate.

```
#include <iostream>
using std::cout;
using std::cin;
int main()
{
        const int SIZE = 50;
        bool found;
        int i, j, pos, num, code[SIZE];

        pos = 0;
        while(pos < SIZE)
        {
                cout << "Enter code: ";
                cin >> num;
                if(num == -1)
                        break;

                found = 0;
                /* The pos variable indicates how many codes have been stored
in the array. The loop checks if the input code is already stored. If it is,
found becomes 1 and the loop terminates. */
                for(j = 0; j < pos; j++)
                {
                        if(code[j] == num)
                        {
                                cout << "Error: Code " << num << " exists.\n";
                                found = 1;
                                break;
                        }
                }
                /* If the code is not stored, we store it and the index
position is incremented. */
```

```
                if(found == 0)
                {
                        code[pos] = num;
                        pos++;
                }
        }
        cout << "\nCodes: ";
        for(i = 0; i < pos; i++)
                cout << code[i] << '\n';
        return 0;
}
```

C.7.8 Write a program that reads 100 integers and stores them in an array. Then, the program should find and display the two different higher values.

```
#include <iostream>
using std::cout;
using std::cin;

int main()
{
        const int SIZE = 100;
        int i, max_1, max_2, arr[SIZE];

        for(i = 0; i < SIZE; i++)
        {
                cout << "Enter number: ";
                cin >> arr[i];
        }
        max_1 = max_2 = arr[0];
        for(i = 1; i < SIZE; i++)
        {
                if(max_1 != arr[i])
                {
                        max_2 = arr[i]; /* We assign that value to max_2, to
compare it with the remaining elements. */
                        break;
                }
        }
        if(i == SIZE)
        {
                cout << "Array contains the same value: " << max_1 << '\n';
                return 0;
        }
        /* Continue with the loop execution from the point the second loop
ended. */
        for(; i < SIZE; i++)
        {
                if(arr[i] > max_1)
                {
                        max_2 = max_1; /* The second higher value becomes equal
to the highest so far. */
                        max_1 = arr[i];
                }
```

```
                else if(arr[i] > max_2 && arr[i] != max_1) /* Search for the
second higher value that is not equal to the first one. */
                        max_2 = arr[i];
        }
        cout << "First_Max: " << max_1 << " Sec_Max: " << max_2 << '\n';
        return 0;
}
```

Comments: The typical approach to find the n-th minimum or maximum element of an array is to sort the array by some sorting algorithm, such as the ones presented in Chapter 12. Then, the element we are searching for is the arr[n-1].

C.7.9 Write a program that declares an array of ten integers and assigns random values within [5, 20] to its elements. Then, the program should check if the array contains duplicated values, and if any, it should delete them. When an element is deleted, the next elements should be shifted one position to the left. The empty positions should be given the value -1. For example, if the array is: {9, 12, 8, 12, 17, 8, 8, 19, 1, 19} it should become: {9, 12, 8, 17, 19, 1, -1, -1, -1, -1}. To remember how to use srand() and rand() read again the example C.6.2.

```
#include <iostream>
#include <cstdlib>
#include <ctime>
int main()
{
        const int SIZE = 10;
        int i, j, k, size, arr[SIZE];

        srand(time(NULL));
        for(i = 0; i < SIZE; i++)
                arr[i] = rand()%16+5;

        size = SIZE;
        for(i = 0; i < size; i++)
        {
                j = i+1;
                while(j < size)
                {
                        if(arr[i] == arr[j])
                        {
                                for(k = j; k < size-1; k++)
                                        arr[k] = arr[k+1]; /* Shift the elements
one position to the left. */
                                size--; /* Since the element is deleted, we
decrement their number. */
                        }
                        else
                                j++;
                }
        }
        for(i = size; i < SIZE; i++)
                arr[i] = -1;
        for(i = 0; i < SIZE; i++)
                std::cout << arr[i] << ' ';
        return 0;
}
```

C.7.10 Write a program that reads the order of preference that 100 tourists answered in the question: "What did you enjoy the most in Greece?"

1. The natural diversity
2. The climate
3. The islands
4. The night life
5. The monuments
6. The people
7. The food

Each answer takes 1–7 points according to its rank order. The first answer takes 7 points, the second one takes 6 points, and the last one takes 1 point. For example, if two tourists answered the following, the program should display:

1ST TOURIST	2ND TOURIST	PROGRAM OUTPUT
5 (7p.)	3 (7p.)	Answer_1 gets 6 points
4 (6p.)	7 (6p.)	Answer_2 gets 8 points
6 (5p.)	2 (5p.)	Answer_3 gets 11 points
3 (4p.)	1 (4p.)	Answer_4 gets 8 points
2 (3p.)	5 (3p.)	Answer_5 gets 10 points
1 (2p.)	4 (2p.)	Answer_6 gets 6 points
7 (1p.)	6 (1p.)	Answer_7 gets 7 points

The program should read valid answers in [1, 7] and check if the answer is already given. If it is, the program should display a message and prompt the user to enter a new one.

```cpp
#include <iostream>
#include <cstring>
using std::cout;
using std::cin;

int main()
{
        const int ANSWERS = 7;
        int i, j, sel, pnts[ANSWERS] = {0}; /* This array holds the points of
each answer. For example, pnts[0] holds the points of the first answer,
pnts[1] holds the points of the second answer and so on. */
        int given_ans[ANSWERS] = {0}; /* This array is used to check if an
answer is already given or not. If an element's value is 1, it means that the
respective answer is chosen. For example, if the user chooses the third
answer, given_ans[2] becomes 1. */
        for(i = 0; i < 100; i++)
        {
                cout << "\nEnter answers of tourist_" << i+1 << ":\n";

                memset(given_ans, 0, sizeof(given_ans)); /* The values must be
zeroed before reading the answers of a new tourist. I know that you don't
know memset(), it just fills a block of memory with a particular value
(e.g., 0). Yes, we could make an iteration loop instead. */
```

```
                    for(j = 0; j < ANSWERS; j++)
                    {
                            while(1) /* Infinite loop until the user enters a valid
answer, not already given. */
                            {
                                    cout << "Answer_" << j+1 << " [1-" << ANSWERS <<
"]: ";

                                    cin >> sel;
                                    if(sel < 1 || sel > ANSWERS)
                                            cout << "Wrong answer ...\n";
                                    else if(given_ans[sel-1] == 1)
                                            cout << "Error: This answer is already
given ...\n";
                                    else
                                            break;
                            }
                            pnts[sel-1] += ANSWERS - j; /* For example, if the first
answer (j = 0) is the fifth choice, then pnts[sel-1] = pnts[5-1] = pnts[4]
+= 7-0 = 7; that is, 7 more points are added to the points of the fifth
choice. */
                            given_ans[sel-1] = 1;
                    }
            }
            cout << "\n***** Answer Results *****\n";
            for(i = 0; i < ANSWERS; i++)
                    cout << "Answer_" << i+1 << " gets " << pnts[i] << " points\n";
            return 0;
}
```

C.7.11 Write a program that simulates an on-line lottery game. Suppose that the winning numbers are 10 and their values are within [0, 100]. However, the program should be written in a way to control the winning numbers. In particular, the "cheat" is that 3 of the winning numbers in each lottery should have also been drawn in the previous one. The program should ask the user if he wants to play, and if the user answers no, the program terminates. The program should output the winning numbers of each lottery. For simplicity, suppose that the same number may appear more than once.

```
#include <iostream>
#include <cstdlib>
#include <ctime>
using std::cout;
using std::cin;

int main()
{
        const int SIZE = 10;
        int i, pos1, pos2, pos3, ans, arr[SIZE];

        srand(time(NULL));
        // First lottery.
        for(i = 0; i < SIZE; i++)
        {
                arr[i] = rand()%101;
                cout << arr[i] << ' ';
        }
```

```
      while(1)
      {
            cout << "\nContinue to play? (0:No): ";
            cin >> ans;
            if(ans == 0)
                  return 0;
            /* We choose three random positions. The numbers stored in
these positions will be "drawn" in the next lottery. */
            pos1 = rand()%SIZE;
            do
            {
                  pos2 = rand()%SIZE;
            } while(pos1 == pos2);

            do
            {
                  pos3 = rand()%SIZE;
            } while((pos1 == pos3) || (pos2 == pos3));

            // Next lottery.
            for(i = 0; i < SIZE; i++)
            {
                  if((i == pos1) || (i == pos2) || (i == pos3))
                  {
                        cout << arr[i] << ' '; // Here is the cheat.
                        continue;
                  }
                  arr[i] = rand()%101;
                  cout << arr[i] << ' ';
            }
      }
      return 0;
}
```

Comments: With this simple example of an "unfair" lottery I just wanted to show you that a betting software can be written in a way to manipulate the winning results. Therefore, **stay away** from betting sites that advertise big profits in on-line lotteries. The big profits they promise are not for you, but for their owners.

TWO-DIMENSIONAL ARRAYS

The form of a two-dimensional array resembles that of a matrix in math; it is an array of elements of the same type arranged in rows and columns. As with one-dimensional arrays we'll use arithmetic types in our examples. As we move on and learn new types, we'll see more application examples, such as in Chapter 10 for storing strings.

Declaration

To declare a two-dimensional array, we must specify its name, its data type, and the number of its rows and columns, like this:

```
data_type array_name[number_of_rows][number_of_columns]
```

The number of its elements is equal to the product of rows multiplied by columns. For example, the statement `double a[20][3];` declares the two-dimensional array a with 60 elements of type `double`.

Accessing Elements

To access an element, we write the name of the array followed by the element's row index and column index enclosed in double brackets. As with one-dimensional arrays, the indexing of rows and columns starts from 0. For example, the statement:

```
int a[3][4];
```

declares a two-dimensional array, whose elements are the `a[0][0]`, `a[0][1]`, ... `a[2][3]`, as shown here:

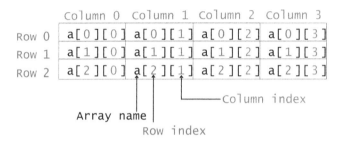

Although a two-dimensional array is visualized as an array with rows and columns, its elements are stored in consecutive memory locations in row-major order, with the elements of row 0 first, followed by the elements of row 1, and so on. For example, the array a consists of 12 integers stored successively in memory, which we access as if they were three arrays of four integers.

 Although we refer to multidimensional arrays, in fact, C++ supports only one-dimensional arrays. Because an element of an array can also be an array we can simulate multidimensional arrays.

For example, the elements of the a array are the `a[0]`, `a[1]`, and `a[2]`, where each one of them is an array of four integers. I'll analyse it more in Chapter 8, when discussing about pointers and two-dimensional arrays. Also, we'll see in exercise C.8.27 how we can treat a two-dimensional array as if it were one-dimensional. In another example, if we write `int a[3][4][5];` a is an array of three elements, where each one is an array of four elements. Each of these four elements is an array of five integers.

As with one-dimensional arrays, when a two-dimensional array is declared, the compiler allocates a memory block in the stack to store the values of its elements. For example, with the declaration `int a[4][5];` the compiler allocates a block of 80 bytes to store the values of its 20 elements. To access an element, we must specify its row index and its column index. Here are some examples:

```
int i = 2, j = 2, a[3][4];
a[0][0] = 100; // The value of the first element becomes 100.
a[i-1][2] = 20; // The value of the seventh element becomes 20.
a[2][j+1] = a[i-2][j-2]; /* The value of the last element becomes equal to
the first element. */
```

 As with one-dimensional arrays, special care is required not exceed the bounds of any dimension.

Consider the two-dimensional integer array a[ROWS][COLS]. Since its elements are stored sequentially in memory, the compiler in order to find the memory address of a[i][j] calculates the row size, that is, row_size = COLS × sizeof(int) and multiplies it by i. Then, it multiplies j by the size of an element, and adds the products to the array's address. Therefore, we have:

```
memory_address = a + (i × row_size) + (j × sizeof(int))
```

 To find the memory address of an element, only the number of columns is required.

Initialization

A two-dimensional array can be initialized when declared, just like a one-dimensional array. The initialization values are assigned in row order, starting from the first row, then the second row, and so on. For example, with the declaration:

```
int arr[3][3] = {{10, 20, 30},
                 {40, 50, 60},
                 {70, 80, 90}};
```

arr[0][0] becomes 10, arr[0][1] becomes 20, arr[0][2] becomes 30, and continue to the next rows. Alternatively, we can omit the inner braces and write:

```
int arr[3][3] = {10, 20, 30, 40, 50, 60, 70, 80, 90};
```

Once the compiler fills one row, it continues with the next one. However, my preference is always to use the inner braces so that the initialization of each row is clearly shown. When using braces, if the initialization list is shorter than the row's elements, the compiler assigns the value 0 to the remaining elements in that row. If it is larger it is illegal. For example, with the declaration:

```
int arr[3][3] = {{10, 20},
                 {40, 50},
                 {70}};
```

the values of arr[0][2], arr[1][2], arr[2][1], and arr[2][2] are initialized to 0.

If we omit the initialization of a row, the compiler initializes its elements to 0. For example, with the declaration:

```
int arr[3][3] = {{10, 20, 30}};
```

the elements of the second and third row are set to 0.

If the inner braces are omitted and the initialization list is shorter than the number of the array elements, the remaining elements are set to 0. For example, with the declaration:

```
int arr[3][3] = {10, 20};
```

arr[0][0] becomes 10, arr[0][1] becomes 20, and the remaining elements are set to 0.

When a two-dimensional array is declared, the number of columns must be specified. However, the number of rows is optional. If it is not specified, the compiler will create a two-dimensional array based on the initialization list. For example, with the declaration:

```
int arr[][3] = {10, 20, 30, 40, 50, 60};
```

since the array has three columns and the initialization values are six, the compiler creates a two-dimensional array of two rows and three columns.

Enough with the initialization lists. Based on what you learned, can you tell me what does the following code output?

```
int arr[][3] = {10, 20, 30, 40, 50, 60, 70};
cout << sizeof(arr)+arr[2][1]+arr[2][2] << '\n';
```

Since the array has three columns and the values are seven, the compiler creates a two-dimensional array of three rows and three columns, that is, an array of nine elements. Since, the initialization list is shorter, the last two, that is, `arr[2][1]` and `arr[2][2]` are set to 0. Therefore, the code outputs 36.

If the initialization value is the same or it can be easily produced, the typical choice to initialize the array is a pair of nested loops. For example, the following program declares a two-dimensional array and assigns the value 60 to its elements.

```
int row, col, arr[5][10];
for(row = 0; row < 5; row++)
      for(col = 0; col < 10; col++)
            arr[row][col] = 60;
```

With the `for` range of C++11 we can write the same code as follows:

```
int arr[5][10];
for(auto& row : arr) // I use auto for the general case.
      for(auto& col : row)
            col = 60;
```

Since we want to change the values of the elements we declare the `row` and `col` as references. The first loop is repeated for the `arr` elements. These elements are arrays of 10 integers. So the type of `row` is a reference to an array of 10 integers. The second loop accesses the elements of the row that the first loop indicates. Therefore, the type of `col` is reference to integer (`int&`). Notice that even if we don't want to change the values of the elements the `row` must be declared as a reference. For example, it is an error to write:

```
int arr[5][10];
for(auto row : arr) // Error.
      for(auto col : row)
            cout << col << '\n';
```

This error is due to the fact that the compiler handles the array name as a pointer, as we'll see in Chapter 8. In particular, because `row` is not declared as a reference, the compiler assumes that the type of `row` is a pointer to the first element of the row, that is, the type is `int*`. Thus, since a pointer itself has no size information about the underlying array, a compilation error occurs. In general, if we want to use the `for` range statement to handle a multidimensional array, all loop control variables, except the last one, must be references.

Vector of Vectors

As with two-dimensional arrays, we can declare a two-dimensional `vector` object. For example:

```
vector<vector<int>> v(5, vector<int>(10));
```

The `v` object is a two-dimensional vector that contains 5 elements, where each element is a vector of 10 integers. For convenience, we can assume that `v` consists of five rows, where each row contains 10 integers. To access an element we use the `[][]` syntax. For example, the following code displays the values of all elements:

```
for(int row = 0; row < v.size(); row++)
        for(int col = 0; col < v[row].size(); col++)
                cout << arr[row][col] << '\n';
```

A two-dimensional `vector` provides the facilities that a simple `vector` object provides. Exercise **C.7.16** is such an example, where the dimensions of the vector will be determined dynamically, during the program execution, and not statically as with the two-dimensional arrays.

EXERCISES

C.7.12 Write a program that creates a 5×5 upper triangular array; it is in array that the elements below the main diagonal should be set to 0. The program should assign random values within [−3, 3] to the remaining elements and display the array. Then, it should display the determinant of the array, that is, the product of the main diagonal's elements. Finally, the program should display the array in reverse form, that is, from the lower-right element to the upper-left one.

```
#include <iostream>
#include <iomanip>
#include <cstdlib>
#include <ctime>
using std::cout;

int main()
{
        const int SIZE = 5;
        int i, j, determ, arr[SIZE][SIZE];

        determ = 1; // Initialize the determinant.
        srand(time(NULL));

        cout << "\nArray elements\n";
        cout << "--------------\n";
        for(i = 0; i < SIZE; i++)
        {
                for(j = 0; j < SIZE; j++)
                {
                        if(i > j)
                                arr[i][j] = 0; /* The elements below the main
diagonal should be set to 0. */
```

```
                else
                        arr[i][j] = rand()%7-3; /* The result of rand()%7 is
an integer in [0, 6]. By subtracting 3, the integer is constrained in [-3, 3]. */
                if(i == j) /* Check if the element belongs in the main
diagonal. */
                        determ *= arr[i][j];

                        cout << std::setw(2) << arr[i][j] << " ";
                }
                cout << '\n';
        }
        cout << "\nDeterminant: " << determ << '\n';
        cout << "\nReverse Order\n";
        cout << "--------------\n";
        for(i = SIZE-1; i >= 0; i--)
        {
                for(j = SIZE-1; j >= 0; j--)
                        cout << std::setw(2) << arr[i][j] << " ";
                cout << '\n';
        }
        return 0;
}
```

C.7.13 Write a program that reads 6 integers and stores them in a 2×3 array (e.g., a). Then, it should read another 6 integers and store them in a second 3×2 array (e.g., b). The program should display the elements of a third 2×2 array (e.g., c), which is the result of c = a×b.

It is reminded from the linear algebra that the product of two matrices is produced by adding the products of the elements of each row of the first matrix with the corresponding elements of each column of the second matrix. Therefore, the outcome of an N×M matrix multiplied with an M×N matrix is an N×N matrix. For example, consider the following a (2×3) and b (3×2) matrices:

$$a = \begin{bmatrix} 1 & -1 & 1 \\ 0 & 2 & 1 \end{bmatrix} \text{ and } b = \begin{bmatrix} 1 & 0 \\ 2 & -2 \\ 2 & 3 \end{bmatrix}$$

The dimension of c = a×b is 2×2, and its elements are:

$$c = \begin{bmatrix} 1\times1+(-1)\times2+1\times2 & 1\times0+(-1)\times(-2)+1\times3 \\ 0\times1+2\times2+1\times2 & 0\times0+2\times(-2)+1\times3 \end{bmatrix} = \begin{bmatrix} 1 & 5 \\ 6 & -1 \end{bmatrix}$$

In math, the value of its element is the outcome of $c_{ij} = \sum_{k=1}^{M} a_{ik} \times b_{kj}$. In programming level, k ranges from 0 to M-1.

```
#include <iostream>
#include <iomanip>
using std::cin;
using std::cout;

int main()
{
        const int N = 2;
        const int M = 3;
        int i, j, k, a[N][M], b[M][N], c[N][N] = {0};
```

```
      for(i = 0; i < N; i++)
      {
            for(j = 0; j < M; j++)
            {
                  cout << "Enter element a[" << i << "]" << "[" <<
j << "]: ";
                  cin >> a[i][j];
            }
      }
      for(i = 0; i < M; i++)
      {
            for(j = 0; j < N; j++)
            {
                  cout << "Enter element b[" << i << "]" << "[" <<
j << "]: ";
                  cin >> b[i][j];
            }
      }
      for(i = 0; i < N; i++)
            for(j = 0; j < N; j++)
                  for(k = 0; k < M; k++)
                        c[i][j] += a[i][k] * b[k][j];

      cout << "\nArray c = a x b\n";
      cout << "----------------\n";
      for(i = 0; i < N; i++)
      {
            for(j = 0; j < N; j++)
                  cout << std::setw(5) << c[i][j];
            cout << '\n';
      }
      return 0;
}
```

C.7.14 Write a program that assigns random values within [0, 20] to the elements of a 6×8 integer array. Then, the program should read the user's choice, and if it is 1, it should read two more integers which correspond to two rows and swap their elements. If it is not 1, the two input integers correspond to columns. The program should check the validity of the two input integers and display the original and final array.

```
#include <iostream>
#include <cstdlib>
#include <ctime>
#include <iomanip>
using std::cin;
using std::cout;
using std::setw;

int main()
{
      const int ROWS = 6;
      const int COLS = 8;
      int i, j, a, b, max, tmp, type, arr[ROWS][COLS];
```

```cpp
    srand(time(NULL));
    for(i = 0; i < ROWS; i++)
    {
            for(j = 0; j < COLS; j++)
            {
                    arr[i][j] = rand()%21;
                    cout << setw(5) << arr[i][j];
            }
            cout << '\n';
    }
    cout << "Enter swap type (1:rows): ";
    cin >> type;
    if(type == 1)
            max = ROWS;
    else
            max = COLS;
    do
    {
            cout << "Enter dim_1[1-" << max << "]: ";
            cin >> a;
    } while(a < 1 || a > max);

    do
    {
            cout << "Enter dim_2[1-" << max << "]: ";
            cin >> b;
    } while(b < 1 || b > max);

    a--; // Subtract 1, since indexing starts from 0.
    b--;
    if(type == 1)
    {
            for(i = 0; i < COLS; i++)
            {
                    tmp = arr[a][i];
                    arr[a][i] = arr[b][i];
                    arr[b][i] = tmp;
            }
    }
    else
    {
            for(i = 0; i < ROWS; i++)
            {
                    tmp = arr[i][a];
                    arr[i][a] = arr[i][b];
                    arr[i][b] = tmp;
            }
    }
    for(i = 0; i < ROWS; i++)
    {
            for(j = 0; j < COLS; j++)
                    cout << setw(5) << arr[i][j];
            cout << '\n';
    }
    return 0;
}
```

C.7.15 In linear algebra, a square matrix is called *Toeplitz* when the elements of each diagonal parallel to the main diagonal are equal. For example, the following 5×5 matrix demonstrates the generic form of a 5×5 *Toeplitz* matrix:

$$t = \begin{bmatrix} a & b & c & d & e \\ f & a & b & c & d \\ g & f & a & b & c \\ h & g & f & a & b \\ i & h & g & f & a \end{bmatrix}$$

Write a program that reads integers and stores them in the first row and first column of a 5×5 array. Then, the program should create the *Toeplitz* matrix and display its elements in algebra form.

```cpp
#include <iostream>
#include <iomanip>
using std::cin;
using std::cout;
using std::setw;

int main()
{
        const int ROWS = 5;
        int i, j, t[ROWS][ROWS];

        cout << "Enter [0][0] element: ";
        cin >> t[0][0];
        // Read the remaining values for the first row.
        for(i = 1; i < ROWS; i++)
        {
                cout << "Enter [0][" << i << "] element: ";
                cin >> t[0][i];
        }
        // Read the remaining values for the first column.
        for(i = 1; i < ROWS; i++)
        {
                cout << "Enter [" << i << "][0] element: ";
                cin >> t[i][0];
        }
        // Create the Toeplitz array,
        for(i = 0; i < ROWS-1; i++)
                for(j = 0; j < ROWS-1; j++)
                        t[i+1][j+1] = t[i][j]; /* We traverse the array t and
make each element equal to the upper left, except the elements of the first
row and column. */
        for(i = 0; i < ROWS; i++)
        {
                for(j = 0; j < ROWS; j++)
                        cout << setw(5) << t[i][j];
                cout << '\n';
        }
        return 0;
}
```

C.7.16 Write a program that reads the number of students and the number of courses and creates a two-dimensional `vector` object. Then, the program should read the grades of the students and store them in the object. The program should display the average, the best, and the worst grade of each student. It should also display the positions in the object which hold the best and worst average grades. If more than one student has the same best or worst average grade, the program should display the first position found. The program should force the user to enter grades within [0, 10] and positive values for the number of students and the courses.

```cpp
#include <iostream>
#include <vector>
using std::cout;
using std::cin;
using std::vector;

int main()
{
        int studs, courses, i, j, min_pos, max_pos;
        float sum, min_grd, max_grd, avg_grd, min_avg_grd, max_avg_grd;

        do
        {
                cout << "Enter number of students: ";
                cin >> studs;

                cout << "Enter number of courses: ";
                cin >> courses;
        } while(studs <= 0 || courses <= 0);

        vector<vector<float>> grd(studs, vector<float>(courses));

        max_avg_grd = -1;
        min_avg_grd = 11;
        for(i = 0; i < studs; i++)
        {
                sum = 0;
                max_grd = -1;
                min_grd = 11;
                for(j = 0; j < courses; j++)
                {
                        do
                        {
                                cout << "Enter grade of student_" << i+1 << " for
lesson_" << j+1 << ": ";
                                cin >> grd[i][j];
                        } while(grd[i][j] < 0 || grd[i][j] > 10);
                        sum += grd[i][j];
                        if(grd[i][j] > max_grd)
                                max_grd = grd[i][j];
                        if(grd[i][j] < min_grd)
                                min_grd = grd[i][j];
                }
                avg_grd = sum/courses;
                if(avg_grd > max_avg_grd)
                {
                        max_avg_grd = avg_grd;
                        max_pos = i;
                }
```

```
                  if(avg_grd < min_avg_grd)
                  {
                          min_avg_grd = avg_grd;
                          min_pos = i;
                  }
                  cout << "Student_" << i+1 << "(Avg:" << avg_grd << " Max:" <<
max_grd << " Min:" << min_grd << ")\n";
          }
          cout << "Student_" << max_pos << " has the higher average " <<
max_avg_grd << " and student_" << min_pos << " has the lower average " <<
min_avg_grd << ".\n";
          return 0;
}
```

C.7.17 Write a program that reads integers and stores them in a square matrix (e.g., 3×3). Then, the program should check whether the array is a magic square, that is, the sum of each row, column, and diagonal is the same.

```cpp
#include <iostream>
using std::cout;
using std::cin;

int main()
{
        const int ROWS = 3;
        const int COLS = 3;
        int i, j, sum, tmp, arr[ROWS][COLS];

        sum = tmp = 0;
        for(i = 0; i < ROWS; i++)
        {
                // We find the sums of the diagonals.
                for(j = 0; j < COLS; j++)
                {
                        cout << "Enter element [" << i << "]" << "[" << j << "]: ";
                        cin >> arr[i][j];
                        if(i == j)
                                sum += arr[i][j];
                        if(i+j == ROWS-1) /* Check if the element belongs in the
secondary diagonal. */
                                tmp += arr[i][j];
                }
        }
        if(sum != tmp)
        {
                cout << "Not magic square -> Sum_main_diag: " << sum <<
"  Sum_sec_diag: " << tmp << '\n';
                return 0;
        }
        for(i = 0; i < ROWS; i++)
        {
                /* Αρχικοποίηση της μεταβλητής που υπολογίζει το άθροισμα των στοιχείων
της κάθε γραμμής. */
                tmp = 0;
                for(j = 0; j < COLS; j++)
                        tmp += arr[i][j];
```

```
                if(sum != tmp)
                {
                        cout << "Not magic square -> Sum_row_" << i+1 << ": " <<
tmp << " Sum_diag: " << sum << '\n';
                        return 0;
                }
        }
        for(i = 0; i < COLS; i++)
        {
                tmp = 0; /* Initialize the variable which calculates the sum of
the elements of each row. */
                for(j = 0; j < ROWS; j++)
                        tmp += arr[j][i];

                if(sum != tmp)
                {
                        cout << "Not magic square -> Sum_col_" << i+1 << ": " <<
tmp << " Sum_diag: " << sum << '\n';
                        return 0;
                }
        }
        cout << "Magic square !!!\n";
        return 0;
}
```

C.7.18 Write a program that simulates a cinema's ticket office. Assume that the cinema has 30 rows of 20 seats each. The program should display a menu to provide the following choices:

1. *Buy a ticket.* The program should allow the viewer to select the row and the seat. If no specific seat is asked, the program should select a random seat. The ticket's price is $6.
2. *Ticket cancellation.* The program should read the row and the seat and cancel the reservation. The refund is $5.
3. *Display the total income and a diagram to show the reserved and free seats.*
4. *Program termination.*

```
#include <iostream>
#include <cstdlib>
#include <iomanip>
using std::cout;
using std::cin;
using std::setw;

int main()
{
        const int ROWS = 30;
        const int COLS = 20;
        bool seats[ROWS][COLS] = {0}; /* We use the seats array to manage the
cinema's seats. If an element is 0, it implies that the seat is free. */
        int i, j, sel, row, col, rsvd_seats, cost;

        rsvd_seats = cost = 0;
        while(1)
        {
                cout << "\nMenu selections\n";
                cout << "---------------\n";
```

```cpp
                cout << "1. Buy Ticket\n";
                cout << "2. Ticket Refund\n";
                cout << "3. Show Information\n";
                cout << "4. Exit\n";
                cout << "\nEnter choice: ";
                cin >> sel;
                switch(sel)
                {
                        case 1:
                            if(rsvd_seats == ROWS*COLS)
                            {
                                    cout << "\nSorry, no free seats\n";
                                    break;
                            }
                            cout << "\nWould you like a specific seat
(No: 0)? ";
                            cin >> sel;
                            if(sel == 0)
                            {
                                    do
                                    {
                                            row = rand() % ROWS; /* Use rand()
to select a random seat. */
                                            col = rand() % COLS;
                                    } while(seats[row][col] == 1);
                            }
                            else
                            {
                                    do
                                    {
                                            cout << "\nEnter row [1-" << ROWS
<< "]: ";
                                            cin >> row;
                                    } while(row < 1 || row > ROWS);

                                    do
                                    {
                                            cout << "Enter seat [1-" << COLS <<
"]: ";
                                            cin >> col;
                                    } while(col < 1 || col > COLS);

                                    row--; /* Subtract 1, since indexing
starts from 0. */
                                    col--;
                            }
                            if(seats[row][col] == 1)
                                    cout << "\nSorry, seat in row_" << row+1
<< " and column_" << col+1 << " is reserved\n";
                            else
                            {
                                    seats[row][col] = 1;
                                    cost += 6;
                                    rsvd_seats++;
                            }
                    break;
```

```
                        case 2:
                                if(rsvd_seats == 0)
                                {
                                        cout << "\nAll seats are free\n";
                                        break;
                                }
                                do
                                {
                                 cout << "\nEnter row [1-" << ROWS << "]: ";
                                        cin >> row;
                                } while(row < 1 || row > ROWS);

                                do
                                {
                                  cout << "Enter seat [1-" << COLS << "]: ";
                                        cin >> col;
                                } while(col < 1 || col > COLS);

                                row--;
                                col--;
                                if(seats[row][col] != 1)
                                        cout << "\nSeat in row_" << row+1 << " and
column_" << col+1 << " is not reserved\n";
                                else
                                {
                                        seats[row][col] = 0;
                                        cost -= 5;
                                        rsvd_seats--;
                                }
                        break;

                        case 3:
                                cout << "\nFree seats: " << ROWS*COLS - rsvd_seats
<< " Income: " << cost << "\n\n";
                                for(i = 0; i < ROWS; i++)
                                {
                                        for(j = 0; j < COLS; j++)
                                        {
                                                if(seats[i][j] == 1)
                                                        cout << setw(2) << 'X';
                                                else
                                                        cout << setw(2) << '#';
                                        }
                                        cout << '\n';
                                }
                        break;

                        case 4:
                        return 0;

                        default:
                                cout << "\nWrong choice\n";
                        break;
                }
        }
        return 0;
}
```

UNSOLVED EXERCISES

U.7.1   Write a program that reads the grades of 100 students and stores them in an array. Then, the program should read two floats (e.g., a and b) and display how many students got a grade within [a, b]. The program should force the user the second number to enter to be greater than the first one.

U.7.2   What is the content of a in the following code?

```
int i, a[3] = {0, 1, 2};
for(i = 1; i < 4; i++)
        a[a[a[3-i]]] = i-1;
```

U.7.3   Write a program that reads ten integers and stores them in an array only if either:

   a. the current position is even, i.e., 0, 2, 4, ..., and the input number is even or
   b. the current position is odd, i.e., 1, 3, 5, ..., and the input number is odd.

   The program should not accept the values 0 and -1 and prompt the user to enter a new value. Once the insertion of the numbers is completed, the unassigned elements should be set to -1. The program should display the array elements before it ends.

U.7.4   Write a program that reads `double` numbers continuously and stores in a `vector` object those with a value more than 5. If the user enters -1 the insertion of numbers should terminate and the program should display the minimum of the values stored.

U.7.5   Write a program that reads 100 integers and stores them in an array. The program should display how many elements have a value greater than the value of the last element and how many elements have a value greater than the average. The first value to enter should be that of the last element.

U.7.6   Write a program that reads integers and stores them in an array of 100 places with the restriction that an input number is stored in the array only if it is less than the last stored. The program should terminate once the array becomes full.

U.7.7   Write a program that reads 100 integers and stores them in an array. Then, the program should rotate the elements one place to the right. For example, if the array were of four elements: 1, -9, 5, 3, the rotated array would be: 3, 1, -9, 5.

U.7.8   Write a program that reads 100 integers and stores them in an array. The program should display the number of the duplicated values. For example, if the array were of five elements {5, 5, 5, 5, 5} the program should display 4 (since number 5 is repeated four times), and if it were {1, -3, 1, 50, -3} the program should display 2 (since numbers 1 and -3 are repeated once), and if it were {3, -1, 22, 13, -7} the program should display 0 (since no number is repeated).

U.7.9   Write a program that reads 100 `double` numbers and stores them in an array. The program should calculate the distance between successive elements and display the minimum one. To calculate the distance of two elements, subtract their values and use the absolute value. For example, if the first four elements are: 5.2, -3.2, 7.5, 12.22, the distances are: $|-3.2-5.2| = 8.4$, $|7.5-(-3.2)| = 10.7$ and $|12.22-7.5| = 4.72$.

U.7.10 Write a program that reads the grades of 100 students and displays the frequency of each grade. The program should also display the grade which is given the most times and the number of its occurrences. Examine the case that more than one grade might be given the same most times. The program should force the user to enter grades within [0, 10]. Assume that the grades are integers.

U.7.11 A parking station for 20 cars charges $6.00 for the first 3 hours. Each extra hour is charged $1.50 (the whole hour is charged even for one extra minute). The maximum charge is $12.00 and the maximum parking time is 24 hours. Write a program that reads the number of the parked cars and the parking time of each car in hours and minutes, and displays the charges in the following form:

```
Car      Time      Charge ($)
1        2.30'        6.00
2        4.30'        9.00
3        3.12'        7.50
4        4.0'         7.50
5        8.0'        12.00
Total                42.00
```

U.7.12 Write a program that reads integers and stores them in a square matrix (e.g., 3×3). Then, the program should check whether the array is upper triangular, lower triangular or both. A square matrix is called upper (lower) triangular if all its elements below (above) the main diagonal are zero.

U.7.13 Write a program that reads integers and stores them in a 3×4 array. Then, the program should find the maximum value of each row and assign that value to all preceding elements in the same row.

U.7.14 Write a program that reads integers and stores them in a square matrix (e.g., 3×3). Then, the program should create and display a new matrix having as rows the columns of the original one and columns the rows of the original one. Use only one array.

U.7.15 Write a program that assigns random values within [1000, 2000] to the elements of the main diagonal of a 5×5 integer array. The program should assign random values to the remaining elements with the restriction that the values of the elements below the main diagonal should be less than those of the main diagonal, and the values of the elements above the main diagonal should be greater than those of the main diagonal.

U.7.16 Write a program that assigns random values within [0, 20] to the elements of a 3×5 integer array, except the last row. The elements of the last row should be assigned with proper values so that the sum of the elements in each column is 50. The program should also store into a one-dimensional array the minimum value of each column of the two-dimensional array and display that array, before it terminates.

U.7.17 Write a program that reads integers and stores them in a 5×5 square matrix. Then, the program should read an integer within [1, 5] (e.g., x) and copy in a second array the elements of the first array, except the elements of the x-row and x-column.

U.7.18 Write a program that reads integers and stores them in a 3×5 array. The program should display the columns whose elements have different values. For example, if the array were:

$$
\begin{bmatrix}
1 & -2 & 2 & 5 & 9 \\
3 & 0 & 2 & 5 & 1 \\
1 & 7 & 2 & -3 & 0
\end{bmatrix}
$$

the program should display the elements of the second and fifth column.

U.7.19 Write a program that simulates a hotel booking software. Assume that the hotel has 10 wings of 50 rooms each. The program should display a menu to provide the following choices:

1. Display the number of available rooms in each wing.
2. Make a reservation. The program should prompt the user to enter a wing number. Then, it reserves the first available room in that wing. If there is no available room, the program should prompt the user to enter a new wing until the reservation is made.
3. Cancel a reservation. The program should prompt the user to enter the wing number and the room number and cancel the reservation.
4. Program termination.

Pointers

8

Pointers are one of the most important parts of the language. It is the mechanism to access memory addresses and manipulate memory directly, and thus, bring you closer to the hardware, which is essential in order to have a more complete understanding of how things work. This chapter uses pointers to numeric variables to introduce you to the pointer concepts. The close relationship between pointers and arrays is presented. You'll also learn how to use arrays of pointers and pointers to functions. Other major applications of pointers, such as passing arguments in functions, to handle strings, to form dynamic data structures, to enable polymorphism, as well as pointers to other types of data will be gradually presented over the next chapters. It is not only that you should learn pointers well in order to handle memory directly and get a practical understanding of memory operations that will certainly prove useful in the future, but also to be able to read huge amounts of real-world code using pointers.

POINTERS AND MEMORY

In modern computers, the main memory consists of millions of consecutively numbered memory cells where each cell stores eight bits of information and is identified by a unique number, called memory address. For example, in a computer with N bytes of memory, the memory address of each cell is a unique number from 0 to N-1, as shown here:

Memory Address	Memory Content
0	
1	
2	
.	
.	
5000	10
5001	0
5002	0
5003	0
.	
n-1	

When a variable is declared, the compiler reserves the required consecutive bytes to store its value. If a variable occupies more than one byte, the variable's address is the address of the first byte. For example, with the declaration int a = 10; the compiler reserves four consecutive unused bytes (e.g., the addresses 5000–5003) and stores the value 10 there, assuming that the less significant byte of the value is stored in the lower address byte (*little-endian* architecture). The compiler associates the name of a variable with its memory address. When the variable is used in the program, the compiler accesses its address. For example, with the statement a = 3; the compiler knows that the memory address of a is 5000 and sets its content to 3.

DOI: 10.1201/9781003230076-8

POINTER DECLARATION

A pointer variable is a variable that can hold a memory address, such as the memory address of another variable. To declare a pointer, we write:

```
data_type *pointer_name;
```

As shown, the `*` character must precede the name of the pointer variable. For example, with the declaration: `int *ptr;`

`ptr` is declared as a pointer variable to type `int`. Therefore, `ptr` can hold the memory address of an `int` variable. In the general case, if the type is *T*, the type of *T** is "pointer to *T*". Pointer variables can be declared together with other variables of the same type. For example:

```
int *p, i, j, k;
```

Note that it is allowed to put the `*` next to the type (e.g., `int* p`). We could say that when we write `int *p;` we give emphasis on the value, that is, `*p` is an integer, while when we write `int* p;` we give emphasis on the type, that is, `p` is a pointer to an integer. Both declarations are valid. The reason I don't prefer the second syntax is because it might be confusing when multiple variables are declared. For example, with the declaration:

```
int* p1, p2;
```

`p1` is declared as pointer, but `p2` as an integer. Also, I prefer to declare the pointer variables first, to distinguish them from the ordinary variables.

As with ordinary variables, when a pointer variable is declared, the compiler allocates memory to store its value. A pointer variable allocates the same size, no matter what is the data type it points to. This value is system dependent. Typically, it is four or eight bytes (for 32-bit and 64-bit system architectures, respectively). Therefore, either we write `char *ptr;` or `float *ptr;` or `double *ptr;` the compiler allocates the same number of bytes for `ptr` (e.g., 4). If you want to find out the size of a pointer variable in your system use the `sizeof` operator (e.g., `cout << sizeof(ptr)`).

POINTER INITIALIZATION

After declaring a pointer variable, we can use it to store the memory address of another variable. To find the address of a variable we use the `&` *address operator* before its name. For example:

```
#include <iostream> // Example 8.1.
int main()
{
        int *ptr, a;

        ptr = &a;
        std::cout << ptr << ' ' << &ptr << '\n';
        return 0;
}
```

With the statement `ptr = &a; ptr` becomes equal, or else "points to" the memory address of a. As we said, the compiler allocates memory to store the value of `ptr`. The program outputs the address of a and the address of `ptr`, in hex. As you see, using pointers we are very close to the hardware and the system's memory. In the general case, if the type is *T* the type of &*T* is "pointer to *T*".

The assignment of an integer value to a pointer variable will probably cause a compilation error. This is logical since a pointer is not an integer. For example:

```
int *ptr;
ptr = 10000; // Potential compilation error.
```

However, in applications that need direct access to hardware addresses (e.g., embedded systems), type cast can be used to allow the assignment. For example:

```
ptr = reinterpret_cast<int*>(10000); // Use a cast operator.
```

A pointer variable can be initialized when declared, provided that the variable that it points to has already been declared. For example:

```
int a, b, *ptr = &a;
```

As a matter of style, I prefer to initialize the pointer variables in separate statements, not together with their declarations, in order to make it clearer. In some examples, I won't do that in order to save space.

The & operator cannot be applied to constants (e.g., &20), expressions (e.g., &(a+b)), and bit fields (we'll discuss them in Chapter 13). It is only applied to objects in memory, such as variables, array elements, and functions.

NULL POINTERS

As with an ordinary variable, the initial value of a pointer variable is the content of its address, that is, the pointer initially points to a "garbage" address. When we want to declare explicitly that the pointer points to nowhere, we assign the value 0. Many prefer to use the macro NULL, instead of 0. The NULL macro is defined in several header files (e.g., cstdlib). A pointer assigned with 0 or NULL is called null pointer and points to nothing. For example, the following program first outputs the initial value of the pointer and then 0:

```
#include <iostream> // Example 8.2
int main()
{
      int *p;

      std::cout << p << '\n';
      p = NULL;
      std::cout << p << '\n';
      return 0;
}
```

Although the value 0 can be used in a pointer context, using NULL makes the code easier to read. For example, the assignment p = 0; may confuse the reader. Is p a numeric variable or a pointer? In contrary, the assignment p = NULL; is more indicative that p is a pointer (however, it is not for sure as you'll see next). The value of a pointer variable can be compared with NULL, as follows:

```
if(p != NULL) // Equivalent to if(p)
if(p == NULL) // Equivalent to if(!p)
```

As a matter of style, the syntax I do not prefer is if(!p).

Because the NULL value is an integer value, its use does not prove for sure that the referred variable is a pointer variable. To eliminate any potential confusion between integers and pointers, C++11 defines the nullptr constant, which represents the null pointer, and it can only be assigned to a pointer variable. For example:

```
int i = NULL; // OK, however i isn't a pointer variable.
int j = nullptr; // Wrong, because j isn't a pointer variable.
double *p = nullptr; // OK, p is a null pointer.
```

Because nullptr is associated only with pointers, this is my preference against the NULL and 0 constants.

USING A POINTER

To access the content of a memory address referenced by a pointer variable we use the * (*indirection or dereference*) operator before its name. Although the same symbol is used, it is other than the multiplication operator. The compiler uses the context to determine whether the dereferencing or the multiplication operator is used. In case you wonder why the standard committee decided to use the same symbol, I don't know for sure, it could be due to the shortage of available characters. The compiler analyses the expression and decides which one is used. Here is an example:

```
#include <iostream> // Example 8.3
int main()
{
        int *ptr, a = 10;

        ptr = &a;
        std::cout << *ptr << '\n';
        *ptr = 20; // Equivalent to a = 20.
        std::cout << a << '\n';
        return 0;
}
```

The expression *ptr is equivalent to the content of the memory address pointed to by ptr. Since ptr points to the address of a, *ptr is an alias for a, that is, equal to a. Therefore, the program first outputs 10, then 20.

 A pointer variable must point to a valid memory address, such as an address of a variable, before being dereferenced.

For example, the following program may crash, because ptr has not been initialized before used in the statement a = *ptr;

```
#include <iostream> // Example 8.4
int main()
{
        int *ptr, a, b = 10;
```

```
        a = *ptr; // ptr has not been initialized.
        std::cout << a << '\n';
        return 0;
}
```

For example, if we add the statement `ptr = &b;` before that, the program is executed successfully; a will be equal to b and the program outputs 10. Typically, in *Unix/Linux* environment, this type of error is indicated with the pop-up runtime message *Segmentation fault*. Similarly, in the following code, since `ptr` has not been initialized, it is wrong to read a value and save it in `*ptr`.

```
int *ptr, i;
cin >> *ptr;
```

If we add the statement `ptr = &i;` before `cin`, the code is fine; the input value is stored into `*ptr`, that is, `i`. Always remember, initialize the pointer before using it, don't let it blowing in the wind. Listen to *Blowing in the Wind* from *Bob Dylan* to bear it in mind.

The `*` and `&` cancel each other when used together. For example, the following program displays three times the address of `i`:

```
#include <iostream> // Example 8.5
int main()
{
        int *ptr, i;

        ptr = &i;
        std::cout << &i << ' ' << *&ptr << ' ' << &*ptr << '\n';
        return 0;
}
```

Because the symbol/* marks the beginning of a comment, in a statement such as a = b/*ptr; whatever follows/* until the */is met is considered comment, so the compilation fails. In that case, leave a space or use parentheses. For example, a = b/ *ptr; or a = b/(*ptr);

Let's see, according to what you've learned so far, can you find the output of the following program?

```
#include <iostream> // Example 8.6
int main()
{
        int *ptr1, i = 4;
        double *ptr2, j = 1.78;

        ptr1 = &i;
        ptr2 = &j;

        *ptr1 = i + *ptr2;
        std::cout << i << ' ' << sizeof(ptr1)*sizeof(ptr2) << ' ' <<
sizeof(*ptr2) << '\n';
        return 0;
}
```

Since `ptr1` points to the address of `i` and `ptr2` to the address of `j`, the statement `*ptr1 = i+*ptr2` is equivalent to `i = i+j`. Since `i` is integer, it becomes 5. As said, the pointer variables allocate the same size no matter the type they point to. If we assume that it is 4 octets and because `ptr2` is a pointer to double, the program displays: 5 16   8

Note that because `sizeof` does not evaluate its operand, it is not necessary for a pointer to have a valid value. For example, we can write:

```
double *p;
cout << sizeof(*p) << '\n';
```

Since `sizeof` knows that the type of *p is `double` it does not need to dereference the pointer.

EXERCISES

C.8.1 Use the `p1` and `p2` pointers and complete the following program to read two float numbers first and then to swap the values they point to. Then, use the same pointers to display the absolute result of the difference of these values. The variables `i` and `j` should be used only once.

```
#include <iostream>
using std::cout;
using std::cin;

int main()
{
        float *p1, *p2, i, j, tmp;
        ...
}
```

Answer:

```
#include <iostream>
using std::cout;
using std::cin;

int main()
{
        float *p1, *p2, i, j, tmp;

        /* The pointers must be initialized before used to store the input
values. */
        p1 = &i;
        p2 = &j;

        cout << "Enter values: ";
        cin >> *p1 >> *p2;

        tmp = *p2;
        *p2 = *p1;
        *p1 = tmp;

        if((*p1-*p2) > 0)
                cout << *p1-*p2 << '\n';
        else
                cout << -(*p1-*p2) << '\n';
        return 0;
}
```

C.8.2 What is the output of the following program?

```cpp
#include <iostream>
int main()
{
        int *ptr1, *ptr2, *ptr3, i = 0, j = 1, k = 2;

        ptr1 = &i;
        i = *ptr1 ?  3 : 4;

        ptr2 = &j;
        j = *ptr2 + *ptr1;

        ptr3 = &k;
        k = *ptr3 + *ptr2;
        std::cout << *ptr1 << ' ' << *ptr2 << ' ' << *ptr3 << '\n';
        return 0;
}
```

Answer: Since ptr1 points to the address of i the expression: *ptr1 = i ? 3 : 4; is equivalent to i = i ? 3 : 4;. Since i is 0, it becomes 4. Since ptr2 points to the address of j, *ptr2 is equal to j, that is, 1. Therefore, j = *ptr2 + *ptr1 = 1+4 = 5. Similarly, since ptr3 points to the address of k, *ptr3 is equal to k, that is, 2. Therefore, k = *ptr3 + *ptr2 = 2+5 = 7. Since the values of *ptr1, *ptr2, and *ptr3 are equal to i, j, and k, respectively, the program displays: 4 5 7

C.8.3 Use the p pointer and a while loop, and complete the following program to display the integers from 1 to 10. The variable i should be used only once.

```cpp
#include <iostream>
int main()
{
        int *p, i;
        ...
}
```

Answer:

```cpp
#include <iostream>
int main()
{
        int *p, i;

        p = &i;
        *p = 1;
        while(*p <= 10)
        {
                std::cout << *p << '\n';
                (*p)++; /* As you'll see next, we must use parentheses for
priority reasons. */
        }
        return 0;
}
```

C.8.4 What is the output of the following program?

```
#include <iostream>
int main()
{
        int *ptr1, *ptr2, i = 10, j = 20;

        ptr1 = &i;
        ptr2 = &j;

        ptr2 = ptr1;
        *ptr1 = *ptr1 + *ptr2;
        *ptr2 *= 2;
        std::cout << *ptr1 + *ptr2 << '\n';
        return 0;
}
```

Answer: The statement `ptr2 = ptr1;` makes `ptr2` to point to the same address that `ptr1` points to, that is, the address of `i`. Therefore, `*ptr2` is equal to `i`. Since both pointers point to the address of `i`, the statement `*ptr1 = *ptr1 + *ptr2;` is equivalent to i = i+i = 10+10 = 20. Similarly, the statement `*ptr2 *= 2;` is equivalent to `*ptr2 = 2*(*ptr2)`; that is, i = 2*i = 2*20 = 40. As a result, the program displays the result of `*ptr1 + *ptr2` = i+i = 40+40, that is, 80.

C.8.5 Use the `p2` pointer and complete the following program to read students' grades continuously until the user enters -1. Use the `p1` pointer to display how many students got a grade within [5, 10] and the `p3` pointer to display the best grade. The variables `sum`, `max`, and `grade` should be used only once.

```
#include <iostream>
int main()
{
        int *p1, sum;
        float *p2, *p3, grade, max;
        ...
}
```

Answer:

```
#include <iostream>
int main()
{
        int *p1, sum;
        float *p2, *p3, grade, max;

        p1 = &sum;
        *p1 = 0;

        p3 = &max;
        *p3 = 0;

        p2 = &grade;
        while(1)
        {
                std::cout << "Enter grade: ";
                std::cin >> *p2;
```

```
                if(*p2 == -1)
                        break;
                if(*p2 >=5 && *p2 <= 10)
                {
                        (*p1)++;
                        if(*p2 > *p3)
                                *p3 = *p2;
                }
        }
        std::cout << *p1 << " students passed (max:" << *p3 << ")\n";
        return 0;
}
```

THE void* POINTER

Sometimes we may need to store or pass to a function the memory address of a variable whose we don't know the type. In such cases, the type void* is used. A void* pointer is a generic pointer in the sense that it can point to a variable of any type. A void* pointer can be assigned to another void* pointer. Also, a non-void* pointer can be assigned to a void* pointer. For example:

```
void *p1, *p2;
int i, j, *p3 = &i;
p1 = &j;
p1 = p3;
p2 = p1;
```

Notice that, except for void*, in order to assign a pointer of one type to a pointer of another type cast is necessary. For example:

```
char *p1;
int *p2;
...
p2 = p1; // Wrong.
p2 = (int*)p1; // Compiled.
```

In general, it'd be better to avoid such castings, as the different sizes of the data types, if, for example, dereferencing occurs, may cause serious problems. If you have to make a cast, it'd be better to use a cast operator (e.g., reinterpret_cast) as we'll see in Chapter 25.

To access a variable using a void* pointer, cast is necessary in order to inform the compiler about the type of the variable. For example:

```
#include <iostream> // Example 8.7
int main()
{
        void *ptr;
        char s[] = "abcd";
        int i = 10;

        ptr = &i;
        *ptr += 20; // Wrong, cast is needed.
        *(int*)ptr += 20; // That's ok now.
        std::cout << i << '\n';
```

```
ptr = s+2;
(*(char*)ptr)++;
std::cout << s << '\n';
return 0;
}
```

To access i, we cast the type of ptr to the type of i using the int* cast. Now, we can change the value of the variable that this generic pointer points to. Therefore, the program displays 30.

Next, ptr points to the s[2] element with value 'c'. ptr is cast to char* and the value of s[2] is incremented. Since it becomes 'd', the program displays abdd. Yes, you are right; since we've not discussed yet about strings and characters it is hard enough to understand this code. I just added another cast example of void* to come back and read it once you learn strings. Note that any pointer can be cast to void* and back again to the original type without any loss of information.

Typically, a void pointer is used as a function parameter in order to pass values of different types or as a function's return type (e.g., memcpy() as we'll see in Chapter 14).

USE OF const QUALIFIER

To prevent a pointer to change the value of the variable it points to, we add the const keyword before its type. For example, the following code won't compile because ptr is not allowed to change the value of i. However, it is allowed to point to some other variable of the same type. Note that the variable does not have to be const. For example:

```
int j, i = 10;
const int *ptr;
ptr = &i; // OK, the variable does not have to be const.
i = 30; // OK, i is not const.
*ptr = 30; // Wrong, it is not allowed to change the value.
ptr = &j; // OK, it is allowed to point to another variable.
```

What exactly is the type of ptr? A practical tip is to read from right to left and read the * as "pointer to". Thus, ptr is a pointer to const int.

To prevent a pointer to point to another variable, we add the const keyword before its name. Thus, we create a const pointer. As with ordinary const variables, the pointer must be initialized when declared. For example, the following code won't compile because ptr is not allowed to point to the address of j. However, it is allowed to change the value of i.

```
int i, j;
int* const ptr = &i; // Initialize the pointer.
ptr = &j; // Wrong.
*ptr = 30; // OK, i becomes 30.
```

What is ptr now? From right to left, it is a const pointer to type int. Note that it is allowed to prevent both actions by using the const keyword twice. For example:

```
int i, j;
const int* const ptr = &i; // Initialize pointer.
ptr = &j; // Wrong.
*ptr = 30; // Wrong.
```

As you see, there are no many things left to do with `ptr`. Essentially, what is left is to test the pointer value. And yes, that's a very rare declaration to see in practice. Here is an example to have in mind for something similar:

```
const char* const days[] = {"Mon", "Tue", "Wed", "Thu", "Fri", "Sat", "Sun"};
```

The outer `const` prevents the modification of the strings, while the inner prevents the pointers to point somewhere else. We'll discuss array of pointers later in this chapter.

Here is a question for you, is the following code correct?

```
const int i = 10;
int *p = &i;
```

Of course not, the second statement won't compile. Why? If allowed, we could use the pointer to change the value of i (e.g., `*p = 2;`) and violate its `const` nature. The address of a `const` variable can only be stored in a pointer to `const`. That is, we must write: `const int *p;`

POINTER ARITHMETIC

Pointer arithmetic refers to the application of some arithmetic operations on pointers. The allowed operations are presented next.

Pointers and Integers

The standard says that adding or subtracting an integer from a pointer is guaranteed to produce reliable results only if the pointer points to an array, otherwise the result is undefined. Suppose that a pointer variable `ptr` points to an element of an array. The addition of a positive integer n in an assignment such as:

```
ptr = ptr + n;
```

increases the pointer's value by *n*size* of the pointer's data type and makes the pointer point to the address of the n-th element after the one it points to. For example, if `ptr` points to the array element `arr[i]` and n is 3, `ptr` will point to `arr[i+3]`. Given the assumptions we've made for the data types in Chapter 2, if `ptr` is declared as a pointer to an array of `int` or `float`, its value is increased by `n*4`, since the size of both types is four bytes. If it is a `char` array, its value is increased by `n*1=n`, while if it is a `double` array, it is increased by `n*8`. After adding the integer to the pointer, the pointer must point to an array element or to the first place past the end which is considered a valid result. If not, the addition invokes undefined behaviour as well as dereferencing the pointer. Let's see the following program:

```
#include <iostream> // Example 8.8
int main()
{
        int *ptr, arr[] = {1, 2, 3};

        ptr = &arr[0];
        *ptr = 10;
        std::cout << "Addr: " << ptr << ' ' << arr[0] << '\n';
```

```
        ptr = ptr+2;
        *ptr = 20;
        std::cout << "Addr: " << ptr << ' ' << arr[2] << '\n';
        return 0;
}
```

Since `ptr` points to the address of `arr[0]`, `arr[0]` becomes `10`. Then, `ptr` is increased by `8`, not by `2`, because `ptr` is declared as a pointer to `int`. Thus, since `ptr` points to `arr[2]`, `arr[2]` becomes `20`. Therefore, the program displays the values `10` and `20` and two addresses with the second being `8` places greater than the first one.

Similar to the addition, subtracting a positive integer from a pointer in an assignment such as:

```
ptr = ptr - n;
```

decreases the pointer's value by *n*size* of its type and makes the pointer point to the address of the n-th element before the one it points to. For example, if we write the following code:

```
ptr = &arr[2];
cout << "Addr: " << ptr << '\n';
ptr = ptr-2;
cout << "Addr: " << ptr << '\n';
```

the second address will be `8` places lower than the first one. As in case of addition, the result is considered valid if the pointer points to an element within the array or to the next place past the end. For example:

```
int arr[] = {10, 20, 30};
int *p1 = arr+3; /* Valid, the pointer points to the next place past the end
of the array. */
int *p2 = arr+8; // Non valid.
int *p3 = arr-1; // Non valid.
```

Although the assignment with the address past the end of the array is valid, as in case of `p1`, do not attempt to dereference this address because it is out of bounds. For example, do not write `*p1 = 2`; the behaviour of the program is unpredictable.

Note that if the pointer does not point to an array element, the use of `++` and `--` operators produce a valid result. The pointer is increased or decreased by the size of the type it points to. For example:

```
#include <iostream> // Example 8.9
int main()
{
        double *ptr, i;

        ptr = &i;
        ptr++;
        std::cout << "Addr: " << ptr << '\n';
        ptr--;
        std::cout << "Addr: " << ptr << '\n';
        return 0;
}
```

The program displays two addresses with the first being `8` places greater than the second one.

As we'll see in next examples, the `++` and `--` operators are often combined with the `*` indirection operator to process array elements. The value of the expression depends on the operator precedence.

Because these combinations are often used, I put them all together for quick reference. For example, let's see the four combinations of * and ++; the same are for --.

i = (*ptr)++; first the value of *ptr is assigned to i and then *ptr is increased by one.

i = *ptr++; first the value of *ptr is assigned to i and then ptr is increased according to its type.

i = ++*ptr; first the value of *ptr is increased by one and then this value is assigned to i.

i = *++ptr; first the value of ptr is increased according to its type and then the value of *ptr is assigned to i.

Subtracting and Comparing Pointers

The result of pointer subtraction is valid only if both pointers point to elements of the same array or in the next place right after the end of the array. The result is the number of elements between them. If the value of the subtracted pointer is greater, the result would be the same with a negative sign. For example, if p1 points to the second element and p2 points to the fifth element of the same array, the result of p2-p1 is 3, while the result of p1-p2 is -3. The type of the result is ptrdiff_t, which is defined in the cstddef file as an alias of some signed integer type (e.g., int).

The result of comparing two pointers with the == and != operators is reliable. Using the relational operators <, <= and >=, the result is valid only if both point to members of the same object (e.g., structure) or to elements of the same array including the next place past the end, otherwise it is undefined. For example, the result of p2 > p1 is 1.

EXERCISES

C.8.6 Use the p1, p2, and p3 pointers and complete the following program to read the grades of a student in three tests. If all grades are greater than or equal to 5, the program should display them in ascending order. Otherwise, the program should display their average. The variables i, j, and k should be used only once.

```
#include <iostream>
int main()
{
        float *p1, *p2, *p3, i, j, k;
        ...
}
```

Answer:

```
#include <iostream>
using std::cout;
using std::cin;

int main()
{
        float *p1, *p2, *p3, i, j, k;

        p1 = &i;
        p2 = &j;
        p3 = &k;

        cout << "Enter grades: ";
        cin >> *p1 >> *p2 >> *p3;
```

```
        if((*p1 >= 5) && (*p2 >= 5) && (*p3 >= 5))
        {
                if(*p1 <= *p2 && *p1 <= *p3)
                {
                        cout << *p1;
                        if(*p2 < *p3)
                                cout << ' ' << *p2 << ' ' << *p3;
                        else
                                cout << ' ' << *p3 << ' ' << *p2;
                }
                else if(*p2 <= *p1 && *p2 <= *p3)
                {
                        cout << *p2;
                        if(*p1 < *p3)
                                cout << ' ' << *p1 << ' ' << *p3;
                        else
                                cout << ' ' << *p3 << ' ' << *p1;
                }
                else
                {
                        cout << *p3;
                        if(*p2 < *p1)
                                cout << ' ' << *p2 << ' ' << *p1;
                        else
                                cout << ' ' << *p1 << ' ' << *p2;
                }
        }
        else
                cout << "Avg: " << (*p1 + *p2 + *p3)/3 << '\n';
        return 0;
}
```

C.8.7 Use the p1, p2, and p3 pointers and complete the following program to read two integers and display the sum of the integers between them. For example, if the user enters 6 and 10, the program should display 24 (7+8+9). The program should force the user to enter numbers less than 100 and the first integer should be less than the second. The variables i, j, and sum should be used only once.

```
#include <iostream>
int main()
{
        int *p1, *p2, *p3, i, j, sum;
        ...
}
```

Answer:

```
#include <iostream>
int main()
{
        int *p1, *p2, *p3, i, j, sum;

        p1 = &i;
        p2 = &j;
        p3 = &sum;
        *p3 = 0;
```

```
        do
        {
                std::cout << "Enter two numbers (a < b < 100): ";
                std::cin >> *p1 >> *p2;
        } while(*p1 >= *p2 || *p2 > 100);

        (*p1)++;
        while(*p1 < *p2)
        {
                *p3 += *p1;
                (*p1)++;
        }
        std::cout << "Sum: " << *p3 << '\n';
        return 0;
}
```

Break time. We reach one of the most important sections. Listen to *Passenger* from *Iggy Pop (Stooges)*, and get on board. Pay extra attention.

POINTERS AND ARRAYS

The elements of an array are stored in successive memory locations, with the first one stored at the lowest memory address. The type of the array defines the distance of its elements in memory. For example, in a char array, the distance is one byte, while in an int array the distance equals the size of int (e.g., four bytes).

 The close relationship between pointers and arrays is based on the fact that the name of an array can be used as a pointer to its first element.

In a similar way, arr+1 can be used as a pointer to the second element, arr+2 as a pointer to the third one, and so on. In general, the following expressions are equivalent:

```
arr == &arr[0]
arr + 1 == &arr[1]
arr + 2 == &arr[2]
...
arr + n == &arr[n]
```

As a result, the following program outputs four times the same value:

```
#include <iostream> // Example 8.10
int main()
{
        int *ptr, arr[5];

        ptr = arr;
        std::cout << ptr << ' ' << &arr[0] << ' ' << arr << ' ' << &arr <<
'\n';
        return 0;
}
```

Notice that although the expression &arr outputs the same value, it is different than the others. This expression evaluates to a pointer to the whole array, whereas, the others evaluate to a pointer to its first element. In particular, the type of &arr is "pointer to an array of five integers", while the type of the others is "pointer to integer". Tough?

And to make it even harder, if we write &arr+1 instead of &arr, what would be the difference with the other values (would be one, four, or something else, ...)? To answer it, use the type of the expression and pointer arithmetic. I won't tell you the answer; give it some thought, run the program, check the output, and try to figure out why is that. If you need an explanation, don't send me an e-mail, I'm out ...

Since the name of an array can be used as a pointer to its first element, its content is equal to the value of its first element. Therefore, *arr is equal to arr[0]. In a similar way, since arr+1 is a pointer to the second element, *(arr+1) is equal to arr[1], and so on. In general, the following expressions are equivalent:

```
*arr == arr[0]
*(arr+1) == arr[1]
*(arr+2) == arr[2]
...
*(arr+n) == arr[n]
```

The parentheses are necessary because the * operator has higher precedence than the + operator. Therefore, the expressions *(arr+n) and *arr + n are evaluated in a different way. For example, consider the following program:

```cpp
#include <iostream> // Example 8.11
int main()
{
        int *ptr, arr[] = {10, 20, 30, 40, 50};

        ptr = arr+1;
        std::cout << *ptr+2 << ' ' << *(ptr+2) << '\n';
        return 0;
}
```

With the statement ptr = arr+1; ptr becomes equal to the address of arr[1], so *ptr is equal to arr[1], that is, 20. Since the * operator has higher precedence than +, *ptr+2 is equal to 20+2 = 22. The value of *(ptr+2) is the content of the address that ptr points to incremented by two integers' positions. Therefore, *(ptr+2) is equal to arr[3]. As a result, the program displays: 22 40

The following program uses array subscripting and pointer arithmetic to display the addresses and the values of arr elements in two different ways:

```cpp
#include <iostream> // Example 8.12
int main()
{
        int i, arr[5] = {10, 20, 30, 40, 50};

        std::cout << "***** Using array notation *****\n";
        for(i = 0; i < 5; i++)
                std::cout << "Addr: " << &arr[i] << " Val: " << arr[i] << '\n';

        std::cout << "\n***** Using pointer notation *****\n";
        for(i = 0; i < 5; i++)
                std::cout << "Addr: " << arr+i << " Val: " << *(arr+i) << '\n';

        return 0;
}
```

The first approach uses the index of the element, while the second one uses the name of the array as a pointer. My preference is to use array subscripting rather than pointer arithmetic. The reason is to get a clearer and less error prone code. In other words, I consider that `arr[i]` is easier to read and safer than `*(arr+i)`. For example, the lack of parentheses introduces a bug, which is not so easy to trace. However, because both ways are quite popular, you must learn and use both of them. In terms of performance, the optimizations that to date advanced compilers make would produce the same efficient code, no matter how you write it.

The important thing to remember is that the compiler converts `arr[i]` to `*(arr+i)`. We could say that `arr[i]` is an elegant shortcut for `*(arr+i)`. You'll encounter a really weird application of this rule in an exercise later on. The trap has been set and is waiting for you!

The following program uses another pointer variable to display the values and the addresses of `arr` elements.

```cpp
#include <iostream> // Example 8.13
int main()
{
        int *ptr, i, arr[5] = {10, 20, 30, 40, 50};

        ptr = arr;
        for(i = 0; i < 5; i++)
        {
                std::cout << "Addr: " << ptr << " Val: " << *ptr << '\n';
                ptr++; /* ptr becomes equal to the memory address of the next
array element. Equivalently, we can write ptr = &arr[i]; */
        }
        return 0;
}
```

The statement `ptr = arr;` makes `ptr` to point to the first element, while each execution of `ptr++;` makes `ptr` to point to the next element. Notice that I don't write `ptr = &arr;` because the type of `&arr` corresponds to a pointer to an array, while `ptr` is a pointer to an integer. It'd be a compilation error.

When the name of an array is used as a pointer, C++ treats it as `const` pointer. Therefore, it is not allowed to change its value and make it point somewhere else. An array is not a modifiable *lvalue*; its value will always be equal to the memory address of its first element.

Therefore, if we write `arr++;` or `arr = &i;` in our last example, the compiler will display an error message for illegal action. Now, you can understand why I told you in Chapter 7 that it is illegal to write `b = a;` in order to copy the elements of the array a into b. However, it is allowed to copy its value in a pointer variable, as we did with `ptr = arr;` and use that pointer to access the array elements.

Although arrays and pointers are closely related, it must be clear to you that an array is not a pointer and vice versa. For example, the declarations `int a[50];` and `int *a;` are quite different. With the first declaration the compiler allocates memory for 50 integers. The array can be filled with different values at different times, but the name a always refers to the same memory address. As said, it is not possible to assign it a new value, that is, it is illegal to write `a = arr`. With the second declaration the compiler allocates memory to store the value of the pointer (e.g., typically 4 bytes). Unlike the array, it is allowed to assign a new value to the pointer and make it point somewhere else, for example, it is legal to write `a = arr;`

Just remember that whenever the name of an array is used in an expression, the compiler converts it to a pointer to the address of its first element. Always? Not always, there are a few exceptions:

a. When it is the operand of the `sizeof` operator. `sizeof` calculates the size of the entire array. Also, when it is the operand of `decltype` and `typeid` operators.
b. As discussed, when the `&` operator is applied to it. It is the array's address that is retrieved. When discussing complex declarations in Chapter 11, we'll see an example of how to declare and initialize a pointer of that type.
c. When initialize a reference to an array. We'll see such an example in Chapter 16.
d. When the array is a literal string initializer used in a declaration.

For more safety when processing an array through pointers, C++11 provides the `begin()` and `end()` functions. Both are declared in the `iterator` file. `begin()` returns a pointer to the first element of the array, while `end()` returns a pointer to the next place past the end. For example, the following program displays the elements with a negative value:

```cpp
#include <iostream> // Example 8.14
#include <iterator>
using namespace std;

int main()
{
        int arr[] = {10, 20, -30, 40, 50};
        int *cur = begin(arr);
        int *fin = end(arr);

        while(cur != fin)
        {
                if(*cur < 0)
                        cout << *cur << '\n';
                cur++;
        }
        return 0;
}
```

By using the pointers returned by `begin()` and `end()` we are sure that we will not access any memory address outside the allowed limits.

Using Pointer with Array Notation

Although a pointer variable is not an array, it can be indexed like an array. For example, the following program subscripts the pointer variable `ptr` as though it were an array to display the values and the addresses of `arr` elements.

```cpp
#include <iostream> // Example 8.15
int main()
{
        int *ptr, i, arr[5] = {10, 20, 30, 40, 50};

        ptr = arr;
        for(i = 0; i < 5; i++)
                std::cout << "Addr: " << &ptr[i] << " Val: " << ptr[i] << '\n';
        return 0;
}
```

Notice that although `arr[i]` and `ptr[i]` access the same element, the compiler gets there in a different way. For example, to access `arr[2]`, it gets the address of `arr`, adds 8 (as said, we assume that the size of `int` is 4 bytes), and goes to the resulting address to get the value. On the other hand, to access `ptr[2]`, it gets the address of `ptr`, retrieves the value that is stored there, adds 8, and goes to that address to get the value. In other words, `arr[2]` resides 8 places after the address of `arr`, while `ptr[2]` resides 8 places after the address that `ptr` points to.

EXERCISES

C.8.8 What is the output of the following program?

```
#include <iostream>
int main()
{
        int i = 5, *p = &i;

        p[0] = 1;
        std::cout << i+p[0] << '\n';
        return 0;
}
```

`Answer:` Since p points to the address of i, we can index it as an array of a single element. Therefore, the statement p[0] = 1; is equivalent to i = 1; and the program displays 2. What would happen if we write p[1] = 1; instead of p[0] = 1?

The statement p[1] = 1; attempts to change the value of an out-of-bound address, which may cause a program crash.

C.8.9 Write a program that reads the daily temperatures of January and stores them in an array. Then, the program should read a temperature and display the first day number with a temperature less than this. Use pointer arithmetic to process the array.

```
#include <iostream>
using std::cout;
using std::cin;

int main()
{
        const int SIZE = 31;
        int i;
        double temp, arr[SIZE];

        for(i = 0; i < SIZE; i++)
        {
                cout << "Enter temperatures: ";
                cin >> *(arr+i);
        }
        cout << "Enter temperature to check: ";
        cin >> temp;
        for(i = 0; i < SIZE; i++)
        { /* The braces are not necessary. I put them to make the code easier
to read. */
                if(*(arr+i) < temp)
                        break;
        }
```

```
        if(i == SIZE)
                cout << "No temperature less than " << temp << '\n';
        else
                cout << "The first temperature less than " << temp << " was "
<< *(arr+i) << " in day " << i+1 << '\n';
        return 0;
}
```

C.8.10 What is the output of the following program?

```
#include <iostream>
int main()
{
        int i, *ptr1, *ptr2, arr[] = {10, 20, 30, 40, 50, 60, 70};

        ptr1 = &arr[2];
        ptr2 = &arr[4];
        for(i = ptr2-ptr1; i < 5; i+=2)
                std::cout << ptr1[i] << ' ';
        return 0;
}
```

Answer: As said, when two pointers that point to the same array are subtracted, the result is the number of elements between them, not their distance in memory. Therefore, although the address of arr[4] is eight places higher than the address of arr[2], the result of ptr2-ptr1 is equal to the difference of their subscripts, that is, 4-2 = 2. Since ptr1 points to arr[2], ptr1[2] corresponds to arr[4] and ptr1[4] to arr[6]. Therefore, the program outputs 50 and 70.

C.8.11 Write a program that reads the grades of ten students, stores them in an array, and displays the best and the worst grade and the positions of their first occurrences in the array. The program should force the user to enter grades within [0, 10]. Use pointer arithmetic to process the array.

```
#include <iostream>
int main()
{
        const int SIZE = 10;
        int i, max_pos, min_pos;
        float *p, max, min, arr[SIZE];

        max = -1;
        min = 11;
        for(i = 0; i < SIZE; i++)
        {
                p = arr+i;

                do
                {
                        std::cout << "Enter grade: ";
                        std::cin >> *p;
                } while(*p > 10 || *p < 0); /* Check if the grade is within
[0, 10]. */
                if(*p > max)
                {
                        max = *p;
                        max_pos = i;
                }
```

```
                    if(*p < min)
                    {
                            min = *p;
                            min_pos = i;
                    }
            }
            std::cout << "Max grade is " << max << " in pos " << max_pos << "\nMin
grade is " << min << " in pos " << min_pos << '\n';
            return 0;
    }
```

C.8.12 Use the `ptr` pointer and complete the following program to read and store the grades of 50 students into `arr` and then display the array's values in reverse order. Use pointer arithmetic to process the array.

```
#include <iostream>
int main()
{
        const int SIZE = 50;
        float *ptr, arr[SIZE];
        ...
}
```

Answer:

```
#include <iostream>
int main()
{
        const int SIZE = 50;
        float *ptr, arr[SIZE];

        ptr = arr;
        while(ptr < arr+SIZE)
        {
                std::cout << "Enter grade: ";
                std::cin >> *ptr;
                ptr++;
        }
        ptr--;
        while(ptr >= arr)
        {
                std::cout << *ptr << '\n';
                ptr--;
        }
        return 0;
}
```

C.8.13 Use the `ptr` pointer and complete the following program to read 50 integers and store into `arr` those with a value within [30, 40]. The program should display how many values are stored in the array. The program should set the value -1 to the remaining elements. Use pointer arithmetic to process the array.

```
#include <iostream>
int main()
{
        const int SIZE = 50;
        int *ptr, i, arr[SIZE];
        ...
}
```

Answer:

```
#include <iostream>
int main()
{
        const int SIZE = 50;
        int *ptr, i, arr[SIZE];

        ptr = arr;
        for(i = 0; i < SIZE; i++)
        {
                std::cout << "Enter number: ";
                std::cin >> *ptr;

                if(*ptr >= 30 && *ptr <= 40)
                        ptr++;
        }
        std::cout << ptr-arr << " elements are stored\n";
        for(; ptr < arr+SIZE; ptr++)
                *ptr = -1;
        return 0;
}
```

C.8.14 How many compilation errors can you detect in the following program?

```
#include <iostream>
int main()
{
        int i, arr[5] = {10, 20, 30, 40, 50};

        for(i = 0; i < 5; i++)
                std::cout << i[arr] << '\n';

        std::cout << 2[arr]-3[arr] << '\n';
        return 0;
}
```

Answer: Did you escape the trap or not? The normal answer to give is that the expression i[arr] is wrong, because arr and not i is declared as an array. For the same reason, the expressions 2[arr] and 3[arr] seem wrong as well. However, the compiler does not complain. Yes, you've read correctly, it is not a typing error; the compiler has no reason to complain about. And now, what shall we do after that concept overturning?

Relax, listen to *Getting Away with It (All Messed Up)* from *James* and wait for the smoke to clear. Nothing is *messed up*, let's see why. As said, the compiler converts i[arr] to *(i+arr), which is equivalent to *(arr+i), equivalent to arr[i]. That is:

```
arr[i] = *(&arr[0]+i) = *(arr+i) = *(i+arr) = i[arr]
```

Thus, 2[arr] is equivalent to arr[2]. Therefore, the program is compiled successfully and displays the values of the array's elements, as well as the difference of arr[2] and arr[3], that is, -10.

In the same "irrational" sense, could we write the following?

```
int *ptr = arr+4;
cout << ptr[-2];
```

Yes, because `ptr[-2]` is converted to `*(ptr-2)`, which is equivalent to `*(arr+4-2)`, that is `arr[2]`, and the program outputs `30`. So, if in a course test or in a job interview you are asked what happens if we write `ptr[-2] = 10;` do not rush to answer that disaster is coming. As long as the resulting element is inside the array, there is no problem; its value becomes `10`.

Needless to say that I'd never recommend use this reverse syntax; I just used it to demonstrate the close relationship between arrays and pointers in a really weird way. Forget what you saw, get it out of your mind, burn the page.

C.8.15 Use the `p1` and `p2` pointers and complete the following program to read and store 50 integers into `arr1` and `arr2` arrays, respectively. Then, the program should display the values of the common elements and their positions in the two arrays, if found. Use pointer arithmetic to process the arrays.

```
#include <iostream>
int main()
{
        const int SIZE = 50;
        int *p1, *p2, arr1[SIZE], arr2[SIZE];
        ...
}
```

Answer:

```
#include <iostream>
using std::cout;
using std::cin;

int main()
{
        const int SIZE = 50;
        int *p1, *p2, arr1[SIZE], arr2[SIZE];

        for(p1 = arr1; p1 < arr1+SIZE; p1++)
        {
                cout << "Enter number: ";
                cin >> *p1;
        }
        cout << "\nSecond array\n";
        for(p2 = arr2; p2 < arr2+SIZE; p2++)
        {
                cout << "Enter number: ";
                cin >> *p2;
        }
        for(p1 = arr1; p1 < arr1+SIZE; p1++)
        {
                for(p2 = arr2; p2 < arr2+SIZE; p2++)
                {
                        if(*p1 == *p2)
                                cout << "Common element:" << *p1 << " found in
positions " << p1-arr1+1 << " and " << p2-arr2+1 << '\n';
                }
        }
        return 0;
}
```

C.8.16 Use the `p1` and `p2` pointers and complete the following program to read the codes of 100 products and store them into `arr`. The program should store a code in the array only if it is not already stored. If the user enters -1, the insertion of codes should terminate. The program should display the codes of the stored products, before it terminates. Use pointer arithmetic to process the array.

```cpp
#include <iostream>
int main()
{
        const int SIZE = 100;
        int *p1, *p2, arr[SIZE];
        ...
}
```

Answer:

```cpp
#include <iostream>
using std::cout;
using std::cin;

int main()
{
        const int SIZE = 100;
        int *p1, *p2, arr[SIZE];

        p1 = arr;
        while(p1 < arr+SIZE)
        {
                cout << "Enter code_" << p1-arr+1 << ": ";
                cin >> *p1;
                if(*p1 == -1)
                        break;

                for(p2 = arr; p2 < p1; p2++) /* Traverse the array to check if
the input code is already stored. */
                {
                        if(*p1 == *p2)
                        {
                                cout << "Error: Code " << *p1 << " exists " <<
'\n';
                                break;
                        }
                }
                // If the code is not stored, increase the pointer.
                if(p2 == p1)
                        p1++;
        }
        // Display the codes.
        for(p2 = arr; p2 < p1; p2++)
                cout << "C:" << *p2 << '\n';
        return 0;
}
```

C.8.17 What is the output of the following program?

```
#include <iostream>
int main()
{
        int a[] = {0, 0, 1, 2, 3}, b[] = {0, 0, 0, 4, 5, 6};
        int *ptr1 = a, *ptr2 = b;

        while(!*ptr1++ && !(*++ptr2))
                ;
        std::cout << *(b+(ptr1-a)) << ' ' << *(a+(ptr2-b)) << '\n';
        return 0;
}
```

Answer: Yes, you need pen and paper to decipher it. It is a tough one, indeed; sorry to be pushing you. Let's trace the iterations:

In the first iteration, since ptr1 points to a[0], *ptr1 is equal to a[0], that is, 0. Thus, the value of !*ptr1 is 1. Next, ptr1 is increased and points to a[1]. Since ptr2 points to b[0], the ++ptr2 makes it point to b[1], so the value of *++ptr2 is b[1], that is, 0. Thus, the value of !(*++ptr2) is 1. Since both terms are true, the loop continues.

Like before, in the second iteration, both terms are true; ptr1 points to a[2] and ptr2 points to b[2]. In the third iteration, since a[2] is 1, the value of !*ptr1 is 0 and when increased it points to a[3]. Pay attention now, here is the key to the answer. Recall from Chapter 4 and the description of the && operator that if an operand is false the rest operands are not evaluated and the value of the expression becomes 0. Therefore, the condition becomes false and the loop terminates. Since ptr2 is not increased, it still points to b[2].

Since ptr1 points to a[3], the result of ptr1-a is 3. Therefore, the expression *(b+(ptr1-a)) is equivalent to *(b+3), that is, b[3]. Similarly, since ptr2 points to b[2] the expression *(a+(ptr2-b)) is equivalent to *(a+2), that is, a[2]. Therefore, the program outputs: 4 1

And to make it even worse, what would be the output if we replace the && operator with the || operator and write:

```
while(!*ptr1++ || !(*++ptr2));
```

If you find it, please let me know…

ARRAY OF POINTERS

An array of pointers is an array whose elements are pointers to the same data type. To declare such an array we add an * before its name. For example, the statement:

```
int *p[3];
```

declares an array of three pointers to integers.

 When you declare an array of pointers, don't enclose its name in parentheses.

For example, the statement:

```
int (*p)[3];
```

declares p as a pointer to an array of three integers and not as an array of three pointers. Don't worry, we'll discuss complex declarations like this one in Chapter 11. The elements of an array of pointers are treated as the ordinary pointers. For example:

```
#include <iostream> // Example 8.16
int main()
{
        int *p[3], i = 10, j = 30;

        p[0] = &i;
        *p[0] = 20;
        p[1] = &j;
        p[2] = p[0];
        std::cout << i+*p[1]+*p[2] << '\n';
        return 0;
}
```

The statement p[0] = &i; makes p[0] to point to the address of i, so *p[0] is equal to i. Thus, i becomes 20. Similarly, *p[1] is equal to j. The statement p[2] = p[0]; makes p2 point to the same address that p[0] points to, that is, the address of i. Thus, *p[2] is equal to i. As a result, the program outputs 70.

Although we'll discuss strings in Chapter 10, an array of pointers is often used in place of a two-dimensional array to handle strings. One reason is to save memory. For example, the declaration:

```
char names[][12] = {"First name", "Second name", "Third"};
```

allocates 12 bytes for each row, no matter what the length of the strings is. On the other hand, if we use an array of pointers:

```
char *names[] = {"First name", "Second name", "Third"};
```

the allocated memory matches the length of each string. The elements of the array are pointers to the respective strings. Because of the diverse right-hand ends, this array is often called a *ragged* string array. Let's make a simple question, what is the size of this names array? Easy, count the characters and answer it. Please, read the answer at the next page only if you are absolutely sure; count carefully.

And because I told you to count the characters you did that? Lucky you are, I didn't choose lengthy strings... Here is the answer. Assuming that each pointer allocates 4 bytes, since the array contains three elements its size is 12 bytes, regardless of the string lengths.

Besides saving memory, the use of an array of pointers to handle strings may improve the performance of the program. Exercise C.10.27 is such an example.

EXERCISES

C.8.18 What is the output of the following program?

```
#include <iostream>
int main()
{
        int *p[3], i, num;

        for(i = 0; i < 3; i++)
        {
                std::cout << "Enter number: ";
                std::cin >> num;
                p[i] = &num;
        }
        for(i = 0; i < 3; i++)
                std::cout << *p[i] << '\n';
        return 0;
}
```

Answer: The statement p[i] = # makes each element of p to point to the address of num. So, since all three pointers point to the same address, their content would be equal to the last value of num. Thus, the second loop outputs three times the last input value.

C.8.19 What is the output of the following program?

```
#include <iostream>
int main()
{
        int *p[3], i, arr[4] = {10, 20, 30, 40};

        for(i = 0; i < 3; i++)
        {
                p[i] = &arr[i]+1;
                std::cout << *p[i] << ' ';
        }
        return 0;
}
```

Answer: The statement p[i] = &arr[i]+1; makes each element of p to point to the address of the next element after arr[i]. Therefore, when i is 0, p[0] points to arr[1], when it is 1, p[1] points to arr[2] and, when it is 2, p[2] points to arr[3]. Therefore, the program displays: 20 30 40.

C.8.20 The converse of the Pythagorean Theorem says that in a triangle with sides of length a, b and c, if:

$a^2 + b^2 = c^2$, the triangle is right
$a^2 + b^2 < c^2$, the triangle is obtuse
$a^2 + b^2 > c^2$, the triangle is acute

Use the array p and complete the following program to read the lengths of a, b, and c sides and display the type of the triangle. The program should force the user to enter a value for c greater than the other two.

```
#include <iostream>
int main()
{
        int a, b, c, *p[3] = {&a, &b, &c};
        // It is not allowed to use again the a, b, c.
}
```

Answer:

```
#include <iostream>
using std::cout;
using std::cin;

int main()
{
        int a, b, c, *p[3] = {&a, &b, &c};

        cout << "Enter length_a and length_b: ";
        cin >> *p[0] >> *p[1];
        do
        {
                cout << "Enter length_c: ";
                cin >> *p[2];
        } while((*p[2] <= *p[0]) || (*p[2] <= *p[1]));

        if((*p[0])*(*p[0]) + (*p[1])*(*p[1]) == (*p[2])*(*p[2]))
                cout << "Right triangle\n";
        else if((*p[0])*(*p[0]) + (*p[1])*(*p[1]) > (*p[2])*(*p[2]))
                cout << "Acute triangle\n";
        else
                cout << "Obtuse triangle\n";
        return 0;
}
```

POINTER TO POINTER

Just like an ordinary variable, when a pointer variable is declared the compiler allocates memory to store its value. Therefore, we can declare another pointer variable to point to this memory address. To declare a pointer to a pointer variable, we use the * twice. For example, the statement:

```
int **pp;
```

declares pp as a pointer to another pointer that points to int.

To use a pointer to a pointer variable, the single * provides access to the address of the second pointer, while the double ** provides access to the content of the address that the second pointer points to. For example:

```
#include <iostream> // Example 8.17
int main()
```

```
{
        int *p, **pp, i = 20;

        p = &i;
        pp = &p;
        std::cout << **pp << '\n';
        return 0;
}
```

Since pp points to the address of p, *pp is equal to p. Since p points to the address of i, **pp is equal to i and the program displays 20.

The most common use of a pointer to a pointer variable is when we want a function to change the value of an argument which is pointer. We'll discuss such examples in Chapter 11. In general, it is allowed to declare a pointer to a pointer to another pointer variable and so on (e.g., int ***p;), but, in practice, it is rarely needed to exceed a depth of two. Let's see an example that combines all together; array, array of pointers and pointer to a pointer:

```
#include <iostream> // Example 8.18
int main()
{
        int a[] = {10, 20, 30}, *p[] = {a, a+1, a+2}, **pp;

        for(pp = p; pp < p+3; pp++)
                std::cout << **pp << ' ';
        return 0;
}
```

Initially, pp points to p[0] which points to the address of a[0]. Therefore, **pp is equal to a[0]. When increased, pp points to p[1] which points to a[1]. As a result, the program displays: 10 20 30.

EXERCISES

C.8.21 What is the output of the following program?

```
#include <iostream>
int main()
{
        int *p, **pp, i = 10, j = 20;

        p = &i;
        pp = &p;
        **pp = j;

        p = &j;
        **pp += 10;
        std::cout << i+j << '\n';
        return 0;
}
```

Answer: Since pp points to p and p points to i, **pp is equal to i. Therefore, the statement **pp = j; is equivalent to i = j = 20. The statement p = &j, makes p point to j, so **pp is equal to j. Therefore, the statement **pp += 10; is equivalent to j = j+10 = 20+10 = 30. As a result, the program displays 50.

C.8.22 What are the values of a elements in the following program?

```
#include <iostream>
int main()
{
        int k = 0, b = 1, c = 2, d = 3, m, a[3];
        int *p[] = {&k, &b, &c, &d};

        for(m = 0; m < 3; m++)
                a[*p[m]] = **(p+m+1);
        return 0;
}
```

Answer: Since p[0] is equal to &k, p[1] is equal to &b, p[2] is equal to &c, and p[3] is equal to &d, the values of *p[0], *p[1], *p[2], and *p[3] are 0, 1, 2, and 3, respectively. In the general case, p+m+1 is a pointer to the p[m+1] element. Let's trace the iterations:

First iteration (m=0): a[*p[0]] = **(p+1) = *p[1] = b, that is, a[0] = 1.
Second iteration (m=1): a[*p[1]] = **(p+2) = *p[2] = c, that is, a[1] = 2.
Third iteration (m=2): a[*p[2]] = **(p+3) = *p[3] = d, that is, a[2] = 3.

C.8.23 Use p1 and complete the following program to read continuously an integer and output the word test as many times as the absolute value of the input number. The program should use p2 to display the total number of the output words. If the user enters 0, the insertion of numbers should terminate. Use only for loops.

```
#include <iostream>
int main()
{
        int **p1, **p2, *p3, *p4, i, num, times;
        ...
}
```

Answer:

```
#include <iostream>
int main()
{
        int **p1, **p2, *p3, *p4, i, num, times;

        p3 = &num;
        p1 = &p3;

        p4 = &times;
        p2 = &p4;

        **p2 = 0;
        for(;;)
        {
                std::cout << "Enter number: ";
                std::cin >> **p1;
                if(**p1 == 0)
                        break;
```

```
            if(**p1 < 0)
                    **p1 = -**p1;
            for(i = 0; i < **p1; i++)
                    std::cout << "test\n";
            **p2 += **p1;
    }
    std::cout << "Total number is " << **p2 << '\n';
    return 0;
}
```

POINTERS AND TWO-DIMENSIONAL ARRAYS

Just as pointers are closely related to one-dimensional arrays, they are also related to multidimensional arrays. In this section, we'll focus on the most common case, that of two-dimensional arrays.

Recall from Chapter 7 that when a two-dimensional array is declared its elements are stored in successive memory locations, starting with the elements of the first row, followed by the elements of the second row, and so on. For example, the following program declares a two-dimensional array and displays the memory addresses of its elements. Their distance is the size of the int type (e.g., 4).

```
#include <iostream> // Example 8.19
int main()
{
        int i, j, a[2][3];

        for(i = 0; i < 2; i++)
                for(j = 0; j < 3; j++)
                        std::cout << "Address of a[" << i << "][" << j << "]:"
<< &a[i][j] << '\n';
        return 0;
}
```

Also remember that C++ treats a two-dimensional array as a one-dimensional array, where each element is an array. For example, the elements of a are the a[0], a[1], and a[2], where each one is an array of three integers. In particular, C++ treats a[0] as an array and by subscripting its name we got its elements, that is, the a[0][0], a[0][1], and a[0][2]. Indeed, if we write sizeof(a[0]), the program outputs 12.

To process a two-dimensional array a[N][M] through pointer arithmetic, we use the name of each array a[0], a[1], ..., a[N-1] as a pointer to the first element of the respective row. For example, since a[0] can be used as a pointer to a[0][0], *a[0] is equal to a[0][0].

Since a[0] points to the first element, a[0]+1 can be used as a pointer to the second element, that is, a[0][1], and a[0]+2 as a pointer to the third element, that is, a[0][2]. In the general case, a[0]+j can be used as a pointer to the a[0][j] element of the first row. So, we have:

- a[0]+j is equivalent to &a[0][j].
- *(a[0]+j) is equivalent to a[0][j].

In a similar way, a[1]+j can be used as a pointer to the a[1][j] element of the second row. So, we have:

- a[1]+j is equivalent to &a[1][j].
- *(a[1]+j) is equivalent to a[1][j].

Therefore, in the general case we have:

- a[i]+j is equivalent to &a[i][j].
- *(a[i]+j) is equivalent to a[i][j].

And because, as we know by now, a[i] is converted to *(a+i) we have:

- *(a+i)+j is equivalent to &a[i][j].
- *(*(a+i)+j) is equivalent to a[i][j].

An example of these equations is that a[0][0] is equivalent to *a[0] and **a. Essentially, when we write a[i][j] the compiler converts it to *(*(a+i)+j). To sum up, the following program uses three ways to display the elements of a two-dimensional array.

```cpp
#include <iostream> // Example 8.20
int main()
{
        int i, j, a[2][3] = {10, 20, 30, 40, 50, 60};

        for(i = 0; i < 2; i++)
                for(j = 0; j < 3; j++)
                {
                        std::cout << "a[" << i << "][" << j << "]:" << a[i][j];
                        std::cout << " a[" << i << "][" << j << "]:" <<
*(a[i]+j);
                        std::cout << " a[" << i << "][" << j << "]:" <<
*(*(a+i)+j) << '\n';
                }
        return 0;
}
```

Needless to say which one is the simplest …

Let's add this. Consider the following declarations:

```cpp
int a[2][3], b[10];
```

My question is: As we say that b can be used as a pointer to b[0], is it correct to say that a can be used as a pointer to a[0][0]?

Because C++ treats a as a one-dimensional array, the answer is no, a can be used as a pointer to the first element, that is, a[0]. Therefore, if we want to assign a to a pointer variable, what should be the type of the pointer? It should be pointer to an array. For example:

```cpp
int (*p)[3]; /* The parentheses are necessary, otherwise the compiler would
interpret p as an array of three pointers to integers. */
p = a;
```

and p points to the first element of the first row of a, that is, a[0][0].

Remember, in a declaration such as int x[5], x "decays" to a pointer, while in a declaration such as int y[5][3], y does not "decay" to a pointer to a pointer, but to a pointer to array.

Make a note of that: the type of the expression &x is a pointer to an array of five inetegrs, while the type of the expression &y is a pointer to an array of five arrays where each array contains three integers.

And if we write p++; where will p point to? Yes, I know, it will point to the *Chapter Exit*, please don't give up, I know that these are difficult concepts. It is normal to feel like this, you don't need this stuff for a plain introduction and use of pointers, but it might be useful if going deeper. Don't forget that pointers are extensively used out there in production code and because you'll certainly meet them you should know how they can be used.

Let's continue, where will p point to? Applying pointer arithmetic and because its type is pointer to an array, it will be incremented by the size of the row and point to the first element of the next row. Consider the following program:

```cpp
#include <iostream> // Example 8.21
int main()
{
        int i, a[2][3] = {10, 20, 30, 40, 50, 60}, (*p)[3];

        for(p = a; p < a+2; p++) // We could write the condition as p < &a[2]
        {
                for(i = 0; i < 3; i++)
                        std::cout << (*p)[i] << ' ';
                std::cout << '\n';
        }
        return 0;
}
```

Notice that the type of p must be pointer to an array. If it were declared as `int*` or `int**` the program wouldn't compile. Each time p is incremented, it points to the first element of the next row and the inner loop displays the elements of that row. What change should we make to display only the elements of a specific row (e.g., the second)?

We'd remove the outer loop and write: p = a+1; or equivalently p = &a[1];. The inner loop remains as is.

What about if we want to declare pointers to each row of the array? We could use an array of pointers. For example:

```cpp
#include <iostream> // Example 8.22
int main()
{
        int i, a[4][2] = {10, 20, 30, 40, 50, 60, 70, 80}, *p[4] = {a[0],
a[1], a[2], a[3]};

        for(i = 0; i < 4; i++)
                std::cout << *(p[i]+1) << ' ';
        return 0;
}
```

When initialized, each p element points to the first element of the respective row of a. For example, p[0] points to a[0][0] and p[0]+1 points to a[0][1]. Therefore, the program displays the values of the second column, that is, 20 40 60 80.

Before finishing a really tough section, the equivalent pointer expressions to access an element of up to a four-dimensional array are:

```cpp
arr[i]          = *(arr+i)
arr[i][j]       = *(*(arr+i)+j)
arr[i][j][k]    = *(*(*(arr+i)+j)+k)
arr[i][j][k][l] = *(*(*(*(arr+i)+j)+k)+l)
```

EXERCISES

C.8.24 What does the following code do?

```
int i, arr[2][5] = {10, 20, 30, 40, 50, 60, 70, 80, 90, 100};
for(i = 0; i < 2; i++)
        *(arr[i]+3) = 0;
```

Answer: In each iteration, `arr[i]` points to the first element of row i. The expression `arr[i]+3` is a pointer to the fourth element of row i. Therefore, `*(arr[i]+3)` is equal to `arr[i][3]`. As a result, the code makes zero the elements of the fourth column, so, `arr[0][3]` and `arr[1][3]` become 0.

C.8.25 What does the following code do?

```
int *ptr, arr[2][5] = {10, 20, 30, 40, 50, 60, 70, 80, 90, 100};
for(ptr = arr[1]+2; ptr < arr[1]+5; ptr++)
        *ptr = 0;
```

Answer: The statement `ptr = arr[1]+2;` makes `ptr` to point to the address of `arr[1][2]`. Since `*ptr` is equal to `arr[1][2]`, the statement `*ptr = 0;` is equivalent to `arr[1][2] = 0;`. The statement `ptr++;` makes `ptr` to point to the next element of the current row. For example, when `ptr` is first increased, it points to the address of `arr[1][3]` and the next increment makes it point to the address of `arr[1][4]`. Therefore, the code makes zero the last three elements of the second row.

C.8.26 And because I'm a "bad character" and want to press you a bit more, what happens if we change the `for` statement to:

```
for(ptr = arr[0]+4; ptr < arr[0]+7; ptr++)
```

Answer: The statement `ptr = arr[0]+4;` makes `ptr` to point to the address of `arr[0][4]`. Therefore, the statement `*ptr = 0;` is equivalent to `arr[0][4] = 0;`. Since each row contains five elements, the addresses beyond `arr[0]+4` don't correspond to array elements. Right?

Don't think so, see why. When `ptr` is incremented and because the array elements are stored in successive memory locations, `ptr` will point to the first element of the next row. In other words, the address of `arr[0]+5` is the same as of `arr[1][0]`. Similarly, the address of `arr[0]+6` is the same as of `arr[1][1]`. Therefore, the code makes zero the value of the last element of the first row and the first two of the next one.

C.8.27 Use the `p` pointer and complete the following program to create an identity 5×5 matrix. In math, an identity matrix has 1s on the main diagonal's elements and 0s everywhere else.

```
#include <iostream>
int main()
{
        const int SIZE = 5;
        int *p, arr[SIZE][SIZE] = {0};
        ...
}
```

Answer:

```
#include <iostream>
int main()
{
        const int SIZE = 5;
        int *p, arr[SIZE][SIZE] = {0};

        for(p = &arr[0][0]; p <= &arr[SIZE-1][SIZE-1]; p++)
        {
                if((p-&arr[0][0])%(SIZE+1) == 0)
                        *p = 1;
        }
        return 0;
}
```

Comments: Since the elements of the array are initialized with 0, it remains to make the elements of the main diagonal equal to 1. The if condition checks if the element is on the diagonal. The form of that condition is based on the observation that the number of elements between two successive diagonal's elements is SIZE. For example, in the 5×5 array, the elements of the diagonal are in positions 0, 6, 12, 18, and 24.

Also, with this example, I want to show you that it is perfectly legal to treat the two-dimensional array as if it were one-dimensional. We exploit the fact that the elements are stored in successive positions in memory.

C.8.28 Write a program that assigns random integers to a 3×5 array and displays the minimum and the maximum value of each row and column. Use pointer arithmetic to process the array.

```
#include <iostream>
#include <iomanip>
#include <cstdlib>
#include <ctime>
using std::cout;
using std::setw;

int main()
{
        const int ROWS = 3;
        const int COLS = 5;
        int i, j, min, max, arr[ROWS][COLS];

        srand(time(NULL));
        for(i = 0; i < ROWS; i++)
        {
                min = max = *arr[i] = rand();
                for(j = 1; j < COLS; j++)
                {
                        *(arr[i]+j) = rand();
                        if(*(arr[i]+j) < min)
                                min = *(arr[i]+j);
                        if(*(arr[i]+j) > max)
                                max = *(arr[i]+j);
                }
                cout << "Row_" << i+1 << ": Min=" << min << " Max=" << max <<
'\n';
        }
```

```
        for(i = 0; i < COLS; i++)
        {
                min = max = *(arr[0]+i);
                for(j = 1; j < ROWS; j++)
                {
                        if(*(arr[j]+i) < min)
                                min = *(arr[j]+i);
                        if(*(arr[j]+i) > max)
                                max = *(arr[j]+i);
                }
                cout << "Col_" << i+1 << ": Min=" << min << " Max=" << max << '\n';
        }
        // Display the array to verify the results.
        for(i = 0; i < ROWS; i++)
        {
                for(j = 0; j < COLS; j++)
                        cout << setw(10) << *(arr[i]+j);
                cout << '\n';
        }
        return 0;
}
```

POINTER TO FUNCTION

Most probably, it'd be better to read this section after reading Chapter 11. However, you may continue and get an idea.

When a function is defined, the compiler allocates memory to store its code. Therefore, every function has an address, as an ordinary variable. A function pointer points to the memory address, where the function's code is stored. We can use this pointer to call the function; however, it is not allowed to change its code. The general syntax to declare a function pointer is:

```
return_type (*pointer_name) (type_param_1 name_1,  type_param_2 name_2,  ...,
type_param_n name_n);
```

The `return_type` specifies the function's return type, while the variables name_1, name_2, ..., name_n indicate the function's parameters, if any. Here are some examples:

```
int (*ptr)(int arr[], int size); /* ptr is declared as a pointer to a
function, which takes as parameters an array of integers and an integer and
returns an integer. */
void (*ptr)(double *arr[]); /* ptr is declared as a pointer to a function,
which takes as parameters an array of pointers to doubles and returns
nothing. */
int test(void (*ptr)(int a)); /* test() returns an integer value and takes as
parameter a pointer to another function, which takes an integer parameter and
returns nothing. */
```

The pointer can only point to functions with the same parameter list and return type as those specified in its declaration. The name of the function pointer must be enclosed in parentheses because the function call operator () has higher precedence than the * operator. For example, the statement:

int *ptr(int a); instead of int (*ptr)(int a); declares a function named ptr, which takes an integer parameter and returns a pointer to an integer.

An easy way to declare a pointer to a function is first to write the function prototype and then replace the function name with an expression of the form (*ptr). Thus, ptr is declared as pointer to a function of that prototype. As we said, to make a pointer to point to a function, the pointer's declaration must match the function's prototype. For example, consider the following program:

```
#include <iostream> // Example 8.23

void test(int a);

int main()
{
        void (*ptr)(int a); /* ptr is declared as a pointer to a function,
which takes an integer parameter and returns nothing. */
        ptr = test; /* ptr points to the address of test(). Alternatively, we
can write ptr = &test. */
        (*ptr)(10); /* Call the function that ptr points to. Alternatively, we
can write ptr(10). */
        return 0;
}

void test(int a)
{
        std::cout << 2*a << '\n';
}
```

 The name of a function can be used as a pointer to its address.

Therefore, the statement ptr = test; makes ptr to point to the address of test(). This statement is allowed, because the declaration of ptr matches the declaration of test(). For example, if we change the return type of test() from void to int, the compilation fails. Note that if we write ptr = &test; the result is the same, because the expression &test is interpreted as a pointer to test(), not as a pointer to a pointer to test(). Of course, we can initialize the function pointer when we declare it. For example: void (*ptr)(int a) = test;

To simplify the declaration we can use the auto keyword. For example: auto ptr = test;. To highlight that ptr is pointer, we can write auto*, that is, auto* ptr = test;. You can store to ptr the address of any function that has the same prototype with test().

To call a function through a pointer we can either use the pointer just as if it were a function name or dereference the pointer. For example, either of: ptr(10); or (*ptr)(10); calls test() and the program displays 20. Although the first form is similar to an ordinary call, my preference is the second one, in order to make clear to the reader that ptr is a pointer to a function, not a function. Also, I prefer to dereference the pointer as we do with ordinary pointers, that is, since ptr points to the function the *ptr is the function. However, when using an array of pointers to functions I usually prefer the first syntax. Because successive calls to a function through a pointer result in equivalent expressions, we can extend the second form and write equivalent expressions such as: (*(*ptr))(10); or (*(*(*ptr)))(10);

The rules for passing arguments are the same as for ordinary calls. For example, if we write (*ptr) ("msg"); the compiler will display an error message for incompatible argument type.

In the next example, we write a function that takes as parameters the grades of two students and returns the greater. The program reads two grades and uses a pointer to call the function and display the greater.

```
#include <iostream> // Example 8.24

float test(float a, float b);
```

```cpp
int main()
{
        float (*ptr)(float a, float b); /* ptr is declared as a pointer to a
function, which takes two float parameters and returns a float. */
        float i, j, max;

        std::cout << "Enter grades: ";
        std::cin >> i >> j;

        ptr = test;
        max = (*ptr)(i, j); // Call the function that ptr points to.
        std::cout << "Max:" << max << '\n';
        return 0;
}

float test(float a, float b)
{
        if(a > b)
                return a;
        else
                return b;
}
```

We could omit the declaration of max and write: cout << "Max:" << (*ptr)(i, j) << '\n';

Function Pointers as Arguments

You may probably wonder, isn't this section too specialised, am I ever going need to pass a function pointer to a function? You are right, I'd most probably wonder the same if I were in your place and skip that section. However, it is almost certain that you need this knowledge in several cases such as to call a library function that accepts such a parameter or to enable the communication of different parts of your program.

Let's discuss about that second case. Several applications need a part of the program (e.g., B) to notify another part (e.g., A) for the emergence of some event. To achieve this, a function of the part A calls a function of the part B and passes to it a pointer to a function in part A. The function in part B copies that pointer into a variable and that variable is used whenever part B wants to notify part A for some event. This communication method is known as *callback* mechanism. For example, in one of my applications, part B was the controller of a serial port and used that callback mechanism to notify the main program (part A) to receive data. Let's see a coding example of this mechanism:

```cpp
#include <iostream> // Example 8.25
#include <cstdlib>
#include <ctime>

void make_rand(void (*ptr)(int evt, int num)); /* Although we could write make_
rand(void ptr(int evt, int num));, I prefer to use the pointer notation. */
void handle_event(int evt, int num);

int main()
{
        srand(time(NULL));
        make_rand(handle_event);
        return 0;
}
```

```
void make_rand(void (*ptr)(int evt, int num))
{
        int i, cnt;

        cnt = 0;
        while(1)
        {
                i = rand();
                cnt++;
                if(i >= 1000 && i <= 2000)
                {
                        (*ptr)(cnt, i);
                        return;
                }
        }
}

void handle_event(int evt, int num)
{
        std::cout << "Times:" << evt << " Num:" << num << '\n';
}
```

At first, the main program (e.g., part A) calls make_rand() (e.g., part B), which takes as parameter a pointer to a function which accepts two integer parameters and returns nothing. Notice, that we just write the name of handle_event(). When the name of a function is not followed by parentheses, the compiler produces a pointer to this function; be careful, it does not call the function. To make sure that you understand the difference, here is an example with two functions a and b:

```
a(b); // The address of b is passed to a.
a(b()); // b is first called, then the return value of b is passed to a.
```

make_rand() generates random integers and, once an integer within [1000, 2000] is generated, it uses the pointer to callback handle_event() and passes as arguments how many numbers were generated and the number in the specified interval. This example has no practical value; I just wanted to show you an implementation example of the callback mechanism. You may find it useful in the future.

Also, the use of a function pointer as an argument can make your function to work in a generic way. Here is an example:

```
#include <iostream> // Example 8.26
#include <vector>
using std::cout;
using std::vector;

int find_val(const vector<int>& v, int (*op)(int a, int b));
int max_val(int a, int b);
int min_val(int a, int b);

int main()
{
        vector<int> vec{3, 8, 12, -5};

        cout << "Max:" << find_val(vec, max_val) << '\n';
        cout << "Min:" << find_val(vec, min_val) << '\n';
        return 0;
}
```

```
int find_val(const vector<int>& v, int (*op)(int a, int b))
{
        int i, res;

        res = v[0];
        for(i = 1; i < v.size(); i++)
        {
                if(op(v[i], res))
                        res = v[i];
        }
        return res;
}

int max_val(int a, int b)
{
        return a > b;
}

int min_val(int a, int b)
{
        return a < b;
}
```

In each call of `find_val()` the address of the respective function is passed and `op` points to that address. The program outputs the maximum and minimum value of the vector elements, that is, `12` and `-5`. As you see, `find_val()` works in a generic way, in the sense that the same function supports both operations. The function can be more generic and work for different types of data (i.e., not only for `int`), as you'll see when you learn about generic programming and function templates in Chapter 16. Instead of passing a function pointer we can pass a function object or a lambda expression, as we'll see in Chapter 26.

ARRAY OF POINTERS TO FUNCTIONS

An array of pointers to functions is nothing more than an array whose elements are function pointers. Notice that all functions must have the same prototype. For example, the statement:

```
void (*ptr[20])(int a);
```

declares an array of 20 elements, where each element is a pointer to a function that takes an integer parameter and returns nothing. In the following program, each element of the array `ptr` is a pointer to a function, which takes two integer parameters and returns an integer.

```
#include <iostream> // Example 8.27

int f1(int a, int b);
int f2(int a, int b);
int f3(int a, int b);

int main()
{
        int (*ptr[3])(int a, int b);
        int i, j, k;
```

```
        ptr[0] = f1; // ptr[0] points to the address of f1.
        ptr[1] = f2;
        ptr[2] = f3;

        std::cout << "Enter numbers: ";
        std::cin >> i >> j;

        if(i > 0 && i < 10)
                k = ptr[0](i, j); /* Call the function that ptr[0] points to.
We could also write k = (*ptr[0])(i, j). */
        else if(i >= 10 && i < 20)
                k = ptr[1](i, j); // Call the function that ptr[1] points to.
        else
                k = ptr[2](i, j); // Call the function that ptr[2] points to.
        std::cout << k << '\n';
        return 0;
}

int f1(int a, int b)
{
        return a+b;
}

int f2(int a, int b)
{
        return a-b;
}

int f3(int a, int b)
{
        return a*b;
}
```

The program reads two integers, checks the first one, and uses a function pointer to call the respective function. The program displays the return value.

An array of function pointers can be initialized when declared, just like an ordinary array. For example, we could write:

```
int (*ptr[3])(int a, int b) = {f1, f2, f3};
```

Suppose that the user enters the values 20 and 10. What does the following statement output?

```
cout << ptr[0](ptr[1](i, j), ptr[2](i, j));
```

The expression ptr[1](i, j) calls f2(), which returns a-b, that is, 10. Similarly, the expression ptr[2](i, j) calls f3(), which returns a*b, that is, 200. Therefore, the expression is translated to ptr[0](10, 200) and the program displays the return value of f1(), that is, 210. When using an array of pointers, I usually prefer to use the pointer name to call the function, first because it is easier to write and read the statement and second because one who reads the code realizes that the call is made through a pointer. For example, I prefer the previous syntax than to write: (*ptr[0])((*ptr[1])(i, j), (*ptr[2])(i, j)).

And because I know that you are curious, I'll show you an implementation example where an array of pointers to functions can improve the program's performance. This example is coming from my experience in the implementation of *Finite State Machines (FSMs)* for network protocols. To give you an idea, an FSM is a mathematical concept using states and events to describe the operation of the protocol. For example, when an event occurs (e.g., data reception from the network card), the program checks the current state of the protocol, the event code, and calls the proper function to process that event. There are several ways to implement an FSM; using the `switch` statement is one of them. For example:

```cpp
const int STATE_1 = 0;
const int STATE_2 = 1;
...

const int EVT_1 = 0;
const int EVT_2 = 1;
...

void evt_received(int evt_code)
{
        switch(state)
        {
              case STATE_1:
                     switch(evt_code)
                     {
                            case EVT_1:
                                   Handle_ST1_Evt1();
                            break;

                            case EVT_2:
                                   Handle_ST1_Evt2();
                            break;

                            ...
                            case EVT_N:
                                   Handle_ST1_EvtN();
                            break;

                            default:
                                   std::cout << "Error: unexpected event_" <<
evt_code << " received at state_" << state << '\n';
                                   break;
                     }
                     break;

              case STATE_2:
                     switch(evt_code)
                     {
                            case EVT_1:
                                   Handle_ST2_Evt1();
                            break;

                            case EVT_2:
                                   Handle_ST2_Evt2();
                            break;

                            ...
                            case EVT_N:
                                   Handle_ST2_EvtN();
                            break;
```

```
                                  default:
                                          std::cout << "Error: unexpected event_" <<
evt_code << " received at state_" << state << '\n';
                                          break;
                                  }
                          break;


                          ...
                          default:
                                  std::cout << "Time to panic: invalid state\n";
                          break;
                  }
}
```

Alternatively, we can declare a two-dimensional array of pointers and use the pointers to call the event handling functions. For example, suppose that each function does not take parameters and returns an integer value. Then, we could declare an array of pointers like this:

```
typedef int (*Func_Ptr)(); /* As we'll see in Ch.11, we use typedef to create
a synonym. */
Func_Ptr func_ptr[MAX_STATES][MAX_EVENTS] = {Handle_ST1_Evt1, Handle_ST1_Evt2,
Handle_ST1_EvtN, Handle_ST2_Evt1, ...};
```

See how much simpler the code becomes:

```
void evt_received(int evt_code)
{
        func_ptr[state][evt_code]();
}
```

Not only the code becomes simpler and easier to read, it is more flexible as well. With the array of pointers, we can easily remove a function (e.g., set the pointer to `nullptr`) or add a new event handling function, if needed. And the most important, we gain in speed, since the proper function is directly called avoiding the time overhead of the `switch` statements.

I've good news and bad news. The good news is that a really tough chapter finished, at last. Close this book and get some rest, because the bad news is that the next chapter is bigger and even harder. Don't be scared, just kidding!

UNSOLVED EXERCISES

U.8.1 Write a program that uses two pointer variables to read two `double` numbers and display the absolute value of their sum.

U.8.2 What is the output of the following program?

```
#include <iostream>
int main()
{
        int *ptr, i = 10, j = 20, k = 30;

        ptr = &i;
        *ptr = 40;
```

```
        ptr = &j;
        *ptr += i;

        ptr = &k;
        *ptr += i + j;
        std::cout << i << ' ' << j << ' ' << k << '\n';
        return 0;
}
```

U.8.3 Write a program that uses a pointer variable to read a `double` number and display its fractional part. For example, if the user enters -7.21, the program should display 0.21.

U.8.4 What is the output of the following program?

```
#include <iostream>
int main()
{
        int i = 10, j = 20, k = 30, *p1 = &i, *p2 = &j, *p3 = &k;

        *p1 = *p2 = *p3;
        k = i+j;
        std::cout << *p3 << '\n';
        return 0;
}
```

U.8.5 Write a program that uses three pointer variables to read three integers and check if they are in successive ascending order (e.g., -5, -4, -3). The program should force the user to enter negative numbers.

U.8.6 What is the output of the following program?

```
#include <iostream>
int main()
{
        int *ptr, i, j = 1, a[] = {j, j+1, j+2, j+3};

        for(i = 0; i < 3; i++)
        {
                ptr = a+i;
                std::cout << a[*ptr] << ' ';
        }
        return 0;
}
```

U.8.7 Write a program that uses three pointer variables to read three integers one after the other. The program should force the user to enter the three numbers in descending order.

U.8.8 What is the output of the following program?

```
#include <iostream>
int main()
{
        int *ptr1, *ptr2, i = 10, j = 20;

        ptr1 = &i;
        *ptr1 = 150;
```

```
                ptr2 = &j;
                *ptr2 = 50;

                ptr2 = ptr1;
                *ptr2 = 250;

                ptr1 = ptr2;
                *ptr1 += *ptr2;
                std::cout << i+j << '\n';
                return 0;
        }
```

U.8.9 Complete the following program by using the `p1` pointer to read 100 integers, the `p2` pointer to display the minimum of those with values less than -5, and the `p3` pointer to display the maximum of those greater than 10. If no value less than -5 or greater than 10 is entered, the program should display an informative message. The variables `num`, `min`, and `max` should be used only once.

```
int main()
{
        int *p1, *p2, *p3, i, num, min, max;
        ...
}
```

U.8.10 What would be the output of C.8.17 if we replace the `&&` operator with the `||` operator?

U.8.11 What are the values of `a` elements in the following program?

```
#include <iostream>
int main()
{
        int i = 0, a[] = {10, 20, 30, 40, 50}, *p = a;

        while(&p[i] < a+5)
        {
                (*(p+i))++;
                p++;
                i++;
        }
        return 0;
}
```

U.8.12 Use `p1`, `p2`, and `temp` and write a loop to reverse the elements of `arr`. Then, use `p1` to display the array elements. For example, the new content of `arr` should be: `2.5 9.4 -3.8 -4.1 1.3`

```
#include <iostream>
int main()
{
        double arr[] = {1.3, -4.1, -3.8, 9.4, 2.5}, temp, *p1 = arr,
*p2 = arr+4;
        ...
}
```

U.8.13 What are the values of a elements in the following program?

```
#include <iostream>
int main()
{
        int *ptr, a[5] = {20};

        for(ptr = a+3; ptr >= a; ptr-=2)
                *ptr = *(ptr-1) + *(ptr+1) + 1;
        return 0;
}
```

U.8.14 Write a program that reads 100 integers and stores them in an array. Then, the program should replace the duplicated values with -99. Use pointer arithmetic to process the array. For example, if the array were {5, 5, 5, 5, 5} the program should make it {5, -99, -99, -99, -99} and if it were {-2, 3, -2, 50, 3} it should make it {-2, 3, -99, 50, -99}.

U.8.15 Use the `ptr` pointer and complete the following program to read and store integers into `arr`, with the restriction to store an input number only if it is less than the last stored number. The value -1 should not be stored in the array. If the user enters 0 or if there is no other free place, the insertion of numbers should terminate (0 is not stored in the array) and the program should display how many numbers were stored in the array. The program should prompt the user to input the numbers, as follows:

```
Enter number_1:
Enter number_2:
...
int main()
{
        int *ptr, arr[100];
        ...
}
```

U.8.16 Use an iterative loop to complete the following program and display the elements of the array in reverse order. It is not allowed to use digits (e.g., to write arr[0], p[1] or p+2).

```
int main()
{
        int *p, arr[] = {10, 20, 30, 40};
        ...
}
```

U.8.17 Use `arr` and complete the following program to read three integers and display the sum of the even numbers. The variables j, k, and m should be used only once.

```
int main()
{
        int *arr[3], i, j, k, m, sum;
        ...
}
```

U.8.18 Write a program that uses two pointers to two-pointer variables to read two integers and swap their values.

U.8.19 What does the following program do?

```
#include <iostream>
int main()
{
        const int COLS = 4;
        int i, arr[][COLS] = {10, 20, 30, 40, 50, 60, 70, 80, 90, 100,
110, 120, 130, 140, 150, 160};

        for(i = 0; i < COLS; i++)
                *(arr[i]+i) = *(arr[i]+COLS-1-i) = 0;
        return 0;
}
```

U.8.20 Write a program that assigns random integers to a 5×5 array and checks if the sum of the elements in the main diagonal is equal to that of its secondary diagonal. Use pointer arithmetic to process the array.

U.8.21 Write a program that reads integers and stores them in a 5×5 array and displays the sum of the elements of the column with the largest sum, as well as the sum of the elements of the row with the largest sum. Use pointer arithmetic to process the array.

Characters

9

Besides the `int`, `float`, and `double` data types we've mostly used in our programs so far, it is time to discuss more about the `char` type. To show you how to work with characters and strings, we assume that the underlying character set relies on the most popular set, the 8-bit ASCII (American Standard Code for Information Interchange) code. As you can see in Annex B, ordinary characters, such as letters and digits, are represented by integers from 0 to 255.

Because the size of the `char` type is too small to represent all the characters of some languages (e.g., Chinese), C++ supports larger types, the `wchar_t`, `char16_t`, and `char32_t` types. In this book, we'll use only the `char` type.

C++ provides a rich set of functions to manage characters. They are declared in the `cctype` file and their operation does not depend on a particular character set. Therefore, they are very useful for writing portable programs. Although we could use them in the next programs, I won't do it, in order to force you to program in more depth.

THE `char` TYPE

Since a character in the ASCII set is represented by an integer between 0 and 255, we can use the `char` type to store its value. Once a character is stored into a variable, it is the character's ASCII value that is actually stored. In the following example:

```
char ch;
ch = 'a';
```

the value of `ch` becomes equal to the ASCII value of the character `'a'`, which is 97. Therefore, the statements `ch = 'a';` and `ch = 97;` are equivalent. Of course, `'a'` is preferable than 97; not only it is easier to read, but your program won't depend on the character set as well.

 Don't forget to enclose a character constant in single quotes.

For example, if you omit them and write `ch = a;` the compiler will treat `a` as an ordinary variable and its value will be assigned into `ch`. If `a` is not declared, the compiler will produce an error message. To display the ASCII value with `cout` we cast the type to `int`. For example:

```
char ch = 'a';
cout << ch << ' ' << (int)ch;
```

DOI: 10.1201/9781003230076-9

The code displays: a 97. What does the following code display?

```
char c = 50, a = 70;
if('c' < 'a')
        cout << a+c;
```

Did the addition confuse you? Are the variables a and c related to 'a' and 'c'? Of course not, and since the ASCII value of a is less than c, the code displays nothing.

 Essentially, when a character appears in an expression, either as constant or variable, C++ treats it as an integer and uses its ASCII value.

Since C++ treats the characters as integers, we can use them in numerical expressions. For example:

```
char ch = 'c';
int i;
ch++; // ch becomes 'd'.
ch = 68; // ch becomes 'D'.
i = ch-3; // i becomes 'A', that is, 65.
```

Handling of characters that represent integers usually confuses novice programmers. For example, the ASCII value of the character 2 it is not 2, but 50. If we want to use the character 2 in our program we write '2', not 2. Similarly, to test if a character is a digit 0-9 we write:

```
if(ch >= '0' && ch <= '9') not if(ch >= 0 && ch <= 9)
```

Alternatively, we can use the isdigit() function declared in cctype to make this test. For example: if(isdigit(ch))

Let's discuss a special sequence of three characters, the *trigraph sequence*. Because, in the past mainly, some systems did not support the following ASCII characters, corresponding trigraph sequences were defined to represent them. All trigraphs begin with ??.

??=	#	??)	]	??!	|
??(	[	??'	^	??>	}
??/	\	??<	{	??-	~

Thus, equivalent C++ programs can be written even if these characters are missing from the keyboard. For example, what is the output of the following program?

```
??=include <iostream> // Example 9.1
int main()
??<
        int a??(2??) = ??<1, 2??>;
        std::cout << (a??(0??) ??! a??(1??));
        return 0;
??>
```

The preprocessor replaces the trigraphs with the corresponding ASCII characters and the program is translated to:

```
#include <iostream>
int main()
{
        int a[2] = {1, 2};
        std::cout << (a[0] | a[1]);
        return 0;
}
```

Therefore, the program outputs 3. C++17 removed trigraphs from the language. However, a compiler may continue to support trigraph substitution.

READING CHARACTERS

There are many ways to read a character from the input stream. The most common is to use the `get()` function, which is a member of the `istream` class. For those who have experience in C, `get()` works similar to `getchar()`. Note that `getchar()` can also be used. `get()` starts reading characters when the user presses the *Enter* key. If it is executed successfully, it returns the character read as `int`. If no more characters are available in the stream, `get()` returns a special constant value defined in `iostream`, named EOF (*End Of File*). This value is different from any valid character value, so it cannot be confused with a regular character. Although EOF is typically -1, it is better to use EOF, so that your program does not depend on the numeric value.

For example, if the user types abc and presses *Enter*, the first call of `get()` returns 'a', the second one returns 'b', the third one 'c', and the fourth one '\n'. If it is called again, the program "stacks" until the user enters new character(s) and presses *Enter* again. The next program displays and counts the input characters until the user presses *Enter*.

```
#include <iostream> // Example 9.2
#include <cstdio>
using std::cin;
using std::cout;

int main()
{
        int ch, sum;

        cout << "Enter characters: ";
        sum = 0;
        while((ch = cin.get()) != '\n' && ch != EOF) /* The inner parentheses
are necessary, because the != operator has greater precedence than =. */
        {
                sum++;
                cout << (char)ch; // Cast the type to display the character.
        }
        cout << '\n' << sum << " characters are read\n";
        return 0;
}
```

`get()` returns one by one the input characters until the '\n' character is met. Each character is stored into `ch` and that value is tested against EOF to determine if it is valid.

Notice that the return type of get() should be stored into an int variable, not char. See why. Suppose that ch is declared as char. If the char type is signed and the character with value 255 is read, it will be stored as -1 into ch. As a result, the condition which tests that value against EOF becomes false and the loop stops reading more characters. If the char type is unsigned and get() returns EOF, EOF won't be stored as -1; therefore, the loop won't terminate.

In case you wonder why we do not read characters with cin in the same way we read numeric values, the reason is that white characters (e.g., spaces, tabs) are skipped by default. For example:

```cpp
#include <iostream> // Example 9.3
int main()
{
        char ch;

        std::cout << "Enter character: ";
        std::cin >> ch;
        if(ch == ' ')
                std::cout << (int)ch;
        return 0;
}
```

Since the white characters are skipped, if the user enters a space and presses Enter, the program neither displays something nor it terminates. To terminate, you must enter a non-white character. This behaviour can change using the noskipws manipulator. That is, if we write:

```cpp
cin >> noskipws >> ch;
```

the white characters are not ignored. So, if the user enters a space the program displays the ASCII value of the space (i.e., 32) and terminates. In the general case where the program is continuously reading characters until the user enters a specific character I prefer get(), because it does not skip the white characters (e.g., the program may require to count all the characters) and it is also easy to check with the EOF, the validity of the character.

An unexpected behaviour that makes many novice programmers wonder why their program is not working properly and make them crazy enough to smash the computer occurs when reading characters after having read numeric values. The following program is such an example. Do you notice any malfunction in the following program when the user enters an integer and presses *Enter*?

```cpp
#include <iostream> // Example 9.4
using std::cout;
using std::cin;

int main()
{
        int i, ch;

        cout << "Enter number: ";
        cin >> i;

        cout << "Enter character: ";
        ch = cin.get();
        cout << i << ' ' << (char)ch << '\n';
        return 0;
}
```

When the user enters an integer and presses *Enter*, the generated new line character is stored in the input queue. get() gets it from there and stores it into the ch variable, without letting the user type any other character. The program displays just the input integer. There are several methods to get rid of the '\n' character. One solution is to add another get() before the second cout, that is, cin.get(); Also, if we reverse the read order, that is, first read the character then the integer, the program will behave normally, because white spaces, such as '\n', are ignored before a numeric value.

EXERCISES

C.9.1 Write a program that reads three characters and checks if they are consecutive in the ASCII character set.

```
#include <iostream>
using namespace std;

int main()
{
        char ch1, ch2, ch3;

        cout << "Enter characters: ";
        cin >> noskipws >> ch1 >> ch2 >> ch3;

        if((ch1+1 == ch2) && (ch2+1 == ch3))
                cout << "Consecutive\n";
        else
                cout << "Not Consecutive\n";
        return 0;
}
```

Comments: If you run the program, don't type a space between the input characters because the space is a character as well (unless the space character is among the characters you want to check).

C.9.2 Write a program that reads two characters and displays the characters between them. For example, if the user enters af or fa, the program should display bcde.

```
#include <iostream>
using namespace std;

int main()
{
        char ch1, ch2;

        cout << "Enter characters: ";
        cin >> noskipws >> ch1 >> ch2;

        if(ch1 < ch2)
        {
                ch1++;
                while(ch1 != ch2)
                {
                        cout << ch1;
                        ch1++;
                }
        }
}
```

```
        else
        {
                ch2++;
                while(ch2 != ch1)
                {
                        cout << ch2;
                        ch2++;
                }
        }
        return 0;
}
```

C.9.3 Write a program that reads a character continuously, and if it is a lowercase letter it should display the respective uppercase, otherwise the input character. If the last two input characters are ':' and 'q', the program should display how many 'w' and 'x' were entered and then terminate. Note that the difference of one lowercase letter from the corresponding uppercase in the ASCII set is 32.

```
#include <iostream>
using namespace std;

int main()
{
        char ch, last_ch;
        int sum1, sum2;

        last_ch = sum1 = sum2 = 0;
        while(1)
        {
                cout << "Enter character: ";
                cin >> noskipws >> ch;

                if(last_ch == ':' && ch == 'q') /* If the last input character
is ':' and the current one is 'q', the insertion of characters should
terminate. */
                        break;
                else if(ch >= 'a' && ch <= 'z')
                        cout << (char)(ch-32) << '\n'; /* Display the respective
uppercase letter. */
                else
                        cout << ch << '\n';

                last_ch = ch; // The last input character is stored in
last_ch.
                if(ch == 'w')
                        sum1++;
                else if(ch == 'x')
                        sum2++;
                cin.get(); /* Extract the '\n' left in the input queue, when
the user presses Enter. */
        }
        cout << "w:" << sum1 << " times and x:" << sum2 << " times\n";
        return 0;
}
```

C.9.4 Write a program that displays all lowercase letters in one line, all uppercase letters in a second line, and all characters that represent the digits 0-9 in a third line. Use one `for` loop.

```cpp
#include <iostream>
int main()
{
        char ch, end_ch;

        end_ch = 'z';
        for(ch = 'a'; ch <= end_ch; ch++)
        {
                std::cout << ch << ' ';
                if(ch == 'z')
                {
                        ch = 'A'-1; /* Subtract 1, so that the ch++ statement in
the next iteration makes it 'A'. */
                        end_ch = 'Z'; /* Change the end character, so that the
loop displays the uppercase letters. */
                        std::cout << '\n';
                }
                else if(ch == 'Z')
                {
                        ch = '0'-1;
                        end_ch = '9';
                        std::cout << '\n';
                }
        }
        return 0;
}
```

C.9.5 According to the ITU-T E.161 international standard, the digits of a phone pad correspond to letters as follows: ABC=2, DEF=3, GHI=4, JKL=5, MNO=6, PQRS=7, TUV=8, WXYZ=9. There is no matching for the digits 0 and 1. Write a program that reads a phone number up to 10 digits, which may include letters and display that number. For example, if the user enters CALL123456, the program should display 2255123456. The program should accept only uppercase letters and digits, otherwise, it should terminate.

```cpp
#include <iostream>
#include <cstdio>
using std::cout;
using std::cin;

int main()
{
        int ch, dig, arr[26] = {2, 2, 2, 3, 3, 3, 4, 4, 4, 5, 5, 5, 6, 6, 6,
7, 7, 7, 7, 8, 8, 8, 9, 9, 9, 9}; /* Initialize an array to make right away
the mapping. */
        dig = 0;
        cout << "Enter digit or letter: ";
        while((ch = cin.get()) != '\n' && ch != EOF)
        {
                if(ch >= 'A' && ch <= 'Z')
                {
                        dig++;
                        cout << arr[ch-'A']; /* The output digit depends on the
value of ch. For example, if the user enters 'I' the output would be
arr[73-65] = 4. */
                }
```

```
                else if(ch >= '0' && ch <= '9')
                {
                        dig++;
                        cout << (char)ch; /* A digit is displayed as is. */
                }
                else
                {
                        cout << "\nError: Not valid character\n";
                        return 0;
                }
                if(dig == 10)
                        break;
        }
        if(dig == 10)
                cout << "\nNumber completed\n";
        return 0;
}
```

C.9.6 Every mobile phone operating in GSM (*2G*) and WCDMA (*3G*) wireless networks is characterized by a unique identifier of 15 digits, called *International Mobile Equipment Identifier* (IMEI). A method to check if the device is really made by the official manufacturer is to compare the IMEI's last digit, called *Luhn digit*, with a check digit. If it is equal, the device is most probably authentic. Otherwise, it is not authentic for sure. The check digit is calculated as follows: first, we calculate the sum of the first IMEI's 14 digits by adding:

   a. The digits in the odd positions.
   b. The double of the digits in the even positions. But, if a digit's doubling is a two-digit number, we add each digit separately. For example, suppose that the value of the checked digit is 8. Its double is 16; therefore, we add to the sum the result of 1+6 = 7, not 16.

If the last digit of the calculated sum is 0, the check digit is 0. If not, we subtract the last digit from 10 and that is the check digit. For example, let's check the IMEI 357683036257378. The algorithm applied in the first 14 digits produces:

```
3 + (2×5) + 7 + (2×6) + 8 + (2×3) + 0 + (2×3) + 6 + (2×2) + 5 + (2×7)+ 3+(2×7) =
3 + (10)  + 7 + (12)  + 8 + (6)   + 0 + (6)   + 6 + (4)   + 5 + (14)  + 3 + (14)  =
3 + (1+0) + 7 + (1+2) + 8 + (6)   + 0 + (6)   + 6 + (4)   + 5 + (1+4) + 3 + (1+4) = 62
```

The check digit is 10-2 = 8, which is equal to the Luhn digit. Therefore, this IMEI is valid.

Write a program that reads the IMEI of a mobile phone (15 digits) and displays a message to indicate if it is authentic or not.

```cpp
#include <iostream>
using std::cout;
using std::cin;

int main()
{
        char chk_dig;
        int i, ch, sum, temp;

        sum = 0;
        cout << "Enter IMEI (15 digits): ";
```

```
        for(i = 1; i < 15; i++) // Read the first 14 IMEI's digits.
        {
                ch = cin.get();
                if((i & 1) == 1) // Check if the digit's position is odd.
                        sum += ch-'0'; /* To find the numeric value of that
digit, the ASCII value of 0 is subtracted. */
                else // The position is even.
                {
                        temp = 2*(ch-'0');
                        if(temp >= 10)
                                temp = (temp/10) + (temp%10); /* If the digit's
doubling produces a two-digit number we calculate the sum of these digits. */
                        sum += temp;
                }
        }
        ch = cin.get(); /* Read the IMEI's last digit, that is, the Luhn
digit. */
        ch = ch-'0';
        chk_dig = sum%10;
        if(chk_dig != 0)
                chk_dig = 10-chk_dig;

        if(ch == chk_dig)
                cout << "*** Valid IMEI ***\n";
        else
                cout << "*** Invalid IMEI ***\n";
        return 0;
}
```

Comments: Since the maximum integer has up to 10 digits, we cannot use cin to read a 15-digit number. Therefore, we use get() to read each digit separately.

As a new test, check the IMEI of your mobile. How you'll find it? Dial *#06#. I hope you won't prove that you have a fake device as I wouldn't like to spoil your mood now, because a tough chapter follows …

UNSOLVED EXERCISES

U.9.1 Write a program that reads characters until the sum of their ASCII values exceeds 500 or the user enters 'q'. The program should display how many characters were read.

U.9.2 Write a program that reads characters and displays how many characters between the first two consecutive '*' are: (a) letters (b) digits, and (c) other than letters and digits. If no two '*' occur, the program should display a related message. For example, if the user enters: 1abc*D2Efg_ #!*345Higkl*mn+op*qr the program should display: Between first two stars (letters:4, digits:1, other:3).

U.9.3 Write a program that reads the digits of a number as characters and displays its value. If the user enters a sign, it should be taken into account. Space characters are allowed only before the number, not between digits. Also, the program should check that the number of digits is up to 10.

U.9.4 Write a program that reads the digits of an IP version 4 address (*IPv4*) as characters and displays a message to indicate if it is valid or not. The form of a valid IPv4 address is x.x.x.x, where each x must be an integer within [0, 255].

Strings

10

Now that you've seen how to use single characters, we may continue with strings. A string is a series of characters stored in consecutive memory locations. C++ supports two ways to handle strings. The first is the same as in C, that is, with an array of characters (*C-style string*). A C-style string must end with a special character, the *null* character, which identifies the end of the string. It is the first character in the ASCII set, its ASCII value is 0 and is denoted by '\0'. We'll also discuss the string class, which is a more flexible and secure approach to handle strings. Because both techniques are quite popular you should know both.

STRING LITERALS

A string literal is a sequence of characters enclosed in double quotes. A string literal is a constant. In particular, C++ treats it as a nameless constant character array. The quotes are not considered part of the string, but serve only to delimit it. In particular, when the compiler encounters a string literal, it allocates memory to store its characters plus the null character to mark its end. For example, if the compiler encounters the string literal "text", it allocates five bytes to store the four characters of the string plus one for the null character. A string literal may be empty. For example, the string literal "" is stored as a single null character.

STORING STRINGS

To store a C-style string in a variable, we use an array of characters. Because a C-style string ends with the null character, to store a string of N characters the size of the array should be N+1 at least. For example, to store a string of up to 4 characters, we write:

```
char str[5];
```

An array can be initialized with a string, when it is declared. For example, with the declaration:

```
char str[5] = "text";
```

the compiler copies the characters of the "text" into the str array and adds the null character. In particular, str[0] becomes 'm', str[1] becomes 'e', and the value of the last element str[4] becomes '\0'. In fact, this declaration is equivalent to:

```
char str[5] = {'t', 'e', 'x', 't', '\0'};
```

Notice that the null character '\0' is one character, not two, since as discussed in Chapter 2, the \ character denotes an escape sequence.

DOI: 10.1201/9781003230076-10

A common error is to confuse the `'\0'` and `'0'` characters. The first is the null character with ASCII code 0, while the second is the zero character with ASCII code 48.

As with an ordinary array, if the number of the characters is less than the size of the array, the remaining elements are initialized to 0. If it is greater, the compilation fails. For example, with the declaration:

```
char str[5] = "te";
```

because the ASCII value of `'\0'` is 0, `str[0]` becomes `'t'`, `str[1]` becomes `'e'` and the rest elements are initialized to 0, or equivalently to `'\0'`. Similarly, with the declaration:

```
char str[5] = {0};
```

all `str` elements are initialized to `'\0'`.

A flexible way to initialize the array is to omit its length and let the compiler compute it. For example, with the declaration:

```
char  str[] = "text";
```

the compiler calculates the length of `"text"` and then allocates five bytes for `str` to store the four characters plus the null character. If we use `sizeof(str)` to output its length, we'll see that it is 5, indeed. Leaving the compiler to compute the length, it is easier and safer, since counting by hand can lead to a calculation error or we may forget to add an extra place for the null character.

 When declaring an array of characters to store a C-style string, don't forget to reserve an extra place for the null character.

If the null character is missing and the program uses a library function to handle the array, such as the ones we'll see later, unpredictable results may arise. This is because functions that work with C-style strings assume that strings are null terminated. In fact, some programmers prefer to emphasize the reservation by adding 1 in the declaration. For example:

```
char  s[SIZE+1];
```

So beware, the declarations `char s[] = "abc";` and `char s[3] = "abc";` are different. In the first case the size of `s` is 4, the null character is stored and we've got a C-style string, while in the second case the size is 3 and we don't have a string.

WRITING STRINGS

There are many ways to display a string. For example, we can use `cout` and pass a pointer to the string. The following code uses the name of the array as a pointer to the first character of the string:

```
char str[] = "Print a message";
cout << str;
```

The code displays the characters of the string beginning from the character that the pointer points to until it encounters the null character. If we want to display a certain number of characters we can use the `write()` function, which is a member of the `ostream` class. For example, if we write: `cout.write(str, 3);` it displays the first three characters, that is, `Pri`. If we don't want to display the string from the beginning we make the pointer point to the desired position. For example, if we write: `cout << str+8;` or equivalently: `cout << &str[8];` it displays the part beginning from the ninth character, that is, `message`. If the null character is encountered, no more characters are printed. For example, if we add the statement: `str[5] = '\0';` before the output, the code displays `Print`.

If we want to split the string in more than one line we can use the `\` character. Note that the string will be displayed in the same line. For example:

```
cout << "This text is displayed \
in the same line\n";
```

Alternatively, because the compiler allows the merging of two or more adjacent literal strings into a single string we can write:

```
cout << "This text is displayed "
"in the same line\n";
```

If the string contains the `"`, we use the escape sequence `\"` to print it. For example:

```
cout << "\"Start\"";
```
and the code displays: `"Start"`

If `cout` does not encounter the null character, it continues past the end of the string until it finds a null character somewhere next in the memory. For example:

```
#include <iostream> // Example 10.1
int main()
{
        char str[10];
        str[0] = 'a';
        str[1] = 'b';
        std::cout << str << '\n';
        return 0;
}
```

The program displays `'a'` and `'b'` and then garbage characters until it finds the null character or an illegal memory access occurs. If we write `char str[10] = {0};` then, because the elements are initialized to `0`, the program would display `ab`.

As we know, to represent some special characters in a literal string, such as `"` or `\`, we must first add one `\`. But if the string contains many such characters, the result string becomes more complex to write and read it. To facilitate the output of such strings, C++11 provides the form of raw processing where each character, like `\`, has no special treatment but is displayed as it is. For example, the `\n` is not interpreted as the new line character, but as two characters the backlash and the n. To represent the character sequence (e.g., `abc`) the character `R` is used with the following syntax `R"(abc)"`. The `"(` and `)"` is the default pair to delimit the sequence and identify it as a raw string. For example, the statement:

```
cout << R"("d:\edu\books?\n")";
```

outputs: `"d:\edu\books?\n"`.

EXERCISES

C.10.1 Is the following code error free?

```cpp
#include <iostream>
int main()
{
        char str1[] = "abc", str2[] = "efg";

        str2[sizeof(str1)] = 'w';
        std::cout << str1[0] << '\n';
        return 0;
}
```

Answer: When str1 is declared the compiler creates an array of four places, to store the 'a', 'b', 'c', and '\0' characters. Similarly, it creates the str2 array with four places, to store the 'e', 'f', 'g', and '\0' characters. The attempt to store the 'w' character in a position that exceeds the length of str2 is wrong. In particular, the assignment str2[4] = 'w' overwrites the data out of str2, which causes unpredictable behaviour. For example, the program may display a, but it may also display w, if str1 is stored right after str2 in memory.

C.10.2 Write a program that creates a string with all lowercase and uppercase letters of the English alphabet.

```cpp
#include <iostream>
int main()
{
        char str[53];
        int i;

        for(i = 0; i < 26; i++)
        {
                str[i] = 'a'+i;
                str[26+i] = 'A'+i;
        }
        str[52] = '\0'; // At the end, we add the null character.
        std::cout << str << '\n';
        return 0;
}
```

Comments: In each iteration, the ASCII value of the respective character is stored in str. For example, in the first iteration (i=0) we have str[0] = 'a'+0 = 'a' = 97 and str[26] = 'A'+0 = 'A' = 65.

C.10.3 The following program stores two strings in two arrays, swaps them, and displays their new content. Is there any error?

```cpp
#include <iostream>
int main()
{
        char temp[100], str1[100] = "Let see", str2[100] = "Is everything
OK?";
```

```
        temp = str1;
        str1 = str2;
        str2 = temp;
        std::cout << str1 << ' ' << str2 << '\n';
        return 0;
}
```

Answer: Recall from Chapter 8 that the name of an array when used as a pointer is a `const` pointer, meaning that it is not allowed to change its value and point to some other address. Therefore, the statement `temp = str1;` is illegal. The same applies for the next two statements, so the program won't compile.

C.10.4 What is the output of the following program?

```
#include <iostream>
int main()
{
        char str[] = "Right'0'Wrong";

        std::cout << str << '\n';
        return 0;
}
```

Answer: Did you answer `Right`? Sorry, it is wrong.

The `'0'` does not represent the null character `'\0'`, but it consists of the `'` character, the zero character, and another `'`. Therefore, the program outputs `Right'0'Wrong`. What would be the output if we had written:

```
char str[] = "Right'\0'Wrong";
```

Since after the first `'` the escape sequence `\0` represents the null character, this time you are right if you answered `Right'`.

POINTERS AND STRING LITERALS

Since a string literal is stored as an array of characters, we can use it also as a pointer to the first character. The purpose of the next statement is to show you this conversion in a really odd way. Although it looks absolutely weird, the string literal is used in two ways, as an array and as a pointer, and it displays twice the fourth character of the string, that is, `'m'`.

```
cout << "example"[3] << ' ' << *("example"+3) << '\n';
```

Don't get stuck with that line, what is really important to understand is that the expressions `"a"` and `'a'` are different. The expression `"a"` is a string literal, which is stored in the memory as an array of two characters, the `'a'` and `'\0'`. Essentially, it is represented by a pointer to that memory. On the other hand, the expression `'a'` is just the character constant `'a'` represented by its ASCII code.

A convenient way to handle a string literal is to declare a pointer variable and make it point to that string. For example:

```
#include <iostream> // Example 10.2
int main()
```

```
{
        const char *ptr = "This is text";
        int i;

        for(i = 0; ptr[i] != '\0'; i++)
                std::cout << *(ptr+i) << ' ' << ptr[i] << '\n';
        return 0;
}
```

With the statement `ptr = "This is text";` the compiler allocates memory to store the string literal and the null character. Then, `ptr` points to the first character of the string, as depicted here.

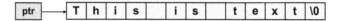

To access the characters of the string, we can use either pointer arithmetic or the pointer as an array and use array subscripting. The program uses both ways to display one by one the characters of the string. The loop is executed until the null character is met.

Because a string literal is constant, since C++11 it is required the pointer type to be `const char*` so that the literal cannot be modified. For example:

```
const char *ptr = "This is text";
*ptr = 'a'; // Illegal.
```

Regarding the declarations:

```
char  ptr[] = "This is text"; and  const char  *ptr = "This is text";
```

although may look similar they have quite different properties as you already know from the section "Pointers and Arrays" in Chapter 8. In particular, the first declaration declares `ptr` as an array of 13 characters (the last one is the null character). We can safely store another string into `ptr`, as long as its length is no more than 13 characters, otherwise the program may behave unpredictably. The second declaration declares `ptr` as a pointer and makes it point to the memory that holds the string literal. As discussed, in the first case we can write `ptr[0] = 'a';` without any concern, while in the second case this statement causes a compilation error. The `ptr` pointer can point to another string during program execution, no matter what its length is. For example:

```
const char *ptr = "First";
ptr = "Second";
std::cout << *ptr << '\n';
```

At first, `ptr` points to the first character of the string literal `"First"`. Then, the statement `ptr = "Second";` makes `ptr` to point to the new memory allocated to store that string. Since `ptr` points to its first character, `*ptr` is equal to `'S'` and the code displays S.

As we've outlined in Chapter 8, a pointer should have been initialized before being used. Consider the following program:

```
#include <iostream> // Example 10.3
int main()
{
        char *ptr;

        ptr[0] = 'a';
        ptr[1] = 'b';
```

```
        ptr[2] = '\0';
        std::cout << ptr << '\n';
        return 0;
}
```

Are the assignment ptr[0] = 'a'; and the next ones correct? Certainly not. Since ptr has not been initialized, writing the 'a', 'b', and '\0' characters somewhere in memory would cause the unpredictable behaviour of the program. Even if the program displays ab, the code is wrong.

 Never ever forget that using an uninitialized pointer variable is a serious error.

Had we declared an array of characters and make ptr to point to its address like:

```
char str[3], *ptr;
ptr = str;
```

the program would have executed successfully.

EXERCISES

C.10.5 What is the output of the following program?

```
#include <iostream>
using std::cout;
int main()
{
        char str1[] = "test", str2[] = "test";

        (str1 == str2) ?  cout << "One\n" : cout << "Two\n";
        return 0;
}
```

Answer: Since the names of the two arrays are used as pointers, the expression str1 == str2 checks if the pointers point to the same address, not if the arrays are the same. Do str1 and str2 point to the memory same address?

Of course not; str1 and str2 have the same content; they are stored in different memory though. Therefore, the program displays Two. What would be the output if we write:

```
(*str1 == *str2) ?  cout << "One\n" : cout << "Two\n";
```

Since str1 can be used as a pointer to its first element, *str1 is equal to 't'. Similarly, *str2 is equal to 't'. Therefore, the program would display One.

C.10.6 What is the output of the following program?

```
#include <iostream>
int main()
```

```
{
        char *p, *q, s[] = "play";

        p = s+1;
        q = s;
        p[1] = 'x';
        *s = 'a';
        std::cout << *q+2 << " " << *(q+2) << '\n';
        return 0;
}
```

Answer: Since p points to the address of the second element of the s array, s[2] changes to 'x'. Also, s[0] becomes 'a'. Because q points to s[0] and the * operator has greater precedence than the + operator, we have *q+2 = 'a'+2. Therefore, the program outputs the ASCII value of the character two places after 'a'. This is 'c' and the program outputs 99. Since the value of *(q+2) is equal to s[2], the program outputs x, as well.

READ STRINGS

There are many ways to read a string. For example, we can use cin to read it:

```
#include <iostream> // Example 10.4
int main()
{
        char str[10];
        int i = 5;

        std::cout << "Enter text: ";
        std::cin >> str; // Danger, be careful.
        std::cout << str << ' ' << i << '\n';
        return 0;
}
```

The program reads a string, stores it into the str array and displays it. By default, cin reads characters until it encounters a white space character (i.e., space, tab, or new line character). Then, it appends a null character at the end of the string. Notice that cin does not check if there is available memory to store all input characters. For example, if the user enters a string with more than ten characters, the first ten will be stored into str, but the rest will be stored into a memory out of the bounds of the array, which causes the unpredictable behaviour of the program. For example, if the value of i is stored into this memory, this value will change. Try it in your system. To avoid a memory overflow, one way is to use the setw(). For example:

```
cin >> setw(10) >> str;
```

Now, the maximum number to be stored is limited to ten. In particular, if the user enters more characters, the first nine will be stored in the first nine positions and the null character in the tenth.

Note that if the user enters many words (e.g., nice day), because cin stops reading characters when it encounters a white character such as the space, only the first word will be stored in the array (e.g., nice). The remaining characters are left in the input queue. To be able to read strings that contain spaces we can use the getline() function, which is a member of the istream class. As we'll see in Chapter 17, to call a function that is a member of a class we write the name of the object (e.g., `cin`) and add the `.` operator. The first argument of `getline()` is a pointer to the memory used to store the characters, while the second specifies the maximum number of characters (e.g., `size`) to be read. This number should not be larger than the size of the allocated memory to prevent overflow. `getline()` stops reading characters when it reads the newline character or when it reads `size-1` characters, whichever comes first. Then, it adds the null character. For example:

```
char str[30];
cin.getline(str, sizeof(str));
```

`getline()` will read a maximum of 29 characters, leaving one place for the null character. The characters will be stored in the `str` array. If the new line character is encountered earlier, `getline()` stops reading. `getline()` extracts the new line character from the input stream and does not store it in the array. If the user enters more characters, the redundant characters are left in the input queue. To make your program independent of the array size, use the `sizeof` operator instead of a fixed value (e.g., 30). Note that there is a version of `getline()` which allows us to specify the character to stop reading. For example:

```
cin.getline(str, sizeof(str), '#');
```

Now, if `getline()` encounters the new line character it won't stop reading. This would allow multiple text lines to be entered. If the # character is read, then it stops reading. Note that an overloaded version of `get()` we saw in Chapter 9 works similarly to `getline()`. Since we are going to use `getline()`, there is no need to describe it.

If we want to find how many characters are read we can use the `gcount()` function. For example:

```
char str[30];
cin.getline(str, sizeof(str));
cout << cin.gcount() << '\n';
```

If the user enters `test`, the code outputs 5.

 The pointer that is passed to `getline()` must point to a memory allocated to store the string.

For example, is the following code correct?

```
char *p, s[10];
p = s;
cin.getline(p, 10);
```

Yes, because p points to an allocated memory. If the statement `p = s;` was missing, the code would be wrong. And, if in `getline()`, instead of 10, we write `sizeof(p)`, would be the same? Of course not, the `sizeof` operator returns the size of the pointer, and not the size of the memory it points to.

An unexpected behaviour that makes many novice programmers wonder why their program does not work correctly arises when the program reads a string after having read a numerical value. We saw something similar in the C.9.4 example. As another example, suppose that the user enters an integer and then presses *Enter*. What does the following program output?

```
#include <iostream> // Example 10.5
using std::cout;
using std::cin;
```

```
int main()
{
        char str[100];
        int num;

        cout << "Enter number: ";
        cin >> num;

        cout << "Enter text: ";
        cin.getline(str, sizeof(str));

        cout << num << ' ' << str;
        return 0;
}
```

The program reads the integer and stores it in num. The new line character generated when *Enter* is pressed is stored in the input queue. Since getline() terminates once the new line character is read, the user cannot enter more characters. Therefore, the program outputs only the input number. A solution is to use cin.get() before getline(), in order to read the new line character.

EXERCISES

C.10.7 What is the output of the following program?

```
#include <iostream>
using std::cout;
using std::cin;

int main()
{
        char *ptr[3], str[100];
        int i;

        for(i = 0; i < 3; i++)
        {
                cout << "Enter text: ";
                cin.getline(str, sizeof(str));
                ptr[i] = str;
        }
        for(i = 0; i < 3; i++)
                cout << *ptr[i] << '\n';
        return 0;
}
```

Answer: The ptr variable is declared as an array of three pointers to character. In each iteration, the statement ptr[i] = str; makes all pointers up to i to point to the first character of the string stored in str array. Since all pointers point to the same address, the second loop displays three times the first character of the last input string.

C.10.8 Complete the following program by using the p pointer and a while loop, so that the program reads a string of less than 100 characters and displays the number of its characters, the number of 'b' occurrences, and the input string after replacing the space character with the new line character and `'a'` with `'p'`.

```
#include <iostream>
int main()
{
        char *p, str[100];
        int cnt;
        ...
}
```

Answer:

```
#include <iostream>
using std::cout;
using std::cin;

int main()
{
        char *p, str[100];
        int cnt;

        p = str;
        cout << "Enter text: ";
        cin.getline(p, sizeof(str));

        cnt = 0;
        while(*p != '\0')
        {
                if(*p == ' ')
                        *p = '\n';
                else if(*p == 'a')
                        *p = 'p';
                else if(*p == 'b')
                        cnt++;
                p++;
        }
        cout << "Len:" << p-str << " Times:" << cnt << "\nText:" << str << '\n';
        return 0;
}
```

Comments: When the loop ends, p points to the null character. Then, we use pointer arithmetic to calculate the length of the string.

C.10.9 Is the following program written correctly? If yes, what does it output?

```
#include <iostream>
int main()
{
        const char *str = "test";

        for(; *str; std::cout << ++str << " ")
                ;
        return 0;
}
```

Answer: As we know, the three expressions of the `for` statement can be any valid expression. Therefore, there is nothing wrong with its syntax. Also, the standalone; means that the body of the loop is empty. The expression `*str` is equivalent to `*str! = 0`. Thus, the loop is executed until the null character is found. In each iteration, the `str` pointer increases and points to the next character. Therefore, the program displays:
`est st t`

C.10.10 What is the output of the following program?

```cpp
#include <iostream>
int main()
{
        const char *str = "Example";
        int *ptr = (int*)str;

        ptr++;
        std::cout << (char*)ptr+3;
        return 0;
}
```

Answer: Since `ptr` is declared as a pointer to `int`, the statement `ptr++;` makes it point to the fifth character of the string. Then, since the type of `ptr` is cast to `char*`, the program displays the part of the string from the eighth character and on. Since the eighth character is the null character, the program displays nothing.

C-STYLE STRING FUNCTIONS

The C++ library has inherited the C string functions. Don't forget that a C-style string ends with the null character. If it is missing their behaviour may be unpredictable. This section presents some of the most used. Although we'll discuss about functions in the next chapter, I think you can understand how they are used. Also, don't forget that a safer approach than using C-style strings is to use the `string` class that we'll see later. However, because lot of existing code uses C-style strings and you'll most probably encounter that code you should learn well both techniques.

The `strlen()` Function

The `strlen()` function is declared in `cstring`:

```cpp
size_t strlen(const char *str);
```

The `size_t` type is defined in the C++ library as an alias of some unsigned integer type (e.g., `unsigned int`). `strlen()` returns the number of characters in the string pointed to by `str`, not counting the null character. For example:

```cpp
int len;
len = strlen("Test"); // len becomes 4.
const char *p = "";
len = strlen(p); // len becomes 0.
char s[] = {'a', 'b', 'c'};
len = strlen(s); /* The result is undefined, because the null character is not
stored in the array. */
```

The pointer is declared as `const`, so that `strlen()` cannot modify the string. Here is an example of how it may be implemented:

```
unsigned int strlen(const char *str)
{
        unsigned int i = 0;

        while(str[i] != '\0') /* We count the characters of the string until
we reach the '\0'. */
                i++;
        return i;
}
```

As an example of using `strlen()` tell me what the following code outputs:

```
char str[] = "Text";
cout << strlen(str+4) << ' ' << strlen("Text"+1) << '\n';
```

Since the name of an array can be used as a pointer to its first element – I do know that I've written it many times, I just want to be sure that you've got it – `str+4` is a pointer to the fifth character of `str`, that is, the null character. Therefore, the first `strlen()` returns `0`. Since the string literal can be used as a pointer, the second `strlen()` returns the number of the characters after the second one. As a result, the code outputs: `0   3`.

The `strcpy()` and `strncpy()` Functions

A very common error is to use the `=` operator to copy strings. For example, see again the C.10.3 exercise or that one:

```
char str[10];
str = "something"; // Wrong.
```

One way to copy C-style strings is to use the `strcpy()` function. It is declared in `cstring`.

```
char *strcpy(char *dest, const char *src);
```

`strcpy()` copies the string pointed to by `src` into the memory pointed to by `dest`. Once the null character is copied, `strcpy()` terminates and returns the `dest` pointer. Since `src` is declared as `const`, `strcpy()` cannot modify the string. If the source and destination strings overlap the behaviour of `strcpy()` and `strncpy()` is undefined. In the following example, `strcpy()` copies the string `"something"` into `str`.

```
char str[10];
strcpy(str, "something");
```

Now, if we write:

```
strcpy(str, "new");
cout << str[6];
```

could you tell me what does it output?

Since `strcpy()` terminates once the null character is copied, the first four elements change and the rest remain the same. Therefore, the code outputs `i`.

If the null character is not found, the copy operation won't perform successfully. For example:

```
char str1[] = "abcd", str2[] = {'e', 'f', 'g'};
strcpy(str1, str2);
```

Since `str2` does not contain the null character, the copy operation won't perform successfully and a runtime error may occur.

 Because `strcpy()` does not check if the string pointed to by `src` fits into the memory pointed to by `dest`, it is the programmer's responsibility to ensure that the destination memory is large enough to hold all characters. Otherwise, the memory past the end of the `dest` will be overwritten causing the unpredictable behaviour of the program.

For example, consider the following program:

```
#include <iostream> // Example 10.6
#include <cstring>
int main()
{
        char c = 'a', str[10];

        strcpy(str, "Longer text. The program may crash");
        std::cout << str << ' ' << c << '\n';
        return 0;
}
```

Since the size of `str` is not large enough to hold the characters of the string, the data past the end of `str` will be overwritten (e.g., c could be stored in that position).

And yes, it is a serious error to pass an uninitialized pointer to `strcpy()`. For example:

```
char *str;
strcpy(str, "test"); // Wrong, str is not initialized.
```

The `strncpy()` function is declared in `cstring`:

```
char *strncpy(char *dest, const char *src, size_t count);
```

`strncpy()` is similar to `strcpy()`, with the difference that only the first `count` characters of the string pointed to by `src` will be copied into `dest`. If the value of `count` is less than or equal to the length of the string that `src` points to, a null character won't be appended to the memory pointed to by `dest`. If it is greater, null characters are appended, up to the value of `count`.

 Since `strncpy()` specifies the maximum number of the copied characters it is safer than `strcpy()`.

Here is an example of `strncpy()`:

```
#include <iostream> // Example 10.7
#include <cstring>
```

```cpp
int main()
{
        char str1[] = "Old text", str2[] = "New", str3[] = "Get";

        strncpy(str1, str2, 3);
        std::cout << str1 << '\n';

        strncpy(str1, str3, 5);
        std::cout << str1 << '\n';
        return 0;
}
```

Since the number 3 is less than the length of the string stored into str2, the first strncpy() copies the first three characters into str1 and does not append a null character. Therefore, the program displays New text. Since the number 5 is greater than the length of the string stored into str3, the second strncpy() copies three characters from str3 into str1 and appends two null characters to reach the value 5. Therefore, the program displays Get.

The strcat() Function

The strcat() function is declared in cstring:

```cpp
char *strcat(char *dest, const char *src);
```

strcat() appends the string pointed to by src to the end of the string pointed to by dest. strcat() appends the null character and returns dest, which points to the resulting string. For example, the following program reads two strings of less than 100 characters and uses strcat() to merge them and store the resulting string into an array.

```cpp
#include <iostream> // Example 10.8
#include <cstring>
using std::cout;
using std::cin;

int main()
{
        char str1[100], str2[100], str3[200] = {0}; /* Store the null
character in str3 for the first strcat(). */

        cout << "Enter first text: ";
        cin.getline(str1, sizeof(str1));

        cout << "Enter second text: ";
        cin.getline(str2, sizeof(str2));

        strcat(str3, str1); // The string contained in str1 is added to str3.
        strcat(str3, str2);
        cout << "The merged text is: " << str3 << '\n';
        return 0;
}
```

 It is the programmer's responsibility to ensure that there is enough room in the memory pointed to by dest to append the string pointed to by src. Otherwise, it is a potential cause of memory overrun with unpredictable results.

For example, consider the following program:

```
#include <iostream> // Example 10.9
#include <cstring>
int main()
{
        char str[20] = "example";

        strcat(str, "not available memory");
        std::cout << "The merged text is: " << str << '\n';
        return 0;
}
```

Since the size of `str` is not large enough to hold the characters of both strings, the data beyond the end of `str` will be overwritten with unpredictable results on the program's operation.

The `strcmp()` and `strncmp()` Functions

The `strcmp()` function is declared in `cstring`:

```
int strcmp(const char *str1, const char *str2);
```

`strcmp()` compares the string pointed to by `str1` with the string pointed to by `str2`. If the strings are identical, `strcmp()` returns 0. If the first string is less than the second, `strcmp()` returns a negative value, whereas, if it is greater it returns a positive value. A string is considered less than another if either one of the following conditions is true:

a. The first n characters of the strings match, but the value of the n+1 character in the first string is less than the value of the n+1 character in the second string.
b. All characters match, but the first string is shorter than the second.

Let's see some examples. The statement `strcmp("onE", "one");` returns a negative value because the ASCII code of the first non-matching character `'E'` is less than the ASCII code of `'e'`. The statement `strcmp("w", "many");` returns a positive value because the ASCII code of the first nonmatching character `'w'` is greater than the ASCII code of `'m'`. The statement `strcmp("some", "something");` returns a negative value because the first four characters match, but the first string is smaller than the second.

A very common error is to use the `==` operator to compare strings. For example, see the C.10.5 exercise once more. Therefore, the `if` condition in the next code:

```
char str[20];
cin.getline(str, sizeof(str));
if(str == "test")
```

does not compare the strings, but the values of `str` and that of the pointer to the literal string. Because the values are different, the condition is always false, no matter what string the user enters.

In Chapter 11, we'll implement the `str_cmp()` function, to see an implementation example of `strcmp()`.

`strncmp()` is similar to `strcmp()`, with the difference that it compares a specific number of characters. It is declared in `cstring`:

```
int strncmp(const char *str1, const char *str2, int count);
```

The parameter `count` specifies the number of the compared characters. As an example of using `strcmp()` and `strncmp()` try the following exercise.

C.10.11 Write a program that reads two strings of less than 100 characters and uses `strcmp()` to compare them. If the strings are different, the program should use `strncmp()` to compare their first three characters and display a related message.

```cpp
#include <iostream>
#include <cstring>
using std::cout;
using std::cin;

int main()
{
        char str1[100], str2[100];
        int k;

        cout << "Enter first text: ";
        cin.getline(str1, sizeof(str1));

        cout << "Enter second text: ";
        cin.getline(str2, sizeof(str2));

        k = strcmp(str1, str2);
        /* We could omit the declaration of k and write: if(strcmp(str1, str2)
== 0) */
        if(k == 0)
                cout << "Same texts\n";
        else
        {
                cout << "Different texts\n";
                if(strncmp(str1, str2, 3) == 0)
                        cout << "But the first 3 chars are the same\n";
        }
        return 0;
}
```

C.10.12 What is the output of the following program?

```cpp
#include <iostream>
#include <cstring>
int main()
{
        char str[5];

        str[0] = 't';
        str[1] = 'e';
        str[2] = 's';
        str[3] = 't';

        if(strcmp(str, "test") == 0)
                std::cout << "One\n";
        else
                std::cout << "Two\n";
        return 0;
}
```

Answer: Did you answer One but Two is displayed? Bad luck, next time …

The str array contains the 't', 'e', 's', and 't' characters, but str[4] is unassigned. On the other hand, the string literal "test" ends with the null character. If the random value of str[4] is not 0 the two contents are different, so, strcmp() returns a non-zero value and the program displays Two.

To continue... If we write char str[5] = {'t', 'e', 's', 't'}; what will be the output? One or Two?

Since the non-initialized elements are set to 0, str[4] becomes '\0' and the program displays One. What about if we change the condition to:

```
if(strcmp(str, "test\0") == 0)
```

No difference, the program displays One.

INTRODUCING THE STRING CLASS

For greater flexibility, convenience, and safety in handling strings, C++ provides the string class. In particular, instead of using an array of characters, we can use an object of the string class to handle the string. The string class is defined in the std namespace. To use it we have to include the string file in our program. The string class provides an extensive set of functions which facilitate string operations, such as copying strings, concatenating strings, comparing strings, and managing the memory they occupy automatically. Let's look at some examples of using string objects:

```
string s1, s2; /* The default constructor is called and two empty strings are
created. */
string s3("Test"); /* The s3 string object is created and it is initialized
with Test. */
s1 = s3; // Assign s3 to s1.
s2 = s1+s3; // Assign the merged strings to s2.
s2 += "More"; // Append the string at the end of s2.
string s4(s1); // The copy constructor initializes s4 with s1.
s3 += '?'; // Append the ? character at the end of s3.
s4 += s3; // Append s3 at the end of s4.
if(s1 == s2) // Compare strings.
if(s1 != s2) // Compare strings.
if(s1 == "Test") // Compare strings.
if(s1 > s2 && s2 <= s3) // Compare strings.
```

As you see, a string object is declared as a variable and not as an array of characters. The result of these actions is that s1 becomes equal to Test, s2 equal to TestTestMore, s3 equal to Test? and s4 equal to TestTest?. These examples show how much easier is to copy, add, or compare strings than to use C-style strings and related functions. For example, see how much easier becomes to compare strings with the last four if than using strcmp(). In fact, as we'll learn in Chapter 18, the string class overloads the respective operators to support these functions. The string class offers several constructors to create objects. We'll discuss about constructors in Chapter 17. I used two of the most common.

Besides simplifying string operations, the great advantage of using a string object is that we do not have to worry about memory issues. The size of the memory is adjusted according to the requirements dynamically, that is, during the execution of the program. In contrast, for C-style strings, the size of the array is determined at compile time and cannot change. For example, although the initial length of s1 was zero, its length dynamically changed in the statement s1 = s3; in order to store s3. The same adjustment happens with the length of s2 in the statement s2 = s1+s3;. To see the difference with the C-style strings, suppose that the s1, s2, and s3 were declared as arrays. Then, the equivalent actions are:

```
strcpy(s2, s1);
strcat(s2, s3);
```

However, as we said, with arrays there is always the risk that the length of the destination array, that is, s2, is not large enough to store all the characters. For example:

```
char s2[10] = "Memory ";
strcat(s2, "Problem");
```

strcat() overwrites the adjacent memory after s2, resulting in unpredictable program behaviour. On the other hand, when using string objects, we are safe. The memory size is adjusted automatically, thus, there is no danger. Of course, there are the strncpy() and strncat() functions which are more safe; however, it is much easier to use string objects. As we'll see in Chapter 18, the string class overloads arithmetic operators, such as the + and =, in order to simplify the syntax of string functions. Memory management is done dynamically, as described for the vector class in Chapter 7. That is, the compiler allocates more memory than needed in order to avoid consecutive memory allocations each time new characters are added. For example, suppose that a character is added sequentially. It would be inefficient to reserve an extra place each time. Also, if this next memory place is in use, then a new block should be allocated and then copy the old content in this new location. To avoid all this, the compiler allocates a block of memory larger than the initial size of the string. If this memory runs out, then the compiler allocates new memory to store the existing content and new characters. The capacity() function returns the size of the allocated memory.

Let's remind the most common ways to read characters and store them in a C-style string.

```
char s[50];
cin >> s; /* Read characters and store them into s, until a white space
character is met. As we said, this approach carries the risk of a buffer
overflow. */
cin.getline(s, 50); /* Read characters and store them into s, until either
the extracted character is the new line character '\n' which is discarded and
not stored in s or 50 characters are stored in s including the null
character. */
cin.getline(s, 50, '?'); /* As previously, with the difference that the
delimiting character is the? , and not the '\n'. */
```

Let's see now how we can read characters and store them in a string object.

```
string s;
cin >> s; /* First, all the white characters that may exist in the input
queue are extracted. Then, characters are read and stored in s until a white
character is met. For example, if the user enters the phrase multiple words
only the word multiple will be stored in s. */
getline(cin, s); /* Read characters and store them into s until the new line
character '\n' is met. The '\n' is discarded and not stored in s. */
getline(cin, s, '?'); /* As previously, with the difference that the
delimiting character is the ?, and not the '\n'. Since the '\n' does not
signal the end of input, we can enter as many lines we want and they'll all
be merged into s. */
```

As we can see, when we use an array, we use the getline() which is a member of the istream class, whereas when we use a string object we use a standalone getline() which is not a class member. Also note that this version does not take a parameter to specify the maximum number of characters to be read, because, as we said, the size of the `string` object is automatically adjusted to fit the string.

The `string` class contains a large number of functions to handle the string. For example, it contains functions to erase, replace, compare, copy all or part of the string. It is also very important that most of these functions are overloaded so that they can work with both `string` objects and C-style strings. Let's look at an example:

```cpp
#include <iostream> // Example 10.10
#include <string>
using std::cout;
using std::cin;
using std::string;

int main()
{
        int i, len;
        string s;

        cout << "Enter string: ";
        getline(cin, s);

        s.append("fin");
        len = s.size(); // Length of the string.
        cout << "L:" << len << " S:" << s << '\n';

        i = s.find('a');
        if(i == -1)
                cout << "Not found\n";
        else
                cout << "Found in position:" << i+1 << '\n';

        for(i = 0; i < len; i++)
        {
                if(s[i] == 'p')
                        s[i] = 'w';
        }
        cout << s << '\n';
        s.resize(2*len, s[0]);
        s.erase(0, 3);
        cout << s << '\n';
        return 0;
}
```

The program reads a string, appends the `fin` at its end, displays its length and the first position of a. Then, it changes all p with w and displays the new string. It then doubles its size and sets the extra characters equal to its first character. Finally, it erases the first three characters and displays it. To access the characters of the string we use the `[]` operator, as with the arrays. In fact, as we'll see in Chapter 18, this operator is overloaded in the `string` class. Also, the `string` class provides the `at()` function, which takes as parameter the location of the element. For example:

```cpp
if(s.at(i) == 'p')
        s.at(i) = 'w';
```

The difference with the `[]` operator is that `at()` checks if the index is within acceptable bounds and if it is not it creates an exception (we'll discuss exceptions in Chapter 22). Therefore, if you care for safety, use at() and check for exceptions. On the other hand, if you are sure that the index will never exceed the limits, use [] for greater speed.

Also, the string class provides the c_str() function, which returns a pointer to a C-style string that contains the characters of the string object. This function is very useful, because we can use functions that require a C-style string as an argument. For example:

```
len = strlen(s.c_str());
```

Another advantage of using the string class is the fact that string objects can be stored in containers (e.g., vector), whereas plain char arrays cannot.

This section does not cover all the capabilities of the string class. It is just to give you an idea of how much easier and safer is to handle strings with the string class. Although in most cases it is the best choice, you should also know how to handle C-style strings for several reasons such as because they are used in many library functions, because you may need to use them or you may meet them in code written by others.

Note that the C++ standard library provides facilities for dealing with the characters sets of all languages. For example, can we write Chinese characters or compare Greek strings? Of course we can, but how to work with different national character sets is beyond the scope of this book. If you need to know, consult your library documentation.

Since C-style strings and string *objects are quite popular, we'll use both of them in the following exercises so that you get familiar with both techniques. When using an array of characters, let's assume that the maximum number of input characters would be less than a reasonable number (e.g., 100).*

EXERCISES

C.10.13 Write a program that reads a string and stores it in a string object. Then, the program should display a message to indicate if it is a palindrome or not, that is, if it can be read the same in either direction. For example, the string level is a palindrome, since it is read the same in both directions.

```
#include <iostream>
#include <string>
using std::cout;
using std::cin;
using std::string;

int main()
{
        int i, diff, len;
        string str;

        cout << "Enter text: ";
        getline(cin, str);
        len = str.size();

        diff = 0;
        for(i = 0; i < len/2; i++)
        {
                if(str[i] != str[len-1-i]) /* If two characters are not the
same, the loop terminates. */
```

```
                {
                        diff = 1;
                        break;
                }
        }
        if(diff == 1)
                cout << str << " is not a palindrome\n";
        else
                cout << str << " is a palindrome\n";
        return 0;
}
```

Comments: The loop compares the characters from the first character up to the middle one with the characters from the last one back to the middle. That's why the loop is executed from 0 up to `len/2`. The last character is stored in `str[len-1]`.

C.10.14 Write a program that reads a string of less than 100 characters, and if it is less than three characters, the user should enter a new one. Then, the program should read a character and check if the string contains the input character three times in a row. The program should display the position of the first triad found.

```cpp
#include <iostream>
#include <cstring>
using std::cout;
using std::cin;

int main()
{
        char ch, str[100];
        int i, len;

        do
        {
                cout << "Enter text (more than 2 chars): ";
                cin.getline(str, sizeof(str));
                len = strlen(str);
        } while(len < 3);

        cout << "Enter character: ";
        ch = cin.get();

        for(i = 0; i <= len-3; i++)
                if(str[i] == ch && str[i+1] == ch && str[i+2] == ch)
                {
                        cout << "There are three successive " << ch << " in
position " << i+1 << '\n';
                        return 0;
                }
        cout << "There aren't three successive " << ch << '\n';
        return 0;
}
```

C.10.15 Write a program that reads a string and stores it in a `string` object. Then, the program should display it after replacing all `'a'` characters that may appear at the beginning and at the end of the string with the space character. For example, if the user enters "aabcdaa", the program should display " bcd   ", while if the input string is "bcdaa", the program should display "bcd   ".

```cpp
#include <iostream>
#include <string>
using std::cout;
using std::cin;
using std::string;

int main()
{
        string str;
        int i, len;

        cout << "Enter text: ";
        getline(cin, str);
        len = str.size();

        for(i = 0; i < len; i++)
        {
                if(str[i] == 'a')
                        str[i] = ' ';
                else
                        break;
        }
        for(i = len-1; i >= 0; i--)
        {
                if(str[i] == 'a')
                        str[i] = ' ';
                else
                        break;
        }
        cout << "New text: " << str << '\n';
        return 0;
}
```

Comments: The first loop compares the characters in the beginning of the string with 'a'. If it is an 'a', it is replaced with the space character, otherwise the loop is terminated. Similarly, the second loop replaces all 'a' characters at the end of the string with the space character.

C.10.16 What is the output of the following program?

```cpp
#include <iostream>
#include <cstring>
int main()
{
        char str[] = "csfbl", *p = str;

        while(*p)
        {
                --*p; /* To make it harder, I could merge the two statements
into --*p++; */
                p++;
        }
        std::cout << p-strlen(str) << '\n';
        return 0;
}
```

Answer: The statement --*p; decreases the content of the address that p points to. For example, in the first iteration, p points to the first character of the string, that is 'c'. Therefore, *p is equal to 'c' and the statement --*p; changes the value of str[0] and makes it equal to the previous character in the ASCII set. Therefore, str[0] becomes 'b'. Next, p is increased and points to the next element of str. In the same way, the next iterations make str[1], str[2], str[3], and str[4] equal to 'r', 'e', 'a', and 'k', respectively.

The loop terminates once p becomes equal to str+5, that is, once the null character is met. Since strlen() returns the length of the string, the expression p-strlen(str) is equivalent to str+5-5 = str. Therefore, the program displays the new string stored into str, that is, break. Indeed, have a break before moving on to the next exercise.

C.10.17 What is the output of the following program?

```cpp
#include <iostream>
#include <cstring>
int main()
{
        char str[] = "Text", *p = str;
        int i;

        for(i = 0; i < strlen(str)-1; i++, p++)
                std::cout << p[i];
        return 0;
}
```

Answer: Since strlen() returns 4, the loop is executed three times. Let's trace the iterations:

First iteration (i = 0): The value of p[0] is displayed, that is, T.

Second iteration (i++ = 1): Since p is incremented by one, p points to the second character of the string, that is, 'e'. Since we handle p as an array, p[0] is 'e' and p[1] is 'x'. Therefore, the program outputs x.

Third iteration (i++ = 2): Now, p points to the third character, that is, 'x'. Therefore, p[0] is 'x', p[1] is 't', and p[2] is equal to '\0'. As a result, the program displays nothing.

To sum up, the program displays: Tx

C.10.18 Write a program that reads a string and stores it in a string object. Then, the program should display the number of appearances of its lowercase letters and its digits. Also, the program should display the lowercase letter, which appears the most times and the number of its appearances. If the string contains more than one letter with the same maximum number of appearances, the program should display the one found first.

```cpp
#include <iostream>
#include <string>
using std::cout;
using std::cin;
using std::string;

int main()
{
        char ch, max_ch;
        int i, max_times, low_let[26] = {0}; /* The size of the array is equal
to the number of the lowercase letters. This array holds the number of the
```

```
appearances of each letter. For example, low_let[0] holds the appearances of
'a', and low_let[25] the appearances of 'z'. */
        int dig[10] = {0}; /* Similarly, dig[0] holds the appearances of digit 0,
and dig[9] the appearances of digit 9. */
        string str;

        cout << "Enter text: ";
        getline(cin, str);

        max_ch = max_times = 0;
        for(i = 0; i < str.size(); i++)
        {
                if((str[i] >= 'a') && (str[i] <= 'z'))
                {
                        ch = str[i]-'a';
                        low_let[ch]++; /* For example, if the character is 'a',
the value of low_let['a'-'a'] = low_let[0], which holds the appearances of
'a', will be incremented by one. */
                        if(low_let[ch] > max_times)
                        {
                                max_times = low_let[ch];
                                max_ch = str[i];
                        }
                }
                else if((str[i] >= '0') && (str[i] <= '9'))
                        dig[str[i]-'0']++;
        }

        cout << "***** Lower case letters appearances\n";
        for(i = 0; i < 26; i++)
                if(low_let[i] != 0) /* Check if the letter appears once at
least. */
                        cout << "Letter " << (char)('a'+i) << " appeared " <<
low_let[i] << " times\n";

        cout << "***** Digits appearances\n";
        for(i = 0; i < 10; i++)
                if(dig[i] != 0)
                        cout << "Digit " << i << " appeared " << dig[i] <<
" times\n";
        if(max_times != 0)
                cout << max_ch << " appears " << max_times << " times\n";
        return 0;
}
```

Comments: If the string contains more than one character, which appears the same most of the times, the program displays the one found first. For example, if the user enters exit1, the output would be: 'e' appears 1 times, because all characters appear once and the character 'e' is the first one.

C.10.19 Write a program that simulates the popular word-guessing game "hangman". The program reads a secret word of less than 30 characters, which is the word to guess. This word is entered by the first player. Then, the second player enters letters one by one. The program should check each letter and inform the player. If the letter is contained in the word, the program should display the letters of the correct guesses in its positions and set the underscore character in the positions of the unknown letters. If it is not contained, the program should display a related message. The game is over if either the player finds the word or 7 incorrect guesses are made. Assume that the second player is not allowed to enter the same letter more than once.

```cpp
#include <iostream>
#include <cstring>
using std::cout;
using std::cin;

int main()
{
        const int ERROR_TRIES = 7;
        char ch, secret[30], hide[30] = {0};
        int i, found, len, error, correct;

        cout << "Enter secret word: ";
        cin.getline(secret, sizeof(secret));
        len = strlen(secret);

        for(i = 0; i < len; i++)
                hide[i] = '_';

        error = correct = 0;
        while(error < ERROR_TRIES)
        {
                cout << "Enter character: ";
                ch = cin.get();
                found = 0;
                for(i = 0; i < len; i++)
                {
                        if(secret[i] == ch)
                        {
                                hide[i] = ch;
                                found = 1;
                                correct++;
                                if(correct == len)
                                {
                                        cout << "Secret word is found !!!\n";
                                        return 0;
                                }
                        }
                }
                if(found == 0)
                {
                        error++;
                        cout << "Error, " << ch << " does not exist. You've got "
<< ERROR_TRIES - error << " more attempts\n";
                }
                else
                        cout << hide << '\n';
                cin.get(); // Discard '\n' from the previous get().
        }
        cout << "Sorry, the secret word was " << secret << '\n';
        return 0;
}
```

C.10.20 Here is just a weird program to show you a syntax example of mixing pointers, function calls, and pointer arithmetic in a single expression. What is the output?

```cpp
#include <iostream>
#include <cstring>
int main()
{
        char str[] = "noteasy";
        std::cout << str+(*(str+3)-1)-str[strlen(str+3)] << '\n';
        return 0;
}
```

Answer: Since the expression `*(str+3)` is equivalent to `str[3]`, that is, `'e'`, the value of `*(str+3)-1` is equal to `str[3]-1`, that is, `'e'-1 = 'd'`. `strlen()` returns the length of the string after the third character, that is, 4. Therefore, the expression is equivalent to `str+'d'-'a' = str+3` and the program outputs easy.

C.10.21 A Universal Product Code (UPC) barcode consists of 12 digits. The last digit is a check digit used for error detection. To calculate its value, we use the first 11 digits, as follows:

a. Add the digits in the odd positions and multiply the result by 3.
b. Add the digits in the even positions to the previous result.
c. Divide the result by 10. Subtract the remainder from 10, and that is the check digit. If the subtraction gives 10 (meaning that the remainder is 0), use 0 as check digit.

For example, let's see if the barcode 123456789015 is correct. The check digit is calculated as follows:

a. 1+3+5+7+9+1 = 26. Multiplied by 3 gives 26*3 = 78.
b. 2+4+6+8+0 = 20. Added to the previous result gives 78+20 = 98.
c. The value of the check digit is 10-(98%10) = 10-8 = 2.

Since the last digit is 5 and the calculated check bit is 2, the barcode is not correct.

Write a program that reads a UPC barcode and checks if it is correct. The program should force the user to enter a valid barcode, meaning that the length of the string should be 12 and it must contain digits only.

```cpp
#include <iostream>
#include <cstring>
using std::cout;
using std::cin;

int main()
{
        char upc[13];
        int i, len, flag, chk_dig, sum;

        while(1)
        {
                cout << "Enter UPC (12 digits): ";
                cin.getline(upc, sizeof(upc));
                len = strlen(upc);
                if(len != 12)
                {
                        cout << "Error: wrong length\n";
                        continue;
                }
```

```
                flag = 1;
                for(i = 0; i < 12; i++)
                {
                        if(upc[i] < '0' || upc[i] > '9')
                        {
                                cout << "Error: only digits allowed\n";
                                flag = 0;
                                break;
                        }
                }
                if(flag == 1)
                        break;
        }
        sum = 0;
        for(i = 0; i < 11; i+=2)
                sum += upc[i]-'0'; /* Subtract '0' to get the numeric value of
the digit character. */
        sum *= 3;
        for(i = 1; i < 11; i+=2)
                sum += upc[i]-'0';

        chk_dig = 10-(sum%10);
        if(chk_dig == 10)
                chk_dig = 0;

        if(chk_dig == (upc[11]-'0'))
                cout << "Valid barcode\n";
        else
                cout << "Wrong check digit. The correct is " << chk_dig << '\n';
        return 0;
}
```

C.10.22 The data compression algorithm Run Length Encoding (RLE) is based on the assumption that a symbol within the data stream may be repeated many times in a row. This repetitive sequence can be replaced by an integer that declares the number of the repetitions and the symbol itself. Write a program that reads a string of less than 100 characters and uses the RLE algorithm to compress it. Don't compress digits and characters that appear once. For example, the string: fffmmmm1234jjjjjjjjjjx should be compressed to: 3f4m123410jx

```
#include <iostream>
#include <cstring>
using std::cout;
using std::cin;

int main()
{
        char str[100];
        int i, len, cnt;

        cout << "Original text: ";
        cin.getline(str, sizeof(str));
        len = strlen(str);

        cout << "Compressed text: ";
        i = 0;
```

```
        while(i < len)
        {
                cnt = 1;
                if(str[i] < '0' || str[i] > '9') /* Digits are not compressed.
*/
                {
                        while(str[i+cnt] == str[i]) /* Check if the current
character, that is str[i], is repeated in the next places. */
                                cnt++;

                        if(cnt == 1)
                                cout << str[i];
                        else
                                cout << cnt << str[i];
                }
                else
                        cout << str[i];

                i += cnt;
        }
        return 0;
}
```

C.10.23 Write a program that reads a string and stores it in a `string` object. Then, the program should display the words that it consists of and their number. Suppose that a word is a sequence of character(s) that does not contain space character(s). For example, if the user enters how   many words   ? (notice that more than one space may be included between the words), the program should display:

```
how
many
words
?
The text contains 4 words
```

```
#include <iostream>
#include <string>
using std::cout;
using std::cin;
using std::string;

int main()
{
        int i, words;
        string str;

        i = words = 0;
        cout << "Enter text: ";
        getline(cin, str);

        if(str[0] != ' ' && str[0] != '\t' && str[0] != '\0') /* If the first
character is other than the space character, it means that a word begins, so
the value of words is incremented. */
                words++;
```

```
        while(str[i] != '\0')
        {
                if(str[i] == ' ' || str[i] == '\t')
                {
                /* Since more than one space character may be included between
words, we check if the next character, that is str[i+1], is also a space
character. If it isn't, it means that a new word begins, so the value of
words is increased. */
                        if(str[i+1] != ' ' && str[i+1] != '\t' && str[i+1] != '\0')
                        {
                                words++;
                                cout << '\n';
                        }
                }
                else
                        cout << str[i];
                i++;
        }
        cout << "\nThe text contains " << words << " words\n";
        return 0;
}
```

C.10.24 What is the output of the following program?

```
#include <iostream>
int main()
{
        const char *arr[] = {"TEXT", "SHOW", "OPTIM", "DAY"};
        const char **ptr1;

        ptr1 = arr;
        std::cout << *++ptr1 << ' ';
        std::cout << *++ptr1+2;
        std::cout << (char)(**++ptr1+1) << '\n';
        return 0;
}
```

Answer: The arr array is declared as an array of pointers to strings. In particular, arr[0] points to "TEXT", arr[1] points to "SHOW", and so on. The statement ptr1 = arr; makes ptr1 to point to the address of arr[0].

The expression ++ptr1 makes ptr1 to point to arr[1]. Since *++ptr1 is equivalent to arr[1], the program displays SHOW.

The expression ++ptr1+2 makes first ptr1 to point to arr[2]. Since *++ptr1 is equivalent to arr[2], the cout statement is translated to cout << ptr[2]+2; and the program skips the first two characters of "OPTIM" and displays TIM.

Like before, the expression ++ptr1+1 makes first ptr1 to point to arr[3]. Therefore, **++ptr1 is equivalent to *arr[3]. What is the value of *arr[3]? Since arr[3] points to the first character of "DAY", *arr[3] is equal to 'D'. Therefore, the value of *arr[3]+1 is 'E' and the program displays E.

As a result, the program displays: SHOW TIME

C.10.25 A simple algorithm to encrypt data is the algorithm of the single transformation. Let's see how it works. In one line, we write the letters of the used alphabet. In a second line, we write the same letters in a different order. This second line constitutes the cryptography key. Note that all key characters must be different from each other. For example, see this figure.

a	b	c	d	e	f	g	h	i	j	k	l	m	n	o	p	q	r	s	t	u	v	w	x	y	z
d	y	p	r	i	a	j	u	h	t	q	w	e	s	f	o	v	c	n	b	l	x	m	k	z	g

Each letter of the original text is substituted with the respective key letter. For example, the word test is encrypted as binb.

Write a program that reads a string of less than 100 characters, the key string of 26 characters, and encrypts the lowercase letters of the input string. Then, the program should decrypt the encrypted string and display it (should be the same with the original string). The program should check that the key characters appear only once.

```cpp
#include <iostream>
#include <cstring>
using std::cout;
using std::cin;

int main()
{
        const int LETTERS = 26;
        bool error;
        char str[100], key[LETTERS+1];
        int i, j, len;

        cout << "Enter text: ";
        cin.getline(str, sizeof(str));
        len = strlen(str);
        do
        {
                error = 0;
                cout << "Enter key (" << LETTERS << " different characters): ";
                cin.getline(key, sizeof(key));
                if(strlen(key) != LETTERS)
                {
                        cout << "Error: Key must be of " << LETTERS <<
" characters\n";
                        error = 1;
                }
                else
                {
                        for(i = 0; i < LETTERS; i++)
                        {
                                for(j=i+1; j < LETTERS; j++)
                                {
                                        if(key[i] == key[j])
                                        {
                                                error = 1;
                                                cout << "Key characters must be
different\n";
                                                break;
                                        }
                                }
                                if(error == 1)
                                        break;
                        }
                }
        } while(error != 0);
```

```
for(i = 0; i < len; i++)
{
        if(str[i] >= 'a' && str[i] <= 'z')
                str[i] = key[str[i]-'a'];
}
cout << "Encrypted text: " << str << '\n';
for(i = 0; i < len; i++)
{
        for(j = 0; j < LETTERS; j++)
        {
                if(str[i] == key[j])
                {
                        str[i] = 'a'+j;
                        break;
                }
        }
}
cout << "Original text: " << str << '\n';
return 0;
}
```

TWO-DIMENSIONAL ARRAYS AND C-STYLE STRINGS

Two-dimensional arrays are often used to store multiple C-style strings. For example, the statement:

```
char str[10][40];
```

declares the `str` array with ten rows. Each row can store a string of up to 40 characters. In case of shorter strings, there is a waste of memory.

We can store string literals in a two-dimensional array when it is declared. For example:

```
char str[3][40] = {"One", "Two", "Three"};
```

the characters of `"One"` are stored in the first row of `str`, the characters of `"Two"` in the second row, and those of `"Three"` in the third row. Since the strings are not large enough to fill the rows, null characters are padded, as depicted here.

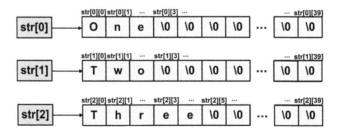

Recall from Chapter 8 and the section "Pointers and Two-Dimensional Arrays" that we can treat each of the elements `str[0]`, `str[1]`, ..., `str[N-1]` of a two-dimensional array `str[N][M]` as a pointer to an array of M elements. For example, str[0] can be used as a pointer to an array of 40 characters, which holds the string One.

Also remember from the section "Array of Pointers" that in order to save memory space we could use an array of pointers instead of a two-dimensional array. For example:

```
const char *str[] = {"One", "Two", "Three"};
```

Although some memory is allocated for the str pointers, the important thing is that the memory allocated for the strings is exactly as needed. Thanks to the close relationship between pointers and arrays, we can subscript str as a two-dimensional array to access a character. For example:

```
for(i = 0; i < 3; i++)
        if(str[i][0] == 'T')
                cout << str[i] << '\n';
```

The loop displays the strings beginning from T. Exercise C.10.27 is another example, where the use of an array of pointers produces more efficient code. Also, do not forget that for a more flexible and safer management of strings we can use the vector class. C.10.28 is such an example. As I have mentioned, it is my intention to show you all these approaches, because they are all quite popular.

EXERCISES

C.10.26 What is the output of the following program?

```
#include <iostream>
#include <cstring>
int main()
{
        char arr[7][10] = {"Monday", "Tuesday", "Wednesday", "Thursday",
"Friday", "Saturday", "Sunday"};
        int i;

        for(i = 0; i < 7; i++)
                if(arr[i][2] == 'n' && *(arr[i]+3) == 'd' && *(*(arr+i)+4) ==
'a')
                        std::cout << arr[i] << " is No." << i+1 << " week
day\n";
        return 0;
}
```

Answer: The characters of "Monday" are stored in the first row of arr, the characters of "Tuesday" in the second row, and so on. Remember that *(arr[i]+3) is equivalent to arr[i][3] and *(*(arr+i)+4) is equivalent to *(arr[i]+4), that is, arr[i][4]. Therefore, the loop checks each row of arr and displays the strings whose third, fourth, and fifth characters are 'n', 'd', and 'a', respectively. Therefore, the program displays:

```
Monday is No.1 week day
Sunday is No.7 week day
```

C.10.27 Write a program that reads 20 names (less than 100 characters each), stores them in an array, and uses an array of pointers to display them in alphabetical order.

```cpp
#include <iostream>
#include <cstring>
using std::cout;
using std::cin;

int main()
{
        const int SIZE = 20;
        char *temp, *ptr[SIZE], str[SIZE][100];
        int i, j;

        for(i = 0; i < SIZE; i++)
        {
                cout << "Enter name: ";
                cin.getline(str[i], sizeof(str[i]));
                ptr[i] = str[i]; /* The elements of the array point to the
input strings. */
        }
        for(i = 0; i < SIZE-1; i++)
        {
                for(j = i+1; j < SIZE; j++)
                {
                        /* If the string pointed to by ptr[j] is less than the
string pointed to by ptr[i], swap the respective pointers. */
                        if(strcmp(ptr[j], ptr[i]) < 0)
                        {
                                temp = ptr[j];
                                ptr[j] = ptr[i];
                                ptr[i] = temp;
                        }
                }
        }
        for(i = 0; i < SIZE; i++)
                cout << ptr[i] << '\n';
        return 0;
}
```

Comments: The main reason I added this exercise is to show you how useful an array of pointers might be. When two strings must be swapped, it is the respective pointers that are swapped, not the strings. As a result, we gain in performance. The sorting algorithm we used is called selection sort and it will be discussed in Chapter 12. The "negative" point in this solution is the potential waste of space. Each row of str allocates 100 characters, even if the string contains less. For a more efficient memory management, see the next exercise. We'll see an alternative way in Chapter 14 with the exercise C.14.6.

C.10.28 Write a program that reads continuously strings and stores in a vector of string elements those that begin with an 'a' and end with 's'. If the user enters end, the insertion of strings should terminate. Then, the program should read a string and display how many times it is contained in the vector.

```cpp
#include <iostream>
#include <string>
#include <vector>
using namespace std;
```

```
int main()
{
        int i, cnt, size;
        string s;
        vector<string> v_str;

        while(1)
        {
                cout << "Enter text: ";
                getline(cin, s);
                if(s == "end")
                        break;
                v_str.push_back(s);
        }
        size = v_str.size();
        if(size == 0)
        {
                cout << "None string is stored\n";
                return 0;
        }
        cout << "Enter text: ";
        getline(cin, s);
        cnt = 0;
        for(i = 0; i < size; i++)
        {
                if(v_str[i] == s)
                        cnt++;
        }
        cout << s << " is stored " << cnt << " times\n";
        return 0;
}
```

Comments: See how much easier is to manage strings using the vector class. We do not need to use a two-dimensional array and we do not care about the size of the memory, since the memory that is reserved for each string is exactly as needed.

UNSOLVED EXERCISES

U.10.1 Write a program that reads three strings of less than 100 characters and stores them in three arrays (e.g., str1, str2, and str3). Then, the program should copy their contents one place right, meaning that the content of str3 should be copied to str1, the content of str1 to str2, and that of str2 to str3.

U.10.2 Write a program that reads a string, stores it in a string object, and if it ends with aa, the program should display it in reverse order.

U.10.3 What is the output of the following program?

```
#include <iostream>
#include <cstring>
int main()
```

```
{
        char str[] = {'t', 'e', 's', 't', '0'}, *p = str;

        *str = str[strlen(str)];
        while(*p)
                std::cout << p++;
        return 0;
}
```

U.10.4 Write a program that reads a string of less than 100 characters and stores it in an array. Then, the program should reverse the stored string and display the new one. For example, if the string code is stored, the program should reverse it and store in the array edoc. Use just one array.

U.10.5 What is the output of the following program?

```
#include <iostream>
int main()
{
        for(const char *p = "mhbd"; *p; std::cout << (char)(*p++++1));
        return 0;
}
```

U.10.6 Write a program that reads a string of less than 100 characters, how many characters are going to be deleted and the position of the first character to be deleted. After the deletion, the rest part of the string should be shifted to the left, a number of places equal to the number of the deleted characters. The program should display the string before it ends. For example, if the input string is test case and the numbers are 4 and 2, the program should display tcase. The program should check the validity of the input numbers in order to assure that the characters are contained in the string.

U.10.7 Write a program that reads two strings of less than 100 characters and displays how many times the second string is contained in the first one. The length of the second string should be less than or equal to the first one.

U.10.8 Write a program that reads a string and stores it in a string object. Then, the program should delete from it all the characters that are not letters, the multiple repetitions of the same letter, and display the new string. For example, if the string jA*8%cr1^c is stored, the program should change its content to jAcr. There is one restriction; don't use a second string object to store the characters that are not deleted.

U.10.9 Modify C.10.23 in order to display the words in reverse order. For example, if the user enters imagine the case, the program should display case the imagine.

U.10.10 Write a program that reads continuously characters and stores them in a string object with the restriction that all stored characters should be different. Also, do not store more than 100 characters. If the user enters q, the insertion of characters should end.

U.10.11 Write ~a program that reads a string of less than eight characters that represents a hexadecimal number (accepted characters: 0-9, a-f, A-F) and displays the corresponding decimal value. For example, if the user enters 1AF, the program should display 431.

U.10.12 Suppose that each lowercase letter has a value as follows. The letters 'a' up to 'i' correspond to units; 'a' has the value 1 and 'i' is 9. The letters 'j' up to 'r' correspond to tens; 'j' has the value 10 and 'r' is 90. The rest correspond to hundreds; 's' has the value 100 and 'z' is 800.

Write a program that reads continuously strings and displays the strings with the largest and smallest value and those values as well, before it ends. For example, the value of cky is 723, while the value of A9m is 40, since the characters 'A' and '9' don't have a value. If more than one string has the same largest or smallest value, the program should display the one entered last. If the user enters ***, the insertion of strings should terminate. To store the strings use string objects.

U.10.13 Write a program that reads two strings of less than 100 characters and removes every occurrence of the second string inside the first one. After each removal, the remaining part of the first string should be shifted to the left, a number of places equal to the characters of the second string. The program should display the first string, before it ends. For example, if the first string is thisthat though and the second is th, the program should display isat ough.

U.10.14 Write a program that reads two strings and stores them in two string objects. The program should display the longest part of the first string that does not contain any character of the second string. For example, if the first string is example and the second one is day, the program should display mple because that part does not contain any character of day.

U.10.15 Write a program that reads an integer and converts it to a string. For example, if the user enters 12345, the program should store the characters '1', '2', '3', '4', and '5' into a string object.

U.10.16 Write a program that reads two strings and stores them in two string objects. The program should display the largest part of the first string that contains exclusively characters from the second string. For example, if the first string is programming and the second string is im, the program should display mmi. Assume that the second string contains different characters.

U.10.17 Write a program that reads an integer in the form of a string and converts the string into that number. For example, if the user enters the string -12345, the program should convert that string to the number -12345, assign it to a numerical variable and display it. Assume that the user enters up to ten digits.

U.10.18 To continue the previous exercise, the program should check if the input string corresponds to a float number and assign that number to a numerical variable. For example, if the user enters the string 12, the program should assign the number 12 to a variable. If the user enters the string -1.234 the assigned value should be -1.234.

U.10.19 Write a program that reads 20 strings (less than 100 characters each) and stores in an array those that begin with an 'a' and end with 's'. Then, the program should read a character and display in which column it occurs most. If there is more than one column with the same most occurrences, the program should display the one found first.

U.10.20 Write a program that reads 20 strings (less than 100 characters each) and stores them in a two-dimensional array. Then, the program should read a string, and if it is found in the array it should be removed. To remove the string, move the strings below that point one row up. In the place of the last row moving up, insert the null character. For example, if the array is:

```
one
two
three
four
...
```

and the user enters two, the new content should be:

```
one
three
four
...
```

U.10.21 Write a program that reads 20 strings (less than 100 characters each) and stores them in a two-dimensional array. Then, the program should:

a. read a column number and display the words that are contained in that column, including those that consist of a single character. In an example with five strings, if the user enters:

```
abcdegm
abcdfpoloo
abcd
abc
abcdkmop
```

and the number 6 as column, the program should display:

```
word_1: gp
word_2: m
```

b. read a row number, except the first one, and if the string in that row contains less than five different lowercase letters, the program should swap that string with the string in the first row.

U.10.22 Write a program that reads the names of 20 bookstores and 500 book titles. Use two two-dimensional arrays to store them. Assume that all names are less than 100 characters. The program should also read for each bookstore the number of copies left in stock for each title. Then, the program should read a book title and display the names of the bookstores that offer this title and the number of copies of that title in those bookstores. Finally, the program should read the name of a bookstore and display its total number of copies left in stock.

U.10.23 The permutation method is an example of symmetric cryptography, in which the sender and the receiver share a common key. The encryption key is an integer of n digits ($n \leq 9$). Each digit must be between 1 and n and appear only once. In the encryption process, the message is divided into segments of size n. For example, suppose that we are using the key 25413 to encrypt the message *This is the end!!* from the classical song of *Doors: The end*. Since the key size is 5, the message is divided into four segments of 5 characters each. If the size of the last segment is less than the key size, padding characters are added. Suppose that the padding character is the *, as shown here.

T	h	i	s		i	s		t	h	e		e	n	d	!	!	*	*	*
h		s	T	i	s	h	t	i			d	n	e	e	!	*	*	!	*

The characters of each segment are rearranged according to the key digits. For example, the second character of the original message is the first one in the encrypted segment, the fifth character goes to the second position, the fourth character in the third position, and so on, as shown in the figure. This process is repeated for each segment.

The recipient uses the same key to decrypt the message. The reverse process takes place. For example, the first character of the first encrypted segment corresponds to the second character of the original message, the second character corresponds to the fifth one, the third character to the fourth one, and so on.

Write a program that reads a string of less than 100 characters, the encryption key (read it as a string), the padding character, and uses that method to encrypt the string. Then, the program should decrypt the message and display it.

Functions

11

A function is an independent block of code that has a name. When it is called its code is executed and when it terminates it may return a value. A function is essentially a small program with its own variables and statements. Writing programs using functions that perform independent tasks is the basis of structured programming. Using functions, a program is divided into smaller parts, making it easier to understand, control, test, and maintain. We could say that functions resemble the different chapters or sections in a book or essay. The author splits the text in separate logical units, so that it becomes easier for the reader to read it.

Functions are reusable. For example, the `sqrt()` function or the functions provided by the `string` class can be used in more than one place in any C++ program. Also, because a function can be called as many times as we want, it is not needed to write the same code, thus the size of the program is reduced. So far, we've written only one function, the `main()`. In this chapter, you'll learn how to write and use your own functions within your programs. We'll also discuss recursion and recursive functions. After reading this chapter and together with what you've learned so far, you'll have enough tools in your hands to start writing some more complex programs. Of course, there are still much more to learn.

FUNCTION DECLARATION

A function declaration, which is also called function prototype, specifies the name of the function, its return type, and an optional list of parameters. The general form of a function declaration is:

```
return_type function_name(parameter_list);
```

The prototype informs the compiler about the type of parameters, their number, and the return type, so that it can check whether the way called in the program matches the prototype. Try to choose descriptive names for your functions. It is much easier to read the code of a function when its name indicates its role. For example, in a function that calculates the sum of some numbers, the name `sum` fits better than `func`, `test`, or `lala`.

Usually, the declarations of functions are put in a separate header file other than their code. For example, the declarations of the library functions reside in several header files. When we are using a library function, we use the `#include` directive to add the file that contains its declaration. For example, to use the `sqrt()` function we have to include the `cmath` file. Otherwise, the compiler will produce an error message for undeclared identifier.

As we'll see later, the declaration may be omitted if the function is defined before called. In that case the definition provides to the compiler the information it needs to process the function call. For simplicity, I'll declare the functions we write in the same file with `main()`.

Return Value

A function may return one value at most. The `return_type` specifies the type of the returned value. A function may return any data type, such as `char`, `double`, `struct`, ... or a pointer to some type. The return type `void` specifies that the function does not return any value.

The only restriction is that it is not allowed to return an array or a function. However, it is allowed to return a pointer to an array or a function. I know that it is too early to see such examples, but I prefer to put them here so that you don't have to search for them elsewhere in this book. A convenient way to specify these return types is to create a synonym. We'll see how to create synonyms in the next section. For example, let's declare a function that returns a pointer to an array of five integers:

```cpp
typedef int arr[5]; /* arr is a synonym for the type array of five integers. */
using arr = int[5]; // Here is an alternative way to declare arr.
arr* f(); // f() returns a pointer to an array of five integers.
```

Here is an example of `f()`:

```cpp
int v[5]; // If the size is not 5 the compiler displays an error message.
arr *f()
{
        return &v;
}
```

C++11 allows us to declare the return type after the list of parameters. For example, the following two statements are equivalent:

```cpp
int f(int a); // Prefix return type.
auto f(int a)->int; // Postfix return type.
```

The `auto` specifier indicates that the return type is added with the `->` after the parameter list. Thus, we can alternatively write:

```cpp
auto f()->int(*)[5];
```

where it is shown that the return type is a pointer to an array of five integers.

Let's see an example of returning a pointer to a function. As previously, we can use a synonym to declare the return type. For example:

```cpp
typedef int (*fp)(); /* fp is a synonym to a pointer to a function that
returns an integer value and does not accept parameters. */
using fp = int(*)(); // Here is an alternative way to declare fp.
fp g(); // g() returns such a pointer type.
```

Here is an example of `g()`:

```cpp
int v() {return 5;}

fp g()
{
        return v;
}
```

```
int main()
{
        fp var;
        var = g();
        cout << (*var)(); // The code outputs 5.
        ...
}
```

If using the C++11 postfix form we can declare g() as follows:

```
auto g()->int(*)();
```

where it is shown that the return type is a pointer to a function that returns an integer value and does not accept parameters.

Usually, the postfix form is used in declarations of function templates when the return type depends on the type of arguments. For example:

```
template <typename T1, typename T2>
auto f(T1 a, T2 b)-> decltype(a*b)
{
        return a*b;
}

int main()
{
        cout << f(10, 1.3); // The code outputs 13.
        ...
}
```

You'll understand this example better after reading about function templates in Chapter 16. When f() is called, T1 is replaced by int, T2 by double, so the return type of f() becomes that of a*b, that is double, and the code outputs 13. As this example shows, when we do not know the types of the arguments that will be passed to f(), and, therefore, we cannot determine the return type, the use of auto and decltype proves to be particularly useful.

Fortunately, C++14 makes easier the syntax and allows us to write a function that uses auto and let the compiler deduce the return type from the return statements according to some rules (e.g., if there are multiple return statements, they must deduce the same type). Thus, we don't have to use the peculiar trailing return type syntax of C++11 and decltype. For example, we can write:

```
template <typename T1, typename T2>
auto f(T1 a, T2 b) // No need to use decltype.
{
        return a*b;
}
```

Another example:

```
auto f(int a)
{
        return a*2.5;
}

int main()
{
        cout << f(3); // The code outputs 7.5.
        ...
}
```

In this example, there is no point in using `auto`. But, for more complex type names its use may be very useful and save us the time and effort that we'd have to deduce it.

The fact that a function is allowed to return one item at most might appear to be a limitation, but this is not true. This item can hold many values. For example, it can be a structure with members used to hold return values or a container (e.g., `vector`). Also, C++11 allows a function to return a list of values inside braces. The list is used to initialize the temporary variable used for the return value. For example:

```cpp
vector<int> f(int a) /* f() returns a vector, which is initialized according
to the value of the argument. */
{
        if(a == 10)
                return {1, 2};
        else if(a == 20)
                return {4, 5, 6};
        else
                return {};
}

int main()
{
        vector<int> v = f(20); /* v is initialized with the values 4, 5, and
6. */
        ...
}
```

Note that if the function returns a basic type (e.g., `int`), the list must contain one value at most.

Don't panic, yes, the examples of this section are difficult to understand since you do not know yet the related concepts. As I said, I put them altogether here so that you can easily find them when you look for similar return type and type deduction examples.

Creating Type Aliases

There are several situations where the creation of type aliases can make our program more flexible and easier to read. To create aliases we can use the `typedef` keyword and since C++11 the `using` keyword. Those specifiers are used to create a synonym for an existing data type. For example, the statement:

```cpp
typedef unsigned int size_t;
```

makes the name `size_t` synonym of the `unsigned int` type. Therefore, the declarations:

```cpp
unsigned int i; and size_t i; are equivalent.
```

The syntax resembles a variable declaration (e.g., as we would declare `size_t`) preceded by the `typedef` keyword. The name is a synonym of the type. For example, the statement:

```cpp
typedef float arr[100];
```

makes `arr` synonym for an array of 100 `floats`. Pay attention, `typedef` (and the same applies to `using`) does not create a variable (i.e., `arr` is not an array variable), neither a new type, just a new name. Therefore, the statement:

```cpp
arr arr1;
```

declares the variable `arr1` as an array of 100 `floats`. If we ever need to make the type of the array `double`, we just change `float` to `double`. The declarations of the variables using `arr` remain as is; we don't have to change them.

Because we create a synonym for an existing type, you may think that this feature is redundant. No, this is not true. For example, if your application is going to run on systems where the data types are system dependent, it is very helpful to use a synonym. For example, the statement:

```
typedef short int size_i;
```

makes the type of all `size_i` variables `short int`. In case these variables must be `int` in another platform, we just change `short int` to `int` and they become `int`. Thus, the use of synonyms helps us to adjust our types very easily in different requirements.

Another common use is to create synonyms of complex types, so that we don't have to repeat them. For example:

```
typedef int (*pcpy)(const char *s1, const char *s2, int len);
```

`pcpy` is a synonym for a pointer to a function that returns an integer and takes two arguments of type `const char*` and an integer argument. To create the synonym, we write the prototype and in place of the function name we put the expression (*pointer_name*). Now, we can use the synonym to declare variables of that type. For example:

```
pcpy p_cpy1, p_cpy2, p_cpy3;
```

As you see, the types of variables are read and written much easier than with the conventional way. Alternatively, instead of creating a synonym to a pointer, although this is the most popular approach, we could create a synonym to the respective function and then declare pointers. For example:

```
typedef int pfunc(const char *s1, const char *s2, int len);
pfunc *p_cpy1, *p_cpy2, *p_cpy3;
```

Usually, the creation of synonyms is put in a header file, so that we can include it in any source file we want and use these new names.

C++11 provides another way to create synonyms by using the `using` keyword. For example, the statement:

```
using pint = int*;
```

makes the name `pint` synonym of the `int*` type. Another example:

```
using fp = void(*)(int);
```

the name `fp` becomes synonym to a pointer type to a function that accepts an `int` and returns nothing. The same declaration with `typedef` would be:

```
typedef void (*p)(int);
```

The `using` syntax looks more intuitive compared to `typedef` as it resembles an ordinary assignment. Also, `using` allows us to create aliases for templates (e.g., we'll see them in Chapter 16), which is something that we cannot do with `typedef`.

Function Parameters

A function may take a list of parameters, separated by commas. Each parameter is preceded by its type. As we'll see later, a function parameter is essentially a variable of the function, which will be initialized with a value when the function is called.

If the function has no parameters we use empty parentheses (). Note that in C when we want to declare that a function does not accept parameters we add the word `void` inside the parentheses. In C the empty parentheses indicate that the function accepts an unknown number of parameters and not any. Because in C++ the empty parentheses indicate that the function does not accept parameters, we can omit the word `void`. Let's see some examples of function declarations:

```
void show(); /* Declare a function that has no parameters and returns
nothing. */
double show(char ch, int a, float b); /* Declare a function that takes a char
parameter, an integer and a float parameter and returns a double value. */
double *show(int *p1, int *p2); /* Declare a function that takes as
parameters two pointers to integers and returns a pointer to double. */
```

Note that we can omit the names of the parameters, the type is enough. For example, we could write:

```
double show(char, int, float);
```

However, my preference is always to use names, so that someone who just reads the prototype or intends to use the function gets an idea about the information being passed to it, in what order and the purpose of each parameter. For example, a function related to the coordinates of a point makes it easier for the reader to understand the purpose and the order of the parameters if declared as:

```
void show(int x, int y); instead of void show(int, int);
```

The type of each parameter must be specified, even if several parameters have the same type. For example, it is illegal to write:

```
void test(int a, b, c);   instead of  void test(int a, int b, int c);
```

FUNCTION DEFINITION

A function definition contains the code of the function. The general form of a function definition is:

```
return_type function_name(parameter_list)
{
      /* Function body */
}
```

The definition of a function is not allowed to split in different files. Also, each function must have a unique definition. If a library function is used, the function has already been defined and compiled. The first line must agree with the function declaration, but it does not have to be identical. For example, the names of the parameters don't have to be the same with the names given in the function declaration. Also, notice that no semicolon; is added at the end. The code, or else the body of the function, is everything enclosed in the two braces. The body of a function can be empty. The function body is executed only if the function is called. The execution of a function terminates if either an exit statement (e.g., `return`) is called or its last statement is executed. Let's see an example of using a function:

```cpp
#include <iostream> // Example 11.1

void test(); // Function declaration.

int main()
{
        test(); // Function call.
        return 0;
}

void test() // Function definition.
{
        // Function body.
        std::cout << "In\n";
}
```

As it will be explained later, the program outputs `In`.

As we said, the function declaration and the function definition are usually put in different files. For example, we can create a file (e.g., `prototype.h`), copy the declaration inside, remove the declaration from the source file, and include the `prototype.h`. By convention, the typical extension to use for our own header files is the `.h`. As discussed in Chapter 1, we enclose our header files in double quotes `""`.

```cpp
#include <iostream>
#include "prototype.h"

int main()
...
```

Note that a function can only be declared without being defined. If the function is not called in the program, the program is compiled normally, but if it is called, an error message will be displayed for undeclared function. Therefore, during the design phase of the program we can add the function declarations to remind us the work we have to do and add the definitions gradually during the development phase.

Although C++ does not require to put function definitions after `main()`, this is my preference, so that the reader first reads `main()`, which is the heart of the program to get an idea about its structure, and then to continue with other functions. If the definition precedes its first call, it is safe to omit the declaration of the function. For example:

```cpp
#include <iostream> // Example 11.2

void test()
{
        std::cout << "In\n";
}

int main()
{
        test();
        return 0;
}
```

Although our programs are short and we could define our functions before `main()`, such a practice is not always applicable. For example, in large applications where the code is split in several files, the function we want to call in a file may be defined in a different file. Then, the existence of a prototype is mandatory, so that the compiler knows how to call this function. Moreover, if there are many functions, the task to put them in correct order so that each of them is defined before being called by another requires effort or it may be impossible. Also, the existence of prototypes allows someone who reads them to get an overview of their functionality. Those reasons are enough to make us always use prototypes.

A function is not allowed to be defined inside another function. However, the declaration of a function can be put inside the body of the calling function. For example:

```cpp
int main()
{
        void test();
        test();
        return 0;
}
```

However, because the declaration of `test()` is visible only inside `main()`, it should be declared in any other function needs to call `test()`. And, if the declaration must change in the future, the programmer should search for and modify all declarations. To avoid that, don't declare functions inside functions.

Typically, a C++ program consists of many files. If we want to use in one file a function defined in another file, we just add its declaration. For example:

```cpp
// first.cpp
int sub(int a, int b) {return a-b;}

// second.cpp
int sub(int a, int b);
...
sub(20, 10);
```

However, the usual practice is to place the function declarations in a header file and include it with the `#include` directive in any file that needs it. Thus, if we have to change the declaration of a function, we'll make that change only in the header file and not in the files that use it. In general, a header file is typically included in many source files. This means that a header should only contain declarations that it is allowed to be duplicated in other files (e.g., numeric constants, function/struct/class declarations, …).

A source file that is compiled by itself together with the header files that it includes is called a *translation unit*. The declaration of every function used in a program must be the same in every translation unit that uses it. As we said, this can be ensured by putting the declaration in a header file and include that file wherever required. Also, every function must be defined only once. If either of these two rules is violated, the linker will produce an error. For example, in the C.11.1 program if we delete the definition of `test()`, a linker error for undefined reference to `test()` will be displayed, because it is not defined what `test()` actually does. If we add another definition of `test()` an error for redefinition of `test()` will be displayed. The distinction between function declaration and function definition allows the separation of the program into parts that can be compiled separately. The declarations allow a part of a program (e.g., header file) to maintain a view of the rest of the program without bothering with the definitions in other parts (e.g., source file).

As mentioned, the main purpose of the functions is to break the functionality of the program into smaller parts so that the program can be written, read, and maintained more easily. Therefore, the size of your functions should be relatively small (e.g., up to 50 lines), so that the reader quickly understands their purpose and how they operate. In this respect, a function should perform a single logical operation.

Also, it is very important for the proper operation and maintenance of the program to avoid *code duplication* as much as possible. Not only it is a waste of time to write the same code more than once, but it carries risks. For example, if the same code snippets are duplicated in several places and you decide to change one of them (e.g., to fix a bug), you have to remember to make the same changes in each individual copy of the same snippet. Even if it is you the same person who duplicated the code it is very easy to forget to make all the adjustments. Much worse if it is someone else who has no clue about the code repetition; a bug may have been fixed in one place and still remain in another place. If each piece of logic resides in a single place, we can avoid this inconsistency and be safe. The function is such a mechanism that may encapsulate common parts and save us from dangerous situations.

COMPLEX DECLARATIONS

Now that we've learned how to define functions, let's make a parenthesis to describe a method for deciphering complex declarations. Always decipher the declaration from inside out. Find the name of the variable and, if it is enclosed in parentheses (), start deciphering from there. Then, continue with the next operator where the precedence order, from high to low, is:

a. the postfix operators. The parentheses () indicate a function, and the brackets indicate [] an array.
b. the prefix operator * indicates "pointer to".

For example, consider the declaration: `int *p[5];`

Let's apply these precedence rules. The variable p is not enclosed in parentheses. Because [] take precedence over * we go right, so we have that p is "an array of five ...", then, go left to * and have "an array of five pointers ...", we add the type and end up with "an array of five pointers to integers".

Let's see another example: `int (*p)[5];`

Now, p is enclosed in parentheses. Deciphering starts inside there, so we go left to * and we have that p is "a pointer to ...", then we go right, so we have "a pointer to an array of five ...", then, go left to add the type and end up with "a pointer to an array of five integers". By the way, here is an example of how to initialize a pointer of that type. Suppose that the array `arr` is declared as `int arr[5];`. To initialize p we write `p = &arr;` or together with the declaration `int (*p)[5] = &arr;`

Another complex declaration: `int *(*p)(int);`

Like before, we start that p is "a pointer to ...", the () take precedence over *, so we go right and have "a pointer to a function with an integer argument ...", then, go left to add the return type and end up with "a pointer to a function with an integer argument that returns a pointer to an integer".

Leave the best for the end: `int *(*p[5])(int*);`

Like before, we start deciphering p inside the parentheses. p is "...", because [] take precedence over *, we go right and have "an array of five ...", then, go left to *, "an array of five pointers ...", then, because () take precedence over * go right and have "an array of five pointers to functions with argument pointer to an integer ...", then, go left to add the return type and end up with the train "an array of five pointers to functions with argument pointer to an integer that returns a pointer to an integer".

With so many left-right zigzagging we feel a little dizzy, just remember, **never drive drunk**. And always fasten your seatbelt or put your helmet on. Also, do not run fast or talk on your cell phone. Drive safe for your own good and for the others.

THE return STATEMENT

The `return` statement is used to terminate immediately the execution of a function. A function can contain as many `return` statements as we need. In some programs so far, we've used the `return` statement to terminate the `main()` function, that is, the program itself when a condition is met. For example, the following program terminates if the user enters 2, otherwise it outputs the input value:

```cpp
#include <iostream> // Example 11.3
int main()
{
        int num;

        while(1)
        {
                std::cout << "Enter number: ";
                std::cin >> num;

                if(num == 2)
                        return 0; // Terminate the program.
                else // else is not needed.
                        std::cout << num << '\n';
        }
        return 0;
}
```

Notice that the last `return` will never be executed, since the first `return` terminates the program. The value returned by `main()` indicates the termination status of the program. The value 0 indicates normal termination, whereas a non-zero value typically indicates an abnormal termination.

If the function returns nothing, we just write `return`. Also, in this case, the `return` statement at the end of the function is unnecessary, since the function will return automatically. In the following example, the `f()` function compares the values of the two parameters and, if they are different, it displays their average. If they are the same, the function terminates.

```cpp
void f(int a, int b)
{
        // Function body.
        if(a == b)
                return;

        cout << (a+b)/2.0;
        // It is not needed to add the return statement.
}
```

If the function is declared to return a value, each `return` statement should be followed by a value. As we'll see later, the value of the executed `return` is returned to the point at which the function was called. The calling function is free to use or discard the returned value. For example, I modified `f()` to return an integer value:

```cpp
int f(int a, int b)
{
        if(a == b)
                return 0;

        cout << (a+b)/2.0;
        return 1;
}
```

Notice that we are allowed to omit the second `return` statement at the end of the function. In that case, the compiler would, most probably, issue a warning message such as *'f': not all control paths return a value* or *control reaches end of non-void function*. The standard says that leaving from a value-returning function (except `main()`) without a `return` statement causes undefined behaviour. The function would return an undefined value, which is undesirable and certainly very dangerous if the calling function uses that return value. So, we must be very careful to make a non-`void` function always return a value through all return paths, otherwise unexpected problems may occur.

The type of the returned value should match the function's return type. If it does not match, the compiler will convert the returned value, if possible, to the return type. For example:

```
int test()
{
        return 4.9;
}
```

Since `test()` is declared to return an `int` value, the returned value is implicitly converted to `int`. Therefore, the function returns `4`.

FUNCTION CALL

A function can be called as many times as needed. When a function is called, the execution of the program continues with the execution of the function's code. In particular, the compiler allocates memory to store the function's parameters and the variables that are declared within its body. Typically, this memory is reserved from a specific part of the memory, called *stack*; however, it might not apply in all cases. For example, parameters are typically passed in system registers for faster access. For simplicity, we assume that the memory is allocated in the stack. Moreover, the compiler allocates memory to store the memory address where the program returns once the function terminates. The allocated memory is automatically released when the function terminates. A more detailed discussion about the actions performed in the memory when a function is called is beyond the scope of this book.

Function Call without Parameters

A call to a function that does not take any parameters is made by writing the function name followed by empty parentheses `()`, which constitute the call operator. The calling function does not pass any data to the called function. In the following program, the calling function, that is, `main()`, calls twice the `test()` function:

```
#include <iostream> // Example 11.4

void test();

int main()
{
        std::cout << "Call_1 ";
        test(); /* Function call. The parentheses are empty, because the
function does not take any parameters. */
        std::cout << "Call_2 ";
        test(); // Second call.
        return 0;
}
```

```
void test()
{
        // Function body.
        for(int i = 0; i < 2; i++)
                std::cout << "In ";
}
```

At the first call of test(), the program continues with the execution of the function body. When test() terminates, the execution of the program returns to the calling point and continues with the execution of the next statement. Therefore, the main program displays Call_2 and calls test() again. As a result, the program displays: Call_1 In In Call_2 In In.

   A common oversight is to omit the parentheses when the function is called.

For example, if you write test the program will compile, but the function won't get called. Recall from Chapter 8 that the compiler treats the name of a function as a pointer; therefore, it permits the statement. However, this statement has no effect; it evaluates the address of the function but does not call it. The compiler may issue a warning message such as *function call missing argument list* or *statement with no effect* to inform the programmer. In the following program, test() returns an integer value.

```
#include <iostream> // Example 11.5

int test();

int main()
{
        int sum;

        sum = test(); // Function call. The returned value is stored in sum.
        std::cout << sum << '\n';
        return 0;
}

int test()
{
        int i = 10, j = 20;
        return i+j;
}
```

test() declares two integer variables with values 10 and 20 and returns their sum. This value is stored into sum and the program displays 30. Note that it is not needed to declare sum; we could write cout << test(); test() is called first and then cout outputs the return value.

Before ending this section, I'd like to point out that the order of the function calls in a compound expression such as: d = a()+ b()* c();
is undefined. That is, these three functions can be called in any order. Don't assume that the b() and c() functions will be called first because of the multiplication's precedence. And, be aware, if any of them changes the value of a variable on which some other variable in another function may depend, the value assigned to d may depend on the evaluation order.

Function Call with Parameters

A call to a function that takes parameters is made by writing the function name followed by a list of arguments, enclosed in parentheses. Using arguments is one way to pass information to a function. Typically, a function needs arguments to perform a task. The difference between *parameter* and *argument* is that the term *parameter* refers to the variables that appear in the definition of the function, while the term *argument* refers to the expressions that appear in the function call. For example, consider the following program:

```cpp
#include <iostream> // Example 11.6

int test(int x, int y);

int main()
{
    int sum, a = 10, b = 20;

    sum = test(a, b); /* The variables a and b become the function's
arguments. */
    std::cout << sum << '\n';
    return 0;
}

int test(int x, int y) /* The variables x and y are the function's
parameters. */
{
    return x+y;
}
```

The argument can be any valid expression, such as constant, variable, math, or logical expression, even another function with a return value. Note that we could omit sum and write: cout << test(a, b); test() is called first, and then cout outputs the return value.

The number of the arguments and their types should match the function declaration. If the arguments are less, the compiler will produce an error message. If the types of the arguments do not match the types of the parameters, the compiler will try to convert implicitly the types of the mismatched arguments to the types of the corresponding parameters. For example, if the mismatched types are arithmetic, the compiler will apply the arithmetic conversions as we saw in Chapter 2. If the compiler succeeds to make the conversion, it may display a warning message to inform the programmer for the type conversion. For example, if a narrowing conversion is applied (e.g., double to int) the compiler will most probably issue a warning. If the conversion is not possible, the compiler will produce an error message. Let's see some examples:

```cpp
test(10.9, b); /* The double type can be converted to int. So, the compiler
will pass the value 10 and the program will be compiled. When a narrowing
conversion is applied and because information may be lost, the compiler will
most probably issue a warning. If you really want to truncate a variable, use
a cast to say it explicitly. */
test(a); // Wrong, smaller number of arguments.
test(a, b, 10); // Wrong, larger number of arguments.
test(a, "Text"); /* Wrong, invalid argument type. Cannot convert from const
char* to int. */
```

Let's return to the program. When it is executed, the compiler allocates eight bytes to store the values of a and b. When test() is called, the compiler allocates another eight bytes to store the values of x and y. Then, the arguments are evaluated and their values are assigned one-to-one to the corresponding memory locations of the parameters x and y. Note that the compiler can evaluate the argument values in any order. Essentially, each function parameter is a variable that is created when the function is called. The initialization value is the value of the corresponding argument. Therefore, x becomes 10 and y becomes 20. When test() terminates, the memory allocated for x and y is automatically released.

Since the memory locations of x and y are different from those of a and b, any changes in the values of x and y have no effect on the values of a and b. This method of passing values is called *call by value*. In other words, the called function always receives the values of the arguments in copies of the original variables. It cannot modify the value of the variable used as an argument; it can only modify the value of its copy. Regarding performance, the call by value cost is the overhead in memory and time to copy the passed arguments.

As we'll see later, an exception to that rule is the arrays. When an array is passed to a function, no copy of the array is made. It is the address of its first element that it is actually passed. The function can access and modify any element of the array.

Change Original Values

If we want the function to be able to modify the value of the original variable, we should pass its address and not its value, as before. How we get the address? You know that, by using a pointer. Let's see an example:

```cpp
#include <iostream> // Example 11.7

void test(int *p, int a);

int main()
{
        int i = 10, j = 20;

        test(&i, j);
        std::cout << i << ' ' << j << '\n';
        return 0;
}

void test(int *p, int a)
{
        *p = 30;
        a = 40;
}
```

Since the type of &i is pointer to int, the call of test() matches the declaration. When test() is called, we have p = &i. Since p points to i, test() may change the value of i. In particular, *p is an alias for i, and the statement *p = 30; changes i from 10 to 30. As it is shown, when a function is called, it is allowed to mix pointers and plain values. The value of j does not change and the program outputs 30 and 20.

Thanks to pointers, since a function cannot return more than one value, we can pass the addresses of the arguments we want to change their values.

Regarding performance, when passing small values (e.g., int) call by value is fine, but when passing large entities (e.g., a vector that contains thousands of elements) it is much more efficient to pass the address and avoid copying the data. In Chapter 16, we'll see an alternative way to pass the address through a reference.

What about if we only want to use the value of the argument and prevent any changes? You know the answer; we make the pointer `const`.

```cpp
void test(const int *p, int a) // We also change the declaration.
{
        if(*p == 10) // Fine.
                *p = 30; // Error.
}
```

One last example to test what you've learned so far. What is the output of the following program? Do not rush to see the answer on the next page. Easy, make no mistake.

```cpp
#include <iostream> // Example 11.8

void test(int *arg);

int var = 100;

int main()
{
        int *ptr, i = 30;

        ptr = &i;
        test(ptr);
        std::cout << *ptr << '\n';
        return 0;
}

void test(int *arg)
{
        arg = &var;
}
```

Easy, who said it is easy? You answered 100, didn't you? *Basket Case* from *Green Day*, play it loud. Let's see the trap.

Because test() accepts the value of ptr as an argument and not its address, it cannot change its value. Therefore, any change in the value of arg does not affect the value of ptr and the program displays 30. We'll discuss the scope of var in a moment.

And how can a function change the value of a pointer? We just pass to the function the address of the pointer, that is, an argument of type pointer to a pointer. For example:

```cpp
#include <iostream> // Example 11.9

void test(int **arg);

int var = 100;

int main()
{
        int *ptr, i = 30;

        ptr = &i;
        test(&ptr); /* The value of &ptr is the memory address of ptr, which
points to the address of i. So, the type of the argument is a pointer to a
pointer to an integer and matches the int** type in the function declaration. */
        std::cout << *ptr << '\n';
        return 0;
}

void test(int **arg)
{
        *arg = &var;
}
```

Since the memory address of ptr is passed to test(), test() may change its value. When test() is called, we have arg = &ptr, so *arg = ptr. Therefore, the statement *arg = &var; is equivalent to ptr = &var; which means that the value of ptr changes and points to the address of var. Therefore, the program displays 100.

I do understand that you might find this example a bit difficult. However, because you'll most probably need to read or write code that changes the value of a pointer, I added here so that it is easy to find and consult it. Enough with the theory, let's have some practice.

EXERCISES

C.11.1 Write two functions that take an integer parameter and return the square and the cube of this number, respectively. The restriction is that the body of the second function consists of a single statement and calls the first. Write a program that reads an integer and uses the functions to display the sum of the number's square and cube.

```cpp
#include <iostream>

int square(int a);
int cube(int a);
```

```
int main()
{
        int i, j, k;

        std::cout << "Enter number: ";
        std::cin >> i;

        j = square(i);
        k = cube(i);
        std::cout << j+k << '\n'; /* We could omit the declarations of j and k
and write cout << square(i)+cube(i); */
        return 0;
}

int square(int a)
{
        return a*a;
}

int cube(int a)
{
        return a*square(a);
}
```

C.11.2 What is the output of the following program?

```
#include <iostream>

void test(int *p1, int *p2);

int main()
{
        int i = 10, j = 20;

        test(&i, &j);
        std::cout << i << ' ' << j << '\n';
        return 0;
}

void test(int *p1, int *p2)
{
        int m, *tmp;

        tmp = p1;
        p1 = &m;
        *p1 = 100;

        *p2 += m;
        p2 = tmp;
        *p2 = 100;
}
```

Answer: When test() is called, we have p1 = &i and p2 = &j. The statements p1 = &m; and *p1 = 100; make m equal to 100. Since p2 points to the address of j, *p2 is 20. Therefore, the statement *p2 += m; makes j equal to 20+100 = 120. Since tmp points to the address of i, the statement p2 = tmp; is equivalent to p2 = &i. Therefore, the statement *p2 = 100; changes the value of i to 100. As a result, the program outputs: 100 120

C.11.3 Write a function that takes as parameters an integer and a character and displays the character as many times as the value of the integer. Also, the function should use the `switch` statement to return the same character if it is `'a'`, `'b'` or `'c'`, otherwise the next character in the ASCII set. Write a program that reads an integer and a character, calls the function, and displays the return value.

```cpp
#include <iostream>
using std::cout;
using std::cin;

char show(int num, char c);

int main()
{
        char c;
        int i;

        cout << "Enter character: ";
        cin >> c;

        cout << "Enter number: ";
        cin >> i;

        c = show(i, c);
        cout << '\n' << c << '\n'; /* We could call show() here and not
before, that is, to write show(i, c) in place of c. */
        return 0;
}

char show(int num, char c)
{
        for(int i = 0; i < num; i++)
                cout << c;

        switch(c)
        {
                case 'a':
                case 'b':
                case 'c':
                return c;

                default:
                return c+1;
        }
}
```

C.11.4 Write a function that takes as parameters three floats and displays their minimum. Also, the function should return the average of those within [1, 2]. If none of them is in [1, 2], it should return -1. Write a program that reads three floats, calls the function, and displays the return value.

```cpp
#include <iostream>

double min_avg(double a, double b, double c);

int main()
{
        double i, j, k, r;
```

```
std::cout << "Enter numbers: ";
std::cin >> i >> j >> k;

r = min_avg(i, j, k);
if(r == -1)
        std::cout << "No value in [1, 2]\n";
else
        std::cout << "Avg:" << r << '\n';
return 0;
}

double min_avg(double a, double b, double c)
{
        int k = 0;
        double sum = 0;

        if(a <= b && a <= c)
                std::cout << "Min:" << a << '\n';
        else if(b < a && b < c)
                std::cout << "Min:" << b << '\n';
        else
                std::cout << "Min:" << c << '\n';

        if(a >= 1 && a <= 2)
        {
                sum += a;
                k++;
        }
        if(b >= 1 && b <= 2)
        {
                sum += b;
                k++;
        }
        if(c >= 1 && c <= 2)
        {
                sum += c;
                k++;
        }
        if(k != 0)
                return sum/k;
        else
                return -1;
}
```

C.11.5 What is the output of the following program?

```
#include <iostream>

int f(int a);

int main()
{
        int i = 10;

        std::cout << f(3-f(2*f(i+1))) << '\n';
        return 0;
}
```

```
int f(int a)
{
        return a+1;
}
```

Answer: Each time `f()` is called it returns the value of its argument incremented by one. The calls are executed inside out. Therefore, since the first call returns 12, the argument in the second call is 24. Since the second call returns 25, the argument in the third call is -22. Therefore, the program displays -21.

C.11.6 Write the `power(double a, int b)` function, which returns the result of a^b. Write a program that reads a float number (e.g., a) and an integer (e.g., b) and uses the function to display the result of a^b.

```
#include <iostream>
using std::cout;
using std::cin;

double power(double a, int b);

int main()
{
        int exp;
        double base;

        cout << "Enter base: ";
        cin >> base;

        cout << "Enter exponent: ";
        cin >> exp;
        cout << base << " power " << exp << " = " << power(base, exp) << '\n';
        return 0;
}

double power(double a, int b)
{
        int i, exp;
        double val;

        val = 1; // Necessary initialization.
        exp = b;
        if(exp < 0) // If the exponent is negative, we make it positive.
                exp = -exp;
        for(i = 0; i < exp; i++)
                val *= a;
        if(b < 0)
                val = 1/val;
        return val;
}
```

Comments: Note that the program does not check extreme conditions such as an overflow case or the use of more efficient algorithms. For example, instead of executing the loop `exp` times we could check if `exp` is even and, if it is, to execute the loop `exp`/2 times, and then square the result. If it is odd, multiply the result once more with a. For example, if `exp` is 8, the loop is executed 4 times $(a^4)^2$. For the same purpose, the C++ library provides the `pow()` function.

C.11.7 Write a function that takes an integer parameter (e.g., n) and returns the result of: $1^3 + 2^3 + 3^3 + \ldots + n^3$. Write a program that reads a positive integer (suppose that the user enters a valid value) and uses the function to display the square root of the result of that expression. Verify that the output value is equal to $n*(n+1)/2$. For the square root write another function that uses the Newton method to find the root of the argument (e.g., n). This method uses some initial guess r_1 for the square root (e.g., n/2) and computes the sequence of values according to $r_{k+1} = 0.5*(r_k + n/r_k)$. If the absolute difference between the new value r_{k+1} and the old value r_k is less than a tolerance (e.g., 0.0001), then the function should return the value of r_{k+1} as the root. For the difference use the `fabs()` library function.

```
#include <iostream>
#include <cmath>

unsigned long long int sum_cube(int n);
double find_root(unsigned long long int n);

int main()
{
        int num;

        std::cout << "Enter number: ";
        std::cin >> num;

        std::cout << find_root(sum_cube(num)) << ' ' << num*(num+1)/2 << '\n';
return 0;
}

unsigned long long int sum_cube(int n)
{
        int i;
        unsigned long long int sum;

        sum = 0;
        for(i = 1; i <= n; i++)
                sum += i*i*i;
        return sum;
}
double find_root(unsigned long long int n)
{
        double old_r, new_r;

        old_r = n/2.0;
        while(1)
        {
                new_r = 0.5*(old_r + n/old_r);
                if(fabs(new_r - old_r) < 0.0001)
                        break;
                old_r = new_r;
        }
        return new_r;
}
```

C.11.8 Write a `void` function that takes as parameters the coefficients of a quadratic equation and returns its real roots, if any. Write a program that reads the coefficients (e.g., a, b, and c) and uses the function to solve the equation. The program should force the user to enter a non-zero value for a. It is reminded from algebra that in order to find the roots of the equation $ax^2 + bx + c = 0$ with $a \neq 0$, the discriminant $D = b^2 - 4ac$ is tested.

    a. If $D > 0$, it has two roots $r_{1,2} = (-b \pm \sqrt{D})/2a$.
    b. If $D = 0$, it has one double root $r = -b/2a$.
    c. If $D < 0$, it has no real root.

```cpp
#include <iostream>
#include <cmath>
using std::cout;
using std::cin;

void find_roots(double a, double b, double c, double *r1, double *r2, int *code);

int main()
{
        int code;
        double a, b, c, r1, r2;

        do
        {
                cout << "Enter coefficients (a<>0): ";
                cin >> a >> b >> c;
        } while(a == 0);

        find_roots(a, b, c, &r1, &r2, &code);
        if(code == 2)
                cout << "Two roots: " << r1 << ' ' << r2 << '\n';
        else if(code == 1)
                cout << "One root: " << r1 << '\n';
        else
                cout << "Not real roots\n";
        return 0;
}

void find_roots(double a, double b, double c, double *r1, double *r2, int *code)
{
        double d;

        d = b*b-4*a*c;
        if(d > 0)
        {
                *code = 2;
                *r1 = (-b+sqrt(d))/(2*a);
                *r2 = (-b-sqrt(d))/(2*a);
        }
        else if(d == 0)
        {
                *code = 1;
                *r1 = *r2 = -b/(2*a);
        }
        else
                *code = 0;
}
```

Comments: Since the return type is void we use pointer parameters, so that the function can return the desired values.

C.11.9 In math, the trapezoidal rule is a technique for approximating the definite integral of a function $f(x)$ within an interval [a, b]. The rule works by adding the areas of the trapezoids that are formed when approximating the function with a polyline, as depicted in the following figure:

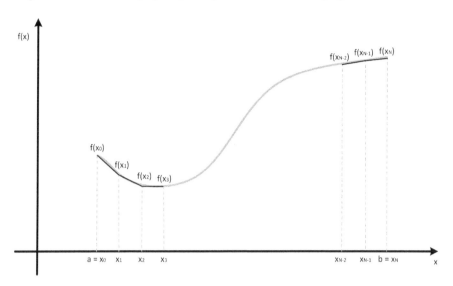

The procedure involves the following steps:

a. Split the interval [a, b] into N subintervals of the same width. Therefore, $x_i = x_0 + \frac{i \times (b-a)}{N}$, $i = 0,...,N$. For larger values of N, the approximation is closer the value of the integral.

b. Calculate the values $f(x_i)$ for $i = 0,...,N$.

c. Calculate the areas of the N trapezoids formed under the polyline and add them. The integral is approximately:

$$\int_a^b f(x) = E_{\tau\rho 1} + \cdots + E_{\tau\rho N} = \frac{(x_1 - x_0) \times (f(x_0) + f(x_1))}{2} + \cdots + \frac{(x_N - x_{N-1}) \times (f(x_{N-1}) + f(x_N))}{2}$$

Write a program that uses the trapezoidal rule to approximate the value of the integral $\int_a^b x^2 = \left[\frac{x^3}{3} \right]_a^b$. The program should read the number N, the limits a and b, and check their validity.

```cpp
#include <iostream>
using std::cout;
using std::cin;

double f(double x);

int main()
{
        int i, a, b, n;
        double step, x, area;

        do
        {
                cout << "Enter number of intervals: ";
                cin >> n;
        } while(n <= 0);
```

```
        do
        {
                cout << "Enter low and up limit (a < b): ";
                cin >> a >> b;
        } while(a >= b);

        step = (double)(b-a)/n;
        x = a;
        area = 0;
        for(i = 0; i < n; i++)
        {
                area += 0.5*step*(f(x)+f(x+step));
                x += step;
        }
        cout << "Calculus = " << area << '\n';
        return 0;
}

double f(double x) /* We're using a function so that if we've to calculate
the integral of another function we just change the code here. */
{
        return x*x;
}
```

STORAGE CLASSES AND VARIABLES SCOPE

Every variable is characterized by three properties: *scope*, *storage class*, and *linkage*. The default properties of a variable depend on the point of its declaration.

The *scope* of a variable is the part of the program in which the variable is accessible, or else, it is visible from the other parts of the program. As we'll see later, the scope of a variable depends on the point of its declaration within the program. In general, it is in scope from the point of its declaration until the end of the scope in which it is declared.

The kind of memory used to store a variable is called its *storage class*. Together with the scope of the variable, the storage class determines the storage duration, simply put, the lifetime of the variable. A variable can have one of the following storage durations: *automatic*, *static*, *dynamic* (we'll explain that in Chapter 14), or *thread* (we don't discuss threads in this book). We'll explain the meaning of automatic and static duration in a moment. Until C++11, the keyword `auto` was used to specify the automatic storage class. As we know, its meaning was changed in C++11 and since then it is used to indicate automatic type deduction. Its former meaning as a storage class specifier is no longer valid. C++98 also used the `register` keyword to indicate automatic storage duration, but it was deprecated in C++11 and removed in C++17.

The *linkage* of a variable concerns the linker and determines whether it can be shared by different parts of the program. A variable with *external linkage* may be shared by different files in the program, while a variable with *internal linkage* is restricted to the file that it is declared; however, it may be shared by the functions in that file. A variable with *no linkage* belongs to a function and cannot be shared.

Local Variables

A variable declared within the body of a function is called *local*. A local variable has *block* scope; its scope is constrained inside the function from the point of its declaration to the end of the block that contains its declaration. This means that the other functions of the program cannot access it. Since a local variable is not visible outside the function in which it is declared, we can use the same name to declare variables in other functions. For example, in the following program, the local variable i declared in main() is different from the local variable i declared in test(), although they have the same name:

```cpp
#include <iostream> // Example 11.10

void test();

int main()
{
        int i = 10;

        test();
        std::cout << "I_main = " << i << '\n';
        return 0;
}

void test()
{
        int i = 200;
        std::cout << "I_test = " << i << '\n';
}
```

Since the variables are different, each has its own value, and the program outputs: I_test = 200 and I_main = 10. What happens if we don't declare i as int in test() and write i = 200;?

Since the two i variables are unrelated, the compiler would issue an error message that the variable i in test() is undeclared.

Note that the parameters of the function are also considered local variables of the function. For example:

```cpp
#include <iostream> // Example 11.11

void test(int i, int j);

int main()
{
        int i = 100, j = 100;

        test(i, j);
        std::cout << i << ' ' << j << '\n';
        return 0;
}

void test(int i, int j)
{
        int a = 2000; // The local variables of the function are a, i and j.
        i = j = a;
}
```

Since the parameters of the function are also local variables, the variables i and j of test() are not related with those of main(). Therefore, the program displays: 100 100

A variable whose lifetime lasts as long as the code runs inside a block and ceases to exist outside that block is called *automatic* and is said to have an *automatic* storage duration. All the variables we have used so far in the programs of this book are automatic.

Each time a function is called, the compiler allocates memory to create its local variables. This memory is automatically released when the function terminates; therefore, a local variable does not retain its value between successive calls. Because a local variable ceases to exist when the function terminates it is an automatic variable. To sum up, the default properties of a local variable is block scope, no linkage, and automatic storage duration. Because the parameters of a function are in effect local variables they have the same properties.

As we said, C++98 supports the `register` storage class specifier, which was removed in C++17. I'll provide some short description in case you meet it. The `register` specifier indicates automatic storage duration; it can be applied to automatic variables and to the parameters of a function. A `register` variable has the same scope, linkage, and lifetime as an automatic variable. Declaring a local variable as `register` (e.g., `register int i;`) is a hint to the compiler that the variable will be used a lot and suggests to save it in a system register for faster access. However, the compiler is free to ignore that hint and store the variable in the main memory as it does with other variables. Modern compilers have been evolved a lot and can determine by themselves whether some variables should be stored in registers or not. As such, C++17 decided that there is no reason to keep it and removed it from the language.

Since the memory of a local variable is released, a function should not return its address. For example:

```cpp
#include <iostream> // Example 11.12

int *test();

int main()
{
        int *ptr, j;

        ptr = test();
        std::cout << *ptr << '\n';

        j = *ptr;
        std::cout << j << '\n';
        return 0;
}

int *test()
{
        int i = 10;
        return &i; // Serious error, don't do it.
}
```

When `test()` is called, the compiler allocates memory for the local variable `i`. Once it terminates, it returns the address of `i`. However, since this memory is released, new data can be stored there and overwrite the value `10`. Therefore, the program may output `10` and a random value, or two random values, instead of `10` and `10`. The behaviour of the program is unpredictable. Most probably, the compiler will warn you with a message such as *returning address of local variable*.

However, as we'll see later, if we declare the variable `i` as `static` we can safely return its address, because the memory allocated for a `static` variable is not released when the function terminates.

 Don't return the address of a local variable unless it is declared as `static`.

Somewhere later, there will be an exercise to test if you digested this rule. Look forward for your answer.

Declare Variables within Block

Although in all the examples of this book we declare the automatic variables at the beginning of the function, we are allowed to declare variables after the { of a compound statement. The general form of a compound statement is { declarations statements }, and that form specifies a block. The scope of a variable declared in a block extends up to the matching}; therefore, it does not conflict with any other variable outside the block having the same name. By default, its storage duration is automatic; the compiler allocates memory to store it when the block is entered and releases that memory when the block is exited. Consider the following program:

```
#include <iostream> // Example 11.13
int main()
{
        int i = 20, num = 10;

        if(num == 10)
        {
                int i; /* Memory for the new i is allocated only if the
condition is true. */
                i = 50;
        } // Release that memory.
        std::cout << i << '\n';
        return 0;
}
```

Because the i variable declared inside the if block is unrelated to the first i, the program displays 20. A reason to declare a variable inside a compound statement instead of the beginning of a function is that memory will be allocated only if needed. This might be useful when writing applications for systems with limited memory. A compound statement is not needed to join a conditional or loop statement; it can exist on its own. For example, the following program outputs 50 and 20.

```
#include <iostream> // Example 11.14
int main()
{
        int i = 20;

        {
                int i = 50; // Allocate memory for that i.
                std::cout << i << '\n';
        } // Release that memory.
        std::cout << i << '\n';
        return 0;
}
```

Global Variables

A variable that is declared outside of any function and types with block scope, such as enumeration, class, or namespace, is called *global*. Its scope extends from the point of its declaration to the end of the file in which it is declared. Therefore, it can be accessed by all functions that follow its declaration. Unlike an automatic variable, a global variable has a permanent lifetime and retains its last assigned value. Memory is reserved for it when the program starts and is released when the program terminates. To sum up, the default properties of a global variable is file scope, external linkage, and static storage duration. To make it clear, static storage duration means that the variable remains in existence permanently until the program terminates.

When the same variable is used in many functions, many programmers tend to declare it as global instead of passing it as an argument in function calls. In fact, a global variable can be used as an alternative way for communicating data between functions. Note that for the better control and understanding of the program, it is very helpful that the name you choose for a global variable describes its role. For example, don't use meaningless names that are often given in local variables (e.g., `i`).

By default, the compiler initializes a global variable or the elements of a composite type (e.g., array) to 0; however, I prefer to do it myself in order to make it clear. Let's see an example of using global variables:

```cpp
#include <iostream> // Example 11.15

void add();
void sub();

int glob = 0; /* Although the compiler initializes it to 0, I prefer to do it
myself. */

int main()
{
        add();
        glob += 2;
        sub();
        std::cout << glob << '\n';
        return 0;
}

void add()
{
        glob++;
}

void sub()
{
        glob--;
}
```

All functions have access to the global `glob` variable, since it is declared before their definitions. The program displays 2.

Although global variables may seem tempting to use, you should better avoid their use. One reason is that it makes more difficult to identify erroneous conditions. For example, if a wrong value is assigned to a global variable, we have to check all the functions that use it in order to identify the guilty one. Also, excessive relying on global variables may have a bad effect on program design and make it more difficult to understand and manage. For example, it'd be more difficult for the reader to correlate each global variable with the functions that use it. In general, in large programs where each file may use hundreds of variables you should keep them as local as possible for the better management and maintenance of the program.

Scope Rules

A local variable may have the same name with a global variable. The scope rule says that when a variable inside a block is named the same with another variable that is already visible, the new declaration hides the old one in that block. For example:

```cpp
#include <iostream> // Example 11.16

void test();
void last(int a);

int a = 100;
```

```cpp
int main()
{
        test();
        a += 50;
        std::cout << a << ' ';
        last(200);
        return 0;
}

void test()
{
        int a = 300;

        if(a == 300)
        {
                int a = 500;
                a++;
                std::cout << a << ' ';
        }
        a += 20;
        std::cout << a << ' ';
}

void last(int a)
{
        a++;
        std::cout << a << '\n';
}
```

The four variables named a are different. Let's apply the scope rule. The a tested in the `if` condition is the one declared in `test()`, while the statement a++; refers to the a declared in the `if` block. Its scope is up to the}, and the next statement a+=20; increases the a of `test()`. Its scope is up to the} at the end of the function. `main()` increases the value of the global a which becomes 150. `last()` increases the local parameter a which becomes 201. As a result, the program outputs: 501 320 150 201. This program is just an example to show you how the scope rule applies when using the same name; it is a bad programming approach. As you see, the code becomes harder to read, confusing, and error prone.

To access a global name we can use the scope resolution operator `::`. Since the global namespace has no name, nothing is added to the left of `::`. For example:

```cpp
int a = 100;
void f()
{
        int a = 300;
        if(::a == 100) // Access the global variable.
        {
                ...
        }
}
```

The scope of names declared in a `for` statement is local, that is, it extends to its end. Thus, we can use the same names many times in a function. For example:

```cpp
void f()
{
        for(int i = 0; i < 5; i++)
        {
                ...
        }
```

```
        for(int i = 10; i > 3; i--) /* If we don't declare i again, the
compiler will display an error message. */
        {
            ...
        }
}
```

Use of extern

A global variable can be visible in more than one source file, that is, it may have external linkage. This is very useful, particularly in large programs, because several source files may need to share the same variable. The `extern` keyword is a storage class specifier that enables a variable to be shared among several files. Typically, such a variable is declared as global in the file used most and the other files refer to it using the `extern` keyword.

We've discussed about the distinction between *declaring* and *defining* a variable in Chapter 2. Let's see again the difference. The statement `int size;` not only declares the type of `size` to be `int`, but defines `size` as well, that is, the compiler allocates memory to store its value. A variable can have only one definition; other files may contain `extern` declarations to access it. For example, to use it in another file we write:

```
// Second file.
extern int size; // Only declaration.
```

Because of the word `extern`, the variable `size` is only declared, that is, the compiler is informed about the name and the type of the variable. The variable is not defined, that is, the compiler does not allocate new memory for it. The word `extern` informs the compiler that the variable `size` is defined somewhere else. The linker will link the reference to `size` with its definition in another file. If we forget the word `extern`, the separate compilation for each file will be successful, but the linker will display an error message that `size` is defined twice. Note that the variable can only be initialized when it is defined, that is, it is wrong to write in the second file:

```
extern int size = 10; // Wrong.
```

`size` can be accessed and modified, if needed, in any of those files that is referred to as `extern`. Since the compiler does not allocate new memory, if the variable is an array we can omit its length in an extern declaration. For example:

```
extern int arr[];
```

Note that the linkage of a `const` global variable, as well as of a `static` one as we'll see below, is internal, that is, the variable can only be used in the file that contains its declaration. For example:

```
const int size = 10; // Internal linkage.
```

If we want it to have an external linkage, we must add the word `extern` to its definition. For example:

```
extern const int size = 10; // External linkage.
```

To use it in another file we write: `extern const int size;`.

Test time. Find the errors in the following example:

```
// first.cpp
int i = 10;
double d;
extern float f;

// second.cpp
int i;
extern int d;
extern float f;
```

All declarations in the second file are wrong. `i` is defined twice, `d` is declared twice with different types, and `f` is declared twice but not defined. As I said, such errors are not detected by the compiler, but by the linker. Note that the errors for `d` and `f` will be detected when used in the program.

Essentially, `extern` is another way for data exchange between functions that reside in different files. Although sharing variables among files is quite popular, care has to be taken, because a wrong assignment in one file may induce unpredictable results in the other files that use it. Also, a program that uses many `extern` variables is more difficult to read and maintain, since the independencies of the `extern` variables make it more complex. Thus, as with global variables, I try to avoid using `extern` variables. We'll see an example of using `extern` variables later in this chapter and in the program of Chapter 27.

Static Variables

As discussed, the memory that is allocated to store a local variable is released when the function terminates. Therefore, there is no guarantee that a local variable would still have its old value when the function is called again. If we want a local variable to retain its value, we should use the `static` storage class specifier. Unlike an ordinary local variable, a `static` variable has static storage duration, that is, it has a permanent lifetime. The memory for a `static` variable is reserved only the first time the function is called. The variable resides at the same memory location throughout program execution, and that memory is not released when the function terminates, but once the program terminates. To sum up, the default properties of a `static` variable declared inside a function is block scope, no linkage, and static storage duration.

A `static` variable is initialized only once, the first time that the function is called. As with a global variable, the initializer must be a constant expression; if it is not explicitly initialized, the default value is `0`. In next calls, it retains its last value and it is not initialized again. For example, consider the following program:

```
#include <iostream> // Example 11.17

void test();

int main()
{
        test();
        test();
        test();
        return 0;
}
```

```cpp
void test()
{
        static int i = 100, arr[1];
        int j = 0;

        i++;
        arr[0] += 2;
        j++;
        std::cout << i << ' ' << arr[0] << ' ' << j << '\n';
}
```

When `test()` is first called, `i` becomes `101`. Since `i` is declared as `static`, it retains its value and the next call of `test()` makes it `102`. Similarly, the third call makes it `103`. Since the elements of a static array are initialised to `0` by default, `arr[0]` becomes `2`, `4`, and `6`, respectively. On the other hand, since `j` is an automatic variable it does not retain its value between `test()` calls. Therefore, the program outputs:

```
101 2 1
102 4 1
103 6 1
```

A `static` variable declared inside a block is initialized only the first time the block is entered. For example:

```cpp
#include <iostream> // Example 11.18

void test(int num);

int main()
{
        test(50);
        test(10);
        test(10);
        return 0;
}

void test(int num)
{
        if (num == 10)
        {
                static int i = 100;
                i++;
                std::cout << i << ' ';
        }
}
```

The program outputs: `101  102`

The use of `static` may improve the performance. For example, if a `const` variable is declared inside a function which is called many times, it'd be more efficient to declare it as `static` as well, so that it is initialized only once. Thus, the function is executed faster. Here is an example:

```cpp
void test()
{
        static const int c = 200;
        ...
}
```

The linkage of a global variable or function is external by default, that is, it may be shared in different files. However, if it is declared as `static`, the linkage changes to internal, which means that it is visible only within the file in which it is defined. For example:

```
#include <iostream>
using namespace std;

static void test(int i);
static int flag;

int main()
{
        ...
}

static void test(int i)
{
        ...
}
```

`flag` and `test()` are visible only within this file, which means that they cannot be accessed by functions in other files. In particular, `flag` has file scope, static storage duration, but internal linkage. The main reason of declaring them as `static` is to hide them from other files, thus, preventing to be used as `extern` when it is not desired. In fact, in a large program split in several files, typically written by different programmers, it is a good idea to declare your functions as `static`. Besides information hiding, another reason is that if the code of a `static` function should be modified later, you won't concern if those changes affect functions in other files (with the exception that a pointer to that function is passed to a function of another file). Also, you don't have to worry if the names you choose are used in other files as well, because, even if it happens, there will be no conflict. Since the linkage is internal, the same names can be reused in other files. Another way to define names with internal linkage, and this is what is recommended, is by using unnamed namespaces, as we'll see in Chapter 25. However, since `static` is used quite extensively in existing code it is good to know how it is used.

Let's see one last example that combines these concepts. Consider the following program which consists of two source files. Both must be compiled and linked to produce the final executable. Can you tell me what does it display?

```
// First file.
#include <iostream> // Example 11.19

void test();
int ext = 10;
static int st = 20;

int main()
{
        test();
        std::cout << ext << ' ' << st << '\n';
        return 0;
}

// Second file.
#include <iostream>

extern int ext;
static int st;
```

```
void test()
{
        st++;
        std::cout << ext << ' ' << st << '\n';
        ext = 30;
}
```

Since the st is declared in the first file as static it does not conflict with the st in the second file (regardless if this second st is declared static or not). Note that the test() is defined in the second file. Since, st is initialized to 0 by default, test() displays 10 and 1. Since test() changes the value of ext to 30, main() displays 30 and 20.

ONE-DIMENSIONAL ARRAY AS ARGUMENT

When a parameter of a function is a one-dimensional array, we write the name of the array followed by a pair of brackets. The length of the array can be omitted; in fact, this is the common practice. I'll explain why later. For example:

```
void test(int arr[]);
```

When passing an array to a function, we write only its name, without brackets. For example:

```
test(arr);
```

 When the name of an array is passed to a function, it is always treated as a pointer. We often say that the name "decays" to a pointer. In effect, the passing argument is the memory address of its first element, not a copy of the array itself. Since no copy of the array is made, the time required to pass an array to a function does not depend on the size of the array.

So remember, when an ordinary variable is passed to a function, the function works with a copy of it. But if an array is passed, no copy is made; the function works with the original array. Why is that decision taken? For better performance, to save memory and time that otherwise would be required to copy all the elements. It is just a pointer to its first element that is passed and the function may access any of its elements. For example:

```
#include <iostream> // Example 11.20

void test(int arr[]);

int main()
{
        int i, a[5] = {10, 20, 30, 40, 50};

        test(a); // Equivalent to test(&a[0]);
        for(i = 0; i < 5; i++)
                std::cout << a[i] << ' ';
        return 0;
}

void test(int arr[])
{
        arr[0] = arr[1] = 0;
}
```

Note that in test() we could use the name a instead of arr, since you know by now that local variables of different functions are not related even if they are named the same. When test() is called, we have arr = a = &a[0]. Therefore, the statements arr[0] = 0; and arr[1] = 0; change the values of the first two elements and the program displays: 0 0 30 40 50

An array parameter can be declared as pointer, as well. For example, the declarations:

```
void test(int arr[]);    and    void test(int *arr);
```

are equivalent. The compiler treats both the same and passes the pointer to the function. Therefore, the second declaration is more accurate, since it clearly states that only a pointer is passed, not a copy of the array. However, my preference is the first one, to show explicitly that the intention is to pass an array. The second declaration is ambiguous; the reader cannot figure out whether the function accepts a number of values or a pointer to a single variable.

Alternatively, we could use pointer arithmetic to access the array elements. For example:

```
void test(int arr[])
{
        *arr = 0; // Equivalent to arr[0] = 0.
        arr++;
        *arr = 0;
}
```

What is really interesting is the statement arr++. Can we change the value of an array? Certainly not, you know from Chapter 8 that when the name of an array is used as pointer it is a const pointer. So, why the compiler allows this statement? Because, as said, although arr is declared as array, it is actually a pointer. Therefore, we can give it a new value. One more example; does the following code compile and, if yes, what is the output?

```
#include <iostream> // Example 11.21

void test(int arr[]);

int main()
{
        int a[3] = {5};

        test(a);
        std::cout << a[0] << '\n' ;
        return 0;
}

void test(int arr[])
{
        int i = 20, b[10];

        arr = b;
        *arr = 10;
        arr = &i;
        *arr = 30;
        std::cout << b[0] << ' ' << i << ' ';
}
```

Of course it compiles, arr is treated as an ordinary pointer. test() outputs 10 and 30. Since test() did not access a[0], the program outputs 5.

And of course, we make sure, as when using an ordinary array, that all the actions we make are within the limits of the array. Note that, if we want, we can pass the whole array instead of the pointer to its first element. We'll see such an example with reference in Chapter 16.

Determining Array End

Although we can use the `sizeof` operator to find the size of an array variable, we cannot use it in a function to find the size of an array parameter. For example, consider the following program:

```cpp
#include <iostream> // Example 11.22

void test(int arr[]);

int main()
{
        int a[] = {1, 2, 3, 4, 5};

        test(a);
        std::cout << "Array = " << sizeof(a) << " bytes\n";
        return 0;
}

void test(int arr[])
{
        std::cout << "Ptr = " << sizeof(arr) << " bytes\n";
}
```

Since an array parameter is treated as a pointer, the `sizeof` operator calculates the size of a pointer variable (e.g., 4), not the actual size of the array. Therefore, the program outputs 4 for the pointer and 20 for the array.

Because it is the pointer that is actually passed to the function, it has no effect if we put the length of the array inside the brackets (e.g., `void test(int arr[5])`). The compiler ignores it; it won't check if the array actually has the indicated length (e.g., 5). Essentially, the passing pointer is a pointer to the first element of an array of unknown length. That's why I strongly recommend leaving the brackets empty; so that you do not create the false impression that the compiler would enforce that only arrays of that specific size (e.g., 5) can be passed as an argument. No, the compiler compiles successfully the program no matter what is the length of the array. An easy way to make known to the function the length of the array is to pass it as an additional argument. For example, we could declare `test()` as follows:

```cpp
void test(int arr[], int size);
```

and write `test(a, 5);` to call it.

Alternatively, we could define a constant, e.g., `const int SIZE = 5;` and use that constant wherever needed instead of passing an additional argument. Another way is to use a special value to indicate the end of the array, provided, of course, that this value wouldn't occur in the array. For example, if an array contains a C-form string it is not needed to pass its length, since the null character indicates its end.

Another way is to pass pointers to the first element and to the next place after the last element. For example, we could declare `test()` as:

```cpp
void test(int *beg, int *end)
{
        while(beg != end)
                std::cout << *beg++ << '\n'; /* The values of the elements are
displayed. */
}
```

and to call it to write: `test(a, a+5);` or use the library functions `begin()` and `end()` and write: `test(begin(a), end(a));`

Use of const

For safety, if we do not want a function to be able to change the values of the array elements, we declare the parameter as `const`. For example, with the declaration:

> void test(const int arr[]); test() may access the elements of arr, but it cannot modify their values. For example, if we write:

```
void test(const int arr[])
{
        arr[0] = 10; // Compilation error.
}
```

the compiler will display an error message. `const` provides security, as we avoid the case of an unintentional change, but also inform those who may read or use our code that no change should be made. Note that this declaration does not oblige us to declare the passed array as constant. It just says that `test()` can treat `arr` as read-only data. Also, if `test()` calls another function (e.g., `f`) and passes the array to it, the array parameter must be also declared as `const`. For example:

```
void test(const int arr[])
{
        f(arr);
}

void f(const int p[])
{
        ...
}
```

If we omit the word `const` in `f()`, the compiler will display an error message similar to *can't convert from const int* to int**. And it makes sense for the compiler to produce an error, since it wants to ensure that `f()` will not change the contents of the array. In general, declaring a pointer argument as `const` (remember, `arr` is treated as a pointer) indicates the programmer's intention that the value of the variable the pointer points to will not change.

Passing a Segment

When passing an array to a function, we can pass a part of it. For example, what does the following program display?

```
#include <iostream> // Example 11.23

void test(int ptr[]);

int main()
{
        int i, arr[6] = {1, 2, 3, 4, 5, 6};

        test(arr+3); // Alternatively, test(&arr[3]).
        for(i = 0; i < 6; i++)
                std::cout << arr[i] << ' ';
        return 0;
}
```

```
void test(int ptr[])
{
        int i, tmp[3] = {10, 20, 30};

        for(i = 0; i < 3; i++)
                ptr[i] = tmp[i];
        *ptr = *(ptr-1);
}
```

When `test()` is called, we have `ptr` = `arr+3`, that is, the part of `arr` from the fourth element and on is passed. Since we use `ptr` as array, `ptr[0]` corresponds to `arr[3]`, `ptr[1]` corresponds to `arr[4]`, and `ptr[2]` to `arr[5]`. Therefore, the loop makes the values of `arr[3]`, `arr[4]`, and `arr[5]` equal to 10, 20, and 30, respectively. Since `ptr` points to `arr[3]`, the statement `*ptr = *(ptr-1);` is equivalent to `arr[3] = arr[2];`. As a result, the program displays: 1 2 3 3 20 30

Let me ask a "weird" question. Could we write the following?

```
void test(int ptr[])
{
        std::cout << ptr[-1] << ' ';
        ...
}
```

Strange as it may seem, the answer is yes. As you already know from Chapter 8, `ptr[-1]` is equivalent to `*(ptr-1)` and, since `ptr` is equal to `arr+3`, it is equivalent to `*(arr+3-1)`, that is, `arr[2]`. If it is certain that elements in the backward direction do exist, yes, it is safe to use negative indexing and access them. Of course, even if you're sure, please don't write such code.

An easy question before finishing, to see that you have fully understood this very important section. Does the following program output the same values? If yes, explain why.

```
#include <iostream> // Example 11.24

void test(const int arr[]);

int main()
{
        int a[10];

        std::cout << "Addr: " << a << '\n';
        test(a);
        return 0;
}

void test(const int arr[])
{
        std::cout << "Addr: " << &arr << '\n';
}
```

Don't hurry to see the answer in the next page, give it some thought.

Not only did you answer yes, but you justified your answer as well? I tricked you once again… watch out for the traps coming next. Don't be angry, listen to *Don't Look Back in Anger* from *Oasis* and check the program again.

main() outputs the address of the a variable. test() outputs the address of the arr variable. Are they the same? Of course not, a and arr are different variables that reside in different memory locations. What is true is that the value of arr is equal to a, that is, if we remove the &, the output values will be the same.

Passing a vector Object

As we said in Chapter 7, for greater safety and flexibility it is better to use the vector class instead of an ordinary array. And of course, we can pass a vector object in a function. For example, try the following exercise.

Write a function that takes as parameters a vector object that contains the students' grades in a test and two grades (e.g., a and b) and returns the average of the grades within [a, b]. Write a program that reads the number of the students, creates a vector object, reads their grades, and stores them in it. Then, it reads the two grades a and b and calls the function to display the average. The program should force the user to enter a value for a less than or equal to b.

```cpp
#include <iostream> // Example 11.25
#include <vector>
using namespace std;

float avg_arr(const vector<float>& v, float min, float max);

int main()
{
        int i, num;
        float a, b, k;

        cout << "Enter number of students: ";
        cin >> num;

        vector<float> grd_v(num);
        for(i = 0; i < num; i++)
        {
                cout << "Enter grade: ";
                cin >> grd_v[i];
        }
        do
        {
                cout << "Enter min and max grades: ";
                cin >> a >> b;
        } while(a > b);

        k = avg_arr(grd_v, a, b);
        if(k == -1)
                cout << "None grade in the indicated set\n";
        else
                cout << "Avg = " << k << '\n';
        return 0;
}
```

```
float avg_arr(const vector<float>& v, float min, float max)
{
        int i, cnt = 0;
        float sum = 0;

        for(i = 0; i < v.size(); i++)
        {
                if(v[i] >= min && v[i] <= max)
                {
                        cnt++;
                        sum += v[i];
                }
        }
        if(cnt == 0)
                return -1;
        else
                return sum/cnt;
}
```

I think the program is clear, except for the & in the vector parameter. When we discuss about references in Chapter 16 you'll understand its role. To give you an idea, if we don't use it the vector will be passed by value and, thus, its elements will be copied, which could be time expensive for a vector with many elements. I used const to show you that we can prevent changes as we do with an ordinary array.

EXERCISES

C.11.10 Does the following program contain any error? If not, what does it output?

```
#include <iostream>
#include <cstring>

char *test();

int main()
{
        char s[100] = "sample";

        strcpy(s, test());
        std::cout << s;
        return 0;
}

char *test()
{
        char str[] = "example";
        return str;
}
```

Answer: You've been warned that you'll encounter such an exercise. Let's see, did you find the error or you answered that it is correct?

When test() is called, the compiler allocates memory for the str array and stores the string into it. This memory location is returned. Remember that the memory of a local variable is released when the function terminates. Most probably, the program won't display example. But, even if it is displayed, the code is not correct.

Always remember, don't return the address of a local variable unless it is declared as static.

If you want to change the contents of an array, the simplest way is to pass the array as an argument. For example, test() is modified like this:

```
void test(char str[])
{
        strcpy(str, "example");
}
```

C.11.11 Write a function that takes as parameters two strings, uses them as pointers, and returns 0 if they are identical or the difference of the first two non-matching characters. Write a program that reads two strings of less than 100 characters and uses the function to display the result of the comparison.

```
#include <iostream>
using std::cout;
using std::cin;

int str_cmp(const char *str1, const char *str2);

int main()
{
        char str1[100], str2[100];
        int i;

        cout << "Enter first text: ";
        cin.getline(str1, sizeof(str1));

        cout << "Enter second text: ";
        cin.getline(str2, sizeof(str2));

        i = str_cmp(str1, str2);
        if(i == 0)
                cout << str1 << " = " << str2 << '\n';
        else if(i < 0)
                cout << str1 << " < " << str2 << '\n';
        else
                cout << str1 << " > " << str2 << '\n';
        return 0;
}

int str_cmp(const char *s1, const char *s2)
{
        while(*s1 == *s2)
        {
                if(*s1 == '\0')
                        return 0;
                s1++;
                s2++;
        }
        return *s1-*s2;
}
```

Comments: If two different characters are found, the loop terminates and the function returns their difference. The str_cmp() function is an implementation example of the strcmp() library function.

C.11.12 What is the output of the following program?

```cpp
#include <iostream>

double *f(double ptr[]);

int main()
{
        int i;
        double a[8] = {0.1, 0.2, 0.3, 0.4, 0.5, 0.6, 0.7, 0.8};

        std::cout << *f(f(f(a))) << '\n';
        for(i = 0; i < 8; i++)
                std::cout << a[i] << '\n';
        return 0;
}

double *f(double ptr[])
{
        (*ptr)++;
        return ptr+2;
}
```

Answer: The $f()$ calls are executed inside out. When $f()$ is first called, we have ptr = a = &a[0]. Therefore, the statement (*ptr)++ is equivalent to a[0]++ and a[0] becomes 1.1.

The return value a+2 is used as an argument in the second call, so f(f(a)) is translated to f(a+2). Therefore, a[2] becomes 1.3. Similarly, the return value a+4 is used as an argument in the third call and a[4] becomes 1.5. Since the last call to f() returns the address of a[6], the * operator is used to display its value, that is, 0.7. As a result, the content of a is: 1.1 0.2 1.3 0.4 1.5 0.6 0.7 0.8

C.11.13 Write a function that calculates the maximum common divisor (MCD) of two positive integers, according to the following *Euclid's* algorithm. Suppose we have the integers a and b, with a > b. If b divides a precisely, this is the MCD. If the remainder r of the division a/b is not 0, then we divide b with r. If the new remainder of the division is 0, then the MCD is r, otherwise this procedure is repeated. Write a program that reads two positive integers (make data validation) and uses the function to calculate their MCD.

```cpp
#include <iostream>
using std::cout;
using std::cin;

int mcd(int a, int b);

int main()
{
        int num1, num2;

        do
        {
                cout << "Enter the bigger number: ";
                cin >> num1;
```

```
                    cout << "Enter the second number (equal or less than the first
one): ";
                    cin >> num2;
        } while((num2 > num1) || (num1 <= 0) || (num2 <= 0));

        cout << "MCD of " << num1 << " and " << num2 << " is " << mcd(num1,
num2) << '\n';
        return 0;
}

int mcd(int a, int b)
{
        int r;

        while(1)
        {
                r = a%b;
                if(r == 0)
                        return b;
                else /* According to the algorithm, we divide b by r, so we
change the values of a and b. */
                {
                        a = b;
                        b = r;
                }
        }
}
```

C.11.14 What is the output of the following program?

```
#include <iostream>

int *test(int *p1, int *p2);

int main()
{
        int arr[] = {1, 2, 3, 4};

        *test(arr, arr+3) = 30;
        std::cout << arr[0] << ' ' << arr[1] << ' ' << arr[2] << ' ' << arr[3]
<< '\n';
        return 0;
}

int *test(int *p1, int *p2)
{
        *(p1+1) = 10;
        *(p2-1) = 20;
        return p1+3;
}
```

Answer: When test() is called, we have p1 = arr, so the pointer p1+1 points to arr[1]. Therefore, the statement *(p1+1) = 10; makes arr[1] equal to 10. Similarly, we have p2 = arr+3, so p2 points to arr[3]. Therefore, the statement *(p2-1) = 20; makes arr[2] equal to 20. Since p1 points to arr, the expression p1+3 returns a pointer to arr[3]. Therefore, arr[3] becomes 30. As a result, the program displays: 1 10 20 30

C.11.15 Write a function that takes as parameter an integer (e.g., N) and calculates the Nth term of the Fibonacci sequence, according to the formula F(N) = F(N-1)+ F(N-2), where F(0) = 0 and F(1) = 1. Write a program that reads an integer N between 2 and 40 and uses the function to display the Nth term.

```cpp
#include <iostream>

unsigned int fib(int num);

int main()
{
        int num;

        do
        {
                std::cout << "Enter a number between 2 and 40: ";
                std::cin >> num;
        } while(num < 2 || num > 40);

        std::cout << "Fib(" << num << ") = " << fib(num) << '\n';
        return 0;
}

unsigned int fib(int num)
{
        unsigned int prev_sum, new_term, sum;

        prev_sum = 1;
        new_term = 0;

        while(num > 1)
        {
                sum = prev_sum + new_term;

                new_term = prev_sum;
                prev_sum = sum;

                num--;
        }
        return sum;
}
```

Comments: Given that F(N) = F(N-1)+ F(N-2), the first terms are: 0, 1, 1, 2, 3, 5, 8, 13, 21, 34, 55, 89, 144, ... For example, F(7) = 13, which is the sum of F(6) and F(5). To calculate the value of a term, we store into prev_sum the last sum, while in new_term the previous one.

C.11.16 Write a function that takes as parameters a character, an integer, and a string and uses it as a pointer to check whether the character exists in the string or not. If not, it should return nullptr. Otherwise, if the integer is 0, it should return a pointer to its first occurrence, otherwise to the last one. Write a program that reads a string of less than 100 characters, a character, and an integer, calls the function and displays the part of the string. For example, if the user enters "bootstrap", 't' and 0, the program should display tstrap. If it is "bootstrap", 't' and 3, the program should display trap.

```cpp
#include <iostream>
using std::cout;
using std::cin;

char *find(char str[], char ch, int f);
```

```
int main()
{
        char *ptr, ch, str[100];
        int flag;

        cout << "Enter text: ";
        cin.getline(str, sizeof(str));

        cout << "Enter character to search: ";
        ch = cin.get();

        cout << "Enter choice (0-first, other-last): ";
        cin >> flag;

        ptr = find(str, ch, flag);
        if(ptr == nullptr)
                cout << ch << "is not included in the text\n";
        else
                cout << "The rest string is " << ptr << '\n';
        return 0;
}

char *find(char str[], char ch, int f)
{
        char *tmp = nullptr; /* Initial value in case the character is not
found. */
        while(*str != '\0')
        {
                if(*str == ch)
                {
                        tmp = str;
                        if(f == 0) /* If the character is found and the choice
is 0, the loop terminates and the function returns the pointer. Otherwise,
tmp points to the place of the last occurrence. */
                                break;
                }
                str++;
        }
        return tmp;
}
```

C.11.17 In math, the bisection method is used to find a root of a continuous function $f(x)$ in a given interval $[x0, x1]$ provided that $f(x0)*f(x1) < 0$. If this applies, the Bolzano's theorem states that the function has one root at least in the interval $(x0, x1)$. The method repeatedly bisects the interval and then selects the subinterval in which the function changes sign, and, therefore, must contain a root. Write a program that implements the bisection method according to the following steps:

1. Read initial $x0$ and $x1$ values so that $f(x0)*f(x1) < 0$.
2. Read a positive number err for root tolerance error.
3. Read the maximum number of bisections (max_steps).
4. Calculate the approximated root $middle = (x0+x1)/2$.
5. If $|f(middle)| <= err$ or $x1-x0$ becomes sufficiently small, that is, $x1-x0 <= 2*err$ or the current number of bisections is greater than the input number (max_steps) then go to Step 7, otherwise go to Step 6.

6. Calculate the product `mul = f(x0)*f(middle)`.
   a. if `mul < 0`, then the root must be in the new subinterval where `x0 = x0` and `x1 = middle`.
   b. if `mul > 0`, then the root must be in the new subinterval where `x0 = middle` and `x1 = x1`.
   Then, go to Step 4.
7. Display `middle` as root.

Apply the bisection method to find the root of $f(x) = x^3 + x - 1$ in a given interval (e.g., [0, 1]).

```cpp
#include <iostream>
#include <cmath>
using std::cout;
using std::cin;

double f(double x);

int main()
{
        int steps, max_steps;
        long double x0, x1, err, middle, mul, tmp;

        do
        {
                cout << "Enter x0: ";
                cin >> x0;

                cout << "Enter x1: ";
                cin >> x1;

                mul = f(x0)*f(x1);
        } while(mul >= 0);

        cout << "Enter positive tolerance: ";
        cin >> err;

        cout << "Enter maximum number of bisections: ";
        cin >> max_steps;

        if(x0 > x1)
        {
                tmp = x1;
                x1 = x0;
                x0 = tmp;
        }
        steps = 0;
        while(1)
        {
                steps++;
                middle = (x0+x1)/2;
                tmp = f(middle);
                if(fabs(tmp) <= err || x1-x0 <= 2*err || steps >= max_steps)
                        break;

                mul = tmp * f(x0);
                if(mul < 0)
                        x1 = middle; // x0 is the same.
```

```
                else if(mul > 0)
                        x0 = middle; // x1 is the same.
        }
        if(steps >= max_steps)
                cout << "Maximum number of bisections is reached. ";
        cout << "Approximated root is " << middle << '\n';
        return 0;
}

double f(double x)
{
        return x*x*x + x - 1;
}
```

C.11.18 Write a `void` function that takes as parameters a `vector` object that contains the prices of some products in a shop and returns the lowest, the highest, and the average of the prices through respective parameters. Write a program that reads continuously prices and stores them in a `vector` object. If the user enters a negative value or zero, the insertion of prices should terminate. The program should use the function to display the lowest, the highest, and the average of the prices.

```
#include <iostream>
#include <vector>
using namespace std;

void stat(const vector<float>& v, float *min, float *max, float *avg);

int main()
{
        int i;
        float min, max, avg, val;
        vector<float> prc_v;

        while(1)
        {
                cout << "Enter price: ";
                cin >> val;
                if(val <= 0)
                        break;
                prc_v.push_back(val);
        }
        if(prc_v.size() == 0) // It means that no value is stored.
                return 0;
        stat(prc_v, &min, &max, &avg);
        cout << "Max=" << max << " Min=" << min << " Avg=" << avg << '\n';
        return 0;
}

void stat(const vector<float>& v, float *min, float *max, float *avg)
{
        int i, size;
        float sum;

        sum = *min = *max = v[0];
        size = v.size();
```

```
        for(i = 1; i < size; i++)
        {
                if(v[i] > *max)
                        *max = v[i];
                if(v[i] < *min)
                        *min = v[i];
                sum += v[i];
        }
        *avg = sum/size;
}
```

C.11.19 What is the output of the following program?

```
#include <iostream>

void swap(const char *s1, const char *s2);

int main()
{
        const char *p[] = {"Shadow", "Play"};

        swap(p[0], p[1]);
        std::cout << p[0] << ' ' << p[1] << '\n';
        return 0;
}

void swap(const char *s1, const char *s2)
{
        const char *p;

        p = s1;
        s1 = s2;
        s2 = p;
}
```

Answer: What kind of play is that, did you answer Play Shadow? Read the answer of the example C.11.8. It is only the song to change; *Shadow Play* from the great *Rory Gallagher*.

As in test() in example C.11.8, swap() takes as arguments the values of the pointers, not their addresses. Therefore, the swapping has no effect and the program displays Shadow Play. What I want you to do is to modify the program in order to output Play Shadow. Let's see, can you do that? To give you a hint, change the type of the parameters to... find it, no more to say.

C.11.20 Write a function that takes as parameter an array and checks if it contains duplicated values. If so, the function should return a pointer to the element which appears the most times, otherwise nullptr. Write a program that reads 100 integers, stores them in an array and uses the function to display the element with the most occurrences. *Note:* if more than one element appears the same most times, the function should return the first found.

```
#include <iostream>

const int *find(const int arr[]);
const int SIZE = 100;
```

```cpp
int main()
{
        const int *ptr;
        int i, arr[SIZE];

        for(i = 0; i < SIZE; i++)
        {
                std::cout << "Enter number: ";
                std::cin >> arr[i];
        }
        ptr = find(arr);
        if(ptr == nullptr)
                std::cout << "No duplicated value is found\n";
        else
                std::cout << "The number " << *ptr <<  " appears the most
times\n";
        return 0;
}

const int *find(const int arr[])
{
        int i, j, cnt, max, pos;

        max = 0;
        for(i = 0; i < SIZE; i++)
        {
                cnt = 0;
                for(j = i+1; j < SIZE; j++)
                {
                        if(arr[i] == arr[j])
                                cnt++;
                }
                if(cnt > max)
                {
                        max = cnt;
                        pos = i;
                }
        }
        if(max == 0)
                return nullptr;
        else
                return arr+pos;
}
```

C.11.21 Write a function that takes as parameters two `vector` objects that contains names and returns a `vector` object that contains the common names. Write a program that reads the number of names, creates two `vector` objects, reads the names, and stores them into the objects. Then, the program should call the function and display the common names. To store the names, use the `string` type.

```cpp
#include <iostream>
#include <vector>
#include <string>
using namespace std;

vector<string> find_same(const vector<string>& v1, const vector<string>& v2);
```

```cpp
int main()
{
        int i, num;

        cout << "Enter number of names: ";
        cin >> num;

        vector<string> v1(num), v2(num);
        for(i = 0; i < num; i++)
        {
                cout << "Enter name_" << i+1 << ": ";
                cin >> v1[i];
                cout << "Enter name_" << i+1 << ": ";
                cin >> v2[i];
        }
        vector<string> v3 = find_same(v1, v2);
        num = v3.size();
        if(num == 0)
                cout << "No common names\n";
        else
        {
                cout << "\nCommon names\n";
                for(i = 0; i < num; i++)
                        cout << v3[i] << '\n';
                /* We could write:
                for(auto& s : v3)
                        cout << s << '\n'; */
        }
        return 0;
}


vector<string> find_same(const vector<string>& v1, const vector<string>& v2)
{
        int i, j, num;
        vector<string> v;

        num = v1.size();
        for(i = 0; i < num; i++)
        {
                for(j = 0; j < num; j++)
                {
                        if(v1[i] == v2[j])
                        {
                                v.push_back(v1[i]);
                                break;  /* Terminate the internal for and check
        the next element. */
                        }
                }
        }
        return v;
}
```

Comments: The use of `vector` may seem difficult to you. Don't worry, it's good to get used to. You'll understand it better when we discuss classes and objects.

C.11.22 During my professional career I used C++ a lot to implement communication protocols. As an example, I'll show you a method to create network data frames.

In order a system to connect to an Internet address, its network card should transmit an IP packet that encapsulates a special TCP segment. Suppose that IPv4 addresses are used. The IPv4 header format is depicted in the following figure:

The TCP header format is depicted in the following figure:

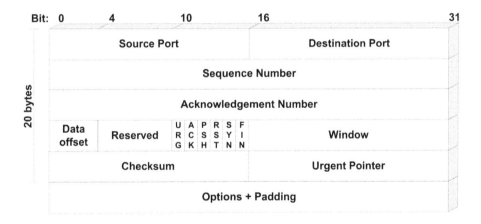

Write a program that reads the source IP address in x.x.x.x format (each x is an integer in [0, 255]), the destination IP address in x.x.x.x format, the TCP destination port (integer in [1, 65535]) and creates an IP packet that encapsulates the proper TCP segment. The program must store the content of the IP packet in hexadecimal format in a user selected text file. Each line must contain 16 bytes. Set the following values in the IPv4 header:

a. Version = 4.
b. IHL = 5.
c. Total Length = total length of the IP packet, including the TCP data.
d. Protocol = 6.
e. Time to Live = 255.
f. Destination Address = destination IP address.
g. Source Address = source IP address.

Set the following values in the TCP header:

    a. `Destination Port` = destination TCP port.
    b. `Source Port` = 1500.
    c. `Window` = the maximum allowed value.
    d. `SYN` bit = 1.

Set the rest fields to `0` and assume that there are no `Options` fields.

The program has one restriction; if the destination IP address starts from 130.140 or 160.170 and the TCP destination port is 80, do not create the IP packet and display a related message.

```cpp
#include <iostream>
#include <iomanip>
using namespace std;


void Build_Pkt(const int IP_src[], const int IP_dst[], int port);
void Show_Frm(const unsigned char pkt[], int len);

int main()
{
        char ch;
        int IP_src[4], IP_dst[4], TCP_dst_port;

        do
        {
                cout << "Enter dst port [1-65535]: ";
                cin >> TCP_dst_port;
        } while(TCP_dst_port < 1 || TCP_dst_port > 65535);

        cout << "Enter dst IP (x.x.x.x): ";
        cin >> IP_dst[0] >> ch >> IP_dst[1] >> ch >> IP_dst[2] >> ch >>
IP_dst[3]; /* ch is used to read the dot. */

        if(TCP_dst_port == 80)
        {
                if(IP_dst[0] == 130 && IP_dst[1] == 140)
                {
                        cout << "It isn't allowed to connect to network
130.140.x.x\n";
                        return 0;
                }
                else if(IP_dst[0] == 160 && IP_dst[1] == 170)
                {
                        cout << "It isn't allowed to connect to network
160.170.x.x\n";
                        return 0;
                }
        }
        cout << "Enter src IP (x.x.x.x): ";
        cin >> IP_src[0] >> ch >> IP_src[1] >> ch >> IP_src[2] >> ch >>
IP_src[3];
```

```
        Build_Pkt(IP_src, IP_dst, TCP_dst_port);
        return 0;
}


void Build_Pkt(const int IP_src[], const int IP_dst[], int port)
{
        unsigned char pkt[40] = {0}; // Initialize all fields to 0.
        int i, j;

        pkt[0] = 0x45; // Version, IHL.
        pkt[8] = 255; // Time to Live.
        pkt[9] = 6; // Protocol = TCP.
        for(i = 12, j = 0; i < 16; i++, j++)
                pkt[i] = IP_src[j]; // IP Source.
        for(i = 16, j = 0; i < 20; i++, j++)
                pkt[i] = IP_dst[j]; // IP Destination.
        pkt[20] = 1500 >> 8; // TCP Source Port.
        pkt[21] = 1500 & 0xFF;
        pkt[22] = port >> 8; // TCP Dest Port.
        pkt[23] = port & 0xFF;
        pkt[33] = 2; // SYN bit.
        pkt[34] = 0xFF; /* The maximum value for the Window field is all 16
bits set to 1. */
        pkt[35] = 0xFF;
        /* The values of the CheckSum and Urgent Pointer are set in positions
36-40, therefore the total length of the IP packet is 40 bytes. */
        pkt[2] = 0; // IP Total Length.
        pkt[3] = 40;

        Show_Frm(pkt, 40);
}


void Show_Frm(const unsigned char pkt[], int len)
{
        for(int i = 0; i < len; i++)
        {
                if(i%16 == 0)
                        cout << '\n';
            cout << setw(2) << setfill('0') << hex << (int)pkt[i] << ' '; /* Each
element is displayed with two hex digits. If the value has one digit, the
digit 0 is added. */
        }
}
```

Comments: Do you have any idea about what this program really does? This program is an oversimplified version of a popular application, almost certainly installed in your computer, the *firewall*. Like this program, a firewall may prevent communication to specific IP addresses and specific applications (e.g., web servers listen to TCP port 80). In fact, the main part of a firewall is nothing more than a sequence of if-else statements.

In a real networking application, this IP packet is encapsulated in a MAC frame; the hardware of the network card encodes the bits of the frame in digital signals (e.g., two different voltage levels to represent 0 and 1) and forwards the frame to the connected router. The router checks the IP destination address; it consults its routing table to determine the next router towards the destination and forwards the frame. This process is repeated for the next router using its own routing table, until the frame eventually reaches the destination. Yes, I understand, it may all seem strange to you, I just tried to introduce you in the fascinating world of Computer Networking.

TWO-DIMENSIONAL ARRAY AS ARGUMENT

The most common way to declare a function that takes as parameter a two-dimensional array is to write the name of the array followed by its dimensions. For example, `test()` takes as parameter a two-dimensional integer array with 5 rows and 10 columns.

```
void test(int arr[5][10]);
```

Because, as discussed in Chapter 7, the compiler is not necessary to know the number of rows to calculate the memory location of an element, the first dimension may be omitted. If you specify it, the compiler will ignore it. For example:

```
void test(int arr[][10]);
```

However, the number of columns must be specified. In the general case, when a multidimensional array is passed to a function, the first dimension may be omitted. All the others must be specified and match the declaration of the array. In this way, the compiler would have the necessary information to make the correct scaling for address arithmetic and access an element. In this example, any array with 10 as second dimension can be passed to the function, but not arrays with dimension other than 10.

Since C++ treats a two-dimensional array as an array of one-dimensional arrays, the compiler actually translates the two-dimensional parameter to a pointer to an array. Therefore, we could equivalently write: `void test(int (*arr)[10]);`. Because the brackets `[]` have greater precedence than `*`, parentheses are necessary, otherwise, `arr` would be interpreted as an array of 10 pointers to integers instead of pointer to an array of 10 integers. Although that declaration is more accurate, my preference is to use the first one and omit the first dimension in order to make it clear that the parameter is a two-dimensional array.

Play some defence now, a burst of questions is coming. Where `arr` points to? It points to the first row of the array. And if we write `arr++` where does it point to? In the next one, since it is increased by the size of the row. And what is the `(*arr)[1]`? It is the second element of the row that `arr` points to. And what does the `(*++arr)[0]`? It increases `arr` to point to the next row and access its first element. And how do we know that the last row of the array is reached? Typically, we either use a constant or pass an argument to declare the total number of rows. End of alert. If you've queries, read again the section "Pointers and Two-Dimensional Arrays" in Chapter 8.

I write it again, the compiler translates the two-dimensional array to a pointer to an array, not to a pointer to pointer as you might expect. Therefore, it is illegal to write `void test(int **arr);`. When we'll discuss the `new` operator in Chapter 14, you'll see in example C.14.5 how we can use a pointer to a pointer variable to create dynamically a two-dimensional array and pass it to a function. Let's summarize how the compiler translates array arguments:

One-dimensional: e.g., `arr[10]` is translated to pointer `*arr`.
Two-dimensional: e.g., `arr[10][20]` is translated to pointer to array `(*arr)[20]`.
Array of pointers: e.g., `*arr[10]` is translated to pointer to pointer `**arr`.

Alternatively, we can treat the array as one-dimensional, but I would not prefer that since accessing the elements is more difficult to understand and prone to errors. Of course, we need to know the dimensions of the array. For example:

```
void f(int *arr, int rows, int cols)
{
        for(int i = 0; i < rows; i++)
```

```
            for(int j = 0; j < cols; j++)
                    cout << arr[i*cols+j] << ' '; /* Complex syntax and
prone to errors. As we already know, it is equivalent to the expression that
the compiler produces when we write arr[i][j]. */
}
```

As with one-dimensional arrays, to pass a two-dimensional array as an argument, we write only its name, without brackets. If we want to pass a row (e.g., i) we pass the pointer to that row (e.g., arr[i]), as we do when passing a one-dimensional array. For example, the following program displays the elements of the first row:

```
#include <iostream> // Example 11.26

const int ROWS = 2;
const int COLS = 3;

void show_row(const int a[]);

int main()
{
        int arr[ROWS][COLS] = {{1, 2, 3}, {4, 5, 6}};

        show_row(arr[0]);
        return 0;
}

void show_row(const int a[])
{
        for(int i = 0; i < COLS; i++)
                std::cout << a[i] << ' ';
}
```

EXERCISES

C.11.23 Write a function that takes as parameter a 3×4 two-dimensional array and returns one array where each element is equal to the sum of the elements of the respective row of the two-dimensional array and another array where each element is equal to the sum of the elements of the respective column of the two-dimensional array. Write a program that reads 12 integers, stores them in a 3×4 two-dimensional array, and uses the function to display the sum of the elements in each row and the sum of the elements in each column as well.

```
#include <iostream>
using std::cout;
using std::cin;

const int ROWS = 3;
const int COLS = 4;

void find_sums(const int arr1[][COLS], int arr2[], int arr3[]);

int main()
{
        int i, j, arr1[ROWS][COLS], arr2[ROWS], arr3[COLS];
```

```
        for(i = 0; i < ROWS; i++)
                for(j = 0; j < COLS; j++)
                {
                        cout << "arr1[" << i << "][" << j << "] = ";
                        cin >> arr1[i][j];
                }

        find_sums(arr1, arr2, arr3);
        for(i = 0; i < ROWS; i++)
                cout << "sum_line_" << i << " = " << arr2[i] << '\n';
        for(i = 0; i < COLS; i++)
                cout << "sum_col_" << i << " = " << arr3[i] << '\n';
        return 0;
}

void find_sums(const int arr1[][COLS], int arr2[], int arr3[])
{
        int i, j, sum;

        for(i = 0; i < ROWS; i++)
        {
                sum = 0;
                for(j = 0; j < COLS; j++)
                        sum += arr1[i][j];
                arr2[i] = sum;
        }
        for(i = 0; i < COLS; i++)
        {
                sum = 0;
                for(j = 0; j < ROWS; j++)
                        sum += arr1[j][i];
                arr3[i] = sum;
        }
}
```

Comments: Since a function cannot return an array, the array that holds the results (e.g., arr3) is declared in main() and passed to the function.

C.11.24 Write a function that takes as parameters an array of names and another name. The function should check if that name is contained in the array. If it is, the function should return a pointer to the position of that name in the array, otherwise nullptr. Write a program that reads the names of 20 students (less than 100 characters each) and stores them in an array. Then, it reads another name and uses the function to check if that name is contained in the array.

```
#include <iostream>
#include <cstring>
using std::cout;
using std::cin;

const int NUM = 20;
const int SIZE = 100;

char *find_name(char name[][SIZE], char str[]);
```

```
int main()
{
        char *ptr, str[SIZE], name[NUM][SIZE]; /* The name array holds the
names of the students. */
        int i;

        for(i = 0; i < NUM; i++)
        {
                cout << "Enter name: ";
                cin.getline(name[i], sizeof(name[i])); /* We use the name[i] as
a pointer to the respective i row of SIZE characters. */
        }
        cout << "Enter name to search: ";
        cin.getline(str, sizeof(str));

        ptr = find_name(name, str);
        if(ptr == nullptr)
                cout << str << " is not contained\n";
        else
                cout << ptr << " is contained\n";
        return 0;
}

char *find_name(char name[][SIZE], char str[])
{
        int i;

        for(i = 0; i < NUM; i++)
                if(strcmp(name[i], str) == 0)
                        return name[i]; /* name[i] points to the first character
of the row that contains the name. */
        return nullptr; /* If this point is reached, the name is not found in
the array. */
}
```

C.11.25 A popular card game among children is a memory matching game. The game starts with a deck of identical pairs of cards face down on a table. The player selects two cards and turns them over. If they match, they remain face up. If not, they are flipped face down. The game ends when all cards are face up.

To simulate that game, write a program that uses the elements of a two-dimensional array as the cards. To test your program, use a 4×4 array and assign the values 1-8 to its elements (cards). Each number must appear twice. Set the values in random positions. An example of the array might be:

$$\begin{bmatrix} 5 & 3 & 4 & 8 \\ 4 & 2 & 6 & 1 \\ 3 & 8 & 7 & 6 \\ 2 & 5 & 1 & 7 \end{bmatrix}$$

The program should prompt the user to select the positions of two cards and display a message to indicate if they match or not. The program ends when all cards are matched.

```
#include <iostream>
#include <cstdlib>
#include <ctime>
using std::cout;
using std::cin;
```

```
const int ROWS = 4;
const int COLS = 4;

void show_board(const int c[][COLS], const int s[][COLS]);
void sel_card(const int c[][COLS], int s[][COLS], int *row, int *col);

int main()
{
      int i, j, m, r, c, r2, c2, cnt, cards[ROWS][COLS], status[ROWS][COLS]
= {0}; /* The status array indicates if a card faces up or down (0 is for
down). */
      cnt = 0; // This variable counts the number of the faced up cards.
      for(i = r = 0; i < ROWS; i++) /* Assign the values 1 to 8,
sequentially. */
      {
            for(j = 0; j < COLS; j+=2)
            {
                  cards[i][j] = cards[i][j+1] = r+1;
                  r++;
            }
      }
      /* Now, shuffle the cards, so that they are placed in random
positions. */
      srand(time(NULL));
      for(i = 0; i < ROWS; i++)
      {
            for(j = 0; j < COLS; j++)
            {
                  c = cards[i][j];
                  m = rand()%ROWS;
                  r = rand()%COLS;
                  cards[i][j] = cards[m][r];
                  cards[m][r] = c;
            }
      }
      show_board(cards, status);
      m = 0;
      while(cnt != ROWS*COLS) /* The game ends when all cards are faced up. */
      {
            sel_card(cards, status, &r, &c);
            cout << "Card_1 = " << cards[r][c] << '\n';

            sel_card(cards, status, &r2, &c2);
            cout << "Card_2 = " << cards[r2][c2] << '\n';

            for(i = 0; i < 18; i++) /* Insert blank line to delete history
and make harder for the player to remember the card positions. */
                  cout << '\n';

            if(cards[r][c] == cards[r2][c2])
            {
                  cout << "Cards matched !!!\n";
                  cnt += 2;
            }
```

```cpp
                else
                {
                        cout << "Sorry. No match !!!\n";
                        status[r][c] = status[r2][c2] = 0; /* Make again the
cards to face down. */
                }
                m++;
                show_board(cards, status);
        }
        cout << "Congrats: You did it in " << m << " tries\n";
        return 0;
}


void show_board(const int c[][COLS], const int s[][COLS])
{
        int i, j;

        for(i = 0; i < ROWS; i++)
        {
                for(j = 0; j < COLS; j++)
                {
                        if(s[i][j] == 1)
                                cout << c[i][j] << ' ';
                        else
                                cout << "* ";
                }
                cout << '\n';
        }
}


void sel_card(const int c[][COLS], int s[][COLS], int *row, int *col)
{
        while(1)
        {
                cout << "Enter row and column: ";
                cin >> *row >> *col;
                (*row)--; /* Subtract 1, because the indexing of the array
starts from 0. */
                (*col)--;
                if(*row >= ROWS  || *row < 0 || *col >= COLS || *col < 0)
                {
                        cout << "Out of bound dimensions\n";
                        continue;
                }
                if(s[*row][*col] == 1)
                {
                        cout << "Error: This card is already flipped\n";
                        continue;
                }
                s[*row][*col] = 1; // Make the card to face up.
                return;
        }
}
```

PASSING DATA TO `main()`

When we run a program from the command line, we'll often need to pass information to it. For example, suppose that the executable file `hello.exe` is stored in the C disk. The command line:

```
C:\>hello 100 200
```

executes the program `hello` and passes the values `100` and `200` to `main()`. To get the data, `main()` must be defined like this:

```
int main(int argc, char *argv[])
```

Although you can use any names, `argc` (*argument count*) and `argv` (*argument vector*) are by convention the typical choice. And because the compiler translates an array parameter to pointer, many prefer to write `**argv` instead of `*argv[]`.

The value of `argc` is equal to the number of the command line arguments, including the name of the program itself. For example, in the previous command line, `argc` is `3`. The arguments should be separated with space(s), to distinguish the values.

The `argv` parameter is an array of pointers to the command line arguments, which are stored as C-style strings. `argv[0]` pointer points to the name of the program, while the other pointers up to `argv[argc-1]` point to the remaining arguments. The last `argv` element is the `argv[argc]`, which is always `nullptr`. In our example, the arguments `hello`, `100`, and `200` are passed to `main()` as strings. In particular, `argv[0]` points to the string `"hello"`, `argv[1]` points to `"100"`, `argv[2]` points to `"200"`, and `argv[3]` is `nullptr`.

The following program checks if the user entered the correct user name and password. Suppose that these are `user` and `pswd`, respectively.

```cpp
#include <iostream> // Example 11.27
#include <cstring>

int main(int argc, char *argv[])
{
        if(argc == 1)
                std::cout << "Error: missing user name and password\n";
        else if(argc == 2)
                std::cout << "Error: missing password\n";
        else if(argc == 3)
        {
                if(strcmp(argv[1], "user") == 0 &&
                        strcmp(argv[2], "pswd") == 0)
                        std::cout << "Valid user. The program " << argv[0] <<
" will be executed ...\n";
                else
                        std::cout << "Wrong input\n";
        }
        else
                std::cout << "Error: too many parameters\n";
        return 0;
}
```

The `if` statements check the value of `argc`. If it is `3`, the program checks if the entered user name and password are correct. If not, the program displays a related message.

EXERCISES

C.11.26 What is the output of the following program?

```cpp
#include <iostream>
int main(int argc, char *argv[])
{
        while(--argc)
                (argc > 1) ?  std::cout << *++argv << ' ' : std::cout << *++argv
<< '\n';
        return 0;
}
```

Answer: `argc` is equal to the number of the command line arguments. If the only argument is the name of the program, `argc` would be `1` and the loop won't be executed because its value becomes `0`. If there are more arguments, the program displays their values, separated by a space, and it adds a new line character after printing the last one.

For example, suppose that the command line arguments are `one` and `two`. So, `argc` would be `3` and the loop condition makes it `2`. Since `(argc > 1)` is true, the program displays the value of `*++argv` and a space. Since `argv` points to `argv[0]`, the expression `++argv` makes it point to `argv[1]`. Therefore, `*++argv` is equivalent to `argv[1]`, and the program outputs `one`. In the next iteration, `argc` becomes `1`, so the program displays the value of `argv[2]`. As a result, the program outputs `two` and a new line character.

Now, answer this one. What would be the output if we write `*argv++` instead of `*++argv`?

Answer: The program would display the name of the program and the command line arguments, but the last one.

C.11.27 The popular `ping` command is used to test the communication between two systems in an IP network. For example, `ping www.ntua.gr`. Write a program that reads the command line argument and checks if it corresponds to a valid destination. To be valid, assume that it should have the form of the example, that is, begin with `"www."`, and the part after the second dot should be two or three characters long (e.g., `gr`).

```cpp
#include <iostream> // Exercise 11.27
#include <cstring>
using std::cout;

int main(int argc, char *argv[])
{
        int i, len;

        if(argc != 2)
        {
                cout << "Wrong number of arguments\n";
                return 0;
        }
        if(strncmp(argv[1], "www.", 4) != 0)
        {
                cout << "Name must begin with www.\n";
                return 0;
        }
```

```
        len = strlen(argv[1]);
        for(i = 4; i < len; i++)
               if(argv[1][i] == '.')
                      break;

        if(i == len)
        {
               cout << "Second.  is missing\n";
               return 0;
        }
        if((len-i-1) != 2 && (len-i-1) != 3)
        {
               cout << "The last part should be two or three characters
long\n";
               return 0;
        }
        cout << "The hostname " << argv[1] << " is valid\n";
        return 0;
}
```

FUNCTIONS WITH VARIABLE NUMBER OF PARAMETERS

A function may accept a variable number of parameters. One way of declaring such a function, which comes from C, is first to put the fixed parameters, that is, those that must always be present in the function call, and then the ... symbol, known as *ellipsis*. In general, ... means "zero or more appearances of something". For example, the declaration:

```
void test(int num, char *str, ...);
```

indicates that test() takes two fixed parameters, an integer and a pointer to a character, which may be followed by a variable number of additional parameters. In practice, you'll rarely need to write functions with a variable number of parameters. It might happen if you want to write a generic function, for example, a function that accepts any number of values and returns their sum.

 A function that accepts a variable number of parameters must have at least one named fixed parameter.

To call such a function, first we write the values of the fixed arguments and then the values of the optional arguments. For example, we could call test() like this:

```
test(3, "example", 5, 8.9, "sample");
```

The data types of the optional arguments are int, float, and char* with values 5, 8.9, and "sample", respectively.

To handle the optional argument list, we use a set of macros defined in the `cstdarg` standard file. Macros are discussed in Chapter 15. For now, assume that their behaviour is similar to functions.

va_list: A variable of type `va_list` is used to point to the optional argument list.

va_start(): The `va_start()` macro takes two parameters. The first one is of type `va_list`, and the second one should be the name of the last fixed parameter. For example, the name of the last fixed parameter in `test()` is `str`. `va_start()` sets the `va_list` argument to point to the first optional argument. `va_start()` must be called before `va_arg()` is used for first time.

va_arg(): The `va_arg()` macro takes two parameters. The first one is of type `va_list` and the second one is the type of an optional argument. For example, the type of the first optional argument in `test()` is `int`. The `va_list` argument must be the one initialized with `va_start()`. `va_arg()` returns the value of the optional argument and advances the `va_list` argument to point to the next optional argument. Therefore, in order to get the values of all optional arguments, we should call `va_arg()` as many times as the number of the optional arguments.

va_end(): The `va_end()` macro takes one parameter of type `va_list`. It must be called to end the processing of the optional argument list.

In the following program, `test()` takes a variable number of parameters of type `char*`. The fixed parameter `num` indicates their number.

```cpp
#include <iostream> // Example 11.28
#include <cstdarg>

void test(int num, ...);

int main()
{
        test(3, "t1", "t2", "t3");
        return 0;
}

void test(int num, ...)
{
        char *str;
        int i;
        va_list arg_ptr;

        va_start(arg_ptr, num); /* va_start() initializes the va_list
variable. In particular, arg_ptr points to the first optional argument.
Notice that the name of the second argument should be the same with the name
of the last fixed parameter in the definition of test(). */
        for(i = 0; i < num; i++)
        {
                str = va_arg(arg_ptr, char*); /* Each call of va_arg() returns
the value of the respective optional argument of type char* and arg_ptr
advances to point to the next optional argument. The second argument is char*,
because it is said that the type of all optional arguments is char*. */
                std::cout << str << ' ';
        }
        va_end(arg_ptr);
}
```

The program outputs the values of the optional arguments: `t1 t2 t3`

The primary difficulty in using a function with a variable argument list is that there is no easy way to determine the number and types of its optional arguments. To find the number, a simple solution is to add a fixed parameter, which declares that number. In the previous example, we used the parameter num. If the arguments are all of the same type, we could use a special value to mark the end of the list. Moreover, the function must somehow be informed about their types. For example, for those who know from C the printf() and scanf() functions, they both use the format string to get the necessary type information to process the argument list. In general, because ... comes from C, it should be used with types that are common in C and C++ and should not be used with other types.

EXERCISE

C.11.28 Write a function that takes a variable parameter list of type double and returns the largest value. Write a program that reads three floats and uses the function to display the largest value.

```
#include <iostream>
#include <cstdarg>

double find_max(int num, ...);

int main()
{
        double i, j, k;

        std::cout << "Enter numbers: ";
        std::cin >> i >> j >> k;

        std::cout << "Max = " << find_max(3, i, j, k) << '\n';
        return 0;
}

double find_max(int num, ...)
{
        int i;
        double max, tmp;
        va_list arg_ptr;

        va_start(arg_ptr, num);
        max = va_arg(arg_ptr, double);
        for(i = 1; i < num; i++)
        {
                tmp = va_arg(arg_ptr, double);
                if(max < tmp)
                        max = tmp;
        }
        va_end(arg_ptr);
        return max;
}
```

Comments: Note that we can use find_max() to find the largest of any number of double arguments, not just 3.

With the C++11 standard we can write a function that accepts a variable number of arguments of a particular type using the standard library type `initializer_list`. This type is defined in the `initializer_list` file and represents an array. As with the `vector` type when declaring an `initializer_list` type we need to specify the type of its elements. The elements of the `initializer_list` are `const`, that is, we cannot change their values. Also, the type supports `begin()` and `end()` functions, similar to those of `vector`, to access its elements. Let's look at an example:

```cpp
#include <iostream> // Example 11.29
#include <initializer_list>
using namespace std;

template <typename T> void show(const initializer_list<T>& lst);

int main()
{
        initializer_list<string> str_lst{"t1", "t2", "t3"};
        show(str_lst);
        show({"t1", "t2", "t3"}); /* When passing a list of values to an
initializer_list parameter, the list must be enclosed in braces. */
        initializer_list<int> int_lst{1, 2, 3};
        show(int_lst);
        show({1, 2, 3});
        return 0;
}

template <typename T> void show(const initializer_list<T>& lst)
{
        for(auto cur = lst.begin(); cur != lst.end(); ++cur)
                std::cout << *cur << ' ';
        cout << '\n';
}
```

The program uses the template `show()` function to display the elements contained in the `initializer_list` parameter. You'll see how it works when we discuss function templates in Chapter 16. For now, it is enough to know that the type T for the `str_lst` variable will be replaced with `string` and for `int_lst` with `int`. As the comment says, when passing a list of values to an `initializer_list` parameter it must be enclosed in braces. Finally, the program displays:

```
t1 t2 t3
t1 t2 t3
1  2  3
1  2  3
```

Note that a function with an `initializer_list` parameter can accept additional ordinary parameters as well. For example:

```cpp
void f(const initializer_list<int>& lst, double d); /* f() accepts an
initializer_list parameter that contains integers and a double value. */
```

and an example of how to call it: `f({1, 2}, 3.4);`

RECURSIVE FUNCTIONS

A function that calls itself is called recursive. For example:

```cpp
#include <iostream> // Example 11.30

void show(int num);

int main()
{
        int i;

        std::cout << "Enter number: ";
        std::cin >> i;
        show(i);
        return 0;
}

void show(int num)
{
        if(num > 1)
                show(num-1);

        std::cout << "val = " << num << '\n';
}
```

To see how recursion works, suppose that the user enters a number greater than 1, e.g., 3, so that show() is called again.

a. In the first call of show(), since num = 3 > 1, show() calls itself with argument num-1 = 3-1 = 2 and the cout is not executed. Since show() is not terminated, the memory allocated for the variable num with value 3 and other information related to the function call is not released.

b. In the second call of show() new memory is allocated for the num variable. Since num = 2 > 1, show() calls again itself with argument num-1 = 2-1 = 1. Like before, cout is not executed and the memory allocated for the new variable num with value 2 is not released.

c. Like before, in the third call of show() new memory is allocated for the num variable. show() is not called again because num is not greater than 1. Therefore, this cout is executed and outputs val = 1. The memory allocated for that num is released.

Next, all unexecuted cout will be executed sequentially, starting from the last one. In each termination of show(), the memory allocated for the respective num and for each particular call is released. Therefore, the program displays:

```
val = 1
val = 2
val = 3
```

 A recursive function must contain a termination condition in order to prevent infinite recursion which generally leads to a program crash.

In our example, this condition was the statement if(num > 1). I say it again, it is very important to ensure that the recursion eventually reaches an end condition in order to avoid infinite recursion and program crash.

Each time a recursive function calls itself, new memory is allocated from the stack to store its automatic variables. In our example, three different num variables were created, each with a different value. A simple way to describe that is to consider that each num is placed on top of the other (e.g., as dirty dishes are piled on top of each other) and at the end of the recursion we access the num created last (e.g., we get the dish at the top of the pile). For static variables no new memory is allocated, that is, all function calls share the same static variables. The information for which part of the code is left unexecuted is also stored in the stack. That code will be executed backwards when the function won't call itself again, that is, when the recursion ends.

In our example, the value of each num is stored in the stack and each cout will be executed in the opposite order from the function calls, that is, from the last one to the first one. This will happen when show() does not call itself again, that is, when num becomes 1.

However, the size of the stack might not be large enough to store the information associated with each function call. For example, if the user enters a large value, say 100000, the execution of the program may terminate abnormally and the message *Stack overflow* appear, which indicates that there is no other available memory in the stack. The default stack size depends on the implementation.

 Be careful when using a recursive function, because if it calls itself many times, its execution may take considerable time and its repeated calls may deplete the stack memory.

In practice, recursion is often used to implement math algorithms or operations in data structures. In general, when an individual task is a smaller version of the original task to be performed, it is a candidate to be implemented using a recursive function. For example, we'll use recursion in Chapter 14 to implement several functions in a binary search tree. However, if you can write equivalent code, it'd be probably a better idea. For example, use an iteration loop instead. Although the recursive code might be easier to read and write, the loop performance would be probably better as it avoids consecutive function calls and memory allocations in the stack.

EXERCISES

C.11.29 What is the output of the following program?

```
#include <iostream>

int a = 4;

int main()
{
    if(a == 0)
        return 0;
    else
    {
        std::cout << a-- << ' ';
        main();
    }
    return 0;
}
```

Answer: Note that main() can be also called recursively. In each call, a is decremented by 1. The program stops calling main() once a becomes 0. Therefore, the program displays: 4 3 2 1

C.11.30 What is the output of the following program?

```cpp
#include <iostream>

int unknown(const int arr[], int num);

int main()
{
        int arr[] = {10, 20, 30, 40};

        std::cout << unknown(arr, 4) << '\n';
        return 0;
}

int unknown(const int arr[], int num)
{
        if(num == 1)
                return arr[0];
        else
                return arr[num-1] + unknown(arr, num-1);
}
```

Answer: When `unknown()` is called, it returns:

```
arr[4-1 = 3] + unknown(arr, 4-1 = 3) =
arr[3] + (arr[3-1] + unknown(arr, 3-1)) =
arr[3] + arr[2] + (arr[2-1] + unknown(arr, 2-1)) =
arr[3] + arr[2] + arr[1] + unknown(arr, 1)
```

The last call of `unknown(arr, 1)` returns `arr[0]`, because `num = 1`. Therefore, the return value is `arr[3]+arr[2]+arr[1]+arr[0]`, that is, the function calculates recursively the sum of the array's elements. Thus, the program outputs `100`.

C.11.31 Write a recursive function that takes as parameter an integer n and returns its factorial, using the formula $n! = n \times (n-1)!$. The factorial of an integer n, where $n >= 1$, is the product of the integers from 1 to n, that is, $1 \times 2 \times 3 \times ... \times n$. The factorial of 0 is 1 $(0!=1)$. Write a program that reads a positive integer and uses the function to display its factorial. Since factorials grow rapidly and may exceed very fast the capacity of the larger type don't enter a large integer

```cpp
#include <iostream>

unsigned long long int fact(int num);

int main()
{
        int num;

        do
        {
                std::cout << "Enter a positive integer: ";
                std::cin >> num;
        } while(num < 0);

        std::cout << "Factorial of " << num << " is " << fact(num) << '\n';
        return 0;
}
```

```
unsigned long long int fact(int num)
{
        if((num == 0) || (num == 1))
                return 1;
        else
                return num * fact(num-1);
}
```

Comments: Notice that for large values of `num` the calls to `fact()` increase; therefore, the time to calculate its factorial also increases. In that case, the alternative solution with the `for` loop in C.6.3 calculates the factorial's number faster.

C.11.32 Write a recursive function that takes as parameter an integer (e.g., N) and returns the Nth term of the *Fibonacci* sequence, using the formula $F(N) = F(N-1) + F(N-2)$, where $F(0) = 0$ and $F(1) = 1$. Write a program that reads an integer N between 2 and 40 and uses the function to display the Nth term.

```
#include <iostream>

unsigned int fib(int num);

int main()
{
        int num;

        do
        {
                std::cout << "Enter a number between 2 and 40: ";
                std::cin >> num;
        } while(num < 2 || num > 40);

        std::cout << "Fib(" << num << ") = " << fib(num) << '\n';
        return 0;
}

unsigned int fib(int num)
{
        if(num == 0)
                return 0;
        else if(num == 1)
                return 1;
        else
                return fib(num-1) + fib(num-2);
}
```

Comments: This recursive solution for calculating Fibonacci numbers is not so efficient, because the calculation of the lower terms is repeated. For example, `fib(5) = fib(4) + fib(3)`. To calculate `fib(4)`, `fib(3)` and `fib(2)` are calculated. However, when the second term `fib(3)` is calculate, the same calculation for `fib(2)` is repeated. As a result, the execution time of `fib()`, especially for large values, increases significantly. Comparing the solutions, the code presented earlier in exercise C.11.15 is executed faster.

C.11.33 What does the following program do?

```cpp
#include <iostream>

int unknown(int num1, int num2);

int main()
{
        int num1, num2, sign;

        std::cout << "Enter numbers: ";
        std::cin >> num1 >> num2;
        sign = 1;

        if((num1 < 0) && (num2 > 0))
        {
                num1 = -num1;
                sign = -1;
        }
        else if((num1 > 0) && (num2 < 0))
        {
                num2 = -num2;
                sign = -1;
        }
        else if((num1 < 0) && (num2 < 0))
        {
                num1 = -num1;
                num2 = -num2;
        }
        if(num1 > num2)
                std::cout << sign*unknown(num1, num2) << '\n';
        else
                std::cout << sign*unknown(num2, num1) << '\n';
        return 0;
}

int unknown(int n1, int n2)
{
        if(n2 == 1)
                return n1;
        else
                return n1 + unknown(n1, n2-1);
}
```

Answer: First, let's see what the function is doing. Suppose that it is called with arguments 10 and 4. The function returns:

```
n1 + unknown(n1, n2-1 = 3) =
n1 + n1 + unknown(n1, n2-1 = 2) =
n1 + n1 + n1 + unknown(n1, n2-1 = 1)
```

The last call of unknown(n1, 1) returns n1, because n2 = 1. Therefore, the function returns:

```
n1+n1+n1+n1 = 4*n1 = n2*n1
```

The `if-else-if` series finds the sign of the product and the absolute values of the integers. The next `if-else` statement is used in order to make the less recursive calls. As a result, the purpose of this program is to calculate the product of the input numbers through the use of a recursive function.

C.11.34 Write a recursive function that takes as parameters a C form string, a character and any other parameter you think is needed and at the end it displays the number of occurrences of the character inside the string. Write a program that reads a string of less than 100 characters and a character and calls the function. Don't rush to see the answer, try it.

```cpp
#include <iostream>
using std::cout;
using std::cin;

void find(const char *p, int ch, int cnt);

int main()
{
        char ch, str[100];

        cout << "Enter text: ";
        cin.getline(str, sizeof(str));

        cout << "Enter character: ";
        ch = cin.get();
        find(str, ch, 0);
        return 0;
}

void find(const char *p, int ch, int cnt)
{
        if(*p == '\0')
                cout << cnt << '\n';
        else
        {
                if(*p == ch)
                        cnt++;
                find(p+1, ch, cnt);
        }
}
```

C.11.35 Sometimes in math it is very difficult to prove some problems that seem quite simple, like the one of the mathematician Lothar Collatz, who first proposed it. Think of a positive integer n and execute the following algorithm:

    a. If it is even, divide it by two (n/2).
    b. If it is odd, triple it and add one (3n+1).

Repeat the same process for each produced number and you'll come to a surprising result: for any integer you choose, you'll always end up with …1!!! For example, if we choose the number 53, the produced numbers are: 53 -> 160 -> 80 -> 40 -> 20 -> 10 -> 5 -> 16 -> 8 -> 4 -> 2 -> 1

This math problem, well known as "Collatz conjecture", remains unsolved, although the use of computing machines confirms that for any positive integer up to 2^{60} we'll eventually reach 1.

What I'm asking you is not to prove the "Collatz conjecture" and contest for the next Fields prize, but just that, to verify it with a simple program. Write a recursive function that takes as parameter a positive integer and displays the produced sequence of numbers.

```cpp
#include <iostream>

int collatz(int n);

int main()
{
        int a;

        do
        {
                std::cout << "Enter a positive integer: ";
                std::cin >> a;
        } while(a <= 0);

        std::cout << "The result is " << collatz(a) << " indeed!!!\n";
        return 0;
}

int collatz(int n)
{
        std::cout << n << '\n';
        if(n == 1)
                return 1;
        else if(n & 1) // If n is odd.
                return collatz(3*n+1);
        else // If n is even.
                return collatz(n/2);
}
```

Comments: Run the program for various positive integers. The result is really impressing. You'll always end up with 1.

UNSOLVED EXERCISES

U.11.1 Write a function that takes as parameters three integers and checks if the sum of the first two numbers is equal to the third one. If it is, the function should return the larger of the first two numbers, otherwise the smaller of the second and the third one. Write a program that reads three integers, calls the function, and displays the return value.

U.11.2 Write a function that takes as parameters two pointers to floats and returns the pointer to the variable with the larger value. Write a program that reads two floats and uses the function to display the larger of them.

U.11.3 Write the functions $f()$ and $g()$, as follows:

$$f(x) = \begin{cases} x+2, & x>0 \\ -3x+7, & x \leq 0 \end{cases} \qquad g(x) = \begin{cases} x^2+2, & x>0 \\ 7x-5, & x \leq 0 \end{cases}$$

Write a program that reads an integer (e.g., x) and uses $f()$ and $g()$ to display the result of $f(g(x))$, with the restriction that $g()$ must be called from inside $f()$.

U.11.4 What does the following function?

```
unsigned int test(const char *str)
{
        const char *ptr = str;

        for(; *str; str++)
                ;
        return str-ptr;
}
```

U.11.5 Write a function that takes as parameters two integers (e.g., a and b), reads 100 integers, and displays the minimum of those within [a, b]. Write a program that reads two integers and calls the function. *Note*: the first argument should be less than the second.

U.11.6 Write a `void` function that takes as parameters two arrays and the number of the elements (e.g., N) to compare. If the N first elements are the same, the function should return 1, 0 otherwise. Write a program that reads 200 `double` numbers and stores them in two arrays of 100 elements each. Then, the program should read the number of the elements to be compared, use the function to compare them and display the result. *Hint*: since the return type is `void` add a pointer argument to return the result of the comparison.

U.11.7 Write a function that returns the value of the polynomial $a_0 + a_1x + a_2x^2 + \ldots + a_nx^n$ for a given x. The function prototype is: `double poly(const vector<double>& a, double x, int n);` where the coefficients of the polynomial are stored into a and n represents its degree. Write a program that reads the degree of a polynomial and its coefficients and stores them in a `vector` object. Then, it reads a value (e.g., x) and uses the function to display the value of the polynomial. The program should restrict the user to input a value for the degree less than 100. To calculate the power of the coefficients, use the function `pow()`, which is declared in `cmath` as: `double pow(double a, double b);`

U.11.8 Write a function that takes as parameter an array and checks if it is sorted. If it is sorted in ascending order, the function should return 1, if in descending order it should return 2, otherwise, another value. Write a program that generates ten random integers in [5, 20], stores them in an array and uses the function to display an informative message if it is sorted or not.

U.11.9 What is the output of the following program?

```
#include <iostream>

void test(int **tmp, int i);

int main()
{
        int **tmp, *ptr, i, arr[] = {10, 20, 30};

        ptr = arr;
        tmp = &ptr;
        for(i = 0; i < 3; i++)
        {
                test(tmp, i);
                std::cout << arr[i] << '\n';
        }
        return 0;
}
```

```
void test(int **tmp, int i)
{
        *(*tmp + i)  += 50;
}
```

U.11.10 Write a `void` function that takes as parameters a `string` object and returns through appropriate parameters the number of its lowercase, uppercase letters, and digits. Write a program that reads a string and stores it into a `string` object. If it begins with `'a'` and ends with `'q'`, the program should call the function and display the return values.

U.11.11 Write a function that takes as parameters two strings and returns a pointer to the longest part in the first string that does not contain any character of the second string. If no part is found, the function should return `nullptr`. Write a program that reads two strings of less than 100 characters, calls the function, and displays that part.

U.11.12 Write a function that takes as parameters three 2×4 two-dimensional arrays, calculates the sum of the first two, and stores that sum into the third one. Write a program that reads 16 integers, stores them in two 2×4 two-dimensional arrays and uses the function to display their sum.

U.11.13 What are the values of the `arr` array in the following program?

```
#include <iostream>

int *test(int p[], int *ptr2);

int main()
{
        int i = 1, arr[] = {1, 2, 3, 4, 5, 6, 7, 8, 9, 10};

        *test(arr+2, &i) = 70;
        return 0;
}

int *test(int p[], int *ptr2)
{
        p[p[2]] = 50;
        return (++p)+*ptr2;
}
```

U.11.14 Write a program that simulates the popular game master-mind. The program should generate a random sequence of four different colours out of six available colours (e.g., red:0, green:1, blue:2, white:3, black:4, and yellow:5). This is the secret sequence. Then, the program should prompt the user to enter sequences of colours in order to find the secret one. For each given sequence, the program should inform the user for the number of the right colours in right places and the number of right colours in wrong places.

   For example, if the secret sequence to be found is: 0 1 2 3 and the user enters the sequence: 5 1 4 2, the program should display: "one right colour in the right place and one right colour in wrong place". If the user makes ten unsuccessful attempts, the program terminates and the user loses.

U.11.15 Write a `void` function that takes as parameters a 3×4 two-dimensional array, a row number, a column number, and uses proper parameters to return the largest value in that row and the smallest value in that column. Write a program that reads 12 integers and stores them in a 3×4 two-dimensional array. Then, the program should read a row number and a column number, and uses the function to display the largest value in that row and the smallest value in that column.

U.11.16 Write a function that takes as parameters a two-dimensional array and an integer and returns a pointer to the row in which that number appears the most times. If the number is not found, the function should return `nullptr`. Write a program that assigns random values to a 5x5 array of integers, it reads an integer and uses the function to display the elements of the row in which it appears the most times. *Note*: if the number appears in more than one row the same most times, the function should return the pointer to the first found.

U.11.17 A parking lot has 200 parking spaces for cars and 40 parking spaces for motos. Write a function (e.g., `find_plate()`) that takes as parameters a two-dimensional array which contains plate numbers of less than ten characters, the plate number of a vehicle, and a third one to specify the vehicle's type (e.g., `1` for cars). If the number is found in the array, the function should return its position in the array, `-1` otherwise.

Write a program that reads continuously plate numbers and their vehicle types. For each plate, the program should call `find_plate()`, and if it returns `-1`, it means that the vehicle is not parked and its plate number should be stored in the first available position of a respective two-dimensional array. Use a two-dimensional plate array for cars and another one for motos. To find an available position, write a second function. If `find_plate()` does not return `-1`, it means that the plate number is found and the program should set `0` to that position in order to free the space and charge it. The parking fee is $10 for the cars and $4 for the motos. If the user enters `end` for plate number, the program should terminate and display the total charge and the number of free spaces.

U.11.18 What is the output of the following program?

```
#include <iostream>

void test(int **tmp);

int main()
{
        int *ptr, arr[] = {5, 10, 15};

        ptr = arr;
        test(&ptr);

        std::cout << *ptr << '\n';
        return 0;
}

void test(int **tmp)
{
        int i;

        i = *(*tmp)++;
        std::cout << i << '\n';

        i = ++(**tmp);
        std::cout << i << '\n';
}
```

U.11.19 Write a program that accepts three command line arguments and displays them in alphabetical ascending order.

U.11.20 Write a program that displays the characters of its command line arguments in reverse order. For example, if the arguments are `one two`, the program should display `owt eno`.

U.11.21 Write a program that accepts as command line arguments the sign of a math operation, two one-digit numbers, and displays the result of the operation. For example, if the arguments are +, 5, -3, the program should display 2. The program should check that the input data are valid.

U.11.22 Write a function that accepts a variable number of pointers to integer arguments and returns the pointer to the largest number. Write a program that reads three integers and uses the function to display the largest value.

U.11.23 What is the output of the following program?

```cpp
#include <iostream>

void test(int val, int *tmp);

int main()
{
        int *ptr, i, arr[] = {5, 10, 15};

        ptr = arr;
        for(i = 0; i < 2; i++)
        {
                test(*ptr, ptr);
                ptr++;
        }
        while(ptr >= arr)
        {
                std::cout << *ptr << ' ';
                ptr--;
        }
        return 0;
}

void test(int val, int *tmp)
{
        std::cout << ++val << ' ' << (*tmp)++ << '\n';
}
```

U.11.24 Write a function (e.g., f()) that takes as parameters an integer (e.g., a) and a pointer to another function (e.g., g()). g() accepts an integer argument, and if that argument is positive it returns the corresponding negative, otherwise it returns the argument as is. If a is even, f() should use the pointer to call g() and display the return value. If it is odd (e.g., 5), it should change it to the next even (e.g., 6) and then call g(). Write a program that reads an integer and uses a pointer variable to call f(). *Note*: re-visit the section "Pointer to Function" in Chapter 8.

U.11.25 Modify the power() function in C.11.6 and use the formula $m^n = m \times m^{n-1}$ to calculate m^n recursively.

U.11.26 In math, a triangular number counts the number of objects needed to form an equilateral triangle, as shown below.

$T_0 = 0$ $T_1 = 1$ $T_2 = 3$ $T_3 = 6$

The T(n) triangular number declares the number of the objects composing the equilateral triangle, and it is equal to the sum of the numbers from 1 to n. Therefore, T(n) is expressed as:

$$T(n) = 1 + 2 + 3 + \ldots + (n-1) + n$$

and in a recursive form: $T(n) = \begin{cases} n, & for\, n = 0 \,or\, n = 1 \\ n + T(n-1), & for\, n > 1 \end{cases}$

Write a program that reads a positive integer (e.g., n) up to 20 and uses a recursive function to display the T(n) triangular number.

U.11.27 What is the output of the following program?

```cpp
#include <iostream>
#include <cstring>

void test(char a, char str[], char *ptr);

int main()
{
        char *tmp, txt[20] = "abcde";

        tmp = txt;
        test(*(tmp+1), txt+3, &txt[1]);
        std::cout << txt << '\n';
        return 0;
}

void test(char a, char str[], char *ptr)
{
        strcpy(str, "1234");
        str[0] = a;
        ptr[2] = *str + 5;
}
```

U.11.28 Write a program that generates ten integers in random and stores them in an array. Then, the program should call a recursive function to check if the array is symmetric, that is, if the value of the first element is equal to the last one, the value of the second one is equal to the value of the last but one, and so on. If the array is not symmetric, the function should return the position of the first element that breaks the symmetry.

U.11.29 Image editing programs often use the *flood fill* algorithm to fill similarly coloured connected areas with a new colour. Suppose that the two-dimensional 8×8 array of Figure a represents the pixels of an image, where 0 corresponds to black colour, 1: white, 2: red, 3: green, and 4: blue. We consider that a pixel is colour-linked to another only if it is adjacent to it and they have the same colour. For example, the similarly coloured areas are shown in Figure b.

```
0 0 0 1 1 1 2 2      0 0 0 1 1 1 2 2      3 3 3 1 1 1 2 2
0 4 4 4 1 1 1 2      0 4 4 4 1 1 1 2      3 4 4 4 1 1 1 2
4 4 4 4 4 2 2 2      4 4 4 4 4 2 2 2      4 4 4 4 4 2 2 2
0 0 3 3 3 3 3 3      0 0 3 3 3 3 3 3      0 0 3 3 3 3 3 3
0 0 0 0 3 3 1 1      0 0 0 0 3 3 1 1      0 0 0 0 3 3 1 1
0 0 3 3 3 1 1 1      0 0 3 3 3 1 1 1      0 0 3 3 3 1 1 1
0 1 1 1 1 1 1 1      0 1 1 1 1 1 1 2      0 1 1 1 1 1 1 2
1 2 2 2 2 2 2 2      1 2 2 2 2 2 2 2      1 2 2 2 2 2 2 2
       (a)                  (b)                  (c)
```

To implement the *flood fill* algorithm, write a recursive `floodfill()` function, which changes the colour (e.g., c) of a pixel at a random location (e.g., i, j) to a new colour and then it changes the colour of its adjacent pixels (i.e., the pixels to its left, right, up, and down) whose colour is also c. Notice that this process should continue recursively on the neighbours of the changed pixels, until there is no other pixel to check. For example, if we choose to change the colour of the pixel in the position 0,0 from black (e.g., 0) to green (e.g., 3), the colour of the top-left area of four pixels changes to green, as shown in Figure c.

Write a program that sets random values at [0, 4] to the elements of an 8×8 array of integers. Then, the program should read the position of a pixel (e.g., i, j) and a new colour and use `floodfill()` to change the existing colour of its similarly coloured area with the new one.

Searching and Sorting Arrays

12

This chapter describes some of the most common algorithms used for searching a value in an array and for sorting the elements of an array in ascending or descending order. For more algorithms, performance analysis, metrics, and best implementations you should read a book that focuses on this subject. The purpose of this chapter is to introduce you in this area and get a feeling of how algorithms can be implemented.

SEARCHING ARRAYS

To check whether a value is stored in an array, we are going to describe the linear and binary search algorithms.

Linear Search Algorithm

The linear search algorithm (also called sequential search) is the simplest algorithm to search for a value in a *non-sorted* array. The searched value is compared with the value of each element until a match is found. In an array of n elements, the maximum number of searches is n, which occurs when the searched value is either the last element or not in the array. In the following program, the linear_search() function implements the linear search algorithm.

EXERCISES

C.12.1 Write a function that searches for a number in an array of doubles. If the number is stored, the function should return the number of its occurrences and the position of its first occurrence, otherwise -1. Write a program that reads up to 100 doubles and stores them in an array. If the user enters -1, the insertion of numbers should terminate. Then, the program should read a double number and use the function to display its occurrences and the position of its first occurrence in the array.

```
#include <iostream>
using std::cout;
using std::cin;

const int SIZE = 100;

int linear_search(const double arr[], int size, double num, int *t);
```

```
int main()
{
      int i, times, pos;
      double num, arr[SIZE];

      for(i = 0; i < SIZE; i++)
      {
            cout << "Enter number: ";
            cin >> num;
            if(num == -1)
                  break;
            arr[i] = num;
      }
      cout << "Enter number to search: ";
      cin >> num;

      pos = linear_search(arr, i, num, &times); /* The variable i indicates
the number of the array's elements. */
      if(pos == -1)
            cout << num << "isn't found\n";
      else
            cout << num << " appears " << times << " times (first pos = "
<< pos << ")\n";
      return 0;
}

int linear_search(const double arr[], int size, double num, int *t)
{
      int i, pos;

      pos = -1;
      *t = 0;
      for(i = 0; i < size; i++)
      {
            if(arr[i] == num)
            {
                  (*t)++;
                  if(pos == -1) /* Store the position of the first
occurrence. */
                        pos = i;
            }
      }
      return pos;
}
```

Comments: Since a function cannot return two values, we use a pointer to return the second value.

C.12.2 Write a function that takes as parameter an integer array and returns the maximum number of the same occurrences. For example, if the array is {1, 10, -3, 5, -3, 8}, the function should return 2 because -3 appears the most times, that is, 2. Write a program that reads ten integers, stores them in an array, and uses the function to display the maximum number of the same occurrences.

```
#include <iostream>
using std::cout;
using std::cin;

const int SIZE = 10;
```

```cpp
int num_occurs(const int arr[]);

int main()
{
        int i, arr[SIZE];

        for(i = 0; i < SIZE; i++)
        {
                cout << "Enter number: ";
                cin >> arr[i];
        }
        cout << "\nMax occurrences is " << num_occurs(arr) << '\n';
        return 0;
}

int num_occurs(const int arr[])
{
        int i, j, k, max_times;

        max_times = 1;
        for(i = 0; i < SIZE; i++)
        {
                k = 1; // Each number appears once at least.
                for(j = i+1; j < SIZE; j++) /* Compare arr[i] with the rest
elements. */
                {
                        if(arr[i] == arr[j])
                                k++;
                }
                if(k > max_times)
                        max_times = k;
        }
        return max_times;
}
```

Binary Search Algorithm

The binary search algorithm is used to search for a value in a *sorted* array (either in ascending or descending order). To understand how the algorithm works, suppose that we are searching for a value in an array sorted in ascending order:

Step 1: We use the variables start and end to indicate the start and the end of the part of the array, in which we are searching for the value. We use the variable middle to store the middle position of that part: middle = (start+end)/2. For example, if we have a sorted array of 100 integers, start should be initialized to 0, end to 99, so middle becomes 49.

Step 2: We compare the value we are searching for with the middle element:

   a. If they are equal, the searched value is found and the algorithm terminates.

   b. If it is greater, the search continues in the part starting from the middle position and up to the end. The value of start becomes start = middle+1 and the algorithm goes back to Step 1.

   c. If it is less, the search continues in the part starting from the start position and up to the middle. The value of end becomes end = middle-1 and the algorithm goes back to Step 1.

In short, the binary search algorithm divides the array into two parts. Then, the searched value is compared with the middle element and the search continues in the proper part. The algorithm terminates if either the searched value is found or `start` becomes greater than `end`. The maximum number of searches in a sorted array of n elements with the binary search algorithm is $\log_2 n$. In the following program, the `binary_search()` function implements the binary search algorithm.

EXERCISES

C.12.3 Write a function that searches for a number in an array of integers. If the number is found, the function should return its position, otherwise -1. Write a program that initializes an array of integers with values sorted in ascending order. The program should read an integer and use the function to display its position in the array.

```cpp
#include <iostream>

int binary_search(const int arr[], int size, int num);

int main()
{
        int num, pos, arr[] = {10, 20, 30, 40, 50, 60, 70};

        std::cout << "Enter number to search: ";
        std::cin >> num;

        pos = binary_search(arr, sizeof(arr)/sizeof(int), num); /* The second
argument calculates in a generic way the number of the elements. */
        if(pos == -1)
                std::cout << num << " isn't found\n";
        else
                std::cout << num << " is found in position " << pos << '\n';
        return 0;
}

int binary_search(const int arr[], int size, int num)
{
        int start, end, middle;

        start = 0;
        end = size-1;
        while(start <= end)
        {
                middle = (start+end)/2;

                if(num < arr[middle])
                        end = middle-1;
                else if(num > arr[middle])
                        start = middle+1;
                else
                        return middle;
        }
        return -1; /* If the execution reaches this point it means that the
number was not found and the function returns -1. */
}
```

Comments: To see how the algorithm works, suppose that the user enters the number 45.

First iteration. The initial value of start is 0 and end is 6. middle becomes (start+end)/2 = 6/2 = 3. Since arr[middle] is 40, less than 45, the next statement to be executed is start = middle+1 = 3+1 = 4.

Second iteration. middle becomes (start+end)/2 = (4+6)/2 = 5. Since arr[middle] is 60, greater than 45, the next statement is end = middle-1 = 4.

Third iteration. middle becomes (start+end)/2 = (4+4)/2 = 4. Since arr[middle] is 50, greater than 45, the next statement is end = middle-1 = 3.

Since start is greater than end, the loop terminates and the function returns -1.

C.12.4 Write a program that reads an integer within [0, 1000] and uses the binary search algorithm to "guess" that number. The program should make questions to determine if the number we are searching for is less or greater than the middle of the examined interval. The answers must be given in the form of 0 (no) or 1 (yes). The program should display in how many tries the number was found.

```cpp
#include <iostream>
using std::cout;
using std::cin;
int main()
{
        int x, ans, low, high, middle, times;

        do
        {
                cout << "Enter number in [0, 1000]: ";
                cin >> x;
        } while(x < 0 || x > 1000);

        times = 1;
        low = 0;
        high = 1000;
        middle = (high+low)/2;
        while(high >= low)
        {
                cout << "Is " << middle << " the hidden number (0 = No, 1 =
Yes)?  ";
                cin >> ans;
                if(ans == 1)
                {
                        cout << "Num = " << " is found in " << times <<
" tries\n";
                        return 0;
                }
                times++;
                cout << "Is the hidden number < " << middle << " (0 = No,
1 = Yes)?   ";
                cin >> ans;
                if(ans == 1)
                {
                        high = middle-1;
                        middle = (high+low)/2;
                }
```

```
            else
            {
                    low = middle+1;
                    middle = (high+low)/2;
            }
        }
        cout << "Num = " << x << " isn't found. You probably gave a wrong
answer\n";
        return 0;
}
```

SORTING ARRAYS

There are several algorithms to sort an array. We are going to describe some of the most popular, the selection sort, the insertion sort, the bubble sort, and the quick sort algorithms.

Selection Sort Algorithm

To describe the algorithm, we'll sort an array in ascending order. At first, we find the element with the smallest value and we swap it with the first element of the array. Therefore, the smallest value is stored in the first position.

Then, we find the smallest value among the rest elements, except the first one. Like before, we swap that element with the second element of the array. Therefore, the second smallest value is stored in the second position. This procedure is repeated with the rest elements and the algorithm terminates once the last two elements are compared.

To sort the array in descending order, the only difference is that we find the largest value instead of the smallest. In the following program, the sel_sort() function implements the selection sort algorithm to sort an array in ascending order.

EXERCISES

C.12.5 Write a function that takes as parameters an array of doubles and uses the selection sort algorithm to sort it in ascending order. Write a program that reads the grades of ten students, stores them in an array, and uses the function to sort it.

```
#include <iostream>

void sel_sort(double arr[]);

const int SIZE = 10;

int main()
{
        int i;
        double grd[SIZE];
```

```
        for(i = 0; i < SIZE; i++)
        {
                std::cout << "Enter grade of stud_" << i+1 << ": ";
                std::cin >> grd[i];
        }
        sel_sort(grd);

        std::cout << "\n***** Sorted array *****\n";
        for(i = 0; i < SIZE; i++)
                std::cout << grd[i] << '\n';
        return 0;
}

void sel_sort(double arr[])
{
        int i, j;
        double tmp;

        for(i = 0; i < SIZE-1; i++)
        {
                for(j = i+1; j < SIZE; j++)
                {
                        if(arr[i] > arr[j])
                        {
                                // Swap values.
                                tmp = arr[i];
                                arr[i] = arr[j];
                                arr[j] = tmp;
                        }
                }
        }
}
```

Comments: In each iteration of the inner loop, `arr[i]` is compared with the elements from `i+1` up to `SIZE-1`. If an element is less than `arr[i]`, their values are swapped. Therefore, in each iteration of the outer loop, the smallest value of the elements from `i` up to `SIZE-1` is stored at `arr[i]`. To sort the array in descending order, we just change the `if` statement to: `if(arr[i] < arr[j])`

C.12.6 To continue the previous exercise, the program should also read the names of the ten students (less than 100 characters each) and display the final rating in ascending order of the given grades. The names should be stored in a `vector` object, which is passed as an extra argument to the `sel_sort()`.

```
#include <iostream>
#include <string>
#include <vector>
using namespace std;

void sel_sort(vector<string>& str, double arr[]);

const int SIZE = 10;

int main()
{
        int i;
        double grd[SIZE];
        vector<string> name(SIZE);
```

```
        for(i = 0; i < SIZE; i++)
        {
                cout << "Enter name: ";
                getline(cin, name[i]);

                cout << "Enter grade: ";
                cin >> grd[i];
                cin.get();
        }
        sel_sort(name, grd);

        cout << "\n***** Final Rating *****\n";
        for(i = 0; i < SIZE; i++)
                cout << name[i] << '\t' << grd[i] << '\n';
        return 0;
}

void sel_sort(vector<string>& str, double arr[])
{
        int i, j;
        double k;
        string tmp;

        for(i = 0; i < SIZE-1; i++)
        {
                for(j = i+1; j < SIZE; j++)
                {
                        if(arr[i] > arr[j])
                        {
                                // Parallel swapping of grades and names.
                                k = arr[i];
                                arr[i] = arr[j];
                                arr[j] = k;

                                tmp = str[j];
                                str[j] = str[i];
                                str[i] = tmp;
                        }
                }
        }
}
```

C.12.7 Write the add_sort() function that inserts a number into a sorted array, so that the array remains sorted. Write a program that reads nine integers, stores them in an array of ten integers, and sorts these nine elements in ascending order. Then, the program should read the last integer, use the add_sort() to insert it in the array and display the sorted array.

```
#include <iostream>
using std::cout;
using std::cin;

void sel_sort(int arr[], int size);
void add_sort(int arr[], int size, int num);
```

```cpp
const int SIZE = 10;

int main()
{
      int i, num, a[SIZE];

      for(i = 0; i < SIZE-1; i++) // Store 9 integers.
      {
            cout << "Enter number: ";
            cin >> a[i];
      }
      sel_sort(a, SIZE-1); // Sort the 9 elements.

      cout << "Insert number in sorted array: ";
      cin >> num;

      add_sort(a, SIZE-1, num); // Insert the last integer in the array.
      for(i = 0; i < SIZE; i++)
            cout << a[i] << '\n';
      return 0;
}

void add_sort(int arr[], int size, int num)
{
      int i, pos;

      if(num <= arr[0])
            pos = 0;
      else if(num >= arr[size-1]) /* If it greater than the last one, store
it in the last position and return. */
      {
            arr[size] = num;
            return;
      }
      else
      {
            for(i = 0; i < size-1; i++)
            {
            /* Check all adjacent pairs up to the last one at positions
SIZE-3 and SIZE-2 to find the position to insert the number. */
                        if(num >= arr[i] && num <= arr[i+1])
                              break;
            }
            pos = i+1;
      }
      for(i = size; i > pos; i--)
            arr[i] = arr[i-1]; /* The elements are shifted one position to
the right, starting from the last position of the array, that is [SIZE-1], up
to the position in which the new number will be inserted. For example, in the
last iteration, i = pos+1, so, arr[pos+1] = arr[pos]. */
      arr[pos] = num; // Store the number.
}

void sel_sort(int arr[], int size)
{
      int i, j, temp;
```

```
        for(i = 0; i < size-1; i++)
        {
                for(j = i+1; j < size; j++)
                {
                        if(arr[i] > arr[j])
                        {
                                // Swap values.
                                temp = arr[i];
                                arr[i] = arr[j];
                                arr[j] = temp;
                        }
                }
        }
}
```

C.12.8 Write a function that takes as parameter a two-dimensional array and sorts its rows in ascending order and another function that sorts its columns in descending order. Write a program that generates 20 random integers and stores them in a 4×5 array. Then, the program should read an integer and if it is 1, the program should call the first function, otherwise the second one.

```
#include <iostream>
#include <iomanip>
#include <cstdlib>
#include <ctime>
using namespace std;

const int ROWS = 4;
const int COLS = 5;

void sort_rows(int arr[][COLS]);
void sort_cols(int arr[][COLS]);

int main()
{
        int i, j, type, arr[ROWS][COLS];

        srand(time(NULL));
        for(i = 0; i < ROWS; i++)
                for(j = 0; j < COLS; j++)
                        arr[i][j] = rand();

        cout << "Enter sort type (1: rows): ";
        cin >> type;
        if(type == 1)
                sort_rows(arr);
        else
                sort_cols(arr);

        for(i = 0; i < ROWS; i++)
        {
                for(j = 0; j < COLS; j++)
                        cout << setw(10) << arr[i][j];
                cout << '\n';
        }
        return 0;
}
```

```c
void sort_rows(int arr[][COLS])
{
        int i, j, k, temp;

        for(i = 0; i < ROWS; i++)
        {
                for(j = 0; j < COLS-1; j++)
                {
                        for(k = j+1; k < COLS; k++)
                        {
                                if(arr[i][j] > arr[i][k])
                                {
                                        temp = arr[i][j];
                                        arr[i][j] = arr[i][k];
                                        arr[i][k] = temp;
                                }
                        }
                }
        }
}

void sort_cols(int arr[][COLS])
{
        int i, j, k, temp;

        for(j = 0; j < COLS; j++)
        {
                for(i = 0; i < ROWS-1; i++)
                {
                        for(k = i+1; k < ROWS; k++)
                        {
                                if(arr[i][j] < arr[k][j])
                                {
                                        temp = arr[i][j];
                                        arr[i][j] = arr[k][j];
                                        arr[k][j] = temp;
                                }
                        }
                }
        }
}
```

Insertion Sort Algorithm

To describe the algorithm, we'll sort an array in ascending order. The operation of the algorithm is based on sequential comparisons between each element (starting from the second and up to the last element) and the elements on its left, which form the "sorted subarray". The elements on its right form the "unsorted subarray". In particular, the most left element of the "unsorted subarray" (i.e., the examined element) is compared against the elements of the "sorted subarray" from right to left, according to that:

Step 1: At first, the examined element is stored in a temporary variable (Figure a).
Step 2a: If it is not less than the most right element of the "sorted subarray", its position does not change and the algorithm continues with the testing of the next most left element.

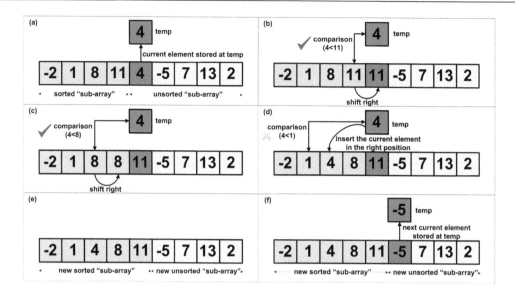

Step 2b: If it is less than the most right element of the "sorted subarray", the latter is shifted one position to the right while the examined element is compared against the most right but one element (Figures b and c). If it is not less, the examined element is stored at the position of the last shifted element, otherwise the same procedure is repeated (the most right but one element is shifted one position to the right and the examined element is compared against the most right but two elements) (Figures c and d). Step 2b terminates either if the examined element is not less than an element of the "sorted subarray" (Figures d and e) or the first element of the "sorted subarray" is reached. Then, Step 1 is repeated for the new most left element (Figures e and f).

The algorithm terminates when the most right element of the "unsorted subarray" is tested.

The algorithm resembles the way that a card player would sort a card game hand, assuming that the player starts with an empty left hand and all cards face down on the table. The player picks up a card with his right hand and inserts it in the correct position in the left hand. To find the correct position, that card is compared against the cards in the left hand, from right to left.

To sort the array in descending order, the only difference is that an element of the "sorted subarray" is shifted one position to the right if it is less than the examined element. In the following program, the `insert_sort()` function implements the insertion sort algorithm to sort an array in ascending order.

EXERCISE

C.12.9 Write a function that takes as parameter an array of integers and uses the insertion sort algorithm to sort it in ascending order. Write a program that reads five integers, stores them in an array, and uses the function to sort it.

```
#include <iostream>

const int SIZE = 5;
```

```
void insert_sort(int arr[]);

int main()
{
        int i, a[SIZE];

        for(i = 0; i < SIZE; i++)
        {
                std::cout << "Enter number: ";
                std::cin >> a[i];
        }
        insert_sort(a);
        std::cout << "\n***** Sorted array *****\n";
        for(i = 0; i < SIZE; i++)
                std::cout << a[i] << '\n';
        return 0;
}

void insert_sort(int arr[])
{
        int i, j, temp;
        for(i = 1; i < SIZE; i++)
        {
                temp = arr[i];
                j = i;
                while((j > 0) && (arr[j-1] > temp))
                {
                        arr[j] = arr[j-1]; /* Shift this element one position to
the right. */

                        j--;
                }
                arr[j] = temp;
        }
}
```

Comments: The `for` loop compares the elements starting from the second one. In each iteration, `temp` holds the examined element. The `while` loop shifts one position to the right the elements being on the left of the examined element and are greater than it. To see how the algorithm works, suppose that the array elements are: 7, 3, 1, 9, 4.

>   *First **for** loop iteration (i = 1 and* `temp = arr[1]` *= 3)*
>   *(j = 1) First **while** loop iteration:* 7 --> 3   1   9   4

So, the array is transformed to: 3   7   1   9   4

>   *Second **for** loop iteration (i = 2 and* `temp = arr[2]` *= 1)*
>   *(j = 2) First **while** loop iteration:* 3   7 --> 1   9   4
>   *(j = 1) Second **while** loop iteration:* 3 --> 7   1   9   4

So, the array is transformed to: 1   3   7   9   4

>   *Third **for** loop iteration (i = 3 and* `temp = arr[3]` *= 9)*
>   *(j = 3)* No shifting takes place because the fourth array element (i.e., `arr[3]` = 9) is greater than the "most right element" (i.e., `arr[2]` = 7).

So, the array remains the same: 1 3 7 9 4

> *Fourth* for *loop iteration* (i = 4 *and* temp = arr[4] = 4)
> (j = 4) *First* while *loop iteration:* 1   3   7   9 --> 4
> (j = 3) *Second* while *loop iteration:* 1   3   7 --> 9   4

The sorting is completed and the array is transformed to: 1   3   4   7   9

To sort the array in descending order, we just change the while statement to:

```
while((j > 0) && (arr[j-1] < temp))
```

in order to shift one position to the right the elements of the "sorted subarray", which are less than the examined element.

Bubble Sort Algorithm

The bubble sort algorithm is based on sequential comparisons between adjacent array elements. Each element "bubbles" up and is stored in the proper position. For example, suppose that we want to sort an array in ascending order.

At first, the last element is compared against the last by one. If it is less, the elements are swapped, so the smaller value "bubbles" up. Then, the last by one element is compared against the last by two. Like before, if it is less, the elements are swapped, so the smaller value keeps "bubbling" up. The comparisons continue up to the beginning of the array, and eventually the smallest value "bubbles" to the top of the array and it is stored at its first position.

This procedure is repeated from the second element and up to the last one, so the second smallest value of the array "bubbles" to the top and stored in the second position. The same is repeated for the part of the array from its third element and up to the last one, and so forth. The algorithm terminates when none element "bubbles" to the top.

To sort the array in descending order, the "bubbling" value is the greatest and not the smallest one. In the following program, the bubble_sort() function implements the bubble sort algorithm to sort an array in ascending order.

EXERCISES

C.12.10 Write a function that takes as parameter an array of integers and uses the bubble sort algorithm to sort it in ascending order. Write a program that reads five integers, stores them in an array, and uses the function to sort it.

```
#include <iostream>

const int SIZE = 5;

void bubble_sort(int arr[]);

int main()
{
        int i, a[SIZE];
```

```
        for(i = 0; i < SIZE; i++)
        {
                std::cout << "Enter number: ";
                std::cin >> a[i];
        }
        bubble_sort(a);

        std::cout << "\n***** Sorted array *****\n";
        for(i = 0; i < SIZE; i++)
                std::cout << a[i] << '\n';
        return 0;
}

void bubble_sort(int arr[])
{
        bool reorder;
        int i, j, temp;

        for(i = 1; i < SIZE; i++)
        {
                reorder = 0;
                for(j = SIZE-1; j >= i; j--)
                {
                        if(arr[j] < arr[j-1])
                        {
                                // Swap values.
                                temp = arr[j];
                                arr[j] = arr[j-1];
                                arr[j-1] = temp;
                                reorder = 1;
                        }
                }
                if(reorder == 0)
                        return;
        }
}
```

Comments: The `reorder` variable checks if the sorting is completed in order to avoid unnecessary iterations. If two elements are swapped, it is set to `1`. Otherwise, the value `0` means that the array is sorted and the function terminates. To see how the algorithm works, suppose that the array elements are: 10, 9, 4, 7, 6.

*First iteration of the outer **for***(i = 1)
  *First iteration of the inner **for**(j = 4)*: 10   9   4   6 <-> 7
  *Second iteration of the inner **for**(j = 3)*: 10   9   4   6   7
  *Third iteration of the inner **for**(j = 2)*: 10   4 <-> 9   6   7
  *Fourth iteration of the inner **for**(j = 1)*: 4 <-> 10   9   6   7

So, the array is transformed to: 4   10   9   6   7

*Second iteration of the outer **for***(i = 2)
  *First iteration of the inner **for**(j = 4)*: 4   10   9   6   7
  *Second iteration of the inner **for**(j = 3)*: 4   10   6 <-> 9   7
  *Third iteration of the inner **for**(j = 2)*: 4   6 <-> 10   9   7

So, the array is transformed to: 4   6   10   9   7

> *Third iteration of the outer* for*(i = 3)*
> *First iteration of the inner* for*(j = 4):* 4   6   10   7 <-> 9
> *Second iteration of the inner* for*(j = 3):* 4   6   7 <-> 10   9

So, the array is transformed to: 4   6   7   10   9

> *Fourth iteration of the outer* for*(i = 4)*
> *First iteration of the inner* for*(j = 4):* 4   6   7   10 <-> 9

The sorting is completed and the array is transformed to: 4   6   7   9   10
To sort the array in descending order, we just change the if statement to:

```
if(arr[j] > arr[j-1])
```

C.12.11 Write a program that reads the names of 50 countries (less than 100 characters each) and the number of tourists visited them on monthly basis. The program should use proper arrays to store the data. Then, the program should read the name of a country and display the annual number of tourists who visited that country. The program should display the five most visited countries (check if more than one country ties in the fifth place) before it ends.

```cpp
#include <iostream>
#include <cstring>
using std::cout;
using std::cin;

const int CNTRS = 50;
const int MONTHS = 12;

void bubble_sort(char str[][100], int arr[]);

int main()
{
        bool flag;
        char cntr[CNTRS][100], str[100];
        int i, j, tmp, tour[CNTRS] = {0};

        for(i = 0; i < CNTRS; i++)
        {
                cout << "Enter name of country_" << i+1 << ": ";
                cin.getline(cntr[i], sizeof(cntr[i]));

                for(j = 0; j < MONTHS; j++)
                {
                        cout << "Enter tourists of month_" << j+1 << ": ";
                        cin >> tmp;
                        tour[i] += tmp; /* This array holds the annual number of
tourists for each country. */
                }
                cin.get();
        }
        cout << "Enter country to search: ";
        cin.getline(str, sizeof(str));
```

```
        flag = 0;
        for(i = 0; i < CNTRS; i++)
        {
                if(strcmp(str, cntr[i]) == 0)
                {
                        flag = 1;
                        cout << tour[i] << " tourists visited " << str << '\n';
                        break;
                }
        }
        if(flag == 0)
                cout << str << " not registered\n";

        bubble_sort(cntr, tour); /* Sort the tourist array and update the
countries array in parallel. */
        cout << "\n***** Tourists in decrease order *****\n";
        for(i = 0; i < 5; i++)
                cout << i+1 << '.' << cntr[i] << '\t' << tour[i] << '\n';

        // Check if more than one country ties in the fifth place.
        while((tour[i] == tour[4]) && i < CNTRS)
        {
                cout << i+1 << '.' << cntr[i] << '\t' << tour[i] << '\n';
                i++;
        }
        return 0;
}

void bubble_sort(char str[][100], int arr[])
{
        bool reorder;
        char temp[100];
        int i, j, k;

        for(i = 1; i < CNTRS; i++)
        {
                reorder = 0;
                for(j = CNTRS-1; j >= i; j--)
                {
                        if(arr[j] > arr[j-1]) /* Parallel swapping of the
tourist numbers and the respective countries. */
                        {
                                k = arr[j];
                                arr[j] = arr[j-1];
                                arr[j-1] = k;

                                strcpy(temp, str[j]);
                                strcpy(str[j], str[j-1]);
                                strcpy(str[j-1], temp);
                                reorder = 1;
                        }
                }
                if(reorder == 0)
                        return;
        }
}
```

Comments: To store the names we could use a `vector` object as in C.12.6, instead of the `cntr` two-dimensional array. As I've mentioned, I chose this way, to get used to both approaches.

Quick Sort Algorithm

The quick sort algorithm is a kind of *divide and conquer* type. It is a particularly popular algorithm and the best choice for a variety of sorting applications. Its operation is based on the partition of the array into two parts and the separate sorting of each part. At first, the element of the partition is selected (i.e., a[i]). The array is reordered according to the following:

    a. a[i] is set in its final position.
    b. no element in the left subarray a[1], ... a[i-1] is greater than a[i].
    c. no element in the right subarray a[i+1], ... a[r] is less than a[i].

This process is recursively repeated for each of the subarrays, until those parts become single elements.

The performance of the algorithm depends on the selection of the partition element. If we are aware of the array content, the best choice is an element that divides the array near the middle. To give you an implementation example, let's sort an array in ascending order. To improve the performance of the algorithm, several methods have been proposed for the optimum selection of the partition element. For simplicity in the implementation, we select the most right element.

We scan the array from left to right until we find an element greater or equal than the partition element. Then, we scan the array from right to left until we find an element less than the partition element. Since those two elements are not in right positions, we swap them. Repeating this procedure, the result is that no element in the left subarray is greater than the partition element and no element in the right subarray is less than the partition element. We use index i for the left scan and index j for the right scan. When the two indexes are met, the rightmost element is swapped with the element indexed by i and the partition is completed. To implement the algorithm we'll use recursion.

```cpp
#include <iostream>

int partition(int a[], int l, int r);
void quick_sort(int a[], int l, int r);

const int SIZE = 7;

int main()
{
        int i, a[SIZE];

        for(i = 0; i < SIZE; i++)
        {
                std::cout << "Enter number: ";
                std::cin >> a[i];
        }
        quick_sort(a, 0, SIZE-1);

        std::cout << "\n***** Sorted array *****\n";
        for(i = 0; i < SIZE; i++)
                std::cout << a[i] << '\n';
        return 0;
}

void quick_sort(int a[], int l, int r)
{
        int i;
```

```
        if(r <= l)
                return;
        i = partition(a, l, r);
        quick_sort(a, l, i-1);
        quick_sort(a, i+1, r);
}

int partition(int a[], int l, int r)
{
        int i, j, v, tmp;

        i = l;
        j = r-1;
        v = a[r];
        while(1)
        {
                while(a[i] < v)
                        i++;
                while(a[j] >= v)
                {
                        if(j == l) /* We check the case that the partition
element is the lower in the examined part. */
                                break;
                        j--;
                }
                if(i >= j)
                        break;
                tmp = a[i];
                a[i] = a[j];
                a[j] = tmp;
        }
        tmp = a[i];
        a[i] = a[r];
        a[r] = tmp;
        return i;
}
```

Comments: To see how the algorithm works, suppose that the user enters the values: 2, 15, 4, 1, 7, 20, 5. Let's trace the first call of partition(). We have i=l=0, j=r-1=5, v=a[6]=5. The first loop performs the left scan and terminates once i becomes 1 (since a[1] > 5). The second loop performs the right scan and terminates once j becomes 3 (since a[3] < 5). The two elements are swapped and the array is transformed to: 2, 1, 4, 15, 7, 20, 5.

Left scan continues and terminates once i becomes 3 (since a[3] > 5). Right scan continues and terminates once j becomes 2 (since a[2] < 5). Because i > j the infinite loop terminates. a[3] and a[6] are swapped and the array is transformed to: 2, 1, 4, 5, 7, 20, 15. Notice that 5 is set in its final position and all elements in its left are less, while all elements in its right are greater. The function returns the value of i, that is, 3. Then, recursion is used to repeat the same procedure for the left subarray (positions 0 to 2) and for the right subarray (positions 4 to 6).

Before finishing this chapter, I'd like to note that although the standard library provides many ready-to-use algorithms (e.g., find()) it is very important to have some experience in implementing algorithms by yourself. Not only because you may need that knowledge either to write your own algorithms or understand code written by others, but also to get an idea about how they are implemented. For example, it is helpful for your programming expertise to know how a sorting algorithm is implemented than just using the sort() function without having any idea. With the implementation examples of this chapter, I tried to give you this feeling of know-how.

UNSOLVED EXERCISES

U.12.1 Write a program that reads the populations of 100 cities and stores them in ascending order in an array when entered. The program should display the array, before it ends. For example, if the users enters 2000 and then 1000, the first two elements should be 1000, 2000. If the next input value is 1500, the first three elements should be 1000, 1500, and 2000.

U.12.2 Write a program that reads the names of 50 students (less than 100 characters each) and stores them in an array. Suppose that the user enters the names in alphabetical order. Use a second array and do the same for another group of 70 students. The program should merge the two arrays into a third one, where all names should be stored in alphabetical order.

U.12.3 Write a program that reads the names of 20 cities (store them in a vector object) and the average monthly temperatures for each city. Then, the program should read a city name and display the warmest month (e.g., 1:Jan–12:Dec) for that city. Also, the program should display for the same city the months with higher temperature than the previous and next month.

U.12.4 Modify C.12.3 so that the program reads a string of less than 100 characters and uses a new version of binary_search() to display its position in the array, if found. Use the following sorted array and the new prototype to modify the function.

```cpp
int binary_search(const char *arr[], int size, const char *str);

int main()
{
        const char *arr[] = {"alpha", "bita", "camma", "delta",
"epsilon", "ita", "omega"};
        char str[100];
        int pos;
        ...
}
```

U.12.5 Write a recursive version of the binary_search() in C.12.3. Use the following prototype to modify the function. Here is an example how to call it:

```cpp
int binary_search(const int arr[], int num, int start, int end);

int main()
{
    ...
    pos = binary_search(arr, num, 0, sizeof(arr)/sizeof(int)-1);
    ...
}
```

U.12.6 Modify sel_sort() of C.12.5 using the p1 and p2 pointers to sort arr in ascending order.

```cpp
void sel_sort(double arr[])
{
        double *p1, *p2, tmp;

        ...
}
```

U.12.7 Write a program that reads the names of ten students (less than 100 characters each), stores them in a two-dimensional array, and uses the bubble sort algorithm to sort the array in alphabetical order. The program should display the array, before it ends.

U.12.8 Write a program that reads the names of ten courses (store them in a vector object) and the grades of 50 students on those courses. The program should display the names of the courses and the average grade next to them, starting with the course with the best average. In case of same average, the program should display the "tied" courses in alphabetical order. To sort the array, use the bubble sort algorithm. Re-visit C.12.6 to see how to use the vector object.

U.12.9 In a music contest, 200 judges vote for the top songs out of 50 songs. Write a program that reads the names of the songs (store them in a vector object) and displays the top five songs. If there is a tie in the fifth place, the program should display the "tied" songs. To vote for a song, the judge enters its title. Each judge can vote up to five songs or less and enter the word end as a song title. Assume that the judge does not vote for the same song more than once. To sort the array, use the selection sort algorithm.

U.12.10 Write a program that reads the prices and the book titles (less than 100 characters each) of two bookstores. Assume that the maximum number of books in each bookstore is 200. If the user enters end for book title, the insertion of books should terminate. The program should display the book titles and prices of both bookstores sorted by price descending order. There is one restriction. If a title is found in both bookstores, the program should display that title once with the price in the first bookstore.

U.12.11 Write a program that reads the names of 1000 candidates, their score, and the name of the school they were accepted. The program should use vector objects to store the names of the candidates and the schools. Then, the program should read a candidate's name and display the school, as well as the score and the names of all candidates accepted in that same school sorted by score descending order. For example if the user enters:

```
P.Smith        2300        CIT
A.Leep         1200        LU
R.Bachir       1600        LU
B.Koong        2800        BPL
```

and then the user enters A.Leep, the program should display LU and:

```
R.Bachir       1600        LU
A.Leep         1200        LU
```

U.12.12 Suppose that 20 firms participate in a contest. Each firm rates the other firms with a grade in [1, 20]. Write a program that reads their names (less than 100 characters) and the grades each firm gives to the others. The program should check that each given grade is in [1, 20] and that it is not already given. Then, the program should calculate the total score for each firm and display the rank list in score descending order.

Structures and Unions

13

This chapter introduces two new types that may be defined by the programmer: *structures* and *unions*. Both help to organize data in a more natural way. Like arrays, structures and unions group a set of values into a single entity. However, their properties are quite different from an array's. The main difference is that, unlike arrays, the members of a structure or union may have *different* types. Also, to access a member of a structure or union, we specify its *name*, not its position. This chapter discusses how to declare structures and unions types, declare variables, and perform operations on them. Essentially, this chapter introduces us to the philosophy of object-oriented programming and will help us to understand the concepts of classes and objects that we'll meet in Chapter 17.

STRUCTURES

Because the concept of the structure is similar to that of the class, which is the fundamental concept of C++, please pay special attention to this chapter so that when we discuss about classes you know the basics.

A structure is a collection of data items used to group information that describes a logical entity. For example, a structure may hold information about a company, such as its name, business core, tax number, number of employees, contact information, and other data or even functions that manage the stored data.

Declare a Structure

To declare a structure we use the `struct` keyword. The general syntax for a structure declaration is:

```
struct structure_tag
{
    Declarations of data members;
    Declarations of functions;
} variable_list;
```

A `struct` declaration creates a type. Since this type is defined by the programmer, it is a *user-defined* type. Although the `structure_tag` is optional, we'll name each structure type we create so that we can use this name, whenever we want, in order to declare respective variables. We'll see another use of the `structure_tag` in Chapter 14 when declaring self-referential structures to form linked lists. In that case it is required to use a structure tag. The *members* or else called *fields* of a structure are used like the ordinary variables. A structure is more versatile than an array, because it may contain elements of different data types. Their logical correlation is that they contain the information needed to describe a particular entity. Also, a structure may contain functions. For simplicity, we'll use structures that contain only variables and not functions. We'll add functions later, when we discuss classes.

DOI: 10.1201/9781003230076-13

As we'll see next, we can declare an optional `variable_list` of that structure type. Don't forget the; at the end. For example, to store information about a company, we declare the type `Company`:

```
struct Company
{
        string name;
        int start_year;
        int field;
        int tax_num;
        int num_empl;
        string addr;
        float balance;
};
```

The first letter of the name is usually in capital. Although members of the same type can be declared in the same line, my preference is to declare them separately to make it easier for the reader to read the stored data.

 The declaration of a structure not followed by a list of variables does not invoke any memory allocation. It just describes the template of the structure.

If a structure tag is used, we can use that tag to declare variables. For example:

```
Company c1, c2;
```

To make it clear, the declaration of the `Company` structure defines a user-defined data type with that name; it does not cause memory allocation, nor is the `Company` a variable. The `Company` just describes what the structure variables will look like when they are declared. The c1 and c2 variables are declared as structures of the type `Company`. Each variable contains its own members and the compiler allocates memory for them. The syntax is as if we were declaring a variable of some basic type (e.g., `int`), we just put the name of the structure type (e.g., `Company`) in the place of `int`. Alternatively, we can declare the variables in the `variable_list`. For example:

```
struct Book
{
        string title;
        int year;
        float price;
} b1, b2;
```

The b1 and b2 variables are declared as structures of the type H HBook. If we declare all the variables we need in the `variable_list`, the tag (i.e., `Book`) may be omitted. However, in order to be able to declare variables whenever we need, my suggestion is always to name the structure and use that tag to declare variables. The typical practice is to put the structure declarations together with other declarations like function prototypes and macros in a header file and use the `#include` directive to include it, when needed. For simplicity, in all next programs, we'll define each structure type with global scope so that all functions may use it. If it is defined inside a function its scope becomes local, so it can only be used in that function.

Each structure (or union) type creates a separate space which specifies its own scope for its members. Therefore, it is allowed to declare ordinary variables with the same names as the members or the tag of a structure. For the same reason, the same member names can be reused in other structures. For example:

```
struct Person
{
        string name;
        int tax_num;
        string addr;
};
```

These three members have no relation with the respective members of the Company type. As another example, check the following declarations:

```
int a;
struct S1 {int a[5]; } s1;
struct S2 {int *a; } s2;
```

Next, you'll learn that we can write s1.a[0] = a; or s2.a = &a; or s2.a = s1.a; without any problem.

Although a structure type is completed with the right brace}, a structure can contain a pointer to an instance of itself because C++ allows the declaration of pointers to incomplete types. For example:

```
struct A
{
        A *p;
};
```

When a structure variable is declared, the compiler allocates memory to store its members in the order in which they are declared. For example, the following program displays how many bytes the variable d allocates.

```
#include <iostream> // Example 13.1

struct Date
{
        int day;
        int month;
        int year;
};

int main()
{
        Date d;

        std::cout << sizeof(d) << '\n';
        return 0;
}
```

For those who know structures from C, a C structure has similar properties to a C++ structure with some differences. One difference is that in C++ the word struct does not need to be added in the declaration of such variables. In C++, the tag can be used like a basic type. This change emphasizes the fact that the declaration of a structure defines a new type. Another difference is that in C++ the structure can also contain functions. However, we will not see such examples of structures, because, as we'll see in Chapter 17, the type that is usually chosen when we want to use functions is the class type and not the structure. There are more differences; those two are the most important.

Let's explain the program. Since d contains three integer members, the allocated memory is 3*4 = 12 bytes. However, the allocated size may be larger than the sizes of the members added together. For example, if we change the type of the day member from int to char, the program may display again 12, not 9 as might expected.

This can happen if the compiler requires that each member is stored in an address multiple of some number (typically four). This requirement may be set for a faster access of the structure members. If we assume that the month member should be stored in an address multiple of four, the compiler would allocate three more bytes, a "hole", right after the day member. In that case, the program would display 12. Holes may exist between members and at the end of the structure, but not at the beginning.

I won't get into details, but if you ever write an application that uses many structures and the memory is limited, keep in mind that the order of the member declarations might affect the alignment and create holes. For example:

```
struct S1
{
        char c;
        double d;
        short s;
};

struct S2
{
        double d;
        short s;
        char c;
};
```

Although the members are the same, reordering the members, from the larger to smaller may save memory. For example, an S1 variable might allocate more bytes than an S2 variable, that is, 24 bytes instead of 16, in case the compiler leaves holes to align the members to the larger type (i.e., double). And if we have an array of S1 elements, the "holes" remain between the successive elements, to keep the alignment.

 To calculate the memory size of a structure variable always use the sizeof operator; don't add the sizes of its members.

Although it is not often used, it is good to know about the offsetof macro. It is defined in cstddef and takes two arguments. The first one is the type of the structure and the second one the name of a member. The macro calculates the number of bytes from the beginning of the structure up to the member. For example, consider the S2 structure. Since C++ guarantees that the address of the first member is the same as the address of the entire structure, the statement:

cout << offsetof(S2, d); outputs 0. If we replace d with s, the code outputs 8. Because a structure may contain holes, if you write an application to run in different platforms and member alignment matters that macro might be useful to check the portability of your program. Note that the use of offsetof imposes restrictions that you should consider before using it.

C++11 provides the alignof operator, which returns the alignment, in bytes, of the indicated type. For example:

```
double d;
cout << alignof(d) << '\n';
```

The code outputs the alignment of the double type (e.g., 8).

C++11 also provides the `alignas` specifier, which can be used to specify the alignment of the type. For example:

```cpp
struct alignas(64) A
{
        int i;
}
cout << alignof(A) << '\n'; // The code outputs 64.
```

Each A variable will be aligned to a boundary of 64 bytes. Note that the number of bytes should be a valid alignment, such as a power of 2.

Initializing a Structure

The most common method to access a structure member is to write the name of the structure variable followed by the `.` operator and the name of the member. For example, the following program displays the values of the b members:

```cpp
#include <iostream> // Example 13.2
#include <string>

struct Book
{
        std::string title;
        int year;
        float price;
};

int main()
{
        Book b;

        b.title = "Literature";
        b.year = 2016;
        b.price = 10.85;
        std::cout << b.title << ' '  << b.year << ' ' << b.price << '\n';
        return 0;
}
```

Besides the . operator, you'll learn next how to use the -> operator to access the members of a structure.

Note that when b is declared its members get initial values. In particular, as with ordinary local variables, arithmetic members are initialized with random values, while class type members are initialized with the default value for the class. For example, the default value for the `string` class is "".

A structure variable can be initialized when it is declared. The declaration is followed by a list of initializers enclosed in braces. The list must appear in the same order as the members of the structure and should match their data types. The list values are separated with a comma and must not be more values than members. Consider the following declaration:

```cpp
Book b = {"Literature", 2016, 10.85};
```

The value of b.title becomes "Literature", b.year becomes 2016 and b.price becomes 10.85.

As with arrays, any unassigned member is given the value 0. For example, with the declaration:

```
Book b = {"Literature"};
```

the values of `year` and `price` members are set to 0.

If the `{}` are empty, the members are initialized with the default values of their types. For example, with the declaration:

```
Book b = {};
```

the value of `b.title` becomes `""` and the values of `b.year` and `b.price` equal to 0.

A structure with automatic storage duration can be initialized by assignment. For example:

```
Book b2 = b1;
```

Note that the initializer (i.e., `b1`) can be any expression of the proper type. For example, we could replace `b1` with a function that returns a structure of type `Book` or write `*p`, where `p` is a pointer to a structure of that type. Alternatively, we can write `Book b2(b1);`. We'll discuss operations on structures in a short.

Finally, a structure variable declared in the `variable_list` can be initialized at the same time. For example:

```
struct Book
{
        string title;
        int year;
        float price;
} b = {"Literature", 2016, 10.8};
```

Since C++11 we can skip the `=` to specify the initial value. For example:

```
Book b1{"Literature", 2016, 10.85};
Book b2{}; /* The structure members are initialized with the default values
according to their types, that is, the numeric members with 0 and the title
with "". */
```

Pointer to a Structure Member

A pointer to a structure member is used like an ordinary pointer. For example, the following code uses pointers to display the values of the b members:

```
int main()
{
        string *p1;
        int *p2;
        float *p3;
        Book b = {"Literature", 2016, 10.8};

        p1 = &b.title;
        p2 = &b.year;
        p3 = &b.price;

        cout << *p1 << ' ' << *p2 << ' ' << *p3 << '\n';
        return 0;
}
```

To make a pointer variable to point to a structure member, its type should be compatible with the type of the member. For example, since the type of the year member is int, p2 is declared as int*.

Structure Operations

Although we cannot use the = operator to copy one array into another, we can use it to copy one structure into another. The structures must be of the same type. Consider the following program:

```
struct Student
{
        int code;
        float grd;
};

int main()
{
        Student s1, s2;

        s1.code = 1234;
        s1.grd = 6.7;
        s2 = s1; // Copy structure.
        ...
}
```

The statement s2 = s1; copies s1 members into s2. It is equivalent to:

```
s2.code = s1.code;
s2.grd = s1.grd;
```

Notice that if s1 and s2 were not variables of the same structure type, the statement s2 = s1; wouldn't compile even if the two types contained the same exact members.

Notice also that if a structure contains an array of characters (e.g., char name[100];), although it is not allowed to write s2.name = s1.name;, once the structure is copied (e.g., s2 = s1) the s1 array is copied to s2. Furthermore, if it contains a pointer member, both pointers will point to the same place after the copy. This can be dangerous. We'll see such examples in the next two sections.

Besides assignment, no other operation can be performed on entire structures. For example, the operators == and != cannot be used to test whether two structures are equal or not. Therefore, it is not allowed to write:

```
if(s1 == s2)      or      if(s1 != s2).
```

To test whether two structures are equal, we should compare their members one by one. For example:

```
if((s1.code == s2.code) && (s1.grd == s2.grd))
```

In the preface I've told you that you might need some luck when programming. Here is an example. One time, I had to compare two structures. The structure did not contain members whose comparison could be dangerous, like floating point members, pointers, or arrays of characters. Because the structure contained many members I decided to use memcmp() (we'll see it in Chapter 14) to save writing, instead of comparing them one by one. I've forgotten, though, that holes, whose values are undetermined, might be added to align the structure. It means that the comparison of the two structures, even if the corresponding members have identical values, could fail because of different values in the holes. Lucky for me, the holes had the same values. Even luckier, I did not have to transfer the application in another platform. Imagine the case, the comparison to work in my platform and fail in customer's, because of different holes there. I'm scared just by the thought that I'd have to look for that bug! Sometimes every programmer needs a shelter of luck, *Gimme Shelter* from *Rolling Stones*.

Structure Containing Arrays

Since a structure may contain any type of data, it may contain one or more arrays. For example, what is the output of the following program?

```cpp
#include <iostream> // Example 13.3
#include <cstring>

struct Student
{
        char name[50];
        float grd[2];
};

int main()
{
        Student s1, s2;

        strcpy(s1.name, "somebody");
        s1.grd[0] = 8.5;
        s1.grd[1] = 7.5;
        std::cout << s1.name << ' ' << s1.name[0] << ' ' << *s1.name << '\n';
        s2 = s1;
        std::cout << s2.name << ' ' << s2.grd[0] << ' ' << s2.grd[1] << '\n';
        return 0;
}
```

As you guess, an array member is treated just like an ordinary array. For example, the statement `strcpy(s1.name, "somebody");` copies the string `somebody` into `name`. The value of `s1.name[0]` becomes `'s'`, `s1.name[1]` becomes `'o'`, and so on.

When using pointer arithmetic to handle the elements of an array, the `*` operator must precede the name of the structure. For example, since `s1.name` can be used as a pointer to its first character, `*s1.name` is equal to `s1.name[0]`, `*(s1.name+1)` is equal to `s1.name[1]`, and so on. As with ordinary arrays, the parentheses must be present for priority reasons. The assignment `s2 = s1;` copies the arrays. Therefore, the program outputs:

```
somebody s s
somebody 8.5 7.5
```

Structure Containing Pointers

A structure may contain one or more pointer members. A pointer member is treated just like an ordinary pointer. For example, what is the output of the following program?

```cpp
#include <iostream> // Example 13.4

struct Student
{
        const char *name;
        float *avg_grd;
};
```

```
int main()
{
        float grd = 8.5;
        Student s1, s2;

        s1.name = "somebody";
        s1.avg_grd = &grd;
        std::cout << s1.name+3 << ' ' << *s1.avg_grd << '\n';

        s2.name = "else";
        s2 = s1;
        grd = 3.4;
        std::cout << s2.name << ' ' << *s2.avg_grd << '\n';
        return 0;
}
```

With the statement s1.name = "somebody"; the compiler allocates memory to store the string "somebody" and then name points to the beginning of that memory. The statement s1.avg_grd = &grd; makes avg_grd to point to the address of grd. To access the content of the memory pointed to by a pointer member, the * operator must precede the name of the structure. Therefore, the program displays: ebody 8.5.

Then, the statement s2 = s1; makes the pointers of s2 to point to the same place as the pointers of s1. Therefore, the program displays: somebody 3.4 (be careful, not else).

The reason I put this statement is to warn you when you copy a structure that contains a pointer. The current value of the pointer of the destination structure (e.g., s2) will be lost. So, pay attention, this may cause a serious problem in your program.

 Be careful when you copy a structure that contains pointers.

Nested Structures

A structure may contain one or more structures. A nested structure must be declared before the declaration of the structure in which it is contained, otherwise the compilation will fail. For example, in the following program, prod contains the nested structures s_date and e_date. s_date holds the production date and e_date the expiration date of a product.

```
#include <iostream> // Example 13.5
#include <string>

struct Date
{
        int day;
        int month;
        int year;
};


struct Product /* Since the type Date is declared, it can be used to declare
nested structures. */
```

```
{
        std::string name;
        double price;
        Date s_date;
        Date e_date;
};

int main()
{
        Product prod;

        prod.name = "product";
        prod.s_date.day = 1;
        prod.s_date.month = 9;
        prod.s_date.year = 2018;

        prod.e_date.day = 1;
        prod.e_date.month = 9;
        prod.e_date.year = 2022;

        prod.price = 7.5;
        std::cout << "The product's life is " << prod.e_date.year - prod.s_
date.year << " years\n";
        return 0;
}
```

Notice that in order to access a member of the nested structure the . operator must be used twice. The program subtracts the respective members and displays the product's life. In general, a structure is allowed to contain a structure which contains another structure, and so on.

Let's see a special case. Suppose that we want to declare two mutually dependent structures, the structure A, which contains a structure of type B, and the structure B, which contains a structure of type A. If we write something like:

```
struct A // Example 13.6
{
        B b;
        ...
};

struct B
{
        A a;
        ...
};
```

the compiler will display an error message for the declaration of b, because it has no idea about B and its size. If we reverse the declarations, the compiler will display the same type of error for the member a and the unknown structure A. One way to overcome this situation is to make b pointer (we change both for similarity):

```
struct B; // Incomplete declaration.
struct A
{
        B *b;
        B b1; // Wrong, the size of the structure is not known yet.
        ...
};
```

```
void f(B *p)
{
        p->k = 10; /* Wrong, the declaration is still incomplete, so the name
of the member is not known. */
};

struct B
{
        int k;
        A *a;
        ...
};
```

Since the compiler knows how much memory to allocate for a pointer, it is not necessary to know the complete declaration of B, when b is declared. To inform the compiler about the existence of B an incomplete declaration is added, also called *forward declaration*. C++ allows the incomplete declaration of a structure as long as the complete declaration comes later in the same scope. Notice that, as the comments in the wrong statements indicate, until the declaration is completed you are not allowed to access a member or to declare a variable.

Bit Fields

A structure may contain fields whose length is specified as a number of bits. A bit field is declared like this:

```
data_type field_name : bits_number;
```

The bit fields can be used just like the other members. The type of a bit field must be integer. Because some compilers may handle the high order bit of a bit field as a sign bit, while others not, declare the bit fields explicitly as signed or unsigned for portability. Here is an example of a structure with several bit fields:

```
struct Person
{
        unsigned int card_id : 4;
        unsigned int tax_id : 6;
        unsigned int age : 3;
};
```

Since the fields are of the same type we could write:

unsigned int card_id: 4, tax_id: 6, age: 3; Since the size of the age field is 3 bits, it can take values between 0 and 7. Similar for the rest fields. To store their values, 4+6+3 = 13 bits are required. Since their type is unsigned int, the compiler allocates four bytes and 4×8-13 = 19 bits remain unused. Note that arrays of bit fields are not allowed.

The main advantage of using bit fields is to save memory space. For example, if we were not using bit fields the compiler would allocate 12 bytes instead of four. Therefore, if we were using the Person structure to store the data of 200.000 persons, we'd save 1.600.000 bytes.

 For better memory saving, declare all bit fields at the beginning of the structure, not among the other members.

Bit fields are often used for the description and access of information encoded in bit level, such as the hardware registers. For example, the information of the register depicted in the following figure could be encoded like this:

bit8	bit7	bit6	bit5	bit4	bit3	bit2	bit1
S	Z		AC		P		CS

```
struct Flags_Reg
{
        unsigned int cs : 1;
        unsigned int p : 1;
        unsigned int ac : 1;
        unsigned int z : 1;
        unsigned int s : 1;
};
```

An alternative way to handle the register value is to use bit operators as we did in exercise C.4.7. Using the structure above, it is much easier to handle the register and assign values to its fields. For example, if we have a `Flags_Reg` variable (e.g., `fr`), to access the ac field we can write:

`unsigned int ac = fr.ac;` while if we use an integer to represent the register value (e.g., `reg`) and manipulate the bits as in Chapter 4 we should write:

```
unsigned int ac = (reg >> 4) & 1;
```

The former syntax makes the code clearer and easier to read. However, as we'll see later, if we want our program to be portable, it'd be better to use bit operators, so that it won't depend on how the compiler allocates the bits.

A bit field may be unnamed. Unnamed fields are typically used for padding. For example, to represent the exact form of the register above, we could add three unnamed fields:

```
struct Flags_Reg
{
        unsigned int cs : 1;
        unsigned int : 1;
        unsigned int p : 1;
        unsigned int : 1;
        unsigned int ac : 1;
        unsigned int : 1;
        unsigned int z : 1;
        unsigned int s : 1;
};
```

The bit fields are packed into storage units (its typical size is 32 bits). To force the compiler to store a bit field at the beginning of the next unit, a bit field of zero length is added before that. For example, in the following structure, if the compiler uses a storage unit of 32-bit, it will allocate three bits for the f field, skip the next 29 bits to the next unit, and allocate four more bits for the k field.

```
struct Test
{
        unsigned int f : 3;
        unsigned int : 0;
        unsigned int k : 4;
};
```

When you assign a value to a bit field, you should make sure that this value fits in the bit field. For example, suppose that the value 2 is assigned to the cs field:

```
Flags_Reg fr;
fr.cs = 2; // Wrong assignment.
```

If we assume that the bit fields are allocated from right to left, cs becomes 0, not 2, because 2 is encoded in two bits (10_2). Notice that the order in which bit fields are allocated, right to left (*little endian*) or left to right (*big endian*), is implementation dependent and may vary from system to system.

 If the operation of your program depends on the order the bits are stored into memory and you plan to run it in different systems, be aware that the allocation order may differ.

Since the memory of a bit field is not allocated like the ordinary variables, it is not allowed to apply the & operator. For example, this statement is wrong:

```
unsigned int *ptr = &fr.cs; // Wrong.
```

Pointer to Structure

A pointer to a structure is used like a pointer to an ordinary variable. Consider the following program:

```
#include <iostream> // Example 13.7
#include <string>

struct Student
{
        std::string name;
        float grd;
};
int main()
{
        Student *ptr, stud;

        ptr = &stud;
        (*ptr).name = "somebody";
        (*ptr).grd = 6.7;

        std::cout << stud.name << ' ' << stud.grd << '\n';
        return 0;
}
```

ptr is declared as a pointer to a structure variable of type Student. The statement ptr = &stud; makes ptr point to the address of stud. In particular, it points to the address of its first member. Since ptr points to the address of stud, *ptr is equivalent to stud. By using the . operator we can access its members. The expression *ptr must be enclosed in parentheses, because the precedence of the . operator is higher than *. That is, the expression *ptr.grd tries to access the grd member of the ptr structure and because ptr is a pointer, the compilation fails.

Alternatively, we can use the `->` operator to access the members of a structure. The `->` operator consists of the `-` and `>` characters. Here is another version of the previous program:

```
int main()
{
        Student *ptr, stud;

        ptr = &stud;
        ptr->name = "somebody";
        ptr->grd = 6.7;
        std::cout << ptr->name << ' ' << ptr->grd << '\n';
        return 0;
}
```

The expression `ptr->name` is equivalent to `(*ptr).name` and the expression `ptr->grd` is equivalent to `(*ptr).grd` (also equivalent to `ptr[0].grd`). Therefore, both programs output: `somebody 6.7`

Between the two ways of using the pointer to access the members of a structure, I find it more expressive and easier to use the `->` operator.

 Pointer arithmetic works the same as for the ordinary pointers. For example, if a structure pointer is increased by one its value will be increased by the size of the structure it points to.

Array of Structures

An array of structures is an array whose elements are structures. Its typical use is to store information about many items, like the data of a company's employees or students' data or the products of a warehouse. In fact, an array of structures may be used as a simple database. For example, with the statement:

```
Student stud[100];
```

the variable `stud` is declared as an array of 100 elements where each element is a structure of type `Student`. An array of structures can be initialized when declared. For example, given the declaration:

```
struct Student
{
        string name;
        int code;
        float grd;
};
```

An initialization example is:

```
Student stud[3] = {{"nick sterg", 150, 7.3},
                   {"john theod", 160, 5.8},
                   {"peter karast", 170, 6.7}};
```

The initialization is done in much the same way as initializing a two-dimensional array. The initial values for the members of each structure are enclosed in braces, separated by comma. For example, `stud[0].name` becomes `"nick sterg"`, `stud[1].code` becomes `160` and `stud[2].grd` becomes `6.7`. The inner braces around each structure can be omitted; however, I prefer to use them to make clearer the initialization of each structure. As usual, the compiler will compute the number of elements if the `[]` is left empty.

As with a simple structure, we can use the {} syntax to initialize all structures. For example, if we write:

```
Student stud[100] = {};
```

the members of each structure are initialized with the default initial values according to their type. That is, the numeric members with 0 and the name with "". We can declare and initialize an array of structures together with the structure declaration. For example:

```
struct Student
{
        string name;
        int code;
        float grd;
} stud[] = {{"nick sterg", 150, 7.3},
                {"john theod", 160, 5.8},
                {"peter karast", 170, 6.7}};
```

The following program uses a loop to store the data of 100 students to an array of students of type Student:

```
#include <iostream> // Example 13.8
#include <string>
using std::cout;
using std::cin;

const int SIZE = 100;

struct Student
{
        std::string name;
        int code;
        float grd;
};

int main()
{
        int i;
        Student stud[SIZE];

        for(i = 0; i < SIZE; i++)
        {
                cout << "\nEnter name: ";
                getline(cin, stud[i].name);

                cout << "Enter code: ";
                cin >> stud[i].code;

                cout << "Enter grade: ";
                cin >> stud[i].grd;

                cout << stud[i].name << ' ' << stud[i].code << ' ' << stud[i].
grd << '\n';
                cin.get(); /* Remove the new line character stored in cin,
after the grade is entered. */
        }
        return 0;
}
```

As with ordinary arrays, we can use pointer notation to access the elements. For example, `*stud` is equivalent to `stud[0]`, `*(stud+1)` equivalent to `stud[1]`, and so on. Therefore, to access the `code` member of the third student, both expressions `stud[2].code` and `(*(stud+2)).code` are acceptable. The parentheses in the second case are required for priority reasons. As with ordinary arrays, my preference is to use array subscripting and not pointer notation in order to get a more readable code.

And as we know instead of an ordinary array we can use a `vector` object. For example:

```cpp
int main()
{
        vector<Student> stud(SIZE);
        ... // The rest of the code is the same.
}
```

Structure as Function Argument

A structure variable can be passed to a function just like any other variable, that is, either the variable itself or its address. Also, a function may return a structure. Consider the following program:

```cpp
#include <iostream> // Example 13.9
#include <string>

struct Student
{
        std::string name;
        int code;
        float grd;
};

Student test(Student s);

int main()
{
        Student st = {"somebody", 20, 5};

        st = test(st); /* According to the function declaration, it must be
called with an argument of type Student. */
        std::cout << st.name << ' ' << st.code << ' ' << st.grd << '\n';
        return 0;
}

Student test(Student s)
{
        s.name = "new";
        s.code = 30;
        s.grd = 7;
        return s;
}
```

When `test()` is called, the values of `st` members are copied to the respective members of `s`. Since `s` and `st` are stored in different memory locations, any changes in the members of `s` don't affect the members of `st`. As you already know by now, even if we were using the name `st` instead of `s`, the result would be the same because they are different variables regardless of naming. Next, the structure that `test()` returns is copied to `st`. Therefore, the program displays: new 30 7

On the other hand, when the address of the structure is passed, the function may change the values of its members. For example, let's change `test()`, in order to modify the members of `st`:

```
void test(Student *ptr);

int main()
{
        ...
        test(&st);
        std::cout << st.name << ' ' << st.code << ' ' << st.grd << '\n';
        ...
}

void test(Student *ptr)
{
        ptr->name = "new";
        ptr->code = 30;
        ptr->grd = 7;
}
```

When `test()` is called, we have `ptr = &st`. Therefore, since `ptr` points to the address of `st`, the function may change the values of its members. As a result, the program displays: `new 30 7`

When a structure is passed to a function, its members are copied to the members of the respective parameter. Notice that if the structure is large or the function is called many times, this copy operation may increase memory requirements and add a time overhead. On the other hand, when the address of the structure is passed to the function through a pointer or reference, the members are not copied.

 For better performance, pass the address of the structure, not the structure itself, even if the function won't change the values of its members.

To prevent the function from changing the values of the members, we declare the pointer or the reference as `const`. For example:

```
void test(const Student *ptr);
```

now, `test()` cannot modify the members of the structure pointed to by `ptr`.

EXERCISES

C.13.1 What is the output of the following program?

```
#include <iostream>

struct Student
{
        char name[50];
        int code;
        float grd;
};
```

```
Student *test(), st;

int main()
{
        Student stud = {"somebody", 1111, 7.5}, *ptr = &stud;

        *ptr = *test();
  std::cout << ptr->name << ' ' << ptr->code << ' ' << ptr->grd << '\n';
        return 0;
}

Student *test()
{
        return &st;
}
```

Answer: Since test() returns the address of st, *test() is equivalent to st. Since ptr points to the address of stud, *ptr is equivalent to stud. Therefore, the expression *ptr = *test(); is equivalent to stud = st; Since the global variable is initialized with zero values, the program outputs: 0 0.

C.13.2 Define the structure type City with members: city name, country name, and population. Write a program that uses this type to read the data of 100 cities and store them in an array. Then, the program should read the name of a country and a number and display the cities of that country whose population is greater than the input number. To read the data of each city write a loop which uses only the following variables:

```
int main()
{
        City *ptr, cities[SIZE];
        ...
}
```

Answer:

```
#include <iostream>
#include <string>
using std::cout;
using std::cin;
using std::string;

const int SIZE = 100;

struct City
{
        string name;
        string cntr;
        int pop;
};

int main()
{
        bool found;
        int i, pop;
        string cntr;
        City *ptr, cities[SIZE];
```

```
        for(ptr = cities; ptr < cities+SIZE; ptr++) /* When ptr increases it
points to the next element of the array, that is, to the next structure. */
        {
                cout << "\nCity: ";
                getline(cin, ptr->name);

                cout << "Country: ";
                cin >> ptr->cntr;

                cout << "Population: ";
                cin >> ptr->pop;
                cin.get();
        }
        cout << "\nEnter country to search: ";
        getline(cin, cntr);

        cout << "Population: ";
        cin >> pop;

        found = 0;
        for(i = 0; i < SIZE; i++)
        {
                if((cities[i].cntr == cntr) && (cities[i].pop > pop))
                {
                        found = 1;
                        cout << cities[i].name << ' ' << cities[i].pop << '\n';
                }
        }
        if(found == 0)
                cout << "\nNone city is found\n";
        return 0;
}
```

C.13.3 Define the structure type Time with members: hours, minutes, and seconds. Write a function that takes as parameter a pointer to an integer and converts that integer to hours, minutes, and seconds. These values should be stored into the members of a structure of type Time, and the function should return that structure. Write a program that reads a number of seconds, calls the function, and displays the members of the returned structure.

```
#include <iostream>

struct Time
{
        int hours;
        int mins;
        int secs;
};

Time mk_time(const int *ptr);

int main()
{
        int secs;
        Time t;

        std::cout << "Enter seconds: ";
        std::cin >> secs;
```

```
        t = mk_time(&secs);
        std::cout << "\nH:" << t.hours << " M:" << t.mins << " S:" << t.secs
<< '\n';
        return 0;
}

Time mk_time(const int *ptr)
{
        Time tmp;

        tmp.hours = *ptr/3600;
        tmp.mins = (*ptr%3600)/60;
        tmp.secs = *ptr%60;
        return tmp;
}
```

Comments: To avoid copying the structure returned from `mk_time()` we could pass the address of a structure variable. For example, we could change the return type to `void` and pass the address of `t` to `mk_time()`. Thus, the function modifies a structure of the calling function instead of declaring and returning a new structure.

```
void mk_time(const int *ptr, struct time *tmp)
{
        tmp->hours = *ptr/3600;
        tmp->mins = (*ptr%3600)/60;
        tmp->secs = *ptr%60;
}
```

C.13.4 Define the structure type `Book` with members: title, code, and price. Write a `void` function that takes as parameters two pointers to structures of type `Book` and returns the structure with the higher code. Check the case of the same codes and print a related message. Write a program that reads and stores the data of `10` books into an array of structures. Then, the program should read two numbers in [1, 10] that represent two structure indexes in the array. The program should check the validity of the input numbers and use the function to display the data of the structure with the higher code.

```
#include <iostream>
#include <string>
using std::cout;
using std::cin;

struct Book
{
        std::string title;
        int code;
        float prc;
};

void max_code(const Book *b1, const Book *b2, Book *fin);

int main()
{
        const int SIZE = 10;
        int i, j;
        Book fin, b[SIZE];
```

```
        for(i = 0; i < SIZE; i++)
        {
                cout << "\nEnter title: ";
                getline(cin, b[i].title);

                cout << "Enter code: ";
                cin >> b[i].code;

                cout << "Enter price: ";
                cin >> b[i].prc;
                cin.get();
        }
        do
        {
                cout << "\nEnter two book numbers [1-" << SIZE << "]: ";
                cin >> i >> j;
        } while((i == j) || i > SIZE || j > SIZE || i < 1 || j < 1);

        i--;
        j--;
        max_code(&b[i], &b[j], &fin);
        if(fin.code != -1)
                cout << "\nN:" << fin.title << " C:"  << fin.code << " P:" <<
fin.prc << '\n';
        else
                cout << "\nBoth books have the same code: " << b[i].code <<
'\n';
        return 0;
}

void max_code(const Book *b1, const Book *b2, Book *fin)
{
        if(b1->code > b2->code)
                *fin = *b1;
        else if(b1->code < b2->code)
                *fin = *b2;
        else
                fin->code = -1;
}
```

C.13.5 Define the structure type `Product` with members: name, code, and price. Write a function that takes as parameters a `vector` of such structures and the code of a product. The function should check if a product in the `vector` has the same code and, if so, it should return a pointer to the respective structure, otherwise `nullptr`. Write a program that uses the type `Product` to read the data of products and store them in a `vector`. If the user enters a negative value for price, the insertion of data should terminate. Then, the program should read the code of a product and use the function to display the product's name and price, if found.

```
#include <iostream>
#include <string>
#include <vector>
using namespace std;
```

```cpp
struct Product
{
        string name;
        int code;
        float prc;
};

const Product *find_prod(const vector<Product>& v, int code);

int main()
{
        const Product *ptr;
        int code;
        float prc;
        Product tmp;
        vector<Product> prod;

        while(1)
        {
                cout << "\nPrice: ";
                cin >> prc;
                if(prc <= 0)
                        break;

                tmp.prc = prc;
                cin.get();
                cout << "Name: ";
                getline(cin, tmp.name);

                cout << "Code: ";
                cin >> tmp.code;
                prod.push_back(tmp);
        }
        if(prod.size() == 0)
        {
                cout << "No product is stored\n";
                return 0;
        }
        cout << "\nEnter code to search: ";
        cin >> code;

        ptr = find_prod(prod, code);
        if(ptr == nullptr)
                cout << "\nNo product with code = " << code << '\n';
        else
                cout << "\nN:" << ptr->name << " C:" << code << " P:" <<
ptr->prc << '\n';
        return 0;
}

const Product *find_prod(const vector<Product>& v, int code)
{
        for(int i = 0; i < v.size(); i++)
        {
                if(v[i].code == code)
```

```
            return &v[i]; /* If the code is found, the function
terminates and the address of that structure is returned. */
        }
        return nullptr; /* If the code reaches that point, it means that the
product is not found and the function returns nullptr. */
}
```

C.13.6 Define the structure type Coord with members the coordinates of a point (e.g., x and y). Define the structure type Rectangle with members two structures of type Coord (e.g., Point_A and Point_B). Write a function that takes as parameters the two endpoints of a rectangle's diagonal. Each endpoint should be a structure of type Coord. The function should calculate and return the area of the rectangle. Write a program that uses the type Rectangle to read the coordinates of a rectangle's diagonal and uses the function to display its area.

```cpp
#include <iostream>
using std::cout;
using std::cin;

struct Coord
{
        double x;
        double y;
};

struct Rectangle
{
        Coord point_A; // First diagonal point.
        Coord point_B; // Second diagonal point.
};

double rect_area(const Coord *c1, const Coord *c2);

int main()
{
        Rectangle rect;

        cout << "Enter the x and y coords of the first point: ";
        cin >> rect.point_A.x >> rect.point_A.y;

        cout << "Enter the x and y coords of the second point: ";
        cin >> rect.point_B.x >> rect.point_B.y;

        cout << "Area:" << rect_area(&rect.point_A, &rect.point_B) << '\n';
        return 0;
}

double rect_area(const Coord *c1, const Coord *c2)
{
        double base, height;

        if(c1->x > c2->x)
                base = c1->x - c2->x;
        else
                base = c2->x - c1->x;
```

```
        if(c1->y > c2->y)
                height = c1->y - c2->y;
        else
                height = c2->y - c1->y;

        return base*height; // Return the area.
}
```

C.13.7 For a complex number z, we have $z = a + bj$, where j is the imaginary unit, a is the real part, and b is the imaginary part. Define the structure type `Complex` with members the float numbers `re` and `im`, which represent the real and imaginary parts of a complex number. Write a function that takes as parameters two structures of type `Complex` and a character, which represents the sign of a math operation. The function should perform the math operation and return the result as a structure of type `Complex`. Write a program that uses the structure `Complex` to read two complex numbers and a math sign (+, -, *, /) and uses the function to display the result of the math operation. If $z_1 = a + bj$ and $z_2 = c + dj$, we have:

$$z = z_1 + z_2 = (a+c)+(b+d)j$$

$$z = z_1 - z_2 = (a-c)+(b-d)j$$

$$z = z_1 \times z_2 = (ac-bd)+(bc+ad)j$$

$$z = \left(\frac{z_1}{z_2}\right) = \left(\frac{ac+bd}{c^2+d^2}\right)+\left(\frac{bc-ad}{c^2+d^2}\right)j$$

```cpp
#include <iostream>
using std::cout;
using std::cin;

struct Complex
{
        double re; // The real part of the complex number.
        double im; // The imaginary part of the complex number.
};

Complex operation(Complex a1, Complex a2, char sign);

int main()
{
        char sign;
        Complex z1, z2, z;

        cout << "Enter real and imaginary part of the first complex number: ";
        cin >> z1.re >> z1.im;
        cout << std::showpos << "z1 = " << z1.re << z1.im << 'j' << '\n';

        cout << "Enter real and imaginary part of the second complex number: ";
        cin >> z2.re >> z2.im;
        cout << "z2 = " << z2.re << z2.im << 'j' << '\n';
```

```
        cout << "Enter sign (+, -, *, /): ";
        cin >> sign;
        if(sign == '+' || sign == '-' || sign == '*' || sign == '/')
        {
                if(sign == '/' && z2.re == 0 && z2.im == 0)
                        cout << "Division by zero is not allowed\n";
                else
                {
                        z = operation(z1, z2, sign);
                        cout << "z = z1" << sign << "z2 = " << z.re << z.im <<
'j' << '\n';
                }
        }
        else
                cout << "Wrong sign\n";
        return 0;
}


Complex operation(Complex a1, Complex a2, char sign)
{
        double div;
        Complex a;

        switch(sign)
        {
                case '+':
                        a.re = a1.re + a2.re;
                        a.im = a1.im + a2.im;
                break;

                case '-':
                        a.re = a1.re - a2.re;
                        a.im = a1.im - a2.im;
                break;

                case '*':
                        a.re = (a1.re*a2.re) - (a1.im*a2.im);
                        a.im = (a1.im*a2.re) + (a1.re*a2.im);
                break;

                case '/':
                        div = (a2.re*a2.re) + (a2.im*a2.im);
                        a.re = ((a1.re*a2.re) + (a1.im*a2.im))/div;
                        a.im = ((a1.im*a2.re) - (a1.re*a2.im))/div;
                break;
        }
        return a;
}
```

Comments: Note that we're using the showpos manipulator, as discussed in Chapter 3, in order to prefix the positive values with +. The reason I did not pass the addresses of the structures to operation() in order to avoid the creation of copies, is to show you an example of a function with parameters structures.

C.13.8 Define the structure type Student with members: name, code, and grade. Write a program that uses this type to read the data of 100 students and store them in an array of such structures. If the user enters -1 for grade, the insertion of data should terminate. Write a function to sort the structures in grade ascending order and another function to display the data of the students who got a better grade than the average grade of all students. The program should call those two functions.

```cpp
#include <iostream>
#include <string>
using std::cout;
using std::cin;

const int SIZE = 100;

struct Student
{
        std::string name;
        int code;
        float grd;
};

void sort_by_grade(Student studs[], int num_studs);
void show_students(const Student studs[], int num_studs, float avg_grd);

int main()
{
        int i;
        float sum_grd;
        Student studs[SIZE];

        sum_grd = 0;
        for(i = 0; i < SIZE; i++)
        {
                cout << "\nGrade [0-10]: ";
                cin >> studs[i].grd;
                if(studs[i].grd == -1)
                        break;

                sum_grd += studs[i].grd;
                cin.get();

                cout << "Name: ";
                getline(cin, studs[i].name);

                cout << "Code: ";
                cin >> studs[i].code;
        }
        if(i == 0)
                return 0;
        sort_by_grade(studs, i); /* Sort the structures in grade ascending
order. The variable i specifies the number of students. */
        show_students(studs, i, sum_grd/i); /* The last argument is the
average grade of all students. */
        return 0;
}

void sort_by_grade(Student studs[], int num_studs)
{
        int i, j;
        Student s;
```

```
        for(i = 0; i < num_studs-1; i++)
        {
                /* In each iteration, the grd member is compared with the
others. If it is less, the structures are swapped. */
                for(j = i+1; j < num_studs; j++)
                {
                        if(studs[i].grd > studs[j].grd)
                        {
                                s = studs[i];
                                studs[i] = studs[j];
                                studs[j] = s;
                        }
                }
        }
}

void show_students(const Student studs[], int num_studs, float avg_grd)
{
        int i;

        for(i = 0; i < num_studs; i++)
                if(studs[i].grd > avg_grd)
                        cout << "\nN:" << studs[i].name << " C:" << studs[i].
code << " G:" << studs[i].grd << '\n';
}
```

C.13.9 Image-editing programs often need to rotate an image by 90°. An image can be treated as a two-dimensional array whose elements represent the pixels of the image. For example, the rotation of the original image (e.g., p[M][N]) to the right produces a new image (e.g., r[M][N]), as shown here:

$$
p = \begin{bmatrix}
p_{0,0} & p_{0,1} & \cdots & p_{0,N-2} & p_{0,N-1} \\
p_{1,0} & p_{1,1} & \cdots & p_{1,N-2} & p_{1,N-1} \\
\cdot & \cdot & \cdot & \cdot & \cdot \\
\cdot & \cdot & \cdot & \cdot & \cdot \\
\cdot & \cdot & \cdot & \cdot & \cdot \\
p_{M-2,0} & p_{M-2,1} & \cdots & p_{M-2,N-2} & p_{M-2,N-1} \\
p_{M-1,0} & p_{M-1,1} & \cdots & p_{M-1,N-2} & p_{M-1,N-1}
\end{bmatrix}
\qquad
r = \begin{bmatrix}
p_{M-1,0} & p_{M-2,0} & \cdots & p_{1,0} & p_{0,0} \\
p_{M-1,1} & p_{M-2,1} & \cdots & p_{1,1} & p_{0,1} \\
\cdot & \cdot & \cdot & \cdot & \cdot \\
\cdot & \cdot & \cdot & \cdot & \cdot \\
\cdot & \cdot & \cdot & \cdot & \cdot \\
p_{M-1,N-2} & p_{M-2,N-2} & \cdots & p_{1,N-2} & p_{0,N-2} \\
p_{M-1,N-1} & p_{M-2,N-1} & \cdots & p_{1,N-1} & p_{0,N-1}
\end{bmatrix}
$$

In particular, the first row of the original image becomes the last column of the new image, the second row becomes the last but one column, up to the last row, which becomes the first column. For example, the image:

$$
p = \begin{bmatrix}
1 & 2 & 3 & 4 & 5 \\
6 & 7 & 8 & 9 & 10 \\
11 & 12 & 13 & 14 & 15
\end{bmatrix}
\quad \text{is transformed to:} \quad
r = \begin{bmatrix}
11 & 6 & 1 \\
12 & 7 & 2 \\
13 & 8 & 3 \\
14 & 9 & 4 \\
15 & 10 & 5
\end{bmatrix}
$$

The colour of each pixel follows the RGB colour model, in which the red, green, and blue colours are mixed together to reproduce a wide range of colours. The colour is expressed as an RGB triplet (r, g, b), in which each component value varies from 0 to 255.

Define the structure type `Pixel` with three integer members named `red`, `green`, and `blue`. Write a program that creates a two-dimensional image (e.g., 3×5) whose elements are structures of type `Pixel`. Initialize the members of each structure with random values within [0, 255]. Then, the program should display the original image, rotate the image by 90° right, and display the rotated image (e.g., 5×3).

Hint: Use a second array to store the rotated image.

```cpp
#include <iostream>
#include <cstdlib>
#include <ctime>
using std::cout;
using std::cin;

const int ROWS = 3;
const int COLS = 5;

struct Pixel // RGB format (Red-Green-Blue).
{
        unsigned char red; // Value in [0, 255].
        unsigned char green;
        unsigned char blue;
};

void rotate_right_90(const Pixel img[][COLS], Pixel tmp[][ROWS]);

int main()
{
        int i, j;
        Pixel img[ROWS][COLS], tmp[COLS][ROWS];

        srand(time(NULL));
        // Create random colours.
        for(i = 0; i < ROWS; i++)
        {
                for(j = 0; j < COLS; j++)
                {
                        img[i][j].red = rand()%256;
                        img[i][j].green = rand()%256;
                        img[i][j].blue = rand()%256;
                }
        }
        cout << "*** Original Image ***\n\n";
        for(i = 0; i < ROWS; i++)
        {
                for(j = 0; j < COLS; j++)
                {
                        cout << '(' << (int)img[i][j].red << ',' <<
(int)img[i][j].green << ',' <<  (int)img[i][j].blue << ") ";
                }
                cout << '\n';
        }
        rotate_right_90(img, tmp);

        cout << "\n*** Rotated Image ***\n\n";
        for(i = 0; i < COLS; i++)
        {
                for(j = 0; j < ROWS; j++)
```

```
                {
                        cout << '(' << (int)tmp[i][j].red << ',' <<
(int)tmp[i][j].green << ',' <<  (int)tmp[i][j].blue << ") ";
                }
                cout << '\n';
        }
        return 0;
}


void rotate_right_90(const Pixel img[][COLS], Pixel tmp[][ROWS])
{
        int i, j, k = 0;

        for(i = ROWS-1; i >= 0; i--)
        {
                for(j = 0; j < COLS; j++)
                {
                        tmp[j][i] = img[k][j];
                }
                k++;
        }
}
```

UNIONS

Like a structure, a union contains one or more members, which may have different types. The properties of unions are almost identical to the properties of structures; the same operations are allowed as on structures. Their difference is that the members of a structure are stored at *different* addresses, while the members of a union are stored at the *same* address. Because the use of a union which contains class members (e.g., `string`) is more complex, I'll describe the properties of the union by using basic types for members.

Union Declaration

The declaration of a union type resembles that of a structure, with the `union` keyword used instead of `struct`. When a union variable is declared, the compiler allocates space only for its largest member. Therefore, its members are all stored in the same memory, overlaying each other. For example, in the following program, the `s` variable allocates eight bytes because its largest member is of type `double`:

```
#include <iostream> // Example 13.10

union Sample
{
        char ch;
        int i;
        double d;
};
```

```cpp
int main()
{
        Sample s;
        std::cout << sizeof(s) << '\n';
        return 0;
}
```

The s union can hold one value, which is of type `char` or `int` or `double`. Since the compiler does not allocate memory for each union member, the main application of a union is to save memory space. For example, unions are often used in embedded systems where memory is limited.

 As with structures, to calculate the memory size of a union variable use the `sizeof` operator.

Since all union members share the same memory, *only* the first member of a union variable can be initialized when it is declared. For example, the compiler would let us write:

```cpp
Sample s = {'x'};
```

but not: `Sample s = {'x', 10, 1.23};`

Access Union Members

The members of a union are accessed in the same way as the members of a structure. However, since they are all stored in the same memory, only the last assigned member has a meaningful value. For example, the following program assigns a value into an s member and displays the other members:

```cpp
#include <iostream> // Example 13.11

union Sample
{
        char ch;
        int i;
        double d;
};

int main()
{
        Sample s;

        s.ch = 'a';
        std::cout << s.ch << ' ' << s.i << ' ' << s.d << '\n';

        s.i = 64;
        std::cout << s.ch << ' ' << s.i << ' ' << s.d << '\n';

        s.d = 12.48;
        std::cout << s.ch << ' ' << s.i << ' ' << s.d << '\n';
        return 0;
}
```

First, the program outputs a and nonsense values for the s.i and s.d members. Next, the value 64 is assigned to i. Since this value is stored in the common space, the value of s.ch is overwritten. Therefore, the program displays 64 and nonsense values for the s.ch and s.d. Next, the value 12.48 is assigned to d. The value of s.i is overwritten and the program outputs 12.48 and nonsense values for the s.ch and s.i.

 When a union member is assigned with a value, any value previously stored in the last assigned member is overwritten.

Let's have a test. What is the output of the following program?

```cpp
#include <iostream> // Example 13.12

union Test
{
        int a, b, c;
};

int main()
{
        Test t;

        t.a = 100;
        t.b = 200;
        t.c = 300;
        std::cout << t.a << ' ' << t.b << ' ' << t.c << '\n';
        std::cout << &t.a << ' ' << &t.b << ' ' << &t.c << '\n';
        return 0;
}
```

Since the members are of the same type and they are all stored in the same memory, once c becomes 300 that would be the value of the other members as well. Therefore, the program displays three times 300. Then, it displays three times the common memory address.

A typical use of unions is to save memory when data can be stored in two or more forms but never simultaneously. For example, suppose that we want to store in an array of 100 structures the preferences of men and women. The preferences of men concern favourite game and movie, while for women television show and book. We could use a structure Person like that:

```cpp
struct Person
{
        char game[SIZE];
        char movie[SIZE];

        char tv_show[SIZE];
        char book[SIZE];
};
```

For simplicity, I'm using fixed size arrays to hold the texts. However, this structure wastes space, since for each person only two of the members are used to store information. To save space, we can use a union with members structures. For example, consider the following program:

```cpp
#include <iostream> // Example 13.13
using std::cout;
using std::cin;
```

```cpp
const int SIZE = 100;

struct Man
{
        char game[SIZE];
        char movie[SIZE];
};

struct Woman
{
        char tv_show[SIZE];
        char book[SIZE];
};

union Data
{
        Man m;
        Woman w;
};

struct Person
{
        int type;
        Data d;
};

int main()
{
        int i, type;
        Person pers_arr[SIZE];

        for(i = 0; i < SIZE; i++)
        {
                cout << "\nSelection (0 for man - 1 for woman): ";
                cin >> type;

                pers_arr[i].type = type;
                cin.get();
                if(type == 0)
                {
                        cout << "Enter favourite game: ";
                        cin.getline(pers_arr[i].d.m.game,
                                sizeof(pers_arr[i].d.m.game));

                        cout << "Enter favourite movie: ";
                        cin.getline(pers_arr[i].d.m.movie,
                                sizeof(pers_arr[i].d.m.movie));

                }
                else if(type == 1)
                {
                        cout << "Enter favourite TV show: ";
                        cin.getline(pers_arr[i].d.w.tv_show,
                                sizeof(pers_arr[i].d.w.tv_show));
```

```
                    cout << "Enter favourite book: ";
                    cin.getline(pers_arr[i].d.w.book,
                            sizeof(pers_arr[i].d.w.book));
            }
      }
      for(i = 0; i < SIZE; i++)
      {
            if(pers_arr[i].type == 0)
            {
                    cout << "\nGame: " << pers_arr[i].d.m.game << '\n';
                    cout << "Show: " << pers_arr[i].d.m.movie << '\n';
            }
            else if(pers_arr[i].type == 1)
            {
                    cout << "\nMovie: " << pers_arr[i].d.w.tv_show << '\n';
                    cout << "Book: " << pers_arr[i].d.w.book << '\n';
            }
      }
      return 0;
}
```

The program reads the sex type and stores the user's preferences in the respective union members. To know which type of structure, that is, `Man` or `Woman`, is contained in each `Person` the member `type` is added. In the second loop, the program checks its value and displays the respective preferences.

 It is the programmer's responsibility to keep track which member of the union contains a meaningful value. A special member may be added (like the `type` above) to indicate what is currently stored in the union.

Another application of unions is to provide multiple views of the same data in order to use the most convenient. For example, in embedded applications, it is often needed to view a register in different ways. Look how we can use a 32-bit register value either in bit level or as a whole:

```
struct Bit_Val
{
      unsigned int CF : 1;
      unsigned int PF : 1;
      /* ... more bit fields. */
};

union Flags_Reg
{
      unsigned int i_val;
      Bit_Val b_val;
};
```

Changing the value of `i_val` alters the values of the bit fields and vice versa. If you ever get involved with such applications, don't forget that the order the bit fields are allocated may differ from system to system.

Unions are often used in the development of communication protocols for the encoding of the exchanged messages. The following exercise is a simple example on how I used a union when developing a protocol for ISDN networks. If you ever get involved with that field, it might be useful.

EXERCISE

C.13.10 In an ISDN network, the SETUP message of the Q.931 signalling protocol is sent by the calling user to the called user to initiate the call establishment procedure. A simplified format of the SETUP message is depicted in the following figure:

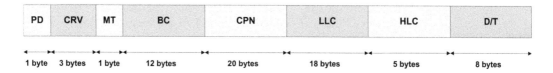

The ALERTING message (see the figure) is sent by the ISDN network to the calling user to indicate that the called user is notified for the incoming call (e.g., ring tone).

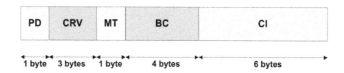

The CONNECT message (see the figure) is sent by the ISDN network to the calling user to indicate that the called user accepted the call (e.g., picks up the phone).

These messages traverse the ISDN switches along the path between the two users. Each node evaluates the content of the received messages. Let's write a program to simulate this message analysis.

Define the structure type Isdn_Msg with member one union. The members of that union are three structures to represent the SETUP, CONNECT, and ALERTING messages. Write a program that reads a byte stream, uses the figures above to parse the data and stores them in the proper union member. To parse the data the program should check the value of the MT field. Its value in the SETUP, CONNECT, and ALERTING messages is 5, 7, and 1, respectively. To get the byte stream the program should read 100 integers in [0, 255] and store them in an array. If the user enters -1, the insertion of data should terminate.

```cpp
#include <iostream>
using std::cout;
using std::cin;

using BYTE = unsigned char;

struct Header
{
    BYTE pd;
    BYTE crv[3];
    BYTE mt;
};
```

```
struct Setup
{
        BYTE bc[12];
        BYTE cpn[20];
        BYTE llc[18];
        BYTE hlc[5];
        BYTE dt[8];
};

struct Connect
{
        BYTE bc[4];
        BYTE ci[6];
};

struct Alerting
{
        BYTE bc[8];
        BYTE pi[4];
        BYTE sig[3];
        BYTE hlc[5];
};

struct Isdn_Msg
{
        Header hdr; // Common header for all messages.
        union
        {
                Setup set;
                Connect con;
                Alerting alrt;
        };
};

int main()
{
        int i, pkt[100];
        Isdn_Msg msg;

        for(i = 0; i < 100; i++)
        {
                cout << "Enter octet: ";
                cin >> pkt[i];
                if(pkt[i] == -1)
                        break;
        }
        msg.hdr.pd = pkt[0];
        for(i = 0; i < 3; i++)
                msg.hdr.crv[i] = pkt[i+1];
        msg.hdr.mt = pkt[4];

        if(msg.hdr.mt == 5) // SETUP
        {
                for(i = 0; i < 12; i++)
                        msg.set.bc[i] = pkt[5+i];
                for(i = 0; i < 20; i++)
                        msg.set.cpn[i] = pkt[17+i];
```

```
                    for(i = 0; i < 18; i++)
                           msg.set.llc[i] = pkt[37+i];
                    for(i = 0; i < 5; i++)
                           msg.set.hlc[i] = pkt[55+i];
                    for(i = 0; i < 8; i++)
                           msg.set.dt[i] = pkt[60+i];
         }
         else if(msg.hdr.mt == 7) // CONNECT
         {
                    for(i = 0; i < 4; i++)
                           msg.con.bc[i] = pkt[5+i];
                    for(i = 0; i < 6; i++)
                           msg.con.ci[i] = pkt[9+i];
         }
         else if(msg.hdr.mt == 1) // ALERT
         {
                    for(i = 0; i < 8; i++)
                           msg.alrt.bc[i] = pkt[5+i];
                    for(i = 0; i < 4; i++)
                           msg.alrt.pi[i] = pkt[13+i];
                    for(i = 0; i < 3; i++)
                           msg.alrt.sig[i] = pkt[17+i];
                    for(i = 0; i < 5; i++)
                           msg.alrt.hlc[i] = pkt[20+i];
         }
         return 0;
}
```

Note that C++17 provides the `variant` class template, which represents a type-safe union. As with unions, a `variant` can store the value of one of a set of alternative types.

UNSOLVED EXERCISES

U.13.1 Define the structure type `Employee` with members: first name, last name, age, and salary. Write a program that uses this type to read the data of 50 employees and store them in an array. The program should display the last name of the employee with the highest salary and the name of the older employee. If more than one employee has the same highest salary or greater age, the program should display the data of the first found.

U.13.2 Add a `void` function in C.13.6 to return through a pointer parameter to a structure of type `Coord` the coordinates of the centre of the rectangle. Modify the main program to test the function.

U.13.3 The following figure depicts the status register of a printer (16 bits). Use bit fields and define the structure `Print_Reg` with the five fields of the figure. Write a program that uses a structure of that type to simulate a printing job of 20 pages, as follows:

1. The `low ink` field is set to `3`, when the `9`th page is print and up to the end of the printing job.
2. The `error code` field is set to `10`, only when the `13`th page is print.
3. The `paper jam` field is set to `1`, only when the `15`th page is print.
4. The `clean` field is set to `1`, only when the last page is print.

Use a loop of 20 iterations to simulate the printing job. Each iteration corresponds to the print of one page. For each printing page, the program should display the value of the status register.

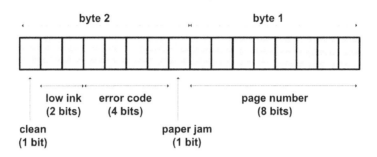

U.13.4 Define the structure type `Circle` with member the radius and the type `Square` with member the length. Write a function that takes as parameters a pointer of type `void*` and an integer parameter. If its value is `0`, the pointer points to a structure of type `Circle`, otherwise to a structure of type `Square`. The function should increase the member of the pointed structure by `5` and return that pointer. Write a program to test the function.

U.13.5 Define the structure type `Student` with members: name and code. Assume that a classroom can be simulated by a two-dimensional array whose elements are structures of type `Student`. Write a program that reads the data of students and stores them in a `3×5` array of structures. Then, the program should read the name of a student and his code and display his position in the array (i.e., row and column), if registered.

U.13.6 Define the structure type `Student` with members: name, code, and grade. Write a program that uses this type to read the data of 100 students and store them in an array sorted by grade in descending order. The sorting must be done during the data insertion.

U.13.7 Define the structure type `Time` with members: hours, minutes, and seconds. Write a function that takes as parameters two pointers to two structures that represent the start time and the end time of a game and returns the game's duration as a structure. Write a program that uses the type `Time` to read the start time of a game and the end time and uses the function to display the game's duration. The user should enter the time in `h:m:s` format.

U.13.8 Rename the function `sort_by_grade()` in C.13.8 to `sort()` and add an extra argument. If it is `0`, the function should sort the students in ascending order by their codes, if it is `1` by their names, and if it is `2` by their grades. Modify the main program to test the function.

U.13.9 Define the structure type `Publisher` with members: name, address, and e-mail. Define the type `Book` with members: title, authors, code, price, and a member of type `Publisher`. Write a program that uses the type `Book` to read the data of 100 books and store them in an array. Then, the program should read a book's code and display the title of the book and the publisher's name, if registered.

U.13.10 Define the structure type `Student` with members: name, code, and grade. Write a program that declares an array of six such structures and initializes the first five with random data sorted by grade in ascending order (e.g., `"A.Smith, 100, 3.2"`, `"B.Jones, 200, 4.7"`, `"K.Lones, 175, 6.4"` ...). Then, the program should read the data of the sixth student and store them in the proper position, so that the array remains sorted.

U.13.11 Define the structure type Car with members: model, price, and manufacture year. Write a program that uses this type to read the data of 100 cars and store them in an array. Then, the program should provide a menu to perform the following operations:

1. *Show model.* The program should read a model and display the related information, if registered. If the user enters '*', the program should show the information of all models.
2. *Show prices.* The program should read a price and show all models that cost more.
3. *Program termination.*

U.13.12 Define the structure type Any_Type with an integer member (e.g., s_type) and a member of type union. The union's members are a structure of type Time (e.g., t) as defined in U.13.7 and a structure of type Student (e.g., s) as defined in U.13.6. Write a program that reads an integer and stores it into the s_type member of a structure variable of type Any_Type. Then, the program should check the value of s_type and read data according to that value. If it is 1 the input data should be stored into the t member, otherwise it should be stored into the s member.

U.13.13 Define the union type Selected_Type with the members named: u_char (of type char), u_int (of type int), u_float (of type float), and u_double (of type double). Define the structure type Var_Type with the members named: type (of type int) and st (union of type Selected_Type). Write a function that takes as parameter a structure of type Var_Type. The function should read a number according to the value of the type member, store that number in the appropriate st member, and display the value of that member. Write a program that prompts the user to enter a number that represents the data type (i.e., 1: char, 2: int, 3: float, 4: double) and then uses the function to read a corresponding value and display it.

Memory Management and Data Structures

14

Memory management is mainly related to memory allocation and release of allocated memory when it is no longer needed. Memory allocation can be performed either *statically* or *dynamically*. In the programs so far, we've mostly used static allocation, that is, the program variables are stored in fixed size memory. In this chapter, you'll learn how to allocate memory dynamically during program execution, in order to form flexible data structures, such as linked lists and binary trees.

MEMORY BLOCKS

When a program runs, it asks for memory resources from the operating system. Various operating systems and compilers use their own models to manage the available memory. Typically, the memory layout of a running program is divided into four parts:

1. The *code* segment, which is used to store the code of the program.
2. The *data* segment, which is used to store the global and static variables.
3. The *stack* segment, which is used to store function's data, such as local variables.
4. The *heap* segment (also called *free store*), which is used for dynamic memory allocation.

Note that this distribution model is a typical choice; each system may define its own. Moreover, each compiler may apply its own optimization policy. For example, the parameters of a function may be stored in system registers for faster access, and not in the stack.

STATIC MEMORY ALLOCATION

In static allocation, the memory is allocated from the stack. The size of the allocated memory is fixed; we must specify its size when writing the program and it cannot change during program execution. For example:

```
int main()
{
        float grades[1000];
        ...
}
```

the compiler allocates 1000×sizeof(float) bytes to store the grades of 1000 students when the program is compiled. This memory is allocated whether or not the program finally uses the array. The length of

DOI: 10.1201/9781003230076-14

the array remains fixed; if we need to store grades for more students, we cannot change it during program execution. If the students proved to be less than 1000, memory is wasted. The only way to change the length of the array is to modify the program and compile it again.

Let's discuss briefly what happens when a function is called. The compiler allocates memory in the stack to store the function's data. As said, system registers may be used; for simplicity, we assume that the allocation occurs in the stack. For example, if the function returns a value, accepts parameters, and uses local variables, the compiler allocates memory to store:

   a. The values of the parameters.
   b. The local variables.
   c. The return value.
   d. The address of the next statement to be executed, when the function terminates.

When the function terminates, the following actions take place:

   a. If the return value is assigned into a variable, it is extracted from the stack and stored into that variable.
   b. The address of the next statement is extracted from the stack and the execution of the program continues with that statement.
   c. The memory allocated to store the function's data is released (except that of the `static` variables).

For example, in the following program, when `test()` is called, the compiler allocates `202×sizeof(int)` bytes in the stack to store the values of `i`, `j`, and `arr` elements:

```cpp
#include <iostream> // Example 14.1

void test(int i, int j);

int main()
{
        float a[1000], b[10];
        test(10, 20);
        return 0;
}

void test(int i, int j)
{
        int arr[200];
}
```

This memory is automatically released when `test()` terminates. Similarly, the memory of `1010×sizeof(float)` bytes allocated for the local variables of `main()` is released when the program terminates.

 If the stack has not enough memory to store the data of a function, the execution of the program would terminate abnormally and the message *Stack overflow* may appear.

This situation may occur when a function allocates large blocks of memory and calls other nested functions with considerable memory needs as well. For example, a recursive function that calls itself many times may cause the exhaustion of the available stack memory.

DYNAMIC MEMORY ALLOCATION

In dynamic allocation, the memory is allocated from the heap during program execution and not at compile time. Unlike static allocation, its size can be dynamically specified. Also, this size may dynamically shrink or grow according to the program's needs. For example, the `vector` class allocates dynamically the memory it needs to store its elements. Dynamic allocation is very common in applications where the user interacts with the program. For example, if the program does not know the number of students, it prompts the user to enter it, and then allocate memory for an array of structures to store their data.

As we said, with static allocation the memory is reserved from the stack. The stack has a fixed size, which is determined by the compiler. Typically, the default stack size is not very large. For example, the following program might not run because of unavailable stack memory:

```cpp
#include <iostream> // Example 14.2
int main()
{
        int arr[10000000]; // Static allocation.
        return 0;
}
```

On the other hand, the size of the heap is usually much larger than the stack size. For example, to allocate the same memory dynamically, we'd write:

```cpp
#include <iostream> // Example 14.3
int main()
{
        int *arr;
        arr = new int[10000000]; // Dynamic allocation.
        delete[] arr; // Release memory.
        return 0;
}
```

The program allocates the required memory from the heap and runs normally. Next, we'll explain how to allocate and release memory.

 The careless management of a dynamically allocated memory may cause serious errors. For example, as we'll see below, memory leaks and access to memory that has already been released are very common errors. So, you need to pay special attention when using it.

The `new` and `new[]` Operators

The most used library function for memory allocation in C is `malloc()`. It can also be used in C++, but C++ provides a better way with the `new` and `new[]` operators. For those who are familiar with `malloc()`/ `free()`, and without getting into details, the general rule is that in C++ we use the `new`/`delete` operators instead. After all, `malloc()` knows nothing about class constructors and `free()` knows nothing about destructors. Let's see how we use the `new` operator to allocate memory. First, we specify the type for which we want to allocate memory, then `new` finds a memory block of the requested size, allocates it, and returns its address, which we assign to a pointer to manage it. For example, the following code allocates memory for an integer, reads a value, and stores it in that memory:

```
int *p;
p = new int;
cin >> *p; /* The value of *p will be equal to the value entered by the user. */
```

If we want, we can initialize the memory allocated for a basic type by enclosing the desired value in parentheses or braces. Otherwise, the initial value is random. For example:

```
double *p;
p = new double{1.2}; // Instead of {} we can use ().
cout << *p; // The value of *p is 1.2.
```

When we attempt to allocate memory, there is a possibility that there is no memory available to satisfy the request. By default, if memory allocation fails the `new` operator throws the `std::bad_alloc` exception. We'll discuss exceptions in Chapter 22 and we'll see how we can catch an exception. If we do not want this exception to be created, we use the `nothrow` constant so in case of failure, the return value is the null pointer. For example, if we have declared the structure type `Student` and we want to allocate memory for a single structure we write:

```
Student *p = new (std::nothrow) Student; /* Declare the pointer and allocate
memory in one step. */
if(p == nullptr)
{
        cout << "Memory allocation error\n";
        exit(EXIT_FAILURE); /* exit() causes the program to terminate. EXIT_
FAILURE is a constant which indicates that an error occurred. */
}
```

 If you choose not to throw an exception, you should check if the allocation was successful. If not, an attempt to use a null pointer would have unpredictable results; the program may crash.

The previous examples are just to see how `new` works. There is no reason to use `new` and a pointer in order to manage a single small data item; we just declare an ordinary variable and that's it. `new` is useful when we want to allocate memory for large chunks of data. In particular, to allocate memory for many items we use the `new[]` operator, where the number of items is declared after their type in brackets. Usually, this number is specified during the execution of the program, since if it was prefixed and was not prohibitively large we could use a fixed size array. For example:

```
int num;
cin >> num;
int *p = new int[num];
```

The `new[]` operator allocates memory for num integers and if the allocation succeeds p will point to the beginning of that memory. The number in `[]` must be an integer. For example, it can be the integer value entered by the user or an integer returned from a function. The initial values of the elements are random. If we want to initialize them with 0 we add empty parentheses or braces:

```
int *p = new int[100]();
```

With C++11 we can specify a list of initial values. For example:

```
int *p = new int[100]{10, 20, 30};
```

The first three elements are initialized with the respective values and the rest with 0. If the initial values are more than the number of elements, a compilation error occurs. Similarly, to allocate memory for 100 structures of type Student we write:

```
Student *p = new Student[100];
```

As we know from Chapter 8, we can use the p pointer with array notation. That is, we can write p[0] instead of *p for the first element, p[1] for the second, and so on. Notice that the pointer does not know the number of elements it points to; this can be the source of major problems. For example, if we allocate memory of 100 integers, we are allowed to write:

```
p[200] = 10; or even p[-10] = 20;
```

and access unrelated memory out of the valid range. The compiler won't prohibit this action; it trusts us that we know what we're doing and will let us access that memory. As we know, disaster is on the way. This kind of bug is particularly hard to find, and the worse is that each time you run the program it may have different error behaviour, which makes more difficult to spot the bug.

Of course, do not forget that, as we've seen in several examples (e.g., C.11.25), instead of new[] we can use a vector object. In that case we can safely access the elements and don't deal with memory allocation and release. The container undertakes those tasks for us. For example:

```
int num;
cin >> num;
vector<int> v(num);
```

In fact, usually I try to avoid using a pointer for memory allocation because its use carries risks; we'll see more below. For example, we may forget to release the memory.

 If you need to allocate memory for a number of elements, it'd be better to use a standard container class (e.g., vector) instead of new[]. Its use is easy, fast, and, most importantly, safe.

Before ending this section, note that it'd be better not to allocate memory for local variables, if you can do it statically. For example:

```
void f()
{
        int *p = new int[1000];
        ...
        delete[] p;
}
```

This code is error prone. For example, the programmer may add somewhere in the function a return statement without first releasing the memory. If it is executed, a memory leak will be created. It is much safer to use an ordinary variable (e.g., int p[1000]), so that memory will be automatically released when the function terminates. In general, in a long-running program repetitive memory leaks can cause serious performance degradation and possibly a program crash.

One more thing to say. Someone might ask why to bother learning about dynamic memory stuff and get the risk of inserting bugs due to pointer misuse when we can use `vector` or another container? Well, there are many answers in this question. One reason is to get experience because there can be situations that you should handle memory by yourself. Another one is to be able to read code written by others that uses such semantics; and there is a lot of code out there. Further, to get an idea about how these containers are implemented. For example, the implementation of `vector` is built on pointers, arrays, and memory operations such as allocation, release, and copy. For these and other reasons, don't even think about skipping this chapter; stay tuned.

Call of `operator` Functions

Without going into details, the use of the `new` and `new[]` operators causes the call of respective `operator` functions. For example, let's look at their simple versions:

```cpp
void* operator new(std::size_t count); // For new.
void* operator new[](std::size_t count); // For new[].
```

The `std::size_t` is a synonym of an integer type defined by the implementation and the `count` parameter indicates the number of bytes to be allocated. For example, the statement:

```cpp
Student *p = new Student; is translated to:

Student *p = operator new(sizeof(Student));
```

that is, the `operator new()` function is called. When we'll discuss operator overloading in Chapter 18, you'll understand how the use of an operator triggers the call of an `operator` function. When `new` is executed, the compiler allocates memory to store an object of that type (e.g., `Student`). It then calls the appropriate constructor to construct the object and returns a pointer to the allocated memory. In the case of `new[]` it allocates memory for a number of objects and, for each object, its constructor is called. Note that C++ allows us to set our own functions to be called when the `new` operator is used. For example, if one of our classes, as we'll see in Chapter 18, has special requirements for memory allocation, we can overload the `new` operator for this class and define our own function. Thus, when an object of that class is created with the `new` operator, our function will be called.

The Placement `new` Operator

With normal `new` operator we cannot specify at which memory address to make the allocation. If we want to specify the address, we can use another version of the `new` operator, the placement `new` operator. This version takes as an argument a pointer to a pre-allocated memory and that memory will be used to construct the item. To use it we include the `new` file. Let's see an example:

```cpp
#include <iostream> // Example 14.4
#include <new>
int main()
{
    int *p1, *p2, *p3, buf1[1], buf2[10];

    buf1[0] = 1;
    p1 = new (buf1) int;
    *p1 = 2; // buf1[0] becomes 2.
```

```
        std::cout << "Addresses: " << buf1 << ' ' << p1; /* Same values are
displayed. */
        p2 = new (buf2) int[10];
        std::cout << "\nAddresses: " << buf2 << ' ' << p2; /* Same values are
displayed. */
        p3 = new (buf1) int;
        *p3 = 3;
        std::cout << "\nValues: " << buf1[0] << ' ' << *p1 << ' ' << *p3;
/* Same values are displayed. */
        return 0;
}
```

The `new` placement does not allocate new memory; it just uses memory space that has already been allocated. In this example, this space is the memory allocated for the `buf1` and `buf2` arrays. Initially, memory is reserved for an integer in `buf1`. That is, the value of `p1` will be the same as the value of `buf1`. Then, memory is reserved for ten integers in `buf2` and `p2` points to the beginning of this memory, so the values of `p2` and `buf2` are the same. Then, `p3` points, like `p1`, to `buf1`. Therefore, the statement `*p3 = 3;` overwrites the content of `buf1`, which was initially 1 and then became 2. Thus, the program outputs the value 3 three times.

The use of the `new` placement causes the call of similar `operator` functions as the ones we saw before, with the difference that they accept an additional parameter, which is the pointer in the memory where the placement will take place. Also note that if the memory is reserved with the `new` placement, as in the previous example, it is wrong to use the `delete` operator to release it. That is, it is an error to write:

```
delete p1; or delete[] p2;
```

The memory for `buf1` and `buf2` is statically allocated, while the `delete` operator, as we'll see below, is used to release dynamically allocated memory.

The `new` placement can be useful in several cases, such as in applications where memory must be reserved from specific memory locations (e.g., hardware-related applications).

The `delete` and `delete[]` Operators

To release the memory that is allocated for one item with the `new` operator we use the `delete` operator. For example:

```
int *p = new int;
...
delete p;
```

Note that the `delete` operator is used to release memory that is dynamically allocated with `new`, and not static. That is, it is wrong to write something like this:

```
int *p, arr[100];
p = arr;
delete p; // Wrong.
```

If the pointer does not point to a valid memory dynamically allocated, it is wrong to use `delete` (or initialize, as you know). For example:

```
int *p;
*p = 10; // Wrong.
delete p; // Wrong.
```

Also, the attempt to release an already released memory or access the memory through a deleted pointer is wrong. For example:

```cpp
int *p = new int;
...
delete p;
*p = 10; // Wrong.
delete p; // Wrong.
```

Notice that the multiple use of `delete` to release the same memory is a serious error, which causes the undefined behaviour of the program.

If the pointer is null, it is safe to apply `delete`. Since a null pointer does not point somewhere, the statement has no effect, nothing happens. For example:

```cpp
int *p = nullptr;
delete p; // OK.
```

Thus, it is not necessary to use an `if` to check before releasing the memory:

```cpp
if(p) // Not necessary.
{
        delete p;
}
```

To release memory that is allocated for many items with the `new[]` operator we use the `delete[]` operator. For example:

```cpp
Student *p = new Student[100];
...
delete[] p;
```

The braces indicate to the compiler that it should release the whole memory, and not just the memory for the item that the pointer points to. If we forget the braces the behaviour is unpredictable. Unfortunately, the compiler most probably won't warn us about this error. Therefore, we need to be very careful not to forget the `[]`.

 We use `delete` to release memory that is allocated with `new` and `delete[]` to release memory that is allocated with `new[]`.

The released memory can be reused for new allocations. Note that if we don't release the memory, it will be released automatically and returned back to the operating system when the program terminates.

Notice that when releasing the memory it does not imply that the value of the pointer will become `nullptr`. For example, its value may be still equal to the address of the allocated memory. In general, in order to avoid disastrous situations it is considered a good practice to reset the value of the pointer to `nullptr`. For example, in large programs, where the same pointer may be used in different parts of the program, it'd be wise, for better control and safety, to make it null pointer when you release the memory. For example:

```cpp
delete[] p; // If it is null, there is no problem; delete has no effect.
p = nullptr;
```

I'll tell you later something that happened to me once. Also, this practice helped me a lot when debugging programs with memory problems.

As with `new` and `new[]`, the use of `delete` and `delete[]` causes the corresponding `operator` functions to be called. For example, let's look at their simple versions:

```
void operator delete(void *ptr);
void operator delete[](void *ptr);
```

For example, the statement `delete p;` causes the call of `delete(p);`. As we'll see in Chapter 17, if p points to memory that is allocated with `new` for an object (e.g., `Student`) the destructor of that object is called, while if it points to memory that is allocated with `new[]` for many objects, the `delete[] p;` causes the call of the destructor of each object starting from the last one. That is, the last element is destroyed first, then the last but one, until the first one.

Note that memory can be dynamically allocated in one function and released in another, provided that the second function has access to that memory (e.g., through a returned pointer). However, as we'll see next, allocating memory in one place, moving around the pointer, and release the memory in another place complicates the management of that memory and also it is a potential source of a memory leak or bug since we can forget to release the memory or release it more than once. Thus, we should try to allocate and release memory in the same function.

As I mentioned, in large programs where the same pointer can be used in different parts of the program, my advice for more safety and better control of the program is to assign it the `nullptr` value when you release the respective memory. Here is an example, similar to what happened to me once.

One time, I used an array of some thousands of pointers to classes. I initialized them with `nullptr` and memory was allocated for some of them during program execution. So far, so good. Once in a while, memory was released in random order. After that, the program was crashing. And the worse part, the program was crashing occasionally, not always. That's the programmer's nightmare, random failures. After days of stress and hard debugging, I concluded that the crash was due to some pointer misuse (… what else?). Here is the buggy code:

```
if(arr[i] != nullptr)
        x = arr[i]->field;
```

The `if` condition didn't let a null pointer to access the member `field` of the class. That's fine, but what about a pointer that used to point to a memory and that memory is later released? Such a pointer is usually called a *dangling* pointer in the sense that it once pointed to a memory that has now been released. For example, suppose that the memory pointed to by some `arr[i]` is released. The condition is still true, because the fact that the memory is released does not mean that `arr[i]` becomes null pointer; it may retain its last value. Therefore, when using `arr[i]` to access the `field` member, the `if` condition was true and the program was crashing. The `nullptr` value must be explicitly assigned, so when I added the statement `arr[i] = nullptr;` after releasing the memory, the problem was solved and we went straight for beers. Cheers!!!

Of course, things could be worse. For example, besides `arr[i]` to use another pointer (e.g., `q[j]`) pointing to the same object. That is, at another point in the program to have the code:

```
if(q[j] != nullptr)
        x = q[j]->field;
```

Making `arr[i]` equal to `nullptr` has no effect on `q[j]`. Thus, I'd have to search in the code to find the right matches of `arr[i]` and `q[j]` pairs and make `q[j]` equal to `nullptr` as well. Nightmare, I do not want to think about it. If, at that time, I had the smart pointers of C++11 at my disposal, I'd have used them and avoid many such dangerous situations. When I heard about them it was too late, I had already burnt my midnight oil, we hear *Too old to rock and roll too young to die* from *Jethro Tull*.

Example of Dynamic Allocation for a Two-Dimensional Array

A typical example of dynamic allocation is for the implementation of two-dimensional arrays. Let's write such a program using a pointer to pointer variable; you may find it useful for future reference, although this does not mean that the following approach is the most efficient. The next program reads the dimensions of a two-dimensional array at run-time, allocates memory for it, reads values, and stores them in its elements. The program emulates a dynamic two-dimensional array using one-dimensional dynamic arrays.

```cpp
#include <iostream> // Example 14.5
using std::cout;
using std::cin;

void set_values(double **arr, int rows, int cols);

int main()
{
        int i, rows, cols;
        double **arr; /* We use a pointer to pointer variable to handle the
two-dimensional array. */
        do
        {
                cout << "Enter dimensions of array[N][M]: ";
                cin >> rows >> cols;
        } while(rows <= 0 || cols <= 0);

        arr = new double*[rows]; /* We allocate memory for 'rows' pointers to
doubles. For example, if rows is 3, we allocate memory for arr[0], arr[1],
and arr[2] pointers. */
        for(i = 0; i < rows; i++) /* Allocate memory to store the elements of
each row. Each row contains 'cols' elements. */
                arr[i] = new double[cols];

        set_values(arr, rows, cols);
        for(i = 0; i < rows; i++)
                delete[] arr[i];
        delete[] arr;
        return 0;
}

void set_values(double **arr, int rows, int cols)
{
        int i, j;

        for(i = 0; i < rows; i++)
                for(j = 0; j < cols; j++)
                {
                        cout << "Set arr[" << i << "][" << j << "]: ";
                        cin >> arr[i][j];
                        cout << "arr[" << i << "][" << j << "] = " << arr[i][j]
<< '\n';
                }
}
```

The program first creates an array of rows pointers, and then, for each element it creates an array of cols elements. That is, each arr[i] is a pointer to the row i that contains cols doubles. The reason

I added the function is to remember how we can pass a pointer to a pointer variable and that we can use array subscripting to handle it. As I said, the above programming approach is not the most efficient. For example, when memory is allocated in that way, the elements most likely won't reside in successive memory locations as happens with an ordinary declaration (e.g., `int arr[100][100]`). Thus, accessing them is not the same fast as with contiguous memory. Also, multiple memory allocations cost in time. The main reason I wrote the program in this way is for educational purposes, to remember how to use an array of pointers and syntax issues.

Alternatively, an easier and more efficient technique is to use a simple pointer and allocate the required memory:

`double *arr = new double[rows*cols];` to access any i, j element we write `arr[i*cols+j]`, as in a two-dimensional array. This way, both the allocation and the release of the memory become much easier.

Also note that if the second dimension is known (e.g., 5), we can write:

`double (*arr)[5] = new double[rows][5];` the memory is contiguous and we can access any i, j element in the ordinary way, that is, we write `arr[i][j]`. And if you want a simpler syntax we can write: `auto arr = new double[rows][5];`

Another approach is to use a two-dimensional vector, as in the C.7.16 exercise. For example:

```
int rows, cols;
cin >> rows >> cols;
vector<vector<double>> v(rows, vector<double>(cols));
set_values(v, rows, cols);

void set_values(vector<vector<double>>& v, int rows, int cols)
{
        for(int i = 0; i < rows; i++)
                for(int j = 0; j < cols; j++)
                        cin >> v[i][j];
}
```

Not only its syntax is simple, but the important thing is that we do not have to deal with issues related to memory management. The `vector` class handles them for us, we don't have to worry. As we said, it is useful to know how to use pointers to allocate and manage memory dynamically, but if some type of the standard library meets your needs, it is better to choose it.

Memory Leaks

One might ask since the allocated memory is automatically returned back to the operating system when the program terminates, do we need to release it? In small programs might not be a big deal, but in case of long-running programs or programs that run forever (e.g., in embedded systems) or programs that run in systems with limited memory, yes, it is essential to release the memory you won't use any more. If you don't do that memory leaks are created, which may cause the gradual degradation of the program's performance, or even worse memory depletion and application collapse.

 Don't forget to release a dynamically allocated memory when you no longer need it, in order to avoid memory leaks.

Let's see an example of memory leak:

```
void f()
{
        int *ptr = new int[10000];
        ...
        ptr = new int[200];
        ...
        delete[] ptr;
}
```

In this example we forget to release the first memory block before the new allocation. This is a memory leak, which occurs every time f() is called.

Another very common example of memory leak is when we allocate memory in one place and forget to release it in another place where it is supposed to do so. For example:

```
double* f(int size)
{
        ...
        return new double[size];
}

void g()
{
        double* p = f(10000);
        /* Do some stuff with p, but then we forget to release the memory
allocated in f(). */
}
```

When g() ends, the local variable p is automatically destroyed, but the memory it points to is not automatically released. We have to do it explicitly by calling delete[] p;. As you guess, in complex and large programs when memory is allocated in one part of the program and released in another part, the programmer may forget to do so and create a memory leak that is difficult to spot. To avoid such memory leaks, try to allocate and release memory in the same function. Also, as we'll see in Chapter 25, a safer practice is the use of smart pointers. That is, if we use a smart pointer in place of p the memory will be released automatically.

Another usual case of memory leak occurs when we assign one pointer to another, but we forget to release the memory to which the pointer originally pointed. For example, find the errors in the following program and fix them:

```
#include <iostream> // Example 14.6
int main()
{
        char *p1, *p2;

        p1 = new char[10];
        p2 = new char[10];
        p1 = p2;
        delete[] p1;

        p2[0] = 'a';
        delete[] p2;
        return 0;
}
```

Let's see the problems:

a. The statement p1 = p2; makes p1 and p2 to point to the same memory. The statement delete[] p1; releases this memory, so, the next statement assigns a value to a non-allocated memory.
b. The statement delete[] p2; releases memory already released.
c. The first block of memory pointed to by p1 was never released.

Note that if we add the statement delete[] p1; before the p1 = p2; the program operates normally.

One more, find the errors in the following program and fix them:

```cpp
#include <iostream> // Example 14.7

struct Test
{
        int *i;
        char *c;
};

int main()
{
        Test *t;
        int i;

        t = new Test;
        t->i = new int[10];
        t->c = new char[10];
        t->i[0] = 'a';
        t->c[5] = 50;
        for(i = 0; i < 10; i++)
                std::cout << t->i[i] << ' ' << t->c[i] << '\n';
        delete t;
        delete[] t->i;
        delete[] t->c;
        return 0;
}
```

Are t->i[0] = 'a' or t->c[5] = 50 wrong? Certainly not, we just assign two integers. What about the loop? Nothing wrong with that, it uses array subscripting to display the existing values. What about the memory release? Well, here is the bug. First we have to release the memory allocated for the members of the structure and then the memory for the entire structure, not the other way around. Therefore, we must move delete t; at the end.

 As we'll see in Chapter 25 another safe practice to avoid problems with the dynamic memory management is to use smart pointers. Once more, using either a container class (e.g., vector) or a smart pointer is a much safer approach than manipulating dynamic memory directly. Then, you don't have to worry about potential dangerous situations, such as dangling pointers and memory leaks. However, you should learn about these operators, how to use them, and the potential hazards because either you'll have to apply them or you'll encounter them in existing code written by others.

MEMORY MANAGEMENT FUNCTIONS

This section discusses briefly the `memcpy()`, `memmove()`, and `memcmp()` functions that are often used for memory management. `memcpy()` is used to copy any type of data from one memory region to another. It is declared in `cstring`:

```
void *memcpy(void *dest, const void *src, size_t size);
```

`memcpy()` copies `size` bytes from the memory pointed to by `src` to the address pointed to by `dest`. If the source and destination addresses overlap, its behaviour is undefined. For example, the following code allocates memory and stores the `"ABCDE"` string in it:

```
char *arr = new char[6]; // Allocate one extra byte for the null character.
memcpy(arr, "ABCDE", 6);
```

The main difference with `strcpy()` is that `strcpy()` stops copying when the null character is met. On the other hand, `memcpy()` does not stop copying until it copies the number of specified bytes. For example, if we have:

```
char str2[6], str1[] = {'a', 'b', 'c', '\0', 'd', 'e'};
```

and write: `memcpy(str2, str1, 6);`

the content of `str2` would be the same as of `str1`.

On the other hand, if we write: `strcpy(str2, str1);`

the content of `str2` would be: `{'a', 'b', 'c', '\0'}`.

`memmove()` is similar to `memcpy()`, except that `memmove()` guarantees that the data will be copied correctly even if the source and destination memory overlap. Because `memcpy()` does not check if the two memory regions overlap, it is executed faster than `memmove()`. Notice that the size of the destination memory should be `size` bytes, at least. If it is not, the extra bytes would be written in a non-allocated memory, which means that the existing data will be overwritten. For example, the next copy is wrong because the size of the destination memory is 3 bytes, while the copied bytes are 6:

```
char str1[3], str2[] = "abcde";
memcpy(str1, str2, sizeof(str2)); // Be careful.
```

 `memcpy()` is often very useful, because it is usually implemented in a way that copying large blocks of data is probably accomplished faster than an iteration loop.

For example, the following code uses `memcpy()` to copy one array to another:

```
int arr1[SIZE], arr2[SIZE];
...
memcpy(arr2, arr1, sizeof(arr1)); /* We use memcpy() instead of an iteration
loop such as:
        for(int i = 0; i < SIZE; i++)
                arr2[i] = arr1[i]; */
```

`memcmp()` is used to compare the data stored in one memory region with the data stored in another. It is declared in `cstring`:

```
int memcmp(const void *ptr1, const void *ptr2, size_t size);
```

`memcmp()` compares `size` bytes of the memory regions pointed to by `ptr1` and `ptr2`. The return value of `memcmp()` is as that of `strcmp()`. Their main difference is that `strcmp()` stops comparing when it encounters the null character in either string. `memcmp()`, on the other hand, stops comparing only when `size` bytes are compared; it does not look for the null character. For example:

```
#include <iostream> // Example 14.8
#include <cstring>
using std::cout;

int main()
{
        char str1[] = {'a', 'b', 'c', '\0', 'd', 'e'};
        char str2[] = {'a', 'b', 'c', '\0', 'd', 'f'};

        if(strcmp(str1, str2) == 0)
                cout << "Same\n";
        else
                cout << "Different\n";

        if(memcmp(str1, str2, sizeof(str1)) == 0)
                cout << "Same\n";
        else
                cout << "Different\n";
        return 0;
}
```

Because `strcmp()` stops comparing when the null character is met, the program displays `Same`. On the contrary, `memcmp()` compares all bytes, and the program displays `Different`.

In the following exercises we could use the `vector` type and get a much simpler code. As I said, the reason I do not do this is to get familiar with dynamic memory management using pointers. This experience will help you if you need to use them or when you encounter existing code written by others to understand what's happening, how they are used, if they are used properly, and potentially fix bugs.

EXERCISES

C.14.1 Does the following program contain errors? If not, what does it display?

```
#include <iostream>
#include <cstring>

void f(char *p);

int main()
{
        char *p1, *p2;
```

```
        p1 = p2 = new char[5];
        strcpy(p1, "test");
        f(p2);
        *p1 = 'm';
        std::cout << p1 << '\n';
        return 0;
}


void f(char *p)
{
        std::cout << p << '\n';
        delete[] p;
}
```

Answer: Once the memory is allocated, p1 and p2 point to the same memory. When f() is called, we have p = p2 and f() displays test. Then, f() releases the memory pointed to by p (that's the same pointed to by p1 and p2). Therefore, the attempt to access this memory with the statement *p1 = 'm'; is wrong. Also, this example shows that we can manage the memory allocated in one function (e.g., main()) into another function (e.g., f()).

C.14.2 Write a function that resizes a dynamically allocated memory that stores integers. The function takes as parameters a pointer to the original memory, the initial memory size, the new size, and returns a pointer to the new memory. The existing data should be copied in the new memory. Write a program that allocates memory dynamically to store an array of ten integers and sets the values 100 up to 109 to its elements. Then, the program should call the function to re-allocate new memory to store 20 integers and display its content.

```
#include <iostream>
#include <cstring>
using std::cout;

int *realloc_mem(int *ptr, int old_size, int new_size);

int main()
{
        int *arr, i;

        arr = new int[10];
        for(i = 0; i < 10; i++)
                arr[i] = i+100;

        arr = realloc_mem(arr, 10, 20); // arr points to the new memory.
        cout << "\n***** Array elements *****\n";
        for(i = 0; i < 20; i++)
                cout << arr[i] << '\n';

        delete[] arr; // Release new memory.
        return 0;
}

int *realloc_mem(int *old_mem, int old_size, int new_size)
{
        int *new_mem;

        // Allocate memory for new_size integers.
        new_mem = new int[new_size];
```

```
        // Copy the existing data to the new memory.
        memcpy(new_mem, old_mem, old_size * sizeof(int));
        delete[] old_mem; // Release old memory.
        return new_mem; // Return the pointer to the new memory.
}
```

Comments: The program displays the values 100–109 for the first ten elements and random values for the next ten, since they are not initialized.

C.14.3 Write a function similar to memcmp(). The program should read two strings of less than 100 characters, the number of the characters to be compared, and use the function to display the result of the comparison.

```
#include <iostream>
#include <cstring>
using std::cout;
using std::cin;

int mem_cmp(const void *ptr1, const void *ptr2, size_t size);

int main()
{
        char str1[100], str2[100];
        int num;

        cout << "Enter first text: ";
        cin.getline(str1, sizeof(str1));

        cout << "Enter second text: ";
        cin.getline(str2, sizeof(str2));

        cout << "Enter characters to compare: ";
        cin >> num;

        cout << mem_cmp(str1, str2, num) << '\n';
        return 0;
}

int mem_cmp(const void *ptr1, const void *ptr2, size_t size)
{
        char *p1, *p2;

        p1 = (char*)ptr1;
        p2 = (char*)ptr2;
        while(size != 0)
        {
                if(*p1 != *p2)
                        return *p1 - *p2;
                p1++;
                p2++;
                size--;
        }
        return 0;
}
```

Comments: The loop compares the characters pointed to by p1 and p2. Since characters are compared, we cast the type void* to char*. If all characters are the same, mem_cmp() returns 0, otherwise the difference of the first two non-matching characters.

C.14.4 Write a function that takes as parameters three pointers to strings and stores the last two strings into the first one. The memory for the first string should have been allocated dynamically. Write a program that reads two strings of less than 100 characters and uses the function to store them into a dynamically allocated memory.

```cpp
#include <iostream>
#include <cstring>
using std::cout;
using std::cin;

void str_cat(char *fin, const char *str1, const char *str2);

int main()
{
        char *fin, str1[100], str2[100];
        int len1, len2;

        cout << "Enter first text: ";
        cin.getline(str1, sizeof(str1));
        len1 = strlen(str1);

        cout << "Enter second text: ";
        cin.getline(str2, sizeof(str2));
        len2 = strlen(str2);
        // Allocate memory to store both strings and the null character.
        fin = new char[len1+len2+1];
        str_cat(fin, str1, str2);
        cout << "Merged text: " << fin << '\n';
        delete[] fin;
        return 0;
}

void str_cat(char *fin, const char *str1, const char *str2)
{
        while(*str1 != '\0') // Or else, while(*str1)
                *fin++ = *str1++;
        // Copy the second string after the first one.
        while(*str2 != '\0') // Or else, while(*str2)
                *fin++ = *str2++;
        *fin = '\0'; // Add the null character.
}
```

Comments: The first loop copies the characters of the string pointed to by `str1` into the memory pointed to by `fin`. Similarly, the next loop adds the characters of the second string. Note that instead of `while` loops, we could use `for` loops. For example:

```cpp
void str_cat(char *fin, const char *str1, const char *str2)
{
        for(;*str1;)
                *fin++ = *str1++;
        for(;*str2;)
                *fin++ = *str2++;
        *fin = '\0';
}
```

How about a more complex solution with a single loop?

```
void str_cat(char *fin, const char *str1, const char *str2)
{
        for(; *str2; *str1?  *fin++ = *str1++ : *fin++ = *str2++)
                ;
        *fin = '\0';
}
```

That's another example of what I consider bad coding style. Don't forget my advice. Write code having simplicity in mind.

C.14.5 Write a function that takes as parameters two arrays of doubles (e.g., a1 and a2) of the same size and their number of elements, and allocates memory to store the elements of a1 that are not contained in a2. The function should return a pointer to that memory. Write a program that reads pairs of doubles and stores them into two arrays of 100 elements (e.g., p1 and p2). If either input value is –1, the insertion of numbers should end. The program should use the function to display the elements of p1 that are not contained in p2.

```
#include <iostream>
#include <cstring>
#include <cstdlib>
using std::cout;
using std::cin;

double *find_diff(const double a1[],const double a2[],int size, int *items);
/* items indicates how many elements are stored in the memory. A pointer is
passed, so that the function may change its value. */

int main()
{
        const int SIZE = 100;
        int i, elems;
        double *p3, j, k, p1[SIZE], p2[SIZE];

        for(i = 0; i < SIZE; i++)
        {
                cout << "Enter numbers: ";
                cin >> j >> k;
                if((j == -1) || (k == -1))
                        break;
                p1[i] = j;
                p2[i] = k;
        }
        elems = 0;
        p3 = find_diff(p1, p2, i, &elems);
        if(elems == 0)
                cout << "\n***** No different elements *****\n";
        else
        {
                for(i = 0; i < elems; i++)
                        cout << p3[i] << '\n';
        }
        delete[] p3;
        return 0;
}
```

```
double *find_diff(const double a1[], const double a2[],int size, int *items)
{
        int i, j, found;
        double *mem;

        mem = new (std::nothrow) double[size]; /* It is just to see an example
with nothrow. */
        if(mem == nullptr)
        {
                cout << "Error: Not available memory\n";
                exit(EXIT_FAILURE);
        }
        for(i = 0; i < size; i++)
        {
                found = 0; /* This variable indicates whether an element of the
first array exists in the second, or not. The value 0 means that it does not
exist. */
                for(j = 0; j < size; j++)
                {
                        if(a2[j] == a1[i])
                        {
                                found = 1;
                                break; /* Since this element exists, we stop
searching. */
                        }
                }
                // If it does not exist, it is stored in the memory.
                if(found == 0)
                {
                        mem[*items] = a1[i];
                        (*items)++;
                }
        }
        return mem;
}
```

C.14.6 Write a program that declares an array of 20 pointers to strings and allocates the exact memory needed to store strings of less than 100 characters. The program should read 20 strings and display the longest one. If more than one string is the longest, the program should display the one found first.

```
#include <iostream>
#include <cstring>
using std::cout;
using std::cin;

const int SIZE = 100;

int main()
{
        char *ptr[SIZE], str[100];
        int i, pos, len, max_len; /* pos is used to indicate the ptr element,
which points to the longest string. max_len holds its length. */
        pos = max_len = 0;
```

```
        for(i = 0; i < SIZE; i++)
        {
                cout << "Enter text: ";
                cin.getline(str, sizeof(str));
                len = strlen(str);
                // Allocate the required memory.
                ptr[i] = new char[len+1];
                // Store the string in the allocated memory.
                strcpy(ptr[i], str);
                /* We compare the length of each string against max_len and if
a longer string is found, we store its position and length. */
                if(len > max_len)
                {
                        pos = i;
                        max_len = len;
                }
        }
        cout << "Longer string: " << ptr[pos] << '\n';
        for(i = 0; i < SIZE; i++)
                delete[] ptr[i];
        return 0;
}
```

Comments: This method of handling the strings is more efficient than the one presented in C.10.27. There is no waste of memory.

C.14.7 Define the structure type `Publisher` with members: name, address, and phone number. Then, define the structure type `Book` with members: title, author, field, code, price, and a pointer to a structure of type `Publisher`. Besides price, all other members must be pointers. Assume that the maximum text length is 100 characters. Write a program that reads the number of books and allocates memory to store their data and the data of the publishers as well. Then, the program should read a book's code and display its title and the name of its publisher, if registered.

```
#include <iostream>
#include <cstring>
using std::cout;
using std::cin;

struct Publisher
{
        char *name;
        char *addr;
        char *phone;
};

struct Book
{
        char *title;
        char *auth;
        char *code;
        Publisher *pub_ptr;
        float prc;
};
```

```cpp
int main()
{
        Book *books_ptr;
        char str[100];
        int i, num, len;

        cout << "Enter number of books: ";
        cin >> num;
        cin.get();

        books_ptr = new Book[num];
        for(i = 0; i < num; i++)
        {
                cout << "\nTitle: ";
                cin.getline(str, sizeof(str));
                len = strlen(str);
                books_ptr[i].title = new char[len+1];
                strcpy(books_ptr[i].title, str);

                cout << "Authors: ";
                cin.getline(str, sizeof(str));
                len = strlen(str);
                books_ptr[i].auth = new char[len+1];
                strcpy(books_ptr[i].auth, str);

                cout << "Code: ";
                cin.getline(str, sizeof(str));
                len = strlen(str);
                books_ptr[i].code = new char[len+1];
                strcpy(books_ptr[i].code, str);

                cout << "Price: ";
                cin >> books_ptr[i].prc;

                cin.get();
                // Allocate memory to store the data of the publishing firm.
                books_ptr[i].pub_ptr = new Publisher;

                cout << "Name: ";
                cin.getline(str, sizeof(str));
                len = strlen(str);
                (books_ptr[i].pub_ptr)->name = new char[len+1];
                strcpy((books_ptr[i].pub_ptr)->name, str);

                cout << "Address: ";
                cin.getline(str, sizeof(str));
                len = strlen(str);
                (books_ptr[i].pub_ptr)->addr = new char[len+1];
                strcpy((books_ptr[i].pub_ptr)->addr, str);

                cout << "Phone: ";
                cin.getline(str, sizeof(str));
                len = strlen(str);
                (books_ptr[i].pub_ptr)->phone = new char[len+1];
                strcpy((books_ptr[i].pub_ptr)->phone, str);
        }
        cout << "\nEnter code to search: ";
        cin.getline(str, sizeof(str));
```

```
for(i = 0; i < num; i++)
{
        if(strcmp(books_ptr[i].code, str) == 0)
        {
                cout << "\nTitle:" << books_ptr[i].title << "\tPublisher:"
<< (books_ptr[i].pub_ptr)->name << '\n';
                break;
        }
}
if(i == num)
        cout << "\nCode isn't registered\n";

for(i = 0; i < num; i++)
{
        delete[] (books_ptr[i].pub_ptr)->name;
        delete[] (books_ptr[i].pub_ptr)->addr;
        delete[] (books_ptr[i].pub_ptr)->phone;

        delete[] books_ptr[i].title;
        delete[] books_ptr[i].auth;
        delete[] books_ptr[i].code;
        delete books_ptr[i].pub_ptr;
}
delete[] books_ptr;
return 0;
}
```

DYNAMIC DATA STRUCTURES

The data structures we've met so far are used for data storage and processing in an easy and fast way. For example, arrays are data structures, which are used for the storage of the same type of data. Structures and unions are also data structures, which can be used for the storage of any type of data. These data structures are static, in the sense that the allocated memory is fixed and cannot be modified during program execution. However, in many applications, it'd be more efficient to use a dynamic data structure, a structure whose size may grow or shrink as needed.

The next sections introduce you to some simple forms of dynamic data structures. The standard library provides many such structures (e.g., list), which we can use in our programs. However, in order to get more familiar with the management of dynamic memory, we are not going to use these ready-to-use tools, but we'll try to implement from the scratch some simple data structures to get a feeling for what is going on behind the scenes.

LINKED LIST

A linked list consists of a chain of linked elements, called *nodes*. Each node is typically represented by a structure, which contains its data and a pointer to the next node in the chain, as depicted in the following figure:

The first node is the head of the list and the last one its tail. The value of the pointer member in the last node must be `nullptr` to indicate the end of the list.

Unlike arrays whose size remains fixed, a linked list is more flexible because its size can be dynamically adjusted to the program's needs. Because we can easily insert and delete nodes at any point of the list, it is much easier to create and maintain a sorted order. On the other hand, to access an array element is very fast; we just use its position as an index. Typically, to access a list node we should start from the head node (leave out the case of storing the nodes' addresses for direct access) and traverse the list serially, whereas arrays provide random access. Therefore, the time to access a node depends on its position in the list. It is fast if the node is close to the beginning, slow if it is near the end. This can make a huge difference to performance.

Insert a Node

A new node can be inserted at any point in the list. To insert a new node, we check the following cases:

1. If the list is empty, the node is inserted at the beginning and becomes the head and the tail of the list. The value of its pointer member is set to `nullptr` since there is no next node in the list.
2. If the list is not empty, we check the following subcases:

   a. If the node is inserted at the beginning of the list, it becomes the new head of the list and its pointer member points to the previous head, which now becomes the second node of the list.
   b. If the node is inserted at the end of the list, it becomes the new tail of the list and the value of its pointer member is set to `nullptr`. The old tail becomes the second to last node and the value of its pointer member changes from `nullptr` to point to the new node.
   c. If the node is inserted after an existing node, the pointer member of the new node must point to the node after the current node and the pointer member of the current node must point to the new node. The following figure depicts how the new node X is inserted between the nodes B and C.

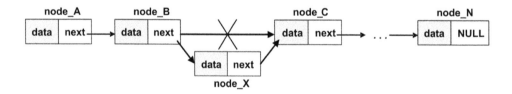

Delete a Node

To delete a node from the list and release the memory it allocates, we check the following cases:

1. If it is the head of the list, we check the following subcases:
   a. If there is a next node, this node becomes the new head of the list.
   b. If there is no next node, the list becomes empty.
2. If it is the tail of the list, the previous node becomes the new tail and its pointer member is set to `nullptr`.

3. If it is an intermediate node, the pointer member of the previous node must point to the node after the one to be deleted. This operation is shown here with the deletion of node C (see the figure).

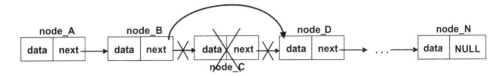

IMPLEMENTATION EXAMPLES

Before creating a linked list, we'll implement two special cases of a linked list, a stack and a queue. Notice that there are various ways to implement these data structures; I tried to implement them in a simple and comprehensible way. In the following examples, each node is a structure of type Node. If you ever need to develop similar data structures, the most part of the code can be reused as is.

As we said, STL provides many classes that implement dynamic data structures. For example, the stack class implements a LIFO (*Last In First Out*) stack. We'll see them briefly in Chapter 26. Here, we'll try to implement some similar functionality of those classes, so that you gain more experience in managing dynamic memory. In the future, this experience may be useful if you don't have ready-to-use classes available and you need to implement your own structures.

Implementing a Stack

In this section, we'll create a LIFO stack, where, as its name indicates, the last inserted node it is the first to get extracted. It is a special case of a linked list with the following restrictions:

a. A new node can be inserted only at the beginning of the stack and becomes its new head.
b. Only the head can be deleted.

A stack like this resembles a stack of dirty dishes. Each new dish is put at the top of the stack and it is the top dish we get to wash.

EXERCISE

C.14.8 Define the structure type Node with members: code, name, grade, and a pointer to a structure of type Node. Create a stack whose nodes are structures of that type. Write a program that displays a menu to perform the following operations:

1. Insert a student. The program should read the student's data and store them in a node, which becomes the new head of the stack.
2. Display the data of the stored students.
3. Display the data of the last inserted student.
4. Delete the last inserted student.
5. Display the total number of the stored students.
6. Program termination.

For simplicity, I chose to handle the stack by using a global pointer. This pointer always points to the head of the stack.

```cpp
#include <iostream>
#include <string>
using std::cout;
using std::cin;
using std::string;

struct Node
{
        string name;
        int code;
        float grd;
        Node *next; /* Pointer to the next node. Notice that the existence of
the structure tag allows us to declare its type. */
};

Node *head; // Global pointer that always points to the head of the stack.

void add_stack(const Node *p);
void show_stack();
void pop();
int size_stack();
void free_stack();

int main()
{
        int sel;
        Node n;

        head = nullptr; /* Initial value for the head pointer, which declares
that the stack is empty. */
        while(1)
        {
                cout << "\nMenu selections\n";
                cout << "---------------\n";

                cout << "1. Add student\n";
                cout << "2. View all students\n";
                cout << "3. View top student\n";
                cout << "4. Delete top student\n";
                cout << "5. Number of students\n";
                cout << "6. Exit\n";

                cout << "\nEnter choice: ";
                cin >> sel;

                switch(sel)
                {
                        case 1:
                                cin.get();
```

```
                        cout << "Name: ";
                        getline(cin, n.name);

                        cout << "Code: ";
                        cin >> n.code;
                        cout << "Grade: ";
                        cin >> n.grd;

                        add_stack(&n);
                break;

                case 2:
                        if(head != nullptr)
                                show_stack();
                        else
                                cout << "\nThe stack is empty\n";
                break;

                case 3:
                        if(head != nullptr)
                                cout << "\nC:" << head->code << " N:" <<
head->name << " G:" << head->grd << '\n';
                        else
                                cout << "\nThe stack is empty\n";
                break;

                case 4:
                        if(head != nullptr)
                                pop();
                        else
                                cout << "\nThe stack is empty\n";
                break;

                case 5:
                        if(head != nullptr)
                                cout << size_stack() << " students exist
in stack\n";
                        else
                                cout << "\nThe stack is empty\n";
                break;

                case 6:
                        if(head != nullptr)
                                free_stack();
                        return 0;

                default:
                        cout << "\nWrong choice\n";
                break;
            }
      }
      return 0;
}
```

```cpp
void add_stack(const Node *p)
{
        Node *new_node;

        new_node = new Node; // Allocate memory to create a new node.
        *new_node = *p; // Copy the student's data into the new node.
        new_node->next = head; /* The new node is inserted at the beginning
of the stack. For example, when the first node is inserted the value of
new_node->next becomes equal to the initial value of head, which is
nullptr. */
        head = new_node; /* head points to the new node, therefore the new
node becomes the new head of the stack. */
}

void show_stack()
{
        Node *p;

        p = head;
        cout << "\n***** Student Data *****\n\n";
        while(p != nullptr)
        {
                cout << "C:" << p->code << " N:" << p->name << " G:" << p->grd
<< '\n';
                p = p->next; /* In each iteration, p points to the next node.
Once it becomes nullptr it means that there is no other node left and the
loop terminates. */
        }
}

void pop()
{
        Node *p;

        p = head->next; /* p points to the next node after the head. This node
will become the new head of the stack. */
        cout << "\nStudent with code " << head->code << " is deleted\n";
        delete head; /* Release the allocated memory. The information about
the next node is not lost, because it was saved in p. */
        head = p; // head points to the new head of the stack.
}

int size_stack()
{
        Node *p;
        int num;

        num = 0;
        p = head;
        while(p != nullptr)
        {
                p = p->next;
                num++; // This variable counts the nodes.
        }
        return num;
}
```

```
void free_stack()
{
        Node *p, *next_node;

        p = head;
        while(p != nullptr)
        {
                next_node = p->next; /* next_node always points to the node
after the one to be deleted. */
                delete p; /* Release the allocated memory. The information
about the next node is not lost, because it was saved in next_node. */
                p = next_node; // p points to the next node.
        }
}
```

Comments:

a. In add_stack() we pass a pointer and not the structure itself, in order to avoid the creation of a structure's copy and make faster the execution of the function.

b. To display immediately the number of the stored students, without traversing the stack, we could remove the size_stack() function and use a variable that would be incremented by one each time a student is inserted in add_stack() and decremented when a student is deleted in pop(). Once the user selects that menu choice, then the program would just display its value. It is much simpler and faster. The reason I added size_stack() is to show you how to traverse the nodes of the stack.

c. If the variable head had been declared locally in main(), we should have passed its address to the functions that need it. For example, add_stack() would change to:

```
void add_stack(const Node *p, Node **head_ptr)
{
        Node *new_node;

        new_node = new Node;
        *new_node = *p;
        new_node->next = *head_ptr;
        *head_ptr = new_node;
}
```

To call it we'd write: add_stack(&n, &head);

Because I think that this code is more complicated, at least for a beginner, I preferred for simplicity to declare head as a global variable and use it directly wherever needed.

Implementing a Queue

In this section, we'll create a FIFO (*First In First Out*) queue, where, as its name indicates, the first inserted node it is the first to get extracted. It is a special case of a linked list with the following restrictions:

a. A new node can be inserted only at the end of the queue and becomes its new tail.

b. Only the head can be deleted.

EXERCISE

C.14.9 Define the structure type `Node` with members: code, name, grade, and a pointer to a structure of type `Node`. Create a queue whose nodes are structures of that type. Write a program that displays a menu to perform the following operations:

1. Insert a student. The program should read the student's data and store them in a node, which becomes the new tail of the queue.
2. Display the data of the stored students.
3. Display the data of the last inserted student.
4. Delete the first inserted student.
5. Program termination.

For simplicity, I chose to handle the queue by using two global pointers. The first one always points to the head of the queue and the second one to its tail.

```cpp
#include <iostream>
#include <string>
using std::cout;
using std::cin;
using std::string;

struct Node
{
        string name;
        int code;
        float grd;
        Node *next;
};

Node *head; // Global pointer that always points to the head of the queue.
Node *tail; // Global pointer that always points to the tail of the queue.

void add_queue(const Node *p);
void show_queue();
void pop();
void free_queue();

int main()
{
        int sel;
        Node n;

        head = nullptr;
        while(1)
        {
                cout << "\nMenu selections\n";
                cout << "---------------\n";
                cout << "1. Add student\n";
                cout << "2. View all students\n";
                cout << "3. View last student\n";
                cout << "4. Delete top student\n";
                cout << "5. Exit\n";
```

```cpp
                cout << "\nEnter choice: ";
                cin >> sel;

                switch(sel)
                {
                        case 1:
                                cin.get();

                                cout << "Name: ";
                                getline(cin, n.name);

                                cout << "Code: ";
                                cin >> n.code;

                                cout << "Grade: ";
                                cin >> n.grd;

                                add_queue(&n);
                        break;

                        case 2:
                                if(head != nullptr)
                                        show_queue();
                                else
                                        cout << "\nThe queue is empty\n";
                        break;

                        case 3:
                                if(head != nullptr)
                                        cout << "\nC:" << tail->code << " N:" <<
tail->name << " G:" << tail->grd << '\n';
                                else
                                        cout << "\nThe queue is empty\n";
                        break;

                        case 4:
                                if(head != nullptr)
                                        pop();
                                else
                                        cout << "\nThe queue is empty\n";
                        break;

                        case 5:
                                if(head != nullptr)
                                        free_queue();
                                return 0;

                        default:
                                cout << "\nWrong choice\n";
                        break;
                }
        }
        return 0;
}

void add_queue(const Node *p)
{
        Node *new_node;
```

```
        new_node = new Node;
        *new_node = *p;
        new_node->next = nullptr;

        if(head == nullptr)
                head = tail = new_node; /* If the queue is empty, both head and
tail pointers point to the new node. */
        else
        {
                tail->next = new_node; /* The new node is inserted at the end
of the queue. */
                tail = new_node; // tail points to the last node.
        }
}
```

Comments: I omit the code of the `show_queue()`, `pop()`, and `free_queue()` functions, because it is the same as the code of `show_stack()`, `pop()`, and `free_stack()` functions in the stack program.

Implementing a Linked List

The following program implements a linked list whose nodes correspond to students. Like before, we use one global pointer to point to the head of the list and another one to point to its tail.

EXERCISES

C.14.10 Define the structure type `Node` with members: code, name, grade, and a pointer to a structure of type `Node`. Create a list whose nodes are structures of that type. Write a program that displays a menu to perform the following operations:

1. Insert a student at the end of the list. The program should read the student's data and store them in a node, which becomes the new tail of the list.
2. Insert a student in a specific place. The program should read the code of a student, locate the corresponding node with that code, and create a new node after that to insert the data of the new student.
3. Display the data of the stored students.
4. Find a student. The program should read the code of a student and display its data, if registered.
5. Modify the grade of a student. The program should read the code of a student and the new grade and modify the existing grade.
6. Delete a student. The program should read the code of a student and remove the node that corresponds to that student, if registered.
7. Program termination.

```
#include <iostream>
#include <string>
using std::cout;
using std::cin;
using std::string;
```

```
struct Node
{
        string name;
        int code;
        float grd;
        Node *next;
};

Node *head; // Global pointer that always points to the head of the list.
Node *tail; // Global pointer that always points to the tail of the list.

void add_list_end(const Node *p);
void add_list(const Node *p, int code);
void show_list();
Node *find_node(int code);
int del_node(int code);
void free_list();

int main()
{
        int k, sel, code;
        float grd;
        Node *p, n;

        head = nullptr;
        while(1)
        {
                cout << "\nMenu selections\n";
                cout << "--------------\n";

                cout << "1. Add student at the end\n";
                cout << "2. Add student\n";
                cout << "3. View all students\n";
                cout << "4. View student\n";
                cout << "5. Modify student\n";
                cout << "6. Delete student\n";
                cout << "7. Exit\n";

                cout << "\nEnter choice: ";
                cin >> sel;

                switch(sel)
                {
                        case 1:
                        case 2: /* To avoid the repetition of the same code we
use the same case to insert data. Then, the if statement checks the user's
choice and calls the respective function. */
                                cin.get();

                                cout << "Name: ";
                                getline(cin, n.name);

                                cout << "Code: ";
                                cin >> n.code;

                                cout << "Grade: ";
                                cin >> n.grd;
```

```
                        if(sel == 1)
                                add_list_end(&n);
                        else
                        {
                                cout << "\nEnter student code after which
the new student will be added: ";
                                cin >> code;
                                add_list(&n, code);
                        }
                break;

                case 3:
                        if(head == nullptr)
                                cout << "\nThe list is empty\n";
                        else
                                show_list();
                break;

                case 4:
                        if(head == nullptr)
                                cout << "\nThe list is empty\n";
                        else
                        {
                                cout << "\nEnter student code to search: ";
                                cin >> code;
                                p = find_node(code);
                                if(p != nullptr)
                                        cout << "\nN:" << p->name << " G:"
<< p->grd << '\n';
                                else
                                        cout << "\nStudent with code " <<
code << " does not exist\n";
                        }
                break;

                case 5:
                        if(head == nullptr)
                                cout << "\nThe list is empty\n";
                        else
                        {
                                cout << "\nEnter student code to modify: ";
                                cin >> code;

                                cout << "Enter new grade: ";
                                cin >> grd;
                                p = find_node(code);
                                if(p != nullptr)
                                        p->grd = grd;
                                else
                                        cout << "\nStudent with code " <<
code << " does not exist\n";
                        }
                break;

                case 6:
                        if(head == nullptr)
                                cout << "\nThe list is empty\n";
```

```
                        else
                        {
                                cout << "\nEnter student code to delete: ";
                                cin >> code;
                                k = del_node(code);
                                if(k == 0)
                                        cout << "\nStudent with code " <<
code << " is deleted\n";
                                else
                                        cout << "\nStudent with code " <<
code << " does not exist\n";
                        }
                        break;

                case 7:
                        if(head != nullptr)
                                free_list();
                        return 0;

                default:
                        cout << "\nWrong choice\n";
                        break;
            }
        }
        return 0;
}


/* For a better understanding of add_list_end(), read the comments of add_queue()
in the previous exercise. */
void add_list_end(const Node *p)
{
        Node *new_node;

        new_node = new Node;
        *new_node = *p;
        new_node->next = nullptr;

        if(head == nullptr)
                head = tail = new_node;
        else
        {
                tail->next = new_node;
                tail = new_node;
        }
}


void add_list(const Node *p, int code)
{
        Node *new_node, *ptr;

        ptr = head;
        /* We traverse the list, until the node with the indicated code is
found. If found, the new node is added after that and the function
terminates. */
```

```
        while(ptr != nullptr)
        {
                if(ptr->code == code)
                {
                        new_node = new Node;
                        *new_node = *p; // Copy the student's data.
                        new_node->next = ptr->next; /* The new node is linked to
the node after the current node. */
                        ptr->next = new_node; /* The current node is linked to
the new node. */
                        if(ptr == tail) /* Check if the new node is added at the
end of the list. If it is, it becomes the new tail. */
                                tail = new_node;
                        return;
                }
                ptr = ptr->next; // Check the next node.
        }
        /* If this point is reached it means that the input code does not
correspond to an existing student. */
        cout << "\nStudent with code " << code << " does not exist\n";
}

void show_list()
{
        Node *p;

        p = head;
        cout << "\n***** Student Data *****\n\n";
        while(p != nullptr)
        {
                cout << "C:" << p->code << " N:" << p->name << " G:" << p->grd <<
'\n';
                p = p->next;
        }
}

Node *find_node(int code)
{
        Node *p;

        p = head;
        while(p != nullptr)
        {
                if(p->code == code)
                        return p;
                p = p->next;
        }
        return nullptr;
}

int del_node(int code)
{
        Node *p, *prev_node; /* prev_node always points to the previous node
from the one that is going to be deleted. */

        p = prev_node = head;
        while(p != nullptr)
```

```
        {
                if(p->code == code)
                {
                        if(p == head)
                                head = p->next; /* If the node is the head of the
list, the next node becomes the new head. If there is no other node, the list
becomes empty and head becomes nullptr. */
                        else
                        {
                                /* p points to the node that will be deleted and
prev_node points to the previous one. This statement links the previous node
with the node after the one to be deleted. */
                                prev_node->next = p->next;
                                if(p == tail) /* Check if the deleted node is the
tail of the list. If it is, the previous node becomes the new tail. */
                                        tail = prev_node;
                        }
                        delete p; // Delete the node.
                        return 0;
                }
                prev_node = p; /* prev_node points to the node that was just
checked and found that it has other code than the input code. */
                p = p->next; /* Now, p points to the next node. Notice that
prev_node always points to the previous node from the one to be examined. */
        }
        return -1;
}

void free_list()
{
        Node *p, *next_node;

        p = head;
        while(p != nullptr)
        {
                next_node = p->next;
                delete p;
                p = next_node;
        }
}
```

Comments: If you want to change the first menu choice and insert the data of the new student at the beginning of the list and not at its end, replace the add_list_end() with the add_stack() presented in the stack program. In that case, the tail pointer is not needed.

C.14.11 Consider the previous linked list. Write a function that takes as parameters the codes of two students and, if they are stored in the list, the function should swap their grades and return 0. If not, the function should return -1.

```
int swap(int code_a, int code_b)
{
        Node *p, *tmp1, *tmp2;
        float grd;

        p = head;
        tmp1 = tmp2 = nullptr;
```

```
      while(p != nullptr)
      {
            if(p->code == code_a)
                  tmp1 = p;
            else if(p->code == code_b)
                  tmp2 = p;

            if(tmp1 && tmp2)
            {
                  grd = tmp1->grd;
                  tmp1->grd = tmp2->grd;
                  tmp2->grd = grd;
                  return 0;
            }
            p = p->next;
      }
      return -1;
}
```

C.14.12 What is the output of the following program?

```
#include <iostream>

struct Node
{
      int i;
      Node *next;
      Node *prev;
};

int main()
{
      Node a = {10}, b = {20}, c = {30}, d = {40};

      a.next = &b;
      a.prev = &d;

      b.next = &c;
      b.prev = &a;

      c.next = &d;
      c.prev = &b;

      d.next = &a;
      d.prev = &c;
      std::cout << a.prev->prev->prev->next->i << '\n';
      return 0;
}
```

Comments: This program is a simple implementation example of another type of list, a circular double linked list, where each node, except the pointer to the next node, contains another pointer to the previous node. Notice that the next pointer of the last node points to the head of the list, while head's prev pointer points to the last node. The program begins with node a, traverses sequentially the d, c, and b nodes, returns back to c and outputs 30. Try now exercise U.14.14.

BINARY SEARCH TREE

To organize data in sorted order, a flexible data structure named *tree* is typically used. This type of structure is met in several real-life examples, like a family tree, an organizational chart, or a computer's folder system. There are many types of trees; here we are going to describe the basic operations in a binary search tree.

Let's present in short some basic concepts. A tree with *root* is a collection of nodes connected with edges. There is only one node with no parent, the top node. That node is named *root*. Each node, except the root, is connected with just one upper node, the *parent* node. The nodes directly connected one level below are its *children*. A tree in which each node has at most two children is called *binary tree*. The two parts are referred to as the left and right subtree. A binary tree where each node has a key and that key:

a. is greater than or equal to the keys in all nodes in its left subtree and
b. is less than or equal to the keys in all nodes in its right subtree

is called *binary search tree*. The main advantage of using that structure is its high performance in critical operations like inserting and searching for a value. Related sorting and search algorithms can be very efficient. The following figure shows an example of a binary search tree.

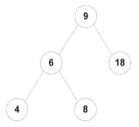

Let's see some implementation examples of the most basic operations in a binary search tree. Suppose that each node is represented by the following structure:

```
struct Node
{
        int key;
        Node *left;
        Node *right;
};
```

We are going to store different keys. The pointers point to the node's children. If a child is missing, the pointer is `nullptr`.

```
#include <iostream> // Example 14.9
#include <cstring>
using std::cout;
using std::cin;
using std::string;

struct Node
{
        int key;
        Node *left;
        Node *right;
};
```

```cpp
Node* add_node(Node *p, int key);
void show_inorder(Node *p);
void delete_tree(Node *p);

int main()
{
        int sel, key;
        Node *root;

        root = nullptr;
        while(1)
        {
                cout << "\nMenu selections\n";
                cout << "---------------\n";
                cout << "1. Add Node\n";
                cout << "2. Show Tree\n";
                cout << "3. Exit\n";

                cout << "\nEnter choice: ";
                cin >> sel;

                switch(sel)
                {
                        case 1:
                                cout << "Key: ";
                                cin >> key;
                                root = add_node(root, key);
                        break;

                        case 2:
                                cout << "Added Keys: ";
                                show_inorder(root);
                        break;

                        case 3:
                                cout << "\nDeleted Keys: ";
                                delete_tree(root);
                        return 0;

                        default:
                                cout << "\nWrong choice\n";
                        break;
                }
        }
        return 0;
}

Node* add_node(Node *p, int key)
{
        if(p == nullptr)
        {
                p = new Node;
                p->left = p->right = nullptr;
                p->key = key;
        }
```

```
        else
        {
                if(key < p->key)
                        p->left = add_node(p->left, key);
                else if(key > p->key)
                        p->right = add_node(p->right, key);
                else
                        cout << "Error: Key(" << key << ") exists\n";
        }
        return p;
}

void show_inorder(Node *p)
{
        if(p == nullptr)
                return;
        show_inorder(p->left);
        cout << p->key << ' ';
        show_inorder(p->right);
}

void delete_tree(Node *p)
{
        if(p == nullptr)
                return;

        delete_tree(p->left);
        delete_tree(p->right);
        cout << p->key << ' ';
        delete p;
}
```

add_node() creates and inserts a new node in the tree, provided that no other node has the same key value. The function compares the inserted key with the key of the examined node and uses recursion to head towards the proper subtree. For example, suppose that the user enters the numbers: 9, 6, 18, 4, and 8.

Insertion of 9: Since root is nullptr, the function creates the root of the tree and assigns the value nullptr to its pointers. The address of the root node is returned to the main program.

Insertion of 6: Because 6 is less than 9, the function is called recursively with argument the p->left pointer. Since it is nullptr, the recursive call creates a new node (at the left of the root) and assigns the value nullptr to its pointers. The address of that new node is returned and p->left becomes equal to that value. The function terminates with the return of the root pointer.

Insertion of 18: Similar to node 6, with the difference that the p->right pointer is used.

Insertion of 4: Because 4 is less than 9, the function is called recursively with argument the p->left pointer. Since it is nullptr and 4 is less than 6, a second recursive call is made with argument the left pointer of node 6. Since it is nullptr, that second call creates a new node and returns its address at the point of the first recursive call. This value is stored in p->left, where p points to node 6. The first call terminates with the return of p. Next, the function terminates with the return of the root pointer.

Insertion of 8: Similar to node 4, with the difference that the argument of the second recursive call is the right pointer of node 6.

In this way, the tree gets the form of binary search tree as shown in the previous figure.

The procedure to insert a key in the tree resembles the procedure to search for a key. Try U.14.16 to write a recursive search function. Alternatively, here is a non-recursive implementation. In fact, this is my preference; remember what we've discussed about recursion performance issues in the respective section of Chapter 11.

```
Node* find_node(Node *p, int key)
{
        if(p == nullptr) /* Check if the tree is empty. We could use the while
condition, I just prefer to make it clear. */
                return nullptr;

        while(p != nullptr)
        {
                if(key < p->key)
                        p = p->left;
                else if(key > p->key)
                        p = p->right;
                else
                        return p;
        }
        return nullptr;
}
```

The code compares the key and the proper subtree is selected. If the lower level is reached, it means that the key is not found. Now that you've seen this method, try U.14.18 to implement add_node() without using recursion. To help you, use the code above to find the node under which the new node must be connected, that is, the parent node. Then, create the new node and connect it with the parent node.

As a new exercise, suppose that the show_inorder() is called. Try to figure out what it is doing and explain how it works. Spend some time, don't rush to look at the answer in the next page.

You turned the page right away, didn't you? Go back and give a try. It's worth to test your skills, to see if you can decode multiple recursions.

Let's see how the function works. In the first recursive call p->left points to node 6. Since it is not nullptr, a second recursive call is made and p->left points to node 4. A third call is made (now p points to 4), and since p->left is nullptr the function returns.

The second recursive call outputs 4 and a new call is made with argument p->right. Since it is nullptr, the function returns. The second recursive call ends and we continue with the first one.

The first call outputs 6 and a new recursive call is made with argument p->right. The recursion is executed where p points to 8. New recursion, which returns because p->left is nullptr. The program outputs 8 and the next recursion returns, because p->right is nullptr.

Where are we? We got lost. If I am not wrong, we were checking the first recursion where p->left points to node 6, and that recursion is just ended. The program outputs 9 and a new recursive call is made with argument p->right. Like before, the program outputs 18 and the function ends, ... at last.

Essentially, show_inorder() performs an in-order tree traversal. In particular, for each traversed node, it first visits the nodes of its left subtree, then the current node, and then the nodes of its right subtree. As a result, the function displays the key values in ascending order.

In the same sense, show_preorder() performs a pre-order tree traversal. In particular, for each traversed node, it first visits the node itself, then the nodes of its left subtree, and then the nodes of its right subtree.

```
void show_preorder(Node *p)
{
        if(p == nullptr)
                return;
        cout << p->key << ' ';
        show_preorder(p->left);
        show_preorder(p->right);
}
```

show_postorder() performs a post-order tree traversal. For each traversed node, it first visits the nodes of its left subtree, then the nodes of its right subtree, and then the current node.

```
void show_postorder(Node *p)
{
        if(p == nullptr)
                return;
        show_postorder(p->left);
        show_postorder(p->right);
        cout << p->key << ' ';
}
```

delete_tree() uses the post-order method to release the allocated memory. For each traversed node, first the memory of the nodes of its two subtrees is released, and then the memory of the node itself. In the previous example, the nodes are released in that order: 4, 8, 6, 18, and 9.

Another method to traverse a tree is to visit the nodes starting from the root and going down in level order. In each level the nodes are visited from left to right. In the previous example, the nodes are visited in that order: 9, 6, 18, 4, and 8. To implement the level order method, we'll write a non-recursive function that uses an array of pointers as a FIFO queue to store the visited nodes. For simplicity, we assume that the tree contains a maximum numbers of nodes.

```
const int MAX_NODES = 200;

void show_levelorder(Node *p)
{
        Node *arr[MAX_NODES] = {0}; /* To simulate a FIFO queue, we use an
array of pointers to the nodes. */
```

```
    int start, end; /* start indicates the node to display its key and end
indicates the last node stored in the queue. */
    if(p == nullptr) // Check if the tree is empty.
            return;

    start = end = 0;
    add_queue(arr, p, &end); // Store the root.

    while((p = pop(arr, &start)) != nullptr)
    {
            cout << p->key << ' ';

            if(p->left)
                    add_queue(arr, p->left, &end);
            if(p->right)
                    add_queue(arr, p->right, &end);
    }
}

void add_queue(Node *arr[], Node *p, int *cnt)
{
        arr[*cnt] = p;
        (*cnt)++;
}

Node* pop(Node *arr[], int *cnt)
{
        Node *tmp;

        tmp = arr[*cnt];
        (*cnt)++;
        return tmp;

        /* Alternatively, without using tmp:
        (*cnt)++;
        return arr[*cnt-1]; */
}
```

Based on that code, try U.14.19. The approach I propose is first to visit all left nodes. Also change the queue to LIFO. For example, consider the nodes of the first program. Initially, the nodes 9, 6, and 4 are stored. We pop the last one and display its key, that is, 4. We pop the last but one, that is 6, and ... your turn now.

EXERCISES

C.14.13 Add a recursive function that displays the smallest key value in the tree.

```
void find_min(Node *p)
{
        if(p == nullptr)
                return;
        if(p->left == nullptr)
```

```
        {
                cout << "Min:" << p->key << '\n';
                return;
        }
        find_min(p->left);
}
```

Comments: In a binary search tree, the smallest value is stored in the most left node. Then, the recursion ends. To find the largest value, just change the pointer to p->right, to find the most right node. Call the function with argument the root pointer, to test its operation. For an alternative non-recursive solution, try U.14.17.

C.14.14 Write a recursive function that counts the nodes of the tree.

```
void tree_nodes(Node *p)
{
        if(p == nullptr)
                return;
        cnt++;
        tree_nodes(p->left);
        tree_nodes(p->right);
}
```

Comments: For simplicity, cnt could be a global variable initialized with 0 and incremented by one each time a node is visited.

C.14.15 Modify the structure that represents the node, in order to store different strings in the tree. For example:

```
struct Node
{
        char *key;
        Node *left;
        Node *right;
};
```

Modify add_node() and delete_tree().

Answer:

```
Node* add_node(Node *p, char key[])
{
        int tmp;

        if(p == nullptr)
        {
                p = new Node;
                p->key = new char[strlen(key)+1];
                strcpy(p->key, key);
                p->left = p->right = nullptr;
        }
        else
        {
                tmp = strcmp(key, p->key);
                if(tmp < 0)
                        p->left = add_node(p->left, key);
```

```
                else if(tmp > 0)
                        p->right = add_node(p->right, key);
                else
                        cout << "Error: Key(" << key << ") exists\n";
        }
        return p;
}

void delete_tree(Node *p)
{
        if(p == nullptr)
                return;

        delete_tree(p->left);
        delete_tree(p->right);
        cout << p->key << '\n';
        delete p->key;
        delete p;
}
```

Before finishing this chapter, I'd like to note that although the standard library provides many ready-to-use algorithms (e.g., sort()) and containers (e.g., list) it is very important to have some experience in implementing algorithms and data structures by yourself. Not only because you may need that knowledge either to write your own applications or understand code written by others, but also to get an idea about how they are implemented. With the implementation examples of the data structures we described in this chapter and the algorithms in Chapter 12, I tried to give you this feeling of know-how. Of course, to learn more about algorithms and data structures, you should read a book that focuses on this subject.

UNSOLVED EXERCISES

U.14.1 Complete the following program to read an integer and a double number and display their sum. Don't use another variable.

```
int main()
{
        int *p1;
        double *p2;
        ...
}
```

U.14.2 Write a program that uses a pointer variable to read three integers and display the greatest. Don't use any other variable.

U.14.3 Use the two pointer variables and complete the following function to return how many products cost less than $20 and how many more than $100.

```
void find(double *arr, int size, int *und20, int *ov100);
```

Write a program that prompts the user to enter the number of the products (i.e., size), their prices, and stores them in a dynamically allocated memory (i.e., arr). Then, the program should use the function to display how many products cost less than $20 and how many more than $100.

U.14.4 Write a program that:

    a. Allocates memory to store a number of integers. The program should prompt the user to enter that number.
    b. The program should read those integers and store them in the allocated memory.
    c. If the user enters -5, the program should release the memory and continue from the first step.
    d. If all integers are entered, the program should display the memory content and terminate.

U.14.5 Use `ptr` and complete the following program to read and display the data of one student.

```
struct Student
{
        char *name;
        int code;
        float grd;
};

int main()
{
        Student *ptr;
        ...
}
```

Then, the program should read a number of students (use extra variables) and use `ptr` to allocate memory and store the data of those students whose name begin with an 'A'. The program should display their data before it ends. Assume that the names are less than 100 characters.

U.14.6 Write a program that reads ten `double` numbers and stores them in a dynamically allocated memory. Then, the program should allocate extra memory of the same size and prompt the user to enter a number, as follows:

    a. If it is 0, the program should store the numbers in that new memory in reverse order.
    b. If it is 1, the program should store first the negatives and then the positives.

Use pointer arithmetic to handle the memory regions. For example, assume that the first memory region contains the numbers:

    -3.2 4 3 -9.1 7 6 -2 15 9 -37. If the user enters 0, the numbers should be stored in the second memory in reverse order: -37 9 15 -2 ... If the user enters 1, it should be stored in that order: -3.2 -9.1 -2 -37 4 3 ...

U.14.7 Use `ptr` and complete the following program to read and display the data of one book. Don't use any other variable. Assume that the length of the input strings is less than 100 characters.

```
struct Book
{
        char *title;
        char *authors;
        int *code;
        double *prc;
};

int main()
{
        Book *ptr;
        ...
}
```

U.14.8 An array in which a large number of elements has zero values is called sparse. An efficient way to store its elements is to put the non-zero elements and its positions in groups of three, in a one-dimensional array. For example, the elements of the array A are stored into B, as follows:

$$A = \begin{bmatrix} 0 & 0 & 6 & 8 \\ 0 & 0 & 0 & -1 \\ -3 & 0 & 0 & 0 \end{bmatrix} \qquad B = \begin{bmatrix} 0 & 2 & 6 & 0 & 3 & 8 & 1 & 3 & -1 & 2 & 0 & -3 \end{bmatrix}$$

Because the element A[0, 2] is 6, the triplet 0 2 6 is stored in B. The rest triplets are generated in the same way. Write a program that reads integers and stores them in a 3×4 array A. Then, the program should allocate memory to create array B and store the triplets in it. The size of the allocated memory should be the exact needed. The program should display the elements of B, before it ends.

U.14.9 Write a program that reads integers continuously until the users enters -1. The program should display only the numbers entered for first time. Here is an example of program execution:

```
Enter number: -20
Output: -20
Enter number: 345
Output: 345
Enter number: -20
Enter number: 432
Output: 432
```

The number -20 does not appear twice.

U.14.10 Write a program that provides a menu to perform the following operations:

1. Intersection. The program reads the common size of two arrays (e.g., A and B) and allocates memory dynamically to store their elements. Then, it reads integers and stores into A those that are not already stored. Then, it does the same for the array B. The program should store the common elements of the two arrays into a third array and display them.
2. Union. The program should store the elements of both arrays A and B into a third array. Notice that a common element should be stored once.
3. Program termination.

U.14.11 Consider the linked list of C.14.10. Write a function that takes as a parameter the code of a student and, if it is stored in the list, the function should return how many nodes are left from this point up to the end of the list. If not, the function should return -1. Don't use the `tail` pointer.

U.14.12 Consider the linked list of C.14.10. Write a `void` function that returns a pointer to the node with the best grade in the list and a pointer to the node with the worst grade. Write a sample program to show how to test the function. *Hint*: Use pointer to pointer function parameters.

U.14.13 A double linked list is a list where each node, except the pointer to the next node, contains another pointer to the previous node. Write a program that generates 100 random integers and creates a double linked list with those integers. Use the following struct to represent the node:

```
struct Node
{
        int num;
        Node *next;
        Node *prev;
};
```

Write the following functions:

a. add_list(int num); it creates a new node with value equal to num.
b. dup_list(void); if all numbers in the list are different it returns nullptr, otherwise a pointer to the first node whose num value is the same with a previous one.
c. del_node(int num); it deletes the node with value equal to num.
d. show_list(void); it displays the num values of the nodes backwards, starting from the end of the list to the beginning.
e. free_list(void); it releases the allocated memory starting from the end of the list to the beginning.

The program should call all these functions in that order, to test their operation.

U.14.14 Write a program that reads the names and the score of some candidates in a contest and inserts them sorted in a linked list. The sorting should be performed when data are entered. The data should be stored in score descending order or in alphabetical order. The program should prompt the user to enter the sorting type (e.g., 1 for alphabetical). If the user enters end for name, the data insertion should terminate and the program should display the list data. Use the following structure to represent the node:

```
struct Node
{
        char name[100];
        int points;
        Node *next;
};
```

For example, if the user has selected sorting in alphabetical order and the list nodes are:

```
Arnesen        350
Santer         280
```

and the user enters the new data Melk and 450, the three list nodes should be in that order:

```
Arnesen        350
Melk           450
Santer         280
```

U.14.15 In the binary search tree program of C.14.9 example, add a recursive function that takes as parameters a pointer to the root and a key value. If the key is found in the tree, the function should return a pointer to that node, nullptr otherwise.

U.14.16 In the binary search tree program of C.14.9 example, add a non-recursive function that takes as parameter a pointer to the root and displays the smallest and the largest key value of the tree.

U.14.17 In the binary search tree program of C.14.9 example, implement add_node() without using recursion. The function should return a pointer to the root.

U.14.18 In the binary search tree program of C.14.9 example, implement show_inorder() without using recursion. Read the hint in that section.

Preprocessor and Macros

15

The preprocessor is a software program, typically integrated into the compiler, which processes a C++ program before it is compiled. Its major capabilities involve file inclusion, macro substitution and conditional compilation. At first, we'll discuss how to define and use macros in a C++ program. Because you may meet macros in code, it is useful to know about their potential hazards and misuses. We'll learn safer alternatives in the next chapter. We'll devote the rest of this chapter to describe preprocessor directives and operators.

SIMPLE MACROS

The behaviour of the preprocessor is controlled by directives. The directives are special commands that begin with the # character and instruct the preprocessor to do something. For example, the `#include` directive instructs the preprocessor to open a specified file and include its contents into the file at the point of the directive. Directives can appear anywhere in the program. A line that contains a single # is legal; it has no effect, though.

We have also discussed the `#define` directive in Chapter 2, which we can use to define a simple macro, that is, a symbolic name associated with a constant value. To define a simple macro we write:

```
#define   macro_name   replacement_characters
```

The `macro_name` must conform to the same naming rules as a variable name. The `replacement_characters` can be any sequence of characters. The macro names are typically in capital letters, in order to distinguish them from program variables. The scope of the name begins from the point of its definition until the end of the file. For example, in the following program:

```
#include <iostream> // Example 15.1

#define LEN 200

int main()
{
      int i, arr[LEN];
      for(i = 0; i < LEN; i++)
            arr[i] = i+LEN;
      return 0;
}
```

the preprocessor replaces each occurrence of LEN with its defined value, that is, 200. A common error is to add a = in the definition. For example, if we write:

```
#define LEN = 200
```

the definition of `arr` expands to `arr[= 200]` and the compilation fails. Another common error is to add a semicolon at the end. For example:

```
#define LEN 200;
```

the definition expands to `arr[200;]` and the compilation fails.

Of course, do not forget, as we discussed in Chapter 2, that when we want to set a constant for a value that is used many times in the program, it is recommended to declare it `const`. In this section, I focus on syntax issues, in case you use `#define` instead or you meet it in existing code.

 If a macro contains operators, enclose it in parentheses.

For example, see what happens if we omit the parentheses:

```
#define NUM 2*5 // Instead of (2*5).
```

a statement like this:

```
#double j = 3.0/NUM;
```

is expanded to: `j = 3.0/2*5 = 7.5;` which assigns the value `7.5` to `j`, not `0.3`, because the division is performed first.

A macro can be defined anywhere in a program, for example, inside a function. The usual practice is to define all macros with global scope at the top of the program, or in a header file, and use the `#include` directive to include it when needed. For example, suppose that we've created the `test.h` file with content:

```
#include <iostream>
#define LEN 200
```

could we write the previous program as follows?

```
#include "test.h"
int main()
{
        ...
}
```

Sure, no problem. It is not mandatory to include explicitly `iostream`. We can include another file, as we did here with `test.h`, and inside there to include `iostream`.

If the name of a macro is part of the name of a variable or contained in a string literal it is not replaced. For example:

```
#include <iostream> // Example 15.2

#define LEN 200

int main()
{
        int BUF_LEN; // No replacement takes place.
        std::cout << "LEN is not used\n"; // No replacement takes place.
        return 0;
}
```

Although simple macros are primarily used to define names for numbers, it can be used for other purposes as well. For example, in the following program:

```cpp
#include <iostream> // Example 15.3

#define test std::cout << "example\n"

int main()
{
        test;
        return 0;
}
```

the preprocessor replaces the test macro and the program displays example.

Notice that it is legal to define a macro with no replacement value. As we'll see later, this kind of macros is typically used for controlling conditional compilation. For example:

```cpp
#define LABEL
```

The name of a macro can be used in the definition of another macro. For example:

```cpp
#define SIZE 200
#define NUM  SIZE
```

Remember that first the preprocessor replaces the macro names with the corresponding values and then the program is compiled.

If you need to extend a macro in several lines (e.g., for better readability), add the backslash character (\) at the end of each line. For example, the following program displays 60:

```cpp
#include <iostream> // Example 15.4

#define NUM \
    10 + \
    20 + \
    30

int main()
{
        std::cout << NUM;
        return 0;
}
```

Notice also that several compilers allow defining a macro name, when the program is compiled. For example:

```cpp
#g++  -DVERSION=3  test.cpp
```

The option -D defines the VERSION macro with value 3. If no value is specified, the default is 1. This ability is very useful, because it is not needed to modify a file to define or change a value.

C++ provides several predefined preprocessing macros. The following table presents some of them. Their names are enclosed in double underscores. Their main purpose is to provide special information about the current compilation.

NAME	DESCRIPTION
__DATE__	It is replaced with the compilation date.
__FILE__	It is replaced with the name of the compiled file.
__LINE__	It is replaced with the line number of the compiled file.
__TIME__	It is replaced with the time of the compilation.
__func__	It is replaced with some text which is defined by the implementation and contains the name of the function.

For example, consider the following program:

```
#include <iostream>  // Example 15.5
int main()
{
        std::cout << "Line " << __LINE__ << " of file " << __FILE__ << " in
function " << __func__ << " is compiled on " << __DATE__ << " at " <<
__TIME__ << '\n';
        return 0;
}
```

When I run the program, the output was:

```
Line 4 of file c:\edu\projects\test.cpp in function main is compiled on Feb 5
2019 at 17:32:52
```

This output is shown each time the program runs. If we recompile and run the program the new compile date and time will be displayed. In case of various versions of the same program, this information might be useful to distinguish the running version. Furthermore, we can use the __LINE__ and __FILE__ macros to locate errors. For example:

```
if(error)
        cout << "Error in line " << __LINE__ << " of file " << __FILE__ << '\n';
```

THE assert() MACRO

For diagnostic purposes, C++ provides the assert() macro. It is declared in the cassert file, as follows:

```
void assert(exp);
```

If exp is true, nothing is displayed. Otherwise, assert() outputs an error message to cerr and calls the std::abort() function. This function terminates the program immediately. The produced message depends on the implementation, but it contains at least the file name and the line number of assert(). For example:

```
assert(a != 0); // Before division, the value of denominator is checked.
c = b/a;
```

assert(), if conditions and directives that we'll see later (e.g., #ifdef) can be used for the same reason, that is, to detect potential bugs during the development phase. Once the program is tested, those checks should be removed, in order not to increase the execution time, particularly in time-critical applications. `if` conditions is the less flexible way, because once removed and the program fails again, it'd take some time to write them again. Using directives (e.g., `#ifdef`) things are much simpler, we just define or not a macro. The same easy is with `assert()`. To disable `assert()` we just define the macro `NDEBUG` before including the `cassert`. If we need to reactivate `assert()` we remove the definition of `NDEBUG`. For example:

```
#define NDEBUG // assert() is ignored.
#include <cassert>
```

One more thing, don't call functions inside `assert()` that are necessary for the correct operation of your program or might create side-effects. For example:

```
assert((len = strlen(str)) > 10);
/* Use of len. */
```

If `NDEBUG` is defined, `assert()` will be ignored, `strlen()` won't be called and `len` won't be updated. The expression `exp` of the `assert()` is checked dynamically, at runtime.

C++11 provides the ability of static assertion with the `static_assert(exp, msg)` statement. Now, the condition is checked statically, at compile time. In particular, `exp` must produce a result at compile time that can be converted to `bool`. For example, `static_assert()` cannot check the `size()` of a vector object. If `exp` evaluates to false, the compilation fails and the message `msg` appears on the screen. If it is true, the assertion does nothing. For example:

```
#int main()
{
        ...
        static_assert(sizeof(int) == 4, "Other size\n");
        ...
}
```

If the size of the `int` type is not 4 bytes, the compilation fails and the corresponding message is displayed on the screen. Since C++17, the `msg` argument is optional. For example: `static_assert(sizeof(int) == 4);` in that case the displayed diagnostic message is platform dependent. One important use of `static_assert` is in generic programming to make assertions about types used as parameters.

Before continue, can you find the errors in the following program?

```
#include <iostream> // Example 15.6

#define LEN20
#define test std::cout << "example\n";

int main()
{
        int arr[LEN] = {10};
        if(arr[0] == 10)
                test;
        else
                std::cout << "Not 10\n";
        return 0;
}
```

Because there is no space between `LEN` and `20`, the compiler will produce an error message for the undeclared variable `LEN`. The second compilation error is due to the `;` at the end of `test`. When `test` is replaced, the second `;` does not let `else` to be associated with the `if` statement.

MACROS WITH PARAMETERS

Besides its simple form, a macro can take parameters and behave like a function. For example, in the following program:

```cpp
#include <iostream> // Example 15.7

#define MIN(a, b) ((a) < (b) ?  (a) : (b))

int main()
{
        int i, j, min;

        std::cout << "Enter numbers: ";
        std::cin >> i >> j;
        min = MIN(i, j);
        std::cout << min << '\n';
        return 0;
}
```

the MIN macro takes two parameters. Once it is met, the preprocessor replaces a with i, b with j, and expands this line to: min = ((i) < (j) ? (i) : (j));

Because a macro can take parameters of any data type, it can be more generic than a function. For example, we could use the same MIN macro to find the minimum of int, char, double, ... and other data types. Also, using a parameterized macro, instead of a function that does the same job, may improve performance, because a function call imposes some runtime overhead due to the storage of context information (e.g., the memory address of the function) and copy of the arguments. On the other hand, a macro invocation does not impose any delay because the preprocessor has expanded it and added its code in the program at compile time. However, the general rule is not to use such macros, because, as you'll see below, their use has many disadvantages and carries risks.

 Don't leave a whitespace after the name of a parameterized macro because the preprocessor will handle the left parenthesis as the beginning of a simple macro definition.

For example, if we write:

```cpp
#define MIN (a, b) ((a) < (b) ? (a) : (b))
```

the compilation will fail because the preprocessor starts the replacement of MIN from the first left parenthesis.

 Because of operators' precedence, always enclose each macro parameter and the macro definition in parentheses.

For example, suppose that we omit the parentheses in the macro definition:

```cpp
#define MIN(a, b) (a) < (b) ? (a) : (b)
```

What would be the output of i in the statement: i = 3*MIN(4, 10);

When the macro is expanded, because multiplication is performed first, the compared values would be 12 and 10, not 4 and 10. As a result, i becomes 10.

See now what happens if we omit the parentheses around the parameters:

```
#define MUL(a, b) (a*b) // Instead of ((a)*(b))
```

a statement like:

```
#int j = MUL(9+1, 8+2); is expanded to: int j = 9+1*8+2 = 19;
```

and j becomes 19, not 100, because the multiplication is performed first.

 Don't use macro arguments with side effects.

For example, the statement: int x = MIN(i++, j); is expanded to:

```
#int x = ((i++) < (j) ? (i++) : (j));
```

As a result, if i is less than j, i will be incremented twice and a wrong value will be assigned to x.

In addition to syntax issues and potential pitfalls, using a macro instead of a function has significant disadvantages. For example, because macros rely on text substitution, you can get into serious trouble when the macro contains complex code, like control-flow constructs. Needless to say, that is much harder to read, maintain, and debug a macro, which contains multiple statements. A macro cannot be overloaded, nor can it be recursive. Because macros are removed during preprocessing, it is not possible to declare a pointer to a macro. Also, when a function is called, the compiler checks the types of the arguments. If an argument has a wrong type and the compiler cannot convert it to the proper type, it produces an error message. On the other hand, the preprocessor does not check the types of the macro arguments, so undesirable values may be passed.

C++ provides better and more secure mechanisms that we can use in place of such macros, such as the inline and the function templates that we'll see in Chapter 16. For example:

```
#template <typename T> inline const T& min(const T& a, const T& b)
{
        return (a < b) ? a : b;
}
```

This definition not only provides the flexibility of the respective macro, but also security by checking the passed arguments when the function is called.

THE # AND ## PREPROCESSOR OPERATORS

The # operator in front of a macro argument instructs the preprocessor to create a string literal having the name of that argument. For example:

```
#include <iostream> // Example 15.8

#define f(s) std::cout << #s << " = " << s << '\n';

int main()
{
        const char *str = "text";
        f(str);
        return 0;
}
```

When the preprocessor expands the f macro, it replaces #s with the name of the argument, that is, str. Therefore, the program displays: str = text

The ## operator is used to merge identifiers together. It is not allowed to appear in the beginning or at the end of the sequence. If the identifier is a macro parameter, the preprocessor first replaces it with the value of the argument and then pasting occurs. For example:

```cpp
#include <iostream> // Example 15.9

#define f(a) s##u##m##a

int sum1(int a, int b);

int main()
{
        int i, j;

        std::cout << "Enter numbers: ";
        std::cin >> i >> j;
        std::cout << f(1)(i, j) << '\n';
        return 0;
}

int sum1(int a, int b)
{
        return a+b;
}
```

When the preprocessor expands the f macro, because the character a has the same name with the argument, the preprocessor replaces a with the value of the argument, that is, 1, and then merges that value with the s, u, and m characters. Therefore, f(1)(i, j) is expanded to sum1(i, j) and the program uses sum1() to display the sum of the two input numbers.

PREPROCESSOR DIRECTIVES AND CONDITIONAL COMPILATION

This section discusses the preprocessor directives that allow the conditional compilation of a part of the program. The conditional compilation can be very useful in many situations, for example, when debugging the program, to monitor the program execution or to maintain multiple versions of the same program.

The #if, #else, #elif, and #endif Directives

The #if and #endif directives are used to define which parts of a program will be compiled, depending on the value of an expression. The general syntax is:

```cpp
#if expression
        ... /* block of statements. */
#endif
```

The expression is a constant integer expression which is not allowed to include sizeof, casts, or enum constants. If its value is true, the preprocessor keeps the block of statements to be compiled.

If not, the block is removed and the compiler won't see it. Notice that if the expression is an undefined identifier, the #if directive evaluates to false. For example:

```
#if NUM
```

If NUM is not defined, the outcome is false, while the value of #if !NUM is true. If NUM is defined with value 0, #if NUM evaluates to false and #if !NUM to true.

The #else directive is used in conjunction with the #if directive to define a block of statements that will be compiled if the value of the expression is false.

```
#if expression
        ... /* block of statements A */
#else
        ... /* block of statements B */
#endif
```

For example, in the following program, the #else part will be compiled because NUM is greater than 0:

```
#include <iostream> // Example 15.10

#define NUM 10

int main()
{
        #if NUM < 0
                std::cout << "Seg_1\n";
        #else
                std::cout << "Seg_2\n";
        #endif
        return 0;
}
```

Therefore, the program displays Seg_2. Notice that if the definition of NUM was missing, the program would display Seg_2, too.

Since nested comments are not allowed, it is not possible to put in comments a part of the program that contains comments. To do that, we can use the #if directive. For example:

```
#if 0
        /* Comment. */
        ...            /* Code. */
        /* Another comment. */
#endif
```

The #elif directive can be used together with #if, #ifdef, and #ifndef directives to define multiple compilation paths. For example:

```
#if expression_A
        ... /* block of statements A */
#elif expression_B
        ... /* block of statements B */
.
.
#else
        ... /* block of statements N */
#endif
```

The second block of statements will be compiled only if the value of `expression_A` is false and the value of `expression_B` is true. Once a `#if` or `#elif` expression is found true, next `#elif` and `#else` directives are discarded. The last `#else` is optional and its block of statements will be compiled only if the previous expressions are all false. In practice, this syntax is often used to support multiple versions of the same program. For example:

```cpp
#include <iostream> // Example 15.11

#define VER_2 1

int main()
{
        int cnt = 0;

        #if VER_1
                cnt = 1;
                std::cout << "Version_1\n";
        #elif VER_2
                cnt = 2;
                std::cout << "Version_2\n";
        #else
                cnt = 3;
                std::cout << "Version_3\n";
        #endif

        std::cout << cnt << '\n';
        return 0;
}
```

Since `VER_1` is not defined and the value of `VER_2` is true, the preprocessor keeps those lines and discards the rest, `cnt` becomes 2 and the program displays: `Version_2` and 2. If we change the value of `VER_2` to 0, the `#elif` expression becomes false and the preprocessor keeps the lines of the `#else` directive. Therefore, the program displays: `Version_3` and 3. If the `#else` directive was missing, the program would display 0.

The #ifdef, #ifndef, and #undef Directives

The `#ifdef` directive is used to check if an identifier is defined as a macro. The general syntax is:

```cpp
#ifdef name
        ... /* block of statements */
#endif
```

The difference with the `#if` directive is that the `#ifdef` directive only checks if the identifier is defined as a macro; it does not evaluate its value. For example:

```cpp
#include <iostream> // Example 15.12

#define VER_1 0

int main()
{
        #ifdef VER_1
                std::cout << "Version_1\n";
```

```
        #else
                std::cout << "Version_2\n";
        #endif
        return 0;
}
```

Since `VER_1` is defined, the program displays `Version_1`.

The `#ifndef` directive is used to check whether an identifier is not defined as a macro. A typical use of the `#ifndef` directive is to prevent multiple inclusions of the same file. Naturally, a large program consists of several source and header files; it is very probable that the same header file is included more than once in a source file. For example, suppose that the `test.cpp` file includes the following files:

```
#// test.cpp
#include "test.h"
#include "one.h"
#include "two.h" // Suppose, that it includes the test.h file.
```

The traditional solution to avoid multiple inclusion of the same file (e.g., `test.h`) is to add the following lines at its beginning:

```
#ifndef SOME_TAG // Use a name not defined somewhere else.
#define SOME_TAG
/* Contents of test.h */
#endif
```

When the first directive that includes `test.h` is met, the preprocessor will include the contents of the `test.h` because the `SOME_TAG` macro is not defined yet. When the preprocessor encounters another directive to include `test.h` (e.g., from `two.h`) it will not include again its content, because `SOME_TAG` has been defined and `#ifndef` evaluates to false. Although you can use any name (e.g., `SOME_TAG`), the common practice is to select a name similar to the name of the header file and with some more characters to avoid a name conflict (e.g., `test_file_h`).

We can use `#ifndef`, not only to avoid multiple inclusions and save some compile time, but also for another reason. If `test.h` contains a type definition (e.g., structure), the compilation will fail because redefinition of the same type is not allowed. For example, suppose that the `test.h` contains the following type:

```
#struct st
{
        ...
};
```

and the `two.h` includes the `test.h`. If `#ifndef` is missing, when `test.cpp` is compiled the definition of `st` will be included twice which causes a compilation error. In fact, this is a violation of the *one definition rule* (*ODR*), which prohibits an entity to be defined more than once in the same compilation unit. This combination of `#ifndef` - `#define` - `#endif` directives is called a `#include` guard. In general, a header file should use this guard to avoid the potential for violation of the ODR.

Furthermore, the use of `#ifndef` prevents endless inclusions. For example, this might happen if one file (e.g., `one.h`) includes a second one (e.g., `sec.h`) and that second one includes the first.

The `#undef` directive cancels the definition of a macro. If the macro has not been defined, `#undef` has no effect. For example:

```
#include <iostream> // Example 15.13

#define NUM 100

int main()
{
        int arr[NUM];
#undef NUM

        std::cout << "Array contains" << NUM << " elements\n";
        return 0;
}
```

Since the directive `#undef NUM` cancels the definition of `NUM`, the compiler will produce an error message in `cout`.

The defined Operator

An alternative way to check if an identifier is defined as a macro is to use the `defined` operator. The `defined` operator is used together with the `#if` or `#elif` directives. If the identifier has been defined, the result is true, false otherwise. For example:

```
#if defined(VER_1) // Equivalent to #ifdef VER_1
...
#endif
```

The parentheses are not necessary; it is a matter of preference. Similarly, the expression: `#if! defined(VER_1)` is equivalent to `#ifndef VER_1`. The advantage over the `#ifdef` and `#ifndef` is that these can be used to check if only one macro is defined or not, while the `defined` operator and the `#if` directive can be used to check multiple macros. See how we are using the `&&` operator to check multiple conditions:

```
#if defined(VER_1) && !defined(VER_2) && defined(VER_3)
...
#endif
```

or use the `||` operator to check if a macro is defined:

```
#if defined(VER_1) || defined(VER_2)
...
#endif
```

As we did in example C.15.11, we can alternatively use the `defined` operator. Suppose that we are writing a program which depends on some external factor, for example, the operating system or the compiler. Instead of writing different versions, we could use conditional compilation. For example:

```
#if defined(UNIX)
...
#elif defined(LINUX)
...
#elif defined(WINDOWS)
...
#endif
```

THE #pragma DIRECTIVE

Most compilers provide the #pragma directive. The #pragma directive is used to request special behaviour from the compiler. The set of commands that can appear in the #pragma directive is different for each compiler. If the command is not supported, the compiler ignores the directive. For example, if a compiler supports the warning command, the directive #pragma warning(disable: 4018) may be used to disable the appearance of the warning message with code 4018.

In another example, if the compiler supports the #pragma once directive we can add it at the beginning of a header file and prevent duplication of its content. However, because #pragma is not standard C++, it'd be better to use the #ifndef directive we saw earlier to prevent multiple inclusion.

EXERCISES

C.15.1 Write a macro that calculates the absolute value of a number. Write a program that reads an integer and uses the macro to display its absolute value.

```
#include <iostream>

#define abs(a) ((a) >= 0 ?  (a) : -(a))

int main()
{
        int i;

        std::cout << "Enter number: ";
        std::cin >> i;
        std::cout << abs(i) << '\n';
        return 0;
}
```

C.15.2 Write a macro that checks whether a number is odd or even. Write a program that reads an integer and uses the macro to display whether it is odd or even.

```
#include <iostream>

#define odd_even(a) (((a) & 1) == 0)

int main()
{
        int i;

        std::cout << "Enter number: ";
        std::cin >> i;
        if(odd_even(i))
                std::cout << "Even\n";
        else
                std::cout << "Odd\n";
        return 0;
}
```

C.15.3 Suppose that the content of test.h is:

```
#include <iostream>

#define TEST

#ifdef TEST
#define f() std::cout << "One ";
#undef TEST
#endif
```

What is the output of the following program?

```
#include "test.h"
int main()
{
        f();
#ifdef TEST
        f();
#endif
        f();
        return 0;
}
```

Answer: The preprocessor replaces the first occurrence of f() with cout and then cancels the definition of TEST. Since TEST is not defined, the preprocessor does not expand the second f() and continues with the third one. Therefore, the program displays: One One

C.15.4 Write a program that reads double numbers continuously and counts either the positives or the negatives depending on the definition of a macro. For example, if the CNT_POS macro is defined, the program should count the positives, otherwise the negatives. If the user enters 0, the insertion of numbers should terminate.

```
#include <iostream>

#define CNT_POS

int main()
{
        int cnt = 0;
        double num = 1;

        while(num != 0)
        {
                std::cout << "Enter number: ";
                std::cin >> num;
                #ifdef CNT_POS
                        if(num > 0)
                                cnt++;
                #else
                        if(num < 0)
                                cnt++;
                #endif
        }
        std::cout << cnt << '\n';
        return 0;
}
```

C.15.5 Write a program that displays One if both VER_1 and VER_2 macros are not defined. Otherwise, if either VER_3 or VER_4 macro is defined, the program should display Two. If nothing from the above happens, it should display Three.

```cpp
#include <iostream>
int main()
{
#if !defined(VER_1) && !defined(VER_2)
        std::cout << "One\n";
#elif defined(VER_3) || defined(VER_4)
        std::cout << "Two\n";
#else
        std::cout << "Three\n";
#endif
        return 0;
}
```

C.15.6 What is the output of the following program?

```cpp
#include <iostream>
#include <cstring>

#define f(text) std::cout << text; if(strlen(text) < 5) return 0;

int main()
{
        f("One");
        f("Two");
        f("Three");
        return 0;
}
```

Answer: The preprocessor expands the first f() to the following lines:

```cpp
std::cout << "One";
if(strlen("One") < 5)
        return 0;
```

When the program runs, the return statement terminates the program because the length of One is 3, less than 5. Therefore, the program displays One.

C.15.7 Write a macro that calculates the greatest of three numbers. Write a program that reads three double numbers and uses the macro to display the greatest.

```cpp
#include <iostream>

#define max(a, b, c) ((a) >= (b) && (a) >= (c) ?  (a) : \
(b) > (a) && (b) > (c) ?  (b) : (c))

int main()
{
        double i, j, k;

        std::cout << "Enter numbers: ";
        std::cin >> i >> j >> k;
        std::cout << max(i, j, k) << '\n';
        return 0;
}
```

C.15.8 What is the output of the following program?

```
#include <iostream>

#define hide(t, r, a, p, i, n) p##a##r##t(i, n)

double show(int a, int b);

int main()
{
        std::cout << (int)hide(w, o, h, s, 1, 2) << '\n';
        return 0;
}

double show(int a, int b)
{
        return (a+b)/2.0;
}
```

Answer: The preprocessor replaces one by one the arguments of the hide() macro. Therefore, the preprocessor substitutes t with w, r with o, and so on. Since the p, a, r, t are replaced by the s, h, o, w and the ## operator merges the operands together, the macro is expanded to show(i, n). Therefore, the program calls show() with arguments 1 and 2, which returns their average, that is, 1.5. Since the return value casts to int, the program displays 1.

C.15.9 Write a macro that calculates the greater of two numbers. Write a program that reads four integers and uses the macro to display the greatest.

```
#include <iostream>

#define max(a, b) ((a) > (b) ?  (a) : (b))

int main()
{
        int i, j, k, l;

        std::cout << "Enter numbers: ";
        std::cin >> i >> j >> k >> l;
        std::cout << max(max(max(i, j), k), l) << '\n';
        return 0;
}
```

Comments: The preprocessor expands the macros from the inner to the outer. Notice, that there are other alternatives, for example, we could write: max(max(i, j), max(k, l));.

C.15.10 What is the output of the following program?

```
#include <iostream>

#define no_main(type, name, text, num) type name() {std::cout << text;
return num;}

no_main(int, main, "No main()", 0)
```

Answer: Leave the best for the end. "Silver alert", `main()` is lost. The program works, though. The preprocessor replaces `type` with `int`, `name` with `main`, `text` with `"No main()"`, and `num` with `0`. Therefore, the preprocessor expands `no_main()` to:

```
int main() {std::cout << "No main()"; return 0;}
```

and the program displays: `No main()`

Notice that if we were using `void` instead of `int` the compilation would fail, because a `void` function cannot return a value.

UNSOLVED EXERCISES

U.15.1 Write a macro that checks whether a number is between two other numbers. Write a program that reads three numbers (e.g., x, a, b) and uses the macro to check if x is within [a, b].

U.15.2 The following macro calculates the absolute value. Find the error(s) in its definition, by giving examples to prove it. Fix the definition.

```
#define abs (a) a > 0 ? a : -a
```

U.15.3 The following macro calculates the minimum of two numbers. It is not correct, though. Pass an expression with the & operator as an argument, to prove the error. Fix the definition.

```
#define MIN(a, b) (a < b ? a : b)
```

U.15.4 Write a macro that takes two arguments and calculates their average. Write a program that reads four integers and uses the macro to display their average.

U.15.5 Write a macro that takes as an argument one character and if it is a lowercase letter it expands to the respective uppercase letter. Write a program that reads a string of less than 100 characters and uses the macro to display its lowercase letters in uppercase.

U.15.6 Write a macro that takes as an argument one character and if it is digit, the macro should evaluate to true, false otherwise. Write a program that reads a string and uses the macro to display how many digits it contains.

U.15.7 What would be the output of the following program when the macro `ONE`:

a. is defined?
b. it is not defined?

Explain why.

```
#include <iostream>

#define ONE 1
#define print(a) std::cout << "x" << #a << "=" << x##a << '\n'

int main()
{
#ifdef ONE
#define TWO ONE+ONE
#else
```

```
#define ONE 2
#define TWO (ONE+ONE)
#endif

        int x1 = 3*(ONE+ONE), x2 = 3*TWO;

        print(1);
        print(2);
        return 0;
}
```

U.15.8 Write a program that reads a string and, based on the definition of a macro, it should display either the number of its lowercase letters or the number of its uppercase letters or the number of its digits. For example, if the macro UL is defined, the program should display the number of the uppercase letters.

U.15.9 Complete the macro SET_BIT to set the bit in position pos, the macro CLEAR_BIT to clear the bit in position pos and the macro CHECK_BIT to display the value of the bit in position pos. Write a program that reads an integer and a bit position and tests the operation of these three macros.

```
#define SET_BIT(a, pos)
#define CLEAR_BIT(a, pos)
#define CHECK_BIT(a, pos)
```

More about Functions

16

In Chapter 11, we learned the basic properties of functions. In this chapter we'll explore some more features, such as default arguments, reference variables, and how to pass function arguments by reference, inline functions, function overloading, and function templates.

DEFAULT ARGUMENTS

A default argument is a value that will be used if the corresponding argument is missing in the function call. For example:

```cpp
#include <iostream> // Example 16.1

int g = 20;
void test(int a, int b = 10, int *p = &g);

int main()
{
        int i = 25;

        test(5);
        test(5, 15);
        test(5, 15, &i);
        return 0;
}

void test(int a, int b, int *p)
{
        std::cout << a+b+(*p) << '\n';
}
```

In the first call of `test()` because no values are passed for the second and third arguments, the default values are used. That is, `b` is initialized with `10` and `p` points to the address of `g`. So, `test()` displays `35`. The second call uses a default value only for the third argument and `test()` displays `40`. In the third call no default value is used and `test()` displays `45`. As you see the default values are used only if the corresponding arguments in the function call are missing. As you know it is not necessary to choose names for the parameters. For example:

```cpp
void test(int, int = 10, int * = &g);
```

Since the `*=` is an operator the space between them is necessary, otherwise the compiler will display an error message.

Usually, the default values are used when the function is mostly called with the same values. The values are specified in the prototype so that the compiler is informed before encountering the function call. The function definition is the same as if there were no default values. So, only the prototype indicates the default values. Notice that if a parameter is declared with a default value, all next parameters to the right must also be declared with default values. For example, the following declarations are not allowed:

```
void test(int a, int b = 10, int *p);  // Wrong.
void test(int a = 20, int b, int *p = &g);  // Wrong.
```

Also, all parameters in a function are allowed to have default values. For example, if we change `test()` to:

```
void test(int a = 30, int b = 10, int *p = &g);
```

and write `test();` the program displays 60.

INLINE FUNCTIONS

Inline function is a feature that C++ provides to improve performance. As we said in Chapter 14, when a function is called, the compiler stores the memory address of the next statement following the function call, it reserves memory from the stack, if needed, to copy the arguments, program control is transferred to the memory address where the code of the function is located, the function is executed, and, when completed, program control returns to the address stored when the function was called. These operations induce a time delay each time the function is called. For example, in the following code, the program control is transferred twice to the function and returns twice from it:

```
void test();

int main()
{
        . . .
        test();
        . . .
        test();
        . . .
        return 0;
}

void test()
{
        for(int i = 0; i < 10; i++)
                cout << "In\n";
}
```

However, if the function is declared as inline we can avoid this time delay and improve the program performance. In particular, what the compiler does is to replace each function call in the program with its code. To make the function inline the keyword `inline` must be used. The common practice is to omit the prototype and put the function definition in the place where the prototype would be inserted. For example, let's declare `test()` as inline and see what the compiler does when it encounters its call:

```
inline void test()
{
        for(int i = 0; i < 10; i++)
                cout << "In\n";
}
```

```
int main()
{
        ...
        {
                for(int i = 0; i < 10; i++)
                        cout << "In\n";
        }
        ...
        {
                for(int i = 0; i < 10; i++)
                        cout << "In\n";
        }
        ...
        return 0;
}
```

As shown, the compiler replaces each test() call with its code and make it "in line" with the rest code. Thus, since the function is not called, the performance of the program is improved. On the other hand, since the code of an inline function is added wherever it is called, the size of the executable program may significantly increase if the function is called many times. This can be a problem in systems with limited memory, such as an embedded system.

As discussed in Chapter 15, macros serve a similar purpose. However, remember their weaknesses and the problems that may occur due to their syntax. Inline functions is a much better alternative; they are more secure as they provide type control and are as simple to declare and use them as an ordinary function.

As for when to declare a function as inline, if the execution time of the function is long compared to the time delay added by the function call mechanism, then the inline declaration will not bring significant improvement. If the execution time is short and the function is called frequently, then the inline declaration may improve the performance. However, the size of the executable file will increase. In general, when making a function inline does not mean that the performance of the program will certainly improve; it may or may not as it depends on the application. Usually, you should consider making inline short functions that are frequently called.

Notice that if you declare a function as inline it does not mean that the compiler will certainly satisfy your request and make the function inline. The inline specifier is just a suggestion to the compiler. That is, the compiler may ignore it and handle the function like an ordinary function. For example, if the compiler considers that its code is too large or complex enough, it may ignore the inline suggestion and use the conventional way to call the function. And yes, a smart compiler may find it more efficient and make a function inline by itself, even if you haven't declared it.

If a function declared as inline is used in many source files, its definition must be available in each source file. All these definitions have to be identical, though. For this reason, the typical approach is to put the definition in a header file, and include that file in each source file that uses the function.

THE ONE DEFINITION RULE

The One Definition Rule (ODR) poses the restriction that variables and functions must be defined only once in the entire program. For example, we saw in Chapter 11 when discussing about extern declarations that if we define a variable in one source file it is an error to define it in another file. The compilation will fail due to the multiple definition of the variable. If we want to use it in the second file, we declare it as extern. The exception to the ODR is the inline functions and inline variables. As we said, the definition of an inline function must appear in every source file that uses it. The inline variables are introduced with C++17. Let's see how it can be used. Suppose that you want to define a variable within a header file:

```
// first.h
int g;
```

If we've multiple source files that include this header file, the compilation will fail due to the multiple definition of the variable. However, if we declare it as inline, then there is no problem. All the definitions refer to the same unique variable. That is, we write: `inline int g;`

Then, the variable can be used in any source file that includes that header file. The semantics of an inline variable are the same as for an inline function. That is, an inline variable can be defined in multiple source files, provided that all definitions are identical, and, second, it must be defined in every source file in which it is used. As in case of inline functions, both are given by including the inline variable in a header file and include that file whenever required. As you already know, to use the same variable in different files we could alternatively use an `extern` declaration.

REFERENCE VARIABLES

A reference variable is an alias for an existing variable. As we know, C++ uses the & operator to get the address of a variable. C++ adds a new property to the & operator to declare reference variables. The compiler checks the context to figure out how it is used. Specifically, to declare a reference variable we add the & before its name and initialize it with an existing variable. For example:

```
int i = 10;
int& r = i;
r = 20; // Equivalent to i = 20.
i = 30; // Equivalent to r = 30.
```

In the declaration of the reference variable r, & is not used as the address operator, but for the declaration of the type. That is, the type of r is `int&`, which means reference to an integer. Essentially, the variable r is an alias, a second name for i; r will always refer to the value and the memory location of i. It is permanently associated with i, that is, it is not allowed to refer to another variable. The common practice is to add the & next to the type (e.g., instead of `int &r = i`), to make it clearer that the two variables have the same value, but also to avoid confusion with the address extraction.

I write it again, especially for those who are coming from C and this syntax may confuse them since they are used to use the & operator to get the memory address (yes, I was confused when I first saw it), a reference is not a pointer to a variable, it is not a copy of the variable, it is the variable itself with another name. That is, when you see a reference to a program, replace it in your head with the name it refers to. Therefore, i will be first 20 and then r becomes 30. A reference variable must be initialized when declared, not after. For example:

```
int& r1; // Wrong.
extern int& r2; // Correct, it has been initialized in another point.
```

As we said in Chapter 4, an *lvalue* is "something" that can be to the left of an assignment. This "something" must refer to an entity for which memory is reserved and it is addressable, such as a variable. So, when we initialize an lvalue reference, the initial value must be an lvalue. We use the lvalue term to describe this type of reference in order to distinguish it from the rvalue reference that you'll see later on. All the references that we'll work with until we meet the rvalue references in this chapter are lvalue references. For a generic type T and a reference T&, the initial value must be an lvalue of type T. For example:

```
int i;
int& r1 = i; // Correct, i is lvalue.
double& r2 = i; // Wrong, it is not the same type.
int& r3 = 10; // Wrong, 10 is not lvalue.
```

For r3, if we make the reference const, that is, write const int& r3 = 10; there will be no problem, because the initial value does not have to be lvalue. Let's see the next program. What does it display?

```
#include <iostream> // Example 16.2
int main()
{
        int i = 10, j = 20;
        int& r = i;

        r = j;
        if(&r == &j)
                std::cout << "Yes\n";
        else
                std::cout << "No\n";
        if(&i == &r)
                std::cout << "Yes\n";
        else
                std::cout << "No\n";
        std::cout << i+r << '\n';
        return 0;
}
```

The statement r = j; does not make r refer to j, it just changes the value of r. Since r refers to i, the statement is equivalent to i = j;. So, the values of i and r become 20. Note that in the if statements the & is used as the address operator. Are the addresses of r and j the same? Of course not, the address of r is the same of i. So, the program displays No, Yes, and 40. Note that if we want to have a pointer to the referred variable, through the reference, we use the & address operator, as we know. For example:

```
int i = 10;
int& r = i;
int* p = &r; // Pointer to the referred variable, that is, pointer to i.
cout << *p; // It outputs 10.
```

We could say that a reference variable resembles a const pointer. Like a const pointer, a reference variable must be initialized when declared and it is permanently associated with that variable, it cannot be bound to another. For example, we could say that the declaration:

int& r = i; is a "disguised" declaration of: int* const p = &i;

where r corresponds to *p. So, remember that a reference always refers to the same variable and will forever be an alias for that variable. The concept of the null reference does not exist. Also, we cannot declare an array of references. That is, you cannot write something like this:

```
int i, j;
int& arr[] = {i, j}; // Wrong.
```

Let's see another example. What is the output?

```cpp
#include <iostream> // Example 16.3
int main()
{
        int *p, i = 10, j = 20;

        p = &i;
        int& r = *p;

        p = &j;
        *p = 30;
        std::cout << r << '\n';
        return 0;
}
```

As we've said, r always refers to the same variable with which it was initialized, that is, to *p, which is equivalent to i. And of course, the value of p may change and point somewhere else without any effect. Therefore, since the value of i does not change, the program displays 10.

Let's see an example, where a reference variable refers to a pointer variable. What does the following program display?

```cpp
#include <iostream> // Example 16.4
int main()
{
        int *p, i = 4, j = 5;
        int*& r = p;

        p = &i;
        *r = 1;
        r = &j;
        *p += i+2;
        std::cout << *p+j << '\n';
        return 0;
}
```

To analyze the declaration of r, reading from right to left, the & operator indicates that r is a reference, and continue left to find the type, that is, reference to int*. Since r refers to p, the statement *r = 1; is equivalent to *p = 1;, so i becomes 1. Similarly, the statement r = &j; is equivalent to p = &j; and the statement *p += i+2; is equivalent to j += i+2;. So, j becomes 8 and the program displays 16.

The purpose of these examples is to show you the syntax and the properties of reference variables. The main use of reference variables is as arguments in function calls, as we'll see later. Also, references become very important in the context of object-oriented programming as we'll see in the next chapters.

References to const

A reference can be associated with a const variable. The reference must be declared as a reference to const. Of course, such a reference cannot be used to change the value of the referred variable. For example:

```cpp
const int a = 10;
const int& r1 = a; // Correct.
r1 = 20; // Wrong, it is not allowed to change the value.
int& r2 = r1; // Wrong, r2 is not a const reference.
```

If the last statement were allowed we could use r2 to change the value referred by r1, that is, the value of a. A reference to const can refer to a non-const variable or constant expression. However, it is not allowed to change the value of the non-const variable through the reference. For example:

```
int a = 10;
const int& r1 = a; // Correct.
const int& r2 = 20; // Correct.
const int& r3 = a*3; // Correct.
a = 30; // Correct, the variable is not const.
r1 = 30; // Wrong, it is not allowed through the reference.
```

References as Function Parameters

As we've learned, when we want a function to change the value of an argument we pass a pointer to the corresponding variable. An alternative way is to pass a reference to it. For example:

```
#include <iostream> // Example 16.5

void test(int& a, int b);

int main()
{
        int i = 10, j = 50;

        test(i, j);
        std::cout << i << ' ' << j << '\n';
        return 0;
}

void test(int& a, int b)
{
        a = 100;
        b = 200;
}
```

When a reference to a variable is passed to a function, it is the memory address of the variable that is actually passed. Thus, the function can access the variable of the calling function. For example, when test() is called, the variable i is passed by reference. In fact, this method of passing data is named *call by reference*. Note that the & operator is only added to the function declaration, not when called. In test(), the variable a refers to i, that is, when a is used it is as if i is used. In other words, a is an alias for i, not a copy of i. On the contrary, as we already know, the variable j is passed by value, that is, b is a copy of j. So, the value of j does not change and the program displays: 100 50

If we do not want the function to be able to change the original value we make the reference const. For example, if we write:

```
void test(const int& a, int b);
```

the statement a = 100; is not allowed. The declaration of a reference-argument as const prevents any change in the value of the referred variable.

Using reference parameters instead of pointers may seem simpler to write and easier to understand. However, my preference in such cases is to use pointers, so that the arguments that their value may change are clearly shown. For example, when using references a call such as f(i, j, k) gives no clue to the reader if f() can change the values of all, of some or none of the arguments. The only way to learn it is to look for the function prototype or its definition. Instead, if we use pointers and write f(&i, j, k), the reader would conclude that f() may only change the value of i. Also, it is very easy to spot the * dereference operator inside the function and find the places where the value of the argument changes. Thus, it is much easier to control the code. On the other hand, when the function receives a pointer and we intend to dereference it we should check that it is not a null pointer, otherwise the program may crash. This cannot happen with references, because a reference always refers to a variable; there is no null reference. Of course, I may prefer pointers because I started programming with C and C does not support references. C uses pointers to access the original data. Had I started with C++, I might have preferred references, because their use is simpler indeed.

In the question when to use a pointer or a reference, what I usually do is to use pointers when passing basic types (e.g., int), structures and unions, and, because C++ often requires using references in class design, I use references when class objects are passed to the function. Of course, this is just my preference, and there might be reasons to make different choices. Regardless of your choice, what is certain is that you should know both ways, because both are quite popular.

And as you already know from Chapter 13, when large entities are passed to the function, such as structures and classes, we choose to pass a reference or pointer even if the function is not going to modify them. The reason is to save the time and memory required to create the copy of the original entity. Thus, the performance of the program is improved. For simple variables, such as basic types, the typical choice is the *call by value*, as long as we do not want the function to modify the original values.

Another example, let's pass a reference to pointer in order to change the value of the pointer. What is the output of the following program?

```
#include <iostream> // Example 16.6

void test(int*& r);

int main()
{
        int i = 10, *p = &i;

        test(p);
        std::cout << *p << '\n';
        return 0;
}

void test(int*& r)
{
        static int b = 20;
        r = &b;
}
```

The parameter r is declared as a reference to type int*. In test(), r is equal to p, so p = &b. Since the value of p changes, the program displays 20. Alternatively, as we know from Chapter 11, to change the value of a pointer we could pass a pointer to pointer variable. In fact, this is my preference. For example:

```
void test(int **r)
{
        static int b = 20;
        *r = &b;
}
```

and write: test(&p); I think that this syntax is simpler and also makes it clearer and easier for the reader to understand that the value of the passed pointer may change. Of course, as I mentioned, I may consider that because I started programming with C. I guess that someone starting with C++ might prefer to use the reference syntax.

Reference as Return Value

See the following program and tell me what it displays:

```cpp
#include <iostream> // Example 16.7

int& test(int& a, int& b);

int main()
{
        int i = 10, j = 20;

        test(test(i, j), j) = 1;
        std::cout << i << ' ' << j << '\n';
        return 0;
}

int& test(int& a, int& b)
{
        a++;
        b += a;
        return a;
}
```

Now that I see it again I should probably have written something easier as a first example. And it is definitely a weird program, since it is the first time we see a function call at the left of =. Let's explain the program. Since references to i and j are passed to test(), the statement a++; is equivalent to i++; and the statement b += a; is equivalent to j += i;. So, the first call of test(), makes i equal to 11 and j equal to 31. Since test() returns i, i is the argument in the second call, so we have test(i, j); again. Essentially, the statement test(test(i, j), j) = 1; is equivalent to:

```cpp
test(i, j);
test(i, j) = 1;
```

Thus, i will be 12 and j will be 43. Since test() returns i, the statement test(test(i, j), j) = 1; is equivalent to i = 1; Therefore, the program displays 1 and 43.

Notice that we are allowed to write the statement test(i, j) = 1; because test() returns a reference. Remember from Chapter 4 that in an assignment, such as, a = 1; the left operand must be a modifiable lvalue, that is, memory must have reserved for it and that memory can be modified. This is true for this statement, because test() returns a reference to i for which memory has been reserved. That is, a returned reference corresponds to an lvalue. If we change the return type from int& to int, the compiler will display an error message similar to «left operand must be lvalue», because the left operand is not now an lvalue.

If we want to prevent such assignments, in order to avoid an unintended change of value, we change the return type from int& to const int&. Now, since the return value is not allowed to change, that is, it is a non-modifiable lvalue, the compiler will display an error message.

Someone might ask, is it common for a function to return a reference? Yes, a very common use of the reference, besides that as a function argument, is as a return value. And why have a function return a reference? The most common case is when we want to use a function call at the left of an assignment, as before with test(). Since a returned reference is an lvalue, it is allowed to do that. For example, as we'll see in Chapter 18, such assignments are very common when overloading operators (e.g., the [] operator). In general, reference return types are used a lot when dealing with classes.

Another reason is for better performance. For example, assume that f() returns an integer. When we write:

```
i = f();
```

the return value of f() may be copied to a temporary memory location and then this value is copied to i. In case that f() returns a reference, no copy is created, the return value is assigned directly to i, since the reference is just a synonym of the referred variable. The memory and time saving is not so significant with basic types, but if the return value is a large entity, such as a large structure, and the function is called many times, it is more efficient to return a reference and avoid a series of copy operations in temporary locations. Of course, an optimizing compiler may skip the temporary copy, but since this is not certain, it'd be better to return the reference to the entity.

 What you should never do is to return a reference to a variable that ceases to exist after the function is terminated.

For example, the following code is not correct:

```
int j = test();

int& test()
{
        int b = 10;
        return b; // Serious error, don't do it.
}
```

Since the variable b ceases to exist after test() terminates, the function returns a reference to a variable that does not exist anymore. What will happen if we attempt to refer to that memory is unpredictable. Essentially, this rule is similar to the one we discussed in Chapter 11 in case a function returns a pointer. Remember, we said never return the address of a local variable unless it is declared as static. That is, if b was declared as static there would be no problem.

Note that if you want to let the compiler deduce the return type you should use auto&, not just auto, to have the compiler deduce a reference type. For example:

```
auto& max(int& a, int& b)
{
        return a > b ?  a : b;
}
```

If you write auto without the &, the compiler will deduce int as return type, not int&.

Pass Array by Reference

If for some reason we want to pass an array to a function and not a pointer to its first element, we can use a reference to the array. One reason could be to enforce that an array of a certain size is passed to the function and not just a pointer to the first element of an array of any size. For example:

```
void f(int (&r)[3]); /* If we print the sizeof(r) we'll see that it is 12
(assume that the int type allocates 4 bytes). */
...
int a1[] = {5, 6, 7};
int a2[] = {5, 6, 7, 8};
f(a1); // Correct.
f(a2); // Wrong.
```

The prototype indicates that a reference to an array of three integers must be passed to the function. Therefore, the second call causes a compilation error, because the a2 array does not contain the expected number of elements. Note that the parentheses around r are required, otherwise the compiler would interpret the type as an array of three references to int. Because arrays of references are not allowed, the compilation would fail.

Another example of using a reference to an array is in function templates. The size of the passed array may vary. For example:

```
template <typename T, int size> void f(T(&r)[size]);
...
int a1[5];
float a2[10];
f(a1);
f(a2);
```

As we'll see later, f() is a function template. When the first call of f() is made, T is replaced by int and size by 5, while in the second call, T is replaced by float and size by 10.

And if you want to declare reference variables in an array here are two examples with one-dimensional and two-dimensional arrays.

```
int a[3];
int (&r)[3] = a; // r refers to an array of three integers.
r[0] = 5; // a[0] becomes 5.

int a[3][4];
int (&r)[4] = a[1]; /* r refers to an array of four integers, which is the
second row of a. */
r[0] = 5; // a[1][0] becomes 5.
```

rvalue References

C++11 introduces a new type of reference, the *rvalue* reference. An rvalue reference refers to a temporary object, which will not be used again after its use. Thus, an rvalue reference can reference the result of an rvalue expression, even though this value is generally temporary. Once an rvalue reference is bound to the result, the lifetime of the memory that is used to hold the result extends as long as the rvalue reference is in scope. Then, that memory is released. To declare an rvalue reference we use two & following the type name. For example:

```
int a = 10, b = 10;
int&& r = a+b;
std::cout << r; // The code outputs 20.
```

The r reference is an alias for the result of the rvalue expression a+b. Note that this example has no real value; it is just to see the syntax of the rvalue reference.

The main purpose of an rvalue reference is, because the object is temporary, to convert a copy operation into a move operation. For example, when copying entities that may contain lot of data (e.g., vector) it would be more efficient, in case the source entity is not used again, instead of copying the data, which not only is unnecessary but also a costly operation, to move them. Fine, but how do we tell the compiler to move data? By using an rvalue reference. For example, consider the following program:

```
#include <iostream> // Example 16.8
#include <string>
using std::cout;
using std::string;
```

```
int main()
{
        string s1("one"), s2;
        s2 = static_cast<string&&>(s1); // Move data.

        cout << s2 << ' ' << s1 << '\n'; // It outputs a single 'one'.
        return 0;
}
```

With `static_cast`, which we'll see in Chapter 25, the type of s1 is casted to `string&&`. As we'll see in Chapter 19, if the referred type (e.g., `string`) overloads the = operator to provide a move assignment operator, then the move operation will be performed. If not, the move operation won't be performed, and the usual copy operation will be performed instead. Since the `string` type provides the move assignment operator, one moves from s1 to s2. The empty string `""` is assigned to s1. Therefore, the program displays a single one. If we don't use an rvalue reference, that is, we write:

```
s2 = s1;
```

instead of the move operation the normal copy operation will be performed and the program will display one twice.

Because the use of `static_cast` makes the code more difficult to read we can alternatively use the `move()` function of the standard library. Essentially, the `move(a)` is equivalent to `static_cast<T&&>(a)`, where `T` is the type of a. That is, despite its name, `move()` does not move its argument (e.g., a), it just returns an rvalue reference to it. I say it again, `move()` neither moves nor copies data; it only performs a type cast to an rvalue reference which when used as an argument, as we'll see in Chapter 19, instructs the compiler to call a move constructor or move assignment operator. So, we can move the data in a more elegant way by writing:

```
s2 = std::move(s1);
```

As said, the idea of the move operation is to apply it to objects whose data will not be used again in our program, such as s1. In general, after calling `move()` we can destroy the source object (e.g., s1) or assign it a new value, but we cannot make assumptions about its initial value or current state. Let's look at an example of swapping values using a function template (we'll discuss them in a short) to better understand the usefulness of moving data:

```
template<typename T> void do_swap(T& a,  T& b)
{
        T tmp = a; // After the assignment to tmp, we have two copies of a.
        a = b; // After the assignment to a, we have two copies of b.
        b = tmp; // After the assignment to b, we have two copies of tmp.
}
```

It'd be more efficient not to copy the data in the assignments but to move them. For example, in the first assignment, there is no reason to have two copies of a. Since the data is stored in `tmp` and a is not going to be used again, there is no reason to keep them in a. To realize the performance gain, consider the case a being a `vector` of several thousand strings, each containing hundreds of characters. The cost of copying and maintaining two copies would be significant. It is more efficient to move the data to the destination (e.g., `tmp`) and then release the resources reserved for the source object (e.g., a).

In the real world, this move operation corresponds to the action of giving away something. For example, when I give a book to someone, (s)he does not get a copy of the book, but (s)he takes my own book, which I no longer have. In other words, property is transferred. And as we said, we instruct the compiler to move data using an rvalue reference. Let's change do_swap() to make the movement:

```cpp
#include <iostream> // Example 16.9
#include <string>
using namespace std;

template<typename T> void do_swap(T& a, T& b);

int main()
{
        string s1("one"), s2("two");
        do_swap(s1, s2);
        cout << s1 << ' ' << s2 << '\n'; // It displays two and one.
        return 0;
}

template<typename T> void do_swap(T& a, T& b)
{
        T tmp = move(a); /* The move constructor of the string class is
called. */
        cout << tmp << ' ' << a << '\n'; // It displays a single one.

        a = move(b); /* The move assignment function of the string class is
called. */
        cout << a << ' ' << b << '\n'; // It displays a single two.

        b = move(tmp);
        cout << b << ' ' << tmp << '\n'; // It displays a single one.
}
```

When do_swap() is called, T will be replaced by the string. As we said, because the string type provides a move constructor and overloads the = operator to move data, the string objects can be moved. For example, do_swap() first outputs one. If we use the previous version of do_swap() it'd display one one, since one won't move from a to tmp. The one remains in a. The same applies for the other assignments, that is, we'll have double appearances of the strings.

Comparing the two do_swap() versions, it is evident that the version of the do_swap() with the rvalue references is a very efficient swap function, much more efficient than being written in the usual way. Of course, in order to be such efficient, the used type (e.g., string) must be able to move data. We'll see similar examples in Chapter 19. If it is not supported, the normal copy operation will be performed.

A last example. Suppose that we want to copy the content of one vector object to another, and the original vector won't be used any more.

```cpp
vector<int> v1(100000);
vector<int> v2;
...
v2 = v1; // Not efficient.
v2 = std::move(v1);
```

Since we are not going to use the content of v1 any more, it is much more efficient to perform a move operation, than to make a needless copy of those thousands of elements. Of course, to move the data, the referred class should provide this ability, and yes, the vector class provides it.

Let's finish with some syntax issues. An rvalue reference must refer to an rvalue, such as a literal string or an expression that returns a value. A function that does not return a reference or expressions with arithmetic, relational, logical, bit, and unary increase/decrease operators are examples of expressions that produce rvalues. An lvalue reference is not allowed to refer to the result of such expressions. In general, in such expressions we can associate a `const` lvalue reference or an rvalue reference. An rvalue reference is not allowed to refer to an lvalue. Let's look at some examples with rvalue and lvalue references:

```cpp
int i;
double f() {return 1.2;}

double&& r1 = f(); // Correct. The return value of f() is rvalue.
int&& r1 = i; /* Wrong. r1 is an rvalue reference, while i is lvalue. */
double& r1 = f(); // Wrong. The return value of f() is not lvalue.
int& r1 = i+10; // Wrong. The result of i+10 is rvalue.
const int& r1 = i+10; /* Correct. It is allowed an lvalue const reference to
refer to an rvalue. */
```

The essential difference between an lvalue and an rvalue reference is that the lvalue reference refers to an entity that will continue to exist, while the rvalue reference refers to an entity that is about to be destroyed. An rvalue reference accesses the object that refers to in the same way as an lvalue reference or an ordinary variable. After all, an rvalue reference, like an lvalue reference, is a synonym of the referred variable. For example:

```cpp
void f(string&& str)
{
        if(str[0] == 't')
        {
        }
}
f("test"); // An rvalue reference may refer to a literal string.
```

Note that if we write:

```cpp
string s("test");
f(s); // Wrong.
```

the compiler will display an error message because an lvalue (e.g., s) cannot be associated with an rvalue reference (e.g., str).

Before ending this tough section, just to remind that we use rvalue references or the `move()` function to perform move operations on objects that we don't need their data any more. The result is performance improvement.

constexpr FUNCTIONS

Sometimes we may want to evaluate the return value of a function (e.g., suppose that a function calculates some value) at compile time rather than performing the same evaluation over and over at runtime. That's the main idea of `constexpr` functions; to improve the performance of the program by performing computations at compile time rather than at runtime.

Since C+11, to declare to the compiler that it is possible to evaluate a function at compile time we use the `constexpr` specifier. However, a `constexpr` function must satisfy several requirements. For example, any given arguments must be constant expressions. Regarding its body, C++11 had posed many restrictions. For example, loops and `if` statements were not allowed. Fortunately, C++14 relaxes the

C++11 restrictions and allows us to write compile-time functions using familiar language constructs. It just poses some few restrictions (e.g., when defining a variable it must be initialized). Let's see an example of a `constexpr` function:

```
constexpr int f(int a) /* Not compiled with C++11, but compiled since C++14. */
{
        int i = 10;

        while(a > i)
        {
                a--;
                i++;
        }
        return (a < 50) ?  i : 20;
}
```

When using the return value of a `constexpr` function for initialization the performance of the program is improved, since that value is computed at compile time and not at runtime. For example:

```
int k = 5;
constexpr int i = f(3);   /* Since the argument is a constant expression, the
value of i will be computed at compile time. */
int i = f(k); /* Since the argument (e.g., k) is not a constant expression,
the value of i will be computed at runtime. */
constexpr int i = f(k);   /* Compilation error. Because k is not constant, the
value of i cannot be computed at compile time. If it was constant there would
be no problem. */
```

As you see, when it is called with a constant argument the `constexpr` function produces a compile-time constant. When called with a non-constant argument, it produces a value at runtime like an ordinary function.

A `constexpr` function can accept references as arguments and return a reference or a pointer. For example:

```
constexpr const int* f(const int& a)
{
        return &a; // Return a pointer.
}
static const int k = 5; /* The memory address of a variable with permanent
lifetime, such as a static or a global variable, is fixed. */
constexpr const int *p = f(k); /* Since the argument is a constant
expression, the value of p will be computed at compile time. */
int i = *p; // i becomes 5.
```

FUNCTION OVERLOADING

Unlike C, C++ allows different functions to have the same name. This feature is called *function overloading* or *function polymorphism* in the sense that a function may have many forms. Function overloading is one of the essential parts of generic programming. An example of the overloading concept is the use of the arithmetic operators. For example, the same + operator can be used to add integers or float numbers or both types. This idea was extended to functions.

The restriction to have many functions with the same name is that each function must have a different *signature*. The signature of a function is determined by the number of its parameters and their types; the names of the parameters don't matter. When an overloaded function is called, the compiler checks the number and the type of the arguments passed to it and determines which version to call. As a consequence, the polymorphism is achieved during the compilation of the program (*static binding*).

Although we can overload functions that perform entirely different tasks, overloading makes sense when used to overload functions that perform similar operations. Thus, there is no need to search for different function names and give the false impression to the reader that they perform different tasks. The same name indicates to the reader that their operation is similar but with different types of data. For example, in the following program the abs_v() function is overloaded three times and the compiler selects the appropriate version:

```cpp
#include <iostream> // Example 16.10

int abs_v(int a);
double abs_v(double a);
void abs_v(int a, int b); // Display the absolute value of the sum.

int main()
{
        int i = -100;
        double j = 1.2345;

        std::cout << abs_v(i) << ' ';
        std::cout << abs_v(j) << ' ';
        abs_v(i, 30);
        return 0;
}

int abs_v(int a)
{
        if(a < 0)
                return -a;
        else
                return a;
}

double abs_v(double a)
{
        if(a < 0)
                return -a;
        else
                return a;
}

void abs_v(int a, int b)
{
        int sum;

        sum = a+b;
        if(sum < 0)
                std::cout << -sum << '\n';
        else
                std::cout << sum << '\n';
}
```

The program displays: 100 1.2345 70. For those who have experience with C, because C does not support overloading, in order to get the same result, we should have defined three functions with different names such as abs(), fabs(), and labs(). Note that the order of the overloaded functions does not affect the selection of the appropriate version.

Notice that only the signature, and not the return type, allows functions to be overloaded. Remember, in order to overload a function, the functions must have different signatures, that is, different number of parameters or types, or both. The compiler does not examine the return types. For example, the signature of the third abs_v() is (int, int). Therefore, if we add the following abs_v():

```
int abs_v(int a, int b);
```

the compiler will display an error message for two versions with the same signature.

Before overloading a function, check if you can get the same result by using default arguments. For example, instead of declaring the following three overloaded functions:

```
int f(int a, int b);
int f(int a, int b, int c);
int f(int a, int b, int c, int d);
```

to calculate the sum of their arguments, we could declare a single function with default arguments. For example:

```
int f(int a, int b = 0, int c = 0, int d = 0);
```

And it is definitely better to declare a single function, because you have to write code for just one and if you ever need to change it you'll make the changes in one place. Also, the compiler allocates memory for one function instead of three.

Ambiguous Situations

There are cases where functions with signatures that look different cannot be overloaded. For example:

```
int f(int a);
int f(int& a);
```

When f() is called (e.g., f(i)), the compiler cannot decide which of the two to call. To avoid this ambiguity, when the compiler examines the signatures it considers that the reference to a type and the type itself have the same signature. Therefore, the compiler will display an error message in the f() call similar to *ambiguous call to overloaded function*.

Ambiguity may also arise if the arguments in the function call do not exactly match any prototype. For example:

```
int f(double a);
void f(char *a);
int f(int a);
int f(long a);
```

What will the compiler do in a call such as f(i) if i is declared as float? When no prototype matches exactly the function call, the compiler applies the conversion rules and, if no ambiguity arises, it selects the closest match. Thus, i is converted to double and the first f() is selected. But what happens if i is unsigned int? Now, since there are three candidate functions to convert i, the compiler does not select any of them and displays an error message for ambiguity in the f() call. What if the last two prototypes are missing and i has been declared as `bool`? The compiler converts i to `double` and selects the first `f()` again. The process to decide which function to use when there are many candidates is called *overload resolution*. A detailed discussion is out of the scope of this book. In short, the ranking from best to worst that the compiler applies to select the most suitable function is:

a. Exact match of arguments.
b. Match using integral promotions as we saw in Chapter 2 (e.g., `short` to `int`) and `float` to `double` promotion.
c. Match using standard conversions (e.g., `int` to `double`).

If there are more than one "best" function, the compiler rejects the call as ambiguous.

Note that the compiler distinguishes between `const` and non-`const` for reference and pointers. For example:

```
void f(const char *a);
void f(char *a);
```

Suppose we write:

```
const char s1[] = "text";
char s2[] = "text";
f(s1); // f(const char *a);
f(s2); // f(char *a);
```

In the first call of `f()` the compiler selects the first version and in the second call it selects the second version. Note that in the second call, since a non-`const` argument can be passed to `const` both versions are candidates, but the compiler selects the second version because it matches exactly.

FUNCTION TEMPLATES

Function templates, why do we need them, are they important? No doubt, templates are the basis for generic programming, that is, to write code that can work with a variety of types. Is it an easy section to read? I'd not say that. Still difficult concepts to learn? Yes, and many more on the way. I know, that's a lot of new stuff, have a break with *More* from *Sisters of Mercy* and prepare yourself to explore this very interesting feature.

A function template allows us to define a function in terms of a generic type(s) so that it can handle different types of data. Each time such a function is called, the compiler checks the type of the arguments and creates a version of the function for that particular types. An example of defining a function template is:

```
template <typename type1, typename type2, ...>
return_type function_name(parameter_list)
```

Let's see how it works. Suppose that we want to create a function that returns the absolute value of a number. Since we do not know the type of the number we have to write different functions or overload one function for all possible types. See now the flexibility that the templates provide us. With templates we do not need to write different versions; we just write a function template in terms of some generic type and that same function can work for a variety of types. This is the concept of *generic programming*.

The following program uses the template `abs()` function to find the absolute value of numbers with different types:

```cpp
#include <iostream> // Example 16.11

template <typename T> T abs(T a);

int main()
{
        int a = -6;
        float b = -1.2;
        double c = 3.4;

        std::cout << abs(a) << ' ' << abs(b) << ' ' << abs(c) << '\n';
        return 0;
}

template <typename T> T abs(T a)
{
        T k;

        if(a < 0)
                k = -a;
        else
                k = a;
        return k;
}
```

Regarding the program design, in a project with multiple source files that may use the same template, the common practice is to put the definition of a function template in a header file and include that file in any file that uses the template. In our examples which consist of a single source file, for simplicity, I'll put the declaration and the definition of the function template in that file.

To declare a function template we write the keyword `template` and inside `<>` the keyword `typename` and the names of the template parameters. Unlike the parameters of an ordinary function which are used to pass values, the parameters of a function template are typically used to pass *types*. Note that we can also use the word `class` instead of the word `typename`. The word `typename` was later added to C++, so you may run into code that uses the word `class`. My preference is the word `typename`, because it makes clear that the `T` parameter corresponds to the name of some type. Also, the word `class` may create the false impression that the type must be a class, which is not true. As for the parameter names you may choose any names you want, as long as they follow the naming rules. The common practice is to use short names that begin with the letter `T` (e.g., `T1`, `T2`).

The template is not a function definition. It is just a blueprint that provides the directions to the compiler about how to define the function. So, when the function is created? Each time the compiler encounters a call to `abs()` it replaces the `T` type with the type of the argument and creates the function. This is referred to as *template argument deduction*. For example, in the first call, it replaces the `T` type with `int` and creates an `int` version of the function. So, the resulting definition is:

```cpp
int abs(int a)
{
        int k;

        if(a < 0)
                k = -a;
        else
                k = a;
        return k;
}
```

Similarly, in the second call, the compiler replaces the `T` type with `float` and the definition of the resulting `float` version is:

```
float abs(float a)
{
        float k;

        if(a < 0)
                k = -a;
        else
                k = a;
        return k;

}
```

The compiler creates a definition of the function template only if it is used in the program. If not used, it will not be defined.

So, we see that in each call the compiler checks the type of the argument; it replaces each appearance of the generic type with it and creates the corresponding version. This type of instantiation is called *implicit instantiation*, in the sense that the compiler creates the function when it encounters the call and deduces the type of the passed arguments. If another function call requires the same instance, the compiler uses the existing instance.

Since the type of the arguments is fixed and known, the compiler instantiates templates at compile time. So, as with function overloading, the polymorphism is achieved at compile time, which means that the use of templates does not induce a delay in the execution time of the program. In other words, templates provide compile time parametric polymorphism. Finally, the program displays: 6   1.2   3.4

We could omit the declaration of `k` and write `abs()` as follows:

```
if(a < 0)
        return -a;
else                      or else: return a < 0 ? -a : a;
        return a;
```

The reason I used `k` is to show you that you can declare a generic type variable, just like an ordinary variable (e.g., `T k`). That is, a template parameter is used like an ordinary data type. For example, we can use its name to construct derived types (e.g., `T*`, `T&`, …).

Note that the use of function templates does not make the size of the executable file shorter. The executable contains the definitions of the three defined functions, just as if we had written them separately. As we said, the advantage of templates is that we do not need to write the same code for different data types. We write the code once in terms of a generic type and that code applies to a variety of types. Thus, the code is easier to read, verified, and maintained, since it appears only at one place. Because templates provide us the ability to write programs that use generic types instead of specific types, we say that C++ supports generic programming. In particular, generic programming gives emphasis on the use of function templates to write generic algorithms that can be applied to containers. For example, to write a generic `sort()` function that sorts the elements of a `vector`:

```
template <typename T> void sort(vector<T>& v);
```

Exercise U.16.2 asks you to implement the `bubble_sort()` algorithm we saw in C.12.10 in a generic way, in order to sort the elements of a `vector` that contains arithmetic elements of any type.

Regarding the parameters of a function template, not all of them have to be generic types. We can mix them with specific types. Here is an example:

```
template <typename T> void f(T a, int b)
```

Like an ordinary function, a function template can be declared as `inline` or `constexpr`. The specifier is added before the return type. For example:

```
inline template <typename T> T abs(T a); // Wrong.
template <typename T> inline T abs(T a); // Correct.
```

Templated Variables

C++14 allows the creation of templated variables. For example:

```
template <typename T> T pi = T(3.14159265359);
```

Typically, a templated variable is used in function templates and classes. For example:

```
template <typename T> T circle_perim(T rad)
{
        return 2*rad*pi<T>;
}
```

The idea behind the templated variables is that, instead of having different variables and initializing expressions for the respective types, it is sometimes useful to vary the type of a variable used for generic purposes. For example, we can write:

```
int rad = 5;
int per = circle_perim(rad);
```

When `circle_perim()` is called, the compiler replaces the `T` type with the type of the `rad` argument and creates the function. Since `T` becomes `int`, `rad` becomes 3 and the function returns 30.

Errors When Using Templates

Try this exercise first. Write a function template that swaps the values of its two arguments. Assume that the arguments are of the same type. Then, write a program to verify the operation of the function.

```
#include <iostream> // Example 16.12

template <typename T> void do_swap(T& a, T& b);

int main()
{
        int a = 1, b = 2;
        double c = 3.4, d = 5.6;

        do_swap(a, b);
        do_swap(c, d);
        std::cout << a << ' ' << b << ' ' << c << ' ' << d << '\n';
        return 0;
}
```

```
template <typename T> void do_swap(T& a, T& b)
{
        T tmp;

        tmp = a;
        a = b;
        b = tmp;
}
```

In the first call of do_swap(), T is replaced with int and in the second call with double. The program displays: 2 1 5.6 3.4

Note that the arguments must have the same type, as the compiler expects to replace T with the same type. That is, if we write:

```
do_swap(a, c); // Wrong.
```

the compiler will display an error message. Someone might wonder, the compiler does not do the usual arithmetic conversions? The answer is no. In particular, it converts an array or function argument to a pointer and it allows to pass to a parameter that is a reference or pointer to const a reference or pointer to non-const. For example:

```
template <typename T> void f(T a);
template <typename T> void g(const T& a);
int arr[10];
f(arr); /* Correct, the array is converted to a pointer to its first element
and the type T becomes int*. */
string s("one");
g(s); /* Correct, it is allowed to pass a non-const reference argument to a
const type. */
```

When you write or use a function template it does not mean that it will work for all types. For example, if you pass an array of characters to do_swap(), the compiler will display error messages for not allowed assignments:

```
char s1[10] = "one";
char s2[10] = "two";
do_swap(s1, s2); // Wrong.
```

One way to solve this problem is to write, as you'll see in the next section, an overloaded version with the corresponding types. For example:

```
void do_swap(char a[], char b[])
{
        char tmp[10];

        strcpy(tmp, a);
        strcpy(a, b);
        strcpy(b, tmp);
}
```

Let me ask you, if instead of character arrays we pass string variables to do_swap(), which is, as we know, a more secure alternative than using strcpy(), will the function work? I do not know, try it.

Also, when writing a function template, the code may not support certain operations for some types or provide meaningless results. For example:

```cpp
template <typename T> int cmp(const T& a, const T& b)
{
        return a < b ?  1 : 2;
}
```

If we pass numeric values to cmp() it will work as expected. But, if we pass two arrays, it will just compare their addresses, not the elements. If we pass a user-defined type, such as a class, cmp() will work only if the class overloads the < operator, as we'll see in Chapter 18. Otherwise, the compiler will display an error message.

Note that errors like the previous ones occur only if the definition of the function template has been created. In this case, the compiler performs the usual checks such as to check the type and number of arguments, the return value and the correct use of the types inside the function. If the function template is not defined, what the compiler can do is to detect syntax errors, such as using an undeclared variable.

Template Parameters with Different Types

The template parameters can have different types. For example, let's write a function template that displays the larger of two numbers:

```cpp
#include <iostream> // Example 16.13

template <typename T1, typename T2> void f(T1 a, T2 b);

int main()
{
        int i = 10, j = 20;
        float k = 1.23;
        double p = 5.64;

        f(i, j); // T1=int, T2=int.
        f(p, i); // T1=double, T2=int.
        f(j, k); // T1=int, T2=float.
        return 0;
}

template <typename T1, typename T2> void f(T1 a, T2 b)
{
        if(a < b)
                std::cout << a << '\n';
        else
                std::cout << b << '\n';
}
```

For example, in the second call, the compiler replaces the T1 type with double, the T2 type with int, and the resulting definition is:

```cpp
void f(double a, int b)
{
        if(a < b)
                std::cout << a << '\n';
        else
                std::cout << b << '\n';
}
```

One problem that may occur when writing a template is that you don't know what type to use in a declaration. For example, let's change `f()` to assign the sum of its arguments to a variable:

```
template <typename T1, typename T2> void f(T1 a, T2 b)
{
        auto sum = a+b;
        ...
}
```

What will be the type of `sum`? Since we do not know in advance how `f()` will be used we cannot specify the type. For example, if `T1` is `double` and `T2` is `int`, `sum` must be declared as `double`. However, if `T1` is `short` and `T2` is `int`, `sum` must be declared as `int`. One way to solve this problem is to use the `auto` specifier. Alternatively, we can use the `decltype` specifier. For example:

```
template <typename T1, typename T2> void f(T1 a, T2 b)
{
        decltype(a+b) sum;
        sum = a+b;
        ...
}
```

The type of `sum` becomes the same as that of `a+b`.

The next plausible question is, and what if the function template returns a value whose type depends on the arguments? For example, what should be the return type in case we want to modify the function and return `sum`? As before, we cannot specify the return type since we do not know which types of arguments will be passed to `f()`. The solution is to use the `auto` specifier as we saw in Chapter 11, when we discussed deduction of return types. See the program:

```
#include <iostream> // Example 16.14

template <typename T1, typename T2>
auto f(T1 a, T2 b)
{
        auto sum = a+b;
        return sum;
}

int main()
{
        int a = 1;
        double b = 2.3;

        auto c = f(a, b);
        std::cout << c << '\n';
        return 0;
}
```

The word `auto` is put in the place of the return type. Absolutely fantastic, what a nice feature is this return type deduction! The type will be deduced from the type of `sum` when the function is called. Thus, the return type becomes `double` and the program displays `3.3`.

Set Types of Template Parameters

There are cases where we may want or we must explicitly specify the type of a template argument. Such a case is when a function returns a value whose type differs from the types of its parameters. For example:

```
template <typename T1, typename T2, typename T3> T1 f(T2 a, T3 b);
```

When we call `f()` we specify the T1 type in `<>`. The T2 and T3 types will be deduced from the values of the arguments. For example, if we write:

```
int i;
double j;
f<int>(i, j); // int f(int, double);
```

the T1 type will be replaced by `int` and the compiler will determine the T2 and T3 types from the types of the corresponding arguments. When multiple template arguments are explicitly set, each argument (e.g., `int`) corresponds to the respective template parameter (e.g., T1) from left to right.

Use of Non-Type Parameters

A function template can accept the following parameters:

a. Types.
b. Integer types (e.g., `int`).
c. Pointers and references to a function or to an object type.
d. Pointer to a class member.
e. Enumeration type.

The number of parameters can be fixed or variable, as we'll see below. The most common parameter is the one we have encountered so far, the type. Let's look at some examples again:

```
template <typename T> void f(T& a);

double d = 2.3;
f<double>(d); // T becomes double.

vector<int> v;
f(v); // T becomes vector<int>.
```

A non-type parameter represents a value instead of a type. The values of the non-type arguments should be able to be determined at compile time. For example, a typical use of integer arguments is when we want to specify the size of a memory:

```
template <typename T, int size> void f(T& a)
{
        T arr[size]; // The size of the array is specified.
        arr[0] = a;
        size = 20; // Wrong.
}

int i = 5;
f<int, 10>(i); /* T becomes int, size becomes 10 and arr[0] becomes equal to i,
that is, 5. */
```

A parameter value is considered constant within the function and we are not allowed to change its value. That is, it is error to write `size = 20`. We'll discuss more about non-type parameters in the corresponding section in Chapter 23.

Default Parameter Values

As with ordinary functions, we can set default values to the parameters of a function template. For example:

```
template <typename T1, typename T2 = int> void f()
{
        T1 i;
        T2 j;
        ...
}
```

If the type of `T2` is omitted, that is, write `f<double>();` the type of `T1` will be `double` and the type of `T2` will be `int`.

We can also specify default values for non-type parameters. For example:

```
template <typename T, int s = 20> void f(){...}
```

If we write `f<int>();` the type of `T` will be `int` and s equal to `20`.

Explicit Instantiation

In addition to the implicit instantiation we can instruct the compiler to create the function definition directly. This type of instantiation is called *explicit instantiation*. An explicit instantiation begins with the word `template` without the `<`. The types are contained inside `<>`. For example, if we add the following statement in the C.16.11 example:

```
template int abs<int>(int a);
```

the compiler will use the `abs()` function template to create directly a definition using the `int` type. Explicit instantiation also occurs if the function is used in the program. For example:

```
double c = 3.4;
cout << abs<double>(c) << '\n';
```

This creates an explicit instantiation for the `double` type. If the specified type does not match with the type of the argument, the compiler will attempt a type conversion. For example, if we write:

```
cout << abs<int>(c) << '\n';
```

the compiler makes an instance of `int` type. Thus, c is converted to `int` and the code outputs `3`. So, be careful with type mismatches, because the compiler may provide an undesirable implicit conversion.

Explicit instantiations may improve the compilation and the linking time of the program, since no instantiations are repeated for the same type(s). Also, in large applications where the use of the same function template in multiple source files may be required, we can avoid the delay caused by its creation by instantiating it explicitly and make it `extern`. For example, if `abs<int>` is defined in one file and we want to use it in a second file we write:

```
extern template int abs<int>(int a); // Second file.
```

With the `extern` declaration the compiler will not redefine the `abs<int>` version in this file. As with ordinary declarations of `extern` variables, the definition of `abs<int>` will be searched in another file. In the same sense, there can be many `extern` declarations for a given function, but only one definition for that instantiation.

Overloading Function Templates

As we said, we write a function template when we want to apply the same code to a variety of types. However, it might be a case that we want to write a function that performs a similar operation, not the same. In such a case we can overload the function template, just as we've learned to do with ordinary functions. For example, suppose we want to write a function template that returns the absolute value of its argument and another one that displays the absolute value of the sum of its arguments:

```cpp
#include <iostream> // Example 16.15

template <typename T> T abs(T a);
template <typename T> void abs(T a, T b, int c = 3);

int main()
{
        int a = 6, b = 3;
        double c = 1.2;

        abs(a, b, -10);
        std::cout << ' ' << abs(c) << '\n';
        return 0;
}

template <typename T> T abs(T a)
{
        return a < 0 ? -a : a;
}

template <typename T> void abs(T a, T b, int c)
{
        T sum;

        sum = a+b+c;
        if(sum < 0)
                std::cout << -sum;
        else
                std::cout << sum;
}
```

As with ordinary overloading, the signatures must be different. The first signature is (T), while the second is (T, T, int). The reason I added the integer parameter c in the second abs() is to show you that, as with ordinary functions, we can have parameters with default values. The program displays: 1 1.2

Explicit Specialization

When writing a function template it might be a case that we want the function to work differently for a particular type. To achieve this we can declare an explicit specialization of the function template. For example, suppose we have declared the following structure:

```
struct Student
{
        string name;
        float grd;
};
```

If we want to swap the contents of the two structures we can use the template do_swap() function we saw earlier in example C.16.12. But if we want to swap only the grades and not the names it won't work. A solution is to supply an explicit specialization of the function template to handle explicitly Student arguments. For example:

```
#include <iostream> // Example 16.16
#include <string>

struct Student
{
        std::string name;
        float grd;
};

template <typename T> void do_swap(T& a, T& b);
template <> void do_swap<Student>(Student& a, Student& b); /* Explicit
specialization. */

int main()
{
        int a = 10, b = 20;
        Student s1 = {"N.Smith", 6.5}, s2 = {"P.Krow", 5.2};

        do_swap(a, b); // Call the function template.
        do_swap(s1, s2); // Call the specialized version.
        std::cout << a << ' ' << b << '\n' << s1.name << ' ' << s1.grd << '\n'
<< s2.name << ' ' << s2.grd << '\n';
        return 0;
}

template <typename T> void do_swap(T& a, T& b)
{
        T tmp;

        tmp = a;
        a = b;
        b = tmp;
}
```

```
template <> void do_swap<Student>(Student& a, Student& b)
{
        float grd;

        grd = a.grd;
        a.grd = b.grd;
        b.grd = grd;
}
```

I guess that the syntax of the specialized version has scared you. Before we discuss it, let me note that it is not necessary to create a specialized version. For example, we could declare a function with a different name (e.g., `swap_studs`) and call it. This is an example of using the same name, which is the typical choice.

As shown, the prototype of the specialized function begins with `template <>` and the name of the specialized type (e.g., `Student`) is enclosed in `<>` after the name of the function. This function will be selected when the type of the argument is `Student`. Because the compiler can deduce from the passed arguments the specialized type, `<Student>` can be omitted and the prototype becomes simpler:

```
template <> void do_swap(Student& a, Student& b);
```

Note that instead of a specialized version we could overload the function template with an ordinary function. Its prototype would be:

```
void do_swap(Student& a, Student& b);
```

In general, a function name may correspond to a simple function, a function template, an explicit specialization of a function template, and overloaded versions of them. The compiler selects the one that fits better to the function call and, if there are many candidates to match, the simple one prevails over the others and the specialized one prevails over the general template.

Let's see an example:

```
template <typename T> void f(T& a);
int f(int& a);
...
int i;
f(i); // Both functions match the call. The compiler selects the simple one.
```

The difference between the explicit specialization and the explicit instantiation we saw earlier is that explicit specialization indicates to the compiler that, if the arguments are of type `Student`, not to use the function template to create a function definition, but to use the specialized definition explicitly defined for the `Student` type. The explicit instantiation instructs the compiler to create instantly a definition for the specific type(s). Let's look at an example with all the cases:

```
...
template <typename T> void do_swap(T& a, T& b);
template <> void do_swap(Student& a, Student& b); // Specialized version.
template void do_swap<int>(int& a, int& b); // Explicit instantiation.

int main()
{
        int i = 10, j = 20;
        double k = 1.23, m = 4.56;
        Student s1, s2;
```

```
do_swap(i, j); // Call the explicitly instantiated version.
do_swap(k, m); // Call the function template.
do_swap(s1, s2); // Call the specialized version.
...
return 0;
}
```

When the compiler encounters the do_swap() declaration for the int type, it creates instantly an int version of the do_swap(). In main(), the compiler checks the do_swap() arguments and selects the appropriate version. For example, in the first call it calls the int version that has already been created, in the second call it creates a double version, and in the third call it selects the specialized version for the Student type.

Templates with Variable Number of Types

C++11 allows us to define a function template that accepts a variable number of parameters of any type. This is called a *variadic* template. Let's look at an example:

```
#include <iostream> // Example 16.17

void f() {std::cout << '\n';}

template <typename T, typename... T_List>
void f(T val, T_List... v_list)
{
        std::cout << val << ' ';
        f(v_list...);
}

int main()
{
        f(2, 3.4, "t1");
        f("t2", "t3");
        return 0;
}
```

In the second version of f() in order to declare that the second parameter accepts a variable number of types we add the ellipsis ... after the word typename. As for the name (e.g., T_List) you can choose any valid name you want. Thus, T_List contains a list of types, while T corresponds to a single type. The ... are also added after the name in the parameter list. v_list contains a list of values that match the list of types in T_List, while val corresponds to a single value of type T.

So, when f() is first called, the T_List parameter contains all the types that match the arguments, that is, int, double, and const char*. The v_list parameter contains the values 2, 3.4, and t1. Similarly, in the second call, T_List contains two types of const char* and v_list the values t2 and t3.

Fine, and how does f() access the values? Note that we cannot index the v_list, that is, to write something like v_list[1] to display the second value. Access is achieved through recursion. In particular, each time f() is called the type of the first argument is assigned to T and the value to val. The remaining types and values remain in T_List and v_list and will be accessed, one at a time, with the next recursive calls of f() until the list of arguments is exhausted. Then, the first version of f() will be called. This is the reason for its existence, so that the recursion ends. In our example, it just changes line so that the arguments of the second f() appear on the next line. Note that in the f() call we add the ... after the name of the argument, in order to expand the list of values contained in v_list.

Let's analyze the call of `f(2, 3.4, "t1");` to understand it better. `T` becomes `int` and `val` equals 2. The other two types remain in `T_List` and the two values in `v_list`. `f()` displays 2 and we have the recursive call of `f(3.4, "t1");` That is, each time, the `v_list` ... argument is replaced with the remaining values. Now, `T` becomes `double` and `val` equals 3.4. The last type remains in `T_List` and its value in `v_list`. `f()` displays 3.4 and the next recursive call is `f("t1");`. Now, `T` becomes `const char*` and `val` equals t1. `f()` displays t1 and because `v_list` is empty, since there are no more arguments, the first version of `f()` is called, which changes line and the recursion ends. To sum up, the program displays:

```
2     3.4     t1
t2    t3
```

In our example the values in each `f()` call are passed by value. If we want to pass arguments of larger size (e.g., classes), then it is more efficient to use `const` references. For example, the declaration of `f()` becomes:

```
template <typename T, typename... T_List>
void f(const T& val, const T_List&... v_list)
```

If we want to learn how many types are in the list we can use the `sizeof` ... operator. For example:

```
template <typename T, typename... T_List>
void f(T val, T_List... v_list)
{
        std::cout << sizeof...(T_List) << ' ' << sizeof...(v_list) << '\n';
        f(v_list...);
}

f(2, 3.4, "t1"); /* The first call of f() displays 2 2, the next 1 1, and the
last 0 0. */
```

Because of their flexibility to accept an arbitrary number of arguments of any type, variadic templates are often used in the standard library.

C++17 provides the ability to compute the result of using a binary operator over all the elements of a parameter pack. For example:

```
template <typename... T_List>
auto sum(T_List... args)
{
        return (... + args);
}
```

The function returns the sum of all passed arguments. For example, if we write:

`sum(1, 2, 3);` the function returns their sum, that is, 6. The return statement is called a *fold expression*. Since three values are passed, the expression (`... + args`) expands to: ((arg1 + arg2) + arg3). This is called *right fold*.

Alternatively, we can use the *left fold*: `return (args + ...);` which expands to:

(arg1 + (arg2 + arg3)).

C++17 introduced the fold expressions to simplify the implementation of variadic templates.

Before we continue with the exercises I'd like to remind you something that I had written in Chapter 1, yes, that was early enough to pay attention. Now that we have come a long way and things are getting harder and harder (yes, this chapter was really difficult), I think you'll give it the proper attention. In addition to error messages, the compiler may issue warnings to inform the programmer about potential malfunction of the program. Although a program that issues only warning messages can be compiled, always check them and fix them if needed in order to avoid problematic situations. In fact, for better control of your program and greater security, I'd suggest that you set the warning level at the maximum level supported by your compiler in order to catch all of them.

EXERCISES

C.16.1 What is the output of the following program?

```cpp
#include <iostream>

void test(int *p, int& r, int a = 2);

int main()
{
        int i = 10, j = 50;

        test(&i, j);
        std::cout << i << ' ' << j << '\n';
        return 0;
}

void test(int *p, int& r, int a)
{
        *p = r;
        p = &r;
        *p = a;
        r += 20;
}
```

Answer: When `test()` is called we have `p = &i` and `r = j`. So, the `*p = r;` makes `i` equal to 50. Then, `p` points to `j`, and the `*p = a;` makes `j` equal to the default value of `a`, that is, 2. Finally, `j` is increased and becomes 22. As a result, the program displays: `50 22`.

C.16.2 Define the structure type `Student` with members name and grade. Write a function that takes as parameters two constant references to `string` objects and returns a reference to the larger one. Overload the function with another function, which takes as parameters two constant references to `Student` types and returns the name of the student with the better grade. Check the case if they are the same. Write a program that verifies the operation of the two functions.

```cpp
#include <iostream>
#include <string>
using std::cout;
using std::string;
```

```cpp
struct Student
{
        string name;
        float grd;
};

const string& cmp(const string& a, const string& b);
string cmp(const Student& a, const Student& b);

int main()
{
        string s1 = "alpha", s2 = "beta";
        Student st1 = {"N.Smith", 6.5}, st2 = {"P.Krow", 5.2};

        string tmp = cmp(s1, s2); /* To see that we can assign the return
value to a simple variable. */
        cout << tmp << '\n';

        tmp = cmp(st1, st2);
        if(tmp == "")
                cout << "Same grades\n";
        else
                cout << tmp << '\n';
        return 0;
}

const string& cmp(const string& a, const string& b)
{
        if(a > b)
                return a;
        else
                return b;
}

string cmp(const Student& a, const Student& b)
{
        if(a.grd > b.grd)
                return a.name;
        else if(a.grd < b.grd)
                return b.name;
        else
                return "";
}
```

C.16.3 Write a `void` function that takes as parameter a reference to a `string` object and another reference that is used to return the number of the digits it contains. The function should convert the lowercase letters to uppercase and vice versa. Write a program that reads a string and, if it ends in `'x'`, it should call the function and display the new string and the number of the digits it contains. If not, the insertion of the string should be repeated. Note that in the ASCII code the difference between a lowercase letter and the respective uppercase is 32.

```cpp
#include <iostream>
#include <string>
using namespace std;

void change(string& s, int& cnt);
```

```cpp
int main()
{
        int dig;
        string str;

        while(1)
        {
                cout << "Enter text ending with x: ";
                getline(cin, str);

                if(str[str.length()-1] == 'x')
                {
                        change(str, dig);
                        cout << str << " contains " << dig << " digits\n";
                        return 0;
                }
        }
        return 0;
}

void change(string& s, int& cnt)
{
        int i;

        cnt = 0;
        for(i = 0 ; i < s.length(); i++)
        {
                if(s[i] >= 'a' && s[i] <= 'z')
                        s[i] -= 32;
                else if(s[i] >= 'A' && s[i] <= 'Z')
                        s[i] += 32;
                else if(s[i] >= '0' && s[i] <= '9')
                        cnt++;
        }
}
```

C.16.4 What is the output of the following program?

```cpp
#include <iostream>

double* test(double *p1, double *p2);
double& test(double& r1, double& r2);

int main()
{
        double a = 1.2, b = 3.4;

        *test(&a, &b) = 5.6;
        std::cout << a << ' ' << b << '\n';

        test(a, b) = 7.8;
        std::cout << a << ' ' << b << '\n';
        return 0;
}
```

```
double* test(double *p1, double *p2)
{
        if(*p1 < *p2)
                return p1;
        else
                return p2;
}

double& test(double& r1, double& r2)
{
        if(r1 < r2)
                return r1;
        else
                return r2;
}
```

Answer: The first version of test() returns the pointer to the parameter with the smaller value, while the second returns the reference. In the first call we have p1 = &a, so *p1 = a = 1.2. Similarly, p2 = &b, so *p2 = b = 3.4. Therefore, test() returns the p1 pointer. Since test() returns the pointer to a, the statement *test(&a, &b) = 5.6; makes a equal to 5.6 and the program displays: 5.6 3.4

In the second call of test(), since r1 = a = 5.6 and r2 = b = 3.4, test() returns a reference to r2. Since test() returns a reference to b, b becomes equal to 7.8 and the program displays: 5.6 7.8.

C.16.5 Write a function template that takes as parameters three numeric values of the same generic type and returns the value of the pair with the largest sum. For example, if the values are 3, 1, 2 the function should return 5. Overload the function with another function template with a void return type, which takes as parameter an array of generic type and returns the maximum and the minimum value of the array through reference parameters of generic type. Write a program that verifies the operation of the two functions.

```
#include <iostream>

const int SIZE = 5;

template <typename T> T find(T a, T b, T c);
template <typename T> void find(T arr[], T& min, T& max);

int main()
{
        int i = 3, j = 1, k = 2;
        double m, n, a[SIZE] = {5.1, 1.1, 2.1, 3.1, 4.1};

        std::cout << "Sum:" << find(i, j, k) << '\n';
        find(a, m, n);
        std::cout << "Min:" << m << " Max:" << n << '\n';
        return 0;
}

template <typename T> T find(T a, T b, T c)
{
        T max;

        max = a+b;
        if(max < a+c)
                max = a+c;
```

```
        if(max < b+c)
                max = b+c;
        return max;
}


template <typename T> void find(T arr[], T& min, T& max)
{
        int i;

        min = max = arr[0];
        for(i = 1; i < SIZE; i++)
        {
                if(arr[i] < min)
                        min = arr[i];
                if(arr[i] > max)
                        max = arr[i];
        }
}
```

C.16.6 Write a function template that takes as parameter a `vector` object with numbers of generic type and returns their average. Overload the function with another function template with a `void` return type, which takes two numeric parameters that may have different types and returns their average through a pointer parameter. Write a program that verifies the operation of the two functions.

```
#include <iostream>
#include <vector>
using std::cout;
using std::vector;

template <typename T> double avg(const vector<T>& v);
template <typename T1, typename T2> void avg(T1 t1, T2 t2, double* p);

int main()
{
        double i;
        vector<int> v = {1, 2, 4};

        avg(1, 2, &i);
        std::cout << "Avg_1:" << avg(v) << '\n';
        std::cout << "Avg_2:" << i << '\n';
        return 0;
}

template <typename T> double avg(const vector<T>& v)
{
        T sum;
        int i, size;

        size = v.size();
        sum = 0;
        for(i = 0; i < size; i++)
                sum += v[i];
        return (double)sum/size;
}
```

```
template <typename T1, typename T2> void avg(T1 t1, T2 t2, double* p)
{
        *p = (t1+t2)/2.0;
}
```

UNSOLVED EXERCISES

U.16.1 Define the `f()` and `g()` functions so that the following program displays `10` and `10`. The only change you are allowed to make in `main()` is in the `f()` and `g()` calls, in order to pass the appropriate arguments.

```
#include <iostream>

??? f(???) // Fill the prototype and the body of the function.
{
        ???
}

??? g(???) // Fill the prototype and the body of the function.
{
        ???
}

int main()
{
        int i = 1, j = 2;

        f() = g() = 10; // Change the way f() and g() are called.
        std::cout << i << ' ' << j << '\n';
        return 0;
}
```

U.16.2 Change the `bubble_sort()` function of C.12.10 to a function template that takes as parameter a `vector` object which contains either numeric elements of generic type or `string` elements and sorts it. Write a program that verifies the operation of the function.

U.16.3 Write a function that takes as parameters two references to `string` objects and a character and returns the string that this character appears most times. Use appropriate return values to handle the cases if it is not contained in either string or it appears the same most times. It is allowed to add one more parameter to the function. Write a program that verifies the operation of the function. The program should display the string that contains the character most times, the number of its appearances and proper messages in case it is not contained or it is contained the same times. For example:

    a. If the strings are `alpha`, `beta`, and we are looking for `a`, the program should display `alpha` and `2`.

    b. If the strings are `alpha`, `betaa`, and we are looking for `a`, the program should display `Same times` and `2`.

    c. If the strings are `alpha`, `betaa`, and we are looking for `c`, the program should display `Not found`.

U.16.4 Write a function template that takes as parameter a `vector` object which contains either numeric elements of generic type or `string` elements and returns the largest. Overload the function with another function template, which takes as parameters two pointers to the same generic numeric type and returns the pointer to the larger value. Write a program that verifies the operation of the two functions.

U.16.5 Write a function template that takes as parameters two references to the same generic numeric type, swaps their values, and returns the reference to the larger value. Overload the function with another function template, which accepts as parameters two arrays of the same size and the same generic numeric type and swaps their elements. Write a program that verifies the operation of the two functions.

Classes and Objects

17

Object-oriented programming introduces new concepts and a different philosophy in program design and development. The most important addition is the concept of class. In fact, the original name of C++ was "C with classes". Essentially, as the name indicates, object-oriented programming involves the use of classes and objects. Key features of object-oriented programming such as data encapsulation, data hiding, and inheritance are based on classes. In this chapter we'll learn how to define classes and create objects and see how the concept of class supports the data encapsulation and data hiding. We'll also discuss constructors and destructors, friend and constant functions, and the `this` pointer.

CLASSES AND OBJECTS

The class type is similar to the structure type. Like a structure, a class is a user-defined type that is used to define the characteristics and operations of an abstract entity. The class enables the programmer to represent real-world entities in a more natural way. A class contains a set of data values that describes the entity according to our needs and can also contain a set of functions that operate on them. This packaging of data values and functions within the class is referred to as *data encapsulation*.

The class is the key building block to represent a concept in a program. For example, to represent a phone call we could define a class that contains related information, such as the calling number, called number, call duration, as well as call establishment, call release, and billing functions. In general, we decide what a class should contain in the context in which we intend to use the class. Since the class translates an abstraction to a user-defined type, the program becomes more descriptive, more elegant, as well as easier to read, write, use, and be maintained. The general syntax for a class declaration is:

```
class class_name
{
        Accessibility: Declarations;
        ...
        Accessibility: Declarations;
};
```

Similar to a named structure, once a class is declared, we can declare variables of this type. These variables are called *objects* or *instances* of the class and they are created based on the specifications set by the class. Each object is a substance of a specific class and the information it contains is stored in its members. The class simply describes the entity; it is a general concept that does not refer to a specific object.

To make it clear, the declaration of a class, like the declaration of a structure, does not create an object. For example, a particular `car` model is an object of the class that describes the `car` entity. We can create and manipulate as many `car` objects as we need in a program, and each of them would have its own properties. In general, we can use classes to model whatever kinds of real-world entities we want and write programs based on them. That's the heart of object-oriented programming.

As with structures, we can pass an object to a function, define a function to return an object, and assign an object to another of the same class. For example, the following program declares the `Student` class,

DOI: 10.1201/9781003230076-17

reads the data of a student, saves it to the corresponding members of an object, and displays it on the screen. The typical practice is to put the class declaration in a header file, which usually is named the same as the name of the class. The implementation of the member functions is placed in one or more code files that make `#include` the header file. Separating the class declaration from the implementation makes the code easier to read and maintain. Let's see the two files:

```cpp
// student.h
#ifndef STUDENT_H
#define STUDENT_H

#include <string>

class Student
{
private:
        int code;
public:
        std::string name;
        float grd;

        void set(int c) {code = c;}
        void show();
};

#endif
```

and then include that file in the source file.

```cpp
// student.cpp
#include <iostream> // Example 17.1
#include "student.h"
using std::cin;
using std::cout;

void Student::show()
{
        cout << "N:" << name << " C:" << code << " G:" << grd << '\n';
}

int main()
{
        int code;
        class Student s; /* s is an object of the class Student. It is not
necessary to add the word class. */

        cout << "Name: ";
        getline(cin, s.name);

        cout << "Grade: ";
        cin >> s.grd;

        cout << "Code: ";
        cin >> code;
        s.set(code);
        s.show();
        return 0;
}
```

For simplicity and to save space, I'll put everything in one file; however, there we'll be some examples to put the class declaration and implementation in different files, as in this example. In order to distinguish a class name from the ordinary names, many programmers, me too, prefer to capitalize the first letter. When an object is declared, the word `class` is not needed, because a class name is a type name by itself. For example, the name `Student` is the name of a new type defined by the user, that is, you (or else the programmer).

A class can also contain objects of other classes that either we or other programmers have created. For example, the `name` field is an object of the `string` library class. So, we are users of the `string` class and we have access, as we'll see in the next section, to the section that the developers of the `string` class decided to make public. By the way, could we use something else instead of a `string` object to store the name? Of course, for example, we could use an array of characters. However, this option sets a limit on the length of the name that can be stored. If we make the array too large, we'd have a waste of memory. Thus, it'd be better to use a `char*` pointer and allocate the exact memory needed to store the name. However, we'll see in examples in later chapters (e.g., C.18.2) that this choice requires effort as code must be added to securely support certain operations. Therefore, it is more convenient, flexible, and safer to use a `string` object and take advantage of the many capabilities offered by this class.

Member Functions

Functions that belong to a class are called member functions. A member function can be defined inside or outside the class. If they are defined inside the class, the declaration of the class may become very large and make it harder for the reader to read it and discriminate its sections and members. To become easier to read the class and get quickly an idea about its functionality, functions are typically defined outside the class in separate source file(s). Actually, this separation makes clear what the class does (function declarations) from how it does it (function definitions). As with structures, to access the members of an object we use the dot (.) and -> operators. That is, we access the functions in the same way as the ordinary data members.

If the function is too short, the common practice is to define it inside the class. Although in our example the code of `show()` is short, I placed its definition outside the class to see how it is defined. Because different classes can have functions with the same name, to define it we use the scope resolution operator `::` and the name of the class to which it belongs. Thus, the compiler knows to which class each function belongs and can compile the code. The `set()` sets the value of the `code` of the object that calls the function (i.e., `s`), while the `show()` displays the values of its fields.

Any function defined inside the class is considered inline. Thus, it is not needed to add the word `inline` to its definition. For example, `set()` is inline. However, as discussed in Chapter 16, it does not necessarily mean that it will be implemented as inline; it's up to the compiler. In general, the common practice is to define inside the class only tiny functions. In the following examples, I'll declare some functions inline and some not, so that you get used to both forms. Note that a function defined outside the class can also be inline by adding the `inline` qualifier to its definition. For example:

```
inline void Student::show()
```

Every time an object is created, the compiler allocates memory for its variables. For example, if we declare the s1 and s2 objects, the memory reserved for s1.grd and s2.grd is different. On contrary, the memory allocated for the functions is the same. For example, the code of show() is stored only in one place, no copies are created every time a new object is declared; and this makes sense, since the code of the functions is the same for all objects. Thus, the statements s1.show() and s2.show() execute the same code and that code is applied to the data of the object that makes the call.

Class Scope

Each class defines within the {} its own scope. The scope of the class members is limited within the class. Therefore, the same names can be used in other classes. For example, a class C may contain its own show():

```
int C::show()
```

Because a member name is not visible outside the class we must use the class name. Using the class name and the scope operator :: the definition of each show() is associated with the corresponding class. When a function is called, the member names refer to the object that called the function. For example, when show() is called, the values of the members of the object that called show() are displayed.

A class member has class scope, that is, it extends from the opening {to the end} of the class declaration. Therefore, a member may refer to another member regardless of the point of its declaration. The rule that a name must be declared before it is used does not apply within the scope of the class. For example:

```
class A
{
public:
        void set(int c) {code = c;}
private:
        int code;
};
```

To know what happens, the compiler first processes all the declarations of the data members (e.g., code) and then the definitions of the functions. This is logical because if the definitions were to be processed in parallel with the members' declarations, the functions would have to be defined in such an order that they refer to members that have already been declared. Because this would make very difficult the design of the class, the compiler first processes all member declarations so that they are visible when the functions are compiled.

The name of the class cannot be reused to declare members. As we'll see next, the exception to this rule is to declare a constructor. For example:

```
class A
{
        A(); // Constructor, that's fine.
        int A(int); // Wrong.
        double A; // Wrong.
};
```

Access Control

It's time to discuss about class accessibility and access specifiers. The members of a class can be public, private, or protected. Private members are accessible only from functions of the same class. They are not allowed to be accessed directly by any function or object outside the class. For example, it is not allowed to write s.code = 1. Instead, the statement code = c; in set() is allowed, because a member function is allowed to access private members. In fact, a member function can access any other member of the same class, regardless of the access specifier, by just using its name. As for the public members, there is no restriction in accessing them, which means that they are accessible from anywhere inside or outside the class. The protected members behave like the private members with the difference that they can be accessed by functions of derived classes, as we'll see in Chapter 20.

The members of a class are private by default. That is, if the word `private` was missing in our example before declaring the `code`, the `code` would be private again. Although unnecessary, my preference is to add it, to make clear the intention to declare specific variables as private. So, we see that a class not only allows the representation of a logical entity by encapsulating data in a type (*data encapsulation*), but it also provides the ability to the programmer to specify which data will be accessible from the external environment and which to be hidden from direct access. This later ability is called *data hiding*. As we'll see later data hiding is very important to ensure the integrity of the object. By saying external environment, I mean the users of the class, that is, programmers who use it in their programs. For example, in the following program, assume that you wrote the `Test` class and gave it to another programmer who uses it to create `Test` objects. Find the errors:

```cpp
#include <iostream> // Example 17.2

class Test
{
private: /* Since the members of a class are private by default, we can omit
the word private. */
        int a;
        void f1();
protected:
        int b;
        void f2();
public:
        int c;
        void f3();
};

void Test::f1()
{
        std::cout << a << ' ' << b << ' ' << c << ' ' << '\n';
}

void Test::f2()
{
        a = 100;
}

void Test::f3()
{
        f1();
}

int main()
{
        Test t;

        t.a = 1;
        t.b = 2;
        t.c = 3;

        t.f1();
        t.f2();
        t.f3();
        return 0;
}
```

Since the a and f1() members have been declared as `private`, it is not allowed to access them from outside the class. Therefore, the statements t.a = 1; and t.f1(); are wrong. The same applies for the `protected` members. Therefore, the statements t.b = 2; and t.f2(); are wrong. Since the access to the `public` members is allowed, the statements t.c = 2; and t.f3(); are acceptable. Finally, since the functions of a class can access its members, the code of f1(), f2(), and f3() is compiled successfully. To put it in another way, f1() can be used directly by the programmer who wrote the class, but not by the programmer who uses the class. So, we remember that access to private and protected members is allowed through functions that are class members and, as we'll see later, through friend functions.

A class may not contain an access specifier, in which case, all members are private by default. Also, specifiers can be used multiple times within the class and in any order. The specified access remains valid until the next specifier or the end of class appears. For example:

```
class A
{
private:
        int a;
public:
        int b;
private:
        int c;
        void f();
};
```

For the better understanding and organization of the class it'd be better not to have repetitive sections. Regarding the order of the sections, when I want to give emphasis to the members that the user of the class has access to, I place the `public` section first. Otherwise, I put `private` first. Typically, the `public` section is put first, because it is the part that interests mostly the user of the class to look at.

Class Design

When we design a class, we declare the members that we do not want to be directly accessible as private (e.g., functions related to the implementation of the class), while we declare the members that we've decided to constitute the interface with the external environment as public. Essentially, the user of a class communicates with the class through its public members. We have already encountered the example C.10.10, whereas users of the `string` class we used public functions (e.g., `size()`) to handle it. We did the same in example C.7.5 to manage the `vector` class.

As another example, in one of my applications, I had implemented the `Protocol` class that simulated the operation of a network protocol. When I finished, I passed it on to another team of developers at the company, which was implementing an application that would use this class to send data in an encrypted form. To communicate with the class, I had placed the `Init()`, `Stop()`, and `Send_Data()` functions in the public section. However, the `Operation()` function and other data (e.g., candidate algorithms for data encryption) that were related to the implementation of the protocol and I wanted to hide them from the users of the class, both for security against mishandling and because there is no reason to publish implementation details, I had placed them in the private section. Data hiding prevents their accidental manipulation and ensures the integrity of the class data and its proper operation. If an error occurs that changes the state of the class data, this error is due to the implementation of the class and not to the way the class is used. Thus, the error search is limited to the class code, resulting in its faster detection.

In principle, the basic idea in the design of a class is to separate the part related to the implementation of the class from the part related to the implementation of its interface with the outside world.

Besides safety, another reason for this separation is that any changes in the implementation of the class (e.g., change the code of Operation()) do not affect the way the class communicates (e.g., not needed to change the code of Init()). We just compile the new class code and link it again to the application. In fact, this should happen, any internal changes do not concern the users of the class, nor of course should they be forced to change their code, that is, they must continue to communicate with the class in the same way they used to communicate. The interface to the outside world should remain the same, as if nothing has changed at all. What should really care the user is the class to operate according to its specification, to be reliable; the task of the user is to learn the services it provides and how to use them through the public interface. For example, are you going to use the string class? Read about it, get familiar with its public members and functions, and learn how to use them. You don't have to worry about the implementation details of the class.

Now that we've discussed about classes we can more easily understand the difference between the object-oriented programming philosophy and the procedural programming. Let's look at the difference with C. C does not support the concept of the class, the closest concept is the structure. However, a C structure is not allowed to contain functions. Therefore, the programmer must define external functions, as in several examples of Chapter 14, in order to manipulate its data. Thus, the functions are scattered in the program and do not form a single unit that we can easily understand and control. Also, the user of the structure has direct access to all of its data, since C does not support the concept of data hiding. In contrast, in C++, the class encapsulates data and functions that handle this data in the same type. Thus, a class unifies the description of an abstract entity and represents it more accurately.

To understand better the difference between the two approaches, consider the C.14.10 program. As you see, several global variables and functions that anyone may use are defined to support the functionality of the list. This program is an example of procedural programming. The emphasis is put on the definition of functions to process the data. In the object-oriented approach, the emphasis is put on the definition of a class type to process the data. For example, we may define the List type to represent the list and put inside there all these variables and functions to manage it. Now, the code becomes more representative, as well as easier to read, write, and be maintained.

```
class List
{
        ...
        Node *head;
        Node *tail;

        void add_list_end(const Node *p);
        void add_list(const Node *p, int code);
        void show_list();
        ...
};
```

The list data are encapsulated inside the List type and it is the programmer's responsibility to specify the access to them.

To sum up, in the public section we place the functions that the user of the class can use in order to communicate with the class, while in the private/protected section the functions that implement the functionality of the class. In other words, to use a class, you need to know its public interface; when writing a class, you need to specify its public interface. Members that are not declared as public should be private or protected. As we'll see in Chapter 20, the decision to make a member protected depends on whether we want to allow direct access to it from within a derived class. If we do, we make it protected; otherwise we make it private. We'll see some simple examples of class design in this book's exercises. I really think that the ability of data encapsulation and data hiding in the same type was a great idea, a very important feature of C++ and object-oriented programming in general.

Wait a minute; we're not done yet. I do not want to create the false impression that the class design is a quite easy task, just decide about the operations you want to support, choose the private, protected and public members and you are done. Even this choice is a difficult decision. For example, wouldn't be safer and easier in order to control the access to have no public members at all and to have only `set()`/`get()` public functions to access the class data? Much worse, think about class creators. When providing a class to the outside world (e.g., `string`) they must have ensured that the public part of the class, as well as the protected in the case of a derived class, is functional and won't change over and over. Any changes the developer of the class makes to the class design should be related to the implementation code, not to the public interface. Imagine the case that programmers who already use the class to be forced to change their code often because in a new version of the class the declarations of the public functions changed or some public members were removed. This is unacceptable.

Also, when designing a class, besides its operations, you have to decide on many of its features, such as what would be the valid values of its members (e.g., in a `Time` class, the valid range for the `hour` member is `0-24`), if the class would overload operators, if it'd be used as a base class, if it'd contain virtual functions, if it'd use the default functions or others you specify, if it'd allow conversion from/to another type, and many more "ifs". Who said the class design is an easy job?

Structures/Unions and Classes

The concept of structure and how to use structure variables is very similar to the class and objects. Indeed, the difference is that the members of a class are private by default, while the members of a structure are public by default. A similar difference, as we'll see in Chapter 19, is that a derived class inherits a base class with private access by default, while a derived structure with public access. Since there is no fundamental difference between them, someone might ask, couldn't we have one single type, `struct` or `class`, and just change the default access if needed? Why have both? Reasonable to wonder, I'm not sure about the answer. I imagine that in the beginning, because the `struct` type pre-existed in C and because object-oriented features were new programming concepts that had not yet spread, Stroustrup would like to introduce a new type in C++ with focus on object-oriented operations. Then, it was decided that the `struct` type would also support object-oriented operations.

The common practice is to use a class when both variables and functions are needed to represent an entity, while the structure is used when only variables are required. Also, if the members are public only, the structure is usually chosen, while if there are private members as well, the class is chosen.

Regarding unions, the union is a special case of the class, whereas we know from Chapter 13, only one of its members has a valid value. As with the structure, the members of a union are public by default. A union supports the properties of the class, but not all. For example, a union may contain `public`, `private`, and `protected` sections. It can also contain member functions including constructors and destructors. However, a union cannot be used as a base class, nor can it inherit another class. Therefore, it cannot contain virtual functions.

`const` Member Functions

In our first example C.17.1, the `show()` function can change the values of the object that calls it. For example, if we add the following statement to its definition:

```
void Student::show()
{
      grd = 2;
      ...
}
```

and write s.show(); the value of grd of the s object becomes 2. If we don't want a function to be able to change the values of the invoking object we add the const keyword at the end of its declaration. The const keyword must also be added in its definition. For example, the declaration of the show() becomes:

```
void show() const; and its definition:
```

```
void Student::show() const
{
        grd = 2; // Wrong.
}
```

If show() attempts to change the value of a member, such as grd, the compiler will display an error message for illegal action.

 For better control of the class operation, it'd be better to declare functions that do not change the values of its members as const.

From inside a const function we can call another const member function, but it is an error to call a non-const function. And this makes sense because the non-const function may modify the object, which removes the applied constness. For example:

```
void Student::show() const
{
        set(5); // Wrong.
}
```

Now, suppose that we add the following member function:

```
float& Student::get() const {return grd;} // Wrong.
```

Is it correct? No, the compiler will not let you do that. You cannot return a plain reference or pointer to a class member. Within a const function, every data member becomes const so that it cannot be modified. Therefore, the reference must be const:

```
const float& Student::get() const {return grd;} // Fine.
```

For example, if you were allowed to return a non-const reference, then you could violate the constness of a const object, that is, to alter an object that must not be modified. For example, to write something like this:

```
const Student s;
s.get() = 10; // The value of s.grd becomes 10.
```

Therefore, the compiler in order to preserve the constness does not allow us to return non-const references to member variables from const functions.

const **Objects**

An object can be declared as const. For example, consider the following program:

```cpp
#include <iostream> // Example 17.3

class Student
{
private:
        int code;
        mutable float grd;
public:
        Student(int c) {code = c;}
        int courses;
        int get_code() {return code;}
        void set_grd(float g) const {grd = g;}
        void show() const {std::cout << grd << '\n';}
};

int main()
{
        const Student s(100);

//      s.get_code(); Wrong. The function must be declared const.
/*      s.courses = 10; Wrong. Assignment is not allowed, the member is read-
only. */
        s.set_grd(5); // OK.
        s.show(); // OK.
        return 0;
}
```

s is a const object, which means that it is not allowed to change the members of s. That is, all member variables of s become const variables. Therefore, we can only call const functions, since they don't permit any change in the values of the members. Calling a non-const function causes a compilation error. If we want to be able to change the value of a member we use the mutable keyword.

As you can see, although set_grd() is declared as const, it can change the value of grd. Note that if show() was not declared as const the compiler would display an error message due to calling a non-const function. If you wonder why the constructor can change the value of the code, the answer is that the object actually becomes const once the constructor completes its construction. Thus, a constructor, we'll discuss about that shortly, is allowed to set values in the members of a const object.

Objects that are const, as well as references or pointers to const objects can only call const member functions.

Friend Functions

As we've learned, a member function can access private members of a class. Is there a way for a non-member function to have access to private members? Yes, provided that it is declared as a friend to the class. In short, a friend function is a non-member function that can access the members of a class regardless of the point of their declaration. That is, a friend function has the same access rights as a member function of the class. To make a function friend it must be declared in the class with the prefix friend. The place does not matter, it can be declared in the private, protected, or public section; the section does not affect its accessibility. But do not forget that, although it is declared in the class, it is not a member of the class.

When defined, because it is not a member of the class, the scope resolution operator :: and the class name are not added. When it comes to declare friend functions, it is a common practice to group them at the beginning or end of the class (I prefer the end) to stand out. Let's look at the following program:

```cpp
#include <iostream> // Example 17.4

class T
{
private:
        int a;
public:
        void show() {std::cout << a << '\n';}
        friend void f(T& t);
};

void f(T& t) // The friend keyword is not added in the definition.
{
        t.a = 10; // It is an error to write a = 10;
}

int main()
{
        T t;

        f(t);
        t.show();
        return 0;
}
```

Since a friend function is not a member of the class we don't add the T:: in the definition of f(). To make it clearer, had we declared the object t1 and write t1.f(t), the compiler would display an error message similar to *f is not a member of T.* For the same reason, because f() is not a member of T we cannot access its members by just using their names. Notice that the `friend` keyword is not added to its definition, unless it is defined inside the class. As we said, although f() is not a member function it has the same access rights as a member function. Thus, it is allowed to access the private member a and the program displays 10.

A friend function can be a global function as in this example or it can be a member of another class. One may ask, is it necessary to declare f() as friend, can't we declare it as an ordinary function outside the class? Of course we can, but since a is private it is not allowed to access it. So, we need to add a public function to the class, which when called to change the value of a. For example:

```cpp
class T
{
...
public:
...
        void set(int i) {a = i;}
};

void f(T& t)
{
        t.set(10);
}
```

To avoid this detour, it is more convenient and simple to make f() friend. Yes, it is simpler, but why not making f() a member of the class at the first place? Yes, we could, this program is just an example to see the properties of a friend function, it has no other practical value. And when a friend function is used?

The most common use is when we want to define a function that accepts as arguments objects of different classes and acts on their private data. We declare the function as friend to each class, so it acts as a link between the classes. Exercise C.17.4 is such an example. Also, we'll see examples in Chapter 18 where friend functions can be useful when overloading operators. Also, we'll see in Chapter 19 that a function which is a member of one class or even the whole class can be friend to another class.

One last thing to say. A function template can also be friend to an ordinary class. In this case, all instantiations of the function template become friends of the class. For example:

```cpp
#include <iostream>

class A
{
private:
        int p;
public:
        A() {p = 20;}
        template <typename T> friend void f(A& a);
};

template <typename T> void f(A& a)
{
        std::cout << a.p;
        a.p += 30;
}

int main()
{
        A a;

        f<int>(a);
        f<double>(a);
        return 0;
}
```

Since the f function template is declared as a friend of the A class, every instance of it is a friend of the A class. Here, we have two f instances and the program outputs first 20 and then 50.

Now that we've discussed friend functions, let's summarize the rules that apply to access class members so that you can find them in one place:

    a. The private members are accessible only by class member functions and friend functions of the class.

    b. The protected members are accessible only by the member functions of the class and its friend functions, as well as by the member functions and the friend functions of the derived classes.

    c. The public members are accessible by any function inside or outside the class.

CONSTRUCTORS AND DESTRUCTORS

A class constructor and destructor are special member functions. In particular:

    a. Whenever an object is created, one of the constructors of the class is invoked.

    b. Whenever an object is destroyed, the destructor of the class is invoked.

Let's discuss about them.

Constructor

The constructor is a special function of the class, which is called whenever an object of this class is created. The declaration of a constructor must follow some rules. In particular, it must have the same name as the class name, it has no return type, it is not allowed to be declared as `const`, it can accept parameters, and it can be overloaded, that is, a class can have many constructors. As with ordinary overloaded functions, the different versions of the constructors must differ in the number or type of their parameters.

Typically, a constructor is used to assign initial values to the members of the object or to allocate memory. For example, in the C.17.1 example, because direct access to the `code` member is not allowed, we cannot write something like this:

```
Student s = {100, "Name", 5.5};
```

Of course, if all members were declared `public`, this declaration would be acceptable, but I refer to the general case where a class contains private members, since data hiding is the main reason for using a class. The `code` is initialized after the creation of s by calling a public member function, such as `set()`. Note that if a member variable of either a basic type (e.g., `int`) or pointer (e.g., `int*`) is not initialized, it will have an arbitrary junk value.

If we want to initialize the members of an object when it is declared we can use the constructor to do it. In fact, this is my preference, that is, I prefer to define a constructor and initialize the members there rather than calling some initialization function, such as `set()`, after the creation of the object. Not only it is more convenient, but it is also safer, especially when creating multiple objects, since we may forget to initialize some of them. When the constructor is used to assign the initial values there is no reason to worry about that.

By the way, this kind of functions (e.g., `set()`) that allow member values to be set from outside the class and respective functions that return their values are often referred to as *setters* and *getters*, respectively.

Note that if a class A contains a member which is an object of another class (e.g., `string name`), its constructor is called first to create the member and then the construction of the A object is completed. Exercise C.17.3 is such an example.

And if something goes wrong with the constructor, how can we handle such a situation? For example:

```
Test::Test(int size)
{
        ...
        p = new int[size];
}
```

What if a negative value is passed to `size`? What we certainly cannot do is to return a special value that indicates the error, because, as we said, a constructor does not return a value. As we'll see in Chapter 22, an easy way is to create an exception that informs the programmer about that error. For example, we can add something like this:

```
if(size < 0)
        throw Negative_Size();
```

Destructor

A class may contain another special function, which is called destructor. The destructor is called automatically when an object of this class is destroyed (e.g., when it goes out of scope) to deal with any cleanup that may be necessary. It must have the same name as the class name preceded by a tilde ~, it has no return type, it does not take parameters, and therefore, it cannot be overloaded. That is, a class can have only one destructor. The ~ complement operator may have been chosen as the symbol for the destructor to imply that the destructor "complements" the constructor.

The reason to define a destructor is when we want to do something when an object is destroyed. If nothing has to be done, then the *default* destructor, as we'll see later, is sufficient. For example, the destructor is typically used to release the memory that the object may have dynamically allocated. We'll see such an example shortly. For now, can you tell me what does the following program output?

```cpp
#include <iostream> // Example 17.5

class Test
{
public:
        int a, b;

        Test();
        Test(int i, int j);
        ~Test();
        void check();
};

Test::Test()
{
        std::cout << "First\n";
}

Test::Test(int i, int j)
{
        std::cout << "Second\n";
        a = i;
        b = j;
}

Test::~Test()
{
        std::cout << "Out\n";
}

void Test::check()
{
        Test t;
}

int main()
{
        Test t1, t2(5, 10);

        std::cout << t1.a << ' ' << t1.b << '\n';
        std::cout << t2.a << ' ' << t2.b << '\n';
        t1.check();
        return 0;
}
```

As we said, the constructor and the destructor do not have a return type. Because there are two overloaded constructors, the compiler selects the appropriate one depending on how each object is created. As we'll see next, a constructor that does not accept any parameters is called a *default* constructor. When the t1 object is created the first constructor is called and the program displays First. The variables a and b of t1 are initialized with garbage values. In fact, it was my intention not to initialize them in order to see that they have garbage values; don't forget to initialize data members otherwise unexpected problems may occur when you use them.

Constructors follow the same overload rules as ordinary functions. The compiler checks the types of arguments to select the appropriate one. Therefore, when t2 is created, the second constructor is called, the values 5 and 10 are passed, and the program displays Second. Then, the program displays the garbage values of a and b of the t1 object and the values 5 and 10 for the respective ones of t2. When check() is called, the t object is created and the first constructor is called. Then, check() terminates and t ceases to exist. Therefore, the destructor of t is automatically called, which displays the message Out.

When the program ends, the destructors of t1 and t2 are called and the program displays Out two more times. Let's see in what order the destructors are called. Because the memory for the variables t1 and t2 is reserved in the stack, the last object created is the first to be destroyed. So, the destructor of t2 will be called first and then that of t1. If we have an array of objects, for example, Test t[10]; the destruction order will be from the last one to the first, that is, t[9]…t[0].

The non-static members of the class are automatically destroyed once the destructor is executed. If a member has a class type, the corresponding destructor for that class will be called. For example, in the C.17.1 example, the destructor of the string class will be called to free the memory reserved for the name member once the s object is destroyed.

Calling the Constructor

First of all, we cannot use an object to call a constructor, as we call a function of the class (e.g., t1.check()), because the object has not yet been created. The constructor is used to create the object. If we want to pass values, the most common way is as we did with the t2 object. We can also call directly the constructor like this:

```
Test t2 = Test(5, 10);
```

t2.a becomes 5 and t2.b becomes 10.

Since C++11 we can use the braces {} to pass the initial values to the constructor. For example:
```
Test t2{5, 10};
```
As we said in Chapter 2 this method is preferable, since the compiler can inform us about incompatible values.

Note that the dynamic creation of an object with the new operator also invokes the constructor. For example:

```
Test *p = new Test(5, 10);
```

In this case, the *p represents the object and the p pointer can be used to manage the object. In general, an initialization statement such as:

```
class_name *p = new class_name(value);
```

invokes the constructor class_name(type_name), where the type_name is the type of the value. To be more precise, as we said in Chapter 14, it first triggers the call of the operator new function to allocate memory for the object, and then invoke the constructor. When we use the delete operator to destroy the object (e.g., delete p) first its destructor will be invoked, and then the memory used for the object will be released.

Similarly, a statement such as:

```
class_name *p = new class_name;
```

invokes the default constructor, that we'll see next. For example:

```
Test *p = new Test;
```

Here is a special case. If a constructor accepts a single argument, it is allowed to initialize an object with a value of the same type as the argument. For example, if the following constructor is defined in class A:

```
A(int v); it is allowed to write: A  a = 20;
```

Such an initialization invokes the constructor. Notice that this feature can cause problems, but it can be disabled, as we'll discuss in Chapter 19.

Calling the Destructor

As we said, the destructor is called automatically when the object goes out of scope or destroyed with the `delete` operator. Consider the following class:

```
class T
{
public:
        T() {};
        ~T() {};
};
```

The question is, can we explicitly call the destructor, that is, can we write something similar to:

```
T t;
t.~T();
```

The answer is yes; we can call it directly, but do not do it, as unexpected errors may occur. You do not need to call the destructor, it will be called automatically. However, I just mention it without further analysis, there may be some special cases where the destructor should be explicitly called.

Another possible question might be, can the destructor be private? Yes, but check the following program:

```
#include <iostream> // Example 17.6

class T
{
private:
        ~T() {std::cout << "Out\n";}
public:
        void end() {delete this;} // The object is destroyed.
        T() {}
};
```

```
int main()
{
        T t; // Wrong.
        T *p;

        p = new T;
        delete p; // Wrong.
        p->end();
        return 0;
}
```

Because the destructor is private, the compiler will display an error message for unauthorized access to a private member when using `delete`. The same error occurs when declaring `t`. If for some reason you want to specify when the object will be destroyed, you can make the destructor private, use a pointer to create the object (e.g., `p`), define a function (e.g., `end()`), and call that function whenever you want (e.g., `p->end()`), in order to release the memory and destroy the object. For example, if you remove the two wrong statements and run the program, it outputs `Out`. The `this` pointer refers to the object itself, we'll discuss that shortly.

Default Constructor and Destructor

The existence of a constructor is essential for the creation of objects. But then, one might ask, how were `Student` objects created in our first example, since no constructor is defined? The answer is that if a class does not contain any constructor, then the compiler automatically provides the default constructor, which has no body. Without this constructor, we would not be able to create `Student` objects. Each time a `Student` object is declared, the compiler calls the default constructor to create the object. The default constructor does not initialize members of basic types (e.g., `int`). It also calls the default constructors of the respective classes for members that are objects. Similarly, if the destructor is not defined, the compiler provides the default destructor, which has no body. For example, the default constructor and destructor for the `Student` class are:

```
Student::Student() {}   and   Student::~Student() {}
```

As you see, both of them take no arguments and do nothing.

 The compiler automatically provides the default constructor only if no other constructor is defined.

For example, if you define the constructor `Student(const string& n, int c, float g);` it is your responsibility to define your own version of the default constructor, if you need it. If you don't, then a declaration such as:

```
Student s;
```

is unacceptable and the compiler will display an error message similar to *No default constructor available*. If you write:

```
Student s("P.Lew", 100, 5.5);
```

there is no problem, since the defined constructor will be called. In addition to the default constructor that does not accept parameters, a constructor with predefined values in all of its arguments is also considered a default constructor. For example:

```
Student(const string& n = "No name", int c = 0, float g = 0);
```

Now, the `Student s;` declaration is acceptable. Note that if you specify such a constructor, it is not allowed to define the default (e.g., `Student()`). Because both can be called without arguments, the `Student s;` declaration would produce a compilation error for ambiguity, since the compiler couldn't determine which of the two to call. To sum up, to create a default constructor, we can use no arguments or default values for all arguments.

As another example of the default constructor, consider the following class:

```
class A
{
private:
        int x, v;
public:
        A(int i, int j = 0) {};
        ...
};
```

See now which declarations are accepted:

```
A a; // Wrong, there is no default constructor.
A a(1, 2); // OK.
A a(1); // OK, the default value of j is used.
```

The default constructor can also be useful when a member of the class is object. For example:

```
class C // Example 17.7
{
public:
        int p;
public:
        C() {};
        C(int m) {p = m;}
        ...
};

class B
{
public:
        C c;
        ...
};

int main()
{
        B b;
        ...
}
```

For the construction of the b object the default constructor of class B is called and for the construction of the c object the default constructor of class C is called. If it was missing, the compiler would display an error message, as it could not construct the c object.

Note that we can also use the C++11 syntax to initialize a member that is object. For example, let's change the declaration of the c object:

```
class B
{
public:
        C c{10}; /* We can also write C c = {10}; Notice that it is not
allowed to use parentheses, that is, it is illegal to write C c(10). */
        . . .
};
```

To create the c object the second constructor will be called, the value 10 is passed, so the value of b.c.p becomes 10.

C++11 supports the assignment of initial values to the members of a class. For example:

```
class A
{
private:
        int x = 10, v = 20; // Initial values.
public:
        A() {};
        A(int i) {x=i;}
        A(int i, int j) {x=i; v=j;}
        . . .
};

A a; // a.x is 10 and a.v is 20.
A a(1); // a.x is 1 and a.v is 20.
A a(1, 2); // a.x is 1 and a.v is 2.
```

When the default constructor is used to create an object of class A, its members are initialized to the specified values, that is, 10 and 20.

Non-Public Constructors

In the question, can a constructor be private, the answer is yes. For example, we can have many public constructors, which all call a private constructor that undertakes to create the object. We'll see that technique with the delegating constructor in Chapter 19. One reason to use a private constructor is when we don't want to expose it to the outside world.

In the similar question, can a constructor be protected, the answer is again yes. For example, in inheritance, a constructor can be declared as protected in the base class in order to prevent the direct creation of base class objects and allow only derived classes to use it. For example, as we'll see in Chapter 20, we can write:

```
class A
{
protected:
        A() {}
};
class B : public A
{
public:
        B() : A() {}
};

A a; // Error.
B b; // OK.
```

Default Functions

Until now, we've learned that the functions that the compiler provides by default for a class `T` are:

a. The default constructor: `T()`.
b. The default copy assignment operator, which is a function declared as:

    `T& operator=(const T&)`. For example, as we'll see in Chapter 18, when we write `t1 = t2;` the `operator=` function is called, which copies the values of the non-static members of `t2` to `t1`. If the member is an array, its elements are copied. The function returns a reference to the left operand.

c. The default destructor: `~T()`.

These are the functions that the compiler will generate for you and call by default, unless you've defined your own versions. In Chapter 19 we'll see more default functions. Notice that there are some special cases where the compiler does not create the default functions. The general rule is that if a class has a member which by definition cannot be constructed, copied, or destroyed, then the compiler deletes, as we'll see in Chapter 19, the corresponding default function. For example, if the class contains a reference or `const` member, the compiler does not generate the copy assignment operator. See the following code and read the comments:

```
class T
{
        ...
        const int r;
        T(int i) : r(i) {} /* r becomes equal to i. We'll see this syntax in
Ch.19. */
};

T t1(10), t2(20);
t1 = t2; /* Compilation error, because the copy assignment operator is
deleted. If you want to make the copy, you'll need to define your own copy
function, as you'll learn in Ch.18. */
```

It makes sense for the compiler to delete the copy function, since it is not allowed to change the value of a `const` variable. Let's have a short test, find the errors in the following program:

```
#include <iostream> // Example 17.8
#include <cstring>

class T
{
private:
        char str[5];
        T(int i, int j) {a=i; b=j;}
public:
        int a, b;

        T() {}
        T(char s[], int i = 0) {strcpy(str, s); a=b=i;}
        ~T(int i) {std::cout << "Out\n";}
};

int main()
{
        T t1(10), t2(), t3("Find the errors\n"), t4(10, 20);
        return 0;
}
```

Constructors, like other functions, are allowed to be defined within the class, so this is not wrong. Is there a constructor that accepts only one integer parameter? No, so the declaration of t1 is wrong. When using the default constructor, a common error is to add parentheses. For example, look at the declaration of t2. This declaration states that t2 is a function, which returns an object of class T.

 A common error when using the default constructor to create an object is to declare it as a function and not as an object.

Let's examine the declaration of t3. The constructor with the predefined integer value is called. The str field is private. Is it allowed to access it by calling strcpy()? Yes, because as we've said, the functions of the class can access its private members. But, is the size of str large enough to hold the characters of the string passed to it? No, that's a serious runtime error, as you already know. Had we declared str as a string variable we'd be safe and we would not care about the length of the argument. Let's go to t4 where you probably gave a wrong answer. Can the program, which is essentially a user of the T class, have direct access to a private member, such as the respective constructor? No, the compiler will display an error message for unauthorized access to a private member, so the t4 declaration is incorrect. One last error. Remember, a class can have only one destructor, which does not accept parameters. Therefore, the declaration of the destructor is incorrect.

Destructor and Memory Release

As we've seen, the destructor of an object with automatic storage duration (e.g., t in example C.17.5) is called automatically when the program exits the block in which the object is defined. If the object has static storage duration, its destructor is called when the program terminates. If the object has been created with the new operator, its destructor will be called when the delete operator is used to free the reserved memory. Also, a program may create temporary objects to perform certain operations; the program calls their destructors when it no longer needs them. For example:

```
Test t;
t = Test(3, 4);
```

First, the default constructor is called and the t object is created. With the next statement, the compiler creates an unnamed temporary object with values 3 and 4 and copies its contents to t, that is, t.a becomes 3 and t.b becomes 4. Then, its destructor is called and this temporary object is destroyed.

Let's see an example that demonstrates the most common use of a destructor, which is to release the memory allocated by members-pointers.

```
#include <iostream> // Example 17.9

class T
{
private:
        int *data;
        int size;
public:
        T(int num);
        ~T();
        void show() const;
};
```

```
T::T(int num)
{
        data = new int[num];
        size = num;
}


T::~T()
{
        delete[] data;
}
void T::show() const
{
        for(int i = 0; i < size; i++)
                std::cout << data[i] << '\n';
}
int main()
{
        T t(10);

        t.show();
        return 0;
}
```

Since the elements have not been initialized with some specific values, the program displays their random values. When an object is destroyed, the memory that has been reserved for it is automatically released, but the memory that may have been reserved by members-pointers is not released. To release this memory, we can use the destructor. And to make it clear, the integers are not stored in the object. The values are stored in the memory reserved by the `new[]` operator and the object uses the `data` field to access this memory. The destructor uses the `delete[]` operator to release the memory. Just to remind, when we use the `new` operator to allocate memory we use the `delete` operator to release it and when we use the `new[]` operator we use the `delete[]` operator to release it. In general, if a class allocates resources (e.g., memory), most likely you need to define a destructor to release them.

 If you allocate memory in the constructor or elsewhere in the implementation of the class do not forget to release it. Typically, the destructor is the best place to do that.

A good programming technique is to try to allocate memory, and in general any kind of resources you need, in the constructor and release in the destructor all the resources that are still owned by the object. It makes easier to control and maintain the program. This technique is typically referred to as *Resource Acquisition is Initialization (RAII)*.

I have a question for you. Is it correct to write the `show()` in the following way? Think about it before you see the answer.

```
void T::show() const
{
        for(int i = 0; i < size; i++)
                cout << data[i] << '\n';
        if(size > 5)
                delete[] data;
}
```

Of course not. If the `if` condition is true, the memory will be released and when the object is destroyed the destructor will attempt to release a memory that has already been released. To avoid such an error, remember what I told you in Chapter 14, that a good practice when releasing memory that may be released elsewhere is to make the respective pointer equal to `nullptr` (e.g., `data = nullptr`). Now, the attempt to release the memory in the destructor will not cause a problem, since, as we know, applying the `delete` operator to a null pointer has no effect.

Another question. Suppose we add the following function:

```
void check(T a)
{
        int i = 10;
}
```

In `main()` we call `check()`, as shown below. Is the code correct? Pay attention, important exercise.

```
int main()
{
        T t(10);

        check(t);
        t.show();
        return 0;
}
```

Although there is no problem in `check()`, since it does not do anything special, its call creates a big problem. Let's see why. When `check()` is called the `t` object is passed by value. The `a` object is a copy of `t`, that is, the `a.data` is equal to `t.data` and the `a.size` equal to `t.size`. When `check()` terminates, the destructor of the `a` object is called and releases the memory that `a.data` points to, which is the same memory that `t.data` points to. So, when `show()` is called, the memory has been released and the program will not work properly. Also, an error occurs when the program ends. Then, the destructor of the `t` object attempts to release a memory that has already been released, which is wrong.

 Be careful when passing an object by value, because if it contains pointer(s) severe problems may occur. In Chapter 18, we'll see that similar problems may occur when copying one object to another.

Fine, and what can we do to avoid this problem? We could pass a reference or a pointer to the object so that no copy is created. For example:

```
void check(const T& a)
{
        int i = 10;
}
```

We continue, see the following program. Are there any errors? If so, fix them and tell me what is the output.

```
#include <iostream> // Example 17.10

class T
{
public:
        ~T() {std::cout << "Out\n";}
};
```

```
T* f()
{
        T t;
        return new T;
}

int main()
{
        delete f();
        return 0;
}
```

A class is allowed to contain only the destructor, `f()` reserves memory for a `T` object and returns it, and `main()` first calls `f()` and then releases the returned memory. I do not see any error. The destructor is called twice, once to destroy the `t` object in `f()` and once when calling `delete` to destroy the object created dynamically in `f()`. So, the program displays `Out` twice.

 In general, because using pointers correctly is not the easiest thing to do, when a class needs dynamic memory, it is safer to use classes that support dynamic memory management instead, such as the `string` and `vector` classes.

Also, the default functions work normally for classes that contain `string` or `vector` members. For example, when we copy an object that has a `vector` member, the copy function of the `vector` class undertakes the copying of the elements it contains. When the object is destroyed, the destructor of the `vector` class undertakes the destruction of its elements. Exercise C.17.5 is such an example.

THE this POINTER

Each member function, with the exception of the static functions as we'll see below, has access to a hidden pointer called `this`. The important thing to remember is that when a member function is called, `this` points to the object that called the function. For example, suppose that the `T` class contains the `f()` and `g()` functions, an integer member named `mem` and `t` is an object of that class. If we write:

```
t.f();
```

the compiler passes the address of the `t` object to `f()` and the `this` pointer in the `f()` is initialized with that address. It is as the compiler interprets the call as:

`f(&t)` and the declaration as `f(T *const this);`

The `this` parameter is defined for us implicitly. Inside the function any direct access to a member is assumed to be an implicit reference through `this`. For example:

```
T::f()
{
        mem = 10; // It is as we've written this->mem = 10;
        g(); // It is as we've written this->g();
}
```

When mem is accessed, the compiler accesses the mem of the object that this points to. That is, the compiler actually translates the access to this->mem. We could write the statement as the comment says, but it is not necessary since the compiler does it for us. The same happens when g() is called.

The most common use of the this pointer is when we want the function to return a pointer to the object that called the function or the object itself. For example, consider the following program:

```cpp
#include <iostream> // Example 17.11

class Test
{
public:
        int a;

        Test(int i) {a = i;}
        Test* cmp(Test* t);
};

Test* Test::cmp(Test* t)
{
        if(t->a > a) // Equivalent to if(t->a > this->a)
                return t;
        else
                return this;
}

int main()
{
        Test *p, t1(5), t2(10);

        p = t1.cmp(&t2);
        std::cout << p->a << '\n';
        return 0;
}
```

The cmp() function takes as an argument a pointer to a Test object and if the value of a of the object that the pointer points to (i.e., t2) is greater than the value of a of the object that called the function (i.e., t1), it returns that pointer. Otherwise, it returns the this pointer, which points to the object that called the function, that is, to t1.

Let's see in this example how the this pointer works. As we said, a non-static member function accesses the object that called that function via an indirect parameter not shown in the parameter list, the this pointer. When the function is called, this is initialized to the address of the invoking object. For example, with t1.cmp() the compiler passes the address of t1 to the unshown this parameter of cmp. To put it simply, just remember this:

When a non-static member function is called, this points to the object that called the function.

Inside a member function, any reference to a non-static member of a class, such as a, implies the use of this to access that member. That is, when cmp() refers to a, it indirectly refers to a of the object that `this` points to. As the comment indicates we can write `this->a` instead of a, but it is not necessary; the compiler makes that translation for us. Also, note that we could omit the variable p and write:

     `t1.cmp(&t2)->a` instead of `p->a`. The program displays `10`.

Many programmers prefer to use the same names for the parameters as the names of the members. We can do that by using the `this` pointer. For example, suppose we have a class `T` with integer members a and b and an appropriate constructor that initializes them:

```
void T::T(int a, int b)
{
        this->a = a; /* If we write a = a, the compiler considers the
argument name. The constructor arguments don't represent the class
members. */
        this->b = b;
}
```

Since `this` holds the address of the current object, we can have the same names for the parameters and the members and use `this` to access the members of the object.

Notice that we cannot change the value of the `this` pointer. For example, it is wrong to write `this = t;` inside `cmp()`. The value of `this` is immutable, it always points to the current object. In particular, for a `const` function its type is `const T*`, so that the function cannot modify the data members of the object. Now you can better understand why the statement `grd = 2;` in the section that we were discussing `const` functions is not allowed. It is translated as `this->grd = 2;` which cannot be compiled since the type of `this` is a pointer to `const`.

Let's do two exercises. Take a piece of paper and hide the answers. Change the `main()` and `cmp()` so that `cmp()` does not return the pointer, but the object with the larger value of a. Use only the variables t1 and t2.

Answer:
`cmp()` changes to:

```
Test Test::cmp(Test *t)
{
        if(t->a > a)
                return *t;
        else
                return *this;
}
```

and `main()` changes to:

```
int main()
{
        Test t1(5), t2(10);

        cout << t1.cmp(&t2).a << '\n';
        return 0;
}
```

Since `this` points to the invoking object, the expression `*this` is equivalent to that object, that is, `t1`. Since `t` points to `t2`, `*t` is equivalent to `t2`.

The second one. Change the `main()` and `cmp()` so that `cmp()` accepts a reference as a parameter and returns a reference to the object with the larger value of a. Use only the variables `t1` and `t2`.

```
Answer:
```
`cmp()` changes to:

```
Test& Test::cmp(Test& t)
{
        if(t.a > a)
                return t;
        else
                return *this;
}
```

and the call of `cmp()` in `main()` changes to: `cout << t1.cmp(t2).a << '\n';`

Another one. Are there any errors in the following program? If not, what is the output?

```
#include <iostream> // Example 17.12

class T
{
private:
        int a;
public:
        T(int i) {a = i;}
        const int* set(int a) const;
};

const int* T::set(int a) const
{
        this->a = a;
        return &((*this).a);
}

int main()
{
        int* p;
        T t;

        p = t.set(10) ;
        std::cout << *p << '\n';
        return 0;
}
```

Yes, there are errors. First, the declaration of t. Since a non-default constructor is defined in T, the default constructor must be defined to make that declaration valid. Let's go to `set()`. Since it is a `const` function, can `set()` change the value of a? Of course not. So, the statement `this->a = a;` is wrong. As we said, the word `const` makes the `this` pointer a pointer to `const`. Is the `return` statement wrong? No, since `*this` corresponds to t, `set()` returns the address of a. Finally, in `main()`, the assignment to p is wrong because its type is not `const int*` as the return type of `set()`.

ARRAY OF OBJECTS

An array of objects is an array whose elements are objects. For example, in the program C.17.1 the statement:

Student s[10]; declares s as an array of ten elements, where each element is a Student object. The default constructor is called for each object created, that is, it is called ten times. In general, we can use the same or different constructors to initialize an array. For example:

```cpp
#include <iostream>  // Example 17.13

class Test
{
public:
        int a, b;
        Test() {a=b=1;}
        Test(int i, int j) {a=i; b=j;}
};

int main()
{
        int i;
        Test t[10] = {Test(1, 2), Test(), Test(5, 6)};

        for(i = 0; i < 10; i++)
                std::cout << t[i].a << ' ' << t[i].b << '\n';
        return 0;
}
```

The second constructor is called for t[0] and t[2], while the default constructor is called for t[1]. Because the initialization list is shorter than the number of elements, the default constructor is called for the remaining seven objects. If it was missing, the compiler would display an error message. The program displays the values of the members of each object.

And if we write: Test *p = new Test[3]; which constructor will be called? The default. How many times? Three, one for each object. How about if the default constructor was missing? In that case, we should use the other constructor. Here is an initialization example:

Test *p = new Test[3]{{1, 2}, {3, 4}, {5, 6}}; /* The a and b of the first object become 1 and 2, respectively. Similarly, for the other two objects. */

When we write delete[] p; which function will be called? The default destructor, again three times. In which order? As we've said, the destructor is called in reverse order from the construction order, that is, p[2] will be destroyed first and p[0] last.

Alternatively, as we know, we can use a vector object with elements of type Test. For example:

```cpp
int main()
{
        int i;
        std::vector<Test> v;
        Test t1(2, 3), t2;

        v.push_back(t1);
        v.push_back(t2);
```

```
        for(i = 0; i < v.size(); i++)
                std::cout << v[i].a << ' ' << v[i].b << '\n';
        return 0;
}
```

CLASS CONSTANTS

When declaring a class we may want to use some constants. We could use global variables, but since they will be used only inside the class it fits to the encapsulation philosophy to define them inside the class. For example, suppose that we want to use a constant to specify the size of an array. Because this constant is the same for all objects, it would be nice to be created only once and shared by all the objects. For example, we'd write something like:

```
class T
{
private:
        const int SIZE = 10;
        int arr[SIZE]; // Wrong.
        ...
};
```

in order the SIZE variable to be created once and shared by all T objects. However, this is not allowed, because the declaration of a class does not create an object to reserve memory for SIZE and store its value, it just describes the structure of the class. What can we do? One way to define a constant within a class is to declare an enumeration. For example:

```
class T
{
private:
        enum {SIZE = 10};
        int arr[SIZE];
        ...
};
```

The enumeration does not create a member of the class. That is, the enumeration is not contained in every object of class T. Simply put, SIZE is a symbolic name and each time the compiler encounters it within the scope of the class, it replaces it with 10.

Another way is to use a static constant. In fact, static members are typically used to define constants. This makes sense, since there is no need to create a copy of the same constant variable each time an object is created. By defining it as static, only one single instance of this constant will be created and shared among the objects. As I've mentioned, I prefer to write the constants in capital letters so that they stand out in the program. For example:

```
#include <iostream> // Example 17.14

class T
{
public:
        static int SIZE = 10; // Wrong, it is not const.
        static const int SIZE = 10; /* OK. We can also use the constexpr
qualifier instead of const. */
        int arr[SIZE];
        void f();
};
```

```
void T::f()
{
        for(int i = 0; i < SIZE; i++)
                arr[i] = i+SIZE;
        std::cout << arr[SIZE-1] << '\n';
}

int main()
{
        T t;
        t.f();
        std::cout << SIZE << '\n'; // Wrong, out of scope.
        return 0;
}
```

Now, only one constant named SIZE is created, which is shared by all T objects. As we'll see in the next section, SIZE is not stored in each object but in the same memory area where other static variables of the program are stored. SIZE is visible within the scope of the class and the call to f() outputs 19. As the comment says, if you try to use it outside of class, the compiler will display an error message. If you use the scope operator and write T::SIZE there will be no problem.

Regarding the initialization there are some restrictions. For example, the type of the static constant must be an integer or enumeration or a constexpr expression and the initial value must also be constant.

```
class T
{
        ...
        static const int PI = 3; // OK.
        static const float PI = 3.14; // Wrong.
        static constexpr float PI = 3.14; // OK.
};
```

The initialization rules are simplified with C++17 and the introduction of the inline variables. It allows us to initialize the variable irrespective of its type. For example, we can write:

```
class T
{
        ...
        static inline const float PI = 3.14; // OK, since C++17.
};
```

The order of the static, inline, and const keywords does not matter.

STATIC MEMBER VARIABLES

When we want to declare a variable in a class that is shared by all the objects of the class we declare it as static. A static variable can be declared in any section and it is accessible by any object. It belongs to the class as a whole, and not to a particular object. To show you an example, let's declare the T class in the test.h file:

```
#ifndef TEST_H
#define TEST_H
```

```
class T
{
private:
        int v;
        double d;
public:
        static int num; // Declare the static variable.
        void set() {v = num;}
};


#endif
```

As with a `static` constant, the compiler allocates memory for a single copy of the `static` variable num, regardless of the number of objects to be created. For example, if we create ten objects the compiler will allocate memory for ten integers v, for ten doubles d, but only for one integer num. The memory reserved for num does not belong to a particular object; it is reserved in a separate area and shared by all T objects. As with a static variable declared within a function, it has permanent lifetime and it is visible only within the class. Let's see the program:

```
#include <iostream> // Example 17.15
#include "test.h"

int T::num = 5; // Define the static variable.

int main()
{
        T t[10];

        t[2].num = 20; // Alternatively, T::num = 20;
        std::cout << t[5].num << '\n';
        return 0;
}
```

As we said, a static constant can be initialized within the class. This is not allowed for a non-constant static variable, though. It must be defined outside the class without the word `static`, using the class name and the scope operator. If you forget the definition, you'll get a compilation error similar to *«T::num undefined reference».*

The memory for such static variables is reserved when the program begins, as with global variables. Thus, num will be defined, that is, memory will be reserved for it, even if no T object is created. Because memory is reserved for a single num, num is common to all objects and the program displays 20. If you do not assign an initial value, that is, write `int T::num;` num becomes 0. Class members (e.g., set()) can access static variables directly, without using the :: operator.

We also see that although the static variable is not a discrete member of the objects, we can use an object, such as t[2] (or pointer or object reference), to access it. In order to make clear that the variable is static, I prefer to use the syntax with the class name and the :: operator (e.g., T::num).

One might ask, couldn't we define a constructor and initialize num there rather than doing this "weird" outside initialization? No we cannot, even if it was allowed, we'd not want to be initialized each time an object is created. Besides, a static member exists even if no object is created. That's why we initialize it outside the class. In fact, the outside statement defines the variable. The line inside the class only declares that num is a static member, it will be defined elsewhere. C++17 relaxes this requirement and simplifies the definition with the introduction of the inline variables. In particular,

C++17 provides the ability to define a static member variable within the class by making it inline. For example:

```
class T
{
        . . .
        static inline int num = 5; // Since C++17.
};
```

Now, we don't have to define it outside the class; making it inline is much more convenient. Also, the fact that it is inline allows us to include that header file in multiple source files without violating the one definition rule.

To sum up, just remember, when you want a variable to be shared by all objects you declare it as static. For example, in one of my applications, where each object represented a tab of an Internet browser, I had declared the members that stored the machine's network addresses (e.g., MAC and IP) as static, because these addresses are common to all the objects. Enough with this chapter, let's go to the exercises.

In some of this book's exercises I use members of type char* *to handle strings. The reason I do this is to gain more experience in using pointers but also to see dangerous situations. Also, lot of code is written out there that uses this type, so it is useful to know how to handle it. As we said, the best choice is the* string *type. Its use is simple, safe, and provides many capabilities.*

EXERCISES

C.17.1 Find the errors in the following code.

```
class T
{
private:
        int a;
public:
        friend int f();
        void r(const T& t) {t.a = a;}
        void g(int b) const {a = b;}
};

int f()
{
        return a;
}
```

Answer: Because the friend function f() is not a member of the class, it cannot access a directly. So, the statement return a; is not acceptable. Because the reference passed to r() is const, it is not allowed to change the members of t. So, the statement t.a = a; is not acceptable. Because g() is declared as const it is not allowed to change the value of a. So, the statement a = b; is not acceptable.

C.17.2 In communication networks, a network can be managed in an object-oriented way. In particular, every element of the network (e.g., router, computer, printer, ...) can be represented by an object.

Define the class PC that represents a computer. The class should contain three string members, in order to store the computer's IP address, the MAC address of its network card, and the IP address of the router to which it is connected. It should also contain two numerical members, in order to store the number of packets transmitted by the network card and the number of packets received. You should decide about the access type of the PC members so that the network administrator can safely configure all three addresses as well as learn the packet values. Write a program that tests the functionality of the PC class.

Answer:

```cpp
#include <iostream>
#include <string>
using std::cout;
using std::string;

class PC
{
private:
        string MAC_addr;
        string IP_addr;
        string gateway_IP_addr;
        unsigned int send_pkts; /* In a real implementation, this value
increases each time the network card sends a packet. */
        unsigned int rcvd_pkts; /* In a real implementation, this value
increases each time the network card receives a packet. */
public:
        PC() {send_pkts = rcvd_pkts = 0;}
        void set_MAC_addr(const string& MAC) {MAC_addr = MAC;}
        void set_IP_addr(const string& IP) {IP_addr = IP;}
        void set_gateway_IP_addr(const string& IP) {gateway_IP_addr = IP;}
        unsigned int get_send_pkts() const {return send_pkts;}
        unsigned int get_rcvd_pkts() const {return rcvd_pkts;}
        void show() const;
};

void PC::show() const
{
        cout << "MAC: " << MAC_addr << " IP: " << IP_addr << " Gateway: " <<
gateway_IP_addr << '\n';
}

int main()
{
        PC pc;

        string s = "1.2.3.4.5.6";
        pc.set_MAC_addr(s);

        s = "200.1.2.3";
        pc.set_IP_addr(s);

        s = "200.1.2.1";
        pc.set_gateway_IP_addr(s);

        pc.show();
        cout << "Send: " << pc.get_send_pkts() << ' ' << "Rcvd: " << pc.get_
rcvd_pkts() << '\n';
        return 0;
}
```

Comments: We declare the members private, so that direct access to them is not allowed. For example, if the send_pkts member was public, its value could accidentally change, so the administrator would read an invalid value. Because the members are declared private, corresponding set/get functions must be declared to access them.

C.17.3 Are there any errors in the following program? If so, fix them and find the output.

```cpp
#include <iostream>
class A
{
public:
        A(int i = 0) {std::cout << "A\n";}
        ~A() {std::cout << "~A\n";}
};

class B
{
public:
        B(int i = 0) {std::cout << "B\n";}
        A a;
        ~B() {std::cout << "~B\n";}
};

int main()
{
        B b[3];
        return 0;
}
```

Answer: In class B, the constructor of A is called to create the a object. I do not see any error. If the default value was missing, the compiler would display an error message in the creation of a, as we said in example C.17.7. Also, if the default value was missing in the constructor of B, the compiler would display an error message in the creation of the b elements. To create b[0], first the constructor of A is executed to create a and then the body of the B constructor continues. Thus, for the three elements of b, the program outputs A B three times. The destruction is done in reverse order. That is, first the destructor of B is called and then the destructor of A for the destruction of a. Thus, the program outputs ~B ~A three times.

C.17.4 Define the class A with an integer private member named data and a constructor that accepts an integer parameter and initializes the data with the parameter's value. Define the class B in the same way as A. Define a friend function that accepts as parameters two constant references to A and B and returns the difference of their data members. Write a program that tests the function.

```cpp
#include <iostream>

class B; /* As in the C.13.6 example we add an incomplete definition of class
B, which is needed to declare f() */

class A
{
private:
        int data;
public:
        A(int i) {data = i;}
        friend int f(const A& a, const B& b);
};
```

```cpp
class B
{
private:
        int data;
public:
        B(int i) {data = i;}
        friend int f(const A& a, const B& b);
};

int f(const A& a, const B& b)
{
        return a.data - b.data;
}

int main()
{
        A a(5);
        B b(3);
        std::cout << f(a, b) << '\n';
        return 0;
}
```

C.17.5 Are there any errors in the following program? If so, fix them and find the output.

```cpp
#include <iostream>
#include <vector>

class A
{
public:
        ~A() {std::cout << "~A\n";}
};

class B
{
public:
        ~B() {std::cout << "~B\n";}
};

class C
{
public:
        std::vector<A> v;
        B *b;
        C& push(A *p) {v.push_back(*p); return *this;}
};

int main()
{
        C c;
        A *p = new A;
        std::cout << &c.push(p) << '\n';
        delete p;
        return 0;
}
```

Answer: Is it fine for a class to define only a destructor? Yes, why not? When p is declared, the default constructor creates an A object. Is the call to push() correct? Yes, no problem. When push() is called the push_back() saves a copy of the passed object in c.v. Then, push() returns the c object, so the program displays its memory address. Then, the memory for the p pointer is released, the destructor of A is called and the program displays ~A. Finally, the default destructor of C is called. Will the destructor of B be called? Of course not, no B object was created, b is just a pointer. Beware now, when v is destroyed, the destructor will be called for every A object it contains. Since it contains only one, the program displays ~A. To sum up, the program has no errors and displays first the memory address of c, and then ~A twice.

C.17.6 Add appropriate functions in class T so that the following program works.

```cpp
#include <iostream>
#include <cstring>

class T
{
private:
        char *s;
        ...
};

int main()
{
        char str[100];

        cout << "Enter text: ";
        cin.getline(str, sizeof(str)); /* Assume that the user inputs a string
with less than 100 characters. */
        T t1(str); // The string should be copied to member s.
        T t2;
        t1.show(); /* show() should display the input string in reverse order.
For example, if the input string is abcd, the program should display dcba.
Also, there is a restriction that the only variable you are allowed to
declare in show () is a pointer. */
        return 0;
}
```

Answer:

```cpp
#include <iostream>
#include <cstring>
using std::cout;
using std::cin;

class T
{
private:
        char *s;
public:
        T(char str[]);
        T();
        ~T();
        void show() const;
};
```

```
T::T()
{
        s = nullptr; /* Initialize the pointer so that there is no problem
when the memory is released. For example, no memory is reserved for t2. */
}

T::T(char str[])
{
        s = new char[strlen(str)+1];
        strcpy(s, str);
}

T::~T()
{
        delete[] s;
}

void T::show() const
{
        for(char *p = s+strlen(s)-1; p >= s; p--)
                cout << *p;
}
```

Answer: Let's explain how we decided to add these functions. Since we see in main() that the objects are created in two ways, we define two constructors. Since s is a pointer, the constructor must allocate memory to copy the string. Therefore, a destructor must be added to release the memory.

C.17.7 Complete the public section of the following class and write a program that reads and stores the data of employees in a vector object that contains elements of type Employee. If the user enters a negative value for salary, the data entry should terminate. Then, the program should read a number and display the data of the employees who have a higher salary than that number. Also, the program should display the data of the employee with the highest salary. Assume that only one employee has the highest salary. There is a restriction not to define a constructor in the class.

```
class Employee
{
private:
        string name;
        float sal;
public:
        ...
};
```

Answer:

```
#include <iostream>
#include <string>
#include <vector>
using namespace std;

class Employee
{
private:
        string name;
        float sal;
```

```
public:
        void set(const string& n, float s);
        float get() const;
        void show() const;
};

void Employee::set(const string& n, float s)
{
        name = n;
        sal = s;
}

float Employee::get() const
{
        return sal;
}

void Employee::show() const
{
        cout << "N:" << name << " S:" << sal << '\n';
}

int main()
{
        int i, pos;
        float base, sal, max_sal;
        string name;
        Employee tmp;
        vector<Employee> empl;

        while(1)
        {
                cout << "\nName: ";
                getline(cin, name);

                cout << "Salary: ";
                cin >> sal;
                if(sal == -1)
                        break;

                tmp.set(name, sal);
                empl.push_back(tmp);
                cin.get(); // Extract the new line character.
        }
        cout << "\nEnter base: ";
        cin >> base;
        max_sal = -1;
        for(i = 0; i < empl.size(); i++)
        {
                sal = empl[i].get();
                if(sal > base)
                        empl[i].show();
                if(sal > max_sal)
                {
                        pos = i;
                        max_sal = sal;
                }
        }
```

```
        if(max_sal != -1)
                empl[pos].show();
        return 0;
}
```

Comments: We need set/get functions to access the private members and the show() function to display the data. Note that there is no need to pass a reference to set(). We could pass a copy of the string by value. As we've said, we use the reference for better performance.

C.17.8 Define the class Rect with private members l and h, which denote the length and width of a rectangle, respectively. Also, define the class Circle with private member r, which denotes the radius of the circle. Each class must contain an appropriate constructor and a public function area(), which returns the area of the corresponding shape.

    a. Define a template function f() that accepts a generic parameter of type Rect or Circle and returns the area of the object. Write a program that tests the function.

Answer:

```
#include <iostream>

class Rect
{
private:
        float l;
        float h;
public:
        Rect(float a, float b) {l=a; h=b;}
        float area() const {return l*h;}
};

class Circle
{
private:
        float r;
public:
        Circle(float a) {r=a;}
        float area() const {return r*r*3.14;}
};

template <typename T> float f(T t)
{
        return t.area();
}

int main()
{
        Rect r(1, 2);
        Circle c(3);

        std::cout << f(r) << ' ' << f(c) << '\n';
        return 0;
}
```

Comments: To initialize the private members we use the constructors.

b. Modify f() so that a pointer to a Rect or Circle object is passed as an argument and return its area. Modify the program accordingly, to test the function.

Answer:

```
template <typename T> float f(T t)
{
        return t->area();
}

int main()
{
        Rect r(1, 2);
        Circle c(3);

        std::cout << f(&r) << ' ' << f(&c) << '\n';
        return 0;
}
```

C.17.9 Complete the public section of the following class and write a program to test the operation of the class. The purpose of the Lifo class is to implement a stack, similar to that of Exercise C.14.8, with the difference that a vector object should be used to store the Node elements and not a linked list.

```
struct Node
{
        string name;
        float grd;
};

class Lifo
{
private:
        vector<Node> vec_n;
public:
        /* Add functions that implement the stack interface. Specifically, the
        push() function that adds an element (that is, a Node object) in the stack (that
        is, in vec_n), the pop() that uses an argument to return the last element added
        in the stack, displays its data and removes it from the stack, the show_all()
        that displays the data of all elements, and the get_nodes() that returns how
        many elements are stored in the stack. Choose which functions to make const. */
};
```

Answer:

```
#include <iostream>
#include <vector>
#include <string>
using std::cout;
using std::string;
using std::vector;

struct Node
{
        string name;
        float grd;
};
```

```cpp
class Lifo
{
private:
        vector<Node> vec_n;
public:
        void push(const Node& n);
        void pop(Node& n);
        void show_all() const;
        int get_nodes() const;
};

void Lifo::push(const Node& n)
{
        vec_n.push_back(n);
}

void Lifo::pop(Node& n)
{
        int size = vec_n.size();
        if(size > 0)
        {
                n = vec_n[size-1];
                vec_n.erase(vec_n.end()-1);
        }
        else
                cout << "Stack is empty\n";
}

void Lifo::show_all() const
{
        int i, size = vec_n.size();
        if(size > 0)
        {
                for(i = 0; i < size; i++)
                        cout << "N:" << vec_n[i].name << " G:" << vec_n[i].grd
<< '\n';
        }
        else
                cout << "Stack is empty\n";
}

int Lifo::get_nodes() const
{
        return vec_n.size();
}

int main()
{
        int i;
        Node n, node[] = {{"Alpha", 1}, {"Beta", 2}, {"Epsilon", 3}};
        Lifo lifo;

        for(i = 0; i < 3; i++)
                lifo.push(node[i]);
```

```
        lifo.show_all();
        lifo.pop(n);
        cout << "\nN:" << n.name << " G:" << n.grd << '\n';
        cout << "\nNodes:" << lifo.get_nodes() << '\n';
        return 0;
}
```

Comments: See the difference of this approach with the solution of C.14.8. In C.14.8, we use external functions to manage the stack. With the object-oriented approach, the functions are contained within the class and the programmer specifies which data will be private and which will be public. Thus, the vector containing the elements of the stack is declared private, in order to prevent access to it, while the functions that constitute the interface of the class are declared public. In place of the vector we could use a dynamically linked list, as in C.14.8. The implementation method only concerns the developer of the class and is not publicly exposed. The user of the class will communicate with it through the public functions that the developer provides. Yes, the object-oriented approach not only yields the concept of the stack more accurately, but it is also safer.

C.17.10 Define the Time class with private members the hr, min, and sec, which denote the time, minutes, and seconds, respectively. The class should contain a constructor to initialize the members with zero values and the inc_hour(), inc_min() and inc_sec() public functions, which increase by one the values of hr, min, and sec, respectively. Also, the class should contain a public show() function to display the values of the members. Define the functions in such a way that the following program works:

```
int main()
{
        Time t(23, 59, 59);

        t.inc_hour().inc_min().inc_sec();
        t.show(); // The program should display 25:1:0
        return 0;
}
```

Answer:

```
#include <iostream>

class Time
{
private:
        int hr;
        int min;
        int sec;
public:
        Time(int h = 0, int m = 0, int s = 0);
        Time& inc_hour();
        Time& inc_min();
        Time& inc_sec();
        void show() const;
};

Time::Time(int h, int m, int s)
{
        hr = h;
        min = m;
        sec = s;
}
```

```
Time& Time::inc_hour()
{
        hr++;
        return *this;
}

Time& Time::inc_min()
{
        min++;
        if(min == 60)
        {
                min = 0;
                hr++;
        }
        return *this;
}

Time& Time::inc_sec()
{
        sec++;
        if(sec == 60)
        {
                sec = 0;
                inc_min();
        }
        return *this;
}

void Time::show() const
{
        std::cout << hr << ':' << min << ':' << sec << '\n';
}
```

Comments: The successive use of the . operator implies that an object must be to its left. Therefore, the functions must return an object and in particular a reference to it, since the changes in the members must be made to the object itself and not to a copy of it. That is, to see if you understood the previous sentence, what will the program display if we change the return type of the three functions from Time& to Time? I do not know, find it yourself.

C.17.11 Complete the public section of the following class and write a program that reads and stores the data of students in a vector object that contains elements of type Student. If the user enters a negative value for grade, the data entry should terminate. Then, the program should call a sort() function that takes as an argument the vector and sorts its elements in ascending order. To sort the elements use the selection sort algorithm of C.12.5. Also, the class should contain a show() function to display the data of the students. There is a restriction to define only three functions in total.

```
class Student
{
private:
        string name;
        float grd;
public:
        ...
};
```

Answer:

```cpp
#include <iostream>
#include <string>
#include <vector>
using namespace std;

class Student
{
private:
        string name;
        float grd;
public:
        Student(const string& n = "", float g = 0);
        friend void sort(vector<Student>& v);
        void show() const;
};

Student::Student(const string& n, float g)
{
        name = n;
        grd = g;
}

void Student::show() const
{
        cout << "N:" << name << " G:" << grd << '\n';
}

void sort(vector<Student>& v)
{
        int i, j, size;
        Student tmp;

        size = v.size();
        for(i = 0; i < size-1; i++)
        {
                for(j = i+1; j < size; j++)
                {
                        if(v[i].grd > v[j].grd)
                        {
                                tmp = v[i];
                                v[i] = v[j];
                                v[j] = tmp;
                        }
                }
        }
}

int main()
{
        int i;
        float grd;
        string name;
        vector<Student> st;
```

```
        while(1)
        {
                cout << "\nName: ";
                getline(cin, name);

                cout << "Grade: ";
                cin >> grd;
                if(grd == -1)
                        break;

                Student tmp(name, grd);
                st.push_back(tmp);
                cin.get();
        }
        sort(st);
        for(i = 0; i < st.size(); i++)
                st[i].show();
        return 0;
}
```

Comments: We need a constructor to create the objects. Since there is a restriction for three functions, the sort function must be declared as friend in order to have access to the private members.

C.17.12 In the area of Networks, there are many commercial applications that simulate network topologies in order to conduct experiments. Let's try a simple example. Write a program that defines the Network class to simulate a network of ten nodes. Assume that the nodes are contained in a 1000×1000 area. The program should create the nodes in random places within this area and store them in a vector object (e.g., node). If the distance between two nodes is less than 200, the nodes are considered neighbours. When a node is created, the constructor of the Node class should store in private members the node identifier, its coordinates, the identifiers of its neighbours, as well as the corresponding distances. After creating the nodes, the program should display the neighbours (i.e., the identifiers) of each node and the distances with them. To calculate the distance use the double sqrt(double a); function, which returns the square root of a and the double pow(double a, double b); which returns the result of a^b. Here is a diagram of the classes.

```
class Node
{
private:
        int id; // The identifier of the node.
        int x, y; // The coordinates of the node.
        ... /* Add appropriate variables to store the identifiers of its
neighbours and the distances with them. */
public:
        Node(int id, int x, int y); /* The x and y coordinates are random
values within the topology. */
        void show_nei() const; /* It shows the distances and the identifiers
of the neighbours, if any. */
        ...
};

class Network
{
private:
        vector<Node> node;
```

```
public:
        void find_nei(); /* It finds the neighbours of each node and stores the
identifier and the distance with each neighbour in corresponding Node members. */
        void show_topology() const; /* It displays the neighbours of each node
and the corresponding distances. */
        ... // Add a constructor to create the nodes.
};

int main()
{
        Network *net;
        ...
}
```

Answer: Let's place the declarations of the classes in the network.h header file.

```
#ifndef NETWORK_H
#define NETWORK_H

#include <vector>
using std::vector;

const int MAX_NODES = 10;

class Node
{
private:
        int id;
        int x, y;
        vector<int> nei_id; // Store the identifiers of the neighbours.
        vector<double> nei_dist; // Store the distances with the neighbours.
public:
        Node(int id, int x, int y);
        void get_coord(int& x, int& y) const;
        void set_nei(int n_id, double dist);
        void show_nei() const;
};

class Network
{
private:
        vector<Node> node;
public:
        Network();
        void find_nei();
        void show_topology() const;
};

#endif
```

Here is the code file.

```
#include <iostream>
#include <cmath>
#include <cstdlib>
#include <ctime>
#include "network.h"
```

```cpp
Node::Node(int id, int x, int y) /* I chose the same parameter names as the
members to remember to use the this pointer. */
{
        this->id = id;
        this->x = x;
        this->y = y;
}


void Node::get_coord(int& x, int& y) const
{
        x = this->x;
        y = this->y;
}


void Node::set_nei(int n_id, double dist)
{
        nei_id.push_back(n_id);
        nei_dist.push_back(dist);
}


void Node::show_nei() const
{
        for(int i = 0; i < nei_id.size(); i++)
                std::cout << id << "->" << nei_id[i] << ":" << nei_dist[i] << '\n';
}


Network::Network()
{
        srand(time(NULL));
        for(int i = 0; i < MAX_NODES; i++)
                node.push_back(Node(i, rand()%1000, rand()%1000));
}


void Network::find_nei()
{
        int i, j, x1, x2, y1, y2;
        double dist;

        for(i = 0; i < MAX_NODES; i++)
        {
                node[i].get_coord(x1, y1);
                for(j = i+1; j < MAX_NODES; j++)
                {
                        node[j].get_coord(x2, y2);
                        dist = sqrt(pow(x1-x2, 2) + pow(y1-y2, 2)); /* We apply
the Pythagorean theorem to calculate the distance. */
                        if(dist < 200) // Store the neighbours.
                        {
                                node[i].set_nei(j, dist);
                                node[j].set_nei(i, dist);
                        }
                }
        }
}
```

```
void Network::show_topology() const
{
        for(int i = 0; i < MAX_NODES; i++)
                node[i].show_nei();
}

int main()
{
        Network *net;

        net = new Network;
        net->find_nei();
        net->show_topology();
        delete net;
        return 0;
}
```

UNSOLVED EXERCISES

U.17.1 Define the Date class with private members the day, mon, and year, which denote the day, month, and year, respectively. Write a program that reads a date in d/m/y format, stores the values in the corresponding members of a Date object, and calls an appropriate function of the class to display them. Do not define a constructor.

U.17.2 Define the WareHouse class, which represents a warehouse. The class should contain two vectors as private members, with the first containing the products' codes and the second one their corresponding quantities. The class should contain the following functions:

    a. void reg(int c, int q); which adds the code c in the codes vector only if it is not already stored and the quantity q in the quantities vector.
    b. void order(int c, int q); which corresponds to an order for the product with code c. The function should check if the code is valid and if there is quantity available and, if so, subtract q from it, otherwise a related message should be displayed.
    c. void show(int c); which checks if the code c is valid, and if yes it displays the available quantity for the respective product, otherwise a related message.
    d. The default constructor.

Write a program that tests the operation of the class.

U.17.3 Define the Book class with private members the title of the book, its code, and its price. It should also contain the following public functions:

    a. void review(float grd); which grades the book with the grade grd. The review() can be called multiple times for the same book. The final score is the average of the grades.
    b. a constructor that accepts as parameters the data of the book and assigns them to the corresponding members of the object.

Add to the class any other function or member you think is needed.
    Write a program that declares an array of five objects and initializes it together with its declaration. To test the operation of the class call the review() of the objects. Then, the program

should read the code of a book and, if the book exists, the program should display its score and price. If the book does not exist or it exists but has not been graded, the program should display a related message.

U.17.4 Complete the public section of the following class and write a program like C.17.7 with the difference that the user will enter the number of employees and will dynamically allocate memory to create `Employee` objects (i.e., no vector is used). Assume that the name of the employee is less than 100 characters.

```
class Employee
{
private:
        char *name; /* The memory for the name member of each object
should be exactly as needed. */
        float sal;
public:
        ...
};

int main()
{
        Employee *empl; /* This pointer should be used to allocate memory
depending on the number of employees that the user will enter. */
        ...
}
```

U.17.5 Define the `Fraction` class with private members the numerator and denominator of a fraction. Add the public functions `add()`, `sub()`, `mul()`, and `div()` to allow the addition, subtraction, multiplication, and division of two fractions, as well as any other function you think is needed for the operation of the class. The results of the operations should be displayed in the form of a fraction. See the following coding example:

```
int main()
{
        Fraction a(4, 9), b(2, 9), c;

        c = a.add(b);
        c.show(); /* In each operation, the program should simplify the
result, if it can be simplified. For example, the program should display
2/3 and not 6/9. Hint, you need to find the maximum common divisor to
make such simplifications. */
        ...
}
```

U.17.6 Define the `Movie` class with private members the title of the movie (e.g., `title`) and public members a member of type `Info` that contains information about the movie, a `vector` object to store the names of the actors (e.g., `v_act`), and a `vector` object to store `Review` elements (e.g., `v_rev`). Define the `Info` class with private members the year the movie is released, the name of the director and the name of the producer. Define the `Review` class with private members the text of the review, the name of the reviewer, and the grade of the reviewer. The program should display a menu to provide the following choices:

1. Add a movie. For each new movie the program should create a `Movie` object. The program should read the title of the movie that will be saved in the `title` member, the names of the actors that will be saved in `v_act` and the information of the movie that will be saved in the `Info` member. Each `Movie` object should be stored in a vector of such elements.

2. Add a review. The program should read the name of the movie to be reviewed, and then the review information that will be saved in the `v_rev` member of the respective `Movie` object.

3. Search for an actor. The program should read an actor's name and check if (s)he has participated in movies. For each participating movie, the program should display its title, information about it (e.g., it is stored in the `Info` field) and review information (e.g., it is stored in the `Review` data of `v_rev`), if any.

4. Program termination.

The functions that each class is allowed to contain are only the constructor(s) and a function (e.g., `show()`) to display the values of its members.

Operator Overloading

18

In Chapter 16, we learned that we can define several functions with the same name, provided that they have different signatures. One of the main goals of C++ was the types that a programmer defines to behave like the basic types. In this chapter, we'll see how C++ achieves this goal, that is, we'll see how we can extend the concept of function overloading to operators so that user defined types, such as classes, to behave like the basic types.

OPERATOR OVERLOADING

Just as a function can be overloaded, an operator can also be overloaded and perform different tasks. In fact, you've already encountered examples of operator overloading. For example, the * operator when applied to two numbers yields their product, while when applied to a pointer it yields the value stored in the address that the pointer points to. The compiler checks the number and type of arguments to determine how to use the operator.

C++ allows us to extend the concept of operator overloading to user defined types. For example, we can overload the + operator to add two objects of our own class type. As a matter of fact, we've seen in Chapter 10 that we can use the + operator to add two string objects or use the < and the == operators to make comparisons. In fact, the string class overloads these operators and many more. This natural way to perform operations reveals the beauty of operator overloading. If applied correctly, it simplifies the programming tasks and leads to an elegant and easy to read and write code. To overload an operator we declare an overloaded function using the operator keyword, as follows:

```
return_type operatorop(parameters)
```

The name of the function is operatorop. The op can be any of the C++ operators (e.g., +, -, ...) with some exceptions. Like any ordinary function, it has a body, return type, and can accept parameters. The number of parameters is the same as the number of the operator's operands. That is, the overloaded function of a binary operator accepts two parameters, while that of a unary operator accepts one. As we said, operator overloading is usually applied to classes so that they operate in a more natural way. For example, the following program defines the Rect class, which contains a function that overloads the + operator:

```cpp
#include <iostream> // Example 18.1

class Rect
{
private:
        float length;
        float height;
public:
        Rect(float l = 0, float h = 0); /* Default constructor with default
values. */
```

DOI: 10.1201/9781003230076-18

```
        Rect operator+(const Rect& r) const;
        float area() const;
        void show() const;
};

Rect::Rect(float l, float h)
{
        length = l;
        height = h;
}

Rect Rect::operator+(const Rect& r) const
{
        Rect tmp;

        tmp.length = length + r.length;
        tmp.height = height + r.height;
        return tmp;
}

float Rect::area() const
{
        return length * height;
}

void Rect::show() const
{
        std::cout << "L:" << length << " H:" << height << '\n';
}

int main()
{
        Rect r1(10, 20), r2(30, 40), r3;

        r3 = r1+r2; // Equivalent to r3 = r1.operator+(r2);
        r3.show();
        return 0;
}
```

Before discussing the operator overloading, let's answer that. Since the length and height members are private, why the compilation does not fail when those members are accessed in the operator+ function (e.g., r.length)? The answer is that C++ allows an object to access all the members of other objects of the same class, including the private members.

When the compiler encounters the r1+r2 statement it examines the types of operands and realizes that it must call the corresponding operator+ function. Specifically, the r1+r2 statement is interpreted as r1.operator+(r2), so the operator+ function of the r1 object is called with argument the r2 object. In general, when the overloaded function of a binary operator is declared in the class, the left operand (e.g., r1) is the object that calls it, while the right operand (e.g., r2) is passed as an argument to the function. Note that if the operator+ function was not declared, the compiler would display an error message for an illegal action, since objects cannot be added. Alternatively, we could explicitly call the function and write r1.operator+(r2). Naturally, the usual use of the operator is an easier to read and write abbreviation of the explicit call. The function returns a new object with dimensions equal to the sum of the corresponding dimensions of the two objects. So, the program displays 40 and 60.

This program demonstrates that C++ operators associated with a class can have a special behaviour when applied to objects of that class. For example, the objects can participate in ordinary expressions (e.g., r1+r2) and behave like the basic types. The conventional way is to define corresponding functions and call them in the usual way. For example, instead of overloading the + operator we can define the add() function:

```
Rect add(const Rect& r1, const Rect& r2)
{
        Rect tmp;

        tmp.length = r1.length + r2.length;
        tmp.height = r1.height + r2.height;
        return tmp;
}

int main()
{
        ...
        r3 = add(r1, r2);
}
```

The benefit of operator overloading is that the operation of the class looks more natural and the program becomes easier to read and write. I also find that it is programmatically more elegant for the class developer to provide such convenient services to class users than making them to implement those services. Yes, it does simplify the work of the class user (e.g., with statements like r1+r2), but it gives a hard time to the class programmer as (s)he has to write the operator functions to support these "natural" operations. After all, as we said, one of the goals of C++ was to make class objects behave like basic types.

Before we continue, did you notice anything strange with the parameters? We said that the number of parameters is the same as the number of the operator's operands. However, we see that the operator+ accepts one parameter, while the + operator accepts two operands. Why's that? If the overloaded function is a class member, the memory address of the first operand (e.g., r1), which actually is the value of the this pointer, is implicitly passed as a "hidden" argument as we saw in Chapter 17 when discussing the this pointer. This is why the overloaded functions that are class members have one parameter less than the number of operands. For example, if the class overloads the ! operator, which is unary, we write operator!() without any parameters. If the overloaded function is not a class member, then it accepts the same number of parameters as its operands.

Some questions to refresh your knowledge. If we did not pass a reference to Rect in operator+ would the output be the same? Yes. And why pass a reference? For efficiency, to save the time and memory required to create a new object and copy r2 to it. And why make the reference const? So that the function cannot change the values of the r members, essentially that of r2. And why the function does not return a reference to the tmp object? Since tmp is a local variable it is destroyed when the function terminates, so the reference would refer to a non-existent object. And why make the function const? So that the function cannot change the values of the members of the object that calls it, that is, r1. A last one, consider the r4 object, could we write r4 = r1+r2+r3?

Sure. Because the + operator is applied from left to right the statement is translated to r4 = r1. operator+(r2+r3); which in turn is translated to r4 = r1.operator+(r2.operator+(r3)); First, r2 is added to r3 and the object that the function returns is added to r1.

Note that when an operator is overloaded it gets a different meaning only for the objects of the class that overloads it. The compiler checks the operand types to decide how to act. For example, in the following code, in the first case it adds the objects, while in the others the integers:

```
int a = 10, b = 20, c;
Rect r1(10, 20), r2(30, 40), r3;
r3 = r1+r2; // Addition of Rect objects.
c = a+b; // Addition of integers.
c = r1.length+r2.length; // Addition of integers.
```

Notice that in an overloaded function the type of at least one operand must be a user defined type, such as a class. You cannot define an overloaded function where all operands are basic types. For example, you cannot define an overloaded function of the == operator with two arguments char* or int.

Try this exercise. In the previous program, add an overloaded function of the > operator that takes as parameter a Rect object (e.g., r) and returns true if the area of the object calling the function is greater than the area of r, false otherwise. Use the area() function to calculate the area. Modify main() to test the operation of the function.

```cpp
bool Rect::operator>(const Rect& r) /* The declaration is added in the
class. */
{
        if(area() > r.area())
                return true;
        else
                return false;
}

int main()
{
        Rect r1(10, 20), r2(30, 40);

        if(r1 > r2)
                std::cout << "Bigger\n";
        else
                std::cout << "Not bigger\n";
        return 0;
}
```

The expression r1 > r2 is translated to r1.operator>(r2), so the function operator> of r1 is called with argument the r2. That is, strange as it may seem, the expressions r1+r2 or r1 > r2 do not perform the usual math operations, but call the corresponding operator functions. Because the function returns false the program displays Not bigger.

Copy Objects that Contain Pointers

Let's now look at the case of copying objects that contain pointer(s). Pay close attention, what is wrong with the following program?

```cpp
#include <iostream> // Example 18.2
#include <cstring>

class T
{
private:
        char *s;
public:
        T(const char str[]);
        ~T();
        void show() const {std::cout << s << '\n';}
};
```

```
T::T(const char str[])
{
        s = new char[strlen(str)+1];
        strcpy(s, str);
}


T::~T()
{
        delete[] s;
}


int main()
{
        T t1("Peter"), t2("Mike");

        t2 = t1;
        t2.show();
        return 0;
}
```

The statement t2 = t1; causes a problem in the operation of the program. Let's see why. The copy operation makes the t2.s pointer to point to the same memory as the t1.s. The memory reserved for t2.s is not released. When the program terminates the destructor of t2 is called, which releases the memory that t2.s points to. Since the t2.s and t1.s point to the same memory, the destructor of t1 attempts to release that memory once more. As we know, the effect of deleting an already released memory is undefined (e.g., it may cause the program to crash).

 If the class contains pointer(s) to memory that has been dynamically allocated, you'll almost certainly need to define your own copy function to avoid problems with the memory.

In such a case the ability of overloading operators proves to be particularly useful. Specifically, to avoid dangerous situations we can overload the = operator in order to define how the copy will be performed. For example:

```
class T
{
public:
        ...
        T& operator=(const T& t);
};


T& T::operator=(const T& t)
{
        /* Something is missing. */
        delete[] s;
        s = new char[strlen(t.s)+1];
        strcpy(s, t.s);
        return *this;
}
```

Now, with the statement t2 = t1; which is equivalent to t2.operator=(t1); first the memory that was allocated for t2.s is released, so it is not wasted, and then new memory is allocated to copy the string pointed to by t1.s. The function returns the invoking object, that is, t2. Thus, the program runs normally and shows Peter. Note that this code is valid for this particular example. But, what happens if we write:

```
t1 = t1; // Now, the code won't work.
```

When the function is called, the common memory pointed to by s and t.s will be released, so it'd be wrong to use t.s to re-allocate new memory and make a copy of something that no longer exists. And how can we fix this problem? Before answering, someone might ask, what is the point of making such an assignment in the first place? Yes, you're right, this self-assignment does not make sense, but in their place could be two pointers (e.g., *p1 = *p2) that you have no clue if they point to the same object. The traditional way to fix it is to check for self-assignment before releasing the memory:

```
T& T::operator=(const T& t)
{
        if(this == &t) // We check for self-assignment (e.g., t1 = t1).
                return *this;
        ...
}
```

 Don't forget to test for self-assignment when overloading the copy assignment operator. If you forget to do that, fatal errors may occur if an object is accidentally assigned to itself.

The if condition compares the address of the invoking object with that of the argument to check if the referred object is itself. If the addresses are the same, the function returns the object and terminates. And why does the function return a reference, could it not just be void? Yes, it could, but, then, we could not use = in chained expressions, such as t1 = t2 = t3;. Because the = operator has right-to-left associativity, this statement is translated to: t1.operator=(t2.operator=(t3)); When t2.operator=(t3) is called, the memory pointed to by t2.s is first released, new memory is then reserved for t2.s and the string pointed to by t3.s is copied to it. The function returns the reference to t2, which becomes the next argument. Thus, the t1.operator=(t2) is now called. Similarly, t2.s is copied to t1.s. Okay, you may find difficult to understand the above now, we'll analyze a similar expression in the next section (e.g., cout << r1 << r2;) and you'll get it. Of course, if you do not want to support chained assignments, you declare it void and you are done. Simply, the usual practice is to return a reference in order to support them.

Another question, will be a problem if instead of the reference to the object we pass the object itself? That is, to write:

```
class T
{
public:
        ...
        T operator=(T t);
};
```

Of course there will be a problem. As we said, the statement t2 = t1; is translated to t2.operator=(t1);. Since t1 is passed by value, t is a copy of t1. That is, the values of the t1 members are copied to the members of t. We'll learn more about this operation when we encounter the copy constructor in Chapter 19. Thus, `t.s` points to the same memory address as the `t1.s`. But, when the function terminates, the destructor of `t` will release that memory. Therefore, the program will not work properly. So, we see once more that when passing references not only we save time and memory but we also avoid dangerous situations.

Since C++11, if we do not want to define another copy function we can disable the default copy function using the `=delete` syntax. For example:

```
class T
{
    ...
    T& operator=(const T&) = delete; /* Disable the default copy
operation. */
};
```

Now, we are not allowed to write `t2 = t1;` it causes a compilation error. We'll see the `=delete` syntax again in Chapter 19.

OVERLOADING RESTRICTIONS

Most operators can be overloaded in the way we saw in the previous examples. Actually, as we'll see below, overloaded operators, with some exceptions, do not have to be member functions. However, there are some restrictions in their use:

a. At least one operand of the overloaded operator must be a user defined type. This rule prevents operator overloading for the basic data types. For example, you cannot overload the + operator to return the difference of two integers instead of their sum.

b. You are not allowed to change the syntax of the operator. For example, you are not allowed to use the addition + operator with just one operand. Similarly, you cannot change the behaviour of ++ from unary to binary. Especially for the operators && and || we know from Chapter 4 that the second operand is not always evaluated due to the *short-circuit* evaluation. This rule does not apply when overloaded, that is, they are treated as ordinary binary operators and both operands are evaluated. In fact, because they are the arguments of the && (or ||) overloaded function they are both evaluated when the function is called, as happens with regular function calls. Therefore, because the familiar short-circuit evaluation that the programmers would expect is not valid any more, it'd be better to avoid overloading them and skip potential bugs.

c. You cannot change the precedence and associativity of the operator. For example, in an expression a*b+c where a, b, and c are objects and the operators * and + are overloaded, the multiplication is performed first and then the addition.

d. You are not allowed to create new operator symbols and then overload them. For example, you are not allowed to declare the `operator^^` function to denote exponentiation, since the ^^ operator does not exist.

e. You are not allowed to overload the following operators:

```
.       .*      ::      ?:      sizeof    typeid    alignas    noexcept
```

f. Most operators can be overloaded either by member or non-members functions. However, the following operators can only be overloaded with non-static member functions:

```
=       ()      []      ->
```

g. Without being a constraint, when an operator is overloaded it is useful for the better understanding and control of the program to perform a function similar to its original purpose. For example, when the + operator is overloaded it'd be better to perform the addition and not some other operation. In the same sense, you should not overload the & address operator. It'd be strange and confusing to use it in a different way than the usual one. In general, unconventional use of operators can be a significant distraction and potential source of errors. Also, if the use of an overloaded operator is not obvious, it'd be probably better to use a function instead, as the function's name indicates its purpose and makes the program easier to read. For example, it'd be better to declare a function with an explanatory name, such as swap(), to swap the dimensions of a Rect object rather than overload the / operator for this task. In general, when an operator is overloaded it should be easy to apply, simplify the programming tasks, and generate comprehensible code.

OVERLOADING EXAMPLES OF
UNARY OPERATORS

We've seen some examples of overloading binary operators, let's see some examples of overloading unary operators, that is, operators that accept one operand. Let's overload the ~ operator to swap the dimensions of the object calling it:

```
void Rect::operator~() // The declaration is added in the class.
{
        int tmp;

        tmp = length;
        length = height;
        height = tmp;
}
```

To test its operation, we write in main():

```
int main()
{
        Rect r(10, 20);

        ~r; // Equivalent to r.operator~();
        r.show(); // The program displays 20 and 10.
        return 0;
}
```

Note that you are free to choose the return value according to your needs. Here is just an example that uses void. For example, when overloading a unary operator it is very common to return a reference to the respective object. Let's change the code:

```
Rect& Rect::operator~()
{
        ...
        return *this;
}
```

Now, we can write in `main()`:

```
int main()
{
        Rect r(10, 20);

        (~r).show(); /* Since the function returns a reference to Rect object,
we can call show(). */
        return 0;
}
```

As I said, when you overload an operator it is very important to make the code easier to read and understand. In this example, someone who reads the code cannot figure out that the ~r expression swaps the dimensions. It'd be better to define a function with a relevant name (e.g., swap) and call that function instead. Here, it is just an example of how to overload a unary operator.

Overloading the ++ and -- Operators

Let's overload the ++ operator, the -- is overloaded in a similar way, to increase the dimensions of the invoking object by one. As we know, the ++ operator can be applied in two ways. Therefore, we'll implement two versions of the function, one for the postfix and one for the prefix increment. For example, with the statement ++r; the function should return the r object after increasing its dimensions, while with r++; to return r before the increment. Fine, but there is a problem. Since both functions have the same name operator++ and do not accept parameters, that is, they both have the same signature, how will the compiler figure out which one to call? To solve this, an integer parameter is added in the postfix version. For example:

```
Rect& Rect::operator++() /* Prefix version (e.g., ++r). The declaration is
added in the class. */
{
        length++;
        height++;
        return *this;
}

Rect Rect::operator++(int) /* Postfix version (e.g., r++). The declaration is
added in the class. */
{
        Rect tmp;

        tmp = *this;
        length++;
        height++;
        return tmp;
}
```

In the postfix version the argument is not used, and therefore its name is not needed. It is just a dummy argument that the compiler uses to distinguish which version to call. Also, the prefix version normally returns a reference to the current object, while the postfix returns a copy of the original object, not a reference. Let's see `main()`:

```
int main()
{
        Rect r1(10, 20), r2, r3;

        r2 = ++r1; // Equivalent to r2 = r1.operator++();
        r1.show(); // The program outputs 11 21
        r2.show(); // The program outputs 11 21

        r3 = r1++; // Equivalent to r3 = r1.operator++(0);
        r1.show(); // The program outputs 12 22
        r3.show(); // The program outputs 11 21
        return 0;
}
```

The equivalent explicit function calls are shown in comments. In the postfix version, the compiler passes the dummy argument (e.g., the value 0). To ask you, let's say that we just want to increase the dimensions of `r1`. Which of the two statements is more efficient?

```
++r1; or r1++;
```

To answer, see again the code of the two functions. The prefix version is more efficient, because the object pointed to by `this` is not copied. In general, the best practice is to support both overloaded versions. As said, the `--` operator is overloaded in the same way, we just replace the increments with decrements in both postfix and prefix versions. A typical use of `++` and `--` overloading is in standard library classes to move iterators. We've already seen such an example when we used the iterators of the `vector` class in Chapter 7.

Overloading the -> and * Operators

Let's see an example of overloading the `->` operator, which can be defined as a unary operator. As mentioned in the overloading restrictions, the overloaded function of the `->` must be a class member:

```
#include <iostream> // Example 18.3

class A
{
public:
        void f() const {std::cout << "One\n";}
};

class T
{
private:
        A a;
public:
        A* operator->();
};

A* T::operator->()
{
        return &a;
}
```

```
int main()
{
      T t;
      t->f(); // Equivalent to (t.operator->())->f();
      return 0;
}
```

Let's see how the program works. To clarify, the program has no practical value; it is just an example of -> overloading. The expression t->f() triggers the call of t.operator->(), which returns a pointer to the a object. Then, f() is called, which displays One. So, this example shows that a T object can access members of the class A in a way similar to a pointer. Note that although -> can be overloaded, its original purpose cannot change. That is, a class member must be specified to the right of -> and the -> is used to access it. Now that we have learned that the operator -> can be overloaded, the expression ptr->field, in the general case, is equivalent to:

```
a) (*ptr).field /* If ptr is a pointer to object or */
b) (ptr.operator())->field /* If ptr is an object of a class that contains an
overloaded operator-> function. If the function returns a pointer the field
member is accessed. If it returns an object that contains an overloaded
operator-> function this function is called again, recursively, until a
pointer is returned to the indicated field member or some other value, in
which case a compilation error will occur.
```

Thus, the return type of operator-> must be a pointer to an object or an object that contains an overloaded operator-> function, which is again called as the comment indicates. Because the syntax of -> does not change, a member name is required after it. For example:

```
A* p = t->; // Wrong.
A* p = t.operator->(); // OK.
```

Although it may seem that the overloading of -> is just a special case rarely needed, it may be useful in certain applications, such as for the implementation of "smart" pointers, which are, as we'll see in Chapter 25, objects that behave like pointers.

To overload the dereference operator we should define the operator* function. Don't forget that it is useful for the better comprehension and maintenance of the program when an operator is overloaded to perform a function similar to its original purpose. Consider the following program:

```
#include <iostream> // Example 18.4

class T
{
private:
      int arr[10];
public:
      int& operator*() const {return arr[0];}
};

int main()
{
      T t;
      *t = 20; // Equivalent to t.operator*() = 20;
      return 0;
}
```

The expression *t = 20; triggers the call of t.operator*(), which returns a reference to arr[0]. Then, its value becomes 20.

Overloading the [] Operator

Although the [] operator is not a conventional unary operator such as ++, I'd like to add an example of its use, because it is a particularly useful operator that is often overloaded. As we saw in the overloading restrictions, the overloaded function of [] must be a class member. Let's look at a simple example of a class that resembles an array:

```cpp
class Array // Example 18.5
{
private:
        int arr[10];
public:
        int& operator[](int i);
};

int& Array::operator[](int i)
{
        return arr[i]; /* For simplicity, it is not checked if the value of i
is within valid range. In exercise U.18.2 you'll be asked to do it. */
}

int main()
{
        Array a;
        a[0] = 5; /* Equivalent to a.operator[](0) = 5. The a.arr[0] becomes
5. */
        return 0;
}
```

Usually, the `operator[]` function is defined to return a reference to the element and not its value, in order to work like [], that is, in both sides of =. For example, if we have an array b, we can write b[3] = i; and i = b[3];. Usually, we want the `operator[]` to support this behaviour. To achieve this, we declare the function to return a reference so that when the operator [] is used at the left of = we can assign a value to a particular element. When the function is called, the value inside the brackets becomes its argument. For example, the statement a[0] = 5; invokes the a.`operator[]`(0), which returns a reference to arr[0]. Thus, the value of a.arr[0] becomes 5.

Note that if the return type was just `int` the compiler would display an error message that the left operand of the assignment is not an lvalue. That is, we could only read the value of an element (e.g., `int` c = a[0];) and not write to it. Also, someone may ask, could we return a pointer and have the same result? That is, could we write?

```cpp
int* Array::operator[](int i)
{
        return &arr[i];
}
```

Yes, why not? But, then you have to dereference the pointer to get to the element. That is, to write: *a[0] = 5; an uglier syntax which makes the code harder to read and write. It is much better to use the reference as return value.

If we don't want to allow changes in the element's value we make the reference `const`. For example:

```cpp
const int& Array::operator[](int i) {return arr[i];}
a[0] = 5; // Wrong, it is not allowed to change the value.
int i = a[0]; // OK.
```

As a matter of fact, a class that overloads the `[]` operator to provide array-like access for both reading and writing typically define two overload variants: `const` and non-`const`. For example:

```
int& Array::operator[](int i) {return arr[i];}
const int& Array::operator[](int i) const {return arr[i];}
```

The first version applies to non-`const` objects and returns a reference, so that you may modify the value of the returned element. For example:

```
Array a;
a[0] = 5; // OK.
int i = a[0]; // OK.
```

The second version applies to a `const` object and returns a `const` reference. Since it cannot appear on the left of an assignment, the constness of the returned element is preserved. For example:

```
const Array a;
a[0] = 5; // Wrong.
int i = a[0]; // OK.
```

Note that for small objects, such as `int`, there is no serious overhead cost to return back by value. That is, instead of `const int&` as return type we could also write:

```
int Array::operator[](int i) const {return arr[i];}
```

Let's have a short test. Add in the `Rect` class an overloaded function of the `==` operator, which takes as a parameter an object of the class `Rect` (e.g., `r`) and returns 1 if both dimensions of the object calling the function are the same as `r`, 2 if one is the same, 3 otherwise. Modify `main()` to test the operation of the function.

```
class Rect
{
        ...
public:
        int operator==(const Rect& r) const;
        ...
};

int Rect::operator==(const Rect& r) const
{
        if(length == r.length && height == r.height)
                return 1;
        else if(length == r.length || height == r.height)
                return 2;
        else
                return 3;
}

int main()
{
        int a;
        Rect r1(10, 20), r2(10, 0);
```

```
a = (r1 == r2); // Equivalent to a = (r1.operator==(r2));
if(a == 1)
        std::cout << "Both the same\n";
else if(a == 2)
        std::cout << "One is the same\n";
else
        std::cout << "Unequal\n";
return 0;
}
```

As we learned, the expression (r1 == r2) does not perform the typical comparison, but it invokes the operator== function of the r1 object with argument the r2 object. Then, we can test its return value as we do with any function. The parentheses are not necessary; I just added them to make it clear that the function will be executed first.

One more, find the errors in the following program.

```
#include <iostream>

class A
{
        int t;
public:
        A(int i) {t = i;}
        void operator+(int i) {t += i;}
};

class B
{
        int t;
public:
        B(int i) {t = i;}
};

int main()
{
        A a1(10), a2;
        B b1(a1.t);

        a2 = a1+5;
        a1+5;
        b1+5;
        5+a1;
        return 0;
}
```

Since a non-default constructor is defined in A, the declaration of a2 is wrong, because no default constructor is defined. The declaration b1(a1.t) is wrong, because the access to the private member t is not allowed. Remember that the `private` label is not needed, since the class members are private by default. The statement a2 = a1+5; is not acceptable, because the overloaded function of the + operator returns nothing. The statement a1+5; is acceptable and adds 5 to the member t of the a1 object. The statement b1+5; is not acceptable, because no overloaded function of the + operator is defined in class B. Finally, the statement 5+a1; is not acceptable, because an A object must be at the left of the operator. To better understand it, 5+a1; is translated to 5.operator(a1); which is not an acceptable expression. We'll see how to handle this situation in the next section.

OVERLOADING WITH NON-MEMBERS FUNCTIONS

As mentioned, most operators can also be overloaded using functions that are not class members. In fact, there are cases where their use is necessary. For example, consider the class A of the previous exercise. As we've seen, the statement a1+5; is acceptable, but not the 5+a1;. To achieve this we must declare a non-member function. Such a function cannot be called by an object. Specifically, the values of the operands are passed as arguments to the function. The restriction is that at least one of the operands must have a class type. In our example, the prototype of the function is:

```
void operator+(int i, A& a);
```

Now, the expression 5+a1; is translated to operator+(5, a1); Let's define it:

```
void operator+(int i, A& a)
{
      a.t += i;
}
```

Is it correct? No, because the t member is private. What did we learn in the previous chapter? How can a non-member function access the private members of a class? We declare it as a friend. Let's see the program:

```
#include <iostream> // Example 18.6

class A
{
      int t;
public:
      A(int i) {t = i;}
      void operator+(int i) {t += i;}
      friend void operator+(int i, A& a);
      void show() const {std::cout << t << '\n';}
};

void operator+(int i, A& a)
{
      a.t += i;
}

int main()
{
      A a(10);

      a+5; // Translated to a.operator+(5).
      a.show(); // The program outputs 15.
      5+a; // Translated to operator+(5, a).
      a.show(); // The program outputs 20.
      return 0;
}
```

Note that it is not necessary to declare the function as friend. We could change its definition to:

```
void operator+(int i, A& a)
{
        a+i; // Equivalent to to a.operator+(i).
}
```

We just change the order of the operands so that the class function is called. In general, when a function is associated with a class, I prefer to declare it as a friend, even if it does not access its private members, in order to make clear the association. Also, if it is ever needed to access the private members, you only have to change the function definition and not the class declaration.

So remember, when we want to overload an operator where the first operand is some basic type (e.g., `int`), the overloaded function cannot be a class member. If we want the function to have access to the private members of the class, we declare it as friend.

Overloading the << Operator

Now that you've seen some examples of operator overloading you can understand what you read in Chapter 3 (yes, it is a long way back) that the << and >> shift operators have been overloaded to output and input data, respectively. For example, `cout` is an object of the `ostream` class, which contains overloaded `operator<<` functions for each of the basic types. That is, one definition with an `int` argument, one with `double`, one with `char*`, and so on. For example, if we write:

```
int a = 10;
cout << a;
```

the `cout.operator<<(int)` function is called, which undertakes to display the integer.

Let's see how we can use `cout` with a user defined type, such as `Rect`. The typical way to display the values of a class is to define a public `show()` function and call it. The question is, could we, instead of `show()`, write something like this and display their values?

```
Rect r(10, 20);
cout << r;
```

Yes we could, provided that the << operator is overloaded. In fact, it is very common to overload the << and use it together with the `cout` object to display the values of an object. See how it works. Since the left operand is an object of the `ostream` class and the right one is an object of the `Rect` class, we must define a function that accepts as arguments two such types. Should that function be friend to the `Rect` class or not? Since the function must have access to the private members in order to display their values, yes it should be friend. Let's see the program:

```
class Rect
{
        ...
public:
        friend void operator<<(ostream& out, const Rect& r);
        ...
};

void operator<<(ostream& out, const Rect& r)
{
        out << r.length << ' ' << r.height << '\n';
}
```

```
int main()
{
        Rect r(10, 20);
        cout << r; // Translated to operator(cout, r).
        return 0;
}
```

Let me ask you, could the reference to `out` be `const`? No, because writing to `out` changes its status. Note that the argument type is reference, because we cannot copy an `ostream` object. Usually, the second parameter is declared as a reference to `const` not only to avoid copying the argument but also because the function does not change its data. Besides `cout`, we can also pass other `ostream` objects (or derived as we'll see in Chapter 20) to the function. For example, the `cerr`, which by default directs the output to the screen. And because `cerr` may be redirected, the output can be sent to a file. We can also pass an `ofstream` object and direct the output to a file. Therefore, we see that depending on the type of the passed `ostream` object, we can use the `operator<<` function to direct the output either to the screen or to a file.

Another question, suppose that the `r1` and `r2` objects have been declared, could we use the above function and write:

```
cout << r1 << r2;
```

To answer that question, we analyse the parts of the statement. The statement is executed from left to right, that is, it is equivalent to: `(cout << r1) << r2;`

Therefore, the `cout << r1`, that is, the call to the `operator<<(cout, r1);` will be executed first. Fine, and what does it return? Nothing, so we cannot continue with the `<< r2` part. What should be the return type? It must be that of the left of `r1`. In particular, it should be a reference to an `ostream` object, so that the execution of the statement can continue. Thus, we change the function definition to:

```
ostream& operator<<(ostream& out, const Rect& r)
{
        out << r.length << ' ' << r.height << '\n';
        return out;
}
```

Because a reference is passed, each time the function is called it always returns the object passed to it, that is, `cout`. Now, the statement `cout << r1 << r2;` runs normally. Specifically, the first part `cout << r1` displays the dimensions of `r1` and it is replaced by the return value, that is, `cout`. So, the original statement becomes `cout << r2` and displays the dimensions of `r2`.

Actually, this is how the `<<` overloaded functions defined in `ostream` work for the various basic data types. In particular, they return a reference to `ostream`. For example, the prototype for displaying integers is similar to:

```
ostream& operator<<(int);
```

Thus, the `<<` operator can be used sequentially in statements such as:

```
int a = 10, b = 20;
cout << a << ' ' << b;
```

The expression `cout << a` triggers a call to `cout.operator<<(int)`, which displays the value of `a` and returns a reference to the invoking object, that is, to `cout`. Thus, the original statement becomes: `cout << ' ' << b;` and we continue accordingly.

And of course, we can format the output as we are used to. For example, to write:

```
cout << "First:" << r1 << "Second:" << r2;
```

When the compiler encounters as a right operand the string, it uses the corresponding ostream definition of the operator<< with a const char* argument to display it, while when it encounters as a right operand the Rect object it uses the definition we saw. Since both definitions return a reference to cout, each part of the statement is replaced by the cout and the execution of the statement proceeds without any problem.

Overloading the >> Operator

To read values, the cin is an object of the istream class, which contains overloaded operator>> functions for every basic type. Its prototype is similar to:

```
istream& operator>>(type&);
```

where type is the type of the input data. Thus, the >> operator can be used sequentially in statements such as:

```
int a, b;
cin >> a >> b;
```

The expression cin >> a triggers a call to cin.operator>>(int&), which reads an integer value, stores it into a, and returns a reference to the invoking object, that is, to cin. Because the argument is reference, cin may change the value of the passed variable. Thus, the original statement becomes cin >> b; and the next value will be read.

Let's see an overloading example of the >> operator to read and store values in a Rect object:

```
class Rect
{
        ...
public:
        friend istream& operator>>(istream& in, Rect& r);
        ...
};

istream& operator>>(istream& in, Rect& r)
{
        cout << "Enter length: ";
        in >> r.length;

        cout << "Enter height: ";
        in >> r.height;
        return in;
}
```

The first parameter is a reference to istream, while the second is a reference to the object that the values will be stored. Because the state of the object will change, the reference cannot be const. As in the case of <<, the function is typically defined to return reference to istream, so that in can be used sequentially in statements such as:

```
Rect r1, r2;
cin >> r1 >> r2;
```

As we said, when we overload an operator we should try to make it behave as much as close to its original purpose. Well, the << and >> are exceptions to this suggestion, as their original use as shift operators has no resemblance with the way that they are used when overloaded.

SUMMARIZING ...

A binary operator can be overloaded with either a non-static class member function that accepts one argument or a non-member function that accepts two arguments. That is, for a binary operator say $, the expression a$b is interpreted as a.operator$(b); or operator$(a, b);. For example, if we want to overload the + operator to add `Rect` objects we can declare in the `Rect` class the function:

```
Rect operator+(const Rect& r);
```

or a function that is not a member. For example:

```
Rect operator+(const Rect& r1, const Rect& r2);
```

which may be also declared as a friend if it is needed to access the private members. The compiler checks how the function is declared and translates the statement accordingly. For example:

```
r3 = r1+r2; /* If it is declared as a member of the class, the statement is
translated as r3 = r1.operator+(r2). */
r3 = r1+r2; /* If not, it is translated as r3 = operator+(r1, r2). */
```

As I said, because I want to make it clear that the function is associated with the class, I prefer to declare it as a member. If it cannot be declared as a member, then you have to resort to the solution of the non-member function and decide whether to be a friend of the class or not. And do not forget, if the function is a member the left operand must be an object. If both functions are defined, the compiler will choose the appropriate one. For example:

```
void operator+(int a, const Rect& r);

class Rect
{
        ...
        void operator+(const Rect& r);
};

r3 = r1+r2; // The member function is chosen.
r3 = 5+r2; // The outer is chosen.
r3 = r2+5; // Wrong.
```

A unary operator can be overloaded with either a non-static class member function that does not accept any argument or a non-member function that accepts one argument. That is, for a unary operator say $, the expression $a is interpreted as a.operator$(); or operator$(a);. If both functions are defined, the compiler will choose the appropriate one. For a postfix operator, the expression a$is interpreted as a.operator$(int); or operator$(a, int);.

And as we said, you are not allowed to change the syntax of the operator. For example:

```
class T
{
        ...
        void operator+(); // Wrong, missing operand.
        void operator*(T&, T&, T&); // Wrong, many operands.
        void operator--(int, int); // Wrong, many operands.
};
```

```
// Non-member functions.
void operator--(T&, int); // OK, postfix decrement.
void operator/(T&); // Wrong, missing operand.
```

Regarding the design of a class, we should think whether to overload operators or not. In general, if overloading an operator simplifies the operation and makes the use of your class easier and safer do it, otherwise do not it. I think this is the most important guideline. The usual candidate operators are:

a. If the class supports input/output operations it makes sense to overload the `<<` and `>>` operators.
b. If the class supports equality tests it makes sense to overload the `==` and `!=` operators.
c. If the class supports comparison tests it makes sense to overload the relational operators (e.g., `<`).
d. If an arithmetic (e.g., `+`) or bit operator is overloaded, it makes sense to overload the corresponding compound operator (e.g., `+=`), in order to provide a choice that the users of the class would expect.
e. A good practice for the return type of the function is to be compatible with the type of the result that the operator normally produces, so that the use of the function matches the typical use of the operator. For example, the return type of functions that overload the logical and relational operators to be `bool`, for arithmetic operators (e.g., `+`) to be that of the type of the class, and for assignment operators (e.g., `=`, `+=`) to be a reference (e.g., reference to `this` or reference to the first argument if the function is defined as non-member), so that we can use the result of the assignment expression in a bigger chained expression. As for the parameters, for operators that normally do not modify their operands (e.g., relational operators) they are usually defined as `const` references to avoid copying the argument and prevent to be modified as well.

Before continuing with the exercises, I'd like to point out that overloading mainly applies to arithmetic and relational operators, but not only to them. For example, overloading the `[]`, `<<`, and `>>` operators is very common. Also, it is very common to overload the `()` call operator and create function objects. You'll see examples with such objects in Chapter 26.

EXERCISES

C.18.1 Consider the `Rect` class of the example C.18.1. Add appropriate functions so that the following program works.

```
int main()
{
        Rect r(10, 20);

        if(r > 1.5) // Compare the area of the r object with 1.5.
                std::cout << "Bigger\n";
        else
                std::cout << "Not bigger\n";

        if(1.5 > r)
                std::cout << "Bigger\n";
        else
                std::cout << "Not bigger\n";
        return 0;
}
```

Answer:

```
class Rect
{
        ...
public:
        bool operator>(double val) const;
        friend bool operator>(double val, const Rect& r);
        ...
};

bool Rect::operator>(double val) const
{
        if(area() > val)
                return true;
        else
                return false;
}

bool operator>(double val, const Rect& r)
{
        if(val > r.area())
                return true;
        else
                return false;
}
```

C.18.2 For a complex number z, we have z = a + bj, where j is the imaginary unit, a is the real part, and b is the imaginary part. Define the Complex_Num class with members the float numbers re and im, which represent the real and imaginary parts of a complex number. Add appropriate functions so that the following program works. Define the constructor inline. If z_1 = a + bj and z_2 = c + dj, it holds that:

$$z = z_1 + z_2 = (a+c)+(b+d)j$$
$$z = z_1 - z_2 = (a-c)+(b-d)j$$
$$z = z_1 \times z_2 = (ac-bd)+(bc+ad)j$$
$$z = \left(\frac{z_1}{z_2}\right) = \left(\frac{ac+bd}{c^2+d^2}\right)+\left(\frac{bc-ad}{c^2+d^2}\right)j$$

```
class Complex_Num
{
private:
        double re; // The real part of the complex number.
        double im; // The imaginary part of the complex number.
public:
        ...
};

int main()
{
        Complex_Num z1(1, 2), z2(3, 4);
        std::cout << z1+z2 << z1-z2 << z1*z2 << z1/z2; /* The result of the
operations should be displayed in different lines. */
        return 0;
}
```

Answer:

```cpp
#include <iostream>
#include <cstdlib>
using namespace std;

class Complex_Num
{
private:
        double re;
        double im;
public:
        Complex_Num(double r=0, double i=0) {re = r; im = i;}
        Complex_Num operator+(const Complex_Num& z) const;
        Complex_Num operator-(const Complex_Num& z) const;
        Complex_Num operator*(const Complex_Num& z) const;
        Complex_Num operator/(const Complex_Num& z) const;
        friend ostream& operator<<(ostream& out, const Complex_Num& z);
};

Complex_Num Complex_Num::operator+(const Complex_Num& z) const
{
        Complex_Num tmp;
        tmp.re = re + z.re;
        tmp.im = im + z.im;
        return tmp;
}

Complex_Num Complex_Num::operator-(const Complex_Num& z) const
{
        Complex_Num tmp;
        tmp.re = re - z.re;
        tmp.im = im - z.im;
        return tmp;
}

Complex_Num Complex_Num::operator*(const Complex_Num& z) const
{
        Complex_Num tmp;
        tmp.re = (re*z.re) - (im*z.im);
        tmp.im = (im*z.re) + (re*z.im);
        return tmp;
}

Complex_Num Complex_Num::operator/(const Complex_Num& z) const
{
        if(z.re == 0 && z.im == 0)
        {
                cout << "Division by zero is not allowed\n";
                exit(EXIT_FAILURE); /* Termination of the program. There are
less "aggressive" ways to handle this error. For example, to create an
exception as we'll see in Ch.22. */
        }
        Complex_Num tmp;
        double div = (z.re*z.re) + (z.im*z.im);
```

```
        tmp.re = ((re*z.re) + (im*z.im))/div;
        tmp.im = ((im*z.re) - (re*z.im))/div;
        return tmp;
}

ostream& operator<<(ostream& out, const Complex_Num& z)
{
        out << showpos << "z = " << z.re << z.im << 'j' << '\n';
        return out;
}
```

Comments: The standard library provides the `complex` class, which supports many operations with complex numbers.

C.18.3 Define the `Time` class with private members the hours (e.g., `hrs`), the minutes (e.g., `mins`), and the seconds (e.g., `secs`). Add appropriate functions so that the following program works.

```
int main()
{
        Time t1, t2(23, 59, 59); /* There is a restriction that the class has
just one constructor. The members of t1 should be initialized with 0. Also,
another restriction is that the constructor's parameters have the same names
as the private members. */
        ++t2; /* The number of seconds increases by one. If the time is
23:59:59, as in the case of t2, the new time becomes 0:0:0. */
        cout << (t1 == t2) << '\n'; /* Compare the two times and if they are
the same, the program should display 1, otherwise 0. For example, with these
values of t1 and t2 the program should display 1. */
        cout << t1; /* The time should be displayed in the h:m:s format. For
example, 0:0:0. */
        return 0;
}
```

Answer:

```
#include <iostream>
using std::cout;
using std::ostream;

class Time
{
private:
        int hrs;
        int mins;
        int secs;
public:
        Time(int hrs=0, int mins=0, int secs=0);
        bool operator==(const Time& t) const;
        void operator++();
        friend ostream& operator<<(ostream& out, const Time& t);
};

Time::Time(int hrs, int mins, int secs)
{
        this->hrs = hrs; /* Due to the restriction about same names we use the
this pointer. */
```

```
        this->mins = mins;
        this->secs = secs;
}

bool Time::operator==(const Time& t) const
{
        if((hrs == t.hrs) && (mins == t.mins) && (secs == t.secs))
                return true;
        else
                return false;
}

void Time::operator++()
{
        secs++;
        if(secs == 60)
        {
                secs = 0;
                mins++;
                if(mins == 60)
                {
                        mins = 0;
                        hrs++;
                        if(hrs == 24)
                                hrs = 0;
                }
        }
}

ostream& operator<<(ostream& out, const Time& t)
{
        out << t.hrs << ':' << t.mins << ':' << t.secs << '\n';
        return out;
}
```

C.18.4 Add appropriate functions in class T so that the following program works.

```
class T
{
private:
        char *s;
        ...
};

int main()
{
        char str[100];

        cout << "Enter text: ";
        cin.getline(str, sizeof(str)); /* Assume that the input string will
have less than 100 characters. */
        T t1(str); // The string should be stored in the s member.

        cout << "Enter text: ";
        cin.getline(str, sizeof(str));
        T t2(str);
```

```
        cout << (t1 == t2) << '\n'; /* If the input strings are the same, the
program should display 0, otherwise a non-zero value. */
        t1+t2; // The t2.s should be added at the end of t1.s.
        t1-'a'; // The 'a' characters of t1.s should be replaced with *.
        t1.show(); /* For example, if the user enters abc and daf the program
should display *bcd*f. */
        return 0;
}
```

Answer:

```
#include <iostream>
#include <cstring>
using std::cout;
using std::cin;

class T
{
private:
        char *s;
public:
        T(char str[]);
        ~T();
        int operator==(const T& t) const;
        void operator+(const T& t);
        void operator-(char ch);
        void show() const {cout << s << '\n';}
};

T::T(char str[])
{
        s = new char[strlen(str)+1];
        strcpy(s, str);
}

T::~T()
{
        delete[] s;
}

int T::operator==(const T& t) const
{
        return strcmp(s, t.s);
}

void T::operator+(const T& t)
{
        char *p;

        p = new char[strlen(s)+strlen(t.s)+1];
        p[0] = '\0';
        strcpy(p, s);
        strcat(p, t.s);
        delete[] s; // Release the old memory.
        s = p; // Now, s points to the new memory.
}
```

```
void T::operator-(char ch)
{
        for(int i = 0; i < strlen(s); i++)
                if(s[i] == ch)
                        s[i] = '*';
}
```

C.18.5 Consider the following Student class. Add any function or member you think is needed so that the following program works. Do not declare any function inline and disable the copy operation, that is, do not allow the statement s1 = s2. There is also the restriction to define up to four functions in total (except main()).

```
class Student
{
private:
        int code; // Student's identifier.
        int courses; // Number of courses.
        float *grd; // Allocate memory to store the grades in all courses.
        ...
public:
        ...
};

int main()
{
        int i;
        Student s1, s2;

        cin >> s1 >> s2; /* The program should read values and store them in
        the code and courses members of the two objects. Then, the program should
        read the grades of each student and store them in the memory pointed to by
        the grd member. */
        i = (s1 > s2); /* The overloaded function should compare the number of
        the passed courses and return 1 if the first student has succeeded in more
        courses, 2 if the second student has succeeded in more courses and 3 if they
        succeeded in the same number of courses. A course is considered passed if its
        grade is >= 5. */
        if(...) /* Check the value of i according to the above. Add code so
        that the program displays the code of the student who has succeeded in most
        courses or Same if they have succeeded in the same number. */
        return 0;
}
```

Answer:

```
#include <iostream>
#include <string>
using std::cout;
using std::cin;
using std::istream;

class Student
{
private:
        int code;
        int courses;
```

```
        float *grd;
        int suc; /* This member is added to hold the number of the passed
courses. */
public:
        ~Student();
        void show() const;
        int operator>(const Student& s) const;
        friend istream& operator>>(istream& in, Student& s);
        Student& operator=(const Student&) = delete; /* Disable the copy
operation. */
};

Student::~Student()
{
        delete[] grd;
}

int Student::operator>(const Student& s) const
{
        if(suc > s.suc)
                return 1;
        else if(suc < s.suc)
                return 2;
        else
                return 3;
}

void Student::show() const
{
        cout << "\nCode:" << code << '\n';
}

istream& operator>>(istream& in, Student& s)
{
        int i;

        cout << "Enter code: ";
        in >> s.code;
        cout << "Enter number of courses: ";
        in >> s.courses;
        s.grd = new float[s.courses];
        s.suc = 0;

        for(i = 0; i < s.courses; i++)
        {
                cout << "Enter grade: ";
                in >> s.grd[i];
                if(s.grd[i] >= 5)
                        s.suc++;
        }
        return in;
}

int main()
{
        int i;
        Student s1, s2;
```

```
        cin >> s1 >> s2;
        i = (s1 > s2);
        if(i == 1)
                s1.show();
        else if(i == 2)
                s2.show();
        else
                cout << "\nSame number of passed courses\n";
        return 0;
}
```

C.18.6 Define the `Triangle` class with members three integers, which correspond to the sides of a triangle (e.g., a, b, and c). Overload the `!=` operator, so that we can compare the perimeters of two triangles (e.g., write a statement such as `t1 != t2;` to compare the perimeters of `t1` and `t2`). Also, overload the `[]` operator, so that new values are assigned to the sides of the triangle (e.g., the statement `t1[0] = 3;` should make the side a of the `t1` object equal to 3, while the statement `t1[1] = 5;` should make the side b equal to 5). Add appropriate functions in the class. Write a program that tests the functionality of the `Triangle` class.

```
#include <iostream>
#include <cstdlib>
using std::cout;

class Triangle
{
private:
        int a;
        int b;
        int c;
public:
        Triangle(int dim1, int dim2, int dim3);
        bool operator!=(const Triangle& t) const;
        int& operator[](int dim);
        void show() const;
};

Triangle::Triangle(int dim1, int dim2, int dim3)
{
        a = dim1;
        b = dim2;
        c = dim3;
}

bool Triangle::operator!=(const Triangle& t) const
{
        if(a+b+c != t.a+t.b+t.c)
                return true;
        else
                return false;
}

int& Triangle::operator[](int dim)
{
        if(dim == 0)
                return a;
```

```
        else if(dim == 1)
                return b;
        else if(dim == 2)
                return c;
        else
        {
                cout << "Error: Wrong index\n";
                exit(EXIT_FAILURE); // Terminate the program.
        }
}

void Triangle::show() const
{
        cout << a << ' ' << b << ' ' << c << '\n';
}

int main()
{
        Triangle t1(1, 2, 3), t2(4, 1, 1);

        if(t1 != t2) // if(t1.operator!=(t2))
                cout << "Different perimeters\n";
        else
                cout << "Same perimeters\n";

        t1[0] = 4; // t1.operator[](0);
        t1[1] = 5;
        t1[2] = 6;
        t1.show();
        return 0;
}
```

Comments: Regarding the design of the class, I declare the sides of the triangle as private members. It is not wrong to make them public, but since the main reason for using a class is to hide data, it is a good practice to declare sensitive information as private. To communicate with the class I declare the public function `show()`. To initialize the members I declare a constructor. Alternatively, I could declare a public function `set()` and call it after the creation of the object to make the initialization. For the reasons mentioned when discussing about the constructor, I prefer to use a constructor. There is no reason to define a destructor, the default is fine. The `operator[]` function works as in example C.18.5. For example, with the statement `t1[0] = 4;` the `operator[]` is called, which returns a reference to a. Thus, a becomes 4. Note that if the return type was `int` the compiler would display an error message that the left operand in the assignment is not lvalue.

C.18.7 Complete the declaration and the definition of the template function `sum()`, so that it can return the sum of the elements of a `vector` containing integers, as well as the sum of the `prc` members of a `vector` containing `Product` objects. Add appropriate functions in the `Product` class so that the following program works.

```
??? sum(???) // Find the prototype.
{
        ...
        for(int i = 0; i < v.size(); i++) /* v may contain integers or
elements of type Product. */
                t = t + v[i]; // Calculate the sum.
        ...
}
```

```
class Product
{
        ...
        int code;
        float prc;
        ...
};

int main()
{
        vector<int> v_i = {1, 2, 3};
        vector<Product> v_p = {Product(100, 5), Product(200, 10), Product(300,
15), Product(400, 20)};

        int i = sum(v_i); /* sum() should return the sum of the v_i elements,
that is, 6. */
        cout << i << '\n'; // The program outputs 6.
        Product p = sum(v_p); /* The value of p.prc should be equal to the sum
of the prc members of the v_p elements, that is, 50. */
        cout << p.prc << '\n'; // The program outputs 50.
        return 0;
}
```

Answer:

```
#include <iostream>
#include <vector>
using namespace std;

template <typename T> T sum(const vector<T>& v)
{
        T t = {0}; /* Assign an initial value. For example, if the type of T
is int, t will become 0. If the type is Product, the constructor will
initialize the members of t to 0. In either case, the initial value 0 is
necessary in order to calculate the sum correctly. */
        for(int i = 0; i < v.size(); i++)
                t = t + v[i];
        return t;
}

class Product
{
        private:
                int code;
        public:
                float prc;
                Product(int c = 0, float p = 0);
                Product& operator+(const Product& p);
};

Product::Product(int c, float p)
{
        code = c;
        prc = p;
}
```

```
Product& Product::operator+(const Product& p)
{
        prc += p.prc;
        return *this;
}
```

Comments: First, let's find the declaration of `sum()`. In `main()` we see that `sum()` returns both `int` and `Product` types. So, we understand that its return type must be generic (e.g., `T`). The argument in both `sum()` calls is `vector` of `int` and `Product` types. Therefore, the type of the `vector` elements must be generic, the same as the return type `T`. As we know, for better performance, we pass a reference, which we make it `const` so that its elements cannot be modified. Thus, we come to the declaration of `sum()`. Let's see its definition. We understand that the type of the `t` variable must be generic and we initialize it with `0`, in order to calculate the sum correctly. `sum()` ends with the return of `t`.

Let's decode the definition of the `Product` class. From the statement `cout << p.prc;` we understand that the `prc` member is public. I declare the `code` private; I could also make it public. From the initialization of `v_p` we understand that we need to add a constructor. We set default zero values, which are needed (basically, `prc` must be set to `0`) when the `t` object is created in `sum()`. Specifically, when `sum(v_p)` is called, `T` will be replaced by `Product` and the object `t` will be created. We come to the calculation of the sum. Okay, when `T` is `int` there is no problem, the sum of integers will be calculated. But, when `T` is `Product` how will the addition be done and what data should be added? We understand that we need to overload the `+` operator and add the `prc` members to calculate their sum. The `operator+` function returns the `t` object and each addition in the `for` loop stores the current sum in `t.prc`.

C.18.8 Consider the following classes `Product` and `Employee`:

```
class Product
{
        private:
                int code;
                float prc; // Price.
        public:
                ...
};


class Employee
{
        private:
                string name;
                float sal; // Salary.
        public:
                ...
};
```

Define the template function `sort()` that takes as parameter a `vector` object (e.g., `v`), which contains either `Product` or `Employee` elements and sorts them. If it contains `Product` elements, the sorting should be done in `prc` increase order. If it contains `Employee` elements, the sorting should be done in name alphabetical order. To sort the elements use the selection sort algorithm of C.12.5. Each class should contain an `inline` constructor, an `inline` function named `show()` to display the values of its members, and the necessary function to compare the elements of `v`. Write a program that declares two `vector` objects with `Product` and `Employee` elements, calls `sort()` and displays their elements.

```
#include <iostream>
#include <string>
#include <vector>
```

```cpp
using std::cout;
using std::string;
using std::vector;

template <typename T> void sort(vector<T>& v);

class Product
{
        private:
                int code;
                float prc;
        public:
                Product(int c = 0, float p = 0) {code = c; prc = p;}
                bool operator>(const Product& p) const;
                void show() const {cout << "C:" << code << " P:" << prc << '\n';}
};

bool Product::operator>(const Product& p) const
{
        if(prc > p.prc)
                return true;
        return false;
}

class Employee
{
        private:
                string name;
                float sal;
        public:
                Employee(const string& n = "", float s = 0) {name = n; sal = s;}
                bool operator>(const Employee& e) const;
                void show() const {cout << "N:" << name << " S:" << sal << '\n';}
};

bool Employee::operator>(const Employee& e) const
{
        if(name > e.name)
                return true;
        return false;
}

int main()
{
        int i;
        vector<Product> v_prd = {Product(10, 3.5), Product(20, 1.5),
Product(30, 2.5)};
        vector<Employee> v_emp = {Employee("Mike", 100), Employee("John",
200), Employee("Nick", 300)};

        sort(v_prd);
        sort(v_emp);
        for(i = 0; i < v_prd.size(); i++)
                v_prd[i].show();
        for(i = 0; i < v_emp.size(); i++)
                v_emp[i].show();
        return 0;
}
```

```
template <typename T> void sort(vector<T>& v)
{
        int i, j, size;
        T tmp; // The constructor of each class will be called.

        size = v.size();
        for(i = 0; i < size-1; i++)
        {
                for(j = i+1; j < size; j++)
                {
                        if(v[i] > v[j]) /* To compare the elements the
overloaded > operator function of each class is called. */
                        {
                                tmp = v[i];
                                v[i] = v[j];
                                v[j] = tmp;
                        }
                }
        }
}
```

UNSOLVED EXERCISES

U.18.1 Modify the following program so that it is compiled and displays:

```
Begin
Show
End

#include <iostream>
using namespace std;
int main()
{
        "Show\n" << cout;
        return 0;
}
```

There is a restriction not to change main(), it should remain the same.

U.18.2 Modify the Array in example C.18.5 to Safe_Arr, to dynamically create a safe array. Add appropriate functions in the class so that the following program works.

```
class Safe_Arr
{
private:
        int *arr; /* This pointer should be used to allocate memory for
size integers. */
        int size; // Number of elements.
public:
        ...
};
```

```
int main()
{
        int i;
        Safe_Arr s_arr(10); /* The size should become equal to the
value of the argument and memory for size integers should be
allocated. */
        s_arr[0] = 10;
        s_arr[30] = 40; /* The class should check if the index has a
valid value. If not, as in this case, the program should display a
related message and terminate. */
        i = s_arr[0];
        std::cout << i << '\n'; // The program should output 10.
        return 0;
}
```

U.18.3 Complete the definition of T according to the comments so that the program works.

```
class T
{
        ...
};

int main()
{
        int a, b;
        T t;

        t >> a >> b; /* The class should read two integer values and
store them in a and b. */
        t << a << b; // The class should display the values of a and b.
        return 0;
}
```

For example, if the user enters 10 and 20, the program should display:

```
Enter number: 10
Enter number: 20
Output number: 10
Output number: 20
```

U.18.4 Consider the Rect class of the example C.18.1. Add appropriate functions so that the following program works.

```
int main()
{
        Rect r1(10, 20), r2(30, 40), r3(50, 60);

        r1 = r2 = r3; /* The dimensions of r1 and r2 should become equal
to that of r3. */
        (r1 += 5).show(); /* The number 5 should be added in both
dimensions of r1 and then show() should be called. */
        return 0;
}
```

U.18.5 Define the Line class that simulates the line $y = ax + b$. The coefficients a and b should be private members of the class. Add appropriate functions so that the following program works.

```
int main()
{
        Line ln1(1, 2), ln2(1, 3);

        cout << (ln1 || ln2) << '\n'; /* The program should check if the
two lines are parallel, that is, if ln1 and ln2 have the same a. If yes,
the function should return true, otherwise false. */
        cout << ln1(2.5); /* Add an overloaded function of (), which
returns the value a*x+b where x is the value of the argument (e.g.,
2.5). For example, the program should display 4.5. */
        return 0;
}
```

U.18.6 Define the `Time` class with private members the hours (e.g., `hrs`) and the minutes (e.g., `mins`). Add appropriate functions so that the following program works.

```
int main()
{
        Time t1(15, 30), t2(11, 30);

        Time t3 = t1+t2; /* t3.hrs becomes 27 and t3.mins becomes 0. */
        t3--; /* The minutes should decrement by one. That is, t3.hrs
becomes 26 and t3.mins becomes 59. */
        ++t1; /* The hours should increment by one. That is, t1.hrs
becomes 16. */
        t2[0] = 18; /* If the index is 0, the hour should change,
otherwise the minutes. That is, t2.hrs becomes 18. */
        cout << t1 << t2 << t3; /* Display the time hold in each object in
h:m format. That is, the program should display 16:30   18:30   26:59. */
        return 0;
}
```

U.18.7 Define the class `Polynomial` that simulates a polynomial of the form $f(x) = ax^2 + bx + c$. The class should contain:

1. The default constructor that initializes the coefficients of the polynomial, that is, a, b, and c to 1. The coefficients should be private members and assume that they are integers.
2. A constructor that initializes the coefficients of the polynomial with values that the user enters.
3. The `show()` function that displays the polynomial in the form ax^2 + bx + c.
4. The `calc(int x)` function that returns the result of the polynomial for the value x.
5. An overloaded function of the + operator, so that additions may be performed between polynomials and integers (e.g., `t1+i`, where `t1` is a `Polynomial` object and `i` is an integer). That is, i should be added to all the coefficients of `t1`.
6. An overloaded function of the + operator, so that additions may be performed between polynomials (e.g., `t1=t2+t3`). That is, the function should return a polynomial with coefficients the sum of the coefficients of `t2` and `t3`.
7. An overloaded function of the [] operator, so that we can assign new values to the coefficients of the polynomial (e.g., with the statement `t1[0] = 3`; the coefficient a of the `t1` object should become 3, while with the statement `t1[1] = 10`; the coefficient b should become 10). If the value of the index is not valid, that is, it is not 0, 1, or 2, the program should terminate.
8. An overloaded function of the == operator, so that we can check if two polynomials are equal, that is, if their respective coefficients are equal.

Write a program that tests the functionality of the `Polynomial` class.

More about Classes

19

In this chapter we'll discuss some more specialized topics regarding the class properties, such as how to perform automatic type conversions with classes, declare static functions in a class, and how to define a constructor with a member initializer list. We'll continue our discussion from Chapter 16 to see how move semantics and rvalue references work. We'll also discuss the copy constructor, friend classes, and nested classes, which are classes declared within other classes.

CONVERSIONS TO CLASS TYPE

As we said in Chapter 17, when a constructor takes a single argument, a value of that argument type can be converted to the class type. That is, the constructor acts as a conversion function. For example, consider the T class:

```
class T
{
private:
       int a;
public:
       T() {}
       T(int i) {a = i;}
       void show() const {cout << a << '\n';}
};
```

Now, we can write:

```
T t;
t = 20;
t.show();
```

The integer value 20 is implicitly converted to a T object. The conversion happens automatically, without using an explicit type cast. Specifically, the compiler uses the T(int) constructor to create a temporary T object and passes the value 20 as argument. Then, the members of the temporary object (in our example it is only a) are copied into t. Thus, the program displays 20.

Implicit conversion also occurs when an integer value is passed to a function that accepts a T object. For example:

```
void f(const T& t)
{
       t.show();
}
...
f(20);
```

`f()` displays the value `20`. Implicit conversion also occurs when a function declared to return a `T` object returns an integer value. For example:

```
T f()
{
        return 20;
}
...
T t = f();
t.show();
```

If we do not want the constructor to operate as a conversion function we precede its declaration with the keyword `explicit`. For example:

```
explicit T(int a);
```

Now, if we write `t = 20`, the compiler will display an error message. However, it is allowed to make a conversion using an explicit type cast. For example:

```
t = static_cast<T>(20);
```

Note that if the constructor is declared as `explicit` and defined outside the class, the word `explicit` is not added to its definition. For example:

```
explicit T::T(int a) {} // Wrong.
T::T(int a) {} // Correct.
```

Let's see an example, where the argument of the constructor is string:

```
#include <iostream> // Example 19.1
#include <string>
using std::cout;
using std::string;

class T
{
private:
        string str;
public:
        T(string s = "") {str = s;}
        void show() const {cout << str << '\n';}
};

int main()
{
        string s = "text";
        T t;

        t = s;
        t.show();
        return 0;
}
```

With the statement `t = s;` the constructor is called to create a temporary object with argument the value of `s`, that is, `text`. Then, the `text` is copied to the `str` member of `t` and the program displays `text`.

You may wonder, don't these implied conversions (e.g., t = s) make the code more difficult to understand? Yes, I agree. My preference is to make clear the creation of the temporary object and not to use the constructor to convert the type. That is, I prefer to write:

t = T("text"); rather than t = s.

Are the implicit conversions safe? No, they are not; due to their automatic nature, an unintended assignment may cause an undesirable conversion and introduce a bug that will change the behaviour of the program. Let's see such an example:

```cpp
#include <iostream> // Example 19.2
#include <string>
using std::string;

class Student
{
private:
        string name;
        int grd[5];
public:
        Student(int g);
        Student(string s);
        int& operator[](int i);
};

Student::Student(string s)
{
        for(int i = 0; i < 5; i++)
                grd[i] = -1;
        name = s;
}

Student::Student(int g)
{
        for(int i = 0; i < 5; i++)
                grd[i] = g;
        name = "none";
}

int& Student::operator[](int i)
{
        return grd[i];
}

int main()
{
        Student s("first");

s = 2; /* The intention is to change the value of an element in the array,
but the programmer made a mistake and didn't specify the element.
Instead, this assignment changes the name to none and the values of the grd
array to 2. */
        return 0;
}
```

The intention of the programmer is to change the value of an element in the array. For example, suppose that you want to make the first grade equal to 2. Instead of writing `s[0] = 2;` which calls the `operator[]` function to change the `grd[0]`, you make a mistake and write `s = 2;` instead. However, with this statement, the compiler uses the `Student(int g);` constructor and converts the value 2 to a temporary object, which is copied to s. So, the value of s.name changes from `first` to `none` and all the elements of the grd array become equal to 2.

Had we made the constructor `explicit`, that is, write `explicit Student(int g);` the compiler would not allow the conversion and produce an error message to inform the programmer. No, I have not made such a mistake to date. But, because there is always a first time for everything, I prefer to declare as `explicit` a constructor that accepts a single argument, in order to protect myself from potential unintended implicit conversions which lead to hard-to-trace bugs. In fact, I'd prefer the standard having made a single-argument constructor `explicit` by default.

CONVERSIONS FROM CLASS TYPE

As a type can be converted to an object, an object (e.g., t) can also be converted to a type. For example:

```
int i = t;
```

This statement is allowed if a conversion function is defined in the class, as follows:

```
operator type();
```

where `type` is the name of the type to which the object will be converted. If this definition is missing the compiler issues an error message since it cannot assign a T object to `int`.

When declaring conversion functions certain rules apply. For example, the conversion function must be a member of the class, with no return type specified in its declaration and take no arguments. The return type is that of `type`. For example, the function prototype for conversion to `int` is:

```
operator int();
```

Also, when the conversion function is declared, explicit conversions are allowed. For example:

```
int i = static_cast<int>(t);
```

Usually, the conversion function does not change the state of the respective object, so it is declared as `const`. Let's see an example where two conversion functions are defined:

```
#include <iostream> // Example 19.3

class T
{
private:
        int a;
        double d;
public:
        T(int i);
        operator int() const; // Conversion function to int.
        operator double() const; // Conversion function to double.
};
```

```
T::T(int i)
{
        a = i;
        d = 1.2;
}


T::operator int() const /* It is an error to add the return type and write
int T::operator int() const. */
{
        return a+2;
}


T::operator double() const
{
        return d+2;
}


int main()
{
        int i;
        double k;

        T t = 3; // The int type is converted to class type.
        i = t; // The int conversion function i = t.int(); is called.
        k = t; // The double conversion function k = t.double() is called.
        std::cout << i << ' ' << static_cast<int>(t) << '\n'; /* The program
displays 5 twice. */
        std::cout << k << ' ' << static_cast<double>(t) << '\n'; /* The program
displays 3.2 twice. */
        return 0;
}
```

Strange as it may seem, you can see that no return type is specified in the declaration of the conversion function. The return type is that of the target type. That is, the `operator int` returns `int`. With the statement `i = t;` the `int` conversion function is called and `i` becomes 5. With the statement `k = t;` the `double` conversion function is called and `k` becomes 3.2. Similarly, with the explicit `static_cast<>` conversions, the corresponding conversion functions are called again. Note that if we do not use explicit conversion and write `cout << t;` the compiler will display an error message since it does not know which of the `int` or `double` conversion function to use.

Again one might ask, don't these implicit automatic conversions make the code harder to understand and less safe since a careless error (e.g., write `i = t` instead of `i = 1`) may lead to an unintended conversion and value assignment? Yes, I agree. My preference is to declare a function in the class that does the same thing and call it rather than using a conversion function. That is, I prefer to write:

```
class T
{
        ...
        int handle_int() {return a+2;}
};
```

and write: `i = t.handle_int();` so that the code is clear. Of course, one might find this less elegant or less convenient and prefer to write `i = t;`. Just remember, that if you decide to use implicit conversion functions, do it with special care.

A popular usage of a conversion function is when checking the state of a stream in a condition. For example:

```
while(cin >> i) {...}
```

As we know, with the `>>` operator a value will be read, stored in `i` and a reference to `cin` is returned. The `istream` class provides an `operator bool` conversion function. Thus, to evaluate the condition, this conversion function is called, which, if the state of `cin` is valid, it returns `true`, otherwise, if an error occurs, it returns `false`.

As with a constructor, if we do not want to allow implicit conversions we can use the word `explicit`. If the conversion function is made `explicit` we must use typecast explicitly to use it. For example:

```
class A
{
        ...
        explicit operator int() const {return 10;}
};

int i;
A a;
i = a; // Wrong.
i = static_cast<int>(a); // Correct, use typecast for explicit conversion.
```

Before we move on to the next section, I'd like to say again that I'm not so fond of using implicit conversions to/from class type, because I prefer things to be clear, simple, and safe. That is what really matters.

POINTER TO A FUNCTION MEMBER

In Chapter 8, we discussed pointers to functions. For example, with `void (*ptr)(int, int); ptr` is declared as a pointer to a function, which takes two integer parameters and returns nothing. Now, let's see how we can declare pointers to functions that are members of a class. For example:

```
#include <iostream> // Example 19.4

class T
{
public:
        void f(int a, int b) {std::cout << a-b << '\n';}
};

typedef void (T::*fptr)(int a, int b);

int main()
{
        T t;

        fptr p; // Pointer declaration.
        p = &T::f; /* This is the syntax to make the pointer point to the
member function. */
        (t.*p)(8, 5); // Call the function through the. * operator.

        T *r = &t;
        (r->*p)(8, 5); // Call the function through the ->* operator.
        return 0;
}
```

To make it easier to write the pointer declaration and the type of the corresponding variables it is more convenient to use the `typedef` statement and create a synonym for the type of the pointer. Fine, but how about the syntax of this declaration? It seems complex. Yes, it might seem, but it is not, as long as we follow the simple method that we've mentioned in Chapters 8 and 11.

As we said, an easy way to declare a pointer to a function is first to write the prototype of the function and then replace the function name with an expression of the form `(*fptr)`. For example, we write the prototype of `f()`, replace `f` with `(*fptr)` and because `f()` is contained in class `T` we add `T::`. Then, we add the `typedef` word.

To remind you, the syntax with `typedef` resembles that of a variable declaration, just preceded by the word `typedef`. For example, we add the word `typedef` to the declaration of `fptr`, and so we can use the `fptr` name in the program. That is, `fptr` is a synonym of the type "pointer to a function member of class `T`, which takes two integer parameters and returns nothing". Using this synonym the declaration of corresponding variables (e.g., `p`) is simplified.

Alternatively, as we know from Chapter 11, we can use the `using` keyword to create a synonym. For example, we can write:

```
using fptr = void (T::*) (int a, int b);
```

Without using synonyms we can declare the p pointer as follows:

```
int main()
{
        void (T::*p)(int a, int b); // Pointer declaration.
        p = &T::f;
        ...
}
```

Alternatively, the declaration becomes very easy with C++11, because we can just use `auto` to deduce the type of the variable for us. For example, we write:

```
auto p = &T::f;
```

As I've told you, it is my intention to show you several alternatives and not just the easiest so that you know how they work in case you may meet them in code written by others.

To make a pointer point to a class member, we apply the `&` operator to the full name of the member. As mentioned in the comments of the program, if the object is used to call the function, we use the `.*` operator, while if a pointer is used, we use the `->*` operator. They must be enclosed in parentheses, because the priority of the call operator `()` is higher. The program displays 3 and 3.

A pointer to a member function may be used to call the function indirectly when we do not know its name. If we know it, there is no reason to use a pointer. That is, we make the call directly by writing `t.f(8, 5);`. So, don't be scared with the example, you may never use such a pointer. But if it happens, this is an example how to use it. The second reason for this example is to discuss the `.*` and `->*` operators, so that you don't wonder about their meaning when you see them in the priority table.

A static member is not associated with an object, so we don't use its full name to declare it. For example:

```
class T
{
public:
        static void f() {}
};

void (T::*p)() = &T::f; // Wrong.
void (*p)() = &T::f; // Correct.
auto p = &T::f;
```

MEMBER INITIALIZATION LIST

As we know, one method to initialize class members is within the body of the constructor. For example:

```
class T
{
private:
        int a;
public:
        double b;
        string s;
        T(int arg1, double arg2);
};

T::T(int arg1, double arg2)
{
        a = arg1;
        b = arg2;
        s = "Text";
}
```

Alternatively, class members can be initialized with a special syntax when the constructor of the class is called. This syntax is called *member initializer list*. For example:

```
T::T(int arg1, double arg2) : s("Text"), a(arg1), b(arg2)
{
}
```

Notice that this member initializer list syntax can only be used with constructors, not with member functions. As shown, a colon: is added and the comma is used to separate the member initializations. First we write the name of the member and then its initial value in parentheses. Thus, Text is stored in s, a becomes arg1 and b becomes arg2. Note that these initializations happen when the object is created and before the body of the constructor is executed.

Although it is logical to think that initializations are made from left to right, that is, first s is initialized and then the rest, the fact is that members are initialized in the order in which they appear in the class declaration, that is, first a, then b, and last s. In general, the initialization order plays no role. But if the value of one member is related to the initialization of another then it may have an effect. For example:

```
class C
{
        ...
        int a;
        int b;
        C(int m) : b(m), a(b) {}
        ...
};

int main()
{
        C c(10);
        ...
}
```

When the c object is created, first a will be initialized with the random value of b and then b will become equal to 10.

 To avoid unintended initializations it is safer to initialize the list members in the same order in which they are declared in the class. In fact, it is better to avoid using members to initialize other members.

A typical use of the member initializer list is to initialize const variables. Recall from Chapter 17 that because the definition of the class does not allocate memory for its members we cannot initialize a const member. However, we can use this syntax and initialize it. For example:

```
class T
{
        ...
        const int k; // It is not allowed to write const int k = 10;
        ...
};

T::T(int arg1, double arg2) : a(arg1), b(arg2), k(10)
{
}
```

When the constructor is called, k becomes 10. As with const members, we can use this syntax to initialize reference variables. For example:

```
int g = 20;
class T
{
        ...
        int &r; // It is not allowed to write int &r = g;
        ...
};

T::T(int arg1, double arg2) : a(arg1), b(arg2), r(g)
{
}
```

 We can use the member initializer list syntax to initialize const members and references.

When the constructor is called, r becomes 20. If the member is pointer, it can also be initialized. For example:

```
class T
{
        ...
        int *p;
        ...
};

T::T(int arg1, double arg2) : p(new int[arg1])
{
}
```

To make clearer the initialization, I prefer to initialize the ordinary variables in the body of the constructor and not all mixed together in the same line. For example:

```
T::T(int arg1, double arg2) : k(10), r(g)
{
        a = arg1;
        b = arg2;
        s = "Text";
}
```

Others prefer to initialize all members in the list. One reason is to avoid compilation errors that may occur with members that require initialization (e.g., const). A second reason is for better performance. For example, in the previous approach, the default constructor of the string class is called first to initialize s with an empty string, and then the copy function is called to assign the Text to it. Yes, it is more efficient to initialize it in the member list since the copy constructor of the string class, as we'll see below, makes directly the initialization. Note that for the basic types (e.g., a) there is no difference in the performance whether the initialization is done in the list or in the body of the constructor.

FORWARDING CONSTRUCTOR

C++11 extends initialization capabilities by providing the forwarding constructor. During the process of creating an object, such a constructor calls another constructor of the class to delegate a task. This is why its common name is *forwarding* or *delegating* constructor. Let's see an example:

```
int n1 = 5;
int n2 = 10;

class T
{
private:
        int x;
public:
        T(int a, int b) {x = a+b;} // Non-forwarding constructor.
        T() : T(n1, n2) {} // Forwarding constructor.
        T(int a) : T(a, n2) {cout << "Delegate\n";} /* Forwarding constructor. */
        void show() const {cout << x;}
};
```

The latter two constructors call the first one. When a forwarding constructor calls a second constructor, the body of that second constructor (e.g., x = a+b;) will be executed first and then its own (e.g., cout << "Delegate\n";). When the execution of its own body is completed, the creation of the object is considered completed. As shown, the syntax of the forwarding constructor is similar to that of the member initialization list except that the list must contain only one item, which is the target constructor. That is, it is not allowed to initialize extra members. For example:

```
T() : T(n1, n2), x(10) {} // Wrong
```

Note that in this example we could use a single constructor with default argument values, I just used three to show you the calling syntax.

Typically, a constructor is called by others when they all need to perform a common set of actions. For example, we could change the class to:

```
class T
{
private:
        int x;
public:
        T(int a, int b) {x = a+b;}
        T() {x = n1+n2;}
        T(int a) {x = a+n2;}
};
```

Comparing the two implementations, I think that it is more readable and also safer for the same code to exist in a single place than to be repeated around, so that if a change needs to be made, you have to edit it once. Thus, forwarding constructors can simplify the construction process and make it safer and easier to control.

Notice that this method of calling the constructor works differently from the explicit call of the constructor inside the body of the function. For example, if you write something like this:

```
T()
{
        T(n1, n2); // Creation of an unnamed object.
}
```

the constructor will not be called as you intended, but a new anonymous temporary object will be created, which will not be used. That is, if we write:

```
int main()
{
        T t;
        t.show();
        return 0;
}
```

the program will display a random value for x and not 15.

COPY CONSTRUCTOR

The copy constructor is a special function that is automatically invoked whenever a new object is created and initialized with an existing object. For example:

```
#include <iostream> // Example 19.5

class T
{
private:
        int a;
public:
        int b;
        T(int i, int j) {a=i; b=j;}
        void show() const {std::cout << a << ' ' << b << '\n';}
};
```

```
int main()
{
        T t1(1, 2);
        T t2(t1); // The default copy constructor is called.
        T t3 = t1; // The default copy constructor is called.

        t2.show();
        t3.show();
        return 0;
}
```

Just as the compiler provides the default constructor if no constructor is defined, the default destructor if no destructor is defined and the default copy function, it provides the default copy constructor if none is defined. Thus, to create the t2 and t3 objects, the default copy constructor is called. And what this constructor does? As its name implies it copies one by one the non-static members of the existing object into the new one. For example, with the statement T t2(t1); the compiler creates the t2 object and calls the copy constructor to copy the members of t1 to t2.

This copy is also called *shallow copy*. The way that each member will be copied depends on its type. The basic types are copied directly, if it is an array its elements are copied and if it is an object the copy constructor of its class is called to make the copy. Similarly, with the T t3 = t1; statement, which is an alternative to T t3(t1);, the copy constructor is called and copies the members of t1 to t3. If the class contains static members they are not affected since they belong to the class and not to an object. The program displays 1 2 twice.

Note that in an ordinary assignment, such as t2 = t1, it is not the copy constructor that is called, but the default copy operator= function, which copies the t1 members to t2. To make it clear, the copy constructor is called when the object is created (e.g., T t2 = t1;), whereas when the object already exists (e.g., t2 = t1;) the copy function is called.

Define Our Copy Constructor

There are some special situations that we need to define our copy constructor. The typical situation is when the class contains pointer(s); we'll see such an example later. Fine, how we declare it? The copy constructor has the same name as the class, it has no return type, and takes as a parameter a reference to an object of the respective class. The usual convention is to declare the reference as const, in the sense that the copy constructor creates a copy of an object without modifying it. If we make it non-const, it would not be allowed to pass a const object, so we could not copy const objects. A reference to const allows both const and non-const objects to be copied. After all, the parameter should be a const reference, because the job of the copy constructor, as its name indicates, is to make a copy, and not to change the original object. In fact, the parameter type for a default copy constructor of any class is a const reference. For example, the prototype of the default copy constructor for the class T is:

```
T(const T&);
```

As an implementation example of our copy constructor, if we add the following in the class definition:

```
T(const T&) {std::cout << "In\n";}
```

this is the copy constructor that will be called. Thus, the program will display In twice and junk values for the members of t2 and t3.

Of course, it is allowed our copy constructor to call another constructor or have an initialization list as we saw earlier. For example:

```
T(const T& t) : T(t.a, t.b) {}
```

Note that if you define a copy constructor, the compiler does not create the default copy constructor. Also, it does not create the default constructor. That is, it is an error to write:

```
class A
{
public:
        A(const A&) {}
};

int main()
{
        A a; // Error, the default constructor is not generated.
        return 0;
}
```

Unless you have a particular reason to define your own copy constructor, don't do it. For example, there is no reason to write:

```
T(const T& t)  : a(t.a), b(t.b) {}
```

in order you to copy the members. Let the default copy constructor do it. Besides simplicity, it is also a safer practice. For example, you may forget to copy a member, so that it gets a random initial value instead of the desired one. Also, if in the future you or someone else adds a new member in the class it is very easy to forget to add its initialization.

Copy Constructor and Function Calls

Besides the initialization cases we saw earlier, the copy constructor is called when a function returns an object or an object is passed to a function by value. For example, suppose that we add the following functions outside the class:

```
T ret_obj(const T& t)
{
        return t;
}

void pass_obj(T t)
{
        t.show();
}
```

and change main() to:

```
int main()
{
        T t1(1, 2), t2(3, 4);

        t1 = ret_obj(t2); // The default copy constructor is called.
        t1.show();
        pass_obj(t1); // The default copy constructor is called.
        return 0;
}
```

When `ret_obj()` returns, the default copy constructor is automatically called, a temporary `T` object is created, the values of `t` are copied to that object, and then the values of that temporary object are copied to `t1`. Note that the C++ standard allows the compiler to perform an optimization and skip the call to the copy constructor in order to avoid creating this temporary object. The compiler is allowed to eliminate this call if certain conditions (a detailed discussion is out of the scope) are met. For example, if the function returns a local automatic variable (not a parameter), the compiler is allowed to perform this optimization and copy directly this value to the variable that holds the result (e.g., `t1`). This optimization is called *Name Return Value Optimization* (NRVO). Here, in our example, this condition is not met, the copy constructor is called and the program displays 3 4.

When `pass_obj()` is called the default copy constructor is called, the values of `t1` are copied to `t` and the program displays 3 4. So, we see that passing an object to a function triggers a call to the copy constructor. As we've said, in order to save memory and time it is more efficient to pass a reference. And if we want to prevent any changes in the object we declare the parameter as `const` reference. We'll analyze it more in the next section.

Let's return to the example of our copy constructor. Someone may ask, can we pass the argument by value? That is, to write:

```
T(T t) {std::cout << "In\n";} // Error.
```

The answer is no. Why? The copy constructor itself is a function. Therefore, when called, if we pass an object as an argument, the compiler will call again the copy constructor to make a copy of the argument. The argument to this new call of the copy constructor is passed by value, so a new call is required, which results to a non-terminating chain of recursive calls to the copy constructor. Thus, the compiler does not allow this to happen and the compilation fails.

Pass Arguments by Reference (Re-Visited)

As we've said, when we pass large entities to a function it is more efficient to make the call by reference (or pass a pointer) rather than by value. Now that we've discussed the copy constructor, let's make a more detailed analysis. Consider the following example:

```
class Student
{
      string name;
      string address;
      ...
};

void f(Student s) {...};

int main()
{
      Student p;
      f(p);
      ...
}
```

When `f()` is called the argument p is passed by value. Let's see what actions this choice causes. As we've said, the default copy constructor of the `Student` class is called to create `s`. Also, for the construction of each `string` member of `s`, the copy constructor of the `string` class is called. When `f()` terminates, the default destructor of the `Student` class is called, as well as the destructor of the `string` class for each `string` object constructed. As you see, many calls for just one passed argument. And we can have many more, if, for example, the `Student` class contains objects of other classes, where the creation of each object triggers a call to the respective copy constructor. And more calls, if, as we'll see when we discuss inheritance, the Student class derives from a base class, which may contain other objects. Then, for the construction of these objects, the respective copy constructors should be called. And if f() is called many times in the program, this number of "hidden" calls is multiplied.

As we know, an alternative way to avoid all these calls to constructors and destructors and, thus, improve performance is to pass the object through a const reference. For example:

```
void f(const Student& s) {...};
```

Now, no new object is created. The const specifier does not allow changes to the passed object, in correspondence to the call by value where any changes are made to a copy of the object.

Copy Constructor and Members Pointers

If the class contains member variables which are pointers, problems may arise if we use the default copy constructor (and the default copy assignment operator, as we know from Chapter 18). For example, consider the following program and try to find out the problem:

```
#include <iostream> // Example 19.6
#include <cstring>

class T
{
private:
        int len;
public:
        char *s;
        T(const char arr[]);
        ~T();
};

T::T(const char str[])
{
        len = strlen(str);
        s = new char[len+1];
        strcpy(s, str);
}

T::~T()
{
        delete[] s;
}

int main()
{
        T t1("text");
        T t2 = t1; // The default copy constructor is called.

        t2.s[0] = 'a';
        std::cout << t1.s << '\n';
        return 0;
}
```

The problem is due to the call of the default copy constructor when t2 is created. Specifically, t2.s becomes equal to t1.s, that is, both pointers point to the same memory. So, when t2.s[0] changes, so does t1.s[0]. Thus, the program displays aext. Besides that, the fact that both pointers point to the same memory creates another error. When t2 is destroyed its destructor is called and the memory that t2.s points to is released, which is the same memory that t1.s points to. So, when t1 is destroyed, its destructor attempts to release the same memory again, which is wrong. And how are these problems fixed?

The solution is to define our own copy constructor. That is, we add the following function in the class:

```
class T
{
public:
        ...
        T(const T& t);
};

T::T(const T& t)
{
        len = t.len;
        s = new char[len+1];
        strcpy(s, t.s);
}
```

Now, when t2 is created this copy constructor is called and the t1 is passed as an argument. That is, the t reference refers to the t1 object. The len member of t1 is copied to t2.len, memory is allocated for t2.s and the t1.s is copied to that memory. This copy is also called *deep copy* in the sense that for each member-pointer of the created object, memory is first allocated and then copy takes place. Now, we copy the real data and not just the pointer to the data as the *shallow copy* does. As a result, the program displays text and not aext as before. Also, since the memory that t1.s points to is different from the memory that t2.s points to, there will be no problem when the destructor of each object is called.

 If the class contains pointer(s), you should define your own copy constructor (and the copy assignment operator) and allocate memory to copy the members of the original object.

For the same reason, remember the example C.18.2, you should define your own copy assignment operator. The difference between the copy constructor and the copy function is that the copy constructor allocates new memory, while the copy function must handle the memory that is already allocated and, if necessary, allocate new one.

In general, whenever you define your own copy constructor, most probably you should define your own copy function as well and vice versa. And don't forget to define the destructor to release the memory. This rule is also known as the *rule of three*, that is, if you define any of these three functions, you should normally declare all of them. Exercise C.19.2 is such an example.

CLASS STATIC FUNCTIONS

A function that is a class member can be declared static using the keyword static. A static member function is not associated with any class object. The word static must be present in the function declaration but not in its definition, if it is defined outside the class. Consider the following program:

```
#include <iostream> // Example 19.7

class T
{
private:
        int code;
```

```
public:
        T(int c);
        static inline int cnt = 0;
        static int get_objs();
};

T::T(int c)
{
        code = c;
        cnt++;
}

int T::get_objs() // We don't add the word static.
{
        return cnt;
}

int main()
{
        T t1(5), t2(6);
        std::cout << t1.get_objs() << ' ' << T::get_objs() << '\n'; /* If
get_objs() was declared in the private section, the compiler would display a
message error for not allowed access. */
        return 0;
}
```

When an object is created the static variable `cnt` increases. The `get_objs()` static function returns this value. So, since two objects are created the program displays 2 twice.

As you see, a static member function is not needed to be called by some object. If it is declared in the public section, as in this example, it can be called using the class name and the `::` scope operator (e.g., `T::get_objs()`). Of course, you can use an object to call it (e.g., `t1`). As the comment says, if it was declared in the private section, the compiler would display an error message for not allowed access. Yet, you can define a public static function which calls it.

Because a static member function is not associated with a particular object, it has not a `this` pointer. Therefore, it cannot be declared as `const` and the use of `this` within its body is not allowed. In fact, like a static member variable, a static member function can be called even if no object of the class is created. For example, let's change `main()` to:

```
int main()
{
        std::cout << T::get_objs() << '\n';
        return 0;
}
```

Since no object has been created, the program outputs 0.

Also, because the function is not associated with a particular object, it can only access static members of the class, since they are not associated with an object as well. For example, if we change the `get_objs()` code to:

```
int T::get_objs() // It is an error to make it const.
{
        std::cout << code << '\n'; // Wrong.
        return cnt; // It is an error to write this->cnt.
}
```

the compiler will display an error message for not allowed access to the `code` member.

MOVE SEMANTICS

Before starting to read this section, I'd suggest to read again the section about the rvalue references in Chapter 16, to refresh your memory. It will make easier for you to understand this section.

One of the most important features that C++11 added is the ability to move an object instead of copying it. Older versions support only the copy operation. As we said in Chapter 16, when we have to copy entities that may contain a lot of data, if we know that the source entity will not be used again, it is much more efficient, instead of copying the data, which is an expensive operation, to move them. For example, the `vector` and `string` classes support move operations. As a move example, consider the `string` class. Each `string` object has a pointer to an array of characters where the characters are stored. The move constructor copies that pointer rather than to allocate new memory and copy the characters to that memory. Let's see a similar example:

```
#include <iostream> // Example 19.8
#include <cstring>

class MyArray
{
private:
        int *p;
        int size;
public:
        MyArray(int s);
        ~MyArray() {delete[] p;}
        MyArray(const MyArray& arr);
        MyArray& operator=(const MyArray& arr);
        const int& operator[](int i) const;
};

MyArray::MyArray(int s)
{
        int i;

        size = s;
        p = new int[size];
        for(i = 0; i < size; i++)
                p[i] = i; // Initial values.
}

MyArray::MyArray(const MyArray& arr)
{
        size = arr.size;
        p = new int[size];
        memcpy(p, arr.p, size * sizeof(int));
}

MyArray& MyArray::operator=(const MyArray& arr)
{
        if(this == &arr)
                return *this;
        delete[] p;
        size = arr.size;
        p = new int[size];
        memcpy(p, arr.p, size * sizeof(int));
        return *this;
}
```

```
const int& MyArray::operator[](int i) const
{
        return p[i]; /* For simplicity, it is not checked if the value of i is
within acceptable limits. */
}

int main()
{
        const int SIZE = 10;
        MyArray arr1(SIZE), arr3(SIZE);

        MyArray arr2 = arr1;
        arr3 = arr2;
        for(int i = 0; i < SIZE; i++)
                std::cout << arr3[i] << '\n';
        return 0;
}
```

Because the class has a pointer member we've made sure to provide our copy constructor and copy assignment operator. The program looks fine, is there any problem? No, but we could improve its performance. How? Let's see the creation of arr2. As we know, the copy constructor is called and the members of arr1 are copied to arr2. Since we won't use again arr1, we do not need to have two copies (arr1 and arr2), that is, we do not need to copy the data of arr1, but move them. The same applies with the assignment of arr2 to arr3. Since we won't use again arr2, it is more efficient to move its data. Well, in this program it does not make a considerable difference in the performance if we move the data, but what about in another application where the objects contain thousands of integers and we have many similar calls? Then, for each call we'd have an unnecessary copy of data. This is the idea of move operations; whenever an entity is temporary and not used any more, it is more efficient to move the data it contains rather than copy them. Let's see another example:

```
MyArray f()
{
        MyArray arr(SIZE);
        ...
        return arr;
}
arr1 = f();
```

Since arr is a local variable which is destroyed when f() terminates, thus we can never reuse it, wouldn't be more efficient to move the data from arr to arr1 and avoid the copy?

Indeed, data moving improves the performance, but how can we move data? The compiler must somehow be able to determine when to copy and when to move data. This decision is based on *rvalue* references. In particular, if we want a user defined type (e.g., MyArray) to support move operations, it must provide a move constructor and an overload function of the = operator to assign the data through movement. You may recall from Chapter 16 that in order to express to the compiler our intention to move data we use rvalue references. Read the comments to understand the additions:

```
class MyArray
{
...
public:
...
        MyArray(MyArray&& a) noexcept; // Move constructor.
        MyArray& operator=(MyArray&& a) noexcept; /* Assign value through
movement. The argument is a rvalue reference. */
};
```

```
MyArray& MyArray::operator=(MyArray&& a) noexcept
{
        if(this == &a) // Check that we don't refer to the same object.
                return *this;

        delete[] p;
        p = a.p; /* Now, no new memory is allocated or data are copied, just
the ownership of the memory is transferred. */
        size = a.size;
        a.p = nullptr; /* Now, the object referred by a has not the property
of the memory. We make a.p equal to nullptr so that the memory is not
released when a is destroyed. As we know, applying delete[] to a nullptr has
no effect. The destructor of the object, to which the memory property was
transferred, will assume to release the memory when it is destroyed. */
        a.size = 0; // I just zero it, to make it clear.
        return *this;
}


MyArray::MyArray(MyArray&& a) noexcept
{
        p = a.p;
        size = a.size;

        a.p = nullptr;
        a.size = 0;
}
```

To distinguish move operations from copy operations, remember that the copy constructor and the copy assignment function take *lvalue* references as parameter, while the move constructor and the move assignment function take *rvalue* references as parameter. Also, these rvalue references are not declared as const, so that the referred entities can be modified. And how we trigger the calls to the move functions? Recall from Chapter 16, that we can use the move() function. move() returns an rvalue reference to its argument. Let's change the program:

```
int main()
{
        const int SIZE = 10;
        MyArray arr1(SIZE), arr3(SIZE);

        MyArray arr2 = std::move(arr1);
        arr3 = std::move(arr2);
        for(int i = 0; i < SIZE; i++)
                std::cout << arr3[i] << '\n';
        return 0;
}
```

If a class (e.g., MyArray) defines both the copy constructor and the move constructor, the compiler checks the types of arguments to call the appropriate one. The same applies for the copy and move functions. That is, it checks whether an lvalue or rvalue reference is passed. Take a look at the following examples to see which function is called (well, in the case of return values the compiler may perform NRVOs, but I refer to the general case):

```
MyArray arr4 = arr3; /* Because arr3 is lvalue the copy constructor is
called. */
arr4 = arr3; /* Because arr3 is lvalue the copy function is called. */
```

```
MyArray f() {...};
arr4 = f(); /* Because f() returns an rvalue the move function is called. */
MyArray arr5 = f(); /* Because f() returns an rvalue the move constructor is
called. */
```

If the move constructor and the move function are not declared in the class, the copy constructor and the copy function will be called instead. For example, in the arr4 = f() statement, if the move function is not defined, the copy function will be called. If we use move() and no move assignment operator is defined, nothing bad happens; the copy assignment operator will be called instead. The same applies with the move constructor. That is, if you use move() to construct an object (e.g., arr2 in the program) and the move constructor does not exist, the copy constructor will be called instead.

Let's see how the program works. In the creation of arr2, since move() returns an rvalue, the move constructor is called, and a is bound to arr1. The type of a is an rvalue reference; this makes sense in order to be bound to the rvalue argument. Also, it makes sense for the compiler to call the move constructor rather than the copy constructor, in order to bind the rvalue argument with the rvalue reference. The move constructor just makes the pointer of the constructed arr2 object to point to the memory that arr1.p points to. In effect, the memory ownership is transferred. As we discussed in Chapter 16, we move an object when it is no longer required. For example, if you use again arr1 (e.g., cout << arr1[0]) unpredictable problems may arise.

Notice that the original pointer must be explicitly set to null, otherwise we'd have two pointers, the pointer of the constructed object (i.e., p) and the pointer of the a object (i.e., a.p), point to the same dynamically allocated memory. Do we want this to happen? Certainly not, we are aware of the dangerous consequences. For example, that same memory will be released twice when the objects are destroyed. Since we don't want bad things to happen, we make the original pointer nullptr. As we know, when a is destroyed applying delete[] to a null pointer has no effect.

Just like a user defined copy constructor typically comes together with a copy assignment operator, a user defined move constructor is typically accompanied by a move assignment operator. This function takes as parameter an rvalue reference. When the right operand of the assignment operator = is an rvalue, the compiler uses the move function rather than the copy function and the rvalue argument is bound to the rvalue reference. Therefore, to continue in our example, arr2 will be passed as an argument to the operator=() move function. As the comments in the code explain, this function moves its data to the calling object, that is, to arr3.

As you see, in both move functions we only copied the pointers, which is nothing compared to the cost of copying entire arrays. To sum up, the move function moves data from the right operand to the left, while the move constructor moves data from its argument (e.g., a) to the newly constructed object.

So, if you want your types (e.g., MyArray) to support move operations for better performance, you need to write your own move functions using rvalue references. As we said, you need to pay extra attention to the code you'll write, so that, after moving, the source object goes into a state that its destructor can handle. For example, if the object contains a pointer that points to an allocated memory (e.g., p), you should assign it explicitly the nullptr value after moving the data, rather than assuming that it will be assigned that value automatically. You must keep in mind that the responsibility for managing the memory now lies to the destination object. When this is destroyed its destructor will release the memory. In general, after a move operation the source object must remain in a valid state where it can be destroyed without any problem.

Before continue, did you notice the existence of the word noexcept? Well, we'll discuss the noexcept keyword in Chapter 22. In brief, it indicates that a function does not throw exceptions. It is recommended that the move constructor and the move assignment operator should be declared as noexcept, assuming that they do not throw exceptions, which is typically true. It is typically true, because the main purpose of the move operations is to steal resources, not to allocate any new memory or perform other operations that might fail. Because a copy function may be called instead of the desired respective move function if the move function is not declared as noexcept, it is very important to declare them as noexcept.

Notice that if you define your own move constructor or move function you should define your own copy constructor and copy function as well. This happens because, by default, the respective default functions are deleted, that is, as we'll see later they become `delete`, and you cannot use them. For example, in the previous program, if we had not defined our own copy function we could not write:

```
arr3 = arr1;
```

the compiler would display an error message similar to *MyArray& MyArray::operator=(const MyArray&) cannot be referenced – it is implicitly declared as deleted.*

Pass Arguments by rvalue References

As you guess, we can pass arguments by rvalue references to functions. Thus, a function can use the reference to move data. Typically, such a function is overloaded, as we saw earlier with the move and copy constructors and assignment operators. That is, there is one version that accepts a `const` lvalue reference and another with an rvalue reference. When the function is called, the compiler checks the type of the argument and selects the appropriate one. Let's see an example with class member overloads:

```cpp
void T::f(const string& s)
{
        string s1 = s; // Copy data.
        ...
}

void T::f(string&& s)
{
        string s1 = move(s); // Move data.
        ...
}

T t;
string s = "Text";
t.f(s); // Since s is lvalue the first version is called.
t.f(move(s)); /* Since move() returns an rvalue reference, the second version
is called. */
t.f("Text"); /* Because the string literal is an rvalue, the second version
is called. */
```

Someone may wonder, why in the second `f()` we are using again `move()`? That is, since the type of s is an rvalue reference couldn't we just write `string s1 = s;` to make the move? Without getting into details, the answer is that the name of a variable is an lvalue, even if the type of that variable is an rvalue reference. That's why we have to use `move()`.

I understand that you may find many of the concepts we have discussed in this chapter (and in the previous ones) very confusing. You are right, many are difficult and complex enough to understand right away. My advice is still the same and won't ever change; write small programs and experiment with them (e.g., add print statements to constructors, assignment functions, destructors, …), to see how they work. I told you, the road to the C++ top is long and paved with many obstacles, in fact, with the continuous evolution of the language, the type of the top is not `const` but `long double`. Don't get surprised if a tough instructor suggests you to listen to *It's a long way to the top if you wanna … pass the C++ course* from *ACDC*.

OBJECTS AS RETURN VALUE

As we've seen in several examples a function may return an object or a reference to it. Let's review again these options. For example, consider the `Student` class:

```
class Student
{
public:
        int code; /* For simplicity, I make the data members public. It
makes easier for me to talk about the structured bindings, as you'll see
next. */
        float grd;

        Student(int c, float g) {code = c; grd = g;}
        Student() {code = 0;}
};
```

Suppose now that we want to write a function that returns the object with the better grade (assume they are different). We declare the arguments as `const`, so that the function cannot modify them.

```
Student max_grd(const Student& s1, const Student& s2)
{
        if(s1.grd > s2.grd)
                return s1;
        else
                return s2;
}
```

Alternatively, the function may return a reference to the object. We just change the prototype, the code remains the same:

```
const Student& max_grd(const Student& s1, const Student& s2);
```

Thus, the following program works with both versions of the function.

```
int main()
{
        Student s1(100, 5), s2(200, 6), max_stud;

        max_stud = max_grd(s1, s2);
        std::cout << max_stud.code << ' ' << max_stud.grd << '\n';
        return 0;
}
```

The question is, which of the two versions is more efficient to choose? Returning a reference does not trigger any call to a copy or move constructor, so, in general, references are preferred. Since both arguments are declared as `const` references, the return type has to be `const` to match. As we've mentioned, when a function returns a reference to an object, the object must continue to exist after the function is terminated, so that the reference can refer to it. Does this rule apply with s1 and s2? Yes, because both are objects of the calling function. For example, if we change the code of max_grd() to:

```
const Student& max_grd(const Student& s1, const Student& s2)
{
        Student s;

        if(s1.grd() > s2.grd())
                s = s1;
        else
                s = s2;
        return s; // Wrong.
}
```

s is a local variable that ceases to exist after the termination of the function. This code causes the unexpected behaviour of the program. Of course, if we change the prototype so that the function does not return a reference but an object there is no problem.

Note that if the class supports move semantics it is efficient to return an object of that class. For example, returning a vector or string object is efficient, because both classes support move semantics.

C++17 allows us to initialize multiple entities with the members of an object. That is, instead of using the max_stud we could write:

```
auto [c, g] = max_grd(s1, s2);
```

The members of the returned structure are bound to the local variables c and g. This mechanism of binding local names to the members of an object is called *structured binding*. A structured binding (e.g., c) is an alias to an existing entity. That is, c and g are aliases for the code and grd members of the returned structure. Their types are the same as of the members. For example, we can write:

```
std::cout << c << ' ' << g << '\n';
```

Note that this binding is allowed, because all members are public. If they weren't public the compilation would fail. In general, if all non-static data members of a class are public, we can bind each non-static data member to a respective name. The number of names must be the same as the number of the non-static members.

Here is another example. Suppose that a function returns a std::pair object (we'll see it in Chapter 26).

```
std::pair<int, float> f() {return std::pair<int, float>(100, 6.5);}
```

The data of a pair object are stored in its first and second members. We can write:

```
std::pair<int, float> p = f();
// Then, use the p.first and p.second members.
```

With the C++17 structure bindings we can write:

```
auto [code, grd] = f();
// Then, use the code and grd.
```

In this case, structured binding makes the code more readable as they allow binding values to names that convey information about their purpose.

We won't get in more details regarding the semantics of the structure bindings. In general, their benefit is the direct access to the members of an entity (e.g., class) and the ability to make the code more readable.

DEFAULT FUNCTIONS

Now that we've discussed about all the constructors and assignment functions, let's summarize the default member functions that the compiler provides automatically when we declare a class. By default, a class T contains:

- a. The constructor: `T()`.
- b. The copy constructor: `T(const T&)`.
- c. The copy function: `T& operator=(const T&)`.
- d. The move constructor (since C++11): `T(T&&)`.
- e. The move function (since C++11): `T& operator=(T&&)`.
- f. The destructor: `~T()`.

These are the functions that the compiler will use by default, unless you've defined your own functions or other circumstances are met. For example, if the class contains a `const` member or a reference, the copy function is not provided. To show you an implementation example, suppose that you've declared the following class:

```
class T
{
private:
        std::string str;
};
```

The actual class that the compiler generates for us is:

```
class T
{
private:
        std::string str;
public:
        T() {}
        ~T() {}
        T(const T& t) : str(t.str) {}
        T(T&& t) noexcept: str(std::move(t.str)) {}
        T& operator=(const T& t)
        {
                str = t.str;
                return *this;
        }
        T& operator=(T&& t) noexcept
        {
                str = std::move(t.str);
                return *this;
        }
};
```

Similar to the default copy constructor and assignment operator the default move functions move all non-static member variables one by one. The compiler can move members of basic types, as well as members that are objects of classes, provided that these classes support move functions. Suppose that the following statements are executed. To refresh your knowledge, read the comments to see which functions are called:

```cpp
T t1, t2; // The default constructor is called twice.
t1 = t2; // The copy assignment operator is called.
t1 = std::move(t2); // The move assignment operator is called.
T t3 = t1; // The copy constructor is called.
T t4 = std::move(t1); // The move constructor is called.
// The destructor is called four times for the t1, t2, t3, and t4 objects.
```

If you write your own functions the following rules apply:

a. If you declare any of those functions, the compiler won't generate the respective default version.
b. If you declare any constructor, the compiler won't generate the default constructor.
c. If you declare any of the copy constructor, copy function, or the destructor, the compiler won't generate the default move constructor or the move function.
d. If you declare a move constructor or move function, the compiler won't generate the default copy constructor or the copy function.

So, when we design a class, we need to consider:

a. Do we need to define our own default constructor? It could be, if the default constructor does not cover our needs or if we've defined another constructor.
b. Do we need to define our own copy constructor or copy function? It could be, if our class contains pointers.
c. Do we need to define our own destructor? It could be, if our class acquires resources (e.g., memory). If needed, most probably we'd have to define our own copy constructor and copy function.
d. Do we need to define our own move constructor or move function? It could be, for better performance.

Typically, if a class needs to define one of the copy function, copy constructor, or destructor, it will most likely need to define the move constructor and the move function. For example, if the class contains pointer(s), besides the first three functions, it is almost certain that you should define the latter two for better performance, to assume ownership of the resources from a temporary object that is ceasing to exist. Thus, the rule of three extends to the *rule of five*, that is, if you define any of these five functions, you should normally declare all of them.

Notice that this rule does not pose the requirement to provide explicit definitions for all five functions. You can use the = `delete` or the = `default` syntax, as we'll see in the next section. On the other hand, don't forget that you may have the option to save the trouble and the risk to introduce bugs when writing your own functions. For example, if you want to implement a dynamic array you can use a `vector` object instead of a pointer. It relieves you from the tasks to define your own functions. And you've seen that it is not an easy task to accomplish. After all, the more code you add the possibility to introduce a bug increases.

Use of =default and =delete

C++11 enables us to prevent the use of a particular default function. To accomplish that we use the =delete syntax. Usually, we use it when we don't want the compiler to create the default copy functions. For example:

```cpp
class T
{
        . . .
        T() {};
        T(const T&) = delete; // Delete copy.
        T& operator=(const T&) = delete; // Delete copy.
};


T t1, t2;
T t3(t2); // Wrong, the copy constructor cannot be called.
t1 = t2; // Wrong, the copy operation is not supported.
```

To give you an example where the use of =delete may be useful, suppose you have an Employee class, which is used to store the data of employees. Since each employee is unique you may want to prevent assignments of one Employee to another in order to avoid overwrites and keep their data safe. To prevent that you can use the =delete syntax to remove the corresponding functions. To go back in the past, before C++11 introduced the =delete, if you wanted to prevent the copy operations, the typical approach was to create your own copy constructor and copy function so that the compiler would not create the default ones. You'd declare them as private so that the compiler would issue an error message if the user of the class attempted to copy objects. Also, to prevent member functions and friend functions of the class to call them, you'd only declare them, not define them, so that if they were called the linker would issue an error message.

Another application of =delete is when we want to prevent an undesired type conversion. For example:

```cpp
class T
{
        . . .
        int a;
        T(int i) {a=i};
        T(double) = delete; // The argument double is not allowed.
        void f(double) {};
        void f(int) = delete; // The argument int is not allowed.
};


T t1(1); // Correct.
T t2(2.3); // Wrong.
t1.f(10); // Wrong.
```

If we had not prevented the passing of a double argument, the constructor would have been called, the conversion would be made, and a become 2. Note that we may use the =delete syntax with ordinary member functions as well. For example, the passing of an integer argument to f() causes a compilation error. Fine, tell me now, what do you think, is the following code correct?

```cpp
class T
{
public:
        ~T() = delete;
};
```

```
int main()
{
        T t;
        return 0;
}
```

Since the destructor is removed, a T object cannot be destroyed. Because the compiler does not allow objects of a type that has no destructor to be created, it issues an error.

C++11 also introduces the =default syntax. This syntax is used when we want to explicitly state that a default function will be used. For example:

```
class T
{
        . . .
        T() = default;
        T(const T&) = default;
};
```

Some may prefer this syntax to make it clear which default functions will be used. Others prefer not to do that, because, their absence implies that they are going to be used anyway. Note that if you want to define an empty default constructor it is better to prefer the =default syntax over the empty {} (e.g., T(){}) for technical reasons, which are beyond the scope of our discussion to analyse.

The =default syntax may be useful when we want to use a default function which due to other conditions is not created automatically. For example, if we declare a move constructor, then the default constructor, the copy constructor, and the copy function are not provided. In that case, we can use this syntax to explicitly declare the default functions we need:

```
class T
{
        . . .
        T(T&&) {};
        T() = default;
        T(const T&) = default;
        T& operator=(const T&) = default;
};
```

If we do not declare the corresponding default functions, each of the following declarations causes a compilation error:

```
T t1;
T t2(t1);
t1 = t2;
```

With the =default syntax, the compiler provides the corresponding default functions and the declarations are compiled successfully.

FRIEND CLASSES

As a function can be friend to a class, a class can be friend to another class. The functions of the friend class may access all the members of the class. An example of using a friend class is when we have two classes and we want one to control the operation of the other. For example, I once had to implement an

IP network management application. I decided to develop a centralized management system, where the Net_Mgt class represents the network administrator, while the System class represents each managed system (e.g., computer). Because I wanted the Net_Mgt class to have access to the private members of System, I've declared Net_Mgt as friend to System. In the following example, the Net_Mgt provides two functions that set the type and the IP address of the managed system.

```
#include <iostream> // Example 19.9
#include <string>
using std::cout;
using std::string;

class System
{
private:
        int type;
        string IP_addr;
public:
        friend class Net_Mgt; /* The Net_Mgt class is declared as friend to
System. */
        enum {PC, Switch, Router};
        void show() const {cout << "T:" << type << " IP:" << IP_addr << '\n';}
};

class Net_Mgt
{
public:
        void set_type(System& s, int type);
        void set_IP(System& s, const string& addr) {s.IP_addr = addr;}
        void show(System& s) const;
};

void Net_Mgt::set_type(System& s, int type)
{
        s.type = type; /* The Net_Mgt class can access the private members of
the System class. */
}

void Net_Mgt::show(System& s) const
{
        s.show();
}

int main()
{
        System s;
        Net_Mgt mgt;

        mgt.set_type(s, System::PC);
        mgt.set_IP(s, "192.168.1.2");
        mgt.show(s);
        return 0;
}
```

Because the functions of the Net_Mgt class refer to members of the System class, I first declare System so that the compiler has the information it needs to process the program. In order for a class to become friend to another, we must declare in it with the prefix friend. The position does not matter, it can be declared in the private, protected or public section. Because Net_Mgt has been declared as friend of System, it may access its private members. That is, if we omit the word `friend` in the declaration of Net_Mgt the compiler won't allow the s.type = type; and s.IP_addr = addr; statements. Also, do not forget that, although Net_Mgt is declared within the System, it is not its member. In case you wonder why I made set_IP() inline and the others not, of course I could make all inline. I'll tell you why I did that in the next section. The program displays T:0 and IP:192.168.1.2.

The purpose of this example is not only to show you how to use a friend class, but also to show you an example where its use provides flexibility in program design. One could say, let's make all System members public so we don't need to use a friend class. Yes, we could, but then we'd lose the safety of data hiding as all the System members would be accessible from the outside world. Another could say, let's add a Net_Mgt object in System, which manages that particular system. Yes, we could, but in this case we'd have a one-to-one relationship, that is, one Net_Mgt object for each System object. By declaring Net_Mgt as friend and passing a System object as an argument to its functions, a single Net_Mgt object can manage all systems, and thus we can implement a centralized management model. As you guess, in a real application, the parameters that a network administrator can configure on a system are many more than just an IP address.

Two classes can become mutually friendly. For example, if we write:

```
class Net_Mgt
{
        friend class System;
        ...
};
```

The System class becomes friend of the Net_Mgt class. Note that the friendship is not transitive. That is, if the System class has its own friend functions, these functions don't have special access to Net_Mgt.

In general, friend classes should associate independent entities that are closely related. In our example, the Net_Mgt entity is not a System entity and vice versa, so the *is-a* model of the public inheritance that we'll see in Chapter 20 does not apply. Similarly, none may be considered as part of the other, so it wouldn't fit to declare either inside the other. The fact that the Net_Mgt controls the state of the System leads to the right choice, to make the Net_Mgt class a friend to the System class.

When you choose a class to become friend to another you need to be careful as all the functions of the friend class will have access to its data. Someone might ask, can we declare as friend some of the functions of a class, and not the entire class? Yes, we can, as we'll see in the next section.

Friend Member Functions

If we do not want to make the entire class friend, we can select which functions to make friend. For example, let's make only the set_IP() friend:

```
class System
{
        ...
        friend void Net_Mgt::set_IP(System& s, const string& addr); /* Only
the set_IP() is declared as a friend function. */
        ...
};
```

As shown, to declare the friend function we need to specify the class in which it belongs. However, this declaration requires a restructuring of the code. Let's see why. In order for the compiler to process this declaration, it must have met the declaration of Net_Mgt in order to be aware of its existence and the presence of set_IP(). So, we need to declare Net_Mgt before System. But, if we do that, the compiler won't have met the declaration of System and won't be able to process the Net_Mgt functions that take a System object as argument. Fine, and how do we overcome this circular dependence? As we did in example C.13.6, by adding a forward declaration of System. The code is restructured as follows:

```
class System; // Forward declaration (incomplete declaration).
class Net_Mgt {...};
class System {...};
```

There is still one problem. When the compiler encounters the inline definition of set_IP() in Net_Mgt it will display an error message because it does not know anything yet about the System class and the members it contains. Therefore, it cannot compile it. This is why I chose to make set_IP() inline. So, that if something similar happens to you, to show you how to solve this problem. The solution is to place the function declarations in the Net_Mgt class and their definitions after the declaration of System. And if you want to make them inline just add the word inline in their definition. Thus, the code is restructured as follows:

```
class System; // Forward declaration
class Net_Mgt {...}; // Function declarations.
class System {...};
// Definitions of Net_Mgt functions.
```

Now, when the compiler encounters the function declarations in Net_Mgt it won't complain, because it is informed from the forward declaration that the System type is a class. Then, when it encounters their definitions it can compile them, because the System has already been declared. Note that even after these changes the program won't compile, because set_type() is no longer friend. Therefore, because the type is a private member, the statement s.type = type; is not acceptable.

NESTED CLASSES

A class can be declared within another class. Such a class is called *nested*. The typical reason to use nested classes is to group together classes that are only used in one place and describe the entity in a more compact form. For example, in an application that manages a company we could declare the Company class and within it nested classes for each department of the company. Consider the following program, where the Mgt_Dpt class is declared inside the Company class:

```
#include <iostream> // Example 19.10

class Company
{
public:
    class Mgt_Dpt
    {
        private:
            int code;
        public:
            Mgt_Dpt(int c, int e) : code(c), empl(e) {}
            int empl;
            void show() const;
    };
```

```
        Company() : tax_id(100), m_ptr(nullptr) {}
        ~Company() {delete m_ptr;}
        void create_dpt(int c, int e);
        void show() const;
private:
        int tax_id;
        Mgt_Dpt *m_ptr; /* Since Mgt_Ptr is already declared, the compiler
won't complain. */
};


void Company::create_dpt(int c, int e)
{
        m_ptr = new Mgt_Dpt(c, e);
}


void Company::show() const
{
        std::cout << "T:" << tax_id;
        m_ptr->show();
}


void Company::Mgt_Dpt::show() const
{
        std::cout << " E:" << empl << " C:" << code << '\n';
}


int main()
{
        Company cmp;

        cmp.create_dpt(1, 5);
        cmp.show();
        return 0;
}
```

Note that it is not needed to declare m_ptr as pointer to access the nested class. We could declare it as Mgt_Dpt object, that is, Mgt_Dpt m_ptr;, and use the . operator instead of ->. I just wanted to show you how to access the nested class using pointer. The program displays T:100 E:5 C:1.

As with member functions, a nested class can be declared inside the enclosing class but defined outside it. For example:

```
class Company
{
public:
        class Mgt_Dpt;
        ...
};
```

To define the nested class we use the name of the enclosing class and the scope operator. For example:

```
class Company::Mgt_Dpt
{
        ...
};
```

Properties of Nested Classes

To discuss the properties of a nested class, let's use the example of Mgt_Dpt. Before that, I'd like to make clear that the declaration of a nested class is not the same as containment, that is, to declare a class object as a member of another class. For example:

```
class A
{
        ...
};

class B
{
        ...
        A a; // Containment.
};
```

Here, the creation of a B object invokes the creation of an A object. In our example, the creation of a Company object does not invoke the creation of an Mgt_Dpt object. That is, a Company object does not contain an Mgt_Dpt object. To make it clear, the nested class just defines a type whose scope is restricted in the enclosing class.

One way to create an Mgt_Dpt object is to call the create_dpt() function. An object of the enclosing class contains only its own members. That is, it is wrong to write:

```
Company cmp;
cmp.empl = 10; // Wrong, empl is not a member of Company.
```

As said, the scope of the Mgt_Dpt type is restricted within the Company. For example, if we were to define the constructor of the Mgt_Dpt outside the class we'd have to use the scope operator and write:

```
Company::Mgt_Dpt::Mgt_Dpt(int c, int e) : code(c), empl(e) {}
```

This syntax indicates that the Mgt_Dpt class is declared within the Company. For a similar reason I defined the show() outside the Mgt_Dpt, to show you the syntax and that there is no name conflict with the show() of the Company. Each show() refers to its own class.

A nested class has no special access privileges to the members of the enclosing class and vice versa, that is, the enclosing class has no special access privileges to the members of the nested class. That is, we follow the same rules to access the members of a nested class as we do with the public, protected, and private members of an ordinary class. For example, since the code is a private member we are not allowed to write: m_ptr->code = 2;

Just as an object of the enclosing class contains only its own members, an object of the nested class contains only its own members. That is, it is wrong to write:

```
void Company::Mgt_Dpt::show()
{
        cout << tax_id; // Wrong.
}
```

Since tax_id is not a member of the Mgt_Dpt class, the compiler will display an error message. And how could the nested class have access to the members of the enclosing class? One way is to pass a pointer to it when an object of the nested class is created. For example, let's change the constructor of `Mgt_Dpt` and pass to it the `this` pointer of the `Company` object:

```
class Mgt_Dpt
{
        private:
                Company *c_ptr;
                ...
        public:
                Mgt_Dpt(Company *p, int c, int e) : c_ptr(p), code(c), empl(e) {}
                ...
};
```

and call the constructor like this:

```
void Company::create_dpt(int c, int e)
{
        m_ptr = new Mgt_Dpt(this, c, e);
}
```

in order to pass the pointer of the `Company` object. This pointer is stored in the `c_ptr` variable, so that it can be used whenever we want to access the members of the enclosing class. For example, we can write:

```
void Company::Mgt_Dpt::show()
{
        cout << c_ptr->tax_id;
}
```

In this way, a function of the nested class may access the members of the enclosing class, even its private members (e.g., `tax_id`).

Access to a Nested Class

As said, a nested class defines a type within the enclosing class. This type can be used by all the members of the enclosing class, regardless of whether it is declared in the public, protected or private part of the enclosing class. However, as with any member, the point of its declaration determines if it can be used from outside the enclosing class. For example, now that `Mgt_Dpt` is declared in the public part the type is accessible from the outside world. That is, if we want to create an `Mgt_Dpt` object we can write:

```
int main()
{
        Company::Mgt_Dpt m_dpt(1, 5);
        m_dpt.show();
}
```

Because `Mgt_Dpt` has a class scope, the scope operator and the name of the enclosing class must be used. However, if `Mgt_Dpt` had been declared in the private or protected part, this declaration would not be allowed and the compiler would issue an error message.

Regarding public inheritance, which we'll discuss in Chapter 20, if the nested class is declared in the public or protected part it is available in the derived class, and therefore the derived class can create objects of the nested class, whereas if it is declared in the private part it is not.

EXERCISES

C.19.1 What is the output of the following program?

```
#include <iostream>

class T
{
public:
        int a;
        T(int i) {a = i;}
        T(const T& t) {std::cout << t.a << ' ';}
};

void f(T p)
{
        p.a = 10;
}

int main()
{
        T *p1, *p2;

        p1 = new T(20);
        p2 = new T(30);

        T r(*p1);
        f(*p2);
        std::cout << '\n' << r.a << ' ' << p1->a << ' ' << p2->a << '\n';
        delete p1;
        delete p2;
        return 0;
}
```

Answer: When r is created the copy constructor for r is called, and the reference t refers to *p1. So, the program displays 20. Since r.a is not initialized it has a random value. For example, if we add the statement a = 1; in the copy constructor, r.a will become 1. Because an object is passed to f() the copy constructor is called, and the reference t refers to *p2. So, the program displays 30 and because *p2 is passed by value the statement p.a = 10; does not affect the value of the a member of *p2. Then, the program displays the random value of r.a, 20, and 30.

C.19.2 Add appropriate functions in class T so that the following program works.

```
class T
{
private:
        char *s;
        ...
};
```

```
int main()
{
        T t1("abc"), t2("def"), t3("gg"), t4("hh"); /* Each string argument
should be copied to the respective s member. */
        t4 = t3 = t1+t2; /* The merging of the strings stored in t1 and t2,
that is the abcdef, should be stored in the s member of both t3 and
t4. */
        T t5(t4);
        t5[2] = 'x'; // The stored string should become abxdef.
        return 0;
}
```

Answer:

```
#include <iostream>
#include <cstring>
#include <cstdlib> // For the exit() function

class T
{
private:
        char *s;
public:
        explicit T(const char str[]);
        T() {s = nullptr;}
        ~T();
        T(const T& t);
        T operator+(const T& t);
        T& operator=(const T& t);
        char& operator[](int i);
};

T::T(const char str[])
{
        s = new char[strlen(str)+1];
        strcpy(s, str);
}

T::~T()
{
        delete[] s;
}

T T::operator+(const T& t) /* Overload of the + operator. It is called
with the t1+t2 statement. The s is the member of t1, while t refers to
t2. */
{
        T tmp;

        tmp.s = new char[strlen(s)+strlen(t.s)+1];
        tmp.s[0] = '\0';
        strcpy(tmp.s, s);
        strcat(tmp.s, t.s);
        return tmp;
}
```

```
T& T::operator=(const T& t) /* Overload of the = operator. First, it is called
with the t3 = t1+t2 statement. The s is the member of t3, while t refers to
the object that the operator+() returns. */
{
        if(this == &t) /* In general, we should check for self-assignment.
It is not needed in this program. */
                return *this;

        delete[] s;
        s = new char[strlen(t.s)+1];
        strcpy(s, t.s);
        return *this;
}

T::T(const T& t) /* The copy constructor is called with the T t5(t4) statement.
The s is the member of t5, while t refers to t4. */
{
        s = new char[strlen(t.s)+1];
        strcpy(s, t.s);
}

char& T::operator[](int i)
{
        if(i < 0 || i >= strlen(s)) /* In general, we should check that we are
not out of the limits. It is not needed in this program. */
                exit(EXIT_FAILURE);
        return s[i];
}
```

Comments: Let's see how we think to add the above functions. Since the s member is a pointer, the constructor must allocate memory to copy the string. Therefore, a destructor must be added to free that memory. To enable the addition of two T objects, an overload function of the + operator must be defined. The function should return an object so that the return value can be assigned to another object. Because the T class contains a pointer we must add an overload function of the = operator to provide deep copy. For the same reason we add the copy constructor to be called when t4 is created. In order for the statement t5[2] = 'x'; to be valid the operator [] must be overloaded and a reference to the element must be returned so that its value may change.

C.19.3 To continue the previous exercise, add a move function and a move constructor. Write a program that demonstrates the operation of both functions.

```
T& T::operator=(T&& t) noexcept
{
        if(this == &t) // For the general case.
                return *this;
        delete[] s;
        s = t.s;
        t.s = nullptr;
        return *this;
}

T::T(T&& t) noexcept
{
        s = t.s;
        t.s = nullptr;
}
```

```cpp
int main()
{
        T t1("abc"), t2("def"), t3("gg");
        T t4 = std::move(t1); // Move constructor.
        t3 = std::move(t2); // Move function.
        return 0;
}
```

Comments: When moving data, `t4.s` points to the memory that `abc` is stored and the `t3.s` points to the memory that `def` is stored. If we do not use `move()` the copy constructor and the copy function will be called, respectively.

C.19.4 Add appropriate functions in class `T` so that the following program works.

```cpp
#include <iostream>
#include <cstring>

class T
{
private:
        double *arr;
public:
        int size;
        ...
};

int main()
{
        T t1(5); /* A constructor should be called, to make size equal to 5
and allocate memory for size numbers. The arr pointer should point to that
memory. Use random numbers to fill the memory. */
        T t2(3);

        T t3 = t1;
        t2 = t1;
        t2 = t2;
        cout << t1 << t2 << t3; /* The program should display the values of
the 5 numbers, which should be the same for all three objects. */
        return 0;
}
```

Answer:

```cpp
#include <iostream>
#include <cstring>
using std::cout;
using std::ostream;

class T
{
private:
        double *arr;
```

```
public:
        int size;
        explicit T(int n);
        ~T();
        T(const T& t);
        T& operator=(const T& t);
        friend ostream& operator<<(ostream& out, const T& t);
};

T::T(int n)
{
        int i;

        size = n;
        arr = new double[size];
        for(i = 0; i < size; i++) // We just store some values.
                arr[i] = i+1;
}


T::~T()
{
        delete[] arr;
}


T::T(const T& t) /* The copy constructor will be called with the
statement T t3 = t1; The size and arr are members of t3, while t refers
to t1. */
{
        size = t.size;
        arr = new double[size];
        memcpy(arr, t.arr, size * sizeof(double));
}


T& T::operator=(const T& t) /* Overload of the = operator. It will be called
with the t2 = t1; and t2 = t2; statements. The size and arr are members of
t2, while t refers to the right operand. In this program, the return type
could be void, I'm using reference for the general case. */
{
        if(this == &t) /* We check if we refer to the same object, with a
statement like t2 = t2; */
                return *this;
        delete[] arr; // Release the old memory.
        size = t.size;
        arr = new double[size];
        memcpy(arr, t.arr, size * sizeof(double));
        return *this;
}

ostream& operator<<(ostream& out, const T& t) /* Use a friend function to
overload the << operator. */
{
        for(int i = 0; i < t.size; i++)
                out << t.arr[i] << ' ';
        out << "\n\n";
        return out;
}
```

UNSOLVED EXERCISES

U.19.1 Add appropriate functions in class T so that the following program works.

```
class T
{
private:
        string *p;
public:
        ...
};

int main()
{
        string s1 = "abcdef", s2 = "abc";
        T t1(s1), t2(s2); /* The constructor should allocate memory for
the p member in order to copy the argument in that memory. */
        t2 = t1; /* Memory should be allocated for the p member of t2 and
copy the abcdef in that memory. */
        T t3(t2);
        t3.show(); // The program should display abcdef.
        return 0;
}
```

To construct a `string` object from an existing one, use the constructor `string(const string& s);`. For example:

```
string s = "abcdef";
string *p = new string(s);
```

U.19.2 Implement a book management application, where the class `Publisher` represents the publishing firm, while the class `Book` represents a published book. The class `Publisher` is allowed to access the private part of `Book`. Do not add another function in the `Book`. In `Publisher`, add the appropriate functions as the comments indicate to make the following program work.

```
class Book
{
private:
        string name; // Name of the book.
        string isbn; // Code of the book.
        string auth; // Name of the author.
public:
        ...
};

class Publisher
{
private:
        string name; // Name of the publishing firm.
        vector<Book> v_book;
public:
        ...
};
```

```
int main()
{
        Publisher pub("Pub");
        pub.set_info("N1", "I1", "A1"); /* set_info() should create a
Book object, store its arguments in the respective private members, and
store that object in v_book.*/
        pub.set_info("N2", "I2", "A2");
        pub.find("I2"); /* find() should take as parameter the isbn of a
book, check if it is contained in the v_book, and if yes, it should
display the name of the publishing firm and the book details. For
example, this code should display Pub N2 I2 A2. */
        return 0;
}
```

U.19.3 Define the class `Team` and the nested class `Player`. The `Team` should contain the `add()` function, which takes as an argument a `Player` object and stores it in a `vector` member (e.g., `v_pl`). Also, it should contain the `show()` function, which takes an integer argument (e.g., `age`) and displays the name of the team, as well as the details of the players who are older than the `age` argument, if any. Finally, it should contain an appropriate constructor. The `Player` should contain up to three functions. Write a program that implements the code as described in the comments to test the operation of the classes.

```
class Team
{
public:
        class Player
        {
                private:
                        string name; // Name of the player.
                        int age; // Age of the player.
                public:
                        ...
        };
        ...
private:
        string name; // Name of the team.
        vector<Player> v_pl;
};

int main()
{
        Team team("T");
        /* Create some Player objects and call the add() to store them in
the v_pl. Then, the program should prompt the user to enter an integer
value that corresponds to the age and pass it as an argument to call
show(). The show() should display the name of the team and the details
of the players who are older, if any. */
        return 0;
}
```

U.19.4 Define the class `Student` and the nested class `Course`. The `Course` class should contain up to three functions (the constructor should be defined outside the class). Add the appropriate functions to the classes to make the following program work.

```cpp
class Student
{
public:
        class Course
        {
                private:
                        int code; // Course code.
                        float grd; // Grade.
                public:
                        ...
        };
        ...
private:
        int code; // Student code.
        vector<Course*> v_crs;
};

int main()
{
        Student st1(10); // The argument is the code of the student.
        Student::Course c1(100, 7.5), c2(200, 3.5), c3(300, 5.5); /* The first
argument is the code of the course and the second one is the grade. */
        st1.add(&c1); // The argument-pointer should be stored in v_crs.
        st1.add(&c2);
        st1.add(&c3);

        Student st2(st1); /* The program should store in st2.v_crs only the
pointers to the Course objects that their grade is >= 5. Then, the program
should sort the pointers in increase order according to the grades of the
respective objects. In this example, the pointer to c3 should be stored in
the first place of st2.v_crs and the pointer to c1 in the second place. To
sort the elements use the sel_sort() of C.12.5. */
        cout << st2; /* The program should display the code of the student and
the details of the courses stored in st2.v_crs. For example, this code should
display 10, then 300 5.5 and then 100 7.5. */
        return 0;
}
```

Inheritance

20

In this chapter we'll discuss one of the most important features of C++, and in general of an object-oriented programming language, the concept of inheritance. Inheritance enables the programmer to reuse existing code rather than to reinvent it. The programmer may derive new classes from existing ones, with the derived class inheriting and expanding the properties of the existing one. Inheritance is a crucial step in the overall program design, since employing code that it has already been used and tested saves considerable time and effort. This chapter describes the public inheritance, which is the most common form. Then, the relationship between the base and derived classes is investigated. Finally, we'll discuss runtime polymorphism as supported by the powerful mechanism of virtual functions. Inheritance and runtime polymorphism are key points in the design and implementation of robust applications.

PUBLIC INHERITANCE

Inheritance is one of the fundamental characteristics of C++, and in general of object-oriented programming. Specifically, inheritance allows a new class to be created from an existing one. The inheriting class is called *derived*, while the existing one is called *base* class. The derived class inherits the characteristics of the base class, that is, inheritance does not remove properties from the base class. The programmer may add new features in the derived class, use the existing ones or modify their behaviour to meet new needs. The general form of declaring a derived class is:

```
class name_of_derived_class : access_type name_of_base_class
```

An object of the derived class contains an object of its base class. The `access_type` determines the access to the members of the base class. If missing, the default access type is `private`. In this chapter, we'll use the `public` type, which is mostly used. In Chapter 21, we'll discuss the `private` and `protected` access types. When the access type is `public`, the functions and the objects of the derived class, as well as the friend functions of the derived class, can access the public members of the base class, but not the private ones. In particular, the derived class can access the private members of the base class only through the public and the protected functions of the base class. Also, the functions of the derived class, as well as its friend functions, can access directly the protected members of the base class, while its objects cannot.

Now that we've learned some inheritance rules for accessibility, let's review the data hiding rules. We already know that direct access to public members is allowed. We are now learning that direct access to its protected members from derived classes is also allowed. In essence, the only members that cannot be directly accessed from outside the class and, thus, provide substantial data hiding are the private ones.

The derived class can be used as a base class to create a new derived class, which in turn can be the base class for a new derived class, and therefore, create a hierarchical chain of classes. For example, a C class can be derived from B class, which in turn can be derived from A, and so on.

The base class contains the general properties of an entity (e.g., `Product`). The derived class is typically a specialization of the base class (e.g., `Book`), which inherits the member variables and functions of the base class and adds its own characteristics. Thus, an object of the derived class, besides its own members, contains a complete sub-object of the base class. For example, consider the following program:

```cpp
#include <iostream> // Example 20.1
#include <string>
using std::cout;
using std::cin;
using std::string;

class Product
{
public:
        string code;
        float prc;

        Product() {cout << "Base Constructor\n";}
        ~Product() {cout << "Base Destructor\n";}
        void show() const {cout << "\nC:" << code << '\n';}
};

class Book : public Product
{
public:
        string title;
        string auth;

        Book() {cout << "Derived Constructor\n";}
        ~Book() {cout << "Derived Destructor\n";}
        void display() const {cout << "T:" << title << " A:" << auth << " P:"
<< prc << '\n';} // The function may access the members of the base class.
};

int main()
{
        Book b;

        cout << "Product Details: ";
        cin >> b.code >> b.prc; // Access the members of the base class.

        cout << "Book Details: ";
        cin >> b.title >> b.auth;

        b.show(); // Call a function of the base class.
        b.display();
        return 0;
}
```

For simplicity, I used only public members. The main advantage of inheritance is that it allows us to use existing code without having to rewrite it. All we have to do is to write the code that implements the derived class. In our example, Book inherited all Product members and functions. We do not have to add them again. That is, a Book object inherits the code and prc members and the show() function. Book also contains its own members and functions.

When a derived object is created, the constructor of the derived class is called first. Then, this constructor calls the constructor of the base class to create the object of the base class contained in the derived object. That is, the derived object contains a base class sub-object. This relationship is also referred to as is-a relationship, in the sense that a derived class object is also a base class object. For example, a Book object is also a Product object.

In particular, the sub-object of the base class must be created first and then the part of the derived object. So, when b is created the constructor of Book first calls the constructor of Product to create the Product sub-object and then continues with the construction of b, that is, the body of the Book constructor is executed. Therefore, the program initially displays:

```
Base Constructor
Derived Constructor
```

In general, as we'll see later, in a hierarchy of classes (e.g., A, B, C, D), when an object of a derived class is created (e.g., D), the constructor of the most base class is called first (e.g., A), then the constructor of its derived class (e.g., B), and so on (e.g., C), until the constructor of the intended class is called (e.g., D). That is, first the A, B, C sub-objects that are contained in the D object are created, and then the D constructor completes the creation of the D object.

Because the Book is produced with public access, b can access the public members of the Product. The program reads the data entered by the user, stores it in Product and Book members and calls functions from both classes to display it. When the derived object is destroyed, the destruction is performed in the reverse order from the construction order, that is, the program first calls the destructor of the derived class and then that of the base class. Thus, the program displays:

```
Derived Destructor
Base Destructor
```

To better illustrate the value of inheritance I'll give you another example. In several of my applications, I often needed to design a windows-based interface to interact with the user. In such cases, inheritance was a valuable help. For example, I used dialogs so that the user could enter data. Did I have to create these dialogs from scratch? Fortunately not, I would never finish. For *Windows* applications, I used as a base class a ready-made class (e.g., *CDialog*) from *Microsoft* libraries, which provided all the resources for managing a dialog box (e.g., to display the dialog and close it when the user presses the OK/Cancel buttons). When I wanted to change the behaviour of the dialog (e.g., when the user selects OK to save the input data in a file), I created a new class (e.g., *CMyDialog*) derived from the base class (e.g., *CDialog*), so that I could take advantage of its functionality without having to write code. I just had to edit my *CMyDialog* class to make the dialog operate as I wish. If you deal with object-oriented programming, be sure that you'll use inheritance to create classes from existing ones either designed by you or by others.

Besides the fact that we do not have to write the same code again, inheritance simplifies the maintenance and upgrade of the program. For example, suppose that we are using the Product class to create other classes. If in the future we need to add a new feature that is relevant to all derived classes we do not have to add it to each one separately. We only add it to the base class and each derived class will inherit it. Also, if there is an error in the base class, we find the error and fix it only there, we do not have to change the code in the derived classes. I think that the concept of class together with the inheritance and the dynamic polymorphism that we'll see below are the most important C++ features and in general of object-oriented programming. Try now to find the errors in the following program:

```cpp
#include <iostream> // Example 20.2

class A
{
private:
        int a;
        void f();
protected:
        int p;
        void g();
};
```

```cpp
class B : public A
{
public:
        int c;
        void h();
};


void A::f()
{
        std::cout << c << '\n';
}


void A::g()
{
        std::cout << a << ' ' << p << '\n';
}


void B::h()
{
        std::cout << p << ' ' << c << '\n';
}


int main()
{
        B b;

        std::cin >> b.a >> b.p;
        b.g();
        b.h();
        return 0;
}
```

First, is it wrong that no class has a constructor? Of course not, the default constructors will be called. Remember, the default constructor of the base class is executed first and then that of the derived. We continue, since the members a and f() are private, objects, and functions of the B class are not allowed to access them. And it makes sense for the C++ standard to prevent this access in order to protect the privacy of the base class members. Otherwise, someone could easily violate the data hiding concept by creating a derived class and use it to access the private members of the base class. Regarding the protected members, remember that for the class itself they behave like the private ones. For a derived class, its functions are allowed to access the protected members of the base class, whereas its objects are not. Therefore, the following statements are not acceptable:

```cpp
cin >> b.a >> b.p; // It is not allowed to access the a and p members.
b.g();
```

Class A does not contain any member named c. The c member is declared in the derived class B, to which class A has no access. Therefore, the following statement is not acceptable:

```cpp
cout << c << '\n'; // In f().
```

And that makes sense. Inheritance does not work reversely, that is, a base class and its objects have no idea about classes derived from it, and, therefore, cannot access their members.

Is-a and Has-a Relationships

As mentioned earlier, public inheritance models better in the program design an *is-a* relationship, that is, a derived class object should also be a base class object. For example, the Book object is also a Product object. The Book class inherits the members of the Product class and might add extra members that apply particularly to books and not to products in general, such as the author.

To better understand the *is-a* relationship, I'll give you an example that does not match that model. Suppose that we have a BookStore class. A bookstore is not a book. Therefore, it'd be better not to derive the Book class from the BookStore class. To clarify that, if you make that derivation, it does not mean that the code won't compile or an error will occur when the program is executed. Nothing prevents you from doing that, but such a program design usually leads to programming problems. Since a bookstore *has* books, the proper approach to associate the classes is the model of the *has-a* relationship. That is, to include a Book object as a member of the BookStore class.

I'll give you some more examples. Suppose that you have defined the Engine class, the Tires class and you want to define the Car class. Since a car *has* an engine and tires, it'd fit to use the *has-a* model and write something like that:

```
class Car
{
        . . .
        Engine eng;
        Tires tir;
};
```

In another example of *has-a* relationship, suppose that you have defined the Date class and you want to define the Employee class. Since an employee *has* date information we'd write:

```
class Employee
{
        . . .
        Date hire_date;
        Date birth_date;
};
```

Now, suppose that you've defined the Shape class and you want to define the Circle class. Since a circle *is* a shape, it'd fit to use the *is-a* model and write something like that:

```
class Circle : public Shape
{
        . . .
};
```

Similarly, suppose that you've defined the BankAccount class and you want to define the CheckingAccount class. Since a checking account *is* a special type of a bank account we'd use inheritance.

What about an Animal class and a Cat class? Since a cat *is* a kind of animal, it is sensible to use inheritance and derive Cat from Animal.

So, when you have to decide whether to add a class as a member or derive from it, the general rule is to see which one of the *has-a* and *is-a* fits better and act accordingly.

Protected Members and Inheritance

In general, when we create a class that might be used as a base class and want to allow access to some of its members from a derived class, we can declare those members protected instead of private. The protected members of the base class are still protected in the derived class. Thus, not only hiding them from the outside world is still achieved, that is, we still keep them *protected*, but we also gain in speed and the code becomes simpler, since a derived class may access them directly. However, we lose in internal security since direct access may cause unwanted side effects to the operation of the base class.

For example, if you have created a class and give it to other developers, they can access the protected members of your class and corrupt their data by simply creating a derived class. So, if you ever place your classes in the outside world, you must take into account the lack of security involved in accessing protected members and decide accordingly. Also, the fact that the protected members may be used in many parts of the program by derived classes makes it more difficult to control the operation of the base class and, therefore, the maintenance of the program. Usually, the best practice is to declare the members private, rather than protected, and provide protected functions where you specify how they can be used and control their operation when called from the derived classes.

Here, I'd like to clarify something about the access of the protected members of the base class from functions of the derived class. This access is permitted only for the protected members of the base sub-object contained in the derived class and not for the protected members of other ordinary base class objects that might be declared in the derived class. I know, the previous sentence was difficult to understand, I did the best I could. Let's look at an example to better understand it:

```cpp
class A
{
protected:
        int p;
};

class B : public A
{
public:
        void f();
};

void B::f()
{
        p = 10; /* Allowed, we refer to the member p of the sub-object of the
A class contained in B. */
        A a;
        a.p = 10; // Wrong, access denied, because a is an ordinary object.
}
```

And it makes sense not to allow the second access. If allowed, we could very easily break the rule that an object is not allowed to access the protected members of a class. How? As in this example, we would create a derived class, declare a base class object (e.g., a) in a member function (e.g., f()) and use it to access the protected members. No, access to the protected members of ordinary objects is still not allowed, only the access to the protected members of the base sub-object is allowed.

Scope and Inheritance

As we know, each class defines its own scope. With inheritance, things are a bit different. Although the base and derived classes are defined in different parts of the program, the scope of the derived class is contained in the scope of the base class. This is why members of the derived class don't have to use the scope operator :: to access members of the base class. When a name is used within a class, the compiler first looks for its declaration in the class scope. If it does not find it, it continues to search in the scope of its base classes, throughout the chain from its direct base class to the top. For example, suppose that the class C is derived from class B, which is derived from class A and only this class contains a public member named p. If we write:

```
C c;
c.p = 10;
```

since c is an object of class C the compiler searches for the declaration of p in it. Because p is not declared in C, the compiler continues the search in its base class, that is, B. Similarly, since p is not declared in B and because B is derived from A, the search continues there, where it is finally found. If the declaration was missing, the compiler would display a related error message.

A logical question one may ask is what if the name p also appears in another class? For example:

```
void g() // Global g().
{
        . . .
}

class A
{
public:
        int p;
        . . .
};

class B : public A
{
public:
        int p;
        . . .
};

class C : public B
{
public:
        int p;
        void f();
        . . .
};

void C::f()
{
        g();
}
```

Of course, it is confusing to use the same name, and you should never make that choice deliberately, because the code becomes more difficult to understand and the possibility of an error increases. However, oversights or circumstances may make it happen. So, what happens if same names are used? As we know from Chapter 11, the names declared in an inner scope hide the names outside of it. Therefore, with the c.p statement we refer to the member p of class C. Because the compiler finds the declaration of p in C it stops searching. If p was not declared in C, it would continue searching in its base class and, therefore, we would be referring to the member p of class B. And what do we do if we want to refer to the member p of another class? We just use the scope resolution operator ::. For example:

```
C c;
c.A::p = 10;
c.B::p = 20;
c.p = 30;
```

Note that the compiler applies the same search procedure to any name, no matter if it is a variable, a function, or something else. For example, suppose it is a function name. If `f()` is called, the compiler searches for the definition of `g()` in the scope of C. If it does not find it, it continues in the scope of B, and then in the scope of A. If it does not find it, it continues to search for a global `g()`, and if it fails again it displays an error message.

Here is another example:

```cpp
class A
{
protected:
        int p;
        ...
};

class B : public A
{
public:
        int p;
        void f() {p = A::p + 10;}
        ...
};
```

`f()` uses the qualified name `A::p` to refer to the base class member, while p refers to the member declared in B.

DERIVED CLASSES AND CONSTRUCTORS

In example C.20.2, we said that if no constructors have been defined, the default constructors are called. In example C.20.1, we saw that the defined constructors are called and as said, because the sub-object of the base class is first created, its own constructor is executed first and then the program continues with the execution of the constructor of the derived class. Let's change the program, add parameters to the two constructors and see how the constructor of the derived class can pass values to the constructor of the base class:

```cpp
#include <iostream> // Example 20.3
#include <string>
using std::cout;
using std::string;

class Product
{
private:
        string code;
        float prc;
public:
        Product(const string& c = "No", float p = 0);
        void show() const;
};

class Book : public Product
{
private:
        string title;
        string auth;
```

```
public:
      Book(const string& c, float p, const string& t, const string& a);
      void display() const;
};

Product::Product(const string& c, float p)
{
      code = c;
      prc = p;
}

void Product::show() const
{
      cout << "C:" << code << " P:" << prc << '\n';
}

Book::Book(const string& c, float p, const string& t, const string& a) :
Product(c, p) /* The constructor of the base class will be called first and
then the following statements will be executed. */
{
      title = t;
      auth = a;
}

void Book::display() const
{
      show();
      cout << "T:" << title << " A:" << auth << '\n';
}

int main()
{
      Book b("AB25", 8.5, "Nice", "Many");

      b.display();
      return 0;
}
```

First, I declared the members private so that the design of the classes resembles that of a real application. As we've said, when an object of a derived class is created, the sub-object of the base class must first be created. And how will this happen? The derived class has to call a base class constructor to initialize the base sub-object.

So, when the b object is created the constructor of the Book class is called and the values of the arguments are passed to the corresponding parameters. For example, c becomes equal to AB25 and p equal to 8.5. Here, to make a parenthesis. As can be seen, literal C-form strings (essentially, as we know, a pointer at the beginning of the string) are passed to the constructor, while the type of the respective parameters is const string&. No problem with this type mismatch? No, because the string class has a constructor with a const char* parameter, and this constructor is automatically called to create a string object and initialize it with the C-form string. The parenthesis closes. After passing the values, the following part of the code is executed:

```
: Product(c, p)
```

which calls the constructor of the base class using the initialization syntax we saw in Chapter 19 and passes to it the values of c and p. If the base class supports multiple constructors we choose the one we want to call. To remember the member initialization syntax, we could alternatively write:

```
Book::Book(const string &c, float p, const string &t, const string &a) :
Product(c, p), title(t), auth(a) {} // Empty body.
```

The constructor of the `Product` class creates the `Product` sub-object of b and stores the values `AB25` and `8.5` in its members. Then, the program proceeds with the construction of the b object and stores the `Nice` and `Many` values in the `title` and `auth` members, respectively. As mentioned in Chapter 19, members are initialized not based on their position in the initialization list, but in the order they are declared in the `Book` class. Finally, the empty body of the `Book` constructor is executed. Note that we could skip the call to the constructor of the base class. That is, to write:

```
Book::Book(const string &c, float p, const string &t, const string &a)
{
        title = t;
        auth = a;
}
```

Because the base class sub-object must be created first, the default constructor of the base class will be called automatically. Remember that a constructor with predefined values in all of its arguments is also considered a default constructor. So, `show()` will display `No` and `0`. Notice that if `Product` did not have a default constructor, for example, we change the declaration to:

```
Product(const string &c, float p);
```

and we wrote the constructor of the `Book` class as before, the compiler would display an error message similar to *'Product': no appropriate default constructor available.*

 Remember, when a program creates a derived class object, the sub-object of the base class is created first. The constructor of the derived class calls a base class constructor. The programmer may use the initialization list syntax to indicate the base class constructor to be called, otherwise, if no constructor is specified, the default base class constructor will be called, if it exists. If it does not exist, the compiler will display an error message. When a derived class object is destroyed, the destructor of the derived class is called first and then that of the base class.

One may ask, instead of using the constructor of the base class to initialize its members couldn't we use the constructor of the derived class to initialize the members of the base class? Yes, we could use it to initialize the public and the protected members. For example:

```
class A
{
private:
        int a1;
protected:
        int a2;
public:
        int a3;
};

class B : public A
{
public:
        B();
};
```

```
B::B()
{
        a1 = 1;  // Wrong.
        a2 = a3 = 2;  // OK.
}
```

Although we can use the constructor of the derived class to initialize base class members I do not prefer this approach. The main reason is that I do not want responsibilities to be confused. I want to know which constructor is responsible for which initializations. Controlling and maintaining code where each constructor can initialize members of base classes becomes difficult and error prone. It is much more convenient and safer to know that each constructor is responsible only for the initialization of its class members. Thus, I prefer a derived class to let the constructor of the base class undertake the initialization of the members of the contained sub-object. After all, the derived constructor cannot initialize the private members of the base class (e.g., a1).

By the way, note that although the non-private members of the base class can be accessed from the derived class, it is not allowed to initialize them in the initialization list of the derived constructor. For example:

```
B::B()  :  a2(2), a3(2)  {}  // Wrong.
```

If we want to initialize them, we should do that within the body of the derived constructor.

Hierarchy of Classes

In a chain of derived classes, each class can use the initialization syntax to pass values to the constructor of its immediate base class. But, pay attention, only to the direct base class and not to another one at a higher level. An exception to this rule is the virtual base classes that we'll see in Chapter 21. For example:

```
#include <iostream>  // Example 20.4
using std::cout;

class A
{
public:
        A(int k) {cout << "A:" << k;}
        ~A() {cout << " ~A\n";}
};

class B : public A
{
public:
        B(int m) : A(m+1) {cout << " B:" << m;}
        ~B() {cout << " ~B";}
};

class C : public B
{
public:
        C(int p) : B(2*p) {cout << " C:" << p << '\n';}
        ~C() {cout << "~C";}
};

int main()
{
        C c(10);
        return 0;
}
```

When the c object is created, the constructor of class C is called, which calls the constructor of class B and passes to it the value 20. In its turn, it calls the constructor of class A, passes to it the value 21 and the body of A constructor is executed. The program displays A:21. Then, the body of B constructor is executed and the program displays B:20. Thus, first the sub-object of class A is created and then the sub-object of class B. That is, the c object contains two sub-objects, one of class A and one of class B. After the construction of these two sub-objects the body of the C constructor is executed and the program displays C:10.

In general, in a hierarchy of classes, a derived object contains a sub-object of its immediate base class and a sub-object for each of its indirect base classes. The destructors are called in the reverse order from which the constructors were called, throughout the hierarchy, from the last derived class to the root. Finally, the program displays:

```
A:21        B:20        C:10
~C          ~B          ~A
```

As mentioned, the constructor of the C class is not allowed to use the above syntax to call directly a class A constructor. What is allowed is to call a constructor only from its direct base class, that is, from B, and a B constructor to call a constructor only from class A. For example, we are not allowed to write:

```
C(int p) : A(p) {} // Wrong.
```

The compiler will display an error message similar to *A is not a direct base of C.*

If we do not want a class to be inherited we use the word `final` introduced by C++11. For example:

```
class A final {...}; // The class A cannot be a base class.
class B {...};
class C : public A {...}; // Wrong.
class D final : public B {...};
class E : public D {...}; // Wrong.
```

The attempt to inherit from class A or D causes a compilation error. We'll discuss more about the word `final` in a short.

SPECIAL RELATIONSHIPS BETWEEN BASE AND DERIVED CLASSES

In this section we'll discuss some special relationships between the base and the derived classes.

Conversions from Derived to Base Class

A special relationship between a base and a derived class is that a pointer or reference to a base class can point or refer to an object of a derived class. Note that type cast is not needed. This conversion is often called *derived-to-base* conversion. For example, consider the classes of example C.20.3:

```
Book b("AB25", 8.5, "Nice", "Many");
Product *p = &b; /* Converting a pointer from a derived class (e.g., &b) to a
pointer to a base class (e.g., p) is allowed. The p pointer points to the
Product sub-object of b.
Product &r = b; // The r reference refers to the Product sub-object of b.
p->show();
r.show();
```

The conversion that the compiler applies is safe, because as we know, a `Book` object contains a `Product` sub-object. If it makes easier for you to understand, change the word "contains" to "is-a", that is, a `Book` object is also a `Product` object. In general, a derived class object or a reference to it can be used in expressions where a base class object is expected. Similarly, we can use a pointer to a derived class object in expressions where a pointer to the base class is expected. However, a reference or pointer to the base class is not allowed to access the members of the derived class. For example, we are not allowed to write:

```
p->display(); // Wrong.
r.display(); // Wrong.
```

Because a pointer or reference to the base class can refer to the derived class (as we said, it points or refers to the base class sub-object contained in the derived object), a function that takes as an argument a pointer or reference to a base class object can also accept a pointer or reference to a derived class object. For example:

```
void f(Product& r) // Example 20.5
{
        r.show();
}
```

Since the argument `r` is a reference to the base class, we can use it to refer to an object of the base or derived class without any concern for the operation of the function. Thus, we can write:

```
Product p("One", 1);
Book b("AB25", 8.5, "Nice", "Many");
f(p);
f(b); // The Book object is also a Product object.
```

As we said, the same applies if the type of the parameter is a pointer to the base class. For example:

```
void f(Product *r)
{
        r->show();
}

Product p("One", 1);
Book b("AB25", 8.5, "Nice", "Many");
f(&p);
f(&b);
```

Note that this property is transitive. That is, if we derive the `ProgrammingBook` class from `Book`, then a pointer or reference to the `Product` class can refer to a `Product` or `Book` or `ProgrammingBook` object.

 Because a derived class object contains a base class sub-object, a pointer or reference to the base class can point to or refer to a derived object.

A derived class object can be used to initialize a base class object. For example:

```
Book b("AB25", 8.5, "Nice", "Many");
Product p(b);
```

Let me ask you this. Does the `Product` class contain a constructor that accepts a `Book` object as a parameter? No. Then, why the declaration of p is allowed? Because, as we said in Chapter 19, the following default copy constructor is automatically called:

```
Product(const Product&);
```

And as we just learned, because the parameter is a reference to the base class it is allowed to refer to a derived class object. Thus, this constructor is called and the members of p are initialized with the values of the `Product` sub-object contained in the b object, that is, with the values AB25 and 8.5, respectively. The derived part of b (e.g., `title`) is ignored; this is often called *object slicing*. Similarly, we can assign a derived class object to a base class object and only the base class members are copied. For example:

```
Book b("AB25", 8.5, "Nice", "Many");
Product p;
p = b;
```

The assignment is translated to p.operator=(b), which invokes the `Product& operator=(const Product&)` function to copy the values of the `Product` sub-object contained in b into the members of p. As we'll see in the next section, the reverse b = p; is not automatically allowed, since a `Product` object is not also a `Book` object.

Finally, we can pass a derived class object in a function that accepts as a parameter a base class object. For example:

```
void f(Product p)
{
        p.show();
}

Book b("AB25", 8.5, "Nice", "Many");
f(b);        // The Book object is also a Product object.
```

When f() is called the copy constructor of `Product` undertakes to copy the `Product` part of b into p. Therefore, f() displays C:AB25 and P:8.5. Like before, the reverse is not allowed, that is, it is not allowed to pass a base class object to a function that expects a derived class object.

 When we assign or initialize a base class object with a derived class object only the members of its base sub-object are copied. The rest part of the derived object is ignored.

Conversions from Base to Derived Class

The reverse conversion *base-to-derived* is not automatically allowed, that is, a reference or pointer to a derived class is not allowed to point to a base class object without type cast. And this is logical, because a base class object does not contain a sub-object of the derived class so that it can be referred or pointed to by a pointer to a derived class. Only the reverse is true, as we saw in the previous section. For example:

```
Product prod("AB25", 8.5);
Book *p = &prod; /* Wrong, it is not allowed to convert a pointer to a base
class (e.g., &prod) to a pointer to a derived class (e.g., p). A Product
object is not a Book object. */
Book &r = prod; // Wrong.
```

But, if we use type cast the code is compiled:

```
Book *p = static_cast<(Book*)>(&prod);
Book &r = static_cast<(Book&)>(prod);
```

However, this operation is not safe, because a `Product` object does not contain a `Book` sub-object. If we try to access members of the derived class, problems in the execution of the program may occur. For example, if we accidentally write:

`p->display();` problems may occur since `display()` is not a member of the `Product` class.

We saw in the previous section that we can assign a derived class object to a base class object. The reverse is not allowed. For example:

```
Book b("AB25", 8.5, "Nice", "Many");
Product p;
b = p;
```

The assignment is translated to `b.operator=(p)`, which invokes the `Book& operator=(const Book&)` function. Because a reference to a derived class cannot automatically refer to a base class object, this code won't compile. One way to make it work is to overload the assignment operator, that is, to define our copy function in the `Book` class to match the argument type. For example:

```
Book& operator=(const Product&) {...}
```

Alternatively, we could define a conversion constructor. For example:

```
Book(const Product&) {...}
```

DERIVED CLASSES AND COPY OPERATIONS

As we've seen, when a derived object is constructed, the contained base class sub-object is first constructed and then its construction is completed. In the same sense, the copy constructor of a derived class must copy the members of the base sub-object as well as the members of the derived class. The same applies for the copy assignment function of the derived class. The following sections describe these operations in more detail.

Define a Copy Constructor in a Derived Class

Let's look at a simple inheritance example with default copy constructors:

```
class A
{
public:
        int r;
        int v;
};
```

```
class B : public A
{
        ...
};

int main()
{
        B b;
        b.r = 10;
        A a = b;
        ...
}
```

When the object a is created, the default copy constructor of the class A will be called and the members of the A sub-object (e.g., r and v) contained in b will be copied to a. That is, a.r will be equal to b.r (i.e., 10) and a.v equal to b.v.

Let's see a more complex example. The following program is an example of how to define your own copy constructors in a derived class and its base class:

```
#include <iostream> // Example 20.6

class A
{
public:
        int a;
        A(int i) : a(i) {}
        A(const A& r) : a(r.a + 1) {}
};

class B : public A
{
private:
        int t;
public:
        B(int i) : A(i), t(i+20) {}
        B(const B& b) : A(b), t(b.t + 1) {}
        void show() const {std::cout << a << ' ' << t << '\n';}
};

int main()
{
        B b1(10);

        B b2 = b1;
        b2.show();
        return 0;
}
```

The constructor of the derived class B calls the constructor of the base class. When the b1 object is created the value of the a member of the A sub-object contained in b1 becomes 10 and the value of b1.t becomes 30.

Let's now look at the calls of the copy constructors to create b2. In general, when we define a copy constructor in a derived class and want to use the defined copy constructor in the base class, we must call it in the initialization list. Thus, when b2 is created, the copy constructor of B is called, which in turn calls the copy constructor of A to handle the A sub-object. In particular, a copy of the A sub-object of b1 should be made, and for that reason the B copy constructor calls the A copy constructor.

To clarify it once more, the fact that there is no A copy constructor that accepts a B reference parameter does not produce a compilation error, because the A copy constructor takes a A reference parameter, and, as we've learned, a base class reference can refer to a derived type. Thus, the A copy constructor uses the A part of the b argument to construct the A sub-object. So, b2.a becomes 11 and b2.t becomes 31. The program displays these values.

Note that if you omit the call to the copy constructor of A, that is, you write:

```
B(const B& b) : t(b.t + 1) {}
```

the compilation fails. The reason is that the compiler knows that it has to create a A sub-object, but it is not specified how to do it. It won't call by itself the copy constructor of A, you have to tell the compiler to do so.

Note that this example has no practical value besides educational purposes; it serves just to see how to call a base class copy constructor from a derived class in case you want to use your own copy constructors. If you do not have a reason to do so, and most probably you won't, let the default copy constructors copy the members and do not define your own. It is dangerous, for example, you can very easily skip copying a member or if you add a new member in the future you may forget to copy it.

Define a Copy Assignment Function in a Derived Class

Like the copy constructor of the derived class, the copy assignment function must copy the members of the base sub-object. Consider the following program:

```
#include <iostream> // Example 20.7

class A
{
public:
        int v;
        A(int i) : v(i) {}
};

class B : public A
{
public:
        int r;
        B(int i) : A(i+5), r(i) {}
        B& operator=(const B& b);
};

B& B::operator=(constB & b)
{
        A::operator=(b); // Copy the members of the base sub-object.
        r = b.r;
        return *this;
}

int main()
{
        B b1(10), b2(20);

        b2 = b1; // Equivalently, b2.operator=(b1).
        std::cout << b2.v << ' ' << b2.r << '\n';
        return 0;
}
```

When b1 is created, b1.v becomes 15 and b1.r becomes 10. When b2 is created, b2.v becomes 25 and b2.r becomes 20. As you can see, B::operator= calls the A::operator= function, that is, the default copy function which copies the values of the members of the A sub-object of b1 to the members of the A sub-object of b2. Thus, b2.v becomes equal to b1.v. If we don't call it, the value of b2.v won't change. Note that we could define our own copy assignment function in class A instead of using the default function. Then, the function copies the values of the members of the derived object (e.g., r = b.r;). Therefore, the program displays 15 10.

As with copy constructors, if you do not have a good reason to define your own copy assignment function, let the default function do the job for greater security and easier control of the program. Otherwise, not only should you copy the members of the derived class, but you should also call the copy functions of all the base classes so that the members of all base sub-objects are copied.

Examples C.20.6 and C.20.7 are simple cases, in the sense that the classes do not contain pointers for which memory must be reserved. Exercise C.20.8 is a more difficult example, where dynamic memory management is needed for the members of the base and derived classes.

FUNCTION REDEFINITION

As we already know, an object of a derived class can use functions of the base class. However, we may need a function of the base class to behave differently in the derived class, which means to have multiple forms of the same function (polymorphism). Thus, the way a particular function behaves may depend on the object that calls it. To achieve polymorphism we must redefine the function in the derived class. There are two situations to explore. The first one is when the functions have the same signature and the second one with different signatures.

Function Redefinition with Same Signature

As an example, consider the C.20.1 program with the Product and Book classes. Let's change the name of the display() function in the Book class to show() and write the following code:

```
void Book::show() const
{
        cout << "T:" << title << " A:" << auth << '\n';
}
```

Now, we have two versions of show(), one in the base class and one in the derived. If we write:

```
Product p("A", 1);
Book b("B", 2, "Nice", "Many");
p.show(); // The Product::show() is called.
b.show(); // The Book::show() is called.
```

the compiler checks the type of the object to decide which of the two versions to call. Essentially, when a base class function is redefined in a derived class, the derived class function hides the base class function. This is logical to happen, because, as it applies with scopes and as we saw in the previous "Scope and Inheritance" section, if a member of a derived class (inner scope) has the same name as a member of a base class (outer scope), then the name of the derived function hides the name of the base function in the scope of the derived class. Thus, the `show()` of the `Book` class hides the `show()` of the `Product` class. With the `b.show()` statement, the compiler searches for the `show()` within the scope of `Book`, finds it, and calls it.

And if we want to call the `show()` of the base class from the derived class could we do that? Yes, we just use the scope resolution operator with the name of the base class. For example:

```
void Book::show()
{
        cout << "T:" << title << " A:" << auth << '\n';
        Product::show(); /* Pay attention, if we write only show() an infinite
recursion will be created. */
}
```

As the comment says, if we write `show()` instead of `Product::show()` the compiler assumes that the `show()` of the `Book` class is called, resulting in the creation of an endless recursion. The scope operator can also be applied when the object is used to call the function. For example:

```
Book b("B", 2, "Nice", "Many");
b.show(); // The Book::show() is called.
b.Product::show(); // The Product::show() is called.
```

Fine, that's clear when an object is used to call the function. But, what happens when a pointer or reference is used to call the function? For example:

```
Book b("B", 2, "Nice", "Many");
Product *p = &b;
p->show(); // Which show() will be called, that of Product or Book?
```

I'll answer briefly now; however, I'll make the same question later on when we discuss virtual functions. Because the type of the pointer is `Product*`, although it points to a `Book` object, the `show()` that will be called is that of the `Product` class.

Function Redefinition with Different Signature

Let's now examine the case where the base class function is declared differently in the derived class. For example:

```
#include <iostream> // Example 20.8

class A
{
public:
        void show() const {std::cout << "A\n";}
};

class B : public A
{
public:
        void show(int k) const {std::cout << k << '\n';}
};
```

```cpp
class C : public B
{
public:
        void show(const char *s) const {std::cout << s << '\n';}
};

int main()
{
        B b;
        b.show(10); // OK.
        b.show(); // Error.

        C c;
        c.show("Test"); // OK.
        c.show(10); // Error.
        c.show(); // Error.
        return 0;
}
```

Redefining a function hides the declarations of all base-class functions of the same name, regardless of the function signatures.

 Redefining a function in a derived class is not a function overloading.

As explained in the previous section, it is not a function overloading because overloaded functions must be defined within the same scope, while the derived class defines a separate scope. Thus, with the declaration of show() in class B we do not have two overloaded versions of show(), but this declaration hides the respective declaration in base class A. In particular, with the statement b.show(); the compiler searches for the name show in B. Once it finds it, it stops searching. Then, because an argument must be passed to show(), the compilation fails. I write it again, the important thing to understand is that the compiler stops searching, it does not keep looking for another version of the show() in the base classes of B that matches the call. Similarly, the declaration of show() in the derived class C hides the respective declarations in the base classes A and B. Therefore, the compiler displays two more error messages. As said, to call the show() of a base class we must use the scope operator and the class name. For example, c.B::show(10);

What about if we want to have overloaded versions of a base class function in a derived class? Could we do that? Yes, we use using declarations. Specifically, we use the using keyword and write the name of the function. The using declaration introduces the function into the scope of the derived class, so the versions are available within the derived class. The compiler checks the signatures to distinguish them. For example:

```cpp
class C : public B
{
public:
        using B::A::show;
        using B::show;
        void show(const char *s) const {std::cout << s << '\n';}
};

int main()
{
        C c;
        c.show("Test"); // The C::show() is called.
```

```
    c.show(10);  // The B::show() is called.
    c.show();  // The A::show() is called.
    return 0;
}
```

Now, the program is compiled successfully. In particular, we have three overloaded versions of `show()` in the scope of `C`. The compiler checks the argument and selects the appropriate version. Thus, the program displays `Test`, `10`, and `A`. Note that the `using` declaration adds all the functions with the same name. For example, if the class `A` contains the overloaded version `int show(int a, int b) {...}`, the `using` declaration adds it as well.

VIRTUAL FUNCTIONS

So, we saw that when we use an object to call a function, the function of the object's class is called. Fine, that's clear.

Let me ask the same question I asked before. Suppose that a derived class function redefines with the same signature a base class function. What happens when we use pointers and references to call that function? For example, consider again the C.20.1 program with the next `show()` instead of the `display()`.

```
void Book::show() const
{
        cout << "T:" << title << " A:" << auth << '\n';
}
```

What do you think the following code displays?

```
Product p("A", 1);
Book b("B", 2, "Nice", "Many");

Product *ptr1 = &p;
ptr1->show();
Product *ptr2 = &b;
ptr2->show();  // Which show() will be called?
Product& ref = b;
ref.show();  // Which show() will be called?
```

In the case of `ptr2->show();` you'd probably answer that since `ptr2` points to `b`, the `show()` of the `Book` class will be called. No, the compiler checks the type of the pointer and decides accordingly. Thus, since `ptr2` is a pointer to the `Product` class the `show()` of that class is called. As you see, the decision about which function to be executed is made when the program is compiled, and this decision won't change. This selection method is called *static binding*. The term *early binding* is also used. Essentially, the function name is associated with the memory address of the code that will be executed each time the function is called. The same applies for references, that is, the compiler uses static binding to select the respective `show()`. As with pointers, the selection is based on the type of the reference, not on the type of the object being referenced. Therefore, the code displays:

```
C:A  P:1;
C:B  P:2;
C:B  P:2;
```

Let's discuss now virtual functions and one of the most important features of C++, the dynamic or else runtime polymorphism. If we declare `show()` as virtual in the base class, the results are different. To declare it as virtual we use the keyword `virtual`. For example:

```
class  Product
{
        . . .
        virtual void show() const;
};

class Book : public Product
{
        . . .
        virtual void show() const;
};
```

 In order for the virtual mechanism to work, the function of the derived class must override the function of the base class.

When a function in a derived class redefines a virtual function of the base class with the same signature, it is called *function overriding*. Regarding the return type, in general, the return type of the virtual function in the derived class should be the same as that of the base class, as well. Strictly speaking, and without getting into details, it should be *covariant* with the classes of the functions. For example, if the return type of the base class function is a pointer or a reference to a class type, the virtual function in the derived class may return a pointer or a reference to a more specialized type than that of the base. If the signatures are the same but the return types are not consistent, the derived class function won't compile.

Notice that if the signatures do not match exactly, the function of the derived class does not override the function of the base class, but it is a new function which hides the one of the base class, as we saw in the previous section. For example, if you use different parameters for the function of the derived class or use different `const` specifiers, then the function of the derived class won't be virtual, which means that the virtual mechanism won't work. We'll discuss again this situation later when we meet the `override` specifier.

Here is the key to runtime polymorphism. When a virtual function is called by a reference or pointer, the selection of the function to be executed is based on the type of the object to which the reference refers to or the pointer points to. Therefore, the previous code displays:

```
C:A      P:1;
T:Nice   A:Many;
T:Nice   A:Many;
```

That is, we can declare a reference or pointer to a base class object, and if it refers or points to a derived object, the function of the derived object is called, provided that it is virtual. For example, consider a hierarchy of classes derived from the `Shape` class that contains a virtual function named `draw()`. It'd be nice if we could declare a reference or pointer to `Shape` and be able to call the `draw()` of each class. Yes, we can do that thanks to the really great concept of the virtual functions.

To explain the mechanism of virtual functions, first we should discuss the *static* and *dynamic* types of a pointer variable. Each pointer has a static type, which is the type of its declaration, and a dynamic type, which is the type of the object it points to. These types may be the same, but they may also be different. For example, the static type of `ptr2` is `Product*`, while its dynamic type is `Book*`. The static type is always the same, while the dynamic type can change if, for example, we change the pointer to point somewhere else. The same applies to references. For example, in the code of example C.20.5, the static type of `r` is `Product&`, while its dynamic type when `f(b)` is called it is the type passed to it, that is, `Book&`. The beauty of runtime polymorphism originates from these types. With virtual functions, the compiler checks the dynamic type of the pointer or reference and decides which function to call.

 When designing a base class, it is a common practice to declare as `virtual` the functions that may be overridden in derived classes, so that those functions are called based on the type of the object that the pointer or the reference refers to.

Let's see another example:

```
class A
{
        . . .
        virtual void f();
};

class B : public A
{
        . . .
        virtual void f();
};

B b;
A* p = &b;
p->f(); // Which f() will be called?
```

Since `p` points to the address of `b`, the `f()` of the `B` class will be called. Note that if `f()` was not declared as `virtual`, the `f()` of the `A` class would be called.

A class function declared as virtual automatically becomes virtual in all classes derived directly or indirectly from that class. That is, the word `virtual` in the declaration of `show()` in the `Book` class is not needed. Although unnecessary, I prefer to add it in order to make it again clear to someone who reads the code. If the function is defined outside the class the word `virtual` is not added. It is only added in the declaration of the function. Note that when you override a function it is useful for the program consistency and readability, the new function to maintain the semantics of the overridden function. That is, a new `draw()` function should provide "draw" services and not used for other purposes.

Any non-static function, except the constructor, can be declared as virtual. Constructors, member static functions, and function templates cannot be virtual. A friend function cannot be declared virtual, as it is not a member of a class. A virtual function must be defined in the class in which it is declared for the first time, unless, as we'll see in Chapter 21, it is declared as a pure virtual function. Note that it is not necessary to be redefined in a derived class that does not need its own version. If not defined, the version defined in the base class is used. If the derived class belongs in a long chain of derivations, the most recently defined version is used.

Dynamic Polymorphism

So, with virtual functions, the decision about which version of the function will be called is not made during the compilation of the program, but during its execution. That is, with virtual functions, polymorphism is achieved dynamically at runtime and not at compile time. This is because the compiler does not know when compiling the program (I refer to the general case and not to the previous code) the type of object that the reference will refer to or the pointer will point to. Here is an example where the type depends on the user choice:

```
int a;
Product *ptr;
cin >> a;
if(a == 1)
        ptr = new Product("A", 1);
else
        ptr = new Book("B", 2, "Nice", "Many");
ptr->show(); /* When compiling the program, the compiler does not know the type
of object that the pointer will point to. It depends on the user's choice. */
```

What the compiler does is to create code, which, while the program runs, binds show() with either the Product::show() or with the Book::show(), depending on the type of the object that ptr points to. Because the function is selected as the program runs, this selection method is called *dynamic binding*. The terms *late binding* or *runtime binding* are also used. Without getting into implementation details, the typical way the compiler handles the virtual functions is for each class to create an array, usually referred to as *vtbl*, which holds the memory addresses of the virtual functions of the class. Indeed, an object with virtual functions allocates more memory than the equivalent object with the same functions declared as non-virtual. When a virtual function is called, the compiler checks the type of the object, finds the function address in the *vtbl* array of the corresponding class, goes to that address, and executes the code found there.

For non-virtual functions the memory address of the code of the called function is known when the program is compiled (static binding), while for virtual functions it is specified when the program runs (dynamic binding).

To make sure that you understand the different processing of a virtual function from a non-virtual, let's look at another example. What does the following program display?

```
#include <iostream> // Example 20.9
using std::cout;

class A
{
public:
        void f() const {cout << "A ";}
        virtual void g() const {cout << "A ";}
        void v() const {cout << "A ";}
};

class B : public A
{
public:
        void f() const {cout << "B ";}
        virtual void g() const {cout << "B ";}
        virtual void v() const {cout << "B ";}
};

int main()
{
        B b;
        A &r = b;
```

```
        r.f();
        r.g();
        r.v();
        return 0;
}
```

When a pointer or reference is used to call a function we check if the function is virtual or not. If not, the binding is static and we look at the type of the pointer or reference. If it is virtual, the binding is dynamic and we look at the type of the object the pointer points to or the reference refers to. Let's apply this rule to the program.

Since `f()` is not virtual, the compiler uses static binding to select which version to call. Because the type of `r` is reference to class A, `A.f()` will be called. Since `g()` is virtual, dynamic binding is used. Because the type of the `b` object referred by `r` is class B, `B.g()` will be called. The declaration of `v()` as virtual in the derived class and not in the base class has no effect. Thus, the binding is static and `A.v()` will be called. As a result, the program displays: A B A

Now, that we've discussed about virtual functions let's sum up. C++ supports:

a. Polymorphism at compile time (e.g., templates).
b. Polymorphism at runtime through virtual functions.

Using the override and Final Specifiers

C++11 introduced the word `override` as a safeguard against mistakes in the declaration of the virtual function in a derived class. For example:

```
class Book : public Product
{
        ...
        void show() override;
        override void show(); // Wrong.
};
```

The word `override` is added at the end of the declaration and explicitly states that the class will override the inherited virtual function. Also, as with the word `virtual`, it is wrong to be added in a definition outside the class. For example:

```
virtual void Book::show() {}; // Wrong.
void Book::show() override {}; // Wrong.
```

The use of the `override` specifier protects us from potential oversights, which may lead to errors that are difficult to spot. For example, what does the following program display?

```
#include <iostream> // Example 20.10
using std::cout;

class A
{
public:
        void f() const {cout << "A ";}
        virtual void g() const {cout << "A ";}
};
```

```
class B : public A
{
public:
        virtual void f() const {cout << "B ";}
        virtual void g(int i) const {cout << i;}
};

int main()
{
        B b;
        A &r = b;

        r.f();
        r.g();
        return 0;
}
```

The programmer forgot to declare f() as virtual in A. The fact that it is declared as virtual in B has no effect. The program is compiled successfully and displays A. If f() was declared virtual, which was the actual intention of the programmer, it would display B. As you can see, such an oversight, which is easy to happen, not only affects the behaviour of the program but also, within a large application, it is an error difficult to spot.

Let's see the declaration of g(). Suppose that you intend to override g() in B, but you made a mistake in the parameter list and added an extra parameter or you forgot to add the const word. Both errors are critical, because, as we said, a derived class function must have the same exact signature in order to override a virtual base class function. The compiler won't inform the programmer about this mismatch, because it allows a derived class function to have a different signature with a virtual base class function, although they have the same name. It just assumes that g() and g(int) are different functions and compiles the program normally. It does not inform the programmer that the g() in B does not override the virtual g() of A. Therefore, the g() of A is called and the program displays A again.

The use of override aids the compiler to spot such kind of errors and inform the programmer. That is, if we write:

```
class B : public A
{
public:
        void f() const override {cout << "B ";} /* Wrong, f() is not virtual. */
        void g(int i) const override {cout << i;} /* Wrong, class A has no
virtual function g(int). */
};
```

In case of f() the compiler would display an error message to indicate that f() is declared to override the virtual function of the base class but there is no such virtual function in A. Thus, the programmer understands that the word virtual is missing in the declaration of f() in A. In case of g() the compiler would display an error similar to *B::g() method with 'override' specifier does not override a base class member*. Thus, the programmer understands that something goes wrong with the declaration of g() in the B class. Since override protects us from potential errors that are difficult to detect, we'll use it from now on when overriding virtual functions. It is not so hard, we just add the override word at the end of the declaration; it may save us from a lot of trouble, especially, in large and complicated class hierarchies.

For more safety it is recommended to use the override specifier when you override a virtual function in a derived class. This enables the compiler to detect mismatches in the function signatures in the base and derived classes. Also, if you ever change the signature of the base class function, it protects you from forgetting to change the function signatures in the derived classes.

We've already seen that we can use the `final` word to prevent a class to be used as a base class. Also, we can use it when we want to prevent a virtual function to be overridden in a derived class. For example:

```
class Book : public Product
{
        . . .
        virtual void show() override final;
};

class Technical_Book : public Book
{
        . . .
        virtual void show(); // Wrong.
};
```

The attempt to override `show()` in classes that have `Book` as base class causes a compilation error. Note that it is not an error to combine `override` and `final` in the declaration; `final` just states that the function is not allowed to be overridden any further. It is also wrong to add the word `final` in a definition outside the class. For example:

```
void Book::show() final {}; // Wrong.
```

Note that the words `override` and `final` are not reserved keywords. For example, you can use them as variable names:

```
int override = 5; // Allowed.
double final = 1.2; // Allowed.
```

When the compiler meets them in the code, it checks the context to figure out how they are used. The reason they are not reserved is because they were used as ordinary variable names in existing code, before they were introduced. Although you are allowed to use them as variable names, it'd be better not to do it, to avoid confusion.

Use of Virtual Functions

A very common use of virtual functions in real applications is in functions that accept as a parameter a reference to an object of the base class. As we know, we can pass a base class object or a derived class object and use the reference to call a virtual function. The virtual function to be called is that of the object being passed. For example:

```
#include <iostream> // Example 20.11

class Shape
{
public:
        virtual void draw() const {std::cout << "Shape ";}
};

class Circle : public Shape
{
public:
        virtual void draw() const override {std::cout << "Circle ";}
};
```

```
void f(const Shape& s)
{
        s.draw();
}

int main()
{
        Circle c;
        f(c);
        return 0;
}
```

As we know, it is allowed to pass in f() a reference or pointer to a derived class object. Because draw() is virtual and s refers to a Circle object the compiler arranges for dynamic binding to the Circle::draw() function. So, the program displays Circle. To realize the strength and flexibility of the runtime polymorphism, as supported by virtual functions, consider a real application which draws shapes. We can add any shape we want derived from Shape, define its own draw() and call f(). Here is the beauty; we don't have to change f(). f() has no idea which type of object is actually passed to it, though, the proper draw() is called. That is, we can extend our program without modifying existing code. No doubt, the virtual mechanism is a very powerful technique for implementing maintainable applications flexible to extensions.

Note that if we pass a pointer to a Circle object, instead of reference, the Circle::draw() function will be again called, with the necessary changes in the code of course. Exercises C.20.4 and C.20.6 are similar examples that demonstrate the flexibility of virtual functions. But, pay attention, if we pass an array, essentially we pass a pointer as you already know, problems may arise. I'll show you such an example in the last section, similar to something once happened to me.

If draw() was not virtual the program would display Shape. And if we change f() to accept an object, that is, we write:

```
void f(Shape s) {s.draw();} what will be the output?
```

Since s is an Shape object, the function Shape::draw() will be called and the program displays Shape. With this example, I want to make it clear once more that when virtual functions are called by objects and not by pointers or references, there is no special treatment. That is, the function of the respective class will be called. In another example, what does the following program output?

```
int main()
{
        Shape sh;
        Circle cir;

        sh.draw();
        cir.draw();
        return 0;
}
```

In each call, the draw() function of the corresponding class is called. Thus, the program displays: Shape Circle. The binding of objects (e.g., sh) to function calls, whether the functions are virtual (e.g., draw()) or not, is static; it happens when the program is compiled, depending on the type of the object.

 The different behaviour of virtual functions happens at runtime when they are called through references or pointers to objects of derived classes and not when called from the objects themselves. When an object is used to call a virtual function, the call is resolved statically at compile time.

Thus, if we change Circle to:

```
class Circle : public Shape
{
public:
        virtual void draw() const override {std::cout << "Circle ";}
        Shape sh;
};
```

and write: cir.sh.draw();
which draw() will be called? That of Circle or Shape? I won't tell you the answer, find it by yourself.

As we said, if a function of the base class may be overridden in a derived class, we declare it virtual. Otherwise, we do not make it virtual, not only to avoid using some extra memory and the overhead to process its call, as we saw earlier with the *vtbl*, but also to make it clear to someone who reads the class design that it is not our intention to be overridden.

Let's look at another example of the usefulness of virtual functions. Suppose we want to manage a collection of Product and Book objects. We cannot use an ordinary array or vector variable to store the objects, because the type of its elements must be the same. However, we can use an array of pointers to Product objects. And because a pointer to a Product object can also point to an object of the derived Book class, we can use this array and appropriate virtual functions to manage both types of objects as we wish. In the general case, thanks to the virtual functions we can use a single array of pointers to manage different types of objects. Let's see the program:

```
int main() // Example 20.12
{
        const int SIZE = 10;

        int i, ch;
        float prc;
        string code, title, auth;
        Product *p[SIZE];

        for(i = 0; i < SIZE; i++)
        {
                cout << "Enter choice (1 for Product): ";
                cin >> ch;

                cout << "Enter code: ";
                cin >> code;
                cout << "Enter price: ";
                cin >> prc;
                if(ch == 1)
                        p[i] = new Product(code, prc);
                else
                {
                        cout << "Enter title: ";
                        cin >> title;
                        cout << "Enter auth: ";
                        cin >> auth;
                        p[i] = new Book(code, prc, title, auth);
                }
        }
```

```
    for(i = 0; i < SIZE; i++)
    {
            p[i]->show(); /* Depending on the type of the object pointed by
the p[i] pointer, the corresponding show() is called. */
            delete p[i];
    }
    return 0;
}
```

If `show()` had not been declared as virtual, the base class `show()` would always have been called. Now, the `show()` that is called depends on the type of the object pointed by the `p[i]` pointer. Alternatively, instead of an array of pointers, we could use a vector of pointers in the base class (e.g., `vector<Product*>`). Exercise C.20.9 is such an example. Another alternative is to use a vector of smart pointers (e.g., `vector<unique_ptr<Product>>`) as we'll see in Chapter 24, so that we don't have to worry about memory misuse (e.g., memory leaks). As you guess, it is important to understand the examples in this section and know how the virtual functions behave in order to exploit their flexibility in your own applications.

Once more, the dynamic binding and the polymorphic behaviour of a function emerges at runtime only if the called function is virtual and its call is made through a pointer or reference.

Call Particular Virtual Function

If for some reason we want to enforce the call of a particular virtual function, we can use the scope operator and the name of its class to achieve that. We've seen several similar examples with plain functions earlier in the section of function redefinition. For example, suppose that we want to call the virtual function of the base class:

```
#include <iostream> // Example 20.13

class A
{
public:
        virtual void f() const {std::cout << "A";}
};

class B : public A
{
public:
        virtual void f() const override;
};

void B::f() const
{
        A::f(); /* To refresh your memory, if you forget to specify the class
name and only write f() the result is infinite recursion. */
}

int main()
{
        B b;
        A &r = b;
        A *p = &b;
```

```
        b.f();
        r.A::f();
        p->A::f();
        return 0;
}
```

Both calls to `f()` through the pointer and the reference identify the particular `f()` of A, so this call will be statically resolved at compile time. Of course, the same applies with the `b.f()` call. The program displays A three times.

Virtual Functions and Access Specifiers

A virtual function can have a different access specifier in a derived class from the specifier in the base class. When we use a base class pointer (or reference) to call the virtual function, the access specifier in the base class determines whether the function is accessible, regardless of the type of the object that the pointer points to. If the virtual function is declared as public in the base class, the function in the derived class can be called through a base class pointer (or reference), regardless of its access specifier in the derived class. For example:

```
#include <iostream> // Example 20.14

class A
{
public:
        virtual void f() const {std::cout << "A" << '\n';}
};

class B : public A
{
private:
        virtual void f() const override {std::cout << "B" << '\n';}
};

int main()
{
        B b;

        A *p = &b;
        b.f(); // Error.
        p->f(); // It outputs B.
        return 0;
}
```

Recall that when we use an object to call a function, the call is resolved at compile time. Because `f()` is private the `b.f();` statement is not allowed. Fine, that's normal, the question is why the `p->f();` is allowed? Because `f()` is overridden and we call it through a pointer, this call is resolved at runtime. What happens is that the access specifier of the virtual function in the base class is applied in all the derived classes. That is, the access specifier of `f()` in the derived class B plays no role. It is meaningful for calls that are resolved statically, at compile time, such as the `b.f();`. If we change the access specifier of `f()` in A from public to either private or protected the `p->f();` won't compile.

Virtual Functions and Predefined Arguments

Similar to an ordinary function, a virtual function can accept predefined arguments. But be careful, when it is called by a base class pointer or reference, the predefined arguments to be used are those of the base class, even if the function of the derived class is called. That is, any default arguments in the function of the derived class have no effect; they will be ignored. For example:

```cpp
#include <iostream> // Example 20.15

class A
{
public:
        virtual void f(int i = 10) const {std::cout << "A:" << i << '\n';}
};

class B : public A
{
public:
        virtual void f(int i = 20) const override {std::cout << "B:" << i <<
'\n';}
};

int main()
{
        B b;
        A &r = b;

        b.f(); // It outputs B:20.
        r.f(); // It outputs B:10.
        return 0;
}
```

The b.f() statement is resolved statically, the f() of the B class is called, so its default argument is used and the program displays B:20. The unexpected outcome arises with the next call r.f(). This call is resolved dynamically. Although the f() of the derived class B is called, the default value of the base class A is used and the program displays B:10. So, we have to be careful, because although we'd expect the derived function to use its own default argument value, it uses that of the base class. To avoid such situations, which may cause problems in the program execution and lead to unexpected results, do not change the default values of the virtual functions in the derived classes. As a matter of fact, it'd be better to avoid using default arguments because if you ever change them in the base class function you may forget to make the same changes in the respective virtual functions of the derived classes.

One might ask, why does this happen, why the compiler does not use the default arguments of each virtual function as the programmer would expect? I guess, the reason has to do with simplicity in implementation and better performance.

Virtual Destructor

A destructor can be virtual. If the class is not to be used as a base class, there is no reason to declare it as virtual. Of course, there will be no compilation error if you do it. However, it indicates to someone who is going to use the class that it is not intended to be used as a base class. But, if it may be used as a base class, you should declare it as virtual. For example, let's change the Book class to understand why:

```cpp
class Book : public Product
{
        ...
        char *n;
        ~Book();
        ...
};
```

```
Book::Book(const string &c, float p, const string &t, const string &a) :
Product(c, p)
{
        n = new char[100];
        ...
}

Book::~Book()
{
        delete[] n;
}

int main()
{
        Product *p = new Book("B", 2, "Nice", "Many");
        delete p; // Which destructor is called?
        return 0;
}
```

When the object is destroyed, which destructor is called? That of the base or the derived class? Since the binding is static the destructor that corresponds to the pointer type is called. Therefore, the default destructor of the `Product` is called. Thus, because the `Book` destructor is not called, the memory reserved for the pointer n will not be released. Things may be much worse than a memory leak; the standard states that if the base class destructor is not virtual, applying `delete` to a base class pointer that points to a derived object results in undefined behaviour. For example, the program may crash or create memory leaks since a half-destroyed object may be out there, with the base part destroyed and the derived part still in life. To ensure that the correct destructor is called for objects of the derived class, the destructor of the base class has to be declared as virtual. For example:

```
class Product
{
        ...
        virtual ~Product() {};
        ...
};
```

When we make the base class destructor virtual, the destructors of all the derived classes become virtual as well. Thus, the binding becomes dynamic and the destructor corresponding to the type of the object pointed by the pointer will be called. Therefore, in our example, the `Book` destructor will be called, which frees the reserved memory. Then, the `Product` destructor will be called.

 Declare a virtual destructor in the base class, even if it has nothing to do, to make sure that the destructors are called in the correct sequence when the derived object is destroyed.

Calls of Virtual Functions within Constructors and Destructors

As we know, the base class sub-object of a derived object is constructed first. When its constructor is executed, the members of the derived part have not yet been initialized. Conversely, with the destruction of a derived object, when the destructor of the base sub-object is executed, the derived part has already been destroyed. That is, when the constructor and the destructor of the base class are executed, the object is partially in life. The question is, what happens if we call a virtual function from inside the constructor or the destructor of the base class? Consider the following program:

```cpp
#include <iostream> // Example 20.16

class A
{
public:
        A() {f();}
        ~A() {f();}
        virtual void f() const {std::cout << "A" << '\n';}
        void test() const {f();}
};

class B : public A
{
public:
        virtual void f() const override {std::cout << "B" << '\n';}
};

int main()
{
        B b;

        b.test(); // It outputs B.
        return 0;
}
```

Before answering the question, first let's see what happens if we call a virtual function from a base class member function. The B class overrides f(), so when we call f() using a b object, we'd expect the f() version of the B class to be called, even if the call to f() originates from inside a base class function. Indeed, when test() is called, the program outputs B. Note that if f() was not declared as virtual the program would display A.

Now let's answer the question and see what happens when we call f() from inside the base constructor. Is B again displayed? If the version in the derived class was called, it'd be very likely to cause a problem in the program execution, since this function may access members of the derived part that have not yet been initialized. Therefore, to avoid such dangerous situations, when a virtual function is called in the constructor of a base class, and because, as we've said, the construction of the object is not yet completed, what the compiler does is to call the version of the function that is in the same class as the executed constructor. Thus, in our example the program outputs A.

Regarding the destructor, because the sub-objects are destructed in the reverse order from their construction order, when the destructor of the base sub-object is executed, the derived part has already been destroyed. Therefore, it'd be again dangerous to call a member function of the derived class. Thus, the compiler calls the f() of the base class and the program outputs A. In total, the program outputs: A B A.

To sum up, a call to a virtual function from inside a constructor or destructor is resolved at compile time and the function that will be called is the one in the same class as the executed constructor or destructor.

Be Careful with Conversions

Before continue with the exercises, I'd like to draw your attention to an error I once made in one of my applications and caused me a lot of trouble. It is one of those errors that don't let you sleep; an overnight thread runs in your head that processes the code and tries to find the error. And the next morning you've got some hair turned into grey due to the overnight stress. To give you a simple example of what happened to me, see the following program:

```cpp
#include <iostream> // Example 20.17

class A
{
public:
        virtual void show() const {std::cout << "A\n";}
};

class B : public A
{
public:
        int a;
        int b;
        virtual void show() const override {std::cout << "B\n";}
};

void f(A* p, int s)
{
        for(int i = 0; i < s; i++)
                p[i].show(); // As we know, it is equivalent to (p+i)->show();
}

int main()
{
        A a[5];
        f(a, 5);

        B b[3];
        f(b, 3);
        return 0;
}
```

My intention was to define a function f(), which takes as an argument an array of objects of base or derived classes and use it to call virtual functions. Sounds fine, why not to do it? The first call of f() does not create any problem. For the second call we know that we can pass a pointer to a derived class without any problem. Because show() is virtual and because, as we know, a pointer is actually passed to f(), the show() that will be called is the show() to which the pointer points to (e.g., p+i), that is, the show() of the B class. Nice, where is the problem?

The problem is that because the size of the B class is larger than A and the value of p+i increases by the size of A, when f() calls the show() of some b element (e.g., b[1]), p+i won't point to the b element that it is supposed to point, but in some other place before that. Thus, the call to show() will cause the program to crash. When I found that bug, I realized what Stroustrup has said: *C makes it easy to shoot yourself in the foot; C++ makes it harder, but when you do it blows your whole leg off* ....

Note that in this program if the B class does not add any new data members (e.g., a and b), that is, if A and B have the same size, then the program does not crash. But, this is just a matter of luck; it is one of the situations that you created a potential bug without knowing that. The bug lives underground and waits for the right signal to explode (e.g., once a new member is added).

To fix the code, I replaced the array with a vector. For example:

```cpp
template <typename T> void f(const vector<T>& v)
{
        for(int i = 0; i < v.size(); i++)
                v[i].show();
}
```

```
int main()
{
        vector<A> a(5);
        f(a);
        vector<B> b(3);
        f(b);
        return 0;
}
```

Now, in each call, the `show()` of the object contained in v is called.

I write it again, do not freak out by some of the concepts we have discussed so far. You are absolutely right, some of them are rather difficult and complicated to understand at first glance. It is very plausible to feel that way. Let's play *Goo goo muck* by *Cramps* and hope you are in a better shape from that on the cover of *Bad music for bad people*.

What is needed is practice, practice, and more practice. Experiment with this book's examples and exercises, write your own programs, try and see, don't be afraid to make errors, learn from them, so that you gradually become familiar with the concepts of the language.

EXERCISES

C.20.1 A web application that runs on a computer supports the layered architecture of the TCP/IP model, in the sense that it uses the services provided by the physical layer, the link layer, the network layer, and the transport layer. Implement this stack of layers in the form of the following hierarchy of classes where the base class is the `Physical` (with an integer member to store the speed of the network card), `Data_Link` (with a `string` member to store the MAC address of the network card), `IP` (with a `string` member to store the IP address of the computer), `Transport` (with a `string` member to store the name of the protocol used for the data transfer), and the last derived class named `Application` (with an integer member to store the port number that the application listens to for incoming communication requests. For example, this number is 80 for an `http` server).

There is a restriction that each class should contain only the mentioned member, which should not be public. The only class that is allowed to contain functions is the `Application`. Specifically, it should contain the `get()` function which reads the initial values and stores them in the respective members of the classes and the `show()` function which displays the values of the members. Implement the classes in such a way so that the following program works.

```
int main()
{
        Application app;
        app.get(); /* The program reads the initial value of each class member
and stores that value into it. */
        app.show(); // The program displays the value of each member class.
        return 0;
}
```

Answer:

```
#include <iostream>
#include <string>
using std::cout;
```

```cpp
using std::cin;
using std::string;

class Physical
{
protected:
        int speed;
};

class Data_Link : public Physical
{
protected:
        string MAC_addr;
};

class Network : public Data_Link
{
protected:
        string IP_addr;
};

class Transport : public Network
{
protected:
        string prtcl;
};

class Application : public Transport
{
protected:
        int port;
public:
        void get();
        void show() const;
};

void Application::get()
{
        cout << "Enter speed: ";
        cin >> speed;
        cout << "Enter MAC_addr: ";
        cin >> MAC_addr;
        cout << "Enter IP_addr: ";
        cin >> IP_addr;
        cout << "Enter transport protocol: ";
        cin >> prtcl;
        cout << "Enter application port: ";
        cin >> port;
}

void Application::show() const
{
        cout << "\nS:" << speed << " MAC:" << MAC_addr << " IP:" << IP_addr <<
" T:" << prtcl << " P:" << port << '\n';
}
```

Comments: Since there is the restriction that each class, besides the `Application`, should not contain any function and its member should not be public, we understand that the members should be declared as protected, so that the functions of the `Application` can access them directly.

C.20.2 Define the class A, from A derive with public access the B, and from B derive with public access the C. Each class should contain a private member of type `string` (e.g., name) and an empty constructor. Add appropriate functions in the classes so that the following program works.

```
int main()
{
        C c("Last", "Sec", "First"); /* The Last should be stored into the
name member of the C class, the Sec in the name of B, and the First in the
name of the A class. */
        A *p = &c;
        p->show(); /* The program should display the name member of C, that is,
Last. */
        return 0;
}
```

Answer:

```
#include <iostream>
#include <string>
using std::cout;
using std::string;

class A
{
private:
        string name;
public:
        A(const string& s) : name(s) {}
        virtual void show() const {cout << name << '\n';}
};

class B : public A
{
private:
        string name;
public:
        B(const string& s1, const string& s2) : A(s2), name(s1) {}
        virtual void show() const {cout << name << '\n';}
};

class C : public B
{
private:
        string name;
public:
        C(const string& s1, const string& s2, const string& s3) : B(s2, s3),
name(s1) {}
        virtual void show() const {cout << name << '\n';}
};
```

Comments: The constructor of the derived class calls the constructor of the base class. Since there is the restriction that it should be empty, each `name` member is initialized in the initialization list. Then, since we see that the `show()` of C is called although the type of p is a pointer to the class A, we understand that we should make the `show()` virtual.

C.20.3 Find the errors in the following program.

```
#include <iostream>

class A
{
private:
        int p;
public:
        A(int a) {p = a;}
};

class B : public A
{
public:
        B(int v) {std::cout << v << '\n';}
        void show(int v) const {std::cout << p+v << '\n';}
};

int main()
{
        B b(10);
        A& r = b;

        r.show(20);
        return 0;
}
```

Answer: The first error is in the definition of `show()`. Since p is a private member, `show()` has no direct access to it. The second error is in the construction of b. Since the constructor of B does not call the constructor of A, the A object cannot be created. For example, if we write `B(int v):A(v)` or define the default constructor there will be no problem. The r may refer to a B object, but because it is declared as a reference to the class A and A does not contain any `show()` it is an error to call it.

C.20.4 Define the class `Product` with protected member the code of the product (e.g., `code`). From `Product` derive with public access the class `Book` with private member the title of the book (e.g., `title`). Each class should contain its own version of `show()`, which displays the member values. Define the function `f()` that takes as arguments two pointers to objects and displays their members. Add appropriate functions in the classes so that the following program works.

```
int main()
{
        Product prod(100); // The code becomes 100.
        Book b("C++", 200); /* The code becomes 200 and the title becomes C++.
The constructor of the Book should call the constructor of Product. */
        ... /* Declare a pointer that points to prod, another one that points
to b and then call f(). */
        return 0;
}
```

```
void f(???? *p1, ???? *p2) /* Find the type of the pointers, it must be the
same. */
{
      p1->show(); /* It should display the code of the Product object, that is,
100. */
      p2->show(); /* It should display the code and the title of the Book
object, that is, 200 and C++. */
}
```

Answer:

```
#include <iostream>
#include <string>
using std::cout;
using std::string;

class Product
{
protected:
      int code;
public:
      Product(int c);
      virtual ~Product() {}; // Not needed, just to get used.
      virtual void show() const;
};

class Book : public Product
{
private:
      string title;
public:
      Book(string t, int c);
      virtual void show() const override;
};

void f(const Product *p1, const Product *p2);

Product::Product(int c)
{
      code = c;
}

void Product::show() const
{
      cout << "C:" << code << '\n';
}

Book::Book(string t, int c) : Product(c)
{
      title = t;
}

void Book::show() const
{
      cout << "C:" << code << " T:" << title << '\n'; /* Since the code is a
protected member we can access it. */
}
```

```
int main()
{
        Product prod(100);
        Book b("C++", 200);

        Product *p1 = &prod;
        Product *p2 = &b;
        f(p1, p2);
        return 0;
}

void f(const Product *p1, const Product *p2)
{
        p1->show();
        p2->show();
}
```

Answer: Since the exercise restricts us that the two pointers in f() must be of the same type and we see that the two calls of show() in f() display the members of both the Product and the Book objects we understand that the show() must be declared as virtual. The type should be a pointer to the base class, so that a pointer to the derived class can be passed (e.g., p2) and the mechanism of the virtual functions comes into effect. If show() was not declared as virtual, the program would call twice the show() of the Product class and display 100 and 200.

C.20.5 What is the output of the following program?

```
#include <iostream>
using std::cout;

class A
{
private:
        int k;
public:
        A() {k = 1;}
        void f() const {cout << k;}
        virtual void v() const {cout << " A.v() ";}
};

class B : public A
{
private:
        int k;
public:
        B() {k = 2;}
        void f() const {cout << k;}
        virtual void v() const override {cout << " B.v() ";}
};

void t1(A a)
{
        a.f();
        a.v();
}
```

```
void t2(A& r)
{
        r.f();
        r.v();
}

int main()
{
        B b;
        t1(b);
        t2(b);
        return 0;
}
```

Answer: When t1() is called only the A part of the b object is passed to the function and copied to a. So, f() displays 1 and then the program displays A.v(). To make it clear, the member k of A has nothing to do with k of B. When t2() is called, r refers to b which is an object of the derived class. Because f() is not virtual the A.f() is called and the program displays 1. On the contrary, because v() is virtual the B.v() is called. To sum up, the program displays: 1   A.v()   1   B.v()

C.20.6 Define the Fruit class with private members the name of the fruit and the number of its calories (e.g., cal). The class must contain an appropriate constructor that initializes its members. From Fruit derive with public access the Apple class with private member the number of the antioxidants (e.g., antiox). The class must contain a constructor to initialize its member and call the constructor of Fruit. Define the function f() which takes as an argument a reference to an object and an integer value and adds them. Write a program according to the following comments.

```
int main()
{
        /* The program should create a Fruit object (e.g., fr) and an Apple
object (e.g., ap). Then, it should call f() twice. The first with argument
fr, and the second with argument ap. */
}

void f(???? &p, int num) // Find the type of the reference.
{
        cout << p+num << '\n'; /* With p+num, if the type of the object is
Fruit, num should be added to the cal member and this new value should be
displayed, while if it is Apple, num should be added to the antiox member and
this new value should be displayed. */
}
```

Answer:

```
#include <iostream>
#include <string>
using std::cout;
using std::string;

class Fruit
{
private:
        string name;
        int cal;
```

```cpp
public:
        Fruit(const string& s, int c) : name(s), cal(c) {}
        virtual ~Fruit() {};
        virtual int operator+(int num);
};

class Apple : public Fruit
{
private:
        int antiox;
public:
        Apple(int ant, const string& name, int cal) : Fruit(name, cal),
antiox(ant) {}
        virtual int operator+(int num) override;
};

int Fruit::operator+(int num)
{
        cal += num;
        return cal;
}


void f(Fruit& p, int num);

int Apple::operator+(int num)
{
        antiox += num;
        return antiox;
}


int main()
{
        Fruit fr("F1", 10);
        Apple ap(20, "F2", 30);

        f(fr, 5); // The program displays 15.
        f(ap, 5); // The program displays 25.
        return 0;
}


void f(Fruit& p, int num)
{
        cout << p+num << '\n';
}
```

Comments: Since we see in f() that an object is added with an integer we understand that the + operator must be overloaded. In order to call the operator+() of the object that p refers to, the function must be declared as virtual in the base class. If it was not declared as virtual, the program would call the operator+() of the Fruit class in the call of f(ap, 5). The reference type in f() is to the base class, so that a reference to a derived class can be passed (e.g., ap) and the mechanism of the virtual functions comes into effect.

C.20.7 What is the output of the following program?

```
#include <iostream>
using std::cout;

class A
{
public:
        A() {cout << "A ";}
        ~A() {cout << "~A ";}
        void f() {cout << "A.f() ";}
        void v() {cout << "A.v() ";}
};

class B : public A
{
public:
        ~B() {cout << "~B ";}
        virtual void f() {cout << "B.f() ";}
};

class C : public B
{
public:
        C() {cout << "C ";}
        virtual ~C() {cout << "~C ";}
        virtual void f() {cout << "C.f() ";}
        void v() {cout << "C.v() ";}
};

int main()
{
        B *p = new C;
        p->f();
        p->v();
        delete p;
        return 0;
}
```

Answer: When the object of the class C is created its constructor is called, which calls the default constructor of B, which in turn calls the constructor of A. Therefore, the program initially displays: A   C. Because f() is declared as virtual in B and p points to an object of C the C.f() will be called. Note that although f() is declared as non-virtual in A, this does not matter since C is derived from B, and the f() in B is declared as virtual. Because v() is not virtual the A.v() is called. When the object is destroyed, because the destructor of B is not virtual, the destructor of C is not called. The fact that it is declared as virtual in C has no effect. Then, the program calls the destructor of A. To sum up, the program displays: A   C   C.f()   A.v()   ~B   ~A

C.20.8 Add appropriate functions in the classes so that the following program works.

```
class A
{
private:
        char *s;
        ...
};
```

```
class B : public A
{
private:
        char *s;
        ...
};

int main()
{
        B b1("abc"); /* The string should be copied into the b1.s member and
in the s member of the A sub-object. */
        B b2(b1);
        B b3; // The s pointers should be initialized to nullptr.
        b3 = b2;
        b3.show(); /* The program should display the strings that the two s
pointers point to, that is, to display abc twice. */
        return 0;
}
```

Answer:

```
#include <iostream>
#include <cstring>

class A
{
private:
        char *s;
public:
        explicit A(const char str[]); // Let's remember explicit.
        A();
        virtual ~A();
        A(const A& a);
        A& operator=(const A& a);
        void show() const;
};

A::A(const char str[])
{
        s = new char[strlen(str)+1];
        strcpy(s, str);
}

A::A()
{
        s = nullptr;
}

A::~A()
{
        delete[] s;
}

A& A::operator=(const A& a)
{
        if(this == &a)
                return *this;
```

```
        delete[] s;
        s = new char[strlen(a.s)+1];
        strcpy(s, a.s);
        return *this;
}


A::A(const A& a)
{
        s = new char[strlen(a.s)+1];
        strcpy(s, a.s);
}


void A::show() const
{
        std::cout << s << '\n';
}


class B : public A
{
private:
        char *s;
public:
        explicit B(const char str[]);
        B();
        virtual ~B();
        B(const B& b);
        B& operator=(const B& b);
        void show() const;
};


B::B(const char str[]) : A(str)
{
        s = new char[strlen(str)+1];
        strcpy(s, str);
}


B::B()
{
        s = nullptr;
}


B::~B()
{
        delete[] s;
}


B& B::operator=(const B& b) // It is called with the b3 = b2; statement.
{
        if(this == &b)
                return *this;

        A::operator=(b); // Copy the base sub-object.
        delete[] s;
        s = new char[strlen(b.s)+1];
        strcpy(s, b.s);
        return *this;
}
```

```
B::B(const B& b) : A(b) /* It is called with the B b2(b1) statement. The copy
constructor of the base class is called. */
{
        s = new char[strlen(b.s)+1];
        strcpy(s, b.s);
}


void B::show() const
{
        std::cout << s << '\n';
        A::show();
}
```

Comments: Since we see that both classes contain a pointer for which memory will be reserved we understand that each one should contain a copy constructor, an overloaded copy function, and a destructor. The copy constructor, the overloaded copy function, and the destructor of the derived class must use their base class counterparts to handle the base class sub-object. This requirement is accomplished with the following actions.

The copy constructor of the derived class calls the copy constructor of the base class in the initialization list (another example is C.20.6). The copy function of the derived class uses the scope operator and calls explicitly the respective operator function of the base class to copy the members of the base sub-object (another example is C.20.7). Finally, when a derived object is destroyed, the destructor of the derived class calls automatically the destructor of the base class.

C.20.9 Define the Company class with private members, the name of the company, the tax number, and the total number of employees. From Company derive with public access the Software_Cmp and Finance_Cmp classes. The Software_Cmp class should contain as private members the name of the main product and the number of the programmers. The Finance_Cmp class should contain as private members the name of the main service and the number of the accountants. All classes should contain a constructor to initialize the respective members and the constructors of the derived classes should not explicitly call the constructor of the base class. Also, each class should have its own version of show(), which displays the registered name and the number of employees. Create three objects (one for each class), store the pointers to these objects in the vector v, and then call the show() of each v element to make sure that the name contained in each class and the respective number of employees are displayed correctly.

```
int main()
{
        vector<Company*> v;
        ...
        return 0;
}
```

Answer:

```
#include <iostream>
#include <string>
#include <vector>
using std::cout;
using std::string;
using std::vector;
```

```cpp
class Company
{
private:
        string cmp_name;
        string tax_num;
        int empl;
public:
        Company(const string& cmp_name, const string& tax_num, int empl);
        Company() {cmp_name = "None"; tax_num = empl = -1;} /* A default
constructor is needed to create the sub-objects of the derived objects. The
exercise does not allow to call the previous constructor. Therefore, in order
to create the base class sub-object contained in the derived object, the
default constructor must be added. */
        virtual ~Company() {};
        virtual void show() const;
};

class Software_Cmp : public Company
{
private:
        string prod;
        int prgr;
public:
        Software_Cmp(const string& prod, int prgr);
        virtual void show() const override;
};

class Finance_Cmp : public Company
{
private:
        string srvc;
        int acnt;
public:
        Finance_Cmp(const string& srvc, int acnt);
        virtual void show() const override;
};

Company::Company(const string& cmp_name, const string& tax_num, int empl)
{
        /* Let's use the this pointer to avoid looking for different parameter
names. */
        this->cmp_name = cmp_name;
        this->tax_num = tax_num;
        this->empl = empl;
}

void Company::show() const
{
        cout << "N:" << cmp_name << " E:" << empl << '\n';
}

Software_Cmp::Software_Cmp(const string& prod, int prgr)
{
        this->prod = prod;
        this->prgr = prgr;
}
```

```
void Software_Cmp::show() const
{
      cout << "N:" << prod << " E:" << prgr << '\n';
}


Finance_Cmp::Finance_Cmp(const string& srvc, int acnt)
{
      this->srvc = srvc;
      this->acnt = acnt;
}


void Finance_Cmp::show() const
{
      cout << "N:" << srvc << " E:" << acnt << '\n';
}

int main()
{
      int i;
      vector<Company*> v;

      Company cmp("Alpha", "12345", 100);
      Software_Cmp sw_cmp("Software_Product", 20);
      Finance_Cmp fin_cmp("Finance_Service", 10);

      v.push_back(&cmp);
      v.push_back(&sw_cmp);
      v.push_back(&fin_cmp);

      for(i = 0; i < v.size(); i++)
            v[i]->show();
      return 0;
}
```

Comments: If show() was not virtual, the program for the v[1] and v[2] elements would display None -1. Using a vector of pointers is an alternative to the array of pointers we used in the example C.20.12.

UNSOLVED EXERCISES

U.20.1 Use public inheritance to define the hierarchy of classes A, B, and C, where the A class is the base. Each class should contain only an integer private member and the public functions get() and show(). Define the classes in such a way that the following program works.

```
int main()
{
      C c;
      c.get(); /* The program should read sequentially three integers
and store them in the respective class members. */
      c.show(); /* The program should display sequentially the values
of the three class members. */
      return 0;
}
```

Suppose that the user enters the values 10, 20, and 30. The program should display:

```
Class_A  input:  10
Class_B  input:  20
Class_C  input:  30
Class_C  output: 30
Class_B  output: 20
Class_C  output: 10
```

U.20.2 Define the classes in such a way that the following program works.

```
class Circle
{
private:
        float rad;
        ...
};

class Sphere : public Circle
{
private:
        string col;
        ...
};

int main()
{
        Sphere sph("Blue", 2); /* Make appropriate calls to constructors,
so that Blue is stored in the col member of Sphere and 2 in the rad
member of Circle. */
        Circle& c = sph;
        c.show(); /* The program should display the colour of the sph
object and its volume according to the type 4/3*pi*r³. In this example,
the program should display Blue and 33.49. */
        return 0;
}
```

U.20.3 In the class hierarchy of exercise C.20.1, change the access type of each data member to private. The Application class should not contain the get() and show() functions. Add a constructor in each class so that the following program works.

```
int main()
{
        Application app(100, "1.2.3.4.5.6", "192.168.1.2", "tcp", 80);
/* The value 100 should be stored in the speed member, the next
argument in the MAC_addr member, the next in IP_addr, the next in
prtcl, and the last argument in the port member. Define appropriate
constructors so that each derived class calls the constructor of its
immediate base. */
        Physical& phy = app;
        phy.print(); /* Add the necessary functions in the appropriate
classes so that the program displays the value of the port, that is,
80. */
        return 0;
}
```

U.20.4 What is the output of the following program?

```cpp
#include <iostream>
using std::cout;

class A
{
public:
        int a;
        A() {}
        A(int i) {a = i;}
        virtual void f() const {cout << " A.f ";}
        void g() const {cout << " A.g ";}
};

class B : public A
{
public:
        B(int i) : A(i) {}
};

class C : public A
{
public:
        void f() const {cout << " C.f ";}
        void g() const {cout << " C.g ";}
};

void t(A* p)
{
        p->f();
        p->g();
}

int main()
{
        B b(10);
        C c;
        cout << b.a + c.a << '\n';
        t(&c);
        return 0;
}
```

U.20.5 Define the Shape class with a non-public member of type string and nothing else. Define the Rect class which is derived from Shape and contains the private members height and length. Add appropriate functions so that the following program works.

```cpp
int main()
{
        Rect r1, r2;
        cin >> r1 >> r2; /* The program should read a string and two
arithmetic values and store them in the respective members of the two
objects. */
        cout << r1+r2; /* The program displays the merging of the strings
and the sum of the respective dimensions. For example, if the user enters
abc, 1, 2 and def, 3, 4, the program should display abcdef, 4, and 6. */
        return 0;
}
```

U.20.6 Define the `Person` class with private member the name of the person (e.g., name). From the `Person` class, derive with public access the `Student` class with private member, the registration number (e.g., code), and the `Employee` class with private member the salary (e.g., sal). Each class should contain only one constructor and its own version of the `show()`, which displays the value of the respective member. Define the `f()` function which accepts as an argument a reference to an object. Implement the classes so that the following program works.

```cpp
int main()
{
        Student st("St", 100); /* The name should become St and the code
100. The constructor of Student should call the constructor of Person. */
        Employee emp("Em", 200); /* The name should become Em and the sal
200. The constructor of Employee should call the constructor of Person. */
        ... /* Call f() with argument the st object and once more with
argument the emp object. */
        return 0;
}


void f(???? &r) // Find the type of r.
{
        r.show(); /* The program should display the values of the private
members. For example, in the first call of f() the program should
display St 100 and in the second call Em 200. */
}
```

U.20.7 Define the `Person` class with a private member to store the name (e.g., name), the `Student` class which is derived from `Person` and contains a private member to store the registration number (e.g., code) and the `Phd_Student` class which is derived from `Student` and contains a private member to store the title of the thesis (e.g., title). Add appropriate functions so that the following program works with the restriction that each class should contain up to two functions (do not define destructors) and one friend function.

```cpp
int main()
{
        Person per("One");
        Student st("Two", 2); // The name should become Two and the code 2.
        Phd_Student phd("Three", 3, "Th"); /* The name should become
Three, the code 3 and the title Th. */
        vector<????> v; /* v is a vector of pointers. Choose the
appropriate type for the pointer. */
        ... // Then, store in v the pointers to the three objects.
        for(int i = 0; i < v.size(); i++)
                cout << *v[i]; /* The program should display the private
member of each class as well as the private member of each base class. */
        return 0;
}
```

For this example, the program should display:

```
One
Two 2
Three 3 Th
```

More about Inheritance

21

In this chapter we'll first discuss about abstract classes and pure virtual functions. Then, we'll discuss about inheritance with private and protected access. Next, we'll see how we can change the access to the members of the base class and make it different from the one specified by the inheritance type. We'll also discuss about multiple inheritance and present some problems that may arise in its use. Finally, we'll discuss about virtual base classes and the properties of static members in inheritance hierarchies.

ABSTRACT CLASSES AND PURE VIRTUAL FUNCTIONS

When we design the classes of an application some classes that seem unrelated may have common data. For example, suppose we want to develop an application that manages right triangles and rectangles. To manage triangles, we could define the `Triangle` class with members the two vertical sides of the triangle. To manage the rectangles, we could define the `Rectangle` class with members the two vertical sides of the rectangle. Also, we could add in both classes a function that displays the dimensions of the shape (e.g., `show()`), a function that calculates its area (e.g., `area()`) and another one for the perimeter (e.g., `perim()`).

To implement the classes, we could use inheritance and make either to be the base class, but since the two shapes are not related, it is an awkward approach. Therefore, it seems better to define the `Rectangle` and `Triangle` classes separately. Yet, this approach still seems inefficient. Both classes have lot in common, but defining them separately ignores this fact.

An elegant-programming approach is to apply the concept of *abstraction*. What's that? We define a third class (e.g., `Shape`), which contains the common members (e.g., the two vertical sides) and functions of the two classes (e.g., `show()`). The `Shape` will be the base class and the other two will inherit it. We declare as virtual the functions that work differently in each class. For example, we make virtual the `area()` since the area of each shape is calculated differently. Since the `Shape` does not represent a shape, it does not need to implement `area()`. But, is it allowed a class to contain a function that is not defined? Yes, C++ gives us this ability by declaring the function as *pure virtual*. To make the function pure virtual we add the curious `= 0` syntax at the end of its declaration. Let's see the program:

```cpp
#include <iostream> // Example 21.1
#include <vector>
#include <cmath>
using std::cout;
using std::cin;
using std::vector;

class Shape
{
protected:
        float l;
        float h;
```

DOI: 10.1201/9781003230076-21

```
public:
        Shape(float len, float hght) {l = len; h = hght;}
        virtual ~Shape() {}; /* As we've said, we add it although it has
nothing to do. */
        void show() {cout << "L:" << l << " H:" << h << '\n';}
        virtual void area() const = 0; // Pure virtual function.
        virtual void perim() const = 0; // Pure virtual function.
};

class Triangle : public Shape
{
public:
        Triangle(float l, float h) : Shape(l, h) {} /* The constructor of the
base class is called. */
        virtual void area() const {cout << "A:" << l*h/2 << '\n';}
        virtual void perim() const {cout << "P:" << l+h+sqrt(l*l+h*h) << '\n';}
// To calculate the hypotenuse we apply the Pythagorean theorem.
};

class Rectangle : public Shape
{
public:
        Rectangle(float l, float h) : Shape(l, h) {}
        virtual void area() const {cout << "A:" << l*h << '\n';}
        virtual void perim() const {cout << "P:" << 2*(l+h) << '\n';}
};

int main()
{
        const int SIZE = 2;

        int i, ch, len, hght;
        vector<Shape*> vec_sh(SIZE);

        for(i = 0; i < SIZE; i++)
        {
                cout << "Enter choice (1 for Triangle): ";
                cin >> ch;
                cout << "Enter length: ";
                cin >> len;
                cout << "Enter height: ";
                cin >> hght;
                if(ch == 1)
                        vec_sh[i] = new Triangle(len, hght);
                else
                        vec_sh[i] = new Rectangle(len, hght);
        }
        for(i = 0; i < SIZE; i++)
        {
                vec_sh[i]->show();
                vec_sh[i]->area();
                vec_sh[i]->perim();
                delete vec_sh[i];
        }
        return 0;
}
```

For convenience, I declared the l and h members as protected so that derived classes may access them directly. As an alternative to the example of C.20.12, in order to manage objects of both Triangle and Rectangle classes with one entity and exploit polymorphism I chose to use a vector of pointers to the base class Shape. As shown, a pure virtual function has no definition. Its purpose is to enable the versions of the function in the derived classes to be called polymorphically.

A class that contains at least one pure virtual function (e.g., Shape) is called *abstract*. An abstract class can contain only pure virtual functions. Notice that it is not allowed to create objects of an abstract class. That is, if we write:

Shape s(1, 2); the compiler will display an error message. The rational of an abstract class is to be used only as base class; it is a concept that represents the common characteristics of related entities.

Since we cannot create an object, it is not allowed to pass it by value in a function or return an object from a function. As for pointers and references to abstract classes it is perfectly legal to use them as parameters or return types. In fact, this is essential in order to exploit the polymorphic behaviour of the virtual functions. Well, a question arises, since we cannot create objects, why does the Shape contain a constructor? It is there to initialize its member variables. And who is going to call it? It will be called by the constructors of the derived classes in order to build the Shape sub-objects they contain.

A pure virtual function not defined in the derived class is still considered to be pure virtual. Thus, the derived class becomes abstract too. For example:

```
class A
{
        . . .
        virtual void f() = 0;
        virtual void g() = 0;
};

class B : public A
{
        . . .
        virtual void g() {}; // f() is still pure virtual.
};

class C : public B
{
        . . .
        virtual void f() {};
};

B b; /* Wrong, B is an abstract class. It is not allowed to create B
objects. */
C c; // Correct.
```

Since g() is not defined in B, B becomes an abstract class, so it is not allowed to create objects of this class.

The programming model based on the concept of abstraction is quite common. To return to this, the common elements resulting from the design of the classes are placed in a base class, while the functions implemented differently in each derived class are declared as pure virtuals. This design avoids duplication of the same code and, thus, facilitates the maintenance and upgrade of the program. In general, abstract classes tend to contain only pure virtual functions (data members are defined in the derived classes) and consequently no constructors (since there are no data members to initialize, it is unlikely to need a constructor). Essentially, an abstract class is a kind of a contract for what a derived class should provide. The abstract class defines "what needs to be implemented", leaving the implementation tasks of the virtual functions to the programmer of each derived class.

PRIVATE AND PROTECTED INHERITANCE

Besides the public inheritance we saw in Chapter 20, a class can be derived with private and protected access. With private inheritance the public and protected members of the base class become private members of the derived class. This means that they are accessible from the functions of the derived class, but not from outside the derived class. For example, consider the following program:

```cpp
#include <iostream> // Example 21.2

class A
{
protected:
        int r;
        void sub(int i) {v-=i;}
public:
        int v;
        A() : v(1), r(2) {};
        void add(int i) {r+=i;}
};

class B : private A
{
public:
        void show();
};

void B::show()
{
        // All the following actions are allowed.
        add(3);
        sub(4);
        std::cout << v+r << '\n';
}

int main()
{
        B b;
        b.show();
        b.add(5); // Illegal action.
        b.sub(6); // Illegal action.
        std::cout << b.v << '\n'; // Illegal action.
        return 0;
}
```

To declare the private inheritance we use the word `private` in the declaration of the derived class. Since the default access type is `private` the word `private` can be omitted. However, my preference is to add it on order to make clear the inheritance type. In the case of a structure type, the default access type is `public`. For example:

```cpp
class B : A {}; // B is derived with private access.
struct B : A {}; // B is derived with public access.
```

Since the B class is derived with private access to the base class A, the members and functions of the A class become private members of the B class. Therefore, the functions of B (e.g., `show()`) may access them, but not its objects (e.g., b).

To derive a class with protected access we use the word `protected` in its declaration. The public and protected members of the base class become protected members of the derived class. Therefore, as with private access, they are accessible from the functions of the derived class, but not from outside. The main difference between private and protected inheritance is when we derive a new class from the derived class. With private inheritance, the second derived class does not have direct access to the members of the base class because they have become private in the first derivation. For example, let's add the class C in the previous program:

```
class C : private B
{
public:
        void f();
};

void C::f() // All the following actions are not allowed.
{
        add(1);
        sub(2);
        cout << v+r << '\n';
}
```

Because the members and functions of the A class have become private members of the B class, it is not allowed to access them directly from class C. On the other hand, if inheritance is protected, access is allowed. For example:

```
#include <iostream> // Example 21.3

class A
{
protected:
        void f() const {std::cout << v << ' ';}
public:
        int v;
        A() : v(10) {};
};

class B : protected A
{
protected:
        int r;
        void g() const {std::cout << r << '\n';}
public:
        B() : r(20) {};
};

class C : protected B
{
public:
        void h();
};

void C::h()// All the following actions are allowed.
{
        v = r = 30;
        g();
        f();
}
```

```
int main()
{
        C c;

        c.h();
        return 0;
}
```

Since the access type is `protected`, the public and protected members of the base class A become protected members of the derived class B. These members, together with the public and protected members of the class B, become protected members of the new derived class C. Therefore, the function `h()` has direct access to the members of both classes. Thus, the program displays 30 30.

Now that we have discussed about all types of inheritance, let's summarize the rules that apply to access the members of the base class, so that you can find them all together in one place. Suppose that the B class is derived from the A class:

a. If A is a private base class, the public and protected members of A become private members of B and they are accessible only from member functions and friend functions of B.

b. If A is a protected base class, the public and protected members of A become protected members of B and they are accessible only from member functions and friend functions of B, as well as from member functions and friend functions of classes derived from B.

c. If A is a public base class, its public members are accessible from any function of B. The protected members of A are accessible from member functions and friend functions of B, as well as from member functions and friend functions of classes derived from B.

The above are summarized in the following table:

MEMBERS OF THE BASE CLASS	PUBLIC INHERITANCE	PROTECTED INHERITANCE	PRIVATE INHERITANCE
The public members become:	public members of the derived class	protected members of the derived class	private members of the derived class
The protected members become:	protected members of the derived class	protected members of the derived class	private members of the derived class
The private members become:	private members of the derived class	private members of the derived class	private members of the derived class

ACCESS REDEFINITION

Sometimes we may want the access of a derived class to one or more members of the base class to be different from the access specified by the inheritance type. Let's look at an example to better understand it:

```
#include <iostream> // Example 21.4

class A
{
private:
        int p;
```

```
protected:
        int v;
public:
        void add(int i) {v+=i;}
        void sub(int i) {v-=i;}
};

class B : public A
{
public:
        void f() {add(1);}
};
```

Because the inheritance type is public, a B object may access the public members of the A class. Suppose that we want to prevent the access to the add() function. Let's see how we can do that:

```
class B : public A
{
private:
        using A::add;
public:
        using A::p; /* Wrong, since p is a private member it is not allowed to
change the access. */
        using A::v; // Correct, A::v becomes public.
        void f() {add(1);}
};
```

As shown, we use the word using and we write the name of the base class followed by the scope resolution operator and the name of the function in the private part. Note that we write just the name of the function, no return type or parameter list. Now, although the A class is inherited with public access, the add() function is inherited with private access. The section where the using declaration is placed also determines the access to the member. That is, since the using declaration of the add() function is placed in the private section of B, only the members and the friend functions of B have access to it. For example, if we write:

```
int main()
{
        B b;

        b.f();
        b.sub(1); // OK.
        b.v = 10; // OK.
        b.add(2); // Wrong.
        return 0;
}
```

The compiler will display an error message, because the access to add() from b is not allowed. Someone may ask, can I use using to change the access of the private members of the base class (e.g., p) to public? The answer is, no, it is not allowed, because private members cannot be accessed in a derived class. A derived class can contain using declarations only for the members it is allowed to access.

The using declaration can also be used in classes derived with private or protected access. For example, let's change the inheritance type of the B class to private. This means that a B object does not have access to the members of the A class. However, we can use `using` declarations and change the access to the members we want.

```
class B : private A
{
public:
        using A::v;
        using A::sub;
        void f() {add(1);}
};
```

Although B is derived with private access, v and sub() become public members for the B class. For example:

```
B b;
b.v = 10;   // OK.
b.sub(1);   // OK.
b.add(2);   // Wrong.
```

Note that a new derived class inherits the members with the new access type specified for them. For example:

```
class C : public B
{
};
```

Since C is derived with public access, a C object may access the public members of the B class. Thus, we can write:

```
C c;
c.v = 10;   // OK.
c.sub(1);   // OK.
```

MULTIPLE INHERITANCE

In Chapter 20, we've seen the *single* inheritance, that is, a derived class derives from a single base class. In this section, we'll discuss about *multiple* inheritance, that is, the ability to derive a class from more than one base class. In general, multiple inheritance is used less frequently than single inheritance. Multiple inheritance is useful when we want to merge data of different, usually unrelated, classes into a third class. However, because complexity increases, it should be used rationally. Let's look at an example and problems that may arise:

```
class A
{
public:
        void show() const {...}
        ...
};

class B
{
public:
        void show() const {...}
        ...
};
```

```
class C : public A, public B
{
        ...
};

int main()
{
        C c;

        c.show(); // Ambiguity, which show() will be called;
        ...
}
```

The C class is derived with public inheritance from the A and B classes. It inherits all the members of both A and B classes. As shown in the declaration of C, the classes are separated by commas and we specify the access specifier for each base class. If it is missing, the compiler assumes that the access is private. For example, if we write:

```
class C : public A, B
```

class B is inherited with private access.

For the construction of the c object, the sub-objects of its base classes are first constructed. The construction order is, from left to right, as the base classes appear in the declaration of the class (e.g., public A, public B). Specifically, when c is created, the default constructor of C is called, which calls the default constructor of A, then that of B, and then the creation of c is completed. That is, the A sub-object is created first and then the B sub-object.

As you'll see in the following sections, the implementation of the multiple inheritance can be more difficult and problem-prone compared to the single inheritance. For example, with multiple inheritance, the same names can be inherited, and as shown in the code above, ambiguity problems may arise. Which show() will be called? That of A or B? Because the compiler does not know which one to call, it will display an error message similar to *call to show() is ambiguous*. Note that there is no problem for a class to inherit multiple members with the same name. The compiler will complain only if we attempt to use a common name, such as show(). To overcome the problem, one solution is to use the scope operator :: and the name of the class that contains the show() that we want to call. For example:

```
c.A::show(); // The show() of A is called.
```

One may ask, could not we rewrite the classes and use a different name? Sure, you can do that. As a matter of fact, you should avoid using the same names when writing classes for use in inheritance. But, you may run into the situation that you are unable to rewrite the class, as when using base classes from a library. Then, you need to qualify the name of the function.

Another solution is to use a using declaration inside the C class to specify from which base class the duplicated member will be selected. For example:

```
class C : public A, public B
{
public:
        using A::show;
        ...
};
```

Now, when we write c.show(); the show() of A will always be called. If you want to call always a certain duplicated member function this option should be preferred against the option to use the qualified name (e.g., c.A::show();). It is simpler and helps you avoid the compilation errors that would otherwise occur if you forget to add the qualified name.

When c is destroyed, the destructors are called in reverse order, that is, first that of C, then that of B, and last that of A. Here is a more difficult example. Consider the following inheritance scheme, where each class contains the default constructor and destructor. In what order will they be called?

```
class A {...};
class B {...};
class C : public B, public A {...};
class D {...};
class E : public D {...};
class F : public E {...};
class G : public F, public C {...};

int main()
{
        G g;
        ...
}
```

The construction order of the sub-objects is D, E, F, B, A, C, G. When g is destroyed, the destructors of the sub-objects are called in reverse order.

Creation of Multiple Base Objects

If in the class hierarchy more than one path exist between a base class and a derived class, multiple sub-objects of the base class are created and, therefore, multiple copies of its members. This may not be desirable. Can we avoid it? We'll answer it later, at first, consider the following program:

```
#include <iostream> // Example 21.5
using std::cout;

class A
{
private:
        int r;
public:
        A(int k) : r(k) {cout << " A()";}
        virtual ~A() {cout << " ~A()";}
        void show_A() const {cout << " A:" << r;}
};

class B : public A
{
private:
        int t;
public:
        B(int m) : A(m), t(m) {cout << " B()";}
        ~B() {cout << " ~B()";}
        void show_B() const;
};

void B::show_B() const
{
        cout << " B:" << t;
        show_A();
}
```

```
class C : public A
{
private:
        int v;
public:
        C(int p) : A(p), v(p) {cout << " C()";}
        ~C() {cout << " ~C()";}
        void show_C() const;
};

void C::show_C() const
{
        cout << " C:" << v;
        show_A();
}

class BC : public B, public C
{
private:
        int z;
public:
        BC(int x) : B(x), C(x+1), z(2*x) {cout << " BC()\n";}
        ~BC() {cout << "~BC()";}
        void show_BC() const {cout << " BC:" << z << '\n';}
};

int main()
{
        BC bc(10);

        bc.show_B();
        bc.show_C();
        bc.show_BC();
        return 0;
}
```

The B and C classes are derived from the A class. The BC class is derived from these two classes. I made the constructors to have parameters so that we remember how the constructor of a derived class can pass values to the constructor of the base class. When the bc object is created the constructor of the BC class is called:

```
BC(int x) : B(x), C(x+1), z(2*x) {cout << " BC()\n";}
```

At first, recall that, as in the class hierarchy of the example C.20.4, a constructor of a derived class can call a constructor only of its direct base classes. An exception to this rule is the virtual base classes, which we'll see below. Now, let's go to the BC constructor. It calls the constructor of the B class and passes to it the value 10. In its turn, it calls the constructor of the A class and passes the same value. So, first the sub-object of the A class is created and r becomes 10. Then, the sub-object of the B class is created and t becomes 10. Then, the constructor of the C class is called and the value 11 is passed to it. It calls the constructor of the A class and passes the same value to it. Thus, the second sub-object of the A class is created and r becomes 11. Then, the sub-object of the C class is created and v becomes 11. Finally, z becomes 20. To sum up, the bc object contains two sub-objects of the A class, one sub-object of the B class and one of the C class.

With multiple inheritance an object of a derived class contains a sub-object for each of its base classes.

As we said, the order in which the objects of the base classes are constructed is from left to right, as the base classes appear in the declaration of the class (e.g., `public B`, `public C`). The order in which the constructors appear in the initialization list does not matter. That is, if we change the order and write:

```
BC(int x) : C(x+1), B(x), z(2*x) {cout << " BC()\n";}
```

the constructor of the B class will be called first again and then that of C.

bc.show_B() calls the show_B() of the B class. It displays the value of t and calls the show_A() of its own A sub-object. Similarly, bc.show_C() calls the show_C() of the C class, which displays the value of v and calls the show_A() of its own A sub-object. The destructors are called in the reverse order from the one that the constructors were called. Finally, the program displays:

```
A()       B()       A()       C()       BC()
B:10      A:10      C:11      A:11      BC:20
~BC()     ~C()      ~A()      ~B()      ~A()
```

As you guess, complications and ambiguities arise from such repeated inheritance. For example, can we write?

```
bc.show_A();
```

No, the compiler will display an error message similar to *BC::show_A() is ambiguous*. The reason is that because there are two sub-objects of the A class, the compiler cannot choose the object to apply show_A(). In the A sub-object of the B class or in the A sub-object of the C class? In our example, I skipped this problem by making show_A() to be called through the functions of the B and C sub-objects. Thus, the compiler calls the show_A() of the A sub-object contained in each class. As we know, another way is to use the `::` scope operator and specify the A sub-object we want. For example:

```
bc.B::show_A(); /* The show_A() of the A sub-object of the B class is called. */
bc.C::show_A(); /* The show_A() of the A sub-object of the C class is called. */
```

Multiple Base Objects and Problems

Let's look at a more realistic example with the creation of multiple base objects and problems that may arise. This time I won't choose different show_ names (e.g., show_A), which is the easy case since it is clear which show_ will be called, but I'll choose the same name show() and use virtual functions for polymorphism. The following program defines the Person class and uses it to derive the Programmer and Author classes. The ProgAuth class is derived from these two classes. Essentially, the program simulates the case of someone being a programmer and a writer.

```
#include <iostream> // Example 21.6
#include <string>
using std::cout;
using std::cin;
using std::string;
```

```cpp
class Person
{
private:
        string name;
        int code;
public:
        Person() {name = "None"; code = 0;}
        Person(const string& n, int c) : name(n), code(c) {}
        virtual ~Person() {}
        virtual void show() const;
};


void Person::show() const
{
        cout << "\nName:" << name << ' ' << "Code:" << code << ' ';
}


class Programmer : public Person
{
private:
        string cmp; // The name of the company (s)he is working at.
public:
        Programmer() {cmp = "Any";}
        Programmer(const string& n, int c, const string& s) : Person(n, c),
cmp(s) {}
        virtual void show() const override;
};


void Programmer::show() const
{
        Person::show();
        cout << "Company:" << cmp;
}


class Author : public Person
{
private:
        int titles; // The number of the books (s)he has written.
public:
        Author() {titles = 0;}
        Author(const string& n, int c, int t) : Person(n, c), titles(t) {}
        virtual void show() const override;
};


void Author::show() const
{
        Person::show();
        cout << "Titles:" << titles;
}


class ProgAuth : public Programmer, public Author
{
};
```

```
int main()
{
        int i;
        Person per("First", 1);
        Programmer pro("Second", 2, "Net");
        Author auth("Third", 3, 5);
        Person *p[3] = {&per, &pro, &auth};

        for(i = 0; i < 3; i++)
                p[i]->show();
        return 0;
}
```

The constructors of the `Programmer` and the `Author` classes use the: syntax to initialize their members and call the constructor of the base class. The `show()` of the derived classes use the name of the base class and the `::` operator to call the base `show()`. Since the `show()` is virtual, the program checks the type of the object that each `p[i]` pointer points to and calls the corresponding `show()`. If `show()` had not been declared as virtual in the base class, the compiler would check the type of the `p` array and because it is a pointer to `Person` it would call the `show()` of `Person` three times. So far so good, this program is essentially another example that demonstrates the behaviour of virtual functions. Let's see now what happens if we add the following code:

```
ProgAuth pro_auth;
pro_auth.show(); // Compilation error.
```

When the `pro_auth` object is created the four default constructors are called. Specifically, the constructor of the `ProgAuth` is called to create the `ProgAuth` object, the `Person` and the `Programmer` constructors to create the corresponding sub-objects, and the `Person` and `Author` constructors to create the corresponding sub-objects. That is, each object of the `ProgAuth` class contains one sub-object of the `Programmer` class, one sub-object of the `Author` class, and two sub-objects of the `Person` class. What would happen if any of the default constructors of the `Person`, `Programmer`, and the `Author` classes was missing? The compiler would issue an error message, because since all these classes have constructors the default constructor is not created automatically, it must be added.

Next point to pay attention. Which `show()` will be called? That of `Programmer` or `Author`? Because the compiler does not know which one to call, it will display an error message similar to *ProgAuth::show() is ambiguous*. One solution is to use the `::` scope operator and the name of the respective class. For example:

```
pro_auth.Programmer::show(); // The show() of Programmer is called.
pro_auth.Author::show(); // The show() of Author is called.
```

Alternatively, another approach is to define a `show()` in the `ProgAuth` class and call from inside there the `show()` we want. For example:

```
class ProgAuth : public Programmer, public Author
{
public:
        virtual void show() const override;
};

void ProgAuth::show() const
{
        Programmer::show();
}
```

Now, we can write: `pro_auth.show();` and the `show()` of the `Programmer` is called.

Suppose now that we want a pointer to the base class to point to a `ProgAuth` object. As we know, we can write:

```
Person *p;
ProgAuth pro_auth;
p = &pro_auth; // Compilation error.
```

However, the compiler will display an error message. Let's see why. Since each of the `Programmer` and `Author` sub-objects is derived from the `Person` class, the `ProgAuth` object also contains two `Person` sub-objects. Normally, as we know, when the address of a derived object is assigned to a pointer to the base class, the pointer points to the address of the base sub-object inside the derived object. But now in the `ProgAuth` object there are two sub-objects of the base class. Which of the two to point to? Because the compiler does not know which address to choose, it displays an error message similar to *Person is an ambiguous base class of ProgAuth*. And how can we solve this problem? We use type cast. For example:

```
Person *p1, *p2;
ProgAuth pro_auth;
p1 = static_cast<Programmer*>(&pro_auth); /* The Person sub-object of the
Programmer sub-object is selected. */
p2 = static_cast<Author*>(&pro_auth); /* The Person sub-object of the Author
sub-object is selected. */
```

The last and the most important question. Since a `ProgAuth` object has two `Person` sub-objects, it will have two names and two codes. Does that make sense? Of course not, someone who is a programmer and a writer should have just one name and one identity like everybody else, not two. And how can we make this possible? The answer is by using virtual base classes. In general, typically, we would want to avoid having multiple sub-objects, so let's see how we can do that.

Virtual Base Classes

The declaration of a base class as virtual allows an object derived from multiple classes which are derived from a common base class to contain just one sub-object of that base class. In other words, to avoid a derived class object to contain more than one sub-objects of the same base class, we declare that base class as virtual. To make the base class virtual we use the word `virtual` in the declaration of the derived classes that inherit it. For example, in the program C.21.5 we write:

```
class B : virtual public A {...};
class C : virtual public A {...};
```

Now, the `B` and `C` sub-objects share a common `A` sub-object. Thus, a `BC` object contains only one `A` sub-object. Therefore, if we write:

```
bc.show_A();
```

the compiler will not display an error message, as in the case of the non-virtual `A` class, because now the `bc` object contains just one `A` sub-object. Thus, no qualification is needed. Note that the words `virtual` and `public` can also be used in reverse order. Note also, that although the same word `virtual` is used to denote virtual classes and virtual functions, these two concepts are different from each other. Now, why it is decided to use the same word and not introduce some new word that better demonstrates the uniqueness of the sub-object (e.g., the word *unique*), I guess that the C++ committee did not want to extend the set of the reserved words and put new restrictions in the selection of names.

 We remember when we want to create a single sub-object of the common base class we make it virtual.

However, with virtual classes the way the constructors are called changes. Let's see why. In our example, the constructors of the B and C classes pass information to the constructor of the A class. No problem, the constructor of each A sub-object is called. But now that we've made the A class virtual we have only one A sub-object. The logical question to make is from which path it will be initialized? From the B or C path? To resolve this issue, C++ disables the passing of information from an intermediate class to the base class, provided that the base class is virtual. That is, the B and C constructors will initialize the members t and v respectively, but the calls to the A constructor are ignored.

Fine, but the A sub-object must be constructed. So, how will it be constructed? The answer is that the responsibility for constructing the sub-object of a virtual base class goes to the constructor of the most distant derived class (e.g., BC). In particular, when the bc object is created the compiler calls the default constructor of A. Is there a default constructor in our example? No, so the compiler will display an error message similar to *A::A default constructor is missing*. Let's add it. The rest of the program remains the same except that we make the A class virtual.

```cpp
#include <iostream> // Example 21.7
using std::cout;

class A
{
        . . .
        A(int k) : r(k) {cout << " A()";}
        A() {cout << " Def_A()"; r = 30;}
        virtual ~A() {cout << " ~A()";}
};

class B : virtual public A
{
        . . .
        B(int m) : A(m), t(m) {cout << " B()";}
        ~B() {cout << " ~B()";}
};

class C : virtual public A
{
        . . .
        C(int p) : A(p), v(p) {cout << " C()";}
        ~C() {cout << " ~C()";}
};

class BC : public B, public C
{
        . . .
        BC(int x) : B(x), C(x+1), z(2*x) {cout << " BC()";}
        ~BC() {cout << " ~BC()";}
};
```

```
int main()
{
        BC bc(10);
        ...
        return 0;
}
```

As we've described, with the creation of the bc object the t member of the B sub-object becomes 10 and the v member of the C sub-object becomes 11. Because A is virtual, the A constructor that will be called is the default constructor. Thus, the r member of the single A sub-object becomes 30. Finally, the program displays:

```
Def_A()     B()         C()         BC()
B:10        A:30        C:11        A:30        BC:20
~BC()       ~C()        ~B()        ~A()
```

But what if we do not want the default constructor of the virtual class to be called and we want to specify some other to be called? We just call it directly. For example:

```
BC(int x) : A(x+5), B(x), C(x+1), z(2*x) {cout << " BC()";}
```

As we learned in Chapter 20, the constructors that are allowed to be included in such an initialization list are only constructors of the immediately preceding base class. Therefore, we would expect that the calls to the B and C constructors are allowed, but not that of A. The exception to this rule is that if a class derives indirectly from a virtual base class, its constructor can be called directly. If A was not virtual, the compiler would issue an error message. So, if we write the BC constructor like this, the program will display:

```
A()         B()         C()         BC()
B:10        A:15        C:11        A:15        BC:20
~BC()       ~C()        ~B()        ~A()
```

If a class derives indirectly from a virtual base class, its constructor is allowed to call directly the constructor of the virtual base class. Otherwise, the default constructor will be called, if it exists. If it does not exist, a compilation error will occur.

To summarize, when we use multiple inheritance, and different paths lead to the creation of multiple sub-objects of a base class, we should ask ourselves if it bothers us to have multiple copies of the same members. If it does not bother us, we do nothing. Otherwise, we need to make the base class virtual. In that case, the construction of the single base sub-object is undertaken by the constructor of the most distant derived class. In general, be aware that using virtual classes is more complex and time consuming for the compiler, so if you can, it'd be better to avoid it.

Object Construction with Multiple Virtual Base Classes

When there is no base virtual class, the sub-objects of the base classes are constructed in the order they appear in the declaration of the derived class. If present, the sub-object of the virtual class is constructed first using the constructor of the most distant derived class and then the objects of the non-virtual base class according to the order in which they appear in the list of the base classes. What if a class has more than one virtual base class? In this case, the sub-objects of the virtual base classes are constructed first from left to right in the order that they appear in the declaration of the class. Then, the sub-objects of the non-virtual classes are constructed. For example:

```
class A {...};
class B {...};
class C {...};
class D {...};
class E : public D, public C, virtual public B, virtual public A {...}

E e1;
E e2(e1);
```

To construct the e1, the constructors are called in the following order. First, the sub-object of B will be constructed, then the sub-object of A, then the sub-object of D, then the sub-object of C, and finally the constructor of E will complete the construction. Note that the same execution order also applies for the default copy constructors (e.g., to create e2), as well as when the members are copied with the default copy function (e.g., e3 = e2). As usual, the destructors are called in reverse order from the constructors, first the destructor of E, last the destructor of B. If the classes B and A are not declared as virtual, the construction order of the sub-objects is D, C, B, and A.

Mixed Virtual and Non-Virtual Base Classes

A base class may be virtual in some derived classes and non-virtual in others. What happens when a new class is derived from them? When a class derives from a base class through virtual and non-virtual paths, the class contains one sub-object of the base class corresponding to all virtual paths and separate sub-objects for each non-virtual path. For example, in the following program, the A class is a virtual base class for the B and C classes and non-virtual for the D and E classes. The F class is derived from the B, C, D, and E classes.

```
#include <iostream> // Example 21.8
using std::cout;

class A
{
public:
      A() {cout << " A()";}
};

class B : virtual public A
{
public:
      B() {cout << " B()";}
};

class C : virtual public A
{
public:
      C() {cout << " C()";}
};
```

```
class D : public A
{
public:
        D() {cout << " D()";}
};

class E : public A
{
public:
        E() {cout << " E()";}
};

class F : public B, public C, public D, public E
{
public:
        F() {cout << " F()";}
};

int main()
{
        F f;
        return 0;
}
```

How many sub-objects of the A class does the f object contain? It contains one sub-object for the B and C classes where the A class is virtual, one sub-object for the D class and one for the E class. The program displays:

```
A()    B()    C()    A()    D()    A()    E()    F()
```

One more question, if in each class we had destructors that display similar messages, what would the program display? Since we know that the destructors are called in the reverse order from that of the constructors the program would display the same output from right (e.g., F) to left.

To sum up, as you've seen, multiple inheritance can introduce programming complexities and be problem-prone to implement and control. If you can avoid it and use single inheritance instead, it is preferable. If not, you need to decide whether to use virtual classes or not.

IHNERITANCE AND STATIC MEMBERS

And an easy section, before we go to the exercises. If a static member is defined in a base class, it is created only once regardless of the number of the classes derived from the base class. The same access rules that apply for the ordinary members, also apply for the static members. Consider the following program:

```
#include <iostream> // Example 21.9

class A
{
public:
        static inline int v = 10;
};
```

```
class B : public A
{
public:
        void f() {v = 20;}
};

class C : public A
{
public:
        void g() {v = 30;}
};

int main()
{
        B b;
        C c;

        b.f();
        c.g();
        std::cout << b.v << ' ' << c.v << '\n'; /* Alternatively, we can write
cout << B::v << ' ' << C::v; */
        return 0;
}
```

Since there is only one instance of v the f() and g() functions change its value sequentially. Thus, the program displays 30 30. If we do not declare v as static, the program will display 20 30, since b.v is a different variable from c.v.

EXERCISES

C.21.1 Find the errors in the following program.

```
#include <iostream>

class A
{
public:
        int p;
        A(int a) {p = a;}
};

class B
{
public:
        int p;
        B() {p = 20;}
        void show(const char str[]) const {std::cout << str << '\n';}
};

class C : public A, public B
{
private:
        int v;
```

```
public:
        C() : v(10) {}
        void show() const {std::cout << v << '\n';}
};

int main()
{
        C c;
        c.p = 10;
        c.show("test");
        return 0;
}
```

Answer: The first error is when c is created. The error is that since no default constructor is defined in A, the A sub-object cannot be constructed. If we had called the existing constructor there would be no problem. For example, C() : A(5), v(10) {}. The second error is when p is accessed. Since both the A and B classes contain a member with the same name p, the compiler does not know which of the two to access. For example, if we had written c.A::p = 10; there would be no problem. The third error is when calling the show(). The show() of the C class hides the show() of the B class. So, if we want to call the show() of the C class we have to write c.show(), while for the show() of the B class we have to write c.B::show("test");

C.21.2 Define the A and B classes and the C class which is derived with public access from A and B. Then, define the D and E classes derived with public access from C. Finally, define the F class derived with public access from D and E. Suppose that an F object is created (e.g., f). Define the classes in such a way that f contains only one sub-object of A and B. In what order do you think the sub-objects of the classes will be created and destroyed? Write a program that implements the above inheritance scheme. Each class should contain a constructor and a destructor that display respective messages so that you can verify your answer about the order in which the objects are created and destroyed.

```
#include <iostream>
using std::cout;

class A
{
public:
        A() {cout << "A()";}
        virtual ~A() {cout << " ~A()";}
};

class B
{
public:
        B() {cout << " B()";}
        virtual ~B() {cout << " ~B()";}
};

class C : virtual public A, virtual public B
{
public:
        C() {cout << " C()";}
        ~C() {cout << " ~C()";}
};
```

```
class D : public C
{
public:
        D() {cout << " D()";}
        ~D() {cout << " ~D()";}
};


class E : public C
{
public:
        E() {cout << " E()";}
        ~E() {cout << " ~E()";}
};


class F : public D, public E
{
public:
        F() {cout << " F()";}
        ~F() {cout << "\n~F()";}
};


int main()
{
        F f;
        return 0;
}
```

Comments: As we know, the destructors are called in the reverse order from that of the constructors. The program displays:

```
A()     B()     C()     D()     C()     E()     F()
~F()    ~E()    ~C()    ~D()    ~C()    ~B()    ~A()
```

C.21.3 Define the abstract class named Person, which contains as private members the name (string type) and the code (int type). Define the Student class derived with public access from Person with a private member holding the grades in five courses (e.g., grd[5]). Then, define the Employee class derived with public access from Person with a private member holding the salary divided in three parts (e.g., fee[3]). Add appropriate functions in the classes so that the following program works.

```
int main()
{
        Person *p;
        Student s; /* The name should be initialized with None and the code
with -1. */
        Employee e; /* The name should be initialized with None and the code
with -1. */
        p = &s;
        (*p)[3] = 5; // The value of s.grd[3] should become 5.
        p = &e;
        (*p)[1] = 100; // The value of e.fee[1] should become 100.
        return 0;
}
```

Answer:

```cpp
#include <iostream>
#include <string>
using std::string;

class Person
{
private:
        string name;
        int code;
public:
        Person(const string& n = "None", int c = -1) : name(n), code(c) {}
        virtual ~Person() {}
        virtual float& operator[](int i) = 0;
};

class Student : public Person
{
private:
        float grd[5];
public:
        virtual float& operator[](int i);
};

class Employee : public Person
{
private:
        float fee[3];
public:
        virtual float& operator[](int i);
};

float& Student::operator[](int i)
{
        return grd[i];
}

float& Employee::operator[](int i)
{
        return fee[i];
}
```

Comments: We check main() to see how to implement the classes. At first, when we read the comments in the creation of the objects we understand that we have to define a default constructor in Person with predefined values. Then, we see that since p points to s, *p corresponds to s. Therefore, the statement (*p)[3] = 5; is equivalent to s[3] = 5;. To allow this statement we conclude that the Student class must overload the [] operator. The operator[] overload function should take as an argument an integer parameter and return a reference to the respective element in the array, so that its value can be modified. Similarly, with the statement (*p)[1] = 100; which is equivalent to e[1] = 100; we conclude that the [] operator must also be overloaded in the Employee class. In order for the operator[] to be called depending on the type of the object pointed by the p pointer, the function must be declared as virtual in the base class. Because the exercise requires the base class to be abstract we declare the function as pure virtual.

C.21.4 Define the `School` class with private member the name of the school. Define the `Programming` and `Network` classes derived with public access from the `School` with a private member, the number of the courses in each field. Define the `Student` class with public access from the `Programming` and `Network` classes with private members the student's name and code. When a `Student` object is created only one sub-object of the `School` class should be created. Add appropriate functions in the classes so that the following program works.

```
int main()
{
        Student s("Univ", "P.Tec", 100, 10, 12); /* The name of the school should
become Univ, the name of the student P.Tec, the code equal to 100, the number
of the Programming courses equal to 10 and the number of the Network courses
equal to 12. Only one sub-subject of the School class should be created. */
        School& p = s;
        p.show(); /* The show() that you'll define in Student should be
called. The program should display all the information, that is, the name of
the school, the number of the courses, and the student's name and code. */
        return 0;
}
```

Answer:

```
#include <iostream>
#include <string>
using std::cout;
using std::string;

class School
{
private:
        string name;
public:
        School(const string& n) : name(n) {}
        School() {}
        virtual ~School() {}
        virtual void show() const;
};

void School::show() const
{
        cout << "School: " << name << '\n';
}

class Programming : virtual public School
{
private:
        int courses;
public:
        Programming(int num) : courses(num) {}
        virtual void show() const;
};

void Programming::show() const
{
        cout << "Prog_Courses: " << courses << '\n';
}
```

```
class Network : virtual public School
{
private:
        int courses;
public:
        Network(int num) : courses(num) {}
        virtual void show() const;
};

void Network::show() const
{
        cout << "Net_Courses: " << courses << '\n';
}

class Student : public Programming, public Network
{
private:
        string name;
        int code;
public:
        Student(const string& sch_n, const string& stud_n, int num, int prg_c,
int prg_n) : School(sch_n), Programming(prg_c), Network(prg_n), name(stud_n),
code(num) {}
        virtual void show() const;
};

void Student::show() const
{
        cout << "Stud:" << name << ' ' << "Code:" << code << '\n';
        Programming::show();
        Network::show();
        School::show();
}
```

Comments: According to the exercise, the base class School should be virtual so that a single object of it is created. The default constructor is added in the School, which the Programming and Network constructors need to call. Since p is a reference to the School and the show() of the Student must be called, we understand that we should define the show() as virtual. To display all the information, we define respective show() in each class, which we call in its body.

C.21.5 Define the Shape class with private members the coordinates of the centre x and y and the pure virtual function area() to calculate the area. Define the Shape2D class derived with public access from the Shape with a private member the name of the shape. Define the Rect class derived with public access from the Shape2D with private members the length and the height of the rectangle. Define the Shape3D class derived with public access from the Shape with a private member the colour of the shape and the pure virtual function vol() to calculate the volume. Define the Sphere class derived with public access from the Shape3D with private member the radius of the sphere. The Rect and Sphere classes should not be abstract. Add appropriate functions in the classes so that the following program works.

```
int main()
{
        Sphere sph(1, 2, "Blue", 3); /* The x member of the Shape sub-object
should become 1, the y member should become 2, the colour of the Shape3D
sub-object should become Blue and the radius of the sph should become 3. */
```

```
        Rect r(4, 5, "Rect", 6, 7); /* The x member of the Shape sub-object
should become 4, the y member should become 5, the name of the Shape2D sub-
object should become Rect, the length of r should become 6 and its height 7. */
        Shape *p[2] = {&sph, &r};
        p[0]->show(); /* The program should display the values of the center x
and y, as well as the area and the volume of the sphere. */
        p[1]->show(); /* The program should display the values of the center x
and y, as well as the area of the rectangle. */
        return 0;
}
```

Answer:

```
#include <iostream>
#include <string>
using std::cout;
using std::string;

class Shape
{
private:
        float cntr_x;
        float cntr_y;
public:
        Shape(float x, float y) : cntr_x(x), cntr_y(y) {}
        virtual ~Shape() {}
        virtual void show() const {cout << "Cx:" << cntr_x << ' ' << "Cy:" <<
cntr_y << '\n';}
        virtual void area() const = 0;
};

class Shape2D : public Shape
{
private:
        string name;
public:
        Shape2D(float x, float y, const string& n) : Shape(x, y), name(n) {}
};

class Rect : public Shape2D
{
private:
        float len;
        float hght;
public:
        Rect(float x, float y, const string& n, float l, float h) :
Shape2D(x, y, n), len(l), hght(h) {}
        virtual void area() const {cout << "\nArea(R):" << len*hght << '\n';}
        virtual void show() const;
};

void Rect::show() const
{
        area();
        Shape::show();
}
```

```
class Shape3D : public Shape
{
private:
        string col;
public:
        Shape3D(float x, float y, const string& n) : Shape(x, y), col(n) {}
        virtual void vol() const = 0;
};

class Sphere : public Shape3D
{
private:
        float rad;
public:
        Sphere(float x, float y, const string& n, float r) : Shape3D(x, y, n),
rad(r) {}
        virtual void area() const {cout << "Area(S):" << 4*3.14*rad*rad << '\n';}
        virtual void vol() const {cout << "Vol(S):" << (4/3.0)*3.14*rad*rad*rad
<< '\n';}
        virtual void show() const;
};

void Sphere::show() const
{
        area();
        vol();
        Shape::show();
}
```

Comments: Since the exercise tells us that the `Rect` and `Sphere` classes are not abstract, we understand that they should implement the pure virtual functions declared in their base classes. Since p is an array of pointers to `Shape` and information contained in the derived classes should be displayed, we understand that the `show()` that we'll define in `Shape` should be virtual. To display the information, we define respective `show()` in `Rect` and `Sphere` and we call the `show()` of the `Shape` in their body.

UNSOLVED EXERCISES

U.21.1 Define the A and B classes and the C class which is derived with public access from A and B. Then, define the D class derived with public access from B. Finally, define the E class derived with public access from C and D. Suppose that an E object is created (e.g., e). Define the classes in such a way that e contains only one sub-object of the B class. In what order do you think the sub-objects of the classes will be created and destroyed? Write a program that implements the above inheritance scheme. Each class should contain a constructor and a destructor that display respective messages so that you can verify your answer about the order in which the objects are created and destroyed. The program should display:

```
B()     A()     C()     D()     E()
~E()    ~D()    ~C()    ~A()    ~B()
```

U.21.2 Define the abstract class named `Product`, which contains the code and the price of the product as protected members. Define the `Book` class derived with public access from the `Product` with the private member the publishing firm (of type `string`). Also, define the `Car` class derived with public access from the `Product` with private member the horsepower. Add appropriate functions in the classes so that the following program works.

```
int main()
{
        Book b(1, 2, "pub"); /* The code should become 1, the price 2,
and the name of the publisher pub. */
        Car c(4, 5, 6); /* The code should become 4, the price 5, and the
horsepower 6. */
        Product& p1 = b;
        Product& p2 = c;
        p1.show(); /* The program should display all the data of the
book, that is, 1, 2, and pub. */
        p2.show(); /* The program should display all the data of the car,
that is, 4, 5, and 6. */
        return 0;
}
```

U.21.3 Write a program that implements a simplified vehicle insurance application. Define the `Vehicle` class with the private member the name of the owner. Assume that the owner owns a car and a motorcycle. Define the `Car` and `Moto` classes with public access from the `Vehicle` with private members, the plate number (of type `string`) and the insurance cost of each vehicle. Define the `Insurance` class derived with public access from the `Car` and `Moto` classes with private member the name of the insurance company. When an `Insurance` object is created a single sub-object of the `Vehicle` class should be created. Define the `f()` function that takes as parameter a `vector` of `Insurance` elements and displays the name of the owner who pays the largest amount, as well as the details of his vehicles and the name of the insurance company. Assume that there is only one owner with the highest total cost. Add appropriate functions in the classes so that the following program works.

```
int main()
{
        vector<Insurance> v;
        Insurance ins1("Alpha", "1.2", 10, "3.4", 20, "Ins_1"),
ins2("Beta", "5.6", 30, "7.8", 40, "Ins_2"); /* In this example, for
ins1, the name of the owner should become Alpha, the plate number of the
car 1.2, the insurance cost 10, the plate number of the motorcycle 3.4,
the insurance cost 20, and the name of the insurance company Ins_1. For
each Insurance object a single Vehicle sub-object should be created.
Create more Insurance objects and store them in v. Then, call f(). For
example, if v contains only these two elements, the program should
display Beta 5.6 7.8 Ins_2, because the total insurance cost is 30+40 =
70, which is greater than 10+20 = 30 of the first owner.*/
        return 0;
}
```

Exceptions

22

In this chapter we'll discuss about exceptions. Exceptions are an integral part of the C++ language. We are using exceptions to catch and identify problems that may occur during the execution of the program (runtime errors). They are used extensively in the standard library to signal errors. It is important to know how the mechanism of the exceptions works, so that you can integrate them in your programs.

EXCEPTIONS

As you guess, when a program is running, errors may occur, which, if not handled properly, can lead to a program crash. The traditional error handling technique is to have scattered code that makes each part of the program responsible to handle its own errors. For example, when we use a function we need to check if it was executed successfully. If it fails, the programmer should have added code to catch the error and handle it. If the function returns a value, the typical way to check for an error is:

```
k = f();
if(k == ERROR_VALUE_1)
{
        ...
}
else if(k == ERROR_VALUE_2)
{
        ...
}
else if(k == ERROR_VALUE_N)
{
        ...
}
else // No error happened.
{
        ...
}
```

Note that if the function does not return a value, we can use a pointer or a reference argument to get back the result. C++ provides the exception mechanism as an alternative error handling technique. Exceptions report errors that occur at runtime. In particular, exceptions allow the detection of errors to be separated from their handling. That is, the error may occur in one part of the program and its handling in another part. The philosophy of the mechanism is to have specific points in the program to handle the errors, and not scattered code to handle them. This makes the code simpler and the error

DOI: 10.1201/9781003230076-22

management easier to read and control. Let's see the syntax of a typical example how to throw and catch exceptions:

```
f()
{
        try
        {
                g();
        }
        catch(type exc_1)
        {
                ...
        }
        catch(type exc_2)
        {
                ...
        }
        catch(...) // catches any type of exception.
        {
                ...
        }
}

g()
{
        ...
        if(error_occurs)
                throw exception; // g() creates an exception.
        ...
}
```

The idea is that if an error occurs in a function (e.g., g()) and the function cannot handle the error, it can use the `throw` statement to create an exception that informs the calling function for the error. In order to catch the exception, the call of the function that can create exceptions must be placed in a block that begins with the `try` statement. The code that handles exceptions is placed right after the `try` statement in one or more blocks that begin with the `catch` keyword. Note that it is not allowed to put any code between the `try` block and the first `catch` block or between successive `catch` blocks; the program won't compile. Each `catch` block specifies the type of the exception it can catch. Because it handles exceptions, the block is also referred to as *exception handler*. The type can be either a basic type or a user-defined type. It is identified by a single parameter within parentheses after the `catch` keyword.

The basic concept of exceptions is when something "exceptional" occurs in one part of the program (e.g., g()), this part to be able to inform another part (e.g., f()) for this "exceptional" event and pass to that part information related to the event. The programmer must determine what this "exceptional" is. For example, a statement that can cause a program to malfunction, such as an attempt to divide by zero, is something "exceptional". Note that the "exceptional" event does not always have to be catastrophic, the programmer should specify its seriousness, it may just be the inability to perform a task. Essentially, creating an exception is a way for the part of the program that cannot handle locally an "exceptional" event (e.g., g()) to forward it to a higher level (e.g., f()) that may be able to handle it.

Catching Exceptions

The `throw` statement creates an exception and its argument specifies the type of the thrown exception. The `throw` terminates the execution of the current function (e.g., g()) and the execution of the program is transferred to the calling function (e.g., `f()`). There, the program examines sequentially the `catch` statements to see if there is one that matches the type of the thrown exception. For example, the statement `throw 20;` creates an exception of type `int` and passes the value 20. If there is a `catch` statement for integer exceptions, such as `catch(int a)`, it will catch the exception, the value of a will become 20 and the code in its block will be executed. Note that if we write `catch(double a)`, the exception will not be caught because the compiler does not perform the usual arithmetic conversions. The conversions it supports are limited. In particular, it supports type conversions ignoring `const` specifiers. For example, a non-`const` integer argument of the `throw` can match a `const` integer argument of the `catch`. It also supports conversions from a derived type to a base class type, as well as the conversion of an array argument or function to the respective pointer.

The `catch` block may contain code to fix the problem, if it can be fixed. If not, the programmer may decide to terminate the program. The remaining blocks are not checked. Note that it is not necessary to declare parameter names, that is, we can write `catch(int)`. Usually, the `throw` argument passed to the `catch` statement provides information related to the exception, so the `catch` parameter is used to hold this information.

The `catch(...)` block is optional and catches all types of exceptions. It catches an exception that it is not caught by any of the previous `catch` blocks. It is a bit like the `default` case in the `switch` statement. Notice that it should be placed at the end of the `catch` blocks. If it is placed in another place, because it catches all the exceptions, the `catch` statements that may exist after that won't be checked. If it is missing, and the exception is not caught by any `catch` statement, then, as we'll see when we discuss about exception forwarding, the exception is passed on towards `main()`, until a matching `catch` block is found. If no block is found to catch the exception, the program terminates.

The `catch(...)` block is particularly useful when we do not know if the calling function throws exceptions. For example, even if we do not know that `g()` or a function that `g()` calls creates exceptions (nor of course their types), we can catch them in the `catch(...)` block. Since the `catch(...)` catches exceptions of any type someone could say why not to use only this block and catch all exceptions rather than wasting time to add separate `catch` blocks for every possible exception type. That is, to write something like this:

```
try
{
        g();
}
catch(...)
{
        ...
}
```

Yes, you can do that, but this approach does not provide any information about the exception in order to handle it properly and identify the problem. If you know possible exception types it is preferable to use separate `catch` blocks that explicitly state which exceptions may be thrown. Then, you can handle each exception, which may need more specific handling, individually. Also, when we discuss about exception objects, we'll see that we can get useful information to aid us in handling and detecting the error.

If no exception is thrown in the `try` block, the `catch` blocks are skipped and the program continues with the statement following the last `catch` block. Let's see an example. The following program reads a password and checks if it is valid:

```
#include <iostream> // Example 22.1
#include <string>
using std::cout;
using std::cin;
using std::string;
```

```cpp
int check_pswd(const string& str);

int main()
{
        string pswd;

        while(1)
        {
                try
                {
                        cout << "Enter password: ";
                        cin >> pswd;
                        if(pswd == "end")
                                break;
                        check_pswd(pswd);
                }
                catch(const char *msg)
                {
                        cout << msg;
                        continue; /* If it was missing, the statement after the
last catch block would be executed. */
                }
                catch(int code)
                {
                        if(code == 10)
                                cout << "Error: Password must contain three
digits at least\n";
                        else if(code == 20)
                                cout << "Error: Password must contain one special
character at least\n";
                        continue;
                }
                catch(...)
                {
                        cout << "Error: Another exception\n";
                        continue;
                }
                cout << "Password " << pswd << " is accepted !!!\n";
        }
        return 0;
}

int check_pswd(const string& str)
{
        bool found;
        int i, len, dig;

        len = str.size();
        if(len < 6)
                throw "Error: Short length\n";

        dig = 0;
        found = false;
        for(i = 0; i < len; i++)
        {
                if(str[i] >= '0' && str[i] <= '9')
                        dig++;
```

```
                if(str[i] == '!' || str[i] == '$' || str[i] == '#')
                        found = true;
        }
        if(dig < 3)
                throw 10;
        if(found == false)
                throw 20;
        return 0;
}
```

Let's see how the program works. Initially, the check_pswd() checks the length of the password. If it is less than six characters, the throw statement creates an exception and passes a literal string to the calling function, that is, to main(). So, the type of the exception is const char*. The throw statement terminates the check_pswd() and the program control is transferred to main(). In general, when an exception is thrown the implementation *unwinds* the function call stack to transfer control to the calling function that has established the means to handle that kind of exception. Since the call to check_pswd() is made inside the try block, the program can catch the exceptions it creates. If the call was made out of the try block, the exceptions could not be caught.

The program now checks if there is a catch statement that matches the exception type. Thus, the const char* block catches the exception and its code is executed. The string "Error: Short length\n" is passed to the msg parameter and it appears on the screen. With the continue statement the program continues with the next iteration of the loop and the user enters a new password. Instead of continue we could have a break or return to end the program or some other approach, such as if the user enters an invalid password three times the program ends. At each catch block, the programmer decides how to handle the exception. Note that if the const char* block did not exist, the exception would have been caught by the catch(...) block and its code would be executed. If neither were present, the program would terminate.

If the password length is acceptable, check_pswd() checks if it contains less than three digits. If yes, it creates an exception of type int. Then, check_pswd() terminates and the int block in main() catches the exception. The code becomes 10 and the program displays the respective message. If the number of the digits is valid, check_pswd() checks if the password contains any of the !, $, or # characters. If not, it creates an exception of type int, in the catch block the code becomes 20, and the program displays the respective message. As before, the continue causes the next loop iteration. Note that, in contrast to return which is allowed to return one data type, throw can return different data types.

If the password is accepted, check_pswd() does not create an exception and returns the value 0. The reason I chose the function to return a value is to show you that a function can create exceptions and return a value as well, which also may indicate if it was executed successfully or not. Then, the program skips the catch blocks and displays the password. The program runs until the user enters the end. Then, the break statement terminates the loop. Yes, I could write a simpler example, I just wanted to show you that the break and continue statements inside a try-catch block work in the usual way.

Here is a simpler example. What does the following program display? Don't rush to see the answer, read the comment below because I want the exact result.

```
#include <iostream> // Example 22.2

void f(int *p);

int main()
{
        try
        {
                int i = 20;
                f(&i);
        }
```

```cpp
        catch(int a)
        {
                std::cout << a << ' ';
        }
        catch(double d)
        {
                std::cout << d << ' ';
        }
        return 0;
}

void f(int *p)
{
        throw *p;
        throw *p/7.0; /* If you don't remember, visit Ch.3 to read about the
precision digits to find out what number is displayed. */
}
```

Did you use a calculator for the 20/7? Did you also go to Chapter 3 to read about precision digits? Fine, but not needed, now listen to *Can't escape* (… from the trap) from *Sound*. As we said, the execution of the `throw` causes the termination of the function. Thus, with the first `throw` the execution of `f()` terminates, the program control goes to `main()`, the program displays 20, and it terminates.

The `try` and `catch` blocks define their own scopes. That is, if a name is to be used in both blocks, then it must be declared outside of them. For example:

```
void f()
{
        int a = 5;
        try
        {
                int i = 20;
                ...
        }
        catch(int)
        {
                a++; // Correct.
                cout << i; // Wrong, i is not in the same scope.
                int j = 20;
        }
        catch(...)
        {
                a--; // Correct.
                cout << j; // Wrong, j is not in the same scope.
        }
}
```

For simplicity, in order to introduce you in the mechanics of throwing and catching exceptions, I used basic types to throw in the exceptions. However, in real programs, the typical choice is to throw class objects, as we'll see later on.

The noexcept Specifier

C++98 provided the ability to specify whether a function may throw exceptions and what their types would be, that is, the exception specifications. For example:

```
void f() throw(int, double);
void g() throw(); // It does not create exceptions.
```

`f()` creates exceptions with `int` and `double` types, while `g()` does not.

Although it seems a useful feature, exception specifications didn't work so well in practice, and was deprecated by C++11. Let's discuss it a bit more to see why. In principle, exception specifications should also include exceptions that may be thrown from other nested function calls. In this example, `f()` informs the reader that it may throw `int` and `double` exceptions. However, `f()` might call another function that calls another function and so on, which might create exceptions. In this case their types must be added as well. If it is you that you write all the functions you know their types and you can add them. But, if these functions are implemented by someone else, as in case of library functions, you need to find the possible exceptions, which might be very difficult or impossible, if, for example, the exceptions are not specified. Anyway, in practice, this feature was found to be problematic and C++11 deprecated that. C++17 finally removed it; it retains `throw()` as a deprecated synonym for the `noexcept` that we'll see next.

C++11 committee considered that it is useful to indicate that a function does not throw exceptions and introduced the `noexcept` specifier for this purpose. In general, if we know that a function does not throw exceptions simplifies the code we have to write when we call it, since we don't have to add code to handle exceptions. It can also enable the compiler to perform some optimizations. For example:

```cpp
void f() noexcept; // It does not throw exceptions.
```

Regarding syntax, in a function that is a member of a class the `noexcept` keyword is added after `const` and before the `final`, `override` or `=0` specifiers in case of a virtual function. If the virtual function is declared as `noexcept`, a function override in a derived class must be `noexcept` as well.

Note that when you declare a function as `noexcept` it may intentionally or unintentionally throw an exception or call another function that throws exceptions. For example, suppose that the A class is defined:

```cpp
void f() noexcept
{
        vector<A> v(1000000);
}
```

The constructor of `vector` may not find available memory for all the elements of `v` and throw an exception, although the function is declared as `noexcept`.

So, the presence of `noexcept` in the declaration of a function just indicates to one who reads the code, as well as to the compiler, that the function does not intend to throw exceptions. However, it does not actually prevent the function from throwing an exception or calling another function that may throw an exception. As a matter of fact, it'd be better to declare a function as `noexcept` only if you know for sure that all the functions that it calls, either directly or indirectly, are also declared as `noexcept`. In practice, the compiler allows a `noexcept` function to contain a `throw` statement or call another function that can throw exceptions. If an exception is thrown, it must be caught somewhere within that function and not rethrown. If it is not caught, the exception will not be propagated to the calling function. Instead, the program terminates. Essentially, the `noexcept` prevents the exception from leaving the function. That is, if we write:

```cpp
void f(int *p) noexcept
{
        if(*p == 10)
                throw *p; // Create an exception.
}
```

The compilation won't fail; note that the compiler may issue a warning message. However, if the `throw` is executed, the exception is not propagated and because it is not caught the program terminates. Of course, you can place the code of the function within a `try` block. For example:

```cpp
void f(int *p) noexcept
{
        try
        {
                ...
        }
        catch(...)
        {
        }
}
```

C++11 also introduces the `noexcept` operator. It is a unary operator, which returns `true` or `false` if its operand may throw an exception or not. Like `sizeof`, `noexcept` does not evaluate the operand. For example:

```
noexcept(f(&i)) /* Since f() is declared not to create exceptions the
operator returns true. */
void h();
noexcept (h()) /* Since h() is not declared not to create exceptions the
operator returns false. */
```

Note that the return value of the `noexcept` operator can be used as an argument in order to declare whether a function may throw or not an exception. For example:

```
void a() noexcept(noexcept(b())) /* If b() does not create exceptions,
neither does a(). If b() may create exceptions, a() may also create
exceptions. */
```

Discussing about Exceptions

Now that you have an idea about the exceptions, let's have a brief discussion about how useful they might be. One might ask, why not to use the traditional technique, that is, to make the function return specific values that correspond to errors and let the calling function to check the return value and handle the errors? Of course we can do that, but it is not always possible. For example, the integer values that a function returns may all be valid and none to be available for error coding. But even if it is possible, these checks should be done after each function call, which, besides being a tedious task, it may significantly increase the size of the program. By placing the function calls in a `try` block, the `catch` blocks are defined only once.

Sometimes we cannot return a value. For example, when we create an object, if an error occurs in the constructor of the class (e.g., wrong initialization values) there is no return value to check. How we'll be informed about the error? Someone might answer, that we could define a private variable in the class that holds the state of the object and each time an object is constructed we can check its value with a public function. If its value, for example, is 0, it means that the construction of the object was successful; otherwise, its value indicates the error code. Instead of doing all this, it is much simpler for the constructor to throw an exception and inform us about the failure. Regarding the destructor, in general, a destructor should not throw exceptions. If it throws, it should catch and handle them by itself, otherwise memory leaks and unpredictable behaviour of the program may occur.

In some situations the error has to be transmitted up a function call chain to the original caller. We'll see in next section that if an error occurs in a nested function (e.g., a() calls b(), which calls c(), which calls d() and the error occurs in d()), we can throw an exception and inform right away the function that made the first call (e.g., a()) about the failure. The traditional approach to use return values from each function to its immediate caller all the way up to the first one (e.g., a()) requires more code and makes the program more illegible, complex, inefficient, and error prone since the programmer may forget to forward some return value.

On the other hand, to be clear, I do not always recommend using exceptions. Yes, separating error detection from handling simplifies and makes the program more readable, but, this is the general rule, it does not necessarily apply in all cases. It's not black or white, that is, never use return codes or never use exceptions.

Each program has its own requirements. For example, if the program accepts user input, and wrong data are entered, this is not a serious problem to throw an exception. The program can simply discard the input and prompt the user to enter new data. In this case, the code that handles the wrong input is combined with the code that handles the overall data input process. After all, the choice of the name *exception* implies that is used to signal exceptional errors and not trivial errors. In another example, when the potential failures are normal, the traditional way of checking the return values with `if-else` conditions can be absolutely sufficient. And of course, you can use return values and exceptions together, there is no one rule that fits in all applications, you decide. If mixing both improves the understanding and maintenance of the code, it could be the best practice.

Also, each programmer may think differently on how to handle an error. For example, you may decide that a particular error is very serious, it cannot be resolved, and so there is no reason to throw an exception. So, you decide to display a diagnostic message or write it to a file and call a function (e.g., `exit()`) to end the program. Of course you can do that, while someone else may decide to throw an exception and let an upper level to deal with the error.

However, in the case of large applications it is very likely that you'll have to use the exception mechanism, if, for example, you are using libraries which throw exceptions. In general, in the development of large applications divided into parts that are implemented separately, by different groups of programmers, for the better control and maintenance of the program, the most flexible, reliable, and effective error management policy for serious errors that occur in different parts and cannot be handled locally is the exceptions, so that the errors may be forwarded and processed at a central point, such as `main()`.

Exceptions with Type Class

Besides the creation of exceptions with basic data types (e.g., `int`), an exception may also throw an object. Typically, this is the usual choice. One advantage of this choice is that we can use different objects to distinguish among different kind of problems that create exceptions. Another advantage is that an object can contain as much information as needed to identify the reasons that caused the exception. For example, let's change the first program so that the exception throws an object:

```cpp
#include <iostream>  // Example 22.3
#include <string>
using std::cout;
using std::cin;
using std::string;

class Err_Rpt
{
private:
        int code;
        string msg;
public:
        Err_Rpt(): code(0), msg("") {}
        Err_Rpt(int c, const char *m) : code(c), msg(m) {}
        void show() const {cout << "C:" << code << ' ' << msg;}
};

int check_pswd(const string& str);

int main()
{
        string pswd;

        while(1)
        {
                try
                {
                        cout << "Enter password: ";
                        cin >> pswd;
```

```
                        check_pswd(pswd);
                        break;
                }
                catch(const Err_Rpt& err)
                {
                        err.show();
                }
                catch(int code)
                {
                        cout << "C:" << code << ' ' << "Error: Password must
contain one special character at least\n";
                }
                catch(...)
                {
                        cout << "Error: Another exception\n";
                }
        }
        cout << "Password " << pswd << " is accepted !!!\n";
        return 0;
}

int check_pswd(const string& str)
{
        bool found;
        int i, len, dig;

        len = str.size();
        if(len < 6)
                throw Err_Rpt(5, "Error: Short length\n"); /* Create an exception
with type an object of the Err_Rpt class. */
        dig = 0;
        found = false;
        for(i = 0; i < len; i++)
        {
                if(str[i] >= '0' && str[i] <= '9')
                        dig++;
                if(str[i] == '!' || str[i] == '$' || str[i] == '#')
                        found = true;
        }
        if(dig < 3)
                throw Err_Rpt(10, "Error: Password must contain three digits at
least\n");
        if(found == false)
                throw 20;
        return 0;
}
```

First, I changed the code so that if the user enters a valid password, the break statement terminates the loop and the program displays it. The continue statements are unnecessary since no code exists after the last catch block. The check_pswd() throws an exception with type int and two others with type an Err_Rpt object. Each object is initialized with values that indicate the type of the error. These exceptions are caught by the respective catch block, which calls the show() of the passed object to display the information contained in its members.

Note that instead of the int exception we could throw another exception of Err_Rpt type. For example, we can write throw Err_Rpt(); where the passed object does not contain any information.

I just wanted to show you an example that combines exceptions of basic and user-defined types. In large applications, where exceptions from different libraries can also be thrown, it is safer to choose your own types rather than basic types (e.g., integer values) to avoid the case that the same exception value is used by some library.

Let me ask you, could we pass an object instead of a reference and write catch(Err_Rpt err); or pass a reference of the basic type and write catch(int& code);. Sure, no problem. In fact, when an exception is thrown, even if a reference is specified, what is really passed is a copy of the object. And so it should be, since the Err_Rpt object does not exist after the end of the check_pswd(). In particular, when an exception object is thrown, because the try block is exited and it will be out of scope, first it is copied to a temporary object and then it is destroyed. That's why there is no problem to throw local objects from inside the try block. Note that in a multi-level exception system, because the object can be copied multiple times until it is finally caught, it'd be better not to contain too much information. The logical question to make is, since the object is copied, why to use a reference? I'll answer it in the next section.

Exceptions and Inheritance

The answer to the previous question is that, as we know from Chapter 20, a reference to the base class can refer to objects of classes derived from it. For example, in the following program we have three classes of exceptions that are related to each other by inheritance:

```cpp
#include <iostream> // Example 22.4

class Err1
{
public:
        virtual void show() const {std::cout << "Err1\n";}
};

class Err2 : public Err1
{
public:
        virtual void show() const override {std::cout << "Err2\n";}
};

class Err3 : public Err2
{
public:
        virtual void show() const override {std::cout << "Err3\n";}
};

void f();

int main()
{
        try
        {
                f();
        }
        catch(const Err1& err)
        {
                err.show();
        }
        return 0;
}
```

```
void f()
{
        throw Err3();
}
```

Since the parameter in the `catch` block is a reference to the base class, it matches any derived class exception. Because `show()` is virtual, the selection of the `show()` to be executed is based on the type of the object to which `err` refers. Thus, the program displays `Err3`. If we did not use a reference, well, you know what happens, the base class copy constructor is called to copy the base class sub-object of the derived object, and the derived part is sliced off. If the diagnostic information regarding the error is in that part it will be lost. Thus, the safe practice is to use references. In our example, if we did not use a reference the `show()` of `Err1` would always be called and the program would display `Err1`, regardless of the object-argument of `throw`.

When throwing exceptions, the best practise is to throw objects. The general rule is to throw the object by value and catch it by reference.

If we want to handle each exception differently, we add separate `catch` statements for each type. But be careful with the order. The order of the `catch` blocks should be in inverse order of derivation, that is, from the last derived class to the base. For example:

```
int main()
{
        int i;

        try
        {
                f();
        }
        catch(const Err3& err)
        {
                i = 3;
        }
        catch(const Err2& err)
        {
                i = 2;
        }
        catch(const Err1& err)
        {
                i = 1;
        }
        return 0;
}
```

If the `Err1&` catch block was placed first, it would catch all `Err1`, `Err2`, and `Err3` exceptions and the value of `i` would always be `1`.

In an inheritance hierarchy of exception classes, the first catch block should refer to the last derived class and the last block to the base class.

Note that if a virtual function is declared in the base class not to throw exceptions, the same must be true when declared in the derived classes. On the other hand, if the virtual function can throw exceptions, we can declare in a derived class that it won't throw. For example:

```cpp
class A
{
public:
        virtual void f() noexcept {};
        virtual void g() {};
};

class B : public A
{
public:
        virtual void f() {}; // Wrong.
        virtual void f() noexcept override {}; // Correct.
        virtual void g() noexcept override {}; // Correct.
};
```

Forwarding Exceptions

The exception handling system can be multilevel. That is, each level handles as many problems as it can and leaves the rest for the higher levels. Thus, if an exception is not caught by the current function, the exception is forwarded to its calling function, and from there to the upper calling function, all the way towards main(), until a catch block is found somewhere in the path that catches the exception. If main() does not catch the exception, the program, by default, aborts. This process is called *stack unwinding*. For example, let's look at the following code:

```cpp
int main()              f()                 g()                    h()
{                       {                   {                      {
...                     ...                 ...                    ...
try                     try                 try                    throw 20;
{                       {                   {                      }
    f();                    g();                h();
}                       }                   }
catch(int)              catch(double)       catch(const char*)
{                       {                   {
    ...                     ...                 ...
}                       }                   }
}                       }                   }
```

The exception in h() is passed on to upper levels and eventually is caught by the catch block of main(), which can handle integer-type exceptions. If instead of throw 20; we write throw 1.2; this exception will be caught by the catch block of f(), while if we write throw "Test"; it will be caught by the catch block of g(). If an A class has been declared and a is its object and we write throw a; this exception will reach main() and because there is no catch block for the A type the program terminates.

This example also demonstrates one very important aspect of the throw mechanism. While return transfers the execution of the program to the first statement following the function call, throw transfers the execution all the way up to the first catch block that can catch the exception.

Rethrowing Exceptions

When a `catch` block catches an exception it may not be able to handle it or decide that it is better a higher level to deal with it. In this case you can rethrow the exception so that it is forwarded to a higher level, more relevant with the type of the exception, to take over its handling. To achieve this we just write `throw`, without any argument. The `throw` must be within a `catch` block or within a function called (directly or indirectly in a call chain) from a `catch` block. Otherwise, the call to `throw` causes the program to terminate. The rethrown exception is the original exception that was caught. For example, in the following program, the initial argument of `throw` is passed all the way up to the `catch` block that will eventually handle the exception:

```cpp
#include <iostream> // Example 22.5

void f();
void g();

int main()
{
        try
        {
                f();
        }
        catch(int a)
        {
                std::cout << "int exception is caught: " << a << '\n';
        }
        return 0;
}

void f()
{
        try
        {
                g();
        }
        catch(int) /* Since the catch block does not use the argument I don't
use a parameter name. */
        {
                std::cout << "int exception is rethrown\n";
                throw; // Rethrow the exception.
        }
        std::cout << "f() terminates\n"; /* Since throw rethrows the
exception, this statement won't be executed. */
}

void g()
{
        throw 10;
}
```

The `int` exception thrown by `g()` is caught by the `catch` block in `f()`. The `f()` rethrows it and it is caught in `main()`. The original argument of `throw` is also passed to `main()`. Therefore, the program displays:

```
int exception is rethrown
int exception is caught: 10
```

By the way, this program is also an example of nested `try` blocks. As we also saw in the previous section, a `try` block, together with its `catch` blocks, can be nested inside another `try` block. In this example, the outer block is that in `main()`, while the inner block is that in `f()`. Each `try` block is associated with its own set of `catch` blocks, which handle the exceptions that may be thrown within it. When an exception is thrown from the inner block, it will be handled by its own `catch` blocks. If none matches the exception type, it will be handled by the `catch` blocks of the outer `try` block. For example, if in `f()` we change the type in the `catch` block from `int` to `double`, then the thrown exception will be propagated to the outer `try` block in `main()`. There, the `catch` block for type `int` catches the exception.

In general, as in an ordinary function, if we want to change the value of the initial argument of the exception we pass a reference to the `catch` block. For example, let's change the `catch` block of `f()`:

```cpp
catch(int& b)
{
        b = 20;
        std::cout << "int exception is rethrown\n";
        throw; // Rethrow the exception.
}
```

Now, the value that will be passed to `main()` when the exception is rethrown is 20.

Exceptions and Memory Management

When a `throw` statement is executed, the memory that has been reserved for all the automatic variables in the path between the `throw` and the `catch` block that catches the exception is released from the stack. If an automatic variable is object, its destructor is called. For example:

```cpp
#include <iostream> // Example 22.6
#include <cstdlib> // for the exit()

class A
{
private:
        int code;
public:
        A(int c) {code = c;}
        ~A() {std::cout << "a_" << code << " is destroyed\n";}
};

void f();
void g();

int main()
{
        try
        {
                f();
        }
        catch(int)
        {
                std::cout << "int exception is caught\n";
                exit(EXIT_FAILURE); // I just used exit() to remember it.
        }
        std::cout << "Program terminates\n";
        return 0;
}
```

```cpp
void f()
{
        A a1(1);

        try
        {
                g();
        }
        catch(double)
        {
                std::cout << "double exception is caught\n";
        }
        std::cout << "f() terminates\n";
}

void g()
{
        A a2(2);
        throw 10;
        std::cout << "g() terminates\n"; /* I put it there just to remember
that since the throw is executed, this statement won't be executed. */
}
```

The int exception thrown by g() is forwarded from f() to main(). The memory allocated in the stack with the calls to f() and g() is released. And so it should be; since their execution has ended there is no reason for this memory to remain reserved. Thus, the memory for the a2 and a1 objects is sequentially released. The exit() terminates the program. Therefore, the program displays:

```
a_2 is destroyed
a_1 is destroyed
int exception is caught
```

What would the program display if instead of throw 10; we write throw 2.3;? Now, the exception is caught by f(). When it terminates, the destructor of a1 is called. Then, the execution continues in main() with the next statement after the catch block. Therefore, the program displays:

```
a_2 is destroyed
double exception is caught
f() terminates
a_1 is destroyed
Program terminates
```

Fine with the release of the memory for the automatic variables, but what about the release of memory dynamically allocated? Take a look at the example below, can you find any problem?

```cpp
void f()
{
        int i, *p = new int[10];

        for(i = 0; i < 10; i++)
        {
                cin >> p[i];
                if(p[i] == -1)
                        throw 10;
        }
        delete[] p;
}
```

If the exception is thrown, the memory reserved for the automatic variables i and p will be released. Notice, however, that the memory pointed to by the p pointer won't be released. That is, we have a memory leak. One way to solve this problem is to add another `delete[] p;` before the `throw`. The point is that it is the responsibility of the programmer to release memory that has been dynamically allocated before throwing the exception. Another way, which relieves the programmer from this responsibility, is to use the smart pointers of the standard library as we'll see in Chapter 24.

 The handling of exceptions in a safe way to ensure that there will be no memory leaks, that the objects are in a valid state, and that the program will continue to run normally, if that is possible, it is a difficult task, which includes techniques that are outside the scope of this book.

Standard Exceptions

The standard library provides several classes of exceptions that we can use in our programs. They reside in the std namespace and they are all derived from the exception class. The exception class is defined in the exception header file. For example, the following program throws such an exception:

```
#include <iostream> // Example 22.7
#include <exception>

void f();

int main()
{
        try
        {
                f();
        }
        catch(std::exception& e)
        {
                std::cout << e.what() << '\n';
        }
        return 0;
}

void f()
{
        throw std::exception();
}
```

The `what()` member function is declared as virtual and it returns a string, which is implementation dependant. Its declaration in the exception class looks like:

```
virtual const char* what() const noexcept;
```

If we want to specify the string to be returned, we can override it in a class derived from the exception and throw an exception of that class. For example:

```
class SomeErr : public std::exception
{
public:
        virtual const char *what() const noexcept override {return "Unexpected
error\n";}
};
```

```
void f()
{
        throw SomeErr();
}
```

As we know, to handle the exception from the derived class, we can still use the same `catch` block with the base class reference. If we want to handle them differently, we just add before that a `catch` block of the `SomeErr` type.

The standard library provides many exception types. Here, we only mention some of them. From the `exception` class the `logic_error` and `runtime_error` classes are derived. These classes, as well as classes derived from them, are defined in the `stdexcept` file. From the `logic_error` class the `domain_error`, `invalid_argument`, `length_error`, and the `out_of_range` classes are derived, which deal with logical errors. Briefly, the `domain_error` is used to indicate the violation of the valid domain of a function (e.g., attempt to calculate the square root of a negative number), the `invalid_argument` is used to indicate unexpected arguments, the `length_error` is used to indicate that there is no enough space (e.g., it is thrown if you add more characters in a `string` object than the maximum allowed length) and the `out_of_range` is used to indicate out of range values (e.g., it is thrown if you index a `vector` object with an out of bounds index). For example, suppose that we have a `Rectangle` class. If a wrong dimension is passed in the constructor we can throw an `out_of_range` exception, like this:

```
Rectangle::Rectangle(double w, double h)
{
        if(w <= 0 || h <= 0)
                throw out_of_range("Wrong dimension");
        ...
}
```

From the `runtime_error` class the `range_error`, `overflow_error`, and `underflow_error` classes are derived, which deal with errors related to the violation of the valid value range or the inability to represent values (e.g., due to overflow) in arithmetic calculations. For more information about the exception types consult a standard library reference.

Let's see the `bad_alloc` exception, which is thrown when the memory allocation with the `new` and `new[]` operator fails, such as because of unavailable memory. The `bad_alloc` class is defined in the `new` file and is derived from the `exception`. For example:

```
#include <iostream> // Example 22.8
#include <cstdlib>
#include <new>

int main()
{
        int num;
        double *p;

        try
        {
                std::cout << "Enter number: ";
                std::cin >> num;
                p = new double[num];
        }
```

```
        catch(const std::bad_alloc& e)
        {
                std::cout << e.what() << '\n';
                exit(EXIT_FAILURE);
        }
        std::cout << "Successful allocation\n";
        delete[] p;
        return 0;
}
```

If the memory allocation fails, the `bad_alloc` exception is thrown, the program displays a corresponding message and terminates. The standard provides the ability for the `new` operator to return a null pointer and not create the `bad_alloc` exception. In this case we write the code in the following way:

```
p = new (std::nothrow) double[num];
if(p == nullptr)
{
        std::cout << "Memory allocation error\n";
        exit(EXIT_FAILURE);
}
```

Handling Uncaught Exceptions

As we've said, an uncaught exception causes, by default, the program to terminate. For example, this can happen if no matching `catch` block is found for a thrown exception or if the function that created the exception is not contained in a `try` block. If an exception is not caught, the `terminate()` library function is called, which, by default, calls the `abort()` function, which then terminates the program. The standard allows us to change the behaviour of `terminate()` and make it call another function instead of `abort()`. To do that, we need to use the `set_terminate()` function. The `terminate()` and `set_terminate()` functions are declared in the `exception` file. The declaration of the `set_terminate()` looks like:

```
typedef void (*terminate_handler)();
terminate_handler set_terminate(terminate_handler p);
```

That is, the `set_terminate()` takes as parameter a pointer to a function that has no parameters and its return type is `void`. It returns the address of the previous terminate handler function, if any. In general, it is not recommended to override the behaviour of `terminate()` unless you want to do a "last" thing before the program exits, such as to output some diagnostic messages to help you spot the problem or return a specific error code to the environment in order to indicate the failure. Notice that the registered function after performing any desired tasks it should terminate the program. If it does not do that and returns to the caller, the behaviour of the program is undefined.

You may wonder why the new terminate function should terminate the program? Remember, `set_terminate()` is designed to handle irrecoverable errors. If there is no code in place to handle these errors, the program is not supposed to resume its normal operation. Unfortunately, it is in some unexpected, erroneous state, which certainly affects badly its operation. Therefore, the only option we have is to terminate its execution. The following program registers a new terminate function, which, in case of an uncaught exception, writes a message and calls `abort()`.

```
#include <iostream> // Example 22.9
#include <exception>
#include <cstdlib>

void end_prg();
void f();
```

```
int main()
{
        std::set_terminate(end_prg); // Set a new terminate function.

        try
        {
                f();
        }
        catch(int)
        {
        }
        return 0;
}

void f()
{
        throw 1.2;
}

void end_prg()
{
        std::cout << "Unhandled exception. Program terminates\n";
        abort();
}
```

Since the exception is not caught, the program calls `terminate()`, which calls the `end_prg()`. The `end_prg()` displays the message and the `abort()` terminates the program.

Recall that we can capture exceptions of unknown types by using the `catch(...)` block. In that case we prevent the program from terminating; however, we still have to handle the exception.

EXERCISES

C.22.1 Write a recursive function that takes as parameter an integer (e.g., `num`) and when it calls itself `num` times throws an `int` expression with code `10`. Write a program that reads an integer, calls the function, and catches the thrown exception.

```
#include <iostream>

void f(int num);

int main()
{
        int i;

        std::cout << "Enter number: ";
        std::cin >> i;

        try
        {
                f(i);
        }
```

```
        catch(int c)
        {
                std::cout << c << '\n';
        }
        return 0;
}

void f(int num)
{
        static int cnt = 0;

        cnt++;
        if(cnt == num)
                throw 10;
        f(num);
}
```

C.22.2 Define the `Account` class with private members, the name of the holder (e.g., name) and the balance of the account (e.g., bal). The class should contain the `create_acnt()` public function which is called after the creation of an `Account` object with arguments the name of the holder and the initial deposit amount. The name must contain only characters. If it does not contain or if the value of the amount is negative, the `create_acnt()` should create an exception with type an object of the `Err_Rpt` class and a related informative message. If the arguments are valid, the program should store them in the `name` and `bal` members, respectively. The program should continuously read names and deposit amounts until they are valid, that is, the `create_acnt()` does not throw an exception. Next, the program should read an amount and call the `deposit()` and `withdraw()` functions. These should be public functions of the `Account`, and take as an argument the amount that will be added or deducted from the account, respectively. If the amount is not valid, the functions should throw an exception of type `Err_Rpt`. If it is valid, the `bal` value should be updated accordingly. Finally, the program should call a public `show()` function, which displays the values of `name` and `bal`.

```
class Err_Rpt
{
public:
        string msg;
        Err_Rpt(const char *m) : msg(m) {}
};
```

Answer:

```
#include <iostream>
#include <string>
using std::cout;
using std::cin;
using std::string;

class Err_Rpt
{
public:
        string msg;
        Err_Rpt(const char *m) : msg(m) {}
};
```

```
class Account
{
private:
        string name;
        double bal;
public:
        void create_acnt(const string& n, double amnt);
        void deposit(double amnt);
        void withdraw(double amnt);
        void show() const {cout << "N:" << name << ' ' << "B:" << bal << '\n';}
};

void Account::create_acnt(const string& n, double amnt)
{
        int i;

        for(i = 0; i < n.size(); i++)
        {
                if((n[i] >= 'a' && n[i] <= 'z') ||
                        (n[i] >= 'A' && n[i] <= 'Z'))
                        continue;
                else
                        throw Err_Rpt("Error: Name must contain letters only\n");
        }
        if(amnt < 0)
                throw Err_Rpt("Error: Not acceptable amount\n");
        name = n;
        bal = amnt;
}

void Account::deposit(double amnt)
{
        if(amnt < 0)
                throw Err_Rpt("Error: Not acceptable amount to deposit\n");
        bal += amnt;
}

void Account::withdraw(double amnt)
{
        if(amnt < 0 || amnt > bal)
                throw Err_Rpt("Error: Not acceptable amount to withdraw\n");
        bal -= amnt;
}

int main()
{
        double amnt;
        string name;
        Account acnt;

        while(1)
        {
                try
                {
                        cout << "Enter initial amount: ";
                        cin >> amnt;
                        cin.get();
```

```
                    cout << "Enter name: ";
                    getline(cin, name);
                    acnt.create_acnt(name, amnt);
                    break;
            }
            catch(const Err_Rpt& err)
            {
                    cout << err.msg;
            }
        }
        try
        {
            cout << "Enter amount to deposit: ";
            cin >> amnt;
            acnt.deposit(amnt);

            cout << "Enter amount to withdraw: ";
            cin >> amnt;
            acnt.withdraw(amnt);
        }
        catch(const Err_Rpt& err)
        {
            cout << err.msg;
            return 0;
        }
        acnt.show();
        return 0;
}
```

C.22.3 Define the `Circle` class with private member the radius of the circle (e.g., `rad`). From the `Circle` class derive with public access the `Ellipse` class with private member the semi-major axis of the ellipse (e.g., `axis`). Define the `f()` function which takes as parameters a reference to an object and an integer value and subtracts them. Add appropriate functions in the classes so that the following program works.

```
int main()
{
        Circle cir(5); // The radius of the circle should become 5.
        Ellipse ell(10, 6); /* The radius of the circle should become 10 and
the axis of the ellipse 6. The constructor of the Ellipse should call the
constructor of the Circle. */
        Circle &r1 = cir, &r2 = ell;
        /* The following calls of f() should be placed in a try-catch section
and if an exception occurs the program should catch it, display a
corresponding message and terminate. */
        f(r1, 3);
        f(r2, 1);
        f(r2, 10);
        return 0;
}

void f(???? &c, int n) // Find the reference type.
{
        ???? tmp = c-n; /* Find the type of tmp. If the type of c is Circle,
the function should make the subtraction and reduce the radius of c by n.
```

If the new value of the radius is negative, the function should create an int exception with code 10. If the type of c is Ellipse, the function should reduce the radius and axis of c by n. If the new value of either the radius or axis is negative, the function should create an int exception with code 10 and 20, respectively.
```
        tmp.show(); /* If no exception is thrown, the program should display
the values  of the tmp members. In this example, in the first call of f(),
the program should display 2 (5-3), in the second call it should display 9
(10-1) and 5 (6-1), while in the third call it must throw an exception with
code 20 since the new value of the axis is negative. */
}
```

Answer:

```cpp
#include <iostream>

class Circle
{
private:
        float rad;
public:
        Circle(float r) {rad = r;}
        virtual ~Circle() {};
        float get() const {return rad;}
        void set(float r) {rad = r;}
        virtual Circle& operator-(int n);
        virtual void show() const;
};

class Ellipse : public Circle
{
private:
        float axis;
public:
        Ellipse(float r, float a) : Circle(r), axis(a) {}
        virtual Ellipse& operator-(int n) override;
        virtual void show() const override;
};

void f(Circle& c, int n);

Circle& Circle::operator-(int n)
{
        rad -= n;
        if(rad < 0)
                throw 10;
        return *this;
}

void Circle::show() const
{
        std::cout << "R:" << rad << '\n';
}
```

```
Ellipse& Ellipse::operator-(int n)
{
        float rad;

        rad = get()-n;
        if(rad < 0)
                throw 10;
        set(rad);
        axis -= n;
        if(axis < 0)
                throw 20;
        return *this;
}

void Ellipse::show() const
{
        std::cout << "R:" << get() << " A:" << axis << '\n';
}

void f(Circle& c, int n)
{
        Circle& tmp = c-n;
        tmp.show();
}

int main()
{
        Circle cir(5);
        Ellipse ell(10, 6);
        Circle &r1 = cir, &r2 = ell;

        try
        {
                f(r1, 3);
                f(r2, 1);
                f(r2, 10);
        }
        catch(int a)
        {
                if(a == 10)
                        std::cout << "Error: negative radius\n";
                else if(a == 20)
                        std::cout << "Error: negative axis\n";
                return 0;
        }
        return 0;
}
```

Comments: Because the rad is a private member and we want the Ellipse to be able to access it, we add public set/get functions in Circle. Since we see in f() that an integer is subtracted from an object we understand that the - operator must be overloaded. In order for the operator-() to be called depending on the type of the object referenced by c, the function must be declared as virtual in the base class. In f(), the c is declared as a reference to the base class, so that a reference to a derived class can be passed (e.g., r2) and exploit the mechanism of the virtual functions. Since the show() can display the values of both Circle and Ellipse members we understand that it must be declared as virtual. Pay attention now to the type of tmp. It must be a reference in the base class so that the show() of the class that the tmp refers is called. The tmp refers to the object returned by the operator-(). If it had not been declared as a reference, the program would always call the show() of the Circle.

UNSOLVED EXERCISES

U.22.1 Define the A and B classes. The B class should contain five A objects as public members. When the third A object is created, the A class should throw an exception with the No message, the program should capture it, display the message, and terminate. How many times the destructor of A is called? Write a program that verifies your answer. The constructor of A should not take parameters.

U.22.2 Define the StrChk class with a private member of type string (e.g., name). Add appropriate functions in the class so that the following program works. In case of exception, use the following Err_Rpt type and the program should display the message contained in msg.

```
class Err_Rpt
{
private:
        string msg;
public:
        Err_Rpt(const char *m) : msg(m) {}
        // Add any function you think it is needed.
};

int main()
{
        /* The following code should be placed in a try-catch block and
    if the Err_Rpt exception occurs the program should capture it, display
    the msg and terminate. */
        StrChk s1("First"), s2("Sec"); /* If the length of the string is
    less than 3, the constructor should throw an exception. Otherwise, the
    argument should be copied into name. */
        StrChk s3 = s1+s2; /* With s1+s2 the name members should be
    merged (e.g., s3.name should become FirstSec). If the length of the new
    string is greater than 10, the program should throw an exception. */
        s3[10] = 'a'; /* If the index is out of bounds, the program
    should throw an exception. That is, in this example, an exception should
    be thrown. */
        /* Experiment with the lengths of the strings, for example, change
    s1 and s2 to test the operation of the program. For example, if you
    change Sec to Second the program should throw the second exception. */
        s3.show();
        return 0;
}
```

Class Templates

23

In Chapter 16, we've discussed about function templates. This chapter introduces you in the basics of class templates. You'll learn how to define and use class templates in your programs. Class templates are a powerful mechanism that allows us to design a class in a general way. Then, we can use the template to define specific versions of the class for different types of data. Both function templates and class templates are used extensively in the standard library to provide generic functions, algorithms, and data structures.

CLASS TEMPLATES

Like function templates, class templates also provide the ability to program in a generic way. With class templates we can define generic purpose classes, that is, classes to which we can pass different types of data, without having to rewrite their code. For example, see again the implementation of the Lifo stack in exercise C.17.9. The type of the elements stored in the stack is Node. If we want to store some other type (e.g., integers), we have to replace all the Node appearances with the new type and re-compile the program. That is, we cannot have two Lifo stacks in the same program, one with Node elements and the other with integers. We need to create a new stack (e.g., Lifo_Int), copy the code of the existing one and change the type from Node to int. If we want to create a new stack with another data type, we have to repeat this process.

To address this inefficiency, C++ introduces the class templates so that we do not have to copy the same code. An example of a class template is the vector class. We'll see more class templates in Chapter 26 when we discuss about the standard template library. A class template is defined in a generic way so that its operation does not depend on a particular type. The type of the elements that each class object will work with is passed as an argument to the generic parameters of the class. So, let's make the Lifo a class template, to see how much more flexible the implementation becomes:

```cpp
#include <iostream> // Example 23.1
#include <string>
#include <vector>
using std::cout;
using std::string;
using std::vector;

template <typename T> class Lifo
{
private:
        vector<T> vec_n;
public:
        void push(const T& t);
        void pop(T& t);
        void show_all() const;
        int get_nodes() const;
};
```

```cpp
template <typename T> void Lifo<T>::push(const T& t)
{
        vec_n.push_back(t);
}

template <typename T> void Lifo<T>::pop(T& t)
{
        int size = vec_n.size();
        if(size > 0)
        {
                t = vec_n[size-1];
                vec_n.erase(vec_n.end()-1);
        }
        else
                cout << "Stack is empty\n";
}

template <typename T> void Lifo<T>::show_all() const
{
        int i, size = vec_n.size();
        if(size > 0)
        {
                for(i = 0; i < size; i++)
                        cout << vec_n[i] << '\n';
        }
        else
                cout << "Stack is empty\n";
}

template <typename T> int Lifo<T>::get_nodes() const
{
        return vec_n.size();
}

int main()
{
        int i;
        string s;

        Lifo<string> lifo_str;
        Lifo<int> lifo_int;

        lifo_str.push("One");
        lifo_str.push("Two");
        lifo_str.push("Three");
        lifo_str.pop(s);
        cout << s << '\n';
        lifo_str.show_all();

        lifo_int.push(1);
        lifo_int.push(2);
        lifo_int.push(3);
        lifo_int.pop(i);
        cout << i << '\n';
        lifo_int.show_all();
        return 0;
}
```

As with ordinary function templates, to declare a class template we use the prefix `template` `<typename T>`. The same applies when we define the functions outside the class. The `T` argument that will be used in the class declaration corresponds to a type name (e.g., `int`, `char*`, `string&`, ...). Instead of the `typename` keyword we can use the `class` keyword; however, this does not mean that the `T` type must be a class. As with function templates, because the `class` word may create this doubt, I prefer to use the `typename` word to make it clear that the `T` argument corresponds to some type. The `T` type can be used like an ordinary data type. For example, you can use it to declare the type of member variables or to specify the return type or the parameters of member functions, either by itself or combined in types such as `T&` or `T*`. As for the name of the argument you can choose any name you want according to the naming rules. Short names that begin with the `T` letter are popular choices.

When we are inside the scope of the class we can refer to the name of the template without specifying the template arguments. For example, if we want to define a default constructor inside the class we do not need to write `Lifo<T>()`, we write `Lifo()`. If it is defined outside the class we write:

```
template <typename T> Lifo<T>::Lifo() {}
```

Note that the `T` is inserted into the external definitions of the functions along with the class name (e.g., `Lifo<T>::`) to identify the class template. If the syntax scares you a bit, I agree with you, I felt the same when I saw it for the first time (... and for the second one). A member function will be defined only if it is used. That is, the compiler compiles only the functions that the program uses. This allows us to pass a type to the class and have the class compiled, linked, and operate normally even if some of its functions cannot work with that type or have other coding errors. Of course, if these functions are eventually used, the compiler will detect these errors. To make it more clear, the definitions of the member functions are templates that will be used by the compiler when needed to be generated. For example, the following:

```
template <typename T> void Lifo<T>::pop(T& t)
{
        . . .
}
```

is not a function definition, it is a template for a function definition. Note that for better readability many prefer to split the function header into two lines like this:

```
template <typename T>
void Lifo<T>::pop(T& t)
{
        . . .
}
```

The compiler will generate and compile its code, only if this function is actually used in the program. If not used, no instance of it is created. Therefore, when testing your entire class template and not a part of it you should ensure that all the member functions are generated and tested.

Since the function templates should be available to any source file that uses the class template, the typical approach is to put their definitions in the same header file that contains the declaration of the class template. In general, the definitions of templates are typically found in header files, which are included to the source files that are using them. In our examples which consist of a single source file, for simplicity, I'll put the declaration of the class template and the definition of its functions in that same file.

Class Template Instantiation

It is important to understand that the class template is not a class definition. It is just an instruction for the compiler on how to define the class. The class is defined when a class instantiation is required to create an object. For example, with the statement:

```
Lifo<int> lifo_int; // It is wrong to write Lifo lifo_int;
```

the compiler replaces the T type with int and defines the "integer" version of the class. Thus, the type of the elements contained in vec_n is int. The Lifo<int> class is called an *implicit instantiation* or *specialization* of the class template. This term distinguishes it from the *explicit instantiation* of a template, which we'll see shortly. Each version of the class template is an independent class. The produced class works like an ordinary class. Notice that I am writing a Lifo<int> class, not Lifo, because this is the class defined for this particular type. The lifo_int is an object of this version, that is, an object of the Lifo<int> class. To make it clearer, it is wrong to write: Lifo lifo_int;. Each object you declare must be an object of a particular version of the class template.

So, a class template is implicitly instantiated only when an object of some type needs to be created. Note that the declaration of a pointer to a particular class type does not cause the template to be instantiated. For example:

```
Lifo<char>* p;
```

This statement declares p as a pointer to type Lifo<char>. Since this declaration does not require the creation of a Lifo<char> object, the class template is not instantiated.

Similarly, when the lifo_string object is declared, the compiler replaces the T type with string and defines the "string" version of the class, that is, Lifo<string>. The Lifo<string> class has nothing to do with the Lifo<int> class, they are two entirely different classes. As you see when an object is declared, the compiler replaces the generic type with the type of the argument and creates the corresponding version of the class. Thus, thanks to the class template we can have different class definitions and respective objects in the same program without having to copy any code. Not only we avoid re-writing similar code, but the program also becomes more flexible, compact, readable, and easier to maintain. Note that a single definition is created for the same type. That is, if we write:

```
Lifo<int> lifo_1;
Lifo<int> lifo_2;
Lifo<int> lifo_3;
```

the Lifo class will be defined only once for the first object and then the compiler will use this instance for the other two objects.

When using templates, it can be more convenient and more readable to create synonyms for the types. For example:

```
using LifoInt = Lifo<int>;
LifoInt lifo_1, lifo_2, lifo_3;
```

As we said, the T parameter is assigned with a type and not a numeric value. For example, in the definition of the Lifo<int> class the value of T becomes int. This is different from the ordinary function templates where the compiler checks the types of the arguments to figure out what kind of function to create. For example:

```
template <typename T> void show(T a) {cout << a << '\n';}
...
int i = 6;
```

```
double j = -1.2;
show(i); /* The compiler checks the type of i and creates the void
show(int a). */
show(j); // Now, it creates the void show(double a).
```

The polymorphism, as in case of function templates, is achieved when compiling the program. Finally, the program displays: Three One Two 3 1 2

Note that besides basic types, we can also pass types that we have defined. As a matter of fact, we've used several times the `vector` class template with our types. As another example, to create a stack with elements of the `Node` class that we defined in the exercise C.17.9 we write:

`Lifo<Node> lifo_n;`. The compiler replaces the T with `Node` and defines the `Lifo<Node>` class. Let me ask you a question, which conceptually is related with the next section, is it allowed to write `lifo_n.show_all()`? Of course not, with the << operator we can display the values of basic data types, but not of the `Node` type. As we know to display the values of its members we should overload the << operator. Do it, to refresh your knowledge.

To sum up, when defining a class template we have to specify the template parameter types. Here is a shorter example:

```
template <typename T> class A
{
private:
        T p;
public:
        A(T val) : p(val) {}
};

A<int> a(10);
```

When the a object is declared T is replaced with `int` and p becomes 10. C++17 relaxes the constraint to specify the type explicitly. In particular, C++17 supports class template argument deduction, which allows us to skip specifying the types if the constructor is able to deduce them. For example, we can write:

```
A a(10); // A<int> is deduced.
```

Misuse of Class Template

When using a class template we must have in mind the way it is designed and not just use it. For example, if we pass the `const char*` type to `Lifo`, does the following code work? If you find any errors fix them.

```
int main() // Example 23.2
{
        string s;

        Lifo<const char*> lifo_str;
        lifo_str.push("One");
        lifo_str.push("Two");
        lifo_str.push("Three");
        lifo_str.pop(s);
        cout << s << '\n';
        return 0;
}
```

The compiler creates a class version for the `const char*` type. Is there a problem with the `push()` calls? No, because the type of the literal string is `const char*` it can be stored in the stack. But what about the `pop()` call? Since the declaration of `pop()` is `pop(const char*& t);` and the type of s is string, the compiler will display an error message for incompatibility of the argument type with the parameter type. Therefore, the program is not compiled. One way to solve this problem is to write:

```
int main()
{
        const char *s = "Test"; // It is not needed to be initialized.
        ...
        lifo_str.pop(s);
        cout << s << ' ';
        return 0;
}
```

Now that the s type has changed there is no problem with the call to `pop()`. In fact, because a reference to the s pointer is passed, `pop()` will change its value and make it point to the place where Three is stored. I intentionally initialized s to make it clear that its value changes, that is, the program displays Three.

Using a Class Template

A class template can be used like an ordinary class. For example, it can be a member of another class, it can be used as a base class in an inheritance relationship, or be the type of an argument in the instantiation of another class template. Let's see an inheritance example:

```
#include <iostream> // Example 23.3

template <typename T> class A
{
private:
        T m;
public:
        A() {m = 10;}
        void show() const {std::cout << m << '\n';}
};

template <typename T> class B : public A<T>
{
};

int main()
{
        B<int> b;
        b.show();
        return 0;
}
```

The declaration of the b object causes the `A<int>` class to be defined, its default constructor is called, and the A sub-object contained in the b object is created. Then, the program calls the `show()` of the base class, which displays 10.

In the following example, the A class template is a member of C:

```
template <typename T> class C
{
        ...
        A<T> a;
};
```

See also this, where an instantiation of the class template is used as a member:

```
template <typename T> class A
{
        ...
public:
        T m;
};

class C
{
        ...
public:
        A<int> a;
};

int main()
{
        C c;
        c.a.m = 10;
        ...
}
```

Here is another example, where the type of the class template is used as an argument to create another class:

```
template <typename T> class A
{
        ...
        T m;
};

A< Lifo<int> > a;
```

The m is an object of the Lifo<int> class. Note that C++98 required to have at least one white space between the two >, so that the compiler is not confused with the >> operator. Since C++11, this is no longer required.

We can also declare a pointer to a specific version of the class template and allocate memory for a respective object. For example:

```
Lifo<int> *p;
p = new Lifo<int>; // Create an object.
```

As with function templates, in large applications where the use of the same class template in multiple code files may be required, we can use the extern keyword so that we don't have to redefine it. For example, if Lifo<int> is defined in a file and we want to use it in a second file we write:

```
extern template class Lifo<int>; // Second file.
```

With the extern declaration the compiler won't redefine the Lifo<int> version in this file. As when using extern with ordinary variables, the definition of the Lifo<int> will be searched in another file.

Finally, a class template can contain friend classes and functions. For example:

```cpp
class A {};

template <typename T> class B
{
        ...
        friend class A;
        friend class Lifo<T>; // This specific version is a friend class.
};
```

We'll discuss about class templates and friends in a short.

Parameters of Different Types

A class template can use more than one type parameter. For example, consider the following program:

```cpp
#include <iostream> // Example 23.4
#include <string>
using std::cout;
using std::string;

template <typename T1, typename T2> class Group
{
private:
        T1 f;
        T2 s;
public:
        Group(T1 t1, T2 t2) {f=t1; s=t2;}
        T1 get_f() const;
        T2 get_s() const {return s;}
};

template <typename T1, typename T2> T1 Group<T1, T2>::get_f() const
{
        return f;
}

int main()
{
        int i, j;

        Group<double, int> g(3.5, 10);
        cout << g.get_f() << ' ' << g.get_s() << '\n';

        Group<int, string> grp[] = {Group<int, string>(10, "Alpha"),
                                    Group<int, string>(20, "Beta"),
                                    Group<int, string>(30, "Gamma")
                               };
        j = sizeof(grp)/sizeof(Group<int, string>);
        for(i = 0; i < j; i++)
                cout << grp[i].get_f() << ' ' << grp[i].get_s() << '\n';
        return 0;
}
```

The compiler in order to define the Group<double, int> class replaces T1 with double and T2 with int. Then, it calls the constructor of the class to create the g object. Thus, the program displays 3.5 and 10.

I could also make the get_f() inline, as I did with get_s(), the reason I did not do it was to show you its syntax. Then, the compiler defines the Group<int, string> class where it replaces T1 with int and T2 with string. The array of grp objects is also declared. The reason I added it is to show you that you can declare an array of class template objects, as well as how to call the constructor of each object. I know it is unnecessary to use the j in the loop. Since the objects are three, I could write i < 3. The reason I did not do it was to see that in order to calculate the size of the memory you can use the sizeof operator in the usual way.

Non-Type Parameters

Like a function template, a class template can take non-type parameters. It is written as a function parameter with the type name followed by the name of the parameter. The most common use of non-type parameters is integer parameters. Typically, they are used when we want to pass values related to numerical sizes and range limits. For example, a common use of an integer argument is when we want to specify the size of a memory. Let's look at such an example:

```
#include <iostream> // Example 23.5

template <typename T, int size> class Grades
{
private:
        T lab[size];
        T theory[size];
public:
        Grades();
};

template <typename T, int size> Grades<T, size>::Grades()
{
        for(int i = 0; i < size; i++)
                lab[i] = theory[i] = 0;
}

int main()
{
        Grades<float, 5> g;
        return 0;
}
```

In the declaration of the class template, the use of typename means that T corresponds to some type, while the second parameter size to an integer value. The compiler in order to define the Grades<float, 5> class replaces T with float and size with 5. Thus, the type of the two lab and theory arrays becomes float and their size equal to 5. It also calls the constructor of the class to create the g object.

Note that there are some restrictions for the non-type parameters. It is allowed to be an integer literal (e.g., 5), an enumeration type, a constant integer expression, a null pointer, a pointer to a class member or a pointer or a reference to an object or to a function. For example, it is wrong to write:

```
int p = 10; // Wrong, p should be a constant.
Grades<float, p> grd;
```

If we declare p as const, there will be no problem. Also, if we write float size the compiler will display an error message. However, we can write float& size or float *size. If you want, you can use the type name of the type parameter as the type of non-type parameter. For example:

```
template <typename T, T size> class Grades {}
```

The name T must appear before used as a type for the non-type parameter, while the choice for the type parameter must be subject to the constraints of the non-type parameters.

Also, there are restrictions on how we can use a non-type parameter inside the template. In particular, it is not allowed to change the value of the argument or access its address. That is, expressions such as size++ or &size are not allowed.

Class Template as Parameter

A class template can take another class template as a parameter. For example:

```cpp
#include <iostream> // Example 23.6

template <typename T> class A
{
private:
        T m;
public:
        void set(T t) {m = t;}
        T get() const {return m;}
};

template <template <typename T> class Test> class C
{
private:
        int k;
        double d;
public:
        Test<int> t1;
        Test<double> t2;
        C() {k=1; d=2.3;}
        void set() {t1.set(k); t2.set(d);}
};

int main()
{
        C<A> c;
        c.set();
        std::cout << c.t1.get() + c.t2.get() << '\n';
        return 0;
}
```

The C template takes as a parameter a class template with type template <typename T>. So, when C<A> is defined, the type of the passed argument, that is A, must match the type of the template parameter Test. Otherwise, the compiler will display an error message. The Test parameter is replaced with the type of the passed argument, that is, with A. Thus, the c object contains the t1 object of the A<int> class and the t2 object of the A<double> class. With the statement c.set(), the set() of each object is called and the respective values are passed. Finally, the program calls the get() of each object and displays the sum of the returned values, that is, 3.3. As with set(), I could declare a get() inside C and do the same job, I did not do it to show you an alternative way. When can a template be used as a parameter? You just saw an example. That is, when the declarations of the members of a class template (e.g., t1) depend on some other template (e.g., Test), which we declare it as a parameter in order to be determined (e.g., A) by the user of the class.

A template parameter can be mixed with ordinary parameters. For example, let's change the declaration of C:

```
template <template <typename T> class Test, typename X, typename Y> class C
{
        ...
        Test<X> t1;
        Test<Y> t2;
};
```

Thus, the types that are used for the t1 and t2 objects become generic. Of course, we should change the declaration of c to:

```
C<A, int, double> c;
```

The Test will be replaced with A, X with int, and Y with double.

Default Parameter Values

In a class template we can specify default values for its parameters. For example:

```
template <typename T1, typename T2 = int> class Group {...}
```

It works similar to the default values for function parameters. For example, if we omit the type of T2 and write Group<double> g; the type of T2 will be int. If a class template provides default values for all its parameters and we want to use all of them we use empty <>. For example:

```
template <typename T1 = string, typename T2 = int> class Group {...}
```

If we write Group<> g; the type of T1 will be string and the type of T2 will be int.
We can also specify default values for non-type parameters. For example:

```
template <typename T, int s = 20> class Grades {...}
```

If we write Grades<int> g; the type of T will be int and s equal to 20.

Static Members

A class template can contain static members. Be careful though, each version of the class contains its own static members. For example:

```
#include <iostream> // Example 23.7

template <typename T> class A
{
public:
        A() {cnt++;}
        static inline int cnt = 0; // Since C++17.
        static int f() {return cnt;}
};

int main()
{
        A<int> a1, a2, a3;
        A<double> d1, d2;
```

```
        std::cout << A<int>::cnt << ' ' << d1.cnt << '\n';
        // A::cnt = 10; Wrong.
        std::cout << a1.f() << ' ' << d2.f() << '\n';
        return 0;
}
```

Each version of the class has its own instances of static members. That is, the A<int>::cnt is different from the A<double>::cnt. All the A<int> objects share the same A<int>::cnt variable and A<int>::f() function, while the A<double> objects share the same A<double>::cnt variable and A<double>::f() function. When the A<int> and A<double> classes are created, the respective cnt variables are initialized to 0. Thus, because three A<int> objects and two A<double> objects are created, the program displays twice 3 and 2. As with static members of non-class templates, to access a static member we can use an object of the class or the scope operator and the name of the specific class. That is, it is wrong to write A::cnt = 10.

Recursive Use

A class template can be used recursively. For example:

```
#include <iostream> // Example 23.8

template <typename T, int n> class Array
{
public:
        T data[n];
};

int main()
{
        Array< Array<int, 10>, 20> arr;
        arr.data[0].data[8] = 3; // Example how to access an element.
        std::cout << sizeof(arr.data[0]) << '\n';
        return 0;
}
```

Initially, the compiler replaces T with int and n with 10 and defines the Array<int, 10> class. The data member of the Array<int, 10> class is an array of 10 integers. Then, it replaces T with this class, that is, arr.data is an array of 20 elements, where each element is an object of the Array<int, 10> class. So, the program displays 40 (assuming that the int type is 4 bytes). The equivalent ordinary array would be declared as: int arr[20][10];

Templates as Members

A class template can be a member of a structure, class, or another class template. For example, the following class template contains a nested class template and a function template:

```
#include <iostream> // Example 23.9

template <typename T1> class A
{
private:
        T1 m;
```

```
public:
        template <typename T2> class B
        {
                private:
                        T2 p;
                public:
                        B() {p = 5;}
                        void show() const {std::cout << p << '\n';}
        };
        A(T1 i) {m = i;}
        B<int> b;
        void show() const {std::cout << m << ' ';}
        template <typename T3> void f(T3 j) const {std::cout << j << '\n';}
};

int main()
{
        A<double> a(1.2);
        a.show();
        a.b.show();
        a.f("text");
        return 0;
}
```

The A class template contains the template of the B class. When a is created, T1 becomes double, and the constructor makes the value of a.m equal to 1.2. The b object of the B<int> class is also created. T2 becomes int, the default constructor B() is called and b.p becomes 5. I also added the f() function template. When called, the compiler checks the type of the argument passed to T3 and creates the definition of f(). Thus, the program displays 1.2 5 text. If we want to define the function template outside the class template, first we write the parameter list of the class and then that of the function. For example:

```
template <typename T1>
        template <typename T3> void A<T1>::f(T3 j)
{
        ...
}
```

Note that a template member function is not allowed to be virtual. For example, it is wrong to write:

```
class A
{
        ...
        template <typename T> virtual void f(const T& t); // Wrong.
};
```

The reason this is not allowed is that the implementation with the array of the virtual functions (*vtbl*) mentioned in Chapter 20 would become more complicated, since every time f() is called with a new type of argument a new entry for the A class would have to be added in the array of its virtual functions.

CLASS TEMPLATE AND FRIENDS

Like an ordinary class, a class template can also have friends. Its friends can be classes, functions, class templates, or function templates. If a class is a friend of a class template, then its member functions become friends to all instantiations of the class template. A friend function can be:

    a. non-template.
    b. template, where an instantiation of the friend function is friend only to the respective instantiation of the class.
    c. template, where all the instantiations of the friend function are friends to each instantiation of the class.

Let's describe in brief these cases.

Non-Template Friend Functions

When a class template contains a non-template friend function, the function becomes friend to all instantiations of the class template. For example:

```cpp
#include <iostream> // Example 23.10

template <typename T> class A
{
private:
        T p;
public:
        A(T i) {p = i;}
        friend void f(A<T>& a);
        friend void g();
};

// Friend function of all A<int> classes.
void f(A<int>& a)
{
        std::cout << a.p << '\n';
}

// Friend function of all A<double> classes.
void f(A<double>& a)
{
        std::cout << a.p << '\n';
}

// Friend function of all A<T> classes.
void g()
{
        A<char> tmp('t');
        std::cout << tmp.p << '\n';
}
```

```
int main()
{
        A<int> a(5);
        A<double> d(2.3);

        f(a);
        f(d);
        g();
        return 0;
}
```

The g() function becomes friend of all instantiations of the A class template. The reason I made f() to take a template parameter is to see how it is associated with the A instances. When the a object is declared, T is replaced with int and the prototype of f() becomes:

```
class A<int>
{
        ...
        friend void f(A<int>& a);
};
```

Thus, the f() with parameter A<int>& becomes a friend function of the A<int> class. Similarly, the f() with parameter A<double>& becomes a friend function of the A<double> class. Note that f() is not a function template. It just takes a template parameter. This is why we need to define explicit specializations of f() for the types we plan to use. If, for example, the definition of f() with parameter A<double>& was missing, the compiler would display an error message in the statement f(d);. To make it more clear, g() has one-to-many friend relationship with class A, that is, it is friend to all instantiations of A, while f() has one-to-one relationship. The program displays 5, 2.3, and t.

Friend Function Template Bound to Class Template

When a class template contains a friend function template, each version of the class can be bound to a matching version of the friend function. Let's see an example, where a class template contains two friend function templates:

```
#include <iostream> // Example 23.11

template <typename T> void f();
template <typename T> void g(T& t);

template <typename T> class A
{
private:
        T p;
        static inline int cnt = 0;
public:
        A(T i) {p=i; cnt++;}
        friend void f<T>();
        friend void g<>(A<T>& t); // We could also write g<A<T>>(A<T>& t);
};

template <typename T> void f()
{
        std::cout << A<T>::cnt << '\n';
}
```

```
template <typename T> void g(T& t)
{
        std::cout << t.p << '\n';
}

int main()
{
        A<int> a1(5), a2(10);
        A<float> d(2.3);

        g(a1); // We could also write g<A<int>>(a1); The program displays 5.
        g(d); // The program displays 2.3.
        f<int>(); // The program displays 2.
        f<float>(); // The program displays 1.
        return 0;
}
```

With template bound friend functions things are more complex than non-template ones. First, we declare their prototypes before defining the class template. Then, we declare them again in the class as friend functions. The <> in their declarations denotes that they are declared as template specializations. The reason I made f() not to take parameters is to see how to use such a function. Because f() does not take parameters, we must use the template syntax <> to indicate the type of its specialization (e.g., f<int>) when we call it. In the case of g(), the <> can be left empty because the type of the template argument can be deduced from the type of the function argument.

When a version of the class template is defined, the respective friend functions bound to that version are also defined. That is, for each instantiation of A there will be one matching instantiation for each friend function. For example, when the A<int> class is defined, the template specializations f<int>() and g<A<int>&>() become friends of the A<int> class. Similarly, when the A<float> class is defined, the f<float>() and g<A<float>&>() functions become its friends. As you see, there is one-to-one friend relationship.

Let's see what happens when they are called. Because f() does not take a parameter from which the compiler would deduce the intended specialization (int or float), we should indicate the type in the <>. Thus, when f<int>() is called, T is replaced with int and the program displays the value of A<int>::cnt. Because two objects of the A<int> class and one object of the A<float> class are created, the value of A<int>::cnt becomes 2 and the value of A<float>::cnt becomes 1. When g() is called, the compiler checks the type of the argument to deduce the specialization. For example, with the statement g(a1); the compiler finds that the type of a1 is A<int> and the program displays the value of a1.p.

Friend Function Template Non-Bound to Class Template

In the previous section we saw that the friend functions are specializations of the templates declared outside the class. We also saw that each instantiation of the class is bound to a matching version of the friend function. For example, an int version of the A class is bound to an int version of the friend function. If we declare the template inside the class, we can create non-bound friend functions, that is, every friend instantiation becomes friend to all the versions of the class and not just to a particular instance as before. For non-bound friends, we use different names in its parameter-types from the names of the parameter-types of the class. Consider the following program:

```
#include <iostream> // Example 23.12

template <typename T> class A
{
private:
        T p;
```

```
public:
        A(T i) {p = i;}
        template <typename V> friend void f(V& v);  /* We use a different type
name (i.e., V) from the type name of the class (i.e., T). */
};

template <typename V> void f(V& v)
{
        std::cout << v.p << '\n';
}

int main()
{
        A<char> a1('r');
        A<int> a2(5);
        A<double> a3(2.3);

        f(a1);
        f(a2);
        f(a3);
        return 0;
}
```

For all instantiations of A, all instantiations of f() are friends. That is, f() has a many-to-many friend relationship with the A class. Therefore, f() may access the p private member of the a1, a2 and a3 objects. Note that an instance of the friend template is created only if the friend function is called in the program. For example, the statement f(a1); causes the instantiation of void f(A<char>& v) and the program displays the value of a1.p. Finally, the program displays r 5 and 2.3.

Class Template as Friend

A class template can be a friend to an ordinary class. In this case, all instantiations of the class template become friends of the class. For example:

```
#include <iostream>  // Example 23.13

class A
{
private:
        int p;
public:
        A() {p = 20;}
        template <typename T> friend class B;
};

template <typename T> class B
{
public:
        void f(const A& a) const {std::cout << a.p;}
};

int main()
{
        A a;
        B<int> b1;
        B<double> b2;
```

```
        b1.f(a);
        b2.f(a);
        return 0;
}
```

Since the B class template is declared as a friend of the A class, every member function of every instantiation of the B template is a friend of the A class. Here, we have two B instantiations and the program outputs 20 twice.

CLASS TEMPLATES SPECIALIZATIONS

You'll encounter many situations where a class template cannot support every conceivable argument type. For example, the comparison functions of a class template may work for passed string types but not for char* types. One option to handle such situations is to define a specialization of the class template, that is, a specialized version which will be used for a specific set of parameter types.

In general, as with function templates, we can define a class template indirectly (*implicit instantiation*), explicitly (*explicit instantiation*), as well as we may have *explicit specializations*. The *partial* specialization of the class template is also supported.

In the examples so far we've used implicit instantiations. As we've said, the compiler creates an implicit instantiation of the class when it needs to create an object. Then, the compiler uses the values of the passed arguments and instantiates the class. For example:

```
Lifo<int> lifo_int; // Implicit instantiation.
```

Besides implicit instantiation we can explicitly instantiate a class without having to create an object of that type. The compiler instantiates the template based on the values of the passed arguments. To instantiate explicitly a class template we write template followed by the template class name and the arguments inside <>. For example:

```
template Lifo<int>; // Explicit instantiation.
```

The compiler defines the Lifo<int> class.

If we want a class template to behave differently for one or more types, we can create explicit specializations of the general template. A specialization is a class definition, not a class template. For example, suppose we want the following A class template to work differently for the char* type.

```
template <typename T> class A
{
private:
        T m;
public:
        A() {m = 20;}
        int cmp() {return m > 10;}
};
```

The following version is an explicit specialization of the general template for the char* type:

```
template <> class A<char*> // Explicit specialization.
{
private:
        char* m;
```

```
public:
        A(char* s) {m = s;}
        int cmp() {return strcmp(m, "text");}
};

int main()
{
        A<int> a1; // The general template is selected.
        A<char*> a2("text"); // The explicit specialization is selected.
        std::cout << a1.cmp() << ' ' << a2.cmp() << '\n';
        return 0;
}
```

As shown, to declare an explicit specialization we write `template <>` and after the name of the class we write the name of the specialized type (e.g., `char*`) inside `<>`. When a specialized definition is available and matches an instantiation request, the compiler uses the specialized version; there is no need to instantiate the general template for that particular type. So, when the a2 object is created, the compiler uses the existing `A<char*>` definition. The statement `a1.cmp()` returns 1, while the `a2.cmp()` returns 0 since the strings are the same. Note that the definition of the specialization must be preceded by the declaration or the definition of the general template. For example:

```
template <typename T> class A; // Just the declaration.
template <> class A<char*> {...}; // Explicit specialization.
A<int> a1; // Wrong, since there is no definition.
A<char*> a2("text"); // Correct.
```

With partial specialization some types may have specific values. For example:

```
template <typename T1, typename T2> class A {...}; // General template.
template <typename T1> class A<T1, int> {...}; // Partial specialization.
```

The partial specialization of a template is still a template. It is a template which will be used for a specific subset of the arguments of the general template. In partial specialization, the `<>` after the `template` keyword contains the types that are not specialized and need to be specified to create an instance. That is, with the second declaration the value of T2 is `int`, while that of T1 is generic. Note that if we specify all the types, we have an explicit specialization. For example:

```
template <> class A<double, int> {...}; // Explicit specialization.
```

The value of T1 is `double`, while that of T2 is `int`. In general, pointers may need to be treated differently than other types, such as objects and references. For example, to compare objects when a pointer type is passed as an argument, the pointers must be dereferenced to make the comparison, otherwise, their addresses will be compared. For this situation, we can partially specialize a general template and create a special version for pointers. For example:

```
template <typename T> class A {...}; // General template.
template <typename T*> class A {...}; // Partial specialization.
```

If a pointer is passed, the compiler uses the partial specialization. Otherwise, it uses the general template. For example:

```
A<int> a; // The general template is used.
A<double*> a; // The partial specialization is used, where T is double.
```

In the second declaration, if the partial specialization was missing, the compiler would use the general template and replace T with `double*`. Now, it uses the specialized template and replaces T with `double`.

When there are many options available, the compiler checks the types being passed and selects the template version that matches them best. For example, consider the following declarations:

```
A<int, float> a; // The general template is used.
A<int, int> a; // The partial specialization is used.
A<double, int> a; // The explicit specialization is used.
```

EXERCISES

C.23.1 Are there any errors in the following program? If not, what does it display?

```
#include <iostream>

class A
{
public:
        void p() const {std::cout << "p\n";}
};

template <typename T> class B
{
private:
        T x;
public:
        int k;
        B(T y) : x(y), k(2) {x.p();}
};

void f(B& r)
{
        std::cout << r.k;
}

int main()
{
        A a;
        B<A*> b(&a);
        f(b);
        return 0;
}
```

Answer: Yes, there are errors. The first error is in the definition of `f()`. There is no `B` class. The programmer must specify the version of the class to which `r` refers (e.g., `B<A*>`). The second error is in the declaration of b. Since the `T` type is replaced with `A*`, the version of the class is:

```
class B<A*>
{
private:
        A* x;
public:
        int k;
        B(A* y) : x(y), k(2) {x.p();}
};
```

Let's see the constructor. The initialization x(y) is correct, x becomes equal to y, that is, x = &a; However, since x is a pointer we should write x->p() and not x.p().

C.23.2 Define the `Employee` class with private members the name (e.g., name) and the salary (e.g., sal) of the employee. From the `Employee` class derive with public access the `Manager` class with private member the name of the department (e.g., dpt). Each class must contain a public show() function to display the values of its members. Next, define the template `Person<T>` class, where T can be a pointer to an `Employee` or `Manager` type. The class should contain a private member of type vector (e.g., v) in which the T objects are stored. To store each object you should define an appropriate add() function. Also, the class should contain a show() function which calls the show() of the objects contained in the vector object to display their elements. Add appropriate functions in the classes so that the following program works.

```
int main()
{
        Employee emp1("First", 1), emp2("Sec", 2); /* name should become equal
to the value of the first argument, and sal with that of the second. */
        Manager mgr1("Prog", "Third", 3), mgr2("Net", "Four", 4); /* dpt should
become equal to the value of the first argument and the constructor of the
Employee class should be called. */
        Person<Employee*> per1;
        per1.add(&emp1); // The argument should be stored in per1.v
        per1.add(&emp2);
        per1.show(); /* The program should display the data of the objects,
that is, First 1 and Sec 2. */
        Person<Manager*> per2;
        per2.add(&mgr1); // The argument should be stored in per2.v
        per2.add(&mgr2);
        per2.show(); /* The program should display the data of the objects,
that is, Third 3 Prog και Four 4 Net. */
        return 0;
}

Answer:

#include <iostream>
#include <vector>
#include <string>
using std::cout;
using std::string;
using std::vector;

class Employee
{
private:
        string name;
        int sal;
public:
        Employee(const string& n, int s) : name(n), sal(s) {}
        void show() const {cout << "N:" << name << " S:" << sal << '\n';} /* Not
needed to be virtual. */
};

class Manager : public Employee
{
private:
        string dpt;
```

```
public:
        Manager(const string& d, const string& n, int s) : Employee(n, s),
dpt(d) {}
        void show() const;
};

void Manager::show() const
{
        Employee::show();
        cout << "D:" << dpt << '\n';
}

template <typename T> class Person
{
private:
        vector<T> v;
public:
        void show() const;
        void add(T t) {v.push_back(t);}
};

template <typename T> void Person<T>::show() const
{
        for(int i = 0; i < v.size(); i++)
                v[i]->show();
}
```

Comments: In the given code we see that `add()` takes as a parameter a pointer to an `Employee` or `Manager` object. So, we understand that the type of the parameter should be generic, the same as that of the `vector` object. As the exercise says, `add()` stores the objects in the `vector` object. The `show()` of the `Person<T>` calls the `show()` of each object contained in the `vector`.

C.23.3 Define the `Circle<T>` class template with private member the radius (e.g., `rad`) of the circle. The type of `rad` should be `T`. Add appropriate functions in the classes so that the following program works.

```
int main()
{
        Circle<int> c1(5), c2; /* The type of rad should become int and
its value equal to the value of the argument. The default initial value
is 0. */
        c2+3; // rad should be increased by 3.
        Circle<int> c3 = c1+c2; /* The c3.rad should become equal to the sum
of c1.rad and c2.rad. */
        Circle<double> c4(1.5);
        c4+1.2; // rad should be increased by 1.2.
        cout << c3 << c4 << '\n'; /* The program should display the values of
c3.rad and c4.rad, that is, 8 and 2.7. */
        return 0;
}
```

Answer:

```
#include <iostream>
using std::cout;
using std::ostream;
```

```
template <typename T> class Circle
{
private:
        T rad;
public:
        Circle<T>(T r = 0) {rad = r;}
        void operator+(T i) {rad += i;}
        Circle<T> operator+(const Circle<T>& c) const;
        template <typename V> friend ostream& operator<<(ostream& out, const
Circle<V>& c);
};

template <typename T> Circle<T> Circle<T>::operator+(const Circle<T>& c)
const
{
        Circle<T> tmp;
        tmp.rad = rad + c.rad;
        return tmp;
}

template <typename V> ostream& operator<<(ostream& out, const Circle<V>& c)
{
        out << c.rad << '\n';
        return out;
}
```

Comments: From the given code we understand that we need to overload operators. We also define a template friend function that can be used by all the versions of the class.

C.23.4 Define the template Map_Key<T1, T2> class with two private members of type T1 and T2. Add appropriate functions in the class so that the following program works.

```
template <typename T1, typename T2> class Map_Key
{
private:
        T1 key;
        T2 val;
public:
        ??? check(???); /* Define the check() which takes as parameter a value
(e.g., k) and checks if the value of the key is the same as k. */
        ??? get(???); /* Define the get() so that it returns the val. */
        // Add any other function you think is needed.
};

int main()
{
        Map_Key<string, int> mk_1("One", 1), mk_2("Two", 2);
        Map_Key<string, int> mk_3 = mk_1 + mk_2;
        /* Declare a vector (e.g., v) of type Map_Key and store mk_1, mk_2,
and mk_3 in it. Then, read a string and check if it is stored in v. If it is,
the program should display the value of val. For example, if the user enters
One, the program should display 1. */
        ...
}
```

Answer:

```cpp
#include <iostream>
#include <string>
#include <vector>
using namespace std;

template <typename T1, typename T2> class Map_Key
{
private:
        T1 key;
        T2 val;
public:
        Map_Key() {};
        Map_Key(const T1& k, const T2& v) : key(k), val(v) {};
        bool check(const T1& k) const {return (key == k) ? true : false;}
        T2 get() const {return val;}
        Map_Key<T1, T2> operator+(const Map_Key& mk) const;
};


template <typename T1, typename T2>
Map_Key<T1, T2> Map_Key<T1, T2>::operator+(const Map_Key& mk) const
{
        Map_Key<T1, T2> tmp;
        tmp.key = key + mk.key;
        tmp.val = val + mk.val;
        return tmp;
}


int main()
{
        int i;
        string s;
        Map_Key<string, int> mk_1("One", 1), mk_2("Two", 2);
        Map_Key<string, int> mk_3 = mk_1 + mk_2;
        vector<Map_Key<string, int>> v;

        v.push_back(mk_1);
        v.push_back(mk_2);
        v.push_back(mk_3);
        cout << "Enter string: ";
        cin >> s;
        for(i = 0; i < v.size(); i++)
        {
                if(v[i].check(s))
                {
                        cout << "Value:" << v[i].get() << '\n';
                        return 0;
                }
        }
        cout << "Not found\n";
        return 0;
}
```

Comments: We tested the program with pairs of string and int types. Try it with other types, as well.

C.23.5 Add appropriate functions in the class template so that the following program works. The purpose of the program is to sort the `size` elements contained in the memory that the `p` pointer points to according to the bubble algorithm. To implement the `bubble_sort()` use the code of C.12.10.

```
#include <iostream>

template <typename T> class Sort_Arr
{
private:
        int size;
        T *p;
public:
        ...
        void bubble_sort(); // Sort the elements.
        void show() const;  // Display the elements.
};

int main()
{
        Sort_Arr<int> sa_1(5); /* The constructor should be called, the size
should become 5 and memory for size numbers should be allocated. The p
pointer should point to that memory. The user should enter the values of the
elements. */
        Sort_Arr<int > sa_2, sa_3;

        sa_3 = sa_2 = sa_1;
        sa_3.bubble_sort();
        sa_3.show();

        Sort_Arr<double> sa_4(5);
        Sort_Arr<double> sa_5(sa_4); /* The copy constructor should be
called. */
        sa_5.bubble_sort();
        sa_5.show();
        sa_5[10] = 1.2; /* If the index is out of bounds, as in this case, the
out_of_range exception should be thrown. */
        return 0;
}
```

Answer:

```
#include <iostream>
#include <cstring>
#include <stdexcept>

template <typename T> class Sort_Arr
{
private:
        int size;
        T *p;
public:
        Sort_Arr();
        Sort_Arr(int s);
        ~Sort_Arr();
        Sort_Arr(const Sort_Arr& s);
        Sort_Arr& operator=(const Sort_Arr& t);
```

```
        T& operator[](int pos) const;
        void bubble_sort();
        void show() const;
};

template <typename T> Sort_Arr<T>::Sort_Arr()
{
        p = nullptr;
}

template <typename T> Sort_Arr<T>::Sort_Arr(int s)
{
        int i;

        size = s;
        p = new T[size];
        for(i = 0; i < size; i++)
        {
                std::cout << "Enter number: ";
                std::cin >> p[i];
        }
}

template <typename T> Sort_Arr<T>::~Sort_Arr()
{
        delete[] p;
}

template <typename T> Sort_Arr<T>& Sort_Arr<T>::operator=(const Sort_Arr<T>& t)
/* Overload the = operator. It will be called twice with the sa_3 = sa_2 =
sa_1; statement. */
{
        if(this == &t) /* Check the self-assignmet for the general case, it is
not needed in this program. */
                return *this;
        delete[] p;
        size = t.size;
        p = new T[size];
        memcpy(p, t.p, size*sizeof(T)); /* Copy size elements. The size of
each element depends on its type and it is equal to sizeof(T). */
        return *this;
}

template <typename T> Sort_Arr<T>::Sort_Arr(const Sort_Arr<T>& t) /* The copy
constructor will be called with the sa_5(sa_4); statement. The size and p are
members of the sa_5, while t refers to sa_4. */
{
        size = t.size;
        p = new T[size];
        memcpy(p, t.p, size*sizeof(T));
}

template <typename T> void Sort_Arr<T>::show() const
{
        for(int i = 0; i < size; i++)
                std::cout << p[i] << '\n';
}
```

```
template <typename T> T& Sort_Arr<T>::operator[](int pos) const
{
        if(pos < 0 || pos > size)
                throw std::out_of_range("Error: out_of_range\n");
        return p[pos];
}

template <typename T> void Sort_Arr<T>::bubble_sort()
{
        bool reorder;
        int i, j;
        T tmp;

        for(i = 1; i < size; i++)
        {
                reorder = 0;
                for(j = size-1; j >= i; j--)
                {
                        if(p[j] < p[j-1])
                        {
                                // Swap values.
                                tmp = p[j];
                                p[j] = p[j-1];
                                p[j-1] = tmp;
                                reorder = 1;
                        }
                }
                if(reorder == 0)
                        return;
        }
}
```

UNSOLVED EXERCISES

U.23.1 Define the Book class with private members the code (e.g., code) and the price (e.g., prc) of the book. Define the CD class with private member the title of the disc (e.g., title). Each class should contain a public show() function to display the values of its members. Next, define the template Shop<T> class, where T can be a CD or Book type. The class should contain a private member of type vector (e.g., v) in which the T objects are stored. To store each object you should define an appropriate add() function. Also, the class should contain a show() function which calls the show() of the objects contained in the vector object to display their elements. Add appropriate functions in the classes so that the following program works.

```
int main()
{
        Shop<Book> s1;
        s1.add(Book(5, 10)); // The argument should be stored in s1.v.
        s1.add(Book(20, 30));
        s1.show(); /* The program should display the data of the objects,
that is, 5 10 and 20 30. */
        Shop<CD> s2;
        s2.add(CD("Music_1")); // The argument should be stored in s2.v.
```

```
        s2.add(CD("Music_2"));
        s2.show(); /* The program should display the data of the objects,
that is, Music_1 and Music_2. */
        return 0;
}
```

U.23.2 Define the template `Stack<T>` class and the `Node` class with private members as in the exercise C.14.8. The purpose of the exercise is to create a stack in which data of generic type can be stored. Add appropriate functions in the classes so that the following program works.

```
template <typename T> class Stack
{
private:
        Node *head;
public:
        ...
};

int main()
{
        Node n1("First", 1, 2), n2("Sec", 3, 4), n3("Third", 5, 6);
        Stack<Node> st1;
        /* The code of the functions of the Stack is similar to the code
of the respective functions in C.14.8. */
        st1.add_stack(n1); /* The add_stack() should add a student in the
stack. */
        st1.add_stack(n2);
        st1.add_stack(n3);
        st1.show_stack(); /* The show_stack() should display the data of
the students. */
        st1.pop(); /* The pop() should display the data of the student
that was extracted from the stack. */
        st1.show_stack(); /* In this example, the program should display
the data of n1, n2. */
        Stack<Node> st2;
        st2.add_stack(n1);
        st2.add_stack(n2);
        cout << ((st1 == st2) ?  "Same\n" : "Different\n"); /* If the two
stacks contain the same number of elements and their names are the same,
as in this example, the program should display Same. */
        return 0;
}
```

Files

24

Real-world programs often need to perform access operations on files. C++ handles file access as it handles standard input and output. In this chapter we'll discuss about text files and binary files, we'll also describe the modes to open a file, the objects that we can use to manage a file, and how we can use them to read and store data in a file.

STREAMS

As we've said, the term *stream* refers to a flow of bytes coming from a source into our program or from our program towards a destination. If the flow is incoming (e.g., from the keyboard) it is called an *input* stream, while if it is outgoing (e.g., to the screen) it is called an *output* stream. In all our programs so far, the input stream is associated with the keyboard, and the output stream with the screen. Larger programs may need additional streams, such as streams associated with disk files or other devices (e.g., sensors, printers, cameras, …).

Until now, we've discussed about the cout and cin objects. For example, cout is associated with the predefined standard output stream (e.g., screen). In particular, since the cout is an object of the ostream class it has members that hold information related to the output format (e.g., field width), as well as a memory buffer for storing the information to be displayed. For example, if we write:

```
cout << "This is a message";
```

the message is stored in this memory, which is managed by the cout. When we say that the cout represents the output stream we basically mean that the information flows, like a stream, from the program, and through the cout object, to the output (e.g., screen). Similarly, when we say that the cin represents the input stream we mean that information flows, like a stream, from the input (e.g., keyboard), and through the cin object, to our program. In this chapter, we'll discuss about streams that are associated with files, that is, the output is directed to a file and, conversely, the input comes from a file.

To read data from a stream (e.g., cin) many programmers prefer expressions such as:

```
while(cin >> a) or while(cin.getline(s, sizeof(s))
```

The two loops work in a similar way. For example, the operator>> function reads a value from the stream, stores it in a, and returns a reference to the stream. If a read error occurs or there is no more data, the condition becomes false and the loop terminates. Now that you've experience you can read again the example C.3.8, to check the integer value entered by the user. As I said, for simplicity in the programs of this book I don't check the state of the stream after each input/output operation. However, in a professional application you should check it.

DOI: 10.1201/9781003230076-24

Stream State

After an operation is performed on a stream (e.g., write data), we should check the state of the stream to see if the operation was successful or not. As shown below, the program can check some specific values (flags) or call the respective functions to determine if an error occurred or not. Each flag is a single bit and they are declared in the `ios_base` class.

FLAG	DESCRIPTION	FUNCTIONS
badbit	Its value becomes 1 if an irrecoverable error occurred.	bad(). Returns true if the value of the badbit is 1.
failbit	Its value becomes 1 if an input/output operation failed.	fail(). Returns true if the value of the badbit or failbit is 1.
eofbit	Its value becomes 1 if the end of file is reached.	eof(). Returns true if the value of the eofbit is 1.
goodbit	Its value becomes 0 if no error occurred, that is, if all three previous values are 0.	good(). Returns true if no error occurred.

There is also the `clear()` function, which takes the value `0` as default argument. For example, the statement `clear();` clears the values of `badbit`, `failbit` and `eofbit`. In the general case, if one of the `badbit`, `failbit`, and `eofbit` is set, and you want to use the stream again, you should clear it in order to reset the state of the stream.

The typical way to check the state of the stream is to use the `operator!` function. For example, to check the state of `cin` we can write:

```
if(!cin)
```

where the condition becomes true if an error has occurred.

BINARY FILES AND TEXT FILES

A *text* file consists of one or more lines that contain readable characters according to a standard format, like the ASCII code. The text file is very easy to read and write as we can use any available editor to process it. Each line ends with the special character(s) the operating system uses to indicate the end of line. In *Windows* systems, for example, the pair of '\r' (Carriage Return) and '\n' (Line Feed) characters, that is, CR/LF, with ASCII codes 13 and 10 respectively, indicate the end of line. Therefore, the new line character '\n' is replaced by '\r' and '\n' when written in the text file. The reverse replacement happens when the file is read. On the other hand, this replacement does not take place in *Unix* systems because the '\n' character indicates the end of line.

Unlike the *text* files, the bytes of a *binary* file don't necessarily represent readable characters. For example, an executable C++ program, an image or a sound file is stored in binary. If you open it, you'll probably see some unintelligible characters. A binary file is not divided into lines and no character translation takes place. In *Windows*, for example, the new line character is not expanded to \r\n when written in the binary file.

Another difference between *text* and *binary* files is that the operating system may add a special character at the end of a text file to mark its end. In *Windows*, for example, the Ctrl+Z character marks the end of a text file. On the other hand, no character has a special significance in a binary file. They are all treated the same.

Storing data in a binary file can save space compared to a text file. For example, suppose that we are using the ASCII character set to write the number 47654 in a text file. Since this number is represented with five characters, the size of the file would be 5 bytes, as shown in the following figure:

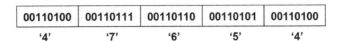

00110100	00110111	00110110	00110101	00110100
'4'	'7'	'6'	'5'	'4'

On the other hand, if this number is stored in binary, the size of the file would be 2 bytes, as shown in the following figure:

10111010	00100110

$47654_{10} = 1011101000100110_{2}$

Binary files might seem a better choice; they have some disadvantages, though. When a binary file is transferred from one system to another the data might not be represented the same, because different systems might store them in different ways. For example, a system may store first the high byte of a number, while some other system the lower byte. Furthermore, because the sizes of the data types may differ from system to system, different number of bytes might be written. For example, a function using `sizeof(int)` to save an integer into a file may write four bytes in one system, eight in another.

FILE INPUT AND OUTPUT

To manage files, C++ provides a variety of useful classes. In particular, the `ofstream` class which derives from `ostream` is used to write data in a file, the `ifstream` class which derives from `istream` is used to read a file, and the `fstream` class which derives from `iostream` which derives from `ostream` and `istream` is used to both write and read a file. These classes inherit the `ios_base` constants and functions we saw earlier in order to check the state of the stream. To use them we include the `fstream` header file.

Let's look at a simple example of writing data into a file. In short, the steps to follow are first to create an `ofstream` object, then to associate it with the file and then use the object, as we use `cout`, to write the data in the file.

```cpp
#include <iostream> // Example 24.1
#include <fstream>
#include <cstdlib> // For exit()

int main()
{
    int i;
    std::ofstream fout; /* fout is an output stream object which has not
been associated yet with a file. */
    fout.open("test.txt"); /* Open a file for writing and associate the
object with it. We could create fout and associate it with the file in one
statement like: ofstream fout("test.txt");  */
    if(fout.is_open() == false) // Alternatively, we can write if(!fout).
    {
        std::cout << "Error: File can not be opened\n";
        exit(EXIT_FAILURE); /* Since the file is not opened, the
program terminates. */
    }
```

```
        for(i = 0; i < 3; i++)
                fout << "Hello_" << i+1 << '\n';
        fout.close(); // Close the file.
        return 0;
}
```

The name of the object can be any valid C++ name (e.g., fout). When we open a file for writing in this way, the program creates the file, if it does not exist. If it exists, its contents are deleted. Next, we'll see how we can write to an existing file without deleting its contents.

If the file exists in the same folder with the executable program, we just put the file name in double quotes. If it does not exist, the file is created in the same folder with the executable. If we want to open a file that is in a different folder from the executable program, then the full path must be specified.

 If the operating system uses the character \ to specify the path, write \\ because, as we saw in Chapter 3, C++ treats \ as the beginning of an escape sequence.

For example, if our program runs in *Windows* and we intend to write in the test.txt file that resides in the d:\dir1\dir2 path, we should write:

```
fout.open("d:\\dir1\\dir2\\test.txt");
```

However, if the program obtains the file name from the command line, it is not needed to add an extra \. For example, we type d:\dir1\dir2\test.txt.

With is_open() we check if the file is opened successfully. If not, the program terminates. For example, is_open() fails when the file path is invalid or we do not have permission to write to the file. Because the ofstream class is derived from the ostream class, its objects can use the ostream functions, such as the overloaded operator<< functions.

If we want to associate the object with a different file we should first close the existing file. For example:

```
fout.close(); // Close the file.
fout.open("new.txt"); // Open a new file.
```

close() closes the file associated with the calling object. All data in memory is written to the file. Also, an open file closes when the associated object ceases to exist, for example, when the program terminates.

Similarly, to read the contents of a file, we need to create an ifstream object, associate it with the file, and use the object, as we use cin, to read its contents. In the following example, suppose that each line of the input file contains the temperatures of an area. The program reads them and displays those within [−5, 5].

```
#include <iostream> // Example 24.2
#include <fstream>
#include <string>
#include <cstdlib>
using namespace std;

int main()
{
        double temp;
        string fname;

        cout << "Enter file name: ";
        cin >> fname;
```

```
        ifstream fin(fname.c_str()); /* Because the type of the parameter in
the constructor is const char*, we pass a C-style string as an argument. */
        if(fin.is_open() == false)
        {
                cout << "Error: File can not be opened\n";
                exit(EXIT_FAILURE);
        }
        while(1)
        {
                fin >> temp;
                if(!fin) /* If an error occurs in reading the data or we reach
the end of the file the operator!() returns true. */
                        break;
                if(temp >= -5 && temp <= 5)
                        cout << temp << '\n';
        }
        fin.close();
        return 0;
}
```

Because the `ifstream` class is derived from the `istream` class, its objects can use the `istream` functions, such as the overloaded `operator>>` functions.

If we want to read and write in a file we have to associate the file with an `fstream` object. The `fstream` class is derived from the `istream` and `ostream` classes, so it inherits their functions. Let's look at an example:

```
#include <iostream> // Example 24.3
#include <fstream>
#include <cstdlib>
#include <string>
using namespace std;

struct Student
{
        string name;
        int code;
        float grd;
};

int main()
{
        Student s1 = {"J.Lee", 100, 5.8}, s2;

        fstream fstr("test.txt", ios_base::in | ios_base::out | ios_base::trunc);
        if(fstr.is_open() == false)
        {
                cout << "Error: File can not be opened\n";
                exit(EXIT_FAILURE);
        }
        fstr << s1.name << ' ' << s1.code << ' ' << s1.grd << '\n';
        fstr.seekg(0);
        fstr >> s2.name >> s2.code >> s2.grd;
        cout << s2.name << ' ' << s2.code << ' ' << s2.grd << '\n';
        fstr.close();
        return 0;
}
```

As we'll see later, the file is opened for both reading and writing; if it exists, its contents are deleted. The reason I chose to use a structure, instead of ordinary variables, is to show you an example of using its members to read/write from/to the file. As you see, we write the data of the structure in the file and with `seekg()`, which we'll discuss about later, we set the file pointer to the beginning of the file, in order to read its contents. To store the information, I used the second structure `s2`. I could use `s1` again, the reason I did not use it is to make the example clearer. The program displays the data of `s2`, which are the same as `s1`, closes the file and terminates. Note that if instead of a structure we use a class with the corresponding members declared public, the code remains the same.

STREAM BUFFER

The `ofstream` class uses a buffer to store data. For each created `ofstream` object, the program allocates respective memory. This memory acts as an intermediary buffer between the program and the file. The data is not written directly to the file, but is stored in this output buffer. When it becomes full, the program flushes the buffer and the data is written to the file. Buffering increases the performance since one large transfer to the disk is much more efficient than many individual transfers. Similarly, buffering also applies when we are using an `ifstream` object to read a file from the disk. That is, the program reads large blocks of data, stores them in the input buffer of the object, and then the data in the buffer are processed. This approach is much faster and more efficient than reading one byte at a time from the disk.

Note that we can flush the output buffer whenever we want. For example, as we saw in Chapter 3, we can use the `flush`, `endl`, `ends`, or `unitbuf` manipulators and flush the buffer. Also, an output stream can be associated with another stream. A write or read operation in this second stream may cause the flushing of the memory in the output stream. For example, the `cin` and `cerr` streams are by default associated with `cout`. Thus, reading from `cin` or writing to `cerr` flushes the buffer of `cout`.

If the program ends abnormally (e.g., crash) the buffer is not flushed. Thus, it is very likely that data which are still in the buffer are not processed (e.g., not printed in the screen). However, this loss can lead us to erroneous conclusions about the operation of the program. For example, when we debug a program that crashed we want to see all the diagnostic messages that have been printed to know which parts of the code have been executed. If some messages do not appear we'd assume that the respective code was not executed which might not be true. The code may have been executed and the messages were not printed because the output buffer was not flushed.

 For the better control of the program, the diagnostic messages related to its operation should be printed directly (e.g., with endl), so that in case the program crashes the programmer has seen them.

CLOSE A FILE

As we said, when we write data to the file, with the buffering approach the data will not be written directly to the file on the disk but to the buffer that is reserved for this purpose. When it is full or the file is closed, the buffer is flushed and the data is stored in the file. Thus, we avoid the often access to the disk, which degrades the performance of the program. The `close()` function is used to close an open file. If the file is open for writing, `close()` stores in the file the data that may be still left in the buffer.

Although an open file is closed automatically when a program terminates normally, it'd be better to close it when you no longer use it. A good reason is that if the file is opened for writing and the program crashes after the file is closed, the file won't be affected.

For example, let's look at the following code:

```
int *p;
ofstream fout("test.txt");
// Write data in the file.
...
// We finished with the data writing, but we did not close the file.
*p = 20; // Wrong action.
```

Because p does not point to a valid address, the program may crash. In that case, data that may be still left in the buffer will be lost. If we had called close() after we've finished with the writing, the buffer would have been flushed and the data would be stored in the file. So, remember to close the file when you no longer need it, to be sure that no data will be lost.

FILE OPEN MODES

When associating a file with a stream object, either by initializing the object with the file name or first create the object and then use the open() function, we can use a second argument, which determines the actions to perform on the file. The ios_base class defines constants that represent the open modes (e.g., ios_base::in). The | bit operator can be used to enable multiple modes, as shown in the following table.

OPEN MODE	ACTION
ios_base::in	Open file for reading.
ios_base::out or ios_base::out | ios_base::trunc	Open file for writing. If the file exists, it will be truncated and its data will be lost. If it does not exist, it will be created.
ios_base::app	Open file for appending. If the file exists, the existing data will be preserved and the new data will be added at its end. If it does not exist, it will be created.
ios_base::in | ios_base::out	Open file for reading and writing.
ios_base::in | ios_base::out | ios_base::trunc	Open file for reading and writing. If the file exists, it will be truncated and its data will be lost. If it does not exist, it will be created.
ios_base::in | ios_base::out | ios_base::app	Open file for reading and appending. If the file exists, the existing data will be preserved and the new data will be added at its end. If it does not exist, it will be created.

There is also the ios_base::ate option, which places the file pointer at the end of the file. The difference between the ios_base::app and ios_base::ate is that the first choice allows you to add data to the end of the file only, while the second just places the file pointer at the end of the file.

To open a text file we choose one of the above modes. To open a binary file we add the constant ios_base::binary. For example, to open a binary file for reading we write ios_base::in | ios_base::binary, while to open it for both reading and writing we write ios_base::in | ios_base::out | ios_base::trunc | ios_base::binary.

As we said, the open mode is an optional argument. If not specified, as in examples C.24.1 and C.24.2, the default mode applies. In particular, the default value for the `ifstream` open() and the constructor is `ios_base::in`, while for `ofstream` open() and the constructor is `ios_base::out`. The default value for the `fstream` open() and the constructor is `ios_base::in | ios_base::out`. Let's look at some examples:

```
ifstream fin("test.txt"); /* The file opens for reading with the default mode
ios_base::in */
ofstream fout("test.txt", ios_base::app); /* The file opens for writing and
appending new data at its end. The existing data are preserved. */
fstream f("test.txt", ios_base::in | ios_base::out | ios_base::trunc); /* The
file opens for reading and writing. The existing data are deleted. */
```

OPEN MULTIPLE FILES

An application may need to open many files. If the files must be open simultaneously, then we must declare separate objects for each file. The number of the files that can be open simultaneously depends on the operating system.

 In applications where many files are opened, it is advisable to close the files you need no more, because the operating system sets a limit to the number of the files that can be opened simultaneously.

When we close a file we can use the respective object for another file, and not declare a new object. Thus, we avoid the allocation of new memory. For example, if we have to open several files sequentially, we do not need to declare separate objects. We can declare a single object and use `open()`, as shown in the following code:

```
ifstream fin;
fin.open(fname1);
/* Use fin to read the file. */
fin.close();
fin.open(fname2);
/* Use the same object to read a new file. */
fin.close();
...
```

FILE PROCESSING

When a file is opened and associated with the respective object, information related to the file is stored in the members of the object. For example, an `ofstream` object contains a pointer member, which indicates the position in the file to write data. Similarly, an `ifstream` object contains a pointer member, which indicates the position in the file to read data.

When a file is opened for reading or writing, the respective pointer points to the beginning of the file. If it opens for appending, it points at the end. When a read or write operation is performed, its value is updated automatically. For example, if a file is opened for reading and 50 characters are read, the value of the pointer changes and points to the location of the file that is 50 bytes from the beginning. If it is opened for writing, the pointer advances a number of places equal to the number of the written bytes. The next write operation will be done at that new position.

To process a file we can use serial and random access. With serial access each read or write operation is performed sequentially. For example, to read the 50th character we have to read the previous 49. With random access, we can move directly to any location within the file. As we'll see below, the seekg() and seekp() functions are used for random access within a file.

Random File Access

For the random access of a file that is associated with an ifstream object we use the seekg() function. There are two versions with the following prototypes:

```
istream& seekg(streamoff offset, ios_base::seekdir origin);
istream& seekg(streampos offset);
```

As we said, an ifstream object contains an input pointer to read the file. The first version of seekg() moves this pointer to a new position that is offset bytes from the position indicated by origin. The streamoff type is a synonym of some integer type. If offset is negative, the pointer moves backwards. The value of origin should be one of the following integer constants of the ios_base class:

ios_base::beg. The pointer is moved offset bytes from the beginning of the file.
ios_base::cur. The pointer is moved offset bytes from its current position.
ios_base::end. The pointer is moved offset bytes from the end of the file.

In the second version, the value of offset indicates in octets from the beginning of the file the new position that the pointer will move. Let's look at some examples:

```
seekg(0, ios_base::end);  // Move to the end of the file.
seekg(20, ios_base::beg); /* Move 20 bytes from the beginning of the file. */
seekg(-5, ios_base::cur); /* Move 5 bytes back from the current position. */
```

If we want to find the current position of the pointer we can use the tellg() function. tellg() returns a streampos value, which represents the current position of the input pointer in bytes from the beginning of the file or -1 if an error occurs. tellg() may be used together with seekg() to return to a previous file location, like this:

```
// Store the location to which we want to return.
streampos old_pos = fin.tellg();
// ... move to another location to read.
fin.seekg(old_pos); // Return back to the first location.
```

Similarly, for the random access of a file that is associated with an ofstream object we use the seekp() and tellp() functions. As we said, an ofstream object contains an output pointer to write data to the file. Note that if seekg() and seekp() are used with text files, care is required with the new line character(s). For example, suppose that the following code writes some text in the first two lines of a text file. If the operating system expands '\n' to '\r' and '\n', the value of offset should be 6 (not 5) in order to move to the beginning of the second line.

```
fout << "text\n";
fout << "another text\n";
/* Move to the beginning of the second line. */
fout.seekp(6, ios_base::beg);
```

It is safer to use seekp() and seekg() with binary rather than text files, because potential translations of the new line character can produce unexpected results.

In case of an `fstream` object the inherited input and output pointers move in tandem. Therefore, the `tellg()` and `tellp()` return the same value.

 If the file is opened for both reading and writing, to switch from reading to writing and vice versa a file positioning function (e.g., `seekp()`) should be first called or the buffer is first flushed (e.g., by `flush`).

If we want to check if `seekg()` or `seekp()` was executed successfully we can use `fail()`. For example:

```
if(fout.fail())
{
        // An error occurred.
}
```

For simplicity, I won't check the return values of the functions I use. That is, I assume that the functions are executed successfully.

END OF FILE

As discussed, the operating system may add a special character at the end of a text file to mark its end, whereas none character marks the end of a `binary` file. In *Dos/Windows* applications, for example, the `Ctrl+Z` character with ASCII value `26` is typically used to mark the end of a `text` file. For example, suppose that the following program runs in such a system:

```cpp
#include <iostream> // Example 24.4
#include <fstream>
#include <cstdlib>
using namespace std;

int main()
{
        int ch;

        fstream fstr("test.txt", ios_base::in | ios_base::out |
ios_base::trunc);
        if(fstr.is_open() == false)
        {
                cout << "Error: is_open() failed\n";
                exit(EXIT_FAILURE);
        }
        fstr << 'a' << 'b' << (char)26 << 'c' << 'd';
        fstr.seekg(0);
        while(1)
        {
                ch = fstr.get();
                if(ch == EOF)
                        break;
                cout << (char)ch;
        }
        fstr.close();
        return 0;
}
```

The loop displays only the characters a and b and the next call of `get()` ends it, since the next character is interpreted as the end of file. On the other hand, if we had added the `binary` mode to create the file as binary, the program would have displayed all the characters since none character has a special significance in a `binary` file.

REDIRECTION

With the inclusion of the `iostream` file we can use the `cin`, `cout`, `cerr`, and `clog` objects. As we know, the `cin` is associated with the standard input device and the `cout` is associated with the standard output device. The `cerr` and `clog` correspond to the standard error stream, which is associated with the standard output device (e.g., screen). Both can be used to display messages. Note that `cerr` is un-buffered, which means that the output appears immediately. Usually, the various operating systems allow the redirection of the `cin` and `cout`. For example, if the name of the executable is `test` and we write in the command line:

```
test >output.txt
```

the data written in `cout` won't be displayed in the screen, but it will be written in the `output.txt` file. Notice that the program does not realize the redirection. To make it clear, the `>output.txt` is not interpreted as an argument of `main()`.

For consistency with the rest programs, we'll continue using `cout` to output all kinds of messages. However, in case of error messages, it'd be better to use `cerr` or `clog` instead of `cout`. If `cout` is redirected, you cannot see the messages until the file is opened. On the other hand, error messages written in `cerr` or `clog` appear real time on the screen, even if `cout` is redirected. For example:

```
if(error_happens)
{
        cerr << "Error happened\n";
        ...
}
else
        cout << "Everything fine\n";
```

If `cout` is not redirected, both messages are displayed on the screen. If it is redirected, the second message is written in the respective file. The first message that informs us about the progress of the program appears on the screen.

Similarly, we can redirect `cin` in order to take the input from a file. For example, if the name of the executable is `test` and we write in the command line:

```
test <input.txt
```

the data read from `cin` won't be read from the keyboard, but from the `input.txt` file. Also, we can combine both redirections. For example:

```
test <input.txt >output.txt
```

The `cin` reads from the `input.txt` file and the `cout` sends the output to the `output.txt`.

WRITE AND READ DATA FROM A TEXT FILE

To handle text files we use the same functions as with the `cout` and `cin` objects, such as the `operator<<()` and `operator>>()` functions. Let's look at an example of writing objects in a file:

```cpp
#include <iostream> // Example 24.5
#include <fstream>
#include <cstdlib>
#include <string>
#include <vector>
using namespace std;

class Student
{
public: // For simplicity, I declare all as public.
        int code;
        string name;
        float grd;
        Student(int c, const string& n, float g) : code(c), name(n), grd(g) {}
};

int main()
{
        int i;
        Student s1(1, "First", 2.5), s2(2, "Sec", 3.5), s3(3, "Third", 4.5);
        vector<Student> v;

        v.push_back(s1);
        v.push_back(s2);
        v.push_back(s3);

        std::ofstream fout("test.txt");
        if(fout.is_open() == false)
        {
                std::cout << "Error: File can not be opened\n";
                exit(EXIT_FAILURE);
        }
        for(i = 0; i < v.size(); i++)
                fout << v[i].code << '\t' << v[i].name << '\t' << v[i].grd << '\n';
        fout.close();
        return 0;
}
```

If we want to specify the format in which the data will be stored in the file we can use the tools we saw in Chapter 3, such as the manipulators. For example, if we want to store the grades with two decimal places we write:

```cpp
fout << fixed << setprecision(2) << v[i].name << '\t' << v[i].code << '\t' <<
v[i].grd << '\n';
```

As when reading from `cin`, the most common functions for reading a file are `operator>>()` functions, `getline()` and `get()`. When using `operator>>()` functions to read from a file and assign the data in appropriate variables, the programmer is supposed to know the type of the stored data and their order in the file. For example, to read the file created in the previous program we need to know that each line contains in that order an integer, a string, and a float number, in order to assign the values to appropriate variables. Also, space(s) are supposed to discriminate the values in the file.

```cpp
#include <iostream> // Example 24.6
#include <fstream>
#include <cstdlib>
#include <string>
using namespace std;

int main()
{
        int code;
        string name;
        float grd;

        ifstream fin("test.txt");
        if(fin.is_open() == false)
        {
                cout << "Error: is_open() failed\n";
                exit(EXIT_FAILURE);
        }
        while(1)
        {
                fin >> code >> name >> grd;
                if(!fin)
                        break;
                cout << code << ' ' << name << ' ' << grd << '\n';
        }
        fin.close();
        return 0;
}
```

The program displays the data of the students stored in the file, that is, the data of s1, s2, and s3. Specifically, in the loop we read the data of each line and store them in the respective variables. If we try to read after the end of the file or if another error occurs, the state of the stream becomes fail, so the `if` condition becomes true and the loop ends. To determine which of the two happened, we can use the `eof()` function. For example, we can add the following code after the loop:

```cpp
if(fin.eof())
        cout << "End of file\n";
else
        cout << "Failed for another reason\n";
```

The message informs us whether the read operation failed because we reached the end of the file or for some other reason.

For simplicity, if something goes wrong during the reading process, I assume that this error is due to the end of the file condition and not for some other reason. However, a robust program should check the reason of failure.

We can also use `getline()`, as we used it with `cin`. For example, the following code uses `getline()` to display the contents of each line without parsing its data:

```
string line;
while(1)
{
        getline(fin, line);
        if(!fin)
                break;
        cout << line << '\n';
}
```

Many programmers place the read statement in the `while` condition, that is, they write:

```
while(getline(fin, line))
        cout << line << '\n';
```

My preference is the infinite loop so that the read statement, as well as the condition that terminates the loop, are clearly visible. Also, if we want, we can use `get()` to read each character of the file one by one. Exercise C.24.5 is such an example.

 If you reach the end of the file and want to access it again, call `clear()` to clear the `eofbit`.

EXERCISES

C.24.1 Change the members of the `Student` class of the example C.24.5 to private and complete the following program, so that it displays the data of the two students.

```
int main()
{
        Student s1(1, "First", 2.5), s2(5, "Second", 7.5);

        fstream fstr("test.txt", ios_base::in | ios_base::out | ios_base::trunc);
/* Open the text file for reading and writing. */
        ...
        fstr << s1 << s2; /* The data of the two students should be stored
into two separate lines. */
        ...
        fstr >> s1 >> s2; /* The program should store the data of each line in
the respective members of s1 and s2. */
        s1.show(); /* Add in the class the show(), which should display the data
of the student. The program should display the initial values of s1 and s2. */
        s2.show();
        return 0;
}
```

Answer:

```
#include <iostream>
#include <fstream>
#include <cstdlib>
```

```
#include <string>
using namespace std;

class Student
{
private:
        int code;
        string name;
        float grd;
public:
        Student(int c, const string& n, float g) : code(c), name(n), grd(g) {}
        friend istream& operator>>(istream& in, Student& s);
        friend ostream& operator<<(ostream& out, const Student& s);
        void show() const {cout << "N:" << name << " C:" << code << " G:" <<
grd << '\n';}

};

istream& operator>>(istream& in, Student& s)
{
        in >> s.name >> s.code >> s.grd;
        return in;
}

ostream& operator<<(ostream& out, const Student& s)
{
        out << s.name << '\t' << s.code << '\t' << s.grd << '\n';
        return out;
}

int main()
{
        Student s1(1, "First", 2.5), s2(5, "Second", 7.5);

        fstream fstr("test.txt", ios_base::in | ios_base::out | ios_base::trunc);
        if(fstr.is_open() == false)
        {
                cout << "Error: File can not be opened\n";
                exit(EXIT_FAILURE);
        }
        fstr << s1 << s2;
        fstr.seekg(0);
        fstr >> s1 >> s2;
        s1.show();
        s2.show();
        fstr.close();
        return 0;
}
```

Comments: To access the private members we declare the overload functions as friends. The functions return references so that the << and >> operators can be used sequentially. Note that the references could be fstream&, I just used the base classes to make it clearer.

C.24.2 Write a program that reads continuously products' codes and their prices and stores them in the test.txt file, as follows:

```
C101   17.5
C102   32.8
. . .
```

If the user enters -1 for price, the insertion of products should terminate. Then, the program should read a product's code and search the file to find and display its price, if found.

```cpp
#include <iostream>
#include <fstream>
#include <cstdlib>
#include <string>
using namespace std;

int main()
{
        bool found;
        string code, tmp;
        double prc;

        fstream fstr("test.txt", ios_base::in | ios_base::out | ios_base::trunc);
        if(fstr.is_open() == false)
        {
                cout << "Error: is_open() failed\n";
                exit(EXIT_FAILURE);
        }
        while(1)
        {
                cout << "Enter price: ";
                cin >> prc;
                if(prc == -1)
                        break;
                cin.get();
                cout << "Enter product code: ";
                getline(cin, code);
                fstr << code << ' ' << prc << '\n';
        }
        cin.get();
        cout << "Enter product code to search for: ";
        getline(cin, tmp);

        found = 0;
        fstr.seekg(0);
        while(1)
        {
                fstr >> code >> prc;
                if(!fstr)
                        break;
                if(code == tmp)
                {
                        found = 1;
                        break; /* Since the product is found we can terminate
the loop. */
                }
        }
        if(found == 0)
                cout << tmp << " code is not listed\n";
        else
                cout << "The price for product " << code << " is " << prc << '\n';
        fstr.close();
        return 0;
}
```

C.24.3 Suppose that each line of the `students.txt` file contains the names of the students and their grades in two lessons, as follows:

```
John        Morne       7       8.12
Sahil       Nehrud      4.5     9
Koon        Lee         2       5.75
```

    Write a program that reads each line of `students.txt` and stores in `suc.txt` the names and grades of the students with average grade greater than or equal to 5, while in `fail.txt` the students with average grade less than 5. The program should display the number of students written in each file.

```cpp
#include <iostream>
#include <fstream>
#include <cstdlib>
#include <string>
using namespace std;

int main()
{
        string fnm, lnm;
        int suc_stud, fail_stud;
        double grd1, grd2;

        ifstream fin("students.txt");
        if(fin.is_open() == false)
        {
                cout << "Error: students.txt can't be loaded\n";
                exit(EXIT_FAILURE);
        }
        ofstream fout_suc("suc.txt");
        if(fout_suc.is_open() == false)
        {
                fin.close();
                cout << "Error: suc.txt can't be created\n";
                exit(EXIT_FAILURE);
        }
        ofstream fout_fail("fail.txt");
        if(fout_fail.is_open() == false)
        {
                fin.close();
                fout_suc.close();
                cout << "Error: fail.txt can't be created\n";
                exit(EXIT_FAILURE);
        }
        suc_stud = fail_stud = 0;
        while(1)
        {
                fin >> fnm >> lnm >> grd1 >> grd2;
                if(!fin)
                        break;
                if((grd1+grd2)/2 >= 5)
                {
                        fout_suc << fnm << ' ' << lnm << ' ' << grd1 << ' ' <<
grd2 << '\n';
                        suc_stud++;
                }
```

```
                else
                {
                        fout_fail << fnm << ' ' << lnm << ' ' << grd1 << ' ' <<
grd2 << '\n';
                        fail_stud++;
                }
        }
        cout << "Fail: " << fail_stud << " Success: " << suc_stud << '\n';
        fin.close();
        fout_suc.close();
        fout_fail.close();
        return 0;
}
```

C.24.4 Write a program that reads the names of two files, compares them line by line, and displays their first common line. If the two files have no common line, the program should display a related message.

```
#include <iostream>
#include <fstream>
#include <cstdlib>
#include <string>
using namespace std;

int main()
{
        bool found;
        string fname, str1, str2;

        cout << "Enter first file: ";
        cin >> fname;
        ifstream fin_f(fname.c_str());
        if(fin_f.is_open() == false)
        {
                cout << "Error: first is_open() failed\n";
                exit(EXIT_FAILURE);
        }
        cout << "Enter second file: ";
        cin >> fname;
        ifstream fin_s(fname.c_str());
        if(fin_s.is_open() == false)
        {
                fin_f.close();
                cout << "Error: second is_open() failed\n";
                exit(EXIT_FAILURE);
        }
        found = 0;
        while(1)
        {
                getline(fin_f, str1);
                getline(fin_s, str2);
                if(!fin_f || !fin_s)
                        break; /* We check if a read error occurred or the end
of a file is reached. In either case, the loop terminates. */
```

```
                if(str1 == str2)
                {
                        cout << "The same line is: " << str1 << '\n';
                        found = 1;
                        break; /* Since a common line is found, exit from the
loop. */
                }
        }
        if(found == 0)
                cout << "There is no common line\n";
        fin_f.close();
        fin_s.close();
        return 0;
}
```

C.24.5 Write a program that reads the name of a file and displays its second line. There is a restriction to use get() and not getline().

```
#include <iostream>
#include <fstream>
#include <cstdlib>
#include <string>
using namespace std;

int main()
{
        int ch, lines;
        string fname;

        cout << "Enter file name: ";
        cin >> fname;
        ifstream fin(fname.c_str());
        if(fin.is_open() == false)
        {
                cout << "Error: is_open() failed\n";
                exit(EXIT_FAILURE);
        }
        cout << "Line contents: ";
        lines = 1;
        while(1)
        {
                ch = fin.get();
                if((!fin) || (lines > 2))
                        break;
                if(lines == 2) /* Only the characters of the second line are
 displayed. */
                        cout << (char)ch;
                if(ch == '\n') /* Once the new line character is read, increment
the variable that counts the lines. */
                        lines++;
        }
        fin.close();
        return 0;
}
```

Comments: Once the program displays the second line, the loop terminates.

C.24.6 A simple way to encrypt data is to XOR them with a secret key. Write a program that reads a key character and the name of a text file and encrypts its content by XORing each character with the key. The encrypted characters should be stored in a second file selected by the user.

```cpp
#include <iostream>
#include <fstream>
#include <cstdlib>
#include <string>
using namespace std;

int main()
{
        int ch, key_ch;
        string fname;

        cout << "Enter input file: ";
        cin >> fname;
        ifstream fin(fname.c_str());
        if(fin.is_open() == false)
        {
                cout << "Error: Input file can't be loaded\n";
                exit(EXIT_FAILURE);
        }
        cout << "Enter output file: ";
        cin >> fname;
        ofstream fout(fname.c_str());
        if(fout.is_open() == false)
        {
                fin.close();
                cout << "Error: Output file can't be created\n";
                exit(EXIT_FAILURE);
        }
        cin.get();
        cout << "Enter key char: ";
        key_ch = cin.get();
        while(1)
        {
                ch = fin.get();
                if(!fin)
                        break;
                fout << (char)(ch ^ key_ch);
        }
        fin.close();
        fout.close();
        return 0;
}
```

Comments: If you rerun the program and give as an input the encrypted file and the same key, the output file would be the same as the original file, because according to the *Boole* algebra we have: (a ^ b) ^ b = a.

C.24.7 Define the class Country with private members: name, capital, and population. Suppose that each line of the country.txt file contains the data of the respective country in the form:

```
name   capital   population
```

Write a program that reads the file and uses the class to store the countries' data in a `vector` of `Country` elements. Then, the program should read a number and display the data of the countries with higher population than this number. Add any function in the class you think is needed.

```cpp
#include <iostream>
#include <fstream>
#include <cstdlib>
#include <string>
#include <vector>
using namespace std;

class Country
{
private:
        string name;
        string capital;
        int pop;
public:
        Country(const string& n = "", const string& c = "", int p = 0) : name(n),
capital(c), pop(p) {}
        void set(const string& n, const string& c, int p);
        int get_pop() const {return pop;}
        void show() const;
};

void Country::set(const string& n, const string& c, int p)
{
        name = n;
        capital = c;
        pop = p;
}

void Country::show() const
{
        cout << name << '\t' << capital << '\t' << pop << '\n';
}

int main()
{
        int i, pop;
        string name, capital;
        Country tmp;
        vector<Country> cntr;

        ifstream fin("country.txt");
        if(fin.is_open() == false)
        {
                cout << "Error: is_open() failed\n";
                exit(EXIT_FAILURE);
        }
        while(1)
        {
                fin >> name >> capital >> pop;
                if(!fin)
                        break;
                tmp.set(name, capital, pop);
                cntr.push_back(tmp);
        }
```

```
        cout << "Enter population: ";
        cin >> pop;
        for(i = 0; i < cntr.size(); i++)
                if(cntr[i].get_pop() >= pop)
                        cntr[i].show();

        fin.close();
        return 0;
}
```

WRITE AND READ DATA FROM A BINARY FILE

The functions used to write and read data to/from a binary file are the `write()` and `read()`, respectively. Although they are primarily used with binary files, they can also be used, with some caution, with text files.

The `write()` Function

The `write()` function is very useful for writing large blocks of data in a single step. Its prototype is:

```
ostream& write(const char *buf, streamsize count);
```

The `buf` argument points to the memory that holds the data to be written in the file. The `streamsize` is a synonym for some integer type. The `count` argument specifies the number of the bytes to be written in the file. For example, to store an array of 1000 integers we write:

```
int arr[1000];
ofstream fout("test.dat", ios_base::out | ios_base::trunc | ios_base::binary);
fout.write((char*)arr, sizeof(arr));
```

To store a `double` number we write:

```
double d = 1.2345;
fout.write((char*)&d, sizeof(double));
```

And to store an object of the `Student` class we write:

```
Student s;
fout.write((char*)&s, sizeof(s));
```

Note that only the data of the object are written to the file, not the functions. As shown in the examples, we should cast the address to `char*`. Also, the best practice is to use the `sizeof` operator to specify the size, in order to make your program platform independent. And if we want to verify that no error occurred, we check the state of the stream. For example:

```
if(!fout)
        cout << "write error\n";
```

The `read()` Function

Like `write()`, `read()` is very useful for reading large blocks of data in a single step. Its prototype is:

```
istream& read(char *buf, streamsize count);
```

The buf argument points to the memory in which the read data will be stored. The count argument specifies how many bytes will be read from the file.

 Because two systems may differ (e.g., in the size of types), there is no guarantee that a file written with the write() function will be read correctly with the read() function in another system.

In the following example, a double number is read and stored into d:

```
double d;
ifstream fin("test.dat", ios_base::in | ios_base::binary);
fin.read((char*)&d, sizeof(d));
```

In the next example, 1000 integers are read and stored into arr:

```
int arr[1000];
fin.read((char*)arr, sizeof(arr));
```

 It is safer to use write() and read() with binary rather than text files, because potential translations of the new line character can produce unexpected results.

For example, suppose that we use write() to write a string of 50 characters in a text file and the value of count is set to 50. If the program runs in *Windows* and the string contains new line character(s), the replacement(s) with the \r\n pair would make its size more than 50; therefore, write() won't write the entire string.

As we'll see in the following examples, write() and read() are very often used with objects that occupy the same amount of memory. As we said, when we store an object in the file only the data members are stored and not its functions. However, be careful with classes that use virtual functions. As we know, with virtual functions, there is a hidden pointer that points to the array which contains the pointers to the virtual functions. This hidden pointer will be stored in the file. Because the next time we run this program this array may be stored in a different memory location, if we read the file, the value of the hidden pointer will change to the one stored in the file. Thus, the pointer will get an invalid value, which may cause the program to crash.

EXERCISES

C.24.8 Write a program that declares an array of 5 integers with values 10, 20, 30, 40, and 50 and writes them in a binary file. Then, the program should read an integer and replace the third stored integer with the input number. The program should read and display the file's content before it ends.

```
#include <iostream>
#include <fstream>
#include <cstdlib>
using namespace std;
```

```
int main()
{
        int i, arr[5] = {10, 20, 30, 40, 50};

        fstream fstr("test.bin", ios_base::in | ios_base::out | ios_base::trunc |
ios_base::binary); /* Open binary file for reading and writing. */
        if(fstr.is_open() == false)
        {
                cout << "Error: is_open() failed\n";
                exit(EXIT_FAILURE);
        }
        fstr.write((char*)arr, sizeof(arr));

        cout << "Enter new value: ";
        cin >> i;
        fstr.seekp(2*sizeof(int)); /* If the integer reserves 4 bytes, seekp()
moves the file pointer 2*sizeof(int) = 8 bytes from the beginning of the file
to get to the third integer. */
        fstr.write((char*)&i, sizeof(int));

        fstr.seekg(0);
        fstr.read((char*)arr, sizeof(arr));
        if(!fstr)
        {
                fstr.close();
                cout << "Error: read() failed\n";
                exit(EXIT_FAILURE);
        }
        cout << "\n***** File contents *****\n";
        for(i = 0; i < 5; i++)
                cout << arr[i] << '\n';

        fstr.close();
        return 0;
}
```

C.24.9 Write a program that reads the titles of 10 books (use an array of 100 characters) and writes them in a binary file selected by the user. First write the size of the title, then the title. Next, the program should read a title and display a message to indicate if it is contained in the file or not.

```
#include <iostream>
#include <fstream>
#include <cstdlib>
#include <string>
#include <cstring>
using namespace std;

int main()
{
        bool found;
        int i, len;
        char title[100], str[100];
        string fname;

        cout << "Enter file name: ";
        cin >> fname;
```

```
        fstream fstr(fname.c_str(), ios_base::in | ios_base::out |
ios_base::trunc | ios_base::binary);
        if(fstr.is_open() == false)
        {
                cout << "Error: is_open() failed\n";
                exit(EXIT_FAILURE);
        }
        cin.get();
        for(i = 0; i < 10; i++)
        {
                cout << "Enter title: ";
                cin.getline(title, sizeof(title));
                len = strlen(title);
                fstr.write((char*)&len, sizeof(int));
                fstr.write(title, len);
        }
        cout << "Enter title to search: ";
        cin.getline(str, sizeof(str));

        found = 0;
        fstr.seekg(0);
        while(1)
        {
                fstr.read((char*)&len, sizeof(int));
                if(!fstr)
                        break;
                fstr.read(title, len);
                if(!fstr)
                        break;
                title[len] = '\0';
                if(strcmp(title, str) == 0)
                {
                        found = 1;
                        break;
                }
        }
        if(found == 0)
                cout << "\nTitle not found\n";
        else
                cout << "\nTitle found\n";
        fstr.close();
        return 0;
}
```

C.24.10 Suppose that the test.bin binary file contains the grades of a student. The number of grades is declared in the beginning of the file. Write a program that reads the grades from the binary file (use the float type) and stores them in a dynamically allocated memory. Then, the program should read a number and display the grades greater than that number.

```
#include <iostream>
#include <fstream>
#include <cstdlib>
using namespace std;
```

```
int main()
{
        int i, grd_num;
        float *grd_arr, grd;

        ifstream fin("test.bin", ios_base::in | ios_base::binary);
        if(fin.is_open() == false)
        {
                cout << "Error: is_open() failed\n";
                exit(EXIT_FAILURE);
        }
        fin.read((char*)&grd_num, sizeof(int));
        if(!fin)
        {
                fin.close();
                cout << "Error: read() failed\n";
                exit(EXIT_FAILURE);
        }
        grd_arr = new float[grd_num]; /* Allocate memory to store the grades. */
        fin.read((char*)grd_arr, grd_num * sizeof(float)); /* Read all grades
and check if they are read successfully. */
        if(fin)
        {
                cout << "Enter grade: ";
                cin >> grd;
                for(i = 0; i < grd_num; i++)
                        if(grd_arr[i] > grd)
                                cout << grd_arr[i] << '\n';
        }
        else
                cout << "Error: read() failed to read grades\n";

        delete[] grd_arr;
        fin.close();
        return 0;
}
```

C.24.11 A common method that an antivirus software uses to identify viruses is the signature-based detection. The signature is a sequence of bytes (e.g., F3 BA 20 63 7A 1B) that identify a particular virus. When a file is scanned, the antivirus software searches the file for signatures that identify the presence of viruses. Write a program that reads a virus signature (e.g., five integers) and checks if it is contained in the binary file test.dat.

```
#include <iostream>
#include <fstream>
#include <cstdlib>
#include <cstring>
using namespace std;

int main()
{
        const int SIZE = 5;
        bool found;
        int i, len, back, buf[SIZE], sign[SIZE];
```

```
        ifstream fin("test.dat", ios_base::in | ios_base::binary);
        if(fin.is_open() == false)
        {
                cout << "Error: is_open() failed\n";
                exit(EXIT_FAILURE);
        }
        cout << "Enter virus signature (" << SIZE << " integers)\n";
        for(i = 0; i < SIZE; i++)
        {
                cout << "Enter number: ";
                cin >> sign[i];
        }
        len = sizeof(sign);
        found = 0;
        back = len - sizeof(int);
        while(1)
        {
                fin.read((char*)buf, SIZE * sizeof(int));
                if(!fin)
                        break;
                if(memcmp(buf, sign, len) == 0)
                {
                        found = 1;
                        break;
                }
                else
                        fin.seekg(-back, ios_base::cur); /* Go back to check the
next group of five. */
        }
        if(found == 1)
                cout << "SOS: Virus found\n";
        else
                cout << "That virus signature isn't found\n";
        fin.close();
        return 0;
}
```

C.24.12 Define the `Employee` structure with members: name (use an array of 100 characters), tax number, and salary. Write a program that uses this type to read the data of 100 employees and store them in an array of such structures. If the user enters `fin` for name, the data insertion should terminate and the program should write the structures in the `test.bin` binary file.

```
#include <iostream>
#include <fstream>
#include <cstdlib>
#include <cstring>
using namespace std;

struct Employee
{
        char name[100];
        int tax_num;
        int salary;
};
```

```cpp
int main()
{
        const int SIZE = 100;
        int i, num_empl;
        Employee empl[SIZE];

        ofstream fout("test.bin", ios_base::out | ios_base::trunc |
ios_base::binary);
        if(fout.is_open() == false)
        {
                cout << "Error: is_open() failed\n";
                exit(EXIT_FAILURE);
        }
        num_empl = 0;
        for(i = 0; i < SIZE; i++)
        {
                cout << "\nEnter full name: ";
                cin.getline(empl[i].name, sizeof(empl[i].name));
                if(strcmp(empl[i].name, "fin") == 0)
                        break;

                cout << "Enter tax number: ";
                cin >> empl[i].tax_num;

                cout << "Enter salary: ";
                cin >> empl[i].salary;

                num_empl++;
                cin.get();
        }
        // Write all structures in a single step.
        fout.write((char*)empl, num_empl * sizeof(Employee));
        fout.close();
        return 0;
}
```

Comments: For the name I use an array of characters and not a `string`, so that the size of each structure stored in the file is the same. Then, as we'll see in the next exercise, we can read them all together with one `read()`.

C.24.13 Suppose that the `test.bin` binary file contains structures of the type `Employee` defined in the previous exercise. Write a program that reads them and copies the employees' data whose salary is more than an amount entered by the user in the `data.bin` binary file. The program should also display the average salary of the employees stored in `data.bin`.

```cpp
#include <iostream>
#include <fstream>
#include <cstdlib>
using namespace std;

struct Employee
{
        char name[100];
        int tax_num;
        int salary;
};
```

```cpp
int main()
{
        int count, amount, sum_sal;
        Employee tmp_emp;

        ifstream fin("test.bin", ios_base::in | ios_base::binary);
        if(fin.is_open() == false)
        {
                cout << "Error: Input file can't be loaded\n";
                exit(EXIT_FAILURE);
        }
        ofstream fout("data.bin", ios_base::out | ios_base::trunc |
ios_base::binary);
        if(fout.is_open() == false)
        {
                fin.close();
                cout << "Error: Output file can't be created\n";
                exit(EXIT_FAILURE);
        }
        cout << "Enter amount: ";
        cin >> amount;
        count = sum_sal = 0;
        while(1)
        {
                fin.read((char*)&tmp_emp, sizeof(Employee));
                if(!fin)
                        break;
                if(tmp_emp.salary > amount)
                {
                        fout.write((char*)&tmp_emp, sizeof(Employee));
                        sum_sal += tmp_emp.salary;
                        count++;
                }
        }
        if(count)
                cout << "Avg:" << (float)sum_sal/count << '\n';
        else
                cout << "No employee gets more than " << amount << '\n';
        fin.close();
        fout.close();
        return 0;
}
```

UNSOLVED EXERCISES

U.24.1 Suppose that the grades.txt text file contains the grades of a number of students. Write a program that reads the file and displays the best and the worst grades, the average grade of those who failed (grade < 5) and the average grade of those who succeeded (grade ≥ 5). Suppose that the grades are within [0, 10].

U.24.2 Write a program that checks if two user selected text files have the same content.

U.24.3 Write a program that finds the sequential doubled words (e.g., "In this this chapter we present...") in a user selected text file and writes them into another text file.

U.24.4 Write a program that reads the names of two text files from the command line and appends the content of the second file into the first one. Then, the program should display the content of the first file.

U.24.5 Write a program that converts the uppercase letters of a user selected text file to lowercase letters and vice versa. *Hint*: call a file positioning function (e.g., seekp()) between successive read and write operations.

U.24.6 Suppose that each line of the students.txt text file contains the name of a student and his grades in three courses. Write a program that reads the file and displays the name of the student with the best average grade. If more than one student has the same best average, the program should display all.

U.24.7 Write a program that reads the name of a text file and copies its content in reverse order, that is, from the last character up to the first one, into a second user selected text file. *Hint*: open the first file as binary.

U.24.8 Write a program that reads the name of a text file from the command line and displays its longest line. Assume that there is no more than one line with the same longer length. The program should also display the occurrences of each digit [0, 9] in the file. Furthermore, the program should read an integer (e.g., x) and display the last x lines of the file. The program should check that the input number is not greater than the number of the total lines. For example, if the user enters 3 the program should display the last three lines of the file. There is one restriction; the program should read each line only once.

U.24.9 Define the Book structure with members: title, author, and price. Suppose that the book.dat binary file contains 100 of those structures. Write a program that reads the sequence number of a book entry (e.g., 25), the new data, and replace the existing data with the new data. Then, the program should read from the file the data of that entry and display them, in order to verify that it was written correctly.

U.24.10 Consider the file book.dat of the previous exercise. Write a program that reads the existing entries and writes them in the book_rvs.dat binary file in reverse order, that is, the last entry should be written first, the last but one written second, and so on.

U.24.11 Suppose that the grades.dat binary file contains the grades of a number of students. The number of students is stored in the beginning of the file. Write a program that reads the file and writes the grades sorted in ascending order in the grd_sort.dat binary file.

U.24.12 The Caesar algorithm is one of the oldest cipher methods used by Julius Caesar to encrypt his messages. According to this algorithm, each character is substituted by the one located in the next three places. For example, if we apply the Caesar algorithm in the English alphabet, the message "Watch out for Ovelix !!!" is encrypted as "Zdwfk rxw iru Ryhola !!!". Notice that the character 'x' is encrypted as 'a' because the substitution continues from the beginning of the alphabet. Similarly, 'y' is replaced by 'b' and 'z' by 'c'. The recipient decrypts the message by substituting each character with the one located three places before it. Write a program that provides a menu to perform the following operations:

1. File Encryption. The program should read the name of a file and the key that will be used to encrypt its content. For example, in the case of Caesar algorithm, the key is 3. The program should encrypt only the lowercase and uppercase characters.
2. File Decryption. The program should read the name of a file and the key that will be used to decrypt its content.
3. Program Termination.

U.24.13 Write a program that can be used as a book library management application. Define the `Book` structure with members: title, authors, and code. Suppose that the `test.bin` binary file exists and contains structures of that type. Write a program that provides a menu to perform the following operations:

1. Add a new book. The program should read the data of a new book and add it at the end of the file.
2. Search for a book. The program should read the title of a book and display its details. If the user enters *, the program should display the details of all books.
3. Modify a book. The program should read the title of a book and its new data and it should replace the existing data with the new one.
4. Delete a book. The program should read the title of a book and set its code equal to -1.
5. Program termination.

Namespaces, Type Cast Operators, and Smart Pointers

25

In this chapter we'll discuss about the namespaces and their most important features. Next, we'll discuss about type identification at runtime and present the operators that the language provides us in order to cast types more securely than the traditional way of the simple type cast. Then, we'll describe an alternative approach to dynamic memory management with the use of smart pointers. Finally, we'll discuss about the `volatile` qualifier.

NAMESPACES

We've discussed about the scope of program elements such as variables and functions. For example, we know that we can use the same name for local variables of different functions. What about names with global scope? Elements that are declared with a global scope, such as global variables, we say that they belong in the global namespace. However, in large programs, where the code is split in many files written by different programmers, the probability of name conflict increases. For example, we may have defined a class named `Queue` in the `queue.h` file and the same name is used in one of the libraries we use (e.g., in the `game.h` file):

```
#include "queue.h"
#include "game.h"
...
```

The compilation will fail due to the multiple definition of the `Queue` class. Of course, if we change the name of our class (e.g., to `My_Queue`) the problem is fixed. However, in the case of using libraries written by others and the same names are chosen, we cannot change them. To avoid such name conflicts, C++ provides an elegant mechanism with the use of namespaces.

A namespace is a named region with its own scope in which we can put the entities of our program (e.g., classes, functions, ...). Namespaces allows us to organize the entities of our program into logical groups and prevent collisions with names declared outside of it. For example, we can create the `Network` namespace and put classes related to network protocols and devices within it. In large applications, where many namespaces are typically used, their use becomes more valuable, because splitting the program into different logical scopes referred to by names (e.g., library for graphics, library for web services, ...) prevents name collisions and facilitates its management, comprehension, and maintenance.

Create a Namespace

To create a namespace we use the `namespace` keyword. For example:

```
namespace A
{
        int var;
        double d = 1.2;
        int f();
        struct S {...};
        class C {...};
} // No semicolon is required.
```

Inside a namespace we can declare the elements we want, such as variables, function declarations and definitions, templates, classes, and objects. The namespace is allowed to be declared in the global namespace or within another namespace, but not within a block (e.g., function). A namespace defines its own scope. The scope of each member extends from the point of its declaration to the end of the namespace. Every name declared within a namespace has the name of the namespace (e.g., A) attached to it. Thus, the names we use in a namespace do not conflict with the same names in other namespaces or in the global namespace. That is, if we create the B namespace that contains a variable named `var` and declare a global variable also named `var` there will be no name conflict between them, that is, between the A::var, B::var, and the global var. This is the main advantage of namespaces, to avoid name conflicts. In large projects involving many programmers, it is common practice to create separate namespaces so that even if the same names are chosen, they will not cause conflicts.

Inside a namespace we can add new elements using the name of the namespace. For example, the following statement extends the scope of the namespace A and adds the declaration of the `g()` function in the elements of A:

```
namespace A
{
        void g();
}
```

As another example, we can use again the A name and add the definition of `f()` later on. For example:

```
namespace A
{
        int f()
        {
                ...
        }
}
```

Alternatively, we can define it, as we define a function outside its class:

```
int A::f()
{
        ...
}
```

Since a namespace defines its own scope, its elements are not visible outside of it. One way to access them is by using the `::` scope operator. For example:

```
A::var = 10;
int i = A::f();
```

Alternatively, we can use `using` declarations and directives as we'll see next.

Names that are declared within a namespace can be accessed without using the scope operator from inside the namespace. For example:

```
namespace A
{
        int f()
        {
                d = 5;
        }
}
```

Build a Namespace

Additions to a namespace can be made to different files than the one in which it was declared. In general, it is a good practice to distinguish the declarations of the elements (e.g., functions) from their implementation, so that when someone reads a namespace may quickly get an idea about its structure and the services it provides, rather than having to search for them among pages of code. For example, in the following namespace we only add the declarations:

```
namespace Network
{
        class Protocol_A {...};
        class Protocol_B {...};
        int setup(...);
        int send_pkts(...);
        int rcv_pkts(...);
        ...
}
```

Thus, the reader may quickly get an idea about the structure and the purpose of the `Network` namespace. In fact, for more clarity, the functions that constitute the communication interface with the user of the namespace I prefer to declare them separately. For example:

```
namespace Network
{
        int setup(...);
}
```

It is common practice to place such blocks that contain only declarations in header files which are then included in the code files they need them. The code files contain the definitions of the functions. Also, for the better understanding and maintenance of the program, I prefer to split the definitions into several blocks (e.g., definitions of classes, definitions of functions) and use the same namespace many times, rather than using it a few times and place large blocks of code inside.

`using` Declarations

In order not to write the name of the namespace all the time, which can be annoying and also the code may become more illegible, especially if the name is large, a more convenient way is to use `using` declarations. A `using` declaration can be placed at global scope as in the examples of this book, within a namespace or a function, even within a statement block. Let's look at an example with the use of the same name:

```
...
int var; // Global variable.
int main()
{
        using A::var;
        using B::var; // It causes compilation error.
        var = 10; // We refer to A::var.
        ::var = 20; // We refer to the global var.

}
```

Now, when we write `var` we refer to `A::var`. Of course, for the other elements of `A` we must add the prefix `A::`. If we make another `var` available from another namespace, the compiler will display an error message for multiple declarations of `var`. If we want to access the `var` of the `B` namespace we must write `B::var`. As we saw in Chapter 11 when a local variable has the same name with a global, the local, that is, `A::var` overrides the global `var`. To refer to the global `var` we use only the `::`, since the global namespace has no name.

The name of a `using` declaration follows the usual scope rules. It is visible from the point of the `using` declaration until the end of the block that contains the declaration. Thus, when the `using` declaration is within a function, the name is only visible within that function. If we put it outside, the name is added to the global namespace. In fact, this is how we place them in the programs of this book. For example:

```
...
using std::cin;
using std::cout;
using A::var;
using A::f; // Suppose that A contains the function f(int, int).

void test();

int main()
{
        cin >> var;
        cout << var;
        ...
}

void test()
{
        var++;
        ...
}
```

In a `using` declaration we write only the name. So, when we want to add a function we only write its name (e.g., `f`). If the `A` namespace contains overloaded versions of `f()` the `using` declaration adds all the versions in the scope of the declaration. Note that if the `using` declaration adds in the same scope a function with the same name and parameter list with an existing one, the compiler will display an error message.

using **Directives**

Unlike the using declaration, a using directive makes all the elements of the namespace available. Thus, we do not need to use the :: operator. For example, we've made the whole std namespace available several times:

```
...
using namespace std;
using namespace A;
...
cin >> var; // Instead of std::cin >> A::var;
string t(vector<string>& v); /* Instead of
std::string t(std::vector<std::string>& v); */
```

Unlike using declarations, if the namespaces that the using directives add contain elements with the same names, the compiler will not display an error message, as long as these names are not used within the scope of the directives. For example, the following program is compiled normally:

```
#include <iostream> // Example 25.1

namespace A
{
        int t = 10;
        void f() {std::cout << t;}
        void g() {}
}

namespace B
{
        int t = 20;
        void f(int) {}
        void g() {}
}

double f(double) {}

using namespace A;
using namespace B;

int main()
{
        // t = 30; Compilation error.
        f(); // The A::f() is called.
        f(10); // The B::f() is called.
        f(1.2); // The global f() is called.
        // g(); Compilation error.
        return 0;
}
```

However, if we try to access a common name (e.g., t) in the same scope of the directives, the compiler will display an error message similar to *reference to t is ambiguous*. That is, if we remove the comments in the assignment of t, the program will not compile. In this case, we have to use the :: operator and the name of the namespace or replace the using directives with using declarations for the elements we want to access.

The same applies for function names. If we use multiple `using` directives that contain the same function name (e.g., `f`), its versions are added to all of its overloaded versions. If a function with the same name and parameter list is declared in the same scope with one of the functions added by a `using` directive (e.g., `g`), the compiler will not display an error message. But if we try to use the function, for example write `g()`, without specifying which one we are referring to, the compiler will issue an error message.

As with the `using` declarations, if the `using` directive is put inside a function, the names of the namespace become available only within that function. For example:

```cpp
int main()
{
        using namespace std;
        ...
}

void test()
{
        cout << "Test\n"; // Wrong, we must write std::cout.
}
```

Here is another example with the same A and B namespaces previously defined:

```cpp
int main()
{
        int t = 30;

        if(t == 30)
        {
                using namespace A;
                f();
        }
        else
        {
                using namespace B;
                f(20);
        }
        return 0;
}
```

The scope of each `using` directive is constrained in the block to which it belongs. Thus, although the A and B namespaces use common names, no conflict occurs, the program is compiled and displays 10.

If we use a `using` directive, the local name overrides the name of the namespace. For example:

```cpp
...
int var;
int main()
{
        using namespace A;

        int var = 10; // It hides the A::var.
        ::var = 20; // We refer to the global var.
        A::var = 30; // We use the :: to refer to the A::var.
}
```

Obviously, it is much easier to read and safer to choose different names. Here it is just an example; I chose the same name to show you how to access it.

To sum up, the `using` declaration makes only one name available, while the `using` directive makes all names available. As I mentioned in Chapter 1, if I don't have to add the namespace many times, I prefer to use the `::` operator. If it is many or only a few names are used from the namespace, I prefer to use separate `using` declarations, so that someone who reads the code can see what elements of the namespace are needed. If many names are used, for more convenience and simplicity in the code, I may use the `using` directive. However, if I am going to use many namespaces, I don't use it, since, if many names are made available, the possibility of name conflicts increases. And if there is no conflict now, it may happen in the future with a new version of the code that may add a common name.

Combine `using` Declarations and `using` Directives

In a namespace we are allowed to use both `using` declarations and directives. For example:

```cpp
namespace C
{
        using std::cout;
        using namespace A;

        void test() {cout << var;}
        ...
}
```

Now, if we want to access the `var` variable of A (e.g., in `test()`) we can write `var` directly since A is contained in C. For the same reason, the statement:

```cpp
using namespace C;
```

makes available all the elements of A and C.

Let's look at another example where their combination prevents conflicts.

```cpp
namespace Name_1
{
        class A {...};
        class B {...};
        ...
}

namespace Name_2
{
        class A {...};
        class B {...};
        ...
}

namespace Name_3
{
        using namespace Name_1; // Makes available all the names of Name_1.
        using namespace Name_2; // Makes available all the names of Name_2.
        using Name_1::A;
        using Name_2::B;
```

```
void f()
{
        A a; // The Name_1::A class is chosen.
        B b; // The Name_2::B class is chosen.
}
...
}
```

The `using` declaration takes precedence over the `using` directive, thus we avoid name conflicts. If the `using` declarations were missing, the compiler would display error messages for ambiguity, as it would not know which of the two classes A and B to choose.

Nested Namespaces

A namespace can be nested in another. For example:

```
void p();
namespace A
{
        int a;
        void f();
        ...
        namespace B
        {
                int b;
                void g();
                ...
        }
        ...
}
```

If we want to make available all the names of B we write: `using namespace A::B;`
Inside the namespaces, the usual scope rules apply. For example:

```
void A::f()
{
        b = 2; // Wrong, there is no b in the A namespace.
        B::b = 2; // Correct.
        B::g(); // Correct.
}

void A::B::g()
{
        f(); // Correct.
        p(); // Correct.
        a = 1; // Correct.
        b = 2; // Correct.
}

void p()
{
        B::b = 2; // Wrong.
        A::B::b = 2; // Correct.
}
```

If we want to add something in the nested namespace, the syntax is to nest the inner namespace within the outer namespace. For example:

```
namespace A
{
        namespace B
        {
                int c;
        }
}
```

If we don't do that and write only:

```
namespace B
{
        int c;
}
```

then, we define a new namespace named B and to access c, we'd write B::c.

C++17 provides an alternative more convenient and easier syntax for nested namespaces, especially as the number of inner levels grows. For example, instead of:

```
namespace A
{
        namespace B
        {
                namespace C
                {
                        int a;
                        void h();
                        ...
                }
        }
}
```

we can write:

```
namespace A::B::C
{
        int a;
        void h();
        ...
}
```

Namespace Aliases

To create a synonym for a namespace we use the = operator. For example, if we want, for convenience, to make a synonym for a long name or for a nested namespace, we write:

```
namespace long_name_for_namespace
{
        ...
}
namespace new_name = long_name_for_namespace;
using namespace new_name;
```

The use of synonyms is helpful in case there are many different implementations of the same namespace. For example, if this namespace implements a library and we want to use different versions of that library, we just change the original value of the synonym and re-compile the program.

Unnamed Namespaces

C++ allows us to skip the name and create an unnamed namespace. The elements of an unnamed namespace are visible from the point of the declaration to the end of the block which contains the declaration (e.g., end of file). If we declare it in the global space, its elements are like the global variables. Since only one unnamed namespace exists in the same file, additional unnamed namespace declarations are extensions of the first one. For example:

```
#include <iostream> // Example 25.2

namespace // Unnamed namespace.
{
        int t;
        void f();
}

namespace // Extension of the unnamed namespace.
{
        void f()
        {
                t++;
        }
}

int main()
{
        t = 10;
        f();
        std::cout << t << '\n';
        return 0;
}
```

The program displays 11. Because the namespace is not named we cannot use `using` declarations or directives to make its elements available in other files. That is, the elements of the unnamed namespace are visible only in the file where it is declared. Essentially, using an unnamed namespace is an alternative approach when we want to declare global variables or functions with internal linkage, that is, to limit their scope only within a specific file. For example, instead of writing:

```
static int t;
static void f();
```

as we did in Chapter 11, we create an unnamed namespace and put these declarations inside there.

```
namespace
{
        int t;
        void f();
        ...
}
```

The linkage of all names declared in an unnamed namespace is internal, that is, they cannot be accessed from another file. The use of `static` declarations for locality comes from C. C++ recommends the use of unnamed namespaces in their place. Because the scope is limited within the file, we can use the same names in another file without fear of creating conflicts. If, for example, we write in a second file:

```
// Second file.
int t;
void f();
```

there will be no conflict between the two t variables. Each t is different and accessible only in its own file. The same happens if we declare these names in another unnamed namespace. The unnamed namespaces in the two files are independent of each other. The names declared in each namespace are local to each file. To sum up, an unnamed namespace ensures the locality of the code and thus we avoid the possibility of name conflicts in different files.

EXERCISES

C.25.1 Find the errors in the following program:

```
#include <iostream>

namespace A
{
        int n;
        void f();
        class C
        {
        public:
                int k;
                int get();
        };
}

namespace A
{
        int C::get()
        {
                cin >> k;
                return k;
        }
}

void f()
{
        n++;
}

int main()
{
        C c;
        using A::n;
        int n;

        n = c.get();
        return 0;
}
```

Answer: Many errors, let's see them. The first is in the definition of `get()`, where `cin` is not declared. So, we write `std::cin`. Because the definition of `f()` is not contained in the namespace, the compiler will display an error message for an undeclared variable `n`. To fix this, we add the declaration inside the A namespace or we write `A::f()` to define it. In `main()`, because n has become available with the `using` declaration, the next re-declaration of n causes a compilation error. Finally, the creation of the c object is not possible, because the C class is not available. To fix this we can add before its declaration the statement `using A::C;` or write `A::C c;`.

C.25.2 Create the A namespace with the `add()` and `sub()` functions, which take two integer parameters and return their sum and difference, respectively. The declaration of the namespace should be put in a header file and the definitions of both functions in a code file. Write a program that reads two numbers, calls the functions, and displays their return values. There is a restriction not to use `using` declarations or directives.

```cpp
// Header file (e.g., code.h)
namespace A
{
        int add(int a, int b);
        int sub(int a, int b);
}


// Code file
#include <iostream>
#include "code.h"

namespace A // Add definitions.
{
        int add(int a, int b)
        {
                return a+b;
        }
        int sub(int a, int b)
        {
                return a-b;
        }
}

int main()
{
        int a, b;

        std::cin >> a >> b;
        std::cout << A::add(a, b) << ' ' << A::sub(a, b) << '\n';
        return 0;
}
```

C.25.3 Create the `Metric` namespace, which contains the `Time` class with private members the `hrs`, `mins`, and `secs`. The class should contain:

    a. a constructor that takes three integer parameters and if their values are valid it assigns them to the corresponding members. Otherwise, it should throw an exception of the `Bad_Value` type that you define.

    b. an overloaded function of the `==` operator, which checks if two `Time` objects have the same values.

    c. a friend `operator<<` function, which takes as parameter an output stream of the `ostream` type (e.g., `out`) and a `Time` object and displays the values of its members in the `out`.

The declaration of the namespace should be done in a header file and the definitions of the functions in a code file. Write a program that checks the operation of the class.

```cpp
// Header file (e.g., metric.h)
#include <iostream>
#include <string>
using std::ostream;
using std::string;


namespace Metric
{
        class Bad_Value
        {
                private:
                        string msg;
                public:
                        Bad_Value(const char *m);
                        void show() const;
        };
        class Time
        {
                private:
                        int hrs, mins, secs;
                public:
                        Time(int h, int m, int s);
                        bool operator==(const Time& t) const;
                        friend ostream& operator<<(ostream& out, const Time& t);
        };
}


// Code file.
#include "metric.h"


namespace Metric
{
        Bad_Value::Bad_Value(const char *m)
        {
                msg = m;
        }
        void Bad_Value::show() const
        {
                std::cout << msg;
        }
}


namespace Metric
{
        Time::Time(int h, int m, int s)
        {
                if(h < 0 || h > 24)
                        throw Bad_Value("Wrong hours\n");
                if(m < 0 || m > 59)
                        throw Bad_Value("Wrong minutes\n");
                if(s < 0 || s > 59)
                        throw Bad_Value("Wrong seconds\n");
```

```
                if(h == 24)
                {
                        if((m != 0) || (s != 0))
                                throw Bad_Value("Wrong time\n");
                }
                hrs = h;
                mins = m;
                secs = s;
        }
        bool Time::operator==(const Time& t) const
        {
                return ((hrs == t.hrs) && (mins == t.mins) && (secs == t.secs));
        }
}

namespace Metric
{
        ostream& operator<<(ostream& out, const Time& t)
        {
                out << "H:" << t.hrs << " M:" << t.mins << " S:" << t.secs;
                return out;
        }
}

int main()
{
        using Metric::Bad_Value;
        using Metric::Time;

        try
        {
                Time t1(1, 2, 3), t2(4, 5, 6);

                std::cout << (t1 == t2) << '\n';
                std::cout << t1;
        }
        catch(const Bad_Value& err)
        {
                err.show();
        }
        return 0;
}
```

RUNTIME TYPE IDENTIFICATION

C++ allows us to determine the type of an object during program execution. To enable type identification at runtime, C++ provides the `dynamic_cast` operator, the `typeid` operator, and the `type_info` structure. Let's describe their basic characteristics.

The `dynamic_cast` Operator

The `dynamic_cast` operator is typically used in a hierarchy of classes and allows us to check if the cast of one type to another is valid. Before we discuss about it, let's look at some examples of type conversions with derived classes, such as the ones we saw in Chapter 20. Suppose that we have the following class hierarchy:

```
class A {...};
class B : public A {...};
class C : public B {...};
```

Now, let's declare the following pointers and make type casts with the traditional way:

```
B *b = new B;
A *a = (A*)b; /* The type cast is safe (as we know we can write directly A
*a = b). */
C *c = (C*)b; // The type cast is not safe.
```

Are the above type casts safe? In the general case of type casts, depending on the class declarations, all may be safe, but those that are guaranteed to be safe are when the pointer being casted points to a derived object. Thus, the first type cast is safe. And it is safe because a B object contains an A sub-object. In fact, as we know from Chapter 20, the casting is not needed. The second is not safe, because the pointer to a base class object (e.g., b) is casted to a pointer to a derived object (e.g., c). Since a B object does not contain a C sub-object it is logical not to be safe, because a c object may contain members that do not exist in b.

As we know, an easy way to find out if a type cast is safe is to check the relationship of the type of the object on the right with the cast type. For example, the first cast is safe because a B object is also an A object, while the second is not safe because a B object is not a C object.

So, we see that although the second cast is not safe, the compiler allows it. This is the main reason why C++ introduces operators for type casts. To set some discipline rules when performing casts so that they are applied with more safety. That is, is there a way to make such type casts and check if they are done safely? Yes, with the help of the `dynamic_cast` operator. The `dynamic_cast` operator only applies to pointers and references to polymorphic classes, that is, there must be at least one virtual function (declared or inherited) in the class to which the pointer points or the reference refers. It takes two operands, a pointer (or reference) to a class type inside <> and the pointer (or reference) to be casted inside (). The types we are casting must be pointers or references to classes within the same class hierarchy. Let's see an example of its syntax with pointer:

```
dynamic_cast<Type*>(p);
```

p is the pointer to be casted. `Type` is the destination type to which p should be cast. The purpose of the `dynamic_cast` is to ensure that the result of the type casting points to a valid object of the target type (e.g., `Type`). If the type conversion is successful, the operator returns a `Type*` pointer. If it fails, it returns a null pointer. If p is the null pointer, the operator returns a null pointer. As we said, this type cast is done at runtime, not at compile time. In fact, the word `dynamic` implies the runtime behaviour. The `dynamic_cast` operator is primarily used to safely downcast, that is, to cast a base class pointer (or reference) to a derived class pointer (or reference). It can also be used for upcasting, that is, to cast a derived class pointer (or reference) to a base class pointer (or reference). Let's look at an example of its use with the type casts we saw earlier:

```
#include <iostream> // Example 25.3

class A
{
public:
        virtual void show() const {std::cout << "A\n";}
};
```

```cpp
class B : public A
{
public:
        virtual void show() const override {std::cout << "B\n";}
};

class C : public B
{
public:
        virtual void show() const override {std::cout << "C\n";}
};

int main()
{
        B *b = new B;

        A *a = dynamic_cast<A*>(b); // Safe cast.
        if(a)
        {
                a->show();
                std::cout << a << ' ' << b << '\n';
        }
        C *c = dynamic_cast<C*>(b); // Not safe cast.
        if(c)
                c->show();
        else
                std::cout << "Error\n";

        delete b;
        return 0;
}
```

The first cast is safe and the `dynamic_cast` operator returns a non-null pointer. Because `show()` is virtual and the a pointer points to an object of the B class, the program displays B. Then, since the a and b pointers point to the same address, the program displays the same value twice. Because the second cast is not safe, the operator returns a null pointer and the program displays `Error`.

As we said, we can apply `dynamic_cast` to a reference. Because in case of failure the notion of null reference does not exist to be returned, the operator throws an exception of type `bad_cast`. This exception is derived from the `exception` class and it is declared in the `typeinfo` file. For example:

```cpp
#include <iostream> // Example 25.4
#include <typeinfo>
int main()
{
        B b;
        B &br = b;

        try
        {
                C &c = dynamic_cast<C&>(br); // Not safe cast.
        }
        catch(std::bad_cast&)
        {
                std::cout << "bad_cast exception is caught\n";
        }
        return 0;
}
```

Because the cast is not safe, the bad_cast exception is thrown, which is captured by the respective catch block.

The typeid Operator

The typeid operator is used to determine the type of an object. It returns a reference to a type_info object which, as its name suggests, holds information about the type of the passed argument. The type_ info class is declared in the typeinfo file. In its usual use, typeid takes as a parameter the name of a class or an expression that is evaluated to an object. If it is a type (e.g., int) the returned value represents the type. If it is an expression that identifies a polymorphic class (a class with at least one virtual function), the returned value represents the dynamic type of the expression. Otherwise, if the expression identifies a non-polymorphic class, the returned value represents the static type of the expression. The type_info class overloads the == and ! = operators so that they can be used to compare types. For example, let's use the previously defined A, B, and C classes:

```
#include <iostream> // Example 25.5
#include <typeinfo>
int main()
{
        B *p = new C;
        C c;
        A& r = c;

        try
        {
                if(typeid(C) == typeid(*p)) /* Compare with the type of the
object that p points to. */
                {
                        p->show();
                        std::cout << typeid(*p).name() << '\n';
                }
                if(typeid(C) == typeid(r)) /* Compare with the type of the
object that r refers to. */
                        r.show();
        }
        catch(std::bad_typeid&)
        {
                std::cout << "bad_typeid exception is caught\n";
        }
        delete p;
        return 0;
}
```

Since the C class is polymorphic, the first if condition checks the type of the object that p points to. Since it points to an object of the C class, the condition is true and the program displays C. Because the C class is polymorphic the type of *p is evaluated at runtime. If p is a null pointer, the typeid(*p) throws the bad_typeid exception. This exception is derived from the exception class and it is declared in the typeinfo file. Also, the type_info class contains the name() function, which returns a C style string that refers to the name of the type and can be used for diagnostic purposes. This string depends on the implementation and it usually contains the name of the class. For example, with the compiler I used the program displays Class C. Then, because the C class is polymorphic the second if condition is true and because show() is virtual the program displays C.

Note that if we make the `show()` non-virtual in classes A and B, the C class is no longer polymorphic, and the `typeid` returns the static type (known at compile time) of the expression. Therefore, the `if` conditions are false and the program displays nothing. In particular, the `typeid(*p)` returns the type of the B class, since this is the static type of *p. Similarly, the `typeid(r)` returns the type of the A class, since this is the static type of r. Note that if p is a null pointer, the operator does not create the `bad_typeid` exception, since it does not need to be a valid pointer to evaluate the type of *p.

Type identification should only be used when necessary. For example, suppose that we have a hierarchy of A, B, and C classes and we want to perform some operations depending on the type of the object to which the reference refers:

```cpp
void f(A& a)
{
        if(typeid(a) == typeid(A))
        {
                . . .
        }
        else if(typeid(a) == typeid(B))
        {
                . . .
        }
        else if(typeid(a) == typeid(C))
        {
                . . .
        }
}
```

Because type identification may involve runtime overhead, this code is not so efficient. Besides that, it is not flexible since every time the class hierarchy changes (e.g., with the addition of a new class) we have to change the `if` clauses. Is there an alternative approach? Of course, we already know it. When our code depends on the type of the object a pointer points to or a reference refers to, the most flexible and efficient approach is to use virtual functions.

As an example of where type identification might be useful consider a class hierarchy where we want to overload the == operator to compare objects. Two objects are the same if they have the same type and the same values in their members. It makes sense for the overload function to take as parameters two references to the base class, so that derived objects can be passed safely. For example:

```cpp
bool operator==(const Base& a, const Base& b)
{
        if(typeid(a) == typeid(b)) // First, compare the types.
        {
                // Then, compare the values of their members.
        }
}
```

TYPE CAST OPERATORS

C++ provides operators that we can use to make type casts with more safety. For example, we saw the `dynamic_cast` operator. The other operators are the `const_cast`, `static_cast`, and `reinterpret_cast`. All of them are processed at compile time. Besides more safety, a second reason for using them is the easy detection of type casts within the program. We just make a search with their name and find them right away. On the contrary, in the traditional way we cannot make such a search. We've to search the code line by line. Next, I'll describe them in brief.

The `const_cast` Operator

The `const_cast` operator is used to add or remove the `const` or `volatile` attribute from a variable. `const_cast` is used with pointers and reference. Its syntax is similar to that of the `dynamic_cast`:

```
const_cast<type_name>(expression);
```

The `type_name` and `expression` should be of the same type, except for the `const` and `volatile` qualifiers. That is, the `const_cast` cannot change the underlying type (e.g., from `const int*` to `double*`). The returned type is that of `type_name`. Typically, it is used to remove the constness of the passed argument. Let's see an example of how it is used:

```
#include <iostream> // Example 25.6
int main()
{
        int *p1, i = 10;

        const int *p2 = &i;
//      It is not allowed to write *p2 = 20.
        p1 = const_cast<int*>(p2);
        *p1 = 20;
        std::cout << i << '\n';
        return 0;
}
```

Suppose that we want to change the value of `i` through a pointer. Since we cannot use `p2` to do that, we use another pointer variable. The use of the `const_cast` operator removes the `const` attribute, thus the `p1` pointer can change the value of `i`. Note that this is still impossible for `p2`. So, the program displays `20`. Of course, we could make the type cast in the traditional way instead of using `const_cast`:

```
p1 = (int*)p2;
```

In another case though, we can accidentally write:

```
double *p3 = (double*)p2;
```

where the compiler will not display an error message to notify us for this unintended action. Had we used the `const_cast` operator instead, that is:

```
double *p3 = const_cast<double*>(p2);
```

the compiler would display an error message because the type of `p2` is not `double*`. Therefore, using `const_cast` is safer than the simple type cast.

Another case where the `const_cast` operator might be useful is if you want to pass a constant argument to a function implemented by someone else (e.g., in a library) and this function takes a non-constant argument. For example:

```
void f(int *p)
{
}
```

Since we cannot change the prototype of `f()` and change the type of p to `const` in order to pass the p2 pointer, we use the `const_cast` operator and pass the p1 pointer. Of course, now `f()` can change the value of *p, and therefore of i.

Before ending the section, notice that you should not use it to change a `const` value. For example:

```
const int i = 10;
int *p = const_cast<int*>(&i);
*p = 20; // The behavior is undefined.
```

The attempt to change the `const` value causes the undefined behaviour of the program.

In the same sense, although you can use `const_cast` to remove the constness of a `const` object you should not do that. If an object is designed to be `const`, it means that it is not expected to be modified. If, for some reason, you have to do it, pay extra attention not to violate the `const` nature of the object, otherwise, you may insert hard to trace bugs.

The `static_cast` Operator

This type of cast is the simplest type. Typically, the `static_cast` operator is used to cast one type to another related type. For example, one pointer type to another in a class hierarchy or a numeric type (e.g., integer) to another (e.g., float). It has the same syntax as the other operators:

```
static_cast<type_name>(expression);
```

The type of the `expression` will be converted to the `type_name`. The operator can be used to convert pointers to related classes, such as to convert a derived class pointer to a base class pointer (*upcast*) and the opposite, that is, to convert a base class pointer to a derived class pointer (*downcast*). For example:

```
class A {...};
class B : public A {...};

A *a1 = new A;
B *b1 = static_cast<B*>(a1); // Not safe.
B *b2 = new B;
A *a2 = static_cast<A*>(b2); // Safe.
```

Let's see the not safe use. As we know, since an A object is not B, the downcast is not safe. However, `static_cast` does not fail, so the programmer is not informed about this risky situation. Recall that in case of the `dynamic_cast` operator, the value of b1 would be the null pointer. Therefore, although `dynamic_cast` adds an overhead due to runtime type checks, whereas `static_cast` does not since it is applied at compile time, the use of `dynamic_cast` is safer because the runtime checks it does protect us from unsafe type casts like this one.

In another example, if we add a third class unrelated to A and B and write:

```
class C {};
C *c = static_cast<C*>(a1);
```

the compiler will display an error message. Note that if we make this unsafe cast in the traditional way, that is:

```
C *c = (C*)a1;
```

the compiler would allow that.

Typically, the static_cast operator is used for numeric conversions. For example:

```
#include <iostream> // Example 25.7
int main()
{
        char c;
        int i = 97, j;
        double d = 3.9;

        c = static_cast<char>(i); // int to char.
        j = static_cast<int>(d); // double to int.
        std::cout << c << ' ' << j << '\n';
        return 0;
}
```

The program displays a and 3.

Also, a common use of static_cast is to cast a void* pointer to the type we want. For example:

```
int i;
void *p1 = &i;
int* p2 = static_cast<int*>(p1); // void* to int*.
```

The reinterpret_cast Operator

The reinterpret_cast operator is typically used to perform casts to unrelated types. It has the same syntax as the other operators:

```
reinterpret_cast<type_name>(expression);
```

It can be used to cast any pointer type to any other pointer type. It also allows the conversion of an integer type to any pointer type and vice versa. For example:

```
int *p = reinterpret_cast<int*>(0xffcc);
```

In the traditional way, this conversion is done as follows:

```
int *p = (int*)(0xffcc);
```

In general, conversions made with this operator are potentially unsafe and should be avoided. That is, it allows you to convert a float to string*, but this can lead to dangerous situations. It is the responsibility of the programmer to ensure that the conversion will not cause problems. For example, dereferencing that pointer may cause a program crash. Similarly, it is not safe to convert a pointer to a class to a pointer to another unrelated class and then use that pointer. But, if, for some reason, you decide to take the risk and make such a conversion, it'd be preferable for the better control of the program to use the `reinterpret_cast` operator, and not the traditional way, so that with a simple search of its name you can quickly identify these dangerous type casts.

SMART POINTERS

A smart pointer is an object that facilitates the management of dynamically allocated memory. It behaves like an ordinary pointer with the difference that it can release the memory that it manages by itself. Thus, we don't have to worry about not to forget to release the allocated memory and create memory leaks. It will be released automatically when no longer is needed. For example, with ordinary pointers the following code may create a memory leak:

```
void f()
{
        int *p = new int[100000];
        ...
        if(error_occurs)
                throw exception();
        ...
        delete[] p;
}
```

If an error occurs, the exception will be created and the memory will not be released, that is, we have a memory leak. Okay, one might say, let's add the `delete[]` and release the memory before throwing the exception. Yes, but it may be needed to do the same in several other places. For example, before each `return` statement which may exist in the ... part of the code or in `catch` blocks that handle thrown exceptions. Believe me, it is not so hard to forget adding the `delete[]` or even worse write `delete` instead of `delete[]`.

Fine, do we have another alternative besides to "remember" to release the memory, that is, is there a way to ensure that the memory will be released even if we forget to do so? Yes, by using smart pointers. If the p pointer were an object and had a destructor, the destructor could release the memory when the object was destroyed. This is the idea behind the smart pointers; to use an object to manage the memory in order to prevent memory leaks. Essentially, a smart pointer is an object of a standard template class which releases the allocated memory when it is destroyed. Thus, we don't have to remember to release the memory; the smart pointer will do it for us. The definitions of the classes are included in the `memory` header file. C++11 introduces the `unique_ptr`, `shared_ptr`, and `weak_ptr` types. We'll describe them in brief.

The `unique_ptr` Type

C++98 supports the `auto_ptr` type. C++11 deprecated its use and introduced the `unique_ptr` type instead. Let's see an example:

```
#include <iostream> // Example 25.8
#include <exception>
#include <memory>
using namespace std;
```

```cpp
class C
{
public:
        double v;
        ~C() {cout << "End\n";}
};

double f(double a, int b);

int main()
{
        double i;
        int j;

        cout << "Enter two numbers: ";
        cin >> i >> j;
        try
        {
                cout << f(i, j) << '\n';
        }
        catch(exception& e)
        {
                cout << e.what() << '\n';
        }
        return 0;
}

double f(double a, int b)
{
        unique_ptr<C> p(new C);
        // Alternatively, unique_ptr<C> p(make_unique<C>());
        if(b == 0)
                throw exception();
        p->v = a/b;
        return (*p).v;
}
```

To create a unique_ptr object we use the usual template syntax. As we've said, smart pointers are template classes. We put in <> the type that the smart pointer points to. When we create a smart pointer we can initialize it with the pointer that the new operator returns. If b is 0, f() creates an exception. The unique_ptr overloads the * and -> operators, so that we can use it as an ordinary pointer. Notice that there is no delete to release the memory. The allocated memory will be released when the p object is destroyed. This happens when p goes out of scope, that is, when the function is terminated, either due to the exception or not. That is, the unique_ptr ensures that the memory will be released even if there is a forced exit from the block. Then, p is destroyed and its destructor will release the memory. Thus, the destructor of C is called and the program displays End in both cases, whether the exception is thrown or not.

C++14 introduces the std::make_unique<>() function template to create a unique_ptr object. In fact, its use is recommended over the new operator. The arguments of the make_unique<T>(...) are the same with the ones used in the new T(...) form. To make easier the syntax we can use the auto identifier. For example:

```cpp
auto p(make_unique<C>());
```

The unique_ptr type supports exclusive ownership, that is, only one unique_ptr pointer can manage the allocated memory. In fact, the word unique implies its role. The memory is released when the unique_ptr object is destroyed. Because a unique_ptr object is the only owner of the memory it cannot be copied. In particular, it does not provide a copy constructor or the copy assignment function. However, as we'll see later, it is allowed to transfer the ownership from one `unique_ptr` object to another. For example:

```
auto p1(make_unique<int>(10));
std::cout << *p1; // It outputs 10.
unique_ptr<int> p2; // unique_ptr that can point to an integer.
unique_ptr<int> p3(p1); // Compilation error.
p2 = p1; // Compilation error.
```

The attempt to copy the object causes a compilation error. The same happens when it is passed by value to a function. For example:

```
int main()
{
        . . .
        unique_ptr<double> p1;
        g(p1);
}

void g(unique_ptr<double> p2)
{
        . . .
}
```

When `g()` is called, because p1 is passed by value, the attempt to make a copy causes a compilation error. How is it fixed? By passing a reference so that no copy is made. For example, what does the following program display?

```
#include <iostream> // Example 25.9
#include <memory>
using namespace std;

void g(unique_ptr<double>& p2);

int main()
{
        auto p1(make_unique<double>(1.2));
        g(p1);
        cout << *p1 << '\n';
        return 0;
}

void g(unique_ptr<double>& p2)
{
        cout << *p2 << '\n';
        *p2 = 3.4;
}
```

The program displays 1.2 and 3.4. Note that there is an exception to the rule that a `unique_ptr` object cannot be copied. We can copy a `unique_ptr` object that is going to be destroyed. For example, the compiler allows the assignment of a `unique_ptr` object returned from a function to another object:

```
#include <iostream> // Example 25.10
#include <memory>
using namespace std;
```

```
unique_ptr<double> f();

int main()
{
        auto p1 = f();
        cout << *p1 << '\n';
        return 0;
}

unique_ptr<double> f()
{
        auto p2(make_unique<double>());
        *p2 = 1.2;
        return p2; /* We could avoid the declaration of p2 and write directly:
return make_unique<double>(1.2); */
}
```

When f() returns, the p1 object takes ownership of the memory that p2 originally owned. And it is logical for the compiler to allow this action, because it knows that p2, since it is a local variable, it will be destroyed, so there will not be two objects pointing to the same memory. The memory will be released when p1 is destroyed. The program displays 1.2.

Let's change f() to return an ordinary pointer and compare the two approaches:

```
void g()
{
        double* p1;
        p1 = f();
        // If we forget to make delete p1; we have a memory leak.
}

double* f()
{
        double* p2 = new double;
        *p2 = 1.2;
        return p2;
}
```

g() is responsible to release the memory allocated in f(). If we forget to release it we have a memory leak. In particular, when f() terminates p1 will be destroyed, but the memory it points to will not be released. And if we change g() to return p1, then the memory should be released by the function that will call g(), and so on. With the use of unique_ptr we don't need to worry about the release of the memory, since the memory will be released when the object that owns it is destroyed.

As we said, we cannot copy a unique_ptr object to another. However, if we want to transfer the ownership to another unique_ptr object and use the object again to point to another location, we can do that by using the move() function. For example:

```
int main()
{
        unique_ptr<double> p1, p2;
        auto p3(make_unique<double>());

        *p3 = 3.4;
        p1 = f();
        p2 = move(p1); /* We use move() to transfer the ownership from p1 to p2.
As we said, if we write p2 = p1; we'll have a compilation error. */
```

```
        p1 = move(p3);  // We transfer the ownership of p3 to p1.
        // cout << *p3 << '\n'; Wrong action.
        cout << *p1 << ' ' << *p2 << '\n';
        return 0;
}
```

The program displays 3.4 and 1.2. Notice that when the ownership is transferred it is the responsibility of the programmer not to use the pointer (e.g., p3) to access the memory originally owned, otherwise a problem will occur in the execution of the program.

Let's see another example of using `unique_ptr` to manage memory allocated for many elements. We'll compare its use with an ordinary pointer:

```
class T
{
private:
        int *p;
public:
        T(int num) {p = new int[num];}
        ~T() {delete[] p;}
};

int main()
{
        T t(100);
        ...
}
```

When using an ordinary pointer (e.g., p) we should not forget to release the memory, otherwise we'll have a memory leak. Also, we should be careful to write `delete[]` and not `delete`. However, if we use a `unique_ptr` object instead, we don't need to worry about such issues. Specifically, we change the class to:

```
class T
{
private:
        unique_ptr<int[]> p;
public:
        T(int num) : p(new int[num]) {} // Older syntax.
        T(int num) : p(make_unique<int[]>(num)) {} // C++14 syntax.
};
```

In the declaration of the `unique_ptr` we put in <> the data type with a pair of empty []. As with an ordinary pointer, to manage the elements, we can use the index notation (e.g., p[0] = 10;). When t is destroyed the p object will also be destroyed. In particular, when p is destroyed, `delete[]` will be called to release the memory. We don't have to do it; the smart pointer will do it for us. Indeed, its use simplifies things and prevents memory leaks.

Of course, never forget the use of `vector<T>` as an alternative. In this example, we could use a `vector` object, which is much more powerful and flexible than using a plain pointer or a `unique_ptr` object.

Note that the `unique_ptr<>` class contains several functions to facilitate the management of the object. I won't describe them, I think that it is enough what you've learned to get an idea. For more information you may consult a reference manual for the standard library.

The `shared_ptr` Type

Similar to `unique_ptr`, to create a `shared_ptr` object we put inside `<>` the type that the pointer will point to. For example:

```
shared_ptr<int> p1;
shared_ptr<vector<int>> p2; // p2 can point to a vector of integers.
shared_ptr<string> p3(new string("test"));
cout << *p3; // This code outputs test.
```

The `shared_ptr` type is used when we want to share the ownership of the memory among several `shared_ptr` objects. That is, many `shared_ptr` objects can manage the same memory. In fact, the word shared implies its role. For example:

```
#include <iostream> // Example 25.11
#include <memory>
using std::shared_ptr;
using std::cout;

int main()
{
        shared_ptr<int> p1(new int);
        shared_ptr<int> p2;
        shared_ptr<int> p3(new int[10]);

        *p1 = 10;
        p2 = p1;
        *p2 = 20;
        p3[0] = 100; // Indexing is supported since C++17.
        cout << *p1 << '\n';
        return 0;
}
```

With the statement p2 = p1, the p1 and p2 objects manage the same memory. Therefore, the program outputs 20.

How the `shared_ptr` works? It has a reference counter which is increased by one each time a `shared_ptr` object points to the same memory. For example, the counter increases when a `shared_ptr` object is used to initialize a new one (e.g., `shared_ptr<int> p4(p1);`) or when used in an assignment (e.g., `p4 = p1;`). It also increases when passed to a function by value. For example:

```
void f()
{
        shared_ptr<int> p(new int);
        g(p);
        ...
}

void g(shared_ptr<int> sp)
{
        ...
}
```

Because the parameter is passed by value the counter becomes 2. When `g()` terminates, the local variable `sp` is destroyed and the counter becomes 1.

When a new value is assigned to the `shared_ptr` pointer or the `shared_ptr` is destroyed (e.g., goes out of scope), the counter decreases by one. When it becomes zero, that is, when the last `shared_ptr` object is destroyed, then the memory it points to is released. For example:

```
shared_ptr<string> p(new string);
shared_ptr<string> q(new string);
p = q; /* Now that p points to a different memory location, the reference
counter for the memory it initially pointed to becomes 0 and that memory is
released. Also, the counter for the memory that q points to increases, since
now p and q point to the same memory. */
```

Note that if we write something similar with ordinary pointers, the original memory won't be released. For example:

```
string *p = new string;
string *q = new string;
p = q; /* The memory that p initially pointed to is not released, that is, we
have a memory leak. */
```

If we want to allocate and initialize memory in one step we can use the `make_shared<T>()` function. In fact, it is recommended for more efficiency. It is defined in the `memory` file and returns a `shared_ptr`, which points to the memory that was allocated. For example:

```
shared_ptr<string> p1 = make_shared<string>("text");
cout << *p1; // It displays text.
shared_ptr<int> p2 = make_shared<int>(10);
int i = *p2; // i becomes 10.
```

When we call `make_shared<T>()` we have to specify in `<>` the type for which memory will be allocated. The argument in `()` is the initialization value. For example, for `p1`, we pass an argument that match one of the `string` constructors. To make easier to write the declaration we can use the `auto` identifier. For example:

```
auto p1 = make_shared<string>("text");
```

To sum up, the important advantage of using smart pointers is that the programmer does not have to remember to release the memory or worry about memory leaks. As for the choice, when we need multiple smart pointers to share the ownership of the same memory we use the `shared_ptr` type, while if we want its exclusive ownership with a single pointer we use the `unique_ptr` type.

The `weak_ptr` Type

The `weak_ptr` is a smart pointer that can refer to a memory managed by a `shared_ptr` object. The association of a `weak_ptr` to a `shared_ptr` does not increase the reference counter. That is, when the last `shared_ptr` object is destroyed, the memory it points to will be released, no matter any associated `weak_ptr` objects. In fact, the word `weak` implies that this pointer is weak in the sense that it does not control the lifetime of the allocated memory, that is, it is not a strong pointer as the `shared_ptr` or the `unique_ptr`. When this pointer could be used? With `weak_ptr` we can first check if the memory it points to is valid, that is, if it still can be managed, and then access it. Let's see an example:

```
#include <iostream> // Example 25.12
#include <memory>
using namespace std;
```

```
int main()
{
        auto sp = make_shared<int>(10);
        weak_ptr<int> wp(sp); /* The reference counter for the allocated
memory is not increased. */

        shared_ptr<int> ptr = wp.lock(); /* Alternatively, we could write:
auto ptr = wp.lock(); ptr and sp point to the same memory. */
        if(ptr)
                cout << *ptr << '\n';
        else
                cout << "Not valid memory\n";
        return 0;
}
```

When `wp` is declared it is initialized with `sp`. That is, `wp` and `sp` point to the same memory allocated for the integer. As we said, the reference counter for this memory does not increase, it remains 1. The direct memory access through `wp` is not allowed. We should first use the `lock()`, which returns a `shared_ptr` object. If the memory pointed by the `weak_ptr` has not been released, the object (e.g., `ptr`) has a valid value and we can safely use it to access the memory. Otherwise, `lock()` returns an empty `shared_ptr` object. That is, with `weak_ptr` and `lock()` we first check if the memory can still be managed and then access it. Thus, the program displays 10. In general, `weak_ptr` is used in advanced cases.

THE `volatile` QUALIFIER

The `volatile` qualifier is rarely used. Typically, it is used in code that communicates with the hardware of the system. It is used to inform the compiler that the value of a variable may change, even if it does not appear to change within the program. In fact, it prevents the compiler from performing optimizations which may be undesirable. Let's look at an example:

```
int out = 0;
while(out != 200)
{
        ... // The value of out does not change from inside the program.
}
```

The condition checks if the value of `out` is other than 200. Because the value of `out` seems to remain the same, an optimizing compiler might replace this loop with an infinite loop, such as `while(1)`. However, if `out` can be modified by a "hidden" entity, such as the system hardware, this optimization would affect the behaviour of the program. To prevent the compiler from optimizing the code we use the `volatile` qualifier in its declaration, that is, `volatile int out;`.

Introduction to Standard Template Library

26

In this chapter we'll make a brief introduction to Standard Template Library (STL) and its most important features. The STL is part of the C++ standard library; it was designed by *Alex Stepanov* and contains a large collection of standard algorithms, iterators, containers, and function objects. All these have been designed in a uniform way based on the principles of generic programming. The classes and algorithms it provides can be used in a wide range of applications and saves us from a lot of work. However, a full description of STL would require a separate book. The next challenge for you is to find a book that focuses on STL and read about it. It is very useful to know the tools it offers; it will make your work simpler, safer, and more flexible. The goal of this chapter is to give you an idea about its features and its design philosophy. We'll briefly discuss about the most important STL components: algorithms, iterators, and containers.

ALGORITHMS

STL provides a great number of algorithms that can be applied to containers. Most of them are declared in the `<algorithm>` file. The design philosophy is to provide a generic way to operate on the data stored in any container, irrespective of how they are stored or the type of the container. For that reason, the STL algorithms have been implemented as function templates in order to operate in a simple, elegant, and generic way, which does not depend on the container to be applied. For example, the same `find()` function can be used to find a value in a `vector` or `set` container or find a value in a `vector` that contains integers and in another that contains `string` elements.

The STL approach is that these functions are not defined as members of the containers, but externally. That is, instead of a separate `find()` for each container, a single non-member `find()` is defined which can be used by all containers. As we'll see later, to accomplish that, STL algorithms use iterators to traverse the container. This practice does not increase the complexity of each container, and also the repetition of similar code is avoided. However, there are cases where the STL defines a function in a container that performs the same task as a non-member function. The reason is that a member function for a particular container may be more efficient than the generic function. In general, whenever a container provides a member function that is functionally equivalent to a generic function, it'd be better to use the former.

When we discuss about iterators, which are generalizations of pointers, we'll see that the STL functions, besides the containers, can also be applied to non-STL containers, such as ordinary arrays. In general, the first two arguments of most functions are iterators that indicate the range of the elements to which the function will be applied. Let's look briefly at some of them.

DOI: 10.1201/9781003230076-26

The `for_each()` Function

The `for_each()` function works with any container. It takes three parameters. The first is an input itera-tor which denotes the initial position (e.g., `first`), the second is an input iterator which denotes the final position without including it (e.g., `last`), and the third is a pointer to a function or, as we'll see next, a function object. The function should take a single parameter of the same type as the type of the container. `for_each()` applies the function in which the pointer points to each of the elements of the container in the specified range, that is, in `[first, last)`. Let's look at an example of its use:

```cpp
#include <iostream> // Example 26.1
#include <vector>
#include <algorithm>

void show(int k);

int main()
{
        std::vector<int> v(3, 30); /* Create a vector of three integers
initialized to 30. */
        v[0] = 20;
        v[1] = 10;
        for_each(v.begin(), v.end(), show);
        return 0;
}

void show(int k)
{
        std::cout << k << '\n';
}
```

Each container provides the `begin()` function, which returns an iterator that points to its first element, and the `end()` function, which returns an iterator that points to the next position after its last element. Recall from Chapter 8 that the name of a function (e.g., `show()`) can be used as a pointer to its address. With `for_each()` the `show()` is called three times, one for each element of the `v` container. Therefore, the program displays 20, 10, and 30. Essentially, `for_each()` works similar to a `for` loop. For example, we could replace it with the following code:

```cpp
vector<int>::iterator it;
for(it = v.begin(); it != v.end(); ++it)
        show(*it);
```

and to make easier the declaration of `it` we can use the `auto` word:

```cpp
for(auto it = v.begin(); it != v.end(); ++it)
        show(*it);
```

The type of the argument in `show()` is the type of the elements in the container. For example, if `v` contains structures of type `Student` the `show()` is declared as:

```cpp
void show(const Student& st);
```

with `const`, so that `show()` cannot change its members.

Let's make a parenthesis here and answer the question of Chapter 6, why some programmers prefer the syntax:

```cpp
for(i = 0; i != 10; ++i)
```

instead of the most common syntax: `for(i = 0; i < 10; i++)`

All the containers of the STL library have iterators which support the != operator. However, some containers may not support comparisons by means of the < operator. In this case, the compilation will fail. And why ++i;. This was answered in Chapter 18, for better performance, in order to avoid the creation of a copy of the object. Thus, these programmers prefer a common syntax for all cases rather than to change it when iterators are to be used.

The find() Function

The find() function works with each container and it is used to search for a value in a container. It takes three parameters. The first two are input iterators (e.g., first, last) that indicate the search range, which is [first, last]. The third is the value to be searched. If the value is found, find() returns an iterator that points to the position of its first occurrence. If not, it returns the value of the second argument (e.g., last). Because, as we'll see next, a pointer also works as an iterator, let's look at an example of its use with an array and a container:

```
#include <iostream>  // Example 26.2
#include <vector>
#include <algorithm>
using namespace std;

int main()
{
        int *p, arr[] = {10, 20, 30, 40, 50};

        p = find(arr, arr+5, 30);
        if(p != arr+5)
                cout << "Element " << *p << " found in position " <<
p-arr+1 << '\n';
        else
                cout << "Element not found\n";

        vector<int> v(arr, arr+5); /* Create a vector with the array elements. */
        vector<int>::iterator it;
        it = find(v.begin(), v.end(), 30);
        if(it != v.end())
                cout << "Element " << *it << " found in position " << it-v.
begin()+1 << '\n';
        else
                cout << "Element not found\n";
        return 0;
}
```

To give you an idea about how find() may be defined in STL, here is an implementation example:

```
template <typename Iterator, typename T>
Iterator find(Iterator start, Iterator end, const T& val)
{
        for(Iterator p = start; p != end; ++p)
                if(*p == val)
                        return p;
        return end;
}
```

In the first call of find() the Iterator type is replaced with int*, while in the second call with the iterator member of the vector class.

The `sort()` Function

The `sort()` function works with containers that contain random access iterators. There are two versions. The first takes two parameters, which are random access iterators (e.g., `first`, `last`) that indicate the sort range, which is [`first`, `last`). `sort()` sorts the elements of basic types in ascending order using the `<` operator. For example, if in C.26.1 we add before `for_each()` the statement:

```
sort(v.begin(), v.end());
```

`sort()` sorts the elements in ascending order and the program displays 10, 20, and 30.

If the elements of the container are user defined types, then the `operator<()` must be defined for that type in order for `sort()` to work. For example, in the following program the `v` container contains structures of the `Student` type:

```
#include <iostream>  // Example 26.3
#include <string>
#include <vector>
#include <algorithm>

struct Student
{
        int code;
        std::string name;
        float grd;
};

bool operator<(const Student& s1, const Student& s2);

int main()
{
        int i;
        Student s[3] = {{10, "C", 3.5}, {20, "A", 2.5}, {30, "B", 4.5}};
        std::vector<Student> v;

        for(i = 0; i < 3; i++)
                v.push_back(s[i]);

        sort(v.begin(), v.end());
        for(i = 0; i < v.size(); i++)
                std::cout << v[i].code << ' ' << v[i].name << ' ' << v[i].grd
<< '\n';
        return 0;
}

bool operator<(const Student& s1, const Student& s2)
{
        if(s1.grd < s2.grd) /* If we want to sort in descending order, one way
is to write if(s2.grd < s1.grd). */
                return true;
        else
                return false;
}
```

The sort() sorts the structures in ascending order according to the grade of each student and the program displays their data.

But what if we want to have multiple ways of sorting and, say, let the user to decide? In this case we use the second version of sort(). This version takes three parameters, where the first two are the same as the first version and the third is a pointer to the function to be used (or a function object), instead of the operator<(), to make the comparison. Its return value must be convertible to bool, with the value true to indicate that the elements are in the right order. For example, let's change the previous program:

```
int main()
{
        . . .
        int sel;
        cout << "Enter sort type (0: grade_order): ";
        cin >> sel;
        if(sel == 0)
                sort(v.begin(), v.end());
        else
                sort(v.begin(), v.end(), name_order);
        . . .
}

bool name_order(const Student& s1, const Student& s2)
{
        if(s1.name < s2.name)
                return true;
        else
                return false;
}
```

Now, if the user does not enter 0, name_order() compares the name members and sorts the structures in alphabetical order.

The count_if() Function

Some STL functions have a second version which applies a function to each element of the container. This second version typically ends with _if. For example, count() and count_if(). The first two parameters of count_if() are input iterators (e.g., first, last) that indicate the range, which is [first, last). The third is a pointer to a function (or a function object), which is applied to each element in [first, last). The return value must be convertible to bool, with the value true to indicate that the element must be counted. count_if() returns the total number of elements for which the function returns a true value. In general, the _if versions are used when we are interested in finding values that meet some criteria. Let's look at an example of its use:

```
#include <iostream> // Example 26.4
#include <vector>
#include <string>
#include <algorithm>
using namespace std;

bool islong(const string& s);
```

```
int main()
{
        vector<string> v = {"First", "Second", "Third"};

        int i = count_if(v.begin(), v.end(), islong);
        cout << i << '\n';
        return 0;
}

bool islong(const string& s)
{
        return (s.size() > 5) ?  true : false;
}
```

islong() accepts one argument whose type is that of the element. It is called three times, for each of the three string objects contained in v. Because only one string has more than five characters, the program displays 1. Note that if we want to compare the size of the string with another value (e.g., 10) we'd have to write another function or define a variable (e.g., size) that we'd change accordingly. Both approaches are not flexible. What we really need is to pass the size as a kind of argument in islong(). We'll see later how we can do that with the function objects.

ITERATORS

An iterator is an object or a simple pointer that points to the elements of the container. The iterator can be used to move through the contents of the container. With iterators we can access the elements of different containers in the same way independent of the stored data types. Thus, the same STL algorithms can be applied to different containers in a uniform way. For example, suppose that we search for a value in a vector<int> object:

```
vector<int> vec;
...
for(i = 0; i < vec.size(); i++)
        if(vec[i] == val) // We search for val.
...
```

Suppose now that we search for a value in a list<int> object, which is a linked list of integers:

```
list<int> lst;
...
for(i = 0; i < lst.size(); i++)
        if(lst[i] == val) // It is not allowed to write lst[i].
...
```

Although it makes sense to use index notation again, we are not allowed to do this because the list container does not provide an overload function of [].

However, with iterators we can write the search code in the same way for both containers. The use of iterators is similar to pointers. For example, suppose that the name of the object (vector or list) is c. In the case of vector<int> we write:

```
vector<int>::iterator it;
for(it = c.begin(); it != c.end(); ++it)
        if(*it == val)
```

While, in the case of `list<int>` we write:

```
list<int>::iterator it;
for(it = c.begin(); it != c.end(); ++it)
        if(*it == val)
```

The only change in the code is the declaration of the iterator, depending on the type of the container. We use the `auto` word and the search code becomes the same:

```
for(auto it = c.begin(); it != c.end(); ++it)
        if(*it == val)
```

That is, by using iterators we can traverse different containers in the same way (e.g., `++it`) and access their elements in the same way (e.g., `*it`), independently of their type and regardless if they reside in consecutive memory locations (e.g., `vector`) or in random places (e.g., `list`).

This is the philosophy of STL, that is, it introduces the concept of iterators and uses them, so that the implementation of each function is done in a generic way, which does not depend on the type of the container. Essentially, the iterators are the link between the containers and the algorithms. Thus, we can have only one `for_each()` for all the containers and not a separate version for each container. As we saw in the previous section, when we call an STL function we pass as arguments iterators of the particular container. For example, the prototype of `find()` is similar to:

```
template<typename InputIterator, typename T>
InputIterator find(InputIterator first, InputIterator last, const T& value);
```

As we'll see later, this prototype indicates that `find()` returns and takes input iterators (or better) as arguments. As we said, the code of an STL function does not depend on the type of the container (e.g., `vector`, `list`, ...), it works the same for each container that is allowed to call it. For example, the code of `find()` is similar to the previous `for` loop and it can be used to find a value in any container. To summarize, passing iterators to an STL function makes it more generic, because the function will work for any container, and this is the philosophy of the STL approach.

Of course, in order to call the STL function, each container should declare an iterator type appropriate to the class. For example, the `vector<int>` class has iterators of type `vector<int>::iterator`. For one class, the iterator may be a simple pointer, while for another it may be an object.

Regardless of the implementation of the iterator, the important thing is that the iterator supports the functions required to access the elements of the container, such as the `*` and `++` operators. Also, if we have two iterators (e.g., p and q) that point to elements of the same container, functions such as assignment (e.g., p = q) and comparison (e.g., p == q) are supported. In addition, each container provides the `begin()` function, which returns an iterator to its first element, and the `end()` which returns an iterator to the next position after its last element. Note that although a pointer is a form of iterator, the reverse is not true, that is, an iterator does not necessarily operate like a pointer. You'll understand why in the next section where you'll see different types of iterators.

Different algorithms may have different requirements for iterators. For example, a search algorithm requires the iterator to support the `++` operator so that it can traverse the elements of the container. It also needs access for reading the values of the elements but not for writing them. That is, if `it` is the iterator it is not necessary to allow a write operation such as `*it = 5`. On the other hand, a sorting algorithm (e.g., `sort()`) requires the iterator to support, besides the `++` operator, the `+` operator for random access to the elements of the container, so that the algorithm can swap any elements. That is, if `it` is the iterator it should be allowed to write `it+5`. Also, this algorithm requires that the iterator can be used for both reading and writing data. So, because there are different requirements in the design of iterators, STL defines different types of iterators. This is the topic of the next section.

TYPES OF ITERATORS

The STL defines five types of iterators and describes each algorithm according to the iterator it needs. Each type has its own properties and supports specific operations. These types are the input, output, forward, bidirectional, and the random access iterator. For example, in the description of `find()` we saw that it takes as arguments two input iterators. All iterators can be dereferenced with the `*` operator and compared with the `==` and `!=` operators. These five types create a form of hierarchy, where each type, with the exception of the output iterator, supports the properties of the previous one and adds its own features. Let's briefly look at their characteristics.

Input Iterator

With an input iterator we can read the values of the container elements sequentially. However, we cannot change their values. For example, if `it` is the iterator we can make the comparison `*it == 2`, but not the assignment `*it = 2`. Therefore, an algorithm that uses an input iterator, such as `find()`, can only read and not change the values of a container. The input iterator supports both forms of the `++` operator (postfix/prefix), that is, `++it` or `it++`, for traversing the elements. The traversing of the container is done only in the forward direction, that is, the iterator does not support the `--` operator to move backwards.

Output Iterator

An output iterator is considered to be the complementary of an input iterator. That is, with an output iterator we can change the values of the container elements, but we cannot read them. For example, if `it` is the iterator we can write `*it = 2`, but we cannot make the comparison `*it == 2`. Therefore, it can be used by an algorithm that requires only to write and not to read values.

Forward Iterator

A forward iterator is considered to be the combination of an input and output iterator. That is, with a forward iterator we can read and change the values of the container elements. Like input and output iterators, a forward iterator uses the `++` operator to traverse the container. As with them, we can move only in the forward direction, one element at a time.

Bidirectional Iterator

With a bidirectional iterator we can read and change the values of the container elements in both directions. It has the same properties with the forward iterator and adds support for both forms of the `--` operator (postfix/prefix) to access the elements in the backward direction. For example, if `it` is the iterator we can write `--it` or `it--`.

Random Access Iterators

Some algorithms, such as the sort algorithm, require the ability to access the elements of the container in a random manner. A random access iterator supports all the properties of a bidirectional iterator and adds features to support random access. Thus, a random access iterator is the most powerful iterator in terms of functionality. For example, if it is the iterator we are allowed to write it+5, it[2] or it -= 3. Essentially, a random access iterator works similar to a pointer. That is, an ordinary pointer meets all the requirements of a random access iterator, and therefore of all iterators.

 An ordinary pointer meets the requirements of any iterator.

Someone might wonder, why do we have these five types? The idea is that, when writing an algorithm, to use the iterator that satisfies its needs. For example, find() does not need to use a random access iterator, but an input iterator. Thus, all containers that contain iterators with the same or higher capabilities than the input iterator can use find(). However, sort() that requires a random access iterator can only be used by containers that support this type of iterator.

Regarding the implementation, an iterator can be represented by a class or an ordinary pointer. For example, a forward iterator can be implemented as an object that accesses sequentially the elements of the container. An STL algorithm works with any iterator implementation that satisfies its requirements. To learn which algorithms a container can use we need to know which kind of iterators it supports. For example, if we read the description of vector we'll see that it supports random access iterators. Therefore, this container can use STL algorithms that work with any type of iterator, since a random access iterator supports the properties of all iterators. Similarly, if we see that some other container supports bidirectional iterators, we understand that this container cannot use algorithms that require random access iterators.

STL ALGORITHMS AND POINTERS

As we've said, iterators are generalization of pointers, while a pointer meets all the requirements of iterators. Therefore, since a pointer is an iterator and the STL algorithms work with iterators, we can apply the STL algorithms to non-STL containers that are based on pointers. For example, we can apply STL algorithms to ordinary arrays. Suppose we want to sort an array of 100 integers (e.g., int a[100]). As we've seen, sort() takes as arguments two random access iterators that specify the sort range. Since a pointer is an iterator we can use pointers as arguments. Thus, the following statement sorts the array in ascending order:

```
sort(arr, arr+100);
```

Another useful STL function is the copy(). It takes as parameters three iterators and it is used to copy the elements of one container to another. The first two parameters are input iterators (e.g., first, last) that indicate the copy range, which is [first, last). The third is an output iterator that indicates the initial position where the data will be copied. The programmer should have ensured that the destination memory is large enough to store the copied data. Since we can use a pointer as an argument we can copy data from or to an array. Let's see an example:

```
int a[] = {10, 20, 30, 40, 50};
vector<int> v(7, 60);
copy(a, a+3, v.begin()+2);
```

This code copies the values of a[0], a[1], and a[2] to the three positions of the vector starting from the v[2] element. Thus, the content of v becomes: 60 60 10 20 30 60 60

PREDEFINED ITERATORS

STL provides some types of predefined iterators, which are declared in the `iterator` file. Their main purpose is to expand the generality of the STL algorithms. In this section we'll briefly present some of them. For example, STL provides the `ostream_iterator`, which is an output iterator that can be used to write data in an output stream. Typically, the `ostream_iterator` and `istream_iterator` are provided as arguments to algorithms. For example:

```cpp
#include <iostream> // Example 26.5
#include <iterator>
int main()
{
        int a[] = {10, 20, 30, 40, 50};
        std::ostream_iterator<int, char> out_it(std::cout, " ");

        copy(a, a+5, out_it);
        return 0;
}
```

The first template argument (e.g., `int`) indicates the type of data to be written to the output stream. The second (e.g., `char`) indicates the character type that the output stream handles. In the constructor of the iterator, the first argument (e.g., `cout`) indicates the output stream. The second indicates the separator between the values (e.g., a space). The program displays the values of the array with a space between them. Note that instead of a named iterator (e.g., `out_it`), we could create an anonymous iterator like this:

```cpp
copy(a, a+5, ostream_iterator<int, char>(cout, " "));
```

Similarly, there is the `istream_iterator`, which is an input iterator that can be used to read data from an input stream. For example:

```cpp
#include <iostream> // Example 26.6
#include <vector>
#include <iterator>
using namespace std;

int main()
{
        vector<int> v(5);

        cout << "Enter 5 integers and then a character: ";
        copy(istream_iterator<int, char>(cin), istream_iterator<int, char>(),
v.begin());
        copy(v.begin(), v.end(), ostream_iterator<int, char>(cout, " "));
        return 0;
}
```

The first template argument (e.g., `int`) indicates the type of data to be read from the input stream. The second (e.g., `char`) indicates the character type used by the input stream. The argument of the constructor (e.g., `cin`) indicates the input stream. If the argument is missing, it corresponds to an iterator that indicates either that there is no other data to read or that a read error occurred. In our example, these two iterators are used to determine the copy range in `copy()`. That is, copying occurs until the end of the input data is met or some other reading error occurs. Thus, when the user enters five integers, the program reads them, stores them in the vector, and when it encounters the character that the user enters (e.g., b) it stops reading since a type incompatibility read error occurred. Then, it displays the contents of the vector.

Another iterator is the `reverse_iterator`, which can be used to display the elements of a container in reverse order, from its end to the beginning. For example, the `vector` class contains the `rbegin()` function which returns a reverse iterator that points to the last element and the `rend()` which returns a reverse iterator that points to the position right before the first element. For example:

```cpp
#include <iostream> // Example 26.7
#include <vector>
#include <algorithm>
using std::cout;
using std::vector;

void show(int k);

int main()
{
        vector<int> v = {1, 2, 3, 4, 5};

        cout << "Reverse order: ";
        for_each(v.rbegin(), v.rend(), show);

        cout << "\nReverse order - again: ";
        vector<int>::reverse_iterator it;
        for(it = v.rbegin(); it != v.rend(); ++it)
                cout << *it << ' ';
        return 0;
}

void show(int k)
{
        cout << k << ' ';
}
```

The first approach uses `for_each()` to display the data in reverse order, while the second approach uses a reverse iterator (e.g., `it`). Note that increasing the reverse iterator (e.g., `++it`) it actually makes it decrement.

When using a copy function, such as `copy()`, we may want to add new elements to the container rather than overwrite existing ones. The three insert iterators `back_insert_iterator`, `front_insert_iterator`, and `insert_iterator` provide this ability. Their type is output iterator.

The `back_insert_iterator` can be used with containers which support insertion of elements at the end. For example, the `vector` container qualifies, since it provides the `push_back()` function. The `front_insert_iterator` can be used with containers which support insertion of elements at the beginning. For example, the `list` container qualifies, since it provides the `push_front()` function. The `insert_iterator` is more general as it can be used with containers which support insertion of elements. That is, it can be used to insert data at any position; the container just needs to support the insert operation. To create the `back_insert_iterator` and `front_insert_iterator` iterators, the template parameter is the data type of the container and the argument of the constructor is the particular container. The `insert_iterator` takes an additional argument in the constructor, which indicates the insert position. Let's look at the following program:

```cpp
#include <iostream> // Example 26.8
#include <vector>
#include <deque>
#include <iterator>
```

```
#include <algorithm>
using namespace std;

void show(int k);

int main()
{
        vector<int> v1(2, 10), v2(3, 20), v3(2, 30);
        deque<int> q1(2, 10), q2(3, 20);

        back_insert_iterator<vector<int>> back_it(v1);
        copy(v2.begin(), v2.end(), back_it);
        cout << "Back iterator: ";
        for_each(v1.begin(), v1.end(), show);

        insert_iterator<vector<int>> ins_it(v1, v1.begin()+2);
        copy(v3.begin(), v3.end(), ins_it);
        cout << "\nInsert iterator: ";
        for_each(v1.begin(), v1.end(), show);

        front_insert_iterator<deque<int>> front_it(q1);
        copy(q2.begin(), q2.end(), front_it);
        cout << "\nFront iterator: ";
        for_each(q1.begin(), q1.end(), show);
        return 0;
}

void show(int k)
{
        cout << k << ' ';
}
```

The first copy() adds the elements of v2 to the end of the vector referenced by the back_it iterator, that is, to v1. The second copy() adds the elements of v3 to the position of the vector indicated by the ins_it iterator, that is, to the third element of v1. Check in the program output that the size of v1 increases dynamically to fit the new data. The third copy() adds the elements of q2 to the beginning of the queue referenced by the front_it iterator, that is, to q1. Finally, the program displays:

```
Back iterator: 10 10 20 20 20
Insert iterator: 10 10 30 30 20 20 20
Front iterator: 20 20 20 10 10
```

Concluding with the predefined iterators we see that their use extends the generality of STL algorithms. For example, copy() can be used not only to copy data from one container to another, but also from one container to an output stream, from an input stream to a container, or even to insert data into a container.

CONTAINERS

A container is a class that stores a collection of objects, which are its elements. Each container manages the storage space for its elements and provides member functions to access them. They are implemented as template classes, which provide a great flexibility in the type of the elements to be stored. The elements can be objects or basic data types. For example, vector<Student> and vector<int>. In general, the decision about which type of container to use in an application does not depend only on the needs of the application, but also on the performance of the operations offered by the container. For example, the `vector` container provides fast access to its elements, but not for an insert operation since the elements after the insert position should be moved in order to make room for the new elements. The containers are divided into three main categories, the sequence containers, container adaptors, and the associative containers.

Sequence Containers

Sequence containers contain objects of the same type that are stored sequentially. The sequential order remains the same, that is, every time the container is traversed the order of the stored objects does not change. Because the layout remains the same, operations such as inserting data at a specific position and deleting data are possible. The `vector`, `deque`, `list` template classes are examples of sequence containers. C++11 added the `array` and `forward_list` classes. We've already seen the `vector` class. The template class `deque` (*double-ended queue*) supports efficient addition/deletion of elements at its beginning and end. The `array` is an easy to use and safer alternative compared to the ordinary array. Like the array, the `array` is of constant length specified at compile time, that is, its dynamic resizing is not allowed. The `forward_list` implements a singly linked list. All these containers, except the `array`, support the addition/deletion of elements at runtime, thus the size of the allocated memory changes dynamically.

The decision about which sequence container to use depends on the requirements of the application. For example, if the application requires insertion/deletion of elements only at the beginning or end, the best option is `deque`. If the application requires more often random access to the elements than insertion/deletion of elements, the best option is `vector`. In general, the `vector` class is typically the better choice; you need a good reason to choose another. Let's have a quick view of `list`.

The list template class

The `list` template class implements a doubly linked list. Each element in the list, except the first and last, is linked to the previous and next element so that the list can be traversed in both directions. Unlike `vector`, `list` does not allow random access to data, but only sequential. That is, we cannot use array notation and write something like `lst[i]`, where `lst` is an object. Comparing the two classes, the advantage of `vector` is that it provides fast access to any element, while `list` provides fast insertion/deletion of elements. For example, to access the tenth element of a `list` we have to visit all the previous elements through the pointer members until we reach it. In contrast, in `vector`, because the elements are stored in contiguous memory locations, access is very fast. On the other hand, the advantage of `list` is that the cost of inserting/deleting an element in any position is of constant time, we just change the values of the respective pointers. In contrast, in `vector`, those operations take more time since the elements should be rearranged. For example, the insertion of a new element requires all the elements after the insertion point to be moved one position at right to make room for the new element.

The iterators that the `list` supports are bidirectionals. Thus, if `it` is an iterator of the list we are not allowed to write `it+5`. To use the `list` we must include the `list` header file. Let's see an example:

```
#include <iostream> // Example 26.9
#include <list>
#include <algorithm>
using namespace std;

void show(int k);

int main()
{
        int arr[5] = {2, 3, 2, 1, 3};
        list<int> lst(3, 1); // List of three integers with value 1.
```

```
        /* If we want to declare an iterator variable we'd write
list<int>::iterator it; For simplicity, we use the auto word. */
        lst.insert(lst.begin(), arr, arr+5);
        cout << "List after insert: ";
        for(auto it = lst.begin(); it != lst.end(); ++it)
                cout << *it << ' ';
        /* We can also use a for-range loop.
        for(const auto& it: lst)
                cout << it << ' '; */

        lst.remove(2);
        cout << "\nList after remove: ";
        for_each(lst.begin(), lst.end(), show);
        lst.unique();
        cout << "\nList after unique: ";
        for_each(lst.begin(), lst.end(), show);

        lst.pop_front();
        lst.push_back(6);
        lst.push_back(5);
        lst.push_front(7);
        lst.sort();
        cout << "\nList after sorting: ";
        for_each(lst.begin(), lst.end(), show);
        return 0;
}

void show(int k)
{
        cout << k << ' ';
}
```

`insert()` inserts elements in the position indicated by the iterator. `remove()` removes all the elements that are equal to the argument. `unique()` removes all duplicate consecutive elements. It keeps only the first element in each group of the same elements. `pop_front()` removes the first element of the list. `push_front()` adds the element at the beginning of the list, while `push_back()` adds it at the end, after its last current element. `sort()` sorts the list. If we use `sort()` first and then `unique()` each element appears only once. The program uses two ways to display the list elements, with iterator and `for_each()`. Finally, the program displays:

```
List after insert: 2  3  2  1  3  1  1  1
List after remove: 3  1  3  1  1  1
List after unique: 3  1  3  1
List after sorting: 1  1  3  5  6  7
```

Note that because the non-member `sort()` we saw earlier requires random access iterators, we cannot use it. So, we use the `sort()` member of the `list`.

Container Adaptors

Container adaptors are implemented on top of other containers and adapt their functionality to their own requirements. A container adaptor provides a limited set of the services of the encapsulated container, tailored to a specific use. For example, the `stack` container, although by default is based on `deque`, it allows the insertion and deletion of elements only at the top of the stack. They have no iterators and do not support access with index notation. The standard container adaptors are the `queue`, `priority_queue`, and `stack` template classes. Let's see them briefly.

The queue template class

The `queue` template class implements a FIFO (*First In First Out*) queue, where elements are inserted into the end of the container and extracted from its front. The implementation supports the basic functionality of a queue. Thus, we can add an element at the end of the queue, remove the first element, find the values of the first and last element, check if the queue is empty, and find the number of the stored elements. Random access to its elements is not supported nor can we traverse the queue. To use `queue` we must include the queue header file. Let's look at an example:

```cpp
#include <iostream> // Example 26.10
#include <queue>
int main()
{
        std::queue<int> q;

        q.push(1);
        q.push(2);
        q.push(3);
        std::cout << "Front: " << q.front();
        std::cout << " End: " << q.back();
        q.pop();
        std::cout << " Size: " << q.size();
        return 0;
}
```

`push()` adds the element at the end of the queue. `front()` returns the value of the first element and `back()` returns the value of the last one. `pop()` removes the first element and `size()` returns the number of the elements in the queue. Therefore, the program displays: `Front: 1 End: 3 Size: 2`

The priority_queue template class

The `priority_queue` template class is similar to `queue`. Their main difference is that in `priority_queue` the elements are sorted according to some priority. The default priority is based on comparing elements using the `<` operator. Therefore, the element stored at the front of the queue is the largest. For example:

```cpp
priority_queue<int> q;
q.push(20);
q.push(10);
q.push(30);
int i = q.top();
```

`top()` returns the first element of the queue, which is `30`. If we want to change the ordering, we add the desired method as the third argument. The second argument indicates the type of the underlying container used to store the elements. For example, if we write:

```cpp
priority_queue<int, vector<int>, greater<int>> q;
```

the sorting will be done in descending order. Thus, the first element will be `10`. We'll discuss later about the `greater<>`.

The stack template class

The `stack` template class implements a LIFO (*Last In First Out*) stack, where elements are inserted and extracted only from one end of the container. The implementation supports the basic functionality of a stack. Thus, we can add an element at the top of the stack, remove the element from the top, find the value of the element at the top, check if the stack is empty, and find the number of the stored elements. Random access to its elements is not supported nor can we traverse the stack. To use the `stack` we must include the `stack` header file. Let's look at an example:

```
#include <iostream> // Example 26.11
#include <stack>
int main()
{
        std::stack<int> s;

        s.push(10);
        s.push(20);
        s.push(30);
        std::cout << "Top: " << s.top();
        s.pop();
        std::cout << " Size: " << s.size();
        return 0;
}
```

`push()` adds the element at the top of the stack. `top()` returns the value of the top element. `pop()` removes the top element and `size()` returns the number of the elements in the stack. Therefore, the program displays: `Top: 30 Size: 2`

Associative Containers

Associative containers associate each element with a key and use the key to find the element in the container. That is, associative containers are designed to find and access its elements by their key, as opposed to sequence containers which are designed to find and access its elements by their position. For example, suppose that each element is a structure which represents a student with members such as name, code, grade, address, contact information, and so on. The key could be the student's code which is unique. The container uses that key to store and locate each element. When we add elements we cannot specify the position in which they will be inserted, because the container applies an algorithm to determine the insert position. The usual way of implementing an associative container is in the form of a binary search tree. The container provides fast access to its elements.

STL provides the `set`, `multiset`, `map`, and `multimap` containers, which store the elements in order. The first two are defined in the `set` file and the other two in the `map` file. In the `set` container the value of each element is identical to its key and each key is unique, while the `multiset` container may contain elements with the same key. In the `map` container the key of each element is associated with mapped data. Each key is unique, while the `multimap` container may contain elements with the same key. STL also provides the `unordered_set`, `unordered_multiset`, `unordered_map`, and `unordered_multimap` containers, which do not store its elements in order. These containers are useful in applications where the elements do not need to be stored in some order. Let's look at two examples with the `set` and `map` containers.

The set template class

The `set` container contains elements, where the value of each element is also the key to identify it. It is useful in applications where we just want to check quickly whether a given value is contained in the container. The values (keys) of the elements are unique in the `set`, that is, each element can appear at most once. The elements are sorted in key order. By default, the container uses the < operator to sort the elements in ascending order; however, we can specify our own comparison method. Typically, the implementation of the `set` container is based on some balanced tree data structure. Searching for an element or inserting a new element execute very fast. The value of an element cannot be modified, it can only be removed. The class supports bidirectional iterators. Let's look at an example:

```
#include <iostream> // Example 26.12
#include <string>
#include <set>
#include <algorithm>
using namespace std;

void show(const string& s);

int main()
{
        set<string> s = {"car", "the", "get", "sea", "sky", "the"};
        set<string>::iterator it;

        cout << "Set after init: ";
        for(it = s.begin(); it != s.end(); ++it)
               cout << *it << ' ';

        s.insert("new");
        cout << "\nSet after insert: ";
        for_each(s.begin(), s.end(), show);

        it = s.find("sky");
        s.erase(it);
        cout << "\nSet after erase: ";
        for_each(s.begin(), s.end(), show);
        return 0;
}

void show(const string& s)
{
        cout << s << ' ';
}
```

When we create a `set` object we specify the type of the key it contains (e.g., `string`). `insert()` inserts the argument into the container. `find()` returns an iterator that points to the position where the argument is stored, if found. `erase()` removes the element indicated by the iterator. Therefore, the program displays:

```
Set after init: car   get   sea   sky   the
Set after insert: car   get   new sea   sky   the
Set after erase: car   get   new sea   the
```

As you see, although `the` appears twice in the list, it is stored only once in the container, since each key must be unique. Also, the output confirms that the elements are stored in ascending order.

The map template class

After `vector`, `map` is probably the second most useful container. The `map` container contains elements that are formed in a combination of a key value and the associated mapped data. It is useful in applications where a key value (e.g., student code) is associated with a set of information (e.g., student data). Given a key value, we can quickly store or retrieve the associated information. Like the `set` container, each element in a map is uniquely identified by its key value, the keys are unique, and the elements are sorted in key order. Also, its implementation is based on some kind of balanced tree. When we create a map object we specify the type of key and the type of data it contains. For example, the declaration:

```
map<int, string> m;
```

creates a map object where the key type is `int` and the data type is `string`. A third argument can be added to indicate the sorting method to be used. The default ordering is ascending. The map class uses the `pair<class K, class T>` template class to group together the key and the data. In particular, if key_type is the key type and `data_type` is the type of the stored data, the type of the combined information is pair<key_type, data_type>. For example, the m object contains pairs of type pair<int, string>. To insert elements into a map object, one method is to create a `pair` object and use the `insert()` function. For example:

```
pair<int, string> p(50, "one"); // The value of the key is 50.
m.insert(p);
```

or create an anonymous `pair` object and write directly:

```
m.insert(pair<int, string> (50, "one"));
```

or, much easier, use the overloaded `[]` operator that takes the key value as an argument and write:

```
m[50] = "one";
```

To access the data of a `pair` object we can use the `first` and second members. For example:

```
pair<int, string> p(50, "one");
cout << p.first << ' ' << p.second;
```

Let's see an example of using the map container:

```
#include <iostream> // Example 26.13
#include <string>
#include <map>
using namespace std;

int main()
{
        map<int, string> m;
        map<int, string>::iterator it;

        m[50] = "one";
        m[40] = "two";
        m[30] = "three";
        m[20] = "four";

        it = m.find(40); /* We could declare here the it iterator and write
        auto it = m.find(40); */
        if(it != m.end())
                cout << "Find: " << it->first << ' ' << it->second << '\n';
```

```
        else
                cout << "Not found\n";

        m.erase(30);
        cout << "Map after erase: ";
        for(it = m.begin(); it != m.end(); ++it)
                cout << it->first << ' ' << it->second << ' ';
        /* Alternatively, we could write:
        for(const auto& item : m)
                cout << item.first << ' ' << item.second << ' ';
         */
        return 0;
}
```

`find()` returns an iterator that points to the position where the key argument is stored, if found. `erase()` removes the element that has the same key value as the argument, if found. Therefore, the program displays:

```
Find: 40   two
Map after erase: 20   four   40 two   50   one
```

Some more examples

In most of the examples we've seen so far we have used basic types (e.g., integers) for a simple demonstration of STL capabilities. However, STL is used a lot to store and manage class objects. For example, let's use the `set` container to create a simple database of students, sorted by grade:

```
#include <iostream> // Example 26.14
#include <string>
#include <set>
#include <algorithm>
using namespace std;

class Student
{
private:
        int code;
        string name;
        float grd;
public:
        Student(int c, string n, float g) : code(c), name(n), grd(g) {}
        Student() : code(0), name("None"), grd(0) {}
        friend bool operator<(const Student& s1, const Student& s2);
        void show() const {cout << "C:" << code << " N:" << name << " G:" <<
grd << '\n';}
};

void display(const Student& s);

int main()
{
        set<Student> s;

        s.insert(Student(200, "two", 3.5));
        s.insert(Student(100, "one", 2.5));
```

```
        s.insert(Student(300, "three", 4.5));
        for_each(s.begin(), s.end(), display);
        return 0;
}

bool operator<(const Student& s1, const Student& s2)
{
        if(s1.grd < s2.grd)
                return true;
        else
                return false;
}

void display(const Student& s)
{
        s.show();
}
```

The program outputs:

```
C:100    N:one     G:2.5
C:200    N:two     G:3.5
C:300    N:three   G:4.5
```

As a second example, let's use the same Student class and the map container to create a simple database of students, where the search key is the student's code:

```
int main()
{
        map<int, Student, greater<int>> m; /* The sorting is done in code
descending order. */
        map<int, Student, greater<int>>::iterator it;

        m[100] = Student(100, "one", 3.5);
        m[200] = Student(200, "two", 4.5);
        m[300] = Student(300, "three", 2.5);

        it = m.find(500);
        if(it != m.end())
                (it->second).show();
        else
                cout << "Not found\n";
        for(it = m.begin(); it != m.end(); ++it)
                (*it).second.show(); // Alternative way, with.  instead of ->
        return 0;
}
```

The program outputs:

```
Not  found
C:300    N:three   G:2.5
C:200    N:two     G:4.5
C:100    N:one     G:3.5
```

FUNCTION OBJECTS

A function object or else functor is an object to which the () call syntax can be applied, similar to a function. To allow this syntax, the class must overload the () call operator by defining the `operator()` function. Let's look at an example:

```
class T
{
        private:
                int a;
        public:
                int operator()(int v) {a=v; return a;}
};

int main()
{
        T t;
        int i = t(20); // i becomes 20.
        ...
}
```

Although `t` is an object, we can "call" the object, as if it were a function. Because such an object behaves like a function it is called a function object. The expression `t(20)` causes the call of the `operator()` function, which returns an integer value. The equivalent expression is `t.operator()(20)`. According to the overloading constraints we saw in Chapter 18, the overload function must be a class member. A class can define many such versions, which should be distinguished by the type or number of its parameters. Note that the list of parameters is added after the empty `()`.

Function objects are often used as arguments in STL algorithms. For example, the third argument of `for_each()`, besides a pointer to a function, can be a functor. And when the use of such an object might be useful? In example C.26.1, `show()` can accept only one argument that represents the value of the element. However, in some applications, we may want to pass more arguments to the function. In such a case, we can pass an object and use its members to provide this additional information to the function. For example, let's change C.26.1 so that not all values are displayed but only those that are less than a certain value.

```
#include <iostream> // Example 26.15
#include <vector>
#include <string>
#include <algorithm>
using namespace std;

template<typename T> class Filter
{
        private:
                T lim;
        public:
                Filter(const T& t) : lim(t) {}
                void operator()(const T& t) const {if(t < lim) cout <<
t << ' ';}
};
```

```
void show(int k);

int main()
{
        vector<int> v = {5, 3, 8, 12, 1};

        cout << "Show all: ";
        for_each(v.begin(), v.end(), show);
        cout << "\nShow less than 6: ";
        for_each(v.begin(), v.end(), Filter<int>(6));
        cout << "\nShow less than 3: ";
        for_each(v.begin(), v.end(), Filter<int>(3));

        vector<string> s{"one", "two", "three"};
        cout << "\nShow less strings: ";
        for_each(s.begin(), s.end(), Filter<string>("test"));
        return 0;
}

void show(int k)
{
        cout << k << ' ';
}
```

show() just displays all the values. When for_each() is called with an object as argument, first the constructor of the class is called and lim becomes equal to the value of the argument, and then operator() displays the values of the elements that are less than lim. That is, operator() is called for each element in the specified range. Thus, we can use for_each() with objects of different values (e.g., 6 and 3). See also that we use the same functor to compare strings. We do not need to create another class. Therefore, the program displays:

```
Show all: 5   3   8 12   1
Show less than 6: 5   3   1
Show less than 3: 1
Show less strings: one
```

This example also demonstrates that using a function object instead of a plain function pointer as an argument, it is much more flexible and powerful since we can use the members of the object to store and use any information we want.

STL provides several predefined function objects. They can be used to provide more flexibility to STL functions that take functions as arguments. For example, sort() by default sorts the elements of the container in ascending order. If we want to change the order to descending we can use the predefined object greater<>. The definitions of these standard function objects are contained in the functional file. For example:

```
#include <iostream>  // Example 26.16
#include <vector>
#include <algorithm>
#include <functional>

void show(int k);

int main()
{
        std::vector<int> v = {5, 3, 8, 12, 1};
        sort(v.begin(), v.end(), std::greater<int>()); /* The constructor of
greater<int> is called to create the object. */
```

```
        for_each(v.begin(), v.end(), show);
        return 0;
}


void show(int k)
{
        std::cout << k << ' ';
}
```

`greater<int>` applies the > operator to compare the elements. Therefore, the program displays: 12 8 5 3 1.

LAMBDA FUNCTIONS

One of the most exciting features that C++11 introduced is the ability to create *lambda* functions. The typical use of lambda functions is as argument in STL functions that accept a function pointer or functor as an argument. As we saw, a functor is more powerful than a function pointer; however, it is required to write some code to support its functionality (e.g., to define a class and overload the () operator). A lambda expression or just lambda often is a more convenient alternative than using a functor or write a function. In particular, a lambda expression may be viewed as an anonymous `inline` function, which is defined just-in-place where we want to use it. Thus, we don't have to define separate functions or functors. For example, let's replace the `Filter` class with a lambda:

```
#include <iostream> // Example 26.17
#include <vector>
#include <string>
#include <algorithm>
using namespace std;

int main()
{
        int i = 6, j = 3;
        string tmp("test");
        vector<int> v = {5, 3, 8, 12, 1};

        cout << "Show less than 6: ";
        for_each(v.begin(), v.end(),
                [i](int a) {if(a < i) cout << a << ' ';});

        cout << "\nShow less than 3: ";
        for_each(v.begin(), v.end(),
                [&j](int a) {if(a < j) cout << a << ' ';});

        vector<string> s{"one", "two", "three"};
        cout << "\nShow less strings: ";
        for_each(s.begin(), s.end(),
                [&tmp](const string& a) {if(a < tmp) cout << a << ' ';});
        return 0;
}
```

As we see, we pass a lambda expression as the third argument. The output of the program is the same as before:

```
Show less than 6: 5   3   1
Show less than 3: 1
Show less strings: one
```

Let's explain the syntax of a lambda expression. In its simplest form it is defined as follows:

```
[capture_clause](parameters) -> return_type
{
        lambda_body;
}
```

The parameter list and the trailing return type are optional parts. A lambda begins with the capture clause `[]`. This part specifies the variables that are captured (e.g., `i`) and whether they are captured by reference or by value. The variables must be in the enclosing scope where the definition of the lambda appears. An empty capture list (e.g., `[]`) indicates that nothing is captured. In this case, the lambda can work only with its arguments and the variables that are declared locally within it. For example, if we did not add `i` in the first call to `for_each()` the compiler would issue an error message. Also, if we try to access `j` within the lambda the compilation fails, because `j` is not contained in the capture list.

The reason I used `i` and `j` differently in the `[]` is to show you the capture modes. Specifically, if an `&` precedes the name of the variable it means that the variable is captured by reference (e.g., `[&j]`), that is, the lambda can change its value. If just the name is used, it means that it is captured by value (e.g., `[i]`), that is, a copy of the local variable is passed to the function. As a matter of fact, the compiler by default, in order to avoid any confusion, does not allow even to change the value of that copy. For example, in the first lambda it is an error to write `i = 10`. Note that it is allowed to mix the modes and capture some by value and others by reference (e.g., `[i, &j]`).

If we write `[&]` it means that all variables in the enclosing scope are captured by reference, while `[=]` means that all are captured by value. Just like an ordinary function, the optional list of arguments (e.g., `a`) is inserted in `()`, while the lambda body is put inside `{}`. A lambda can use names that are defined outside the function in which it is contained. Thus, it can use `cout`.

If the lambda does not have a `return` statement, the return type is `void`. Otherwise, the return type is deduced from the type of the `return` expression. If there are multiple `return` statements, then all must return a value of the same type. Alternatively, a trailing return type can be used (e.g., `[i]() -> int {...}`).

The syntax of a lambda expression supports many more options than those in this simple example. Actually, it can be quite complicated. However, once you get familiar with the syntax details, you may feel more comfortable using lambdas as arguments instead of defining separate functions or functors.

Using lambdas can be convenient, but also harder to understand. In general, a lambda should be kept simple in order to avoid confusion. To make the code easier to read, we can name the lambda expression in order to state its purpose and also to make it available for further use in the program. For example:

```
auto show_less = [i](int a) {if(a < i) cout << a << ' ';};
for_each(v.begin(), v.end(), show_less);
```

The `auto` keyword makes the compiler to find the type of `show_less` from the right side of `=`, which is, a lambda expression. Without getting into details, it is good to know that a lambda expression evaluates to a function object. That is, when the compiler meets a lambda expression, it generates a class type, and the lambda results in an `operator()` function. Thus, the type of `show_less` is the type of the class that the compiler internally generated.

Lambdas are often used as an argument in STL algorithms, when the default behaviour is not the desirable. For example, the following code uses a lambda expression to sort the names in descending alphabetical order and then displays them.

```
vector<string> s{"one", "two", "three"};
sort(s.begin(), s.end(),
       [](const string& a, const string& b) {return a > b;});
for(auto& x : s)
       cout << x << '\n';
```

In C++11, the parameters of the lambda function need to be declared with specific types. C++14 relaxes this restriction, allowing lambda parameters to be declared with the auto specifier. Thus, we can write generic lambdas. For example:

```
auto f = [](auto a, auto b) {return a+b;};
```

Also, C++14 allows the initialization of the captured variables. Note that the capture variable does not need to be an existing variable, which means that we can declare new variables and use them inside the lambda body. For example:

```
auto f = [x = 10]() {return x+10;};
cout << f(); // outputs 20.
```

As I said in the beginning of this chapter, its purpose was just to give you an idea of the general principles and capabilities of the STL. The next stop on your C++ trip is to read a related reference book to get familiar with the lots of useful services and tools that the STL offers.

Application Example

27

The code of a program can extend from a few lines to millions of lines, as in the case of large commercial applications. In large applications, the common practice is different groups of programmers to undertake different parts of the project. With the responsibility of each group being limited to specific code files, the implementation, testing, control, and the management of the overall application becomes faster and easier. In this chapter, we'll discuss briefly about how to organize a program and see a simple application example related to the implementation of communication protocols.

PROGRAM STRUCTURE

There are several books with focus on how to organize a program. Here, we'll just have a very brief discussion. First, we break down the application requirements into separate modules. This partitioning facilitates the project management and the understanding of the program structure. Then, we define the interactions between the different modules, their dependencies, and how these modules communicate with each other. A communication example is the *callback* mechanism as we saw in Chapter 8. The services of each module are mapped to programming concepts, such as functions and classes, which are defined in corresponding code files.

For each module there must be a detailed description of its purpose, the services it provides, and the way it operates, in order to facilitate its maintenance, upgrade, and better understanding. The latter is very important in case of changes in the programming team, as with the addition of new members. Each module consists of code files, where each file implements a subset of the services provided by the module. Each file should contain the necessary information about the types it uses. All files are compiled separately and the linker, as we said in Chapter 1, undertakes to link the produced code.

For each module, we choose the functions that may be shared by other modules and put their declarations in a header file, which represents the module's interface file. For example, a module might be implemented as a library and provide a header file which contains the functions that will be the communication interface with the outside world. The functionality of each module and the respective software tasks should be as independent as possible from each other, so that different groups of programmers may work in parallel to implement them.

As for program elements, the common practice is to put namespaces, definitions of `inline` functions, constants, enumerations, type synonyms, macros, templates, declarations of types, and functions in header files, which are protected against multiple inclusion with the `#ifndef` directive as we saw in Chapter 15. We can use one header file or many files. Definitions of variables and functions are placed in code files. As for the `extern` variables, many prefer to place them in header files. Others, like me, put them in the code files which use them, in order to make it clear. When put in header files there is no indication of where they are used.

One Header File

A simple way to organize a program consisting of many files is to place the definitions (e.g., functions, classes, …) in the code files where they are used and all the declarations in a single header file. This header file is included in each code file. By convention, the extension of a header file is .h. Yes, for a small-size program, this approach might be convenient, since we'd have only one place to search for declarations and edit. However, it is not an efficient approach for large programs. One reason is that every time its contents change all the code files have to be re-compiled, which is time consuming for a large application. Also, changes in this file by many programmers are a source of risk for potential errors. And of course, its large size makes quite difficult tasks such as to read it, use it, understand, and maintain.

Many Header Files

An alternative approach is each code file to have its own header file. The header file facilitates one who reads it to get quickly an idea what part of the program the code file implements and about the services it provides. In large programs this way of organizing files is the best way. It is very helpful for the better control, understanding, and maintenance of the program the services that the code files provide to be split into more than one header files. If there is a change in one header file, only the code files that include it are compiled again.

The declarations are placed in the header files and the definitions in the respective code files. Common information used in more than one code file is put in a header file which is included in the code files that need it. The advantage of having a common file is that if we need to make a change we do not need to look in different files to make that change, we'll do it in one place. For example, the declaration of a class used in many code files is placed in a header file, which is included in any code file that uses it. The functions of the class can be defined in the code files that use them in the same way as when we have a single code file, that is, with the class name and the :: operator.

APPLICATION EXAMPLE

Because in my working experience I was deeply involved with the development of network protocols, I decided to implement a simple protocol to show you an example of a larger application. The purpose of the program is not to understand the details of the implementation, but to get an idea of the object-oriented design approach and how the different program files communicate. Also, if you ever decide to get involved with the area of communication protocols, this example might help you for start.

At first, what is a network protocol? Simply put, it is a set of rules that enables system communication. A protocol may be implemented in hardware, software, or both. Typically, its operation is based on the standard defined by an international organization. A protocol example is the famous *Internet Protocol* (*IP*). It is specified by the *IETF* organization in *RFC 791* standard. A protocol standard specifies, among others, the information exchanged between systems, the format of the exchanging messages, their significance, and the message handling procedures. Typically, the guideline for the implementation of a protocol is a finite-state machine that models the protocol operation in terms of states and events.

Let's describe the protocol we are going to implement. It is an oversimplified version of the *ITU-T Q.931* signaling protocol. *Q.931* protocol is designed for the establishment, maintenance, and release of calls in an ISDN network. When the calling user dials the number of the called user a message named SETUP is created. The SETUP message is routed through the ISDN network to reach the called user. If the called user accepts the call (e.g., picks up the phone) a message named CONNECT is transmitted back to the calling user. The called user responds with CONNECT_ACK and the call establishment procedure ends. A circuit is reserved along the path between the two parties to serve the data transfer. Now, the two parties can communicate. If either party closes the connection (e.g., hangs up), a message named RELEASE is transmitted to the other party and the circuit is released.

The application provides a menu of choices and simulates the message exchange between the two parties in order to establish and release calls. Each message is identified by a unique code and contains specific information. For example, the code of the SETUP message is 5 and it contains several information elements, such as the phone number of the calling user. Having the object-oriented philosophy in mind, we represent each call by an object. Each call is identified by a unique number, which is named CRV (*Call Reference Value*). For simplicity, let's assume that each message contains only its code and the CRV.

The usual choice for the name of the file that contains main() is the name of the application, for example, prtcl.cpp. We split the functionality of the program into several modules. Each of the following source files represents a module:

prtcl.cpp. It contains functions which implement the interface with the upper and lower layer. It parses and forwards the messages it receives to the *fsm.cpp*. The concept of layers is described in *Open Systems Interconnection* (*OSI*) model, a reference model which describes how an application that runs in system A can communicate, through a network, with another application than runs in system B. A layer may be implemented in software or hardware. For example, the lower layer might be the driver of the network card or the card itself, while the upper layer might be an application which provides the means to communicate with another system (e.g., web browser). In our program, the upper layer is a simple console application which provides a menu of some choices to the user.

fsm.cpp. It contains the function which implements the protocol finite state machine. Each call is in a certain state. For example, when the SETUP message is sent (i.e., to establish the call), the call goes to the CALL_INIT state. If in this state, the CONNECT message (sent by the called user) is received, the call goes to the ACTIVE state, which means that the call is established. When the RELEASE message is sent (i.e., to release the established call), the call goes to the RELEASE_INIT state, and when the RELEASE_COMPLETE message (sent by the called user) is received, the call is released.

send.cpp. It contains the function which create messages and send them to the lower layers. Also, here we simulate the side of the called side by sending the CONNECT and RELEASE_COMPLETE replies.

As we said, we put the common information used in many code files in one header file. Let's name it general.h. To avoid multiple inclusion we use the #ifndef directive.

```cpp
/* general.h */
#ifndef general_h
#define general_h

#include <iostream>
#include <vector>
#include <map>
using std::cout;
using std::cin;
using std::map;
using std::vector;

#define LOOPBACK_MODE

// Message codes according to the ITU-T standard.
const int SETUP = 0x5;
const int CONNECT = 0x7;
const int RELEASE = 0x4D;
const int RELEASE_COMPLETE = 0x5A;
```

```
struct Msg /* This structure is used as an argument in function calls. */
{
        int code;
        int CRV;
        int call_index;
        /* Normally, the structure contains many more members that correspond
to the information elements conveyed by each message. */
};


class Call // Each call is represented by a Call object.
{
private:
        int CRV; // It holds the identifier of the call.
        int state; // It holds the state of the call.
        /* Normally, the class contains many more members related to the
call, such as the phone numbers of the two parties and the duration of the
call. */
public:
        Call(int crv);
        int fsm(Msg *p);
        int send_msg(Msg *p);
};


class Prtcl
{
private:
        vector<Call> calls; // We use a vector to store the calls.
        map<int, int> map_CRV; /* Mapping of the key, which is the CRV value
of each call with the position of the object in the vector. Thus, we find the
position of the object that corresponds to a CRV value. */
public:
        int handle_up_msg(Msg *p); /* It is used for communication with the
upper layer. */
        int handle_low_msg(int data[]); /* It is used for communication with
the lower layer. */
        int find_call(int CRV) const;
        void show() const {cout << "\nCalls: " << calls.size() << '\n';} /* As
you see we can define the function in the header file. It displays the number
of the established calls. */
};


#endif
```

With the object-oriented approach it makes sense each call to be represented by a respective object. In our example, each call is represented by an object of the Call class. Also, it simplifies the design to have another class to manage the calls. In our example, the Prtcl class manages the calls and provides the functions with communication with the outside world, that is, with the upper and lower layers. To store the calls we use a vector. Let's see the prtcl.cpp.

```
#include "general.h"
#include "fsm.h"

Prtcl prtcl; /* I declare it as global, to show you how to use it as extern
in other files. */
```

```cpp
int main()
{
        int CRV, index, num, sel;
        Msg msg;

        CRV = 100; // Just, an initial value.
        while(1)
        {
                cout << "\nOperations\n";
                cout << "------------\n";

                cout << "1. Establish Call\n";
                cout << "2. Release Call\n";
                cout << "3. Show Calls\n";
                cout << "4. Exit\n";

                cout << "\nEnter choice: ";
                cin >> sel;

                switch(sel)
                {
                        case 1:
                                msg.code = SETUP;
                                msg.CRV = CRV; // Call identifier.
                                CRV++; /* For simplicity, the CRV of each call is
incremented by one. */
                                prtcl.handle_up_msg(&msg); /* In a real
application, the user enters information related to the call, such as the
phone number of the called user. */
                                break;

                        case 2:
                                cout << "Enter CRV of the call to be released: ";
                                cin >> num;
                                index = prtcl.find_call(num); /* We find the
call, that is, the object, with the same CRV as the one entered by the
user. */
                                if(index != -1)
                                {
                                        msg.code = RELEASE;
                                        msg.CRV = num;
                                        msg.call_index = index;
                                        prtcl.handle_up_msg(&msg); /* Activate the
call release procedure. */
                                }
                                else
                                        cout << "Non existing call\n";
                        break;

                        case 3:
                                prtcl.show();
                        break;

                        case 4:
                        return 0;
```

```
                              default:
                                      cout << "\nWrong choice\n";
                              break;
                      }
              }
              return 0;
      }


      int Prtcl::handle_up_msg(Msg *p) /* Handle the message coming from the upper
      layer. */
      {
              int index;

              if(p->code == SETUP)
              {
                      Call c(p->CRV); // Create an object to manage the call.
                      calls.push_back(c); // Store the object.
                      index = calls.size()-1;
                      map_CRV[p->CRV] = index; /* Map the CRV to the position of the
      object in the vector. */
                      calls[index].fsm(p); /* Forward the message to the object that
      manages the call. */
              }
              else if(p->code == RELEASE)
              {
                      index = p->call_index;
                      calls[index].fsm(p);
              }
              else
              {
                      cout << "Upper message_" << p->code << " not supported\n";
                      return -1;
              }
              return 0;
      }


      int Prtcl::handle_low_msg(int data[]) /* Handle the message coming from the
      lower layer. */
      {
              int ret, index;
              Msg msg; /* The information coming from the lower layer is stored in
      the Msg members. */
              index = find_call(data[0]); /* We find the call, that is, the object
      which has the same CRV with the CRV contained in the message. */
              if(index == -1)
              {
                      cout << "Non existing call\n";
                      return -1;
              }
              msg.code = data[1];
              switch(msg.code)
              {
                      case CONNECT:
                              calls[index].fsm(&msg); /* Forward the message to the
      object that manages the call. */
                      break;
```

```
        case RELEASE_COMPLETE:
                ret = calls[index].fsm(&msg); /* Here is an example to
check the return value. The respective object is deleted. */
                if(ret == CLEAR_CALL)
                {
                        calls.erase(calls.begin()+index);
                        map_CRV.erase(data[0]);
                }
        break;

        default:
                cout << "Received message_" << msg.code << " not
supported\n";
            return -1;
    }
    return 0;
}

int Prtcl::find_call(int CRV) const /* To find the object we use map_CRV
which maps the CRV with its position in the vector. */
{
    auto it = map_CRV.find(CRV);
    if(it != map_CRV.end())
            return it->second;
    return -1;
}
```

The `handle_up_msg()` is called when a message from the upper layer is received. In our example, the upper level corresponds to the application menu which provides some operations to perform. For example, if the user selects the call setup option, a new object is created to manage the call and the SETUP message is supposed to be sent to the called user. In a real application, this message is created when the calling user initiates communication with the called user (e.g., dials the number), then the network card transmits it to the physical medium (e.g., optical fiber), and the message traverses the ISDN network to reach the destination.

The `handle_low_msg()` is called when a message from the lower layer is received. For example, in a real application, the message is received from the network card, it is passed to the driver of the card, and the driver forwards it to the application to handle it. In our example, the message is contained in the `data` array. In a real application, because the `handle_low_msg()` and `handle_up_msg()` are called asynchronously and access the same resources, I put them in two threads and use semaphores to synchronize them. STL provides classes for multi-thread programming. Think of a thread as a separate program executed in parallel with the main program. In this book we don't discuss about threads, I just give some hints in case someone is involved with something similar in the future.

Next files are the `fsm.cpp` and `fsm.h`. These files implement the state machine of the protocol. For example, when the SETUP message is received in the IDLE state, the call state changes to CALL_INIT and the message is forwarded to `send.cpp` for transmission. When the call is in CALL_INIT state and the CONNECT message is received, the state changes to ACTIVE, which means that the call has been established. To release the call, the call state changes from ACTIVE to RELEASE_INIT and the RELEASE message is forwarded to `send.cpp` for transmission. When the RELEASE_COMPLETE message is received, the call is released and the respective object is deleted from the vector. For simplicity, I'm using the `switch` statement. However, my typical choice is to use an array of pointers to functions, as in the example of the respective section in Chapter 8, in order to improve performance.

```
#include "general.h"
#include "fsm.h"
```

```
Call::Call(int crv)
{
        CRV = crv;
        state = IDLE;
}

int Call::fsm(Msg *p)
{
        switch(state)
        {
                case IDLE:
                        if(p->code == SETUP)
                        {
                                state = CALL_INIT;
                                send_msg(p);
                        }
                        else
                        {
                                cout << "Unexpected message_" << p->code << " in
state_" << state << '\n';
                                return UNKNOWN_MSG;
                        }
                break;

                case CALL_INIT:
                        if(p->code == CONNECT)
                        {
                                cout << "\nCall with CRV " << CRV << " is
established\n";
                                state = ACTIVE;
                        }
                break;

                case ACTIVE:
                        if(p->code == RELEASE)
                        {
                                state = RELEASE_INIT;
                                send_msg(p);
                        }
                break;

                case RELEASE_INIT:
                        if(p->code == RELEASE_COMPLETE)
                        {
                                cout << "\nCall with CRV " << CRV << " is
released\n";
                                return CLEAR_CALL;
                        }
                break;

                default:
                        cout << "Not supported state\n";
                return UNKNOWN_STATE;
        }
        return 0;
}
```

```
/* fsm.h */
#ifndef fsm_h
#define fsm_h

// Call states.
enum fsm_states {IDLE = 1, CALL_INIT, ACTIVE, RELEASE_INIT};

// Return values.
const int CLEAR_CALL = 1;
const int UNKNOWN_MSG = 2;
const int UNKNOWN_STATE = 3;

#endif
```

Next file is the send.cpp. Each message is created according to the protocol specification and it is passed to the lower layer. This lower layer might be the driver of the network card which forwards the message to the card for transmission in the network. As we said, for simplicity, we assume that each message contains only its code and the CRV.

```
#include "general.h"

extern Prtcl prtcl;

int Call::send_msg(Msg *p)
{
        int data[2]; /* Since the message contains only its code and the CRV,
its size is set to 2. The exercise C.11.22 shows an example of how to create
a message. */
        data[0] = CRV;
        data[1] = p->code;

        switch(data[1])
        {
                case SETUP:
                break;

                case RELEASE:
                break;

                default:
                        cout << "Unexpected message " << data[1] << " for
transmission\n";
                        return -1;
        }
#ifndef LOOPBACK_MODE
        /* In a real application, here is the place where we typically call a
function of the lower layer (e.g., a function of the driver) with arguments
the data array and its length for transmission in the network. */
        cout << "Only loopback tests are supported\n";
#else
        switch(data[1])
        {
                case SETUP:
                        data[0] = CRV;
                        data[1] = CONNECT; /* We simulate the scenario that the
other party accepted the call and the message CONNECT is received to complete
the call establishment. */
                        break;
```

```
            case RELEASE:
                    data[0] = CRV;
                    data[1] = RELEASE_COMPLETE; /* We simulate the scenario
that the other party closed the connection and the message RELEASE_COMPLETE
is received to complete the release of the call. */
                    break;
        }
        prtcl.handle_low_msg(data);
#endif
        return 0;
}
```

If you ever are assigned to implement a network protocol here are some advices. Suppose that you implement the A side. You create and send messages to the B side. The question is, how could you verify that your code handles properly the responses supposed to receive from the B side? If you can find an application in the market that simulates the B side, it is fine, get it and use it to test your code. But what if you cannot find one? For example, I was involved with the development of a protocol where the B side was a switching node of a wireless network and I could not find an application to simulate its operation. The company I used to work for was a small one and could not afford the cost to buy a real node. So, what I did?

I did what you just saw. That is, I defined the LOOPBACK_MODE macro and added code to simulate the B side into the same application. As a result, I managed to test the most part of the code and fix bugs locally in my office, before going to the customer's premises to deliver the software. Of course, the operation of the protocol was thoroughly tested when integrated into the customer's network platform, but most tests had already been performed. Thus, thanks to the loopback testing, the integration phase completed earlier than expected saving time and money for the company. For your information, the customer was a manufacturer of network equipment (e.g., switches) looking for systems that would simulate the behaviour of many subscribers (e.g., establish thousands of calls in parallel and send data) in order to evaluate the performance of its equipment before selling it to the network operators.

In another application, I implemented the application that simulates the B side in another system and used a network service (e.g., sockets) to communicate with that system and test the implementation of the A side. Of course, with both approaches, the simulation code should be written with special care, because in case it contains errors, it will lead you to the wrong conclusion that the A side is not written correctly. For this reason, the code of the B simulator should be written step by step, first to support some basic tests and gradually add more functionality to support more complex tests.

So far, all our programs consist of a single source file. How can we create a program that consists of several files? It depends on the compiler you use. For example, the Integrated Development Environment (IDE) of the *Microsoft Visual Studio* that I am using provides a menu option similar to *File->New->Project* to create the program and *Project->Add_New_Item* to add files. The source files can be compiled separately or all together with the *Build* command. An example of running the program is:

```
Enter choice: 1
Call with CRV 100 is established
Enter choice: 1
Call with CRV 101 is established
Enter choice: 2
Enter CRV of the call to be released: 100
Call with CRV 100 is released
```

Epilogue

To all of you who have endured reading this book and finally reached at the end and still insist on getting involved with programming, I welcome you with *Space Oddity* from *David Bowie* and all my wishes for a successful career in the "programming" space. On the other hand, if you have not yet decided whether to stay in or leave the programming area listen to *Should I Stay or Should I Go* by *The Clash* and decide. What really matters in life is to find out something that satisfies you, to do something that pleases you and makes you happy. Good luck!

Annex A: Precedence Table

Table A.1 lists C++ operators from the highest to the lowest order of precedence. Operators listed in the same line have the same precedence. The last column indicates the order in which operators of the same precedence are evaluated.

TABLE A.1 Precedence Table

PRECEDENCE	OPERATORS	ASSOCIATIVITY
1	`::` (scope operator)	Left to right
2	`.` (member access)	
	`->` (member access)	
	`[]` (subscripting)	
	`()` (function call)	
	`type()`, `type{}` (type cast, e.g., `int(a)`)	
	`++`(postfix)	
	`--`(postfix)	
	`typeid`	
	`dynamic_cast<type>(expression)`	
	`static_cast<type>(expression)`	
	`reinterpret_cast<type>(expression)`	
	`const_cast<type>(expression)`	
3	`sizeof`	Right to left
	`sizeof...`	
	`alignof`	
	`++` (prefix)	
	`--` (prefix)	
	`~`	
	`!`	
	`+` (unary)	
	`-` (unary)	
	`&` (address)	
	`*` (dereference)	
	`new`	
	`new[]`	
	`delete`	
	`delete[]`	
	`noexcept`	
	`(type)` (type cast, e.g., `(int)a)`)	
4	`.*` (member selection)	Left to right
	`->*` (member selection)	
5	`*` (multiplication) `/` `%`	Left to right
6	`+` (addition) `-` (subtraction)	Left to right
7	`<<` `>>`	Left to right
8	`<` `<=` `>` `>=`	Left to right
9	`==` `!=`	Left to right
10	`&`	Left to right
11	`^`	Left to right

(Continued)

TABLE A.1   Precedence Table *(Continued)*

PRECEDENCE	OPERATORS	ASSOCIATIVITY
12	`|`	Left to right
13	`&&`	Left to right
14	`||`	Left to right
15	`?:  =  +=  -=  *=  /=  %=  &=  ^=` `|=  <<=  >>=  throw`	Right to left
16	`,  (comma)`	Left to right

Annex B: ASCII Table

This annex presents the standard (0–127) and extended (128–255) ASCII character sets.

Dec	Hex	Name	Char	Ctrl-char	Dec	Hex	Char	Dec	Hex	Char	Dec	Hex	Char
0	0	Null	NUL	CTRL-@	32	20	Space	64	40	@	96	60	`
1	1	Start of heading	SOH	CTRL-A	33	21	!	65	41	A	97	61	a
2	2	Start of text	STX	CTRL-B	34	22	"	66	42	B	98	62	b
3	3	End of text	ETX	CTRL-C	35	23	#	67	43	C	99	63	c
4	4	End of xmit	EOT	CTRL-D	36	24	$	68	44	D	100	64	d
5	5	Enquiry	ENQ	CTRL-E	37	25	%	69	45	E	101	65	e
6	6	Acknowledge	ACK	CTRL-F	38	26	&	70	46	F	102	66	f
7	7	Bell	BEL	CTRL-G	39	27	'	71	47	G	103	67	g
8	8	Backspace	BS	CTRL-H	40	28	(	72	48	H	104	68	h
9	9	Horizontal tab	HT	CTRL-I	41	29	)	73	49	I	105	69	i
10	0A	Line feed	LF	CTRL-J	42	2A	*	74	4A	J	106	6A	j
11	0B	Vertical tab	VT	CTRL-K	43	2B	+	75	4B	K	107	6B	k
12	0C	Form feed	FF	CTRL-L	44	2C	,	76	4C	L	108	6C	l
13	0D	Carriage feed	CR	CTRL-M	45	2D	-	77	4D	M	109	6D	m
14	0E	Shift out	SO	CTRL-N	46	2E	.	78	4E	N	110	6E	n
15	0F	Shift in	SI	CTRL-O	47	2F	/	79	4F	O	111	6F	o
16	10	Data line escape	DLE	CTRL-P	48	30	0	80	50	P	112	70	p
17	11	Device control 1	DC1	CTRL-Q	49	31	1	81	51	Q	113	71	q
18	12	Device control 2	DC2	CTRL-R	50	32	2	82	52	R	114	72	r
19	13	Device control 3	DC3	CTRL-S	51	33	3	83	53	S	115	73	s
20	14	Device control 4	DC4	CTRL-T	52	34	4	84	54	T	116	74	t
21	15	Neg acknowledge	NAK	CTRL-U	53	35	5	85	55	U	117	75	u
22	16	Synchronous idle	SYN	CTRL-V	54	36	6	86	56	V	118	76	v
23	17	End of xmit block	ETB	CTRL-W	55	37	7	87	57	W	119	77	w
24	18	Cancel	CAN	CTRL-X	56	38	8	88	58	X	120	78	x
25	19	End of medium	EM	CTRL-Y	57	39	9	89	59	Y	121	79	y
26	1A	Substitute	SUB	CTRL-Z	58	3A	:	90	5A	Z	122	7A	z
27	1B	Escape	ESC	CTRL-[	59	3B	;	91	5B	[	123	7B	{
28	1C	File separator	FS	CTRL-\	60	3C	<	92	5C	\	124	7C		
29	1D	Group separator	GS	CTRL-]	61	3D	=	93	5D	]	125	7D	}
30	1E	Record separator	RS	CTRL-^	62	3E	>	94	5E	^	126	7E	~
31	1F	Unit separator	US	CTRL-_	63	3F	?	95	5F	_	127	7F	DEL

Dec	Hex	Char	Dec	Hex	Char	Dec	Hex	Char	Dec	Hex	Char
128	80	Ç	160	A0	á	192	C0	└	224	E0	α
129	81	ü	161	A1	í	193	C1	┴	225	E1	ß
130	82	é	162	A2	ó	194	C2	┬	226	E2	Γ
131	83	â	163	A3	ú	195	C3	├	227	E3	π
132	84	ä	164	A4	ñ	196	C4	─	228	E4	Σ
133	85	à	165	A5	Ñ	197	C5	┼	229	E5	σ
134	86	å	166	A6	ª	198	C6	╞	230	E6	µ
135	87	ç	167	A7	º	199	C7	╟	231	E7	τ
136	88	ê	168	A8	¿	200	C8	╚	232	E8	Φ
137	89	ë	169	A9	⌐	201	C9	╔	233	E9	Θ
138	8A	è	170	AA	¬	202	CA	╩	234	EA	Ω
139	8B	ï	171	AB	½	203	CB	╦	235	EB	δ
140	8C	î	172	AC	¼	204	CC	╠	236	EC	∞
141	8D	ì	173	AD	¡	205	CD	=	237	ED	φ
142	8E	Ä	174	AE	«	206	CE	╬	238	EE	ε
143	8F	Å	175	AF	»	207	CF	╧	239	EF	∩
144	90	É	176	B0	░	208	D0	╨	240	F0	≡
145	91	æ	177	B1	▒	209	D1	╤	241	F1	±
146	92	Æ	178	B2	▓	210	D2	╥	242	F2	≥
147	93	ô	179	B3	│	211	D3	╙	243	F3	≤
148	94	ö	180	B4	┤	212	D4	Ö	244	F4	⌠
149	95	ò	181	B5	╡	213	D5	╒	245	F5	⌡
150	96	û	182	B6	╢	214	D6	╓	246	F6	÷
151	97	ù	183	B7	╖	215	D7	╫	247	F7	≈
152	98	ÿ	184	B8	╕	216	D8	╪	248	F8	°
153	99	Ö	185	B9	╣	217	D9	┘	249	F9	·
154	9A	Ü	186	BA	║	218	DA	┌	250	FA	·
155	9B	¢	187	BB	╗	219	DB	█	251	FB	√
156	9C	£	188	BC	╝	220	DC	▄	252	FC	ⁿ
157	9D	¥	189	BD	╜	221	DD	▌	253	FD	²
158	9E	Pts	190	BE	╛	222	DE	▐	254	FE	■
159	9F	ƒ	191	BF	┐	223	DF	▀	255	FF	

Annex C: Hexadecimal System

This annex provides a brief description of the hexadecimal system. The base of the hexadecimal system is the number 16. The numbers 0-9 are the same of the decimal system. The numbers 10-15 are represented by the letters A to F. The correspondence of the hexadecimal system to the binary and decimal systems is depicted in Table C.1.

TABLE C.1   Hexadecimal System

HEXADECIMAL	BINARY	DECIMAL
0	0000	0
1	0001	1
2	0010	2
3	0011	3
4	0100	4
5	0101	5
6	0110	6
7	0111	7
8	1000	8
9	1001	9
A	1010	10
B	1011	11
C	1100	12
D	1101	13
E	1110	14
F	1111	15

As shown, each hexadecimal digit (0 to F) is represented with four binary digits. For example, the hexadecimal number F4A is written in binary as: 1111 0100 1010.

To find the decimal value of a hexadecimal number that consists of n digits (e.g., $d_{n-1}\ldots d_2 d_1 d_0$), we apply the formula:

$$\text{Decimal} = \sum_{i=0}^{n-1}\left(d_i \times 16^i\right)$$

For example, the decimal value of F4A is: $(A \times 16^0) + (4 \times 16^1) + (F \times 16^2) = 10 + 64 + 3840 = 3914$.

Bibliography

"C++ Primer", S. Lippman, J. Lajoie, B. Moo, 5th edition, Addison-Wesley, 2012.

"The C++ Programming Language", B. Stroustrup, 4th edition, Addison-Wesley, 2013.

"Programming Principles and Practice Using C++", B. Stroustrup, 2nd edition, Addison-Wesley, 2014.

"C: From Theory to Practice", G. Tselikis and N. Tselikas, 2nd edition, CRC Press/Taylor and Francis Group, 2017.

"C Programming Language", B. Kernighan and D. Ritchie, 2nd edition, Prentice Hall, 1988.

Index

#

#, 453
#(operator), 459
##, 459
#define, 26, 453
#elif, 461
#else, 461
#endif, 461
#if, 460
#ifdef, 462
#ifndef, 463
#include, 3, 453
#pragma, 465
#undef, 464

_

__DATE__, 456
__FILE__, 456
__func__, 456
__LINE__, 456
__TIME__, 456

.

.cpp, 2
.exe, 9
.h, 3
.o, 8
.obj, 8

A

a.out, 9
abort(), 456, 736
Abstract classes, 691
Access specifiers, 512
Address of variable, 170
adjustfield, 34
Algorithms (STL), 835
Alias (Type), 268
alignas, 369
alignof, 369
and, 62
and_eq, 62
ANSI C, 1
argc, 324
Argument (function), 277
argv, 324
Arithmetic constants, 20
Arithmetic conversions, 21
Arithmetic operators, 47
Array (one-dimensional), 133
    access elements, 134

and pointers, 183
C-style strings, 227
declaration, 133
function argument, 298
initialization, 136
of objects, 536
of pointers, 193
of pointers to functions, 208
of structures, 378
search, 343
sort, 348
structure member, 372
two-dimensional, 152
two-dimensional and pointers, 199
array<>, 847
ASCII set, 875
asm, 12
assert(), 456
Assignment, 45
Associative containers, 850
    map, 851
    set, 850
Associativity, 67
auto, 18, 266, 288
Auto
    in for-range, 137
    return type, 266
    variable type, 18
auto_ptr, 826
Automatic variables, 16, 289

B

back_insert_iterator, 845
bad(), 774
bad_alloc, 735
badbit, 774
Base class (inheritance)
    abstract, 689
    private, 692
    protected, 692
    public, 637
    virtual, 703
basefield, 34
Basic data types, 12
begin(), 140
Bidirectional iterator, 842
Binary files, 774
Binary operators, 47
Binary search, 345
Binary search trees, 441
Bit fields, 375
Bit operators, 59
bitand, 62
bitor, 62

Block, 4, 288, 291
bool, 13
boolalpha
    flag, 34
    manipulator, 36
Braces, 4, 17
Brackets, 133, 152
break, 88, 103
Bubble sort, 356
Bug, 10

C

C, 1
C++, 1
Callback mechanism, 206
Call by reference, 477
Call by value, 278
case, 88
Cast
    const_cast<>, 823
    C-style, 23
    dynamic_cast<>, 818
    static_cast<>, 824
catch, 718
cerr, 778, 783
char, 13, 217
char16_t, 12
char32_t, 12
Character, 217
    \ (escape), 32
    array of, 227
    ASCII set, 875
    null, 227
    output, 217
    read, 219
    trigraph sequence, 218
    variable, 13
cin, 39
Class, 509
    abstract classes, 689
    access to class members, 512
    and structures/unions, 516
    assignment of initial values to
            members, 527
    base classes, 637
    class design, 514
    const functions, 516
    conversion from class type, 598
    conversion to class type, 595
    data encapsulation, 509, 513
    data hiding, 513, 637, 640
    declaration, 509
    derived classes, 637
    derived classes and constructors, 644
    friend classes, 622
    friend functions, 518
    friend member functions, 624
    inline functions, 511
    member functions, 511
    members with constant
            values, 537
    nested class, 625

    objects, 509
    predefined functions, 528, 619
    relationship between base and derived
            class, 648
    scope of class, 512
    static functions, 610
    static members, 538
    template, 745
    virtual base classes, 703
clog, 783
close(), 776
Close file, 778
Command line arguments, 324
Comments, 6
Compilation errors, 9
Compile program, 7
compl, 62
complex, 581
Complex declarations, 273
Compound statement, 4,
    72, 291
Conditional compilation, 460
Conditional operator, 85
const
    class function, 516
    function argument, 301
    member, 537
    object, 518
    pointer, 178
    reference, 476
    variable, 24
const_cast<>, 823
constexpr, 26, 484
Constants
    #define, 26
    arithmetic, 20
    character, 20
    const, 24
    pass to functions, 301
    pointer, 178
    string, 227
    within class, 537
Constructor, 520
    call constructor, 523
    default, 525
    delegating, 604
    explicit, 596
    member initialization
            list, 602
Container adaptors, 848
    priority_queue, 849
    queue, 849
    stack, 850
Containers, 846
    adaptors, 848
    associative, 850
    sequence, 847
continue, 105
Conversions
    arithmetic, 21
    disable, 596
    explicit, 23, 822
    from class type, 598

implicit, 21
    to class type, 595
Copy
    deep, 610
    predefined function, 528
    shallow, 606
copy(), 843
Copy assignment function, 528
    in derived class, 653
Copy constructor, 605
    in derived class, 651
Copy disable, 565, 621
count_if(), 839
cout, 31

D

Dangling else, 76
Dangling pointer, 411
Data hiding, 513, 637, 640
Data input, 39
Data output, 31
Data types, 12
Debugging, 10
dec
    flag, 34
    manipulator, 36
Declaration
    array, 133
    class, 509
    enumeration, 57
    function, 265
    pointer, 170
    pointer to pointer, 196
    structure, 365
    two-dimensional array, 152
    union, 393
    variable, 15
    variable in switch, 92
decltype, 19, 267, 494
Deep copy, 610
default, 89
Default
    class functions, 528, 619
    constructor, 525
    destructor, 525
    function arguments, 471
    iterators, 844
    macros, 456
defined, 464
Definition
    class template, 747
    of function, 270
    of function inside class, 511
    of function outside class, 511
Delegating constructor, 604
delete, 409
delete[], 409
deque<>, 847
Dereference pointer, 172
Derived class, 637
Destructor, 521
    and memory release, 529

call of, 524
    default, 525
    virtual, 668
Directives
    #define, 26, 453
    #elif, 461
    #else, 461
    #endif, 461
    #if, 460
    #ifdef, 462
    #ifndef, 463
    #include, 3, 453
    #pragma, 465
    #undef, 464
    using, 809
Disable conversion, 596
do-while, 125
double, 14
Dynamic binding, 660
dynamic_cast<>, 818
Dynamic data structures, 425
    binary tree, 441
    queue, 431
    single linked list, 434
    stack, 427
Dynamic memory allocation, 405
Dynamic pointer type, 658
Dynamic reference type, 659
Dynamic polymorphism, 659

E

Early binding, 657
Ellipsis …, 326
else, 74
Encapsulation, 509, 513
end(), 140
endl, 36
ends, 36
enum, 57
Enumerations, 57
EOF, 219
eof(), 774, 785
eofbit, 774
Escape sequences, 32
Exceptions, 717
    and inheritance, 728
    and memory management, 732
    catch, 718
    catch exceptions, 718
    create exception, 718
    exception specifications, 723
    forward exceptions, 730
    handle uncaught exceptions, 736
    noexcept, 723
    rethrow exception, 731
    standard exceptions, 734
    throw, 718
    try, 718
    with type class, 726
    within constructor, 725
    within destructor, 725
exit(), 406

EXIT_FAILURE, 406
explicit, 596
Explicit conversions, 23
export, 12
extern, 294
External linkage, 288, 294

F

fabs(), 15
fail(), 774, 782
failbit, 774
[[fallthrough]], 91
false, 13
FIFO, 431, 849
Files, 773
    binary, 774
    close, 778
    end of, 782
    executable, 9
    open, 779
    processing, 780
    redirection, 783
    text, 774
    write and read from binary file, 794
    write and read from text file, 784
fill(), 38
final, 648, 663
find(), 837
fixed
    flag, 34
    manipulator, 36
flags(), 38
float, 14
floatfield, 34
flush, 36
Flush output memory, 778
fmtflags, 34
Fold expression, 501
for, 99
for_each(), 836
Format flags, 33
Forward declaration, 375
Forward iterator, 842
forward_list<>, 847
free(), 405
Free store, 403
Friend classes, 622
Friend functions, 518
front_insert_iterator, 845
fstream, 775, 777
Function arguments, 277
    array, 298
    command line, 324
    default, 471
    in main(), 324
    object, 531
    pass by reference, 477
    pass by value, 278
    pointer, 278
    structure, 380
    two-dimensional array, 318
    variable number, 326

Functions, 265
    arguments, 277
    array of pointers to functions, 208
    body, 270
    call, 275
    call by reference, 477
    call by value, 278
    call with parameters, 277
    call without parameters, 275
    const member, 516
    constexpr, 484
    constructor, 520
    copy assignment, 528
    copy constructor, 605
    declaration, 265
    default arguments, 471
    definition, 270
    destructor, 520
    final, 648, 663
    friend functions, 518
    inline, 511
    main(), 4
    move assignment, 619
    noexcept, 723
    overloading, 485
    overriding, 658
    parameters, 270
    parameters in main(), 324
    pointer to function, 204
    prototype, 265
    pure virtuals, 689
    recursive, 330
    return, 274
    return from function, 266
    signature, 486
    static class functions, 610
    static functions, 297
    stream state functions, 774
    template functions, 488
    variable number of parameters, 326
    virtual, 657
Functor, 855

G

g++, 7
Generic programming, 485
get(), 219
getchar(), 219
getline(), 234
global namespace, 293, 805
global scope, 291
global variable, 291
good(), 774
goodbit(), 774
goto, 128
greater<>, 856

H

Has-a relationship, 641
Header files, 3
Heap, 403

hex
    flag, 34
    manipulator, 36
Hexadecimal
    number, 20
    system, 877
Hide data, 513, 637, 640
Hierarchy of classes, 647

I

if, 71
ifstream, 775
Identifier, 11
Implicit conversions, 21
#include, 3, 453
Incomplete class declaration, 625
Incomplete structure declaration, 375
Indirection operator, 180
Infinite loop, 101, 103, 118
Inheritance, 637
    access redefinition, 694
    and protected members, 641
    and scope, 642
    and static members, 858
    class hierarchy, 707
    define copy assignment function in derived
            class, 653
    define copy constructor in derived
            class, 651
    derived classes and constructors, 644
    derived classes and copy operations, 651
    final, 648, 663
    multiple inheritance, 696
    private inheritance, 692
    protected inheritance, 693
    public inheritance, 637
    relationships between base and derived
            class, 648
    virtual base classes, 703
Initial value of variable, 16
Initialization
    member initialization list, 602
    of array, 136
    of constant, 24
    of object, 521, 527
    of reference, 474
    of structure members, 369
    of two-dimensional array, 154
    of variable, 17
    within class, 527
inline
    functions, 472
    variables, 474
Input iterator, 842
Input stream, 39, 773
insert_iterator, 845
Insertion sort, 353
Integer variables, 13
internal
    flag, 34
    manipulator, 36
Internal linkage, 288, 294, 814

ios_base, 33
    flags, 34
    functions, 38
    manipulators, 36
<iostream>, 3
isdigit(), 218
Is-a relationship, 641
is_open(), 776
istream, 39
istream_iterator, 844
Iteration loops, 99
    do-while, 125
    for, 99
    for-range, 137
    nested, 112
    while, 117
Iterators, 840
    access, 841
    bidirectional, 842
    forward, 842
    input, 842
    output, 842
    predefined, 844
    random access, 842

K

Keywords, 11
    and, 62
    and_eq, 62
    alignas, 369
    alignof, 369
    asm, 12
    auto, 18, 266, 288
    bitand, 62
    bitor, 62
    bool, 13
    break, 88, 103
    case, 88
    catch, 718
    char, 13, 217
    char16_t, 12
    char32_t, 12
    class, 509, 58
    compl, 62
    const, 24
    const_cast<>, 823
    constexpr, 26, 484
    continue, 105
    decltype, 19, 267, 494
    default, 89
    delete, 409
    do, 125
    double, 14
    dynamic_cast<>, 818
    else, 74
    enum, 57
    explicit, 596
    export, 12
    extern, 294
    false, 13
    final, 648, 663
    float, 14

for, 99
friend, 518, 622
goto, 128
if, 71
inline, 472
int, 13
long, 13
mutable, 518
namespace, 805
new, 405
not, 62
not_eq, 62
operator, 559
or, 62
or_eq, 62
override, 661
private, 512, 692
protected, 512, 692
public, 512, 637
register, 288, 290
reinterpret_cast, 822
return, 274, 4
short, 13
signed, 13
sizeof, 55
static, 295
static_cast<>, 824
struct, 365
switch, 88
template, 489
this, 532
thread_local, 12
throw, 718
true, 13
try, 718
typedef, 268
typeid, 821
typename, 489
union, 393
unsigned, 13
using, 808, 809, 268
virtual, 657, 703
void, 177, 266
volatile, 833
wchar_t, 13
while, 117
xor, 62
xor_eq, 62

L

Lambda expressions, 857
Language versions, 2
Late binding, 660
left
    flag, 34
    manipulator, 36
LIFO, 427
Linear search, 343
Linkage, 288
Linked list, 425, 434
Linker, 8
Literals

    binary, 20
    character, 20
    hexadecimal, 20
    integer, 20
    octal, 20
    string, 227
list<>, 847
Local variables, 288
Logical operators, 51
long, 13
long double, 14
long long int, 12
Loops, 99
Lvalue, 46, 185, 474, 614
Lvalue reference, 474

M

Macros, 453
    alternative choices, 459
    assert, 456
    predefined, 456
    simple, 453
    static_assert(), 457
    with parameters, 458
main(), 4
make_shared<>(), 832
make_unique<>(), 827
malloc(), 405
Manage dynamic memory (functions), 416
Manipulators, 36
map<>, 851
memcmp(), 417, 371
memcpy(), 416
memmove(), 416
Member initialization list, 602
Memory allocation
    dynamic, 405
        new placement, 409
        static, 403
Memory blocks, 403
Memory leaks, 413
memset(), 150
move(), 482, 829
Move constructor, 619
Move semantics, 612
multimap<>, 850
Multiple inheritance, 696
    multiple virtual base classes, 705
    virtual and non-virtual base classes, 706
    virtual base classes, 703
multiset<>, 850
mutable, 518

N

Name conflicts, 297, 463, 805
Name return value optimization
            (NRVO), 608
Namespaces, 805
    alias, 813
    build, 807
    creation, 806

global, 293, 805, 808
    nested, 812
    unnamed, 814
    using declarations, 808
    using directives, 809
Naming variables, 11
Narrowing conversion, 23
NDEBUG, 457
Nested class, 625
    access, 628
    declaration, 625
    properties, 627
Nested loop, 112
Nested namespace, 812
Nested structure, 373
new, 405
new[], 405
noboolalpha, 36
noexcept, 723
noshowbase, 36
noshowpoint, 36
noshowpos, 36
noskipws, 36
NOT, 52
not, 62
not_eq, 62
nothrow, 406, 736
nounitbuf, 36
nouppercase, 36
NULL, 171
Null character, 227
Null pointer, 171
Null statement, 72, 102
nullptr, 172, 411

O

Object, 509
    array of, 536
    class, 509
    const, 518
    creation, 521
    destruction, 521
    function argument, 531
    function (functor), 855
    initialization, 521, 527
    pointer to, 523
    return from function, 617
    slicing, 650
    temporary, 529, 595
Object oriented programming, 1
oct
    flag, 34
    manipulator, 36
octal constants, 20
offsetof, 368
One definition rule, 463
One dimensional array, 133
ofstream, 775
open(), 779
Open files, 779, 780
Operator overloading, 559
    binary, 559, 561, 577

examples with unary
        operators, 566
    operator =, 563
    operator [], 570
    operator <<, 574
    operator >>, 576
    operator ++ and --, 567
    operator -> and *, 568
    restrictions, 565
    unary, 577
    with non-members functions, 573
Operator precedence, 67, 873
Operators
    .*, 600
    ->*(pointer to member), 600
    *(dereference pointer), 172
    ->(pointer to member), 378
    [](access element), 134
    address of (&), 170
    alternative representations, 62
    arithmetic, 47
    assignment operator (=), 45
    associativity, 67, 873
    bitwise, 59
    comma (,), 54
    compound, 50
    conditional (?:), 85
    const_cast<>, 823
    decrement (--), 48
    delete, 409
    delete[], 409
    dot (.), 369
    dynamic_cast<>, 818
    increment (++), 48
    logical, 51
    new, 405
    new[], 405
    noexcept, 723
    not operator (!), 52
    overloading, 459
    precedence, 67, 873
    preprocessor, 581
    reinterpret_cast<>, 822
    relational, 49
    resolution scope operator (::), 5
    shift, 61
    sizeof, 55
    sizeof..., 501
    static_cast<>, 824
    typeid, 821
or, 62
or_eq, 62
ostream, 31
ostream_iterator, 844
out_of_range, 735
Output iterator, 842
Output stream, 31, 773
Overloading function, 485
    create ambiguities, 487
Overloading function
        templates, 497
override, 661
Overriding function, 658

P

pair<>, 852
Pass arguments, 277
    by lvalue reference, 477
    by rvalue reference, 484
    by value, 278
Pass arrays, 298
Pointers, 169
    and arrays, 183
    and dynamic memory allocation, 405
    and integers, 179
    and iterators, 843
    and memory release, 409
    and string literals, 231
    and two-dimensional arrays, 199
    array of, 193
    array of pointers to functions, 208
    const, 178
    dangling, 411
    declaration, 170
    dereference, 172
    dynamic type, 658
    NULL, 171
    null pointer, 171
    pointer arithmetic, 179
    pointer initialization, 170
    smart pointers, 826
    static type, 658
    subtraction and comparison, 181
    this, 532
    to derived class, 648
    to function, 204
    to function member, 600
    to object, 523
    to pointer, 196
    to structure, 377
    to structure member, 370
    to void, 177
Polymorphism
    dynamic, 659
    function overloading, 485
    static, 486
    virtual functions, 657
pow(), 284
#pragma, 465
Precedence, 67, 873
precision(), 38
Preprocessor, 453
    directives, 460
    operators, 459
printf(), 31
priority_queue<>, 849
private
    access specifier, 512
    base class specifier, 692
Private class member, 512
Private inheritance, 692
Program, 2
    comments, 6
    compilation, 7
    compile errors, 9
    execution, 9
    life-cycle, 2
    linking, 8
    writing style, 5
Program with many files, 861
protected
    access specifier, 512
    base class specifier, 692
Protected class member, 512
Protected inheritance, 692
Prototype (function), 265
ptrdiff_t, 181
public
    access specifier, 512
    base class specifier, 637
Public class member, 512
Public inheritance, 637
Pure virtual functions, 689

Q

Queue, 431
queue<>, 849
Quick sort, 360

R

rand(), 101
RAND_MAX, 101
Random file access, 781
Random number, 101
range-based for loop, 137
range_error, 735
Raw strings, 229
rbegin(), 845
read(), 794
Recursion, 330
Redirection, 783
References
    function argument, 477
    dynamic type, 659
    lvalue, 474
    pass array, 480
    return type, 479
    rvalue, 481
    rvalue and member functions, 614
    static type, 659
    to const, 476
    to pointer, 476
    variables, 474
register, 288, 290
reinterpret_cast<>, 822
Relational operators, 49
Release dynamic memory, 409
rend(), 845
resetiosflags(), 36
Resource Acquisition is Initialization (RAII), 530
return, 274, 4
Return type deduction, 267
Return value, 266
reverse_iterator, 845
right
    flag, 34
    manipulator, 36

Rule of five, 620
Rule of three, 610
Runtime error, 9
Runtime type identification, 818
    dynamic_cast<>, 818
    type_info, 821
    typeid, 821
Rvalue, 46
Rvalue reference, 481

S

scanf(), 40
scientific
    flag, 34
    manipulator, 36
Scientific notation, 21
Scope
    class, 512
    enumerator, 57
    global, 291
    local, 289
    namespaces, 805
    scope operator ::, 5
    variable, 288
Scope variable rules, 292
Search algorithms
    binary search, 345
    linear search, 343
Self-assignment, 564
seekg(), 781
seekp(), 781
Selection sort, 348
Sequence containers, 847
    array, 847
    deque, 847
    forward_list, 847
    list, 847
    vector, 138
Serial file access, 781
set<>, 850
setbase(), 36
setf(), 34
setfill(), 36
setiosflags(), 36
setprecision(), 36
set_terminate(), 736
setw(), 36
Shallow copy, 606
shared _ ptr, 831
Shift operators, 61
short, 13
Short-circuit evaluation, 52
showbase
    flag, 34
    manipulator, 36
showpoint
    flag, 34
    manipulator, 36
showpos
    flag, 34
    manipulator, 36
signed, 13

Single linked list, 425
sizeof, 55
sizeof..., 501
size_t, 55
skipws
    flag, 34
    manipulator, 36
Smart pointers, 826
    auto_ptr, 826
    shared_ptr, 831
    unique_ptr, 826
    weak_ptr, 832
sort(), 838
Sort array algorithms, 348
    bubble sort, 356
    insertion sort, 353
    quick sort, 360
    selection sort, 348
Source files, 2
Specializations
    class template, 762
    function template, 498
sqrt(), 286
srand(), 101
Stack, 275, 403
    dynamic data structure, 427
    overflow, 404
stack<>, 850
Standard exceptions, 734
    bad_alloc, 735
    bad_cast, 820
    domain_error, 735
    invalid_argument, 735
    length_error, 735
    logic_error, 735
    out_of_range, 735
    overflow_error, 735
    range_error, 735
    runtime_error, 735
    underflow_error, 735
Standard library algorithms, 835
    copy(), 843
    count_if(), 839
    find(), 837
    for_each(), 836
    sort(), 838
Standard template library, 835
    algorithms, 835
    algorithms and pointers, 843
    containers, 846
    function objects, 855
    iterators, 840
    lambda expressions, 857
    predefined iterators, 844
Statement
    break, 88, 103
    continue, 105
    do-while, 125
    for, 99
    goto, 128
    if-else, 71
    return, 274
    switch, 88

throw, 718
try-catch, 718
while, 117
Static
    class function, 610
    class variable, 538
    function, 297
    memory allocation, 403
    variable, 295
static_assert(), 457
Static binding, 657
static_cast<>, 824
Static pointer type, 805
Static reference type, 806
Static type control, 15
stdin, 39
stdout, 31
Storage classes, 288
strcat(), 241
strcmp(), 242
strcpy(), 239
Stream flags, 774
Streams, 773
string, 244
    append(), 246
    at(), 246
    c_str(), 247
    capacity(), 246
    erase(), 246
    find(), 246
    getline(), 245
    resize(), 246
    size(), 246
Strings, 227
    and pointers, 232
    and two-dimensional arrays, 258
    C-style, 227
    C-style functions, 238
    literals, 227
    literals and pointers, 231
    output, 228
    read, 234
    store, 227
    raw-style, 229
    string class, 244
strlen(), 238
strncmp(), 242
strncpy(), 239
Structure bindings, 618
Structures, 365
    access members, 369, 378
    and classes, 516
    array of, 378
    as function argument, 380
    bit-fields, 375
    declaration, 365
    incomplete declaration, 374
    initialization of structure members, 369
    members, 365
    naming, 365
    operations between structures, 371
    pointer to structure, 377
    pointer to structure member, 370

which contains array, 372
which contains pointer, 372
which contains structure, 373
switch, 88

T

tellg(), 781
tellp(), 781
Template classes, 745
    as members, 756
    as parameter, 754
    default parameter values, 755
    examples, 750
    instantiation, 748
    recursive use, 756
    specializations, 762
    static members, 755
    template parameters with different types, 752
    use of non-type parameters, 753
Template classes and friend functions, 758
    bound template friend functions, 759
    non-template friend functions, 758
    non-bound template friend functions, 760
Template functions, 488
    default parameter values, 496
    explicit instantiation, 496
    explicit specialization, 498
    implicit instantiation, 490
    overload template function, 497
    parameters with different types, 493
    set types of template parameters, 495
    templated variables, 491
    use of non-type parameters, 495
    variable number of types, 500
terminate(), 736
Ternary operator, 85
this, 532
thread_local, 12
throw, 718
time(), 101
Trailing return type, 267
Translation unit, 272
Trigraph sequence, 218
true, 13
try, 718
Two dimensional arrays, 152
    access, 153
    and pointers, 199
    declaration, 152
    initialization, 154
Type alias, 268
Type cast, 23, 822
Type sizes, 13
typedef, 268
typeid, 821
typeinfo, 821
typename, 489

U

Unary operators, 47
Undefined behaviour, 10

underflow_error, 735
unique_ptr<>, 826
Unions, 393
    access to union members, 394
    and classes, 516
    declaration, 393
unitbuf
    flag, 34
    manipulator, 36
Unnamed namespace, 814
unordered_map<>, 850
unordered_multimap<>, 850
unordered_multiset<>, 850
unordered_set<>, 850
unsetf(), 34, 37
Unsigned variables, 13
uppercase
    flag, 34
    manipulator, 36
using
    declaration, 808
    directive, 809
    type alias, 268

V

va_start(), 327
va_arg(), 327
va_end(), 327
va_list(), 327
Value assignment, 17
Variables, 11
    address, 170
    arithmetic conversions, 21
    assignment, 17
    automatic, 16, 289
    C-style strings, 227
    constant, 24
    declaration, 15
    definition, 17, 294
    enumeration, 57
    extern, 294
    floating-point, 14
    global, 291
    initial value, 16
    integers, 13
    local, 288
    naming, 11
    output, 31
    register, 288, 290
    scope, 288
    size, 13
    static, 295

    storage classes, 288
    type casts, 23, 822
    types, 12
    unsigned, 13
    volatile, 833
Variadic templates, 500
vector<>, 138
    at(), 139
    begin(), 140
    capacity(), 140
    end(), 140
    erase(), 140
    insert(), 141
    iterator, 140
    push_back(), 140
    size(), 140
    swap(), 141
Vector of vector, 156
Virtual and non-virtual base classes, 706
Virtual base classes, 703
Virtual destructor, 668
Virtual functions, 657
    and access specifiers, 667
    and dynamic polymorphism, 659
    and predefined arguments, 667
    call of within constructors and destructors, 669
    declaration, 658
    final, 648, 663
    function table (vtbl), 660
    override, 661
    pure virtual functions, 689
void
    pointer, 177
    return type, 266
volatile, 833

W

wchar_t, 13
weak_ptr, 832
what(), 734
while, 117
White characters, 40
width(), 38
write(), 794
ws, 36

X

XOR, 60
xor, 62
xor_eq, 62